ANTIQUES & COLLECTIBLES

2015 PRICE GUIDE • Eric Bradley

Published by

Krause Publications, a division of F+W Media, Inc.
700 East State Street • Iola, WI 54990-0001
715-445-2214 • 888-457-2873
www.krausebooks.com

To order books or other products call toll-free 1-800-258-0929
or visit us online at www.krausebooks.com

ISSN: 1536-2884

ISBN-13: 978-1-4402-4091-1
ISBN-10: 1-4402-4091-4

Cover Design by Sharon Bartsch
Designed by Jana Tappa
Edited by Eric Bradley

Printed in the United States of America

FRONT COVER, CLOCKWISE FROM TOP:
Vintage gas/service station island metal Mobiloil display, pre-1938,
$500-$1,200 (Victorian Casino Auctions)
Pennsylvania Star of Bethlehem quilt, 75" x 77", $152 (Pook & Pook, Inc.)
Late Victorian enamel, ruby, diamond and gold snake bracelet, 6-1/2" x 3/4",
$7,187 (Heritage Auctions)
Trumpet-shaped Quezal shade with purple hooked feather design, signed,
2-1/4" fitter x 6-3/4" h., $1,778 (James D. Julia, Inc.)
George III terrestrial globe, J & W Cary, London, circa 1815, 46" h. x 29" dia.,
$21,250 (Heritage Auctions)
"Moon Over Miami" (20th Century Fox, 1941), one sheet, Style B poster,
27" x 41", $15,535 (Heritage Auctions)

BACK COVER:
1930s Coca-Cola cardboard sign, 12" x 15", $180 (Morphy Auctions)
Cigar store Indian princess, circa 1880, attributed to New York workshop of
Samual Robb or Thomas Brooks, 83" h., $747,000 (Guyette, Schmidt and
Deeter)

Contents

LISTINGS

Introduction

Antique Trader Antiques & Collectibles Price Guide is a book entirely devoted to making you a better collector. As the No. 1 selling reference book of its kind, this big volume is overflowing with a broad range of items collected today – and each entry is illustrated with a full-color photograph to help you know what you're looking at. If you're new to collectibles, your curiosity piqued after catching the latest episode of "Antiques Roadshow," "American Pickers" or "Pawn Stars," then you've come to the right place.

Eric Bradley

As you'll see in the following pages, there's no telling what precious objects might appeal to collectors. From carnival glass to firearms, kitchenware to quilts, every year we scan the spectrum of the hobby for examples of the most popular collectibles trading hands. This year's book is overflowing with color photographs to help you focus your collecting interests or teach you something new about the things you already own. The art and objects collectors are interested in changes over time, and these trends are influenced by several factors. Condition aside, the more unusual something is, it seems there is no end to the prices some collectors are willing to pay for it. A few trends surfaced during the last year, and we were surprised to see the number of categories on the move. From our vantage point, the collectibles hobby is certainly seeing an exciting resurgence of new buyers and those curious about what they already own or have inherited.

Here are our annual picks of some of the hottest areas in the hobby:

Regional U.S. paintings

Advertising signs in all condition

Vintage Colt pistols

Americana

Fine and contemporary art by well-known artists

Celebrity memorabilia

Sports memorabilia

Jewelry (especially large colored diamonds and gemstones)

First edition children's books (signed first editions even more so)

Scientific models and instruments

Pre-1970 comics in excellent condition

Abraham Lincoln memorabilia

U.S. coins

Curiosities or vintage objects that defy classification

These picks are influenced by a number of conditions, but last year three important factors rose to the surface as the chief influence behind auction prices:

Fresh to Market Makes a Difference

Collectors love a chance to be the first to tap into a collection, even if the collection has been fabled in story and song for many decades. Privately held, single-owner collections are commanding strong prices. When these collections come to market, collectors acutely feel the double-edge sword. Although it's troubling to realize these massive, carefully curated collections may likely never be assembled again, it's gratifying to see other collectors enjoy rare objects for the first time in decades. Perhaps that's why prices realized for these collections are on the climb.

Eric Bradley is a public relations associate at Heritage Auctions, ha.com, the world's third largest auction house and the world's largest collectibles auctioneer; editor of Antique Trader Antiques & Collectibles Price Guide, *America's No. 1 selling reference book on collectibles; and author of* Mantiques: A Manly Guide to Cool Stuff. *He is the former editor of* Antique Trader *magazine and an award-winning investigative journalist with a degree in economics. Bradley's work has received press from* The New York Times *and* The Wall Street Journal. *He served as a featured guest speaker on investing with antiques. He lives in Dallas with his wife, Kelly, and their three children, Patrick, Olivia, and Megan.*

"One-of-a-Kind" Means More Now Than Ever Before

Unique items are more highly sought after than ever. The term "rare" is bandied about these days with little care to its accuracy. Most of the time, the term "rare" is used to describe an item of which no more than 10 examples are known to exist. Dedicated collectors know rare when they see it, and they show plenty of enthusiasm when such an object is discovered at a show, shop, flea market, or auction. Several indicators show this trend has no intention of slowing. This "best or nothing" mentality at the top of the market has introduced new pressure on buyers, but sellers must tread carefully as well. Collectors who are ready to sell should thoughtfully study prices realized across a variety of platforms to best decide where and how to dispose of a collection.

Condition is Still King

With the exception of advertising signs, it seems condition is the No. 1 arbiter of value. Even a common collectible in near-mint to mint condition demands a higher price on the market these days. Serious collectors have picked a side in the "quantity vs. quality" debate, and quality won out. This doesn't mean you should never consider purchasing an item in excellent to very good condition. Just know that your resale price may be closer to what you paid the first time around, rather than the windfalls you see on reality TV shows. Top-shelf collectors are willing to pay what it takes to own the prime examples and this is something to keep in mind when you're ready to make big purchases: Buy the best you can afford.

While all these factors affect what people sell, dealers, auctioneers, and shop owners are changing how people collect. It's easier than ever to start a collection or sell what you've got, and this means a host of new services to help. Here are three major developments from the past year:

Americana is hot. Stoneware jar, circa 1825, salt-glazed, James Miller (active 1797-1827), Alexandria, Virginia, or Georgetown, D.C., reversed "3" gallon capacity mark, ovid form with single incised ring below flanged flat-top rim, slightly arched tab-like handles, crudely beaded foot, brushed and slip-trailed cobalt spread-wing shield-breast Federal eagle decoration on one side, additional cobalt across top of handles, 12-1/4" h. x 7-1/4" dia. rim........**$75,750**

Jeffrey S. Evans & Associates

1. eBay's new mobile app has revolutionized the auction service provider, making it easier than ever to snap a photo, type a description and post an item for sale from anywhere in the world. This in turn has encouraged auctioneers and other auction service providers to embrace mobile computing as the new frontier in collecting.

2. Dealers faced with increased competition have turned their Facebook, email and Instagram accounts into storefronts. An innovative picker I know sends an email filled with photos and brief descriptions of his wares to his customer list every Tuesday at 7 p.m. Few items are priced more than $200 and few items ever appear twice. Adapting emerging technology is a great way dealers are reaching new collectors. Several new services now hold "flash sales" on Facebook pages, in which customers compete in real time to lay claim to an antique posted on the business' page. Some dealer consortiums are now holding "virtual shows" on their websites to introduce collectors to new and interesting things.

3. Shop owners are re-imagining "quitting time." The standard Monday-Friday, 9:00 to 5:00 open hours for traditional shops no longer serve working couples juggling demanding careers. Shops are increasingly extending their hours to as late as 9:00 p.m. some evenings. Some offer wine pairings or craft beer samplings to attract customers. A shop owner in Wisconsin reached out to his local library system to host special talks on pop culture collectibles. He also hosts movie screenings at his store or lets shoppers' children play video games on vintage consoles while parents shop. Researching before you start collecting and selling is one of the smartest moves you can make

for the long-term health of your collection and your pocketbook. Here are a few other tips to consider to start you on your way:

HEAD OUT – Visit shops, shows, auctions, and flea markets. Take the time to chat with the clerk behind the counter or the auctioneer behind the podium. Most everyone collects something and you might be surprised at how gratifying it can be to learn something new about your interests.

JOIN A COLLECTING CLUB – Active clubs issue newsletters filled with practical information on fakes and reproductions as well as offer an instant marketplace for hard-to-find items.

READ, READ, READ – From pottery and porcelain to Star Wars figures, reference books are available on thousands of topics. Take the time to build a strong reference library and you'll avoid costly missteps, scams, and dishonest sellers.

And that's where this reference guide comes in. In this year's edition we've expanded and updated the most popular sections and added new ones, too. You'll notice special attention is drawn to the very best items pursued by collectors as **Top Lots!** Special features show why some categories are irresistible to collectors. We've also been on the road – like many of you – meeting dealers, auctioneers, collectors, and show managers who gave us the scoop on what's really happening in the hobby. You'll see their smiling faces along with their top tips, opinions, and observations under the header "Inside Intel" located in various chapters across this new edition. We hope this helps you get to know the people behind the prices as well as teach you something new about the precious objects you collect.

A book of this magnitude is a team project and many thanks is owed to editor Mary Sieber; Antoinette Rahn, editor, online editor, and content manager of *Antique Trader* magazine; Karen Knapstein, print editor of *Antique Trader* magazine; designer Jana Tappa; Editorial Director Paul Kennedy; and several specialists and contributors. Ever the professionals, they work year round to make this book the best it can be. Their patience, hard work, and great ideas are always focused on one goal: selecting the topics, images and features our readers will find the most fascinating. We hope you enjoy the results. As always, we welcome your thoughts and comments on this and future editions. Feel free to reach out at ATpriceguide@fwmedia.com.

— *Eric Bradley*

Antique Trader.

ABOUT ANTIQUETRADER.COM

We think you'll be impressed with the layout, sections, and information in this year's annual. Because the antiques world (like everything else) is constantly changing, I invite you to visit AntiqueTrader.com and make it your main portal into the world of antiques.

Like our magazine, AntiqueTrader.com's team of collectors, dealers and bloggers share information daily on events, auctions, new discoveries, and tips on how to buy more for less. Here's what you'll find at AntiqueTrader.com:

Free eNewsletters: Get a recap of the world of antiques sent to your inbox every week.

Free classified ads: Discover inventory (great and small) from around the world offered to buy, sell or trade.

Expert Q&A columns: Learn how to value and sell your collections online and for the best prices.

The Internet's largest free antiques library: Dig into thousands of articles on research, prices, show reports, auction results, and more.

Blogs: Get vital how-to information about topics that include selling online, buying more for less, restoring pieces, spotting fakes and reproductions, displaying your collections, and finding hidden gems in your town!

Show guides: Check out the Internet's most visited antiques events calendar for links to more than 1,000 auctions, flea markets, conventions, and antiques shows worldwide.

Advertising

ADVERTISING ITEMS, with the exception of glass and ceramics, is the most diverse category in all of collectibles. Before the days of mass media, advertisers relied on colorful product labels, containers, store displays, signs, posters, and novelty items to help set their product or service apart from competitors.

In the United States, advertising became an art form during the boom years after World War II until well into the mid-1970s. The rise of the middle class and freely flowing dollars left us with a plethora of items to collect. These items represent the work of America's skilled and talented writers and commercial illustrators and give us an entertaining look into everyday life of the 19th and 20th centuries.

Interestingly, this demand is rippling through other categories, and a good example is toys. Vintage toys featuring company logos, slogans, ad characters and the like seem to be fetching higher prices compared to their non-branded counterparts. Marx toy gas pumps, tin toys, and even pull toys are enjoying more crossover appeal than ever before.

The arrival of large, carefully curated collections at auctions and at specialty shows is also renewing interest in advertising items. During the last two years alone, we've seen massive collections of tobacco tins, coffee tins, talcum powder containers, rarely seen syrup dispensers, and Coca-Cola memorabilia offered at auction. These large sales are increasingly offering grouped lots of up to 20 items, offering collectors the opportunity to purchase an interesting assortment of advertising items at one time.

The most popular pieces are sought after for one chief reason: eye appeal, according to William Morford, owner of William Morford Investment Grade Collectibles at Auction. Modern values "depend on the subject matter and the graphics – how powerful it is," he says. One of Morford's top lots during a spring 2014 auction was an unusual Marathon Motor Oil figural gallon can in the form of an early oil well from the Transcontinental Oil Co. of Pittsburgh. It had everything going for it: It is scarce, has good form, bright graphics, and – at 15-1/4" tall – it displays very nicely. The oil can hammered for an impressive $4,200 against a $100 opening bid.

"The advanced collector who has the resources knows it's a smarter move to buy the best ... and it's leaving all the lower end stuff behind. It's like the larger economy: Walmart and Target aren't doing so well, but Cartier and Tiffany are doing just fine," he says.

Wright & McGill Co.'s Eagle brand fishing tackle sign, paper lithography, excellent condition, 16" x 57" (13-1/8" x 54-1/4" visible). **$600**

William Morford Investment Grade Collectibles

ADVERTISING

Morford said another emerging trend is the popularity of male-centric items bringing higher than expected prices at auction. "Hunting, fishing, oil, gas, and cars, gambling – pretty much all of them are popular now," he adds. "The cutesy stuff, the flowery stuff doesn't seem to have the same audience right now."

The most heavily collected advertising pieces remain signs, especially those with porcelain graphics. Lately this segment also has become dominated by items in exceptional condition and by obscure examples. However, unlike other segments, some auctioneers are reporting interest in signs in poor condition, even if sale prices are low. It seems new collectors entering the hobby are seeking rusty, chipped examples made popular on television programs such as "American Pickers."

To learn more detailed information on advertising signs, see *Picker's Pocket Guide to Signs* (Krause Publications, 2014).

Durham-Duplex Safe Razor early tin litho sign by American Art Works for Durham Duplex razors and sharpening strops, multicolor lithography, excellent condition, 6-1/8" x 27-1/4".........................**$1,700**

William Morford Investment Grade Collectibles

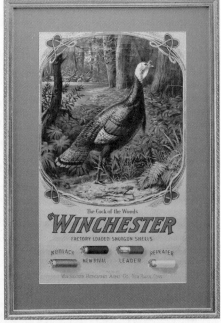

Poster, Winchester Repeating Arms Co. featuring Chesapeake retriever, circa 1906-1907, captioned "Self-Loading Shotguns For Fowl, Bird or Trap Shooting," very good to excellent condition, 15" w. x 25-7/8" h................ **$3,851**

James D. Julia Auctioneers

Poster, Winchester Repeating Arms Co., circa 1905, captioned "The Cock of the Woods," very good condition, 14-1/2" w. x 24-1/2" h...............**$4,740**

James D. Julia Auctioneers

Sign, Wincarnis Tonic and Nerve Restorative, circa 1904, porcelain enamel, 69" x 37". Wincarnis was a popular British drink that was founded in 1888. A smaller version of this sign was reproduced in the late 1980s. **$5,000**

Heritage Auctions

Early heavy porcelain sign for Selz brand shoes with image of company's feet characters, original Ingram-Richardson label on backside, excellent condition, 24" h. x 36" w.............................. **$950**

William Morford Investment Grade Collectibles

Large early, heavy enameled porcelain sign for Texaco Golden motor oil promoting company's crankcase service, excellent condition, 30" x 30"..................... **$1,300**

William Morford Investment Grade Collectibles

ADVERTISING

Ward's Lime-Crush figural lime soda fountain syrup dispenser with ceramic ball-type pump mechanism, near excellent condition, 13-1/2" h............. **$2,073**

James D. Julia Auctioneers

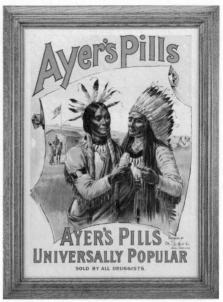

Poster, Ayer's Pills with Native Americans, stone lithograph, very good condition with professional restoration, scarce and iconic example from "Golden Age" of American lithography, 29" w. x 41" h. **$6,517**

James D. Julia Auctioneers

Hanging light, National Cigar Stand, circa 1910, stained glass pool table light in form of U.S. capitol, milk glass and stained glass, displays variety of cigar ads, both front and rear milk glass panels feature embossed lettering in blue, red stripes and white stars that reads "National Cigar Stand," milk glass side panels read "Black and White 5¢ Cigar" and "Lord Carver 10¢ / 3 for 25¢," very good to excellent condition, 23" w. x 21-1/2" h. x 11" d. **$1,066**

James D. Julia Auctioneers

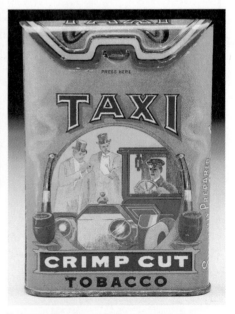

Pocket tin, Taxi Crimp Cut Tobacco, vertical, embossed roll top, taxicab graphics on both sides, considered a Holy Grail to tobacco tin collectors, near excellent condition, 4-1/4" h. **$3,792**

James D. Julia Auctioneers

Two scarce veterinary-themed cardboard signs, OH Mfg. Co., Lyndon, Vermont, "Standard Worm Balls" and "Arabian Scratches and Gall Salve," excellent condition, each 7-1/4" h. x 12-3/8" w. **$425**

William Morford Investment Grade Collectibles

TOP LOT!

Store display, Edison Mazda Lamps, electrified, working, two reverse on glass panels in metal housing, one side illustrates uniformed theater ushers holding colossal bulbs and other panel recommends them "For good light at low cost," very good condition, 20-1/2" w. x 13" h. x 7" d. **$1,007**

James D. Julia Auctioneers

Marathon Motor Oil important early hand-soldered figural tin litho one-gallon can in shape of early oil well, made by Transcontinental Oil Co., Pittsburgh, excellent condition, scarce, 15-1/4" h. x 6-1/2" w. x 6-1/2" d. **$4,200**

William Morford Investment Grade Collectibles

Early celluloid bridge game scorer advertising United States Tires with graphic monkey image on backside (turning counting wheels changes eyes and mouth of monkey on back), 2-1/4" x 3".............. **$70**

William Morford Investment Grade Collectibles

Eveready Flashlights three-piece cardboard holiday window display with Santa, marked Nov. 21, 1934, created as battery-powered motion display with Santa's hand waving Eveready flashlight, made by National Carbon Co., Jersey City, New Jersey, good condition, 20-1/2" w. x 13" h. x 7" d................**$177**

James D. Julia Auctioneers

Air Race Motor Oil early one-quart tin litho solder seam picture can for Deep Rock Oil Co.'s Air Race brand motor oil with airplane image, excellent condition, 5-5/8" h. x 4" dia. **$700**

William Morford Investment Grade Collectibles

Pocket tin, Luxura upright, made by Booker Tobacco Co. of Lynchburg, Virginia, interior scene with burgundy curtains and hookah pipe, near excellent condition, 4" h. **$2,488**

James D. Julia Auctioneers

Pocket tin, Cardinal Cut Plug, made by Myers Cox & Co., Dubuque, Iowa, red cardinal on front, near excellent condition, scarce, 4-1/2" h. **$1,896**

James D. Julia Auctioneers

Peerless Autos early cardboard advertising sign for The Peerless Eight automobile with hand colored-racing image, Walker Litho Co., Boston, very good condition, 17-1/8" x 24-5/8" (13-3/8" x 20-3/4" visible). Peerless, a Cleveland, Ohio automaker, was known for building high-quality precision luxury automobiles and hired racecar driver Barney Oldfield, who went on to set world speed records driving its Green Dragon racecar. **$3,500**

William Morford Investment Grade Collectibles

Sign, circa 1894-1907, Shenandoah Valley of Virginia, self-framed chromolithograph on tin, for Horsey & Atwell Outfitters, Winchester and Woodstock, 19" l. x 13" w... **$920**

Jeffrey S. Evans & Associates

Circus Club Marshmallows, set of six different tin litho product tins for Harry Horne Co.'s "Circus Club" mallow puffs, Toronto, Canada, each with circus animal image, 6 oz. size. **$1,050**

William Morford Investment Grade Collectibles

ADVERTISING

INSIDE INTEL

SIGNS

HOT: Feed signs are hot. Just about any farm sign, feed signs, implement or anything farm-related is in demand these days. Milk, bread, and especially ice cream signs are hot, too. The better the sign, the more [money] it brings. The sign makers all went out of business, but their signs last forever.

NOT: Coke has cooled off a bit, but when you find the good stuff you don't pass it up. There're a lot more reproductions out there now – a lot more. People look at the real stuff and say, "Wow, look at all the repros." When we tell them they're real, they tell us they can buy a repro around the corner for $20. Well, sure you can, but they're not ever going to be worth any more than $20.

— *Ron Garrett*
Collector/dealer, signs and advertising displays
Gilmer, Texas

Early celluloid advertising pocket mirror with branded Jell-O girl, scarce, excellent condition, 2-3/4" x 1-3/4".**$4,500**

William Morford Investment Grade Collectibles

Owl Cigar early two-sided cardboard die-cut sign, excellent condition, 11-1/2" x 7-3/4"................................**$775**

William Morford Investment Grade Collectibles

Early celluloid advertising pocket mirror for Western Ohio Creamery Co., Greenville, Ohio, with multicolor graphic image of farm girl feeding cows, scarce, excellent condition, 1-3/4" h. x 2-3/4" w. ... **$300**

William Morford Investment Grade Collectibles

Tray, Jacob Leinenkugel Brewing Co., Chippewa Falls, Wisconsin, tin litho promoting Chippewa's Pride brand, American Art Works, excellent condition, 13-1/2"..............**$100**

William Morford Investment Grade Collectibles

Figural metal tire-shaped advertising pocket knife for Pirelli's Superflex brand tires, excellent condition, 3-1/8" l. x 1" w. **$600**

William Morford Investment Grade Collectibles

Liberty Motor Oil early tin litho two-gallon motor oil can for Liberty brand, Radbill Oil Co., Philadelphia, images of Statue of Liberty all around, very good condition, 9" x 9-1/2" x 6-5/8"................................ **$210**

William Morford Investment Grade Collectibles

Five different cardboard boxes for rubber canning jar rings: Kamo; Excelsior; Tulip; Victor; and Farm & Home brands, excellent condition, approximately 3-1/4" x 3-1/8" x 1-1/4"...................... **$100**

William Morford Investment Grade Collectibles

Tin, Powow Brand Salted Peanuts, 11 lb. capacity, made by F. M. Hoyt & Co., Amesbury, Massachusetts, American Indian Chief graphic, excellent condition, 8-1/4" dia. x 9-5/8" h................................... **$1,422**

James D. Julia Auctioneers

Great Puff Tobacco early cloth 1 oz. tobacco pouch, full, sealed, never opened, by B. Leidersdorf Co., Milwaukee, wraparound label, Series 1902 tax stamp, 3-1/2" x 2-1/4" x 1"............................. **$450**

William Morford Investment Grade Collectibles

Tin cafe clock to promote beverage St. Raphael Quinquina, windup brass clock movement, early 20th century, good condition, 19" dia. **$151**

James D. Julia Auctioneers

Heinz products brass-trimmed leather-bound salesman's presentation catalog with several fold-out sections that feature large multicolor graphic images of product jars, crocks, cans, bottles, etc., circa 1910, excellent condition, 11-1/2" x 8-1/2" x 1-1/2".................. **$525**

William Morford Investment Grade Collectibles

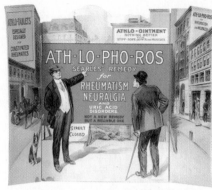

Athlo Medicines early cardboard tri-fold stand-up display advertising "Ath-lo" brand patent medicine products, with multicolor lithography (American Litho Co., New York), excellent condition, 18-7/8" x 28-1/2". **$675**

William Morford Investment Grade Collectibles

Two early tin litho spice tins: Oak Hill 2 oz. nutmeg by Hall Co., Brockton, Massachusetts, excellent condition, 4-1/2" h. x 1-1/2" dia.; White Villa brand 2 oz. turmeric by White Villa Grocers, Cincinnati and Dayton, Ohio, excellent condition, 3-3/4" h. x 2-1/4" w. x 1-1/4" d. **$40**

William Morford Investment Grade Collectibles

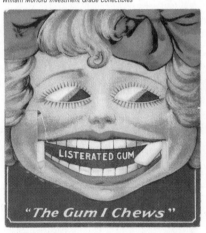

Early tin litho countertop display for Buss brand auto fuses, excellent condition, 7-1/4" x 8-5/8" x 3-1/8". **$625**

William Morford Investment Grade Collectibles

Listerated brand chewing gum early cardboard mechanical advertisement (squeezing card from top and bottom creates an animated up and down chewing motion in child's mouth, while at same time changing her eyes), excellent condition, 4" h. x 3-7/8" w. **$70**

William Morford Investment Grade Collectibles

Early unusual three-way tin litho store sign for Star brand chewing tobacco with image of early tobacco plug, with tin vertical strips on front side that show three different messages when viewed from varying angles: views show words STAR TOBACCO, CHEW, and SOLD HERE, with printed text advertising on backside, excellent condition, 4-1/4" x 18-1/5". **$2,700**

William Morford Investment Grade Collectibles

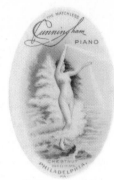

Early tin litho one-quart crimp seam motor oil picture can from Golden West Oil Co., San Antonio, Texas, excellent condition, 5-5/8" x 4" dia. **$3,300**

William Morford Investment Grade Collectibles

Pearlicross Spice early tin litho tin, allspice, for Pearlicross brand, York, Pennsylvania, with multicolor graphic image, same on both sides, excellent condition, 3-1/4" h. x 2-3/8 w. x 1-3/8" d. **$550**

William Morford Investment Grade Collectibles

Early celluloid advertising pocket mirror for Cunningham Pianos, Philadelphia, with image of nude in ocean waves, excellent condition, 2-3/4" h. x 1-3/4" w. **$650**

William Morford Investment Grade Collectibles

Large tin-over-cardboard advertising button-style sign for DuPont Co.'s Peters brand sporting ammunition, excellent condition, 8-3/4" dia. **$775**

William Morford Investment Grade Collectibles

Two-piece cardboard product box for Babe Ruth brand athletic underwear, circa 1920s, with image of famous slugger, excellent condition, 12-3/4" h. x 9-7/8 w. x 2-1/2" d. **$300**

William Morford Investment Grade Collectibles

Baby Rice Pop Corn unusual early tin litho one-pound tin with multicolor graphics, different images both sides, full, sealed can, excellent condition, 4-5/8 h. x 3-3/8" dia. **$575**

William Morford Investment Grade Collectibles

Match holder, Detroit Stove Works Co.'s "Crown Jewel" brand stoves, large, heavy figural cast iron with embossing, excellent condition, 5-1/2" x 6-3/4" x 5-1/2" **$200**

William Morford Investment Grade Collectibles

Two early wooden cigar boxes with multicolor graphic labels: "American Editors" (8-1/2" x 6-7/8" x 5-1/4") with *New York Herald, Tribune* and *Sun* newspaper editors pictured under respective mastheads, and "Hattie Tom" (7-3/4" x 8-3/8" x 5-1/8") with image of Indian princess, excellent condition. **$40**

William Morford Investment Grade Collectibles

Early cardboard hanger sign on heavy cardstock for A No.1 Co. Chocolate Brownies penny candies, with images of Palmer Cox Brownie characters, excellent condition, 8-3/8" h. x 8-1/2" w. **$1,000**

William Morford Investment Grade Collectibles

Set of 10 Heinz pickles early cardboard die-cut bookmarks promoting various Heinz Co. products, excellent condition, sizes range from 7/8" x 3-5/8" to 5-1/8" x 1-3/4". **$230**

William Morford Investment Grade Collectibles

Auto Service celluloid pocket mirror with multicolor graphic image of nude and cherubs, scarce, excellent condition, 2-1/8" dia. **$650**

William Morford Investment Grade Collectibles

Five Log Cabin Syrup and nut tins: Towle's Log Cabin Syrup – "Express Office," 4-5/8" w. x 4-5/8" h.; Towle's Log Cabin Syrup – "Frontier Jail," 3-5/8" w. x 3-5/8" h.; Towle's Log Cabin Syrup – "Home Sweet Home" later version with scenes on side panels, 3-5/8" w. x 3-5/8" h.; Towle's Log Cabin Syrup – "Home Sweet Home" 1919-1927 early version without printing on sides, 3-5/8" w. x 3-5/8" h.; and "The Nut House" peanut log cabin tin, 2-1/2" w. x 2-1/4" h. **$91**

James D. Julia Auctioneers

Pair of large, early driving gloves with advertising on each for Buick motorcars, heavy, canvas-type cloth material, 24" l. x 8-1/4" w. **$650**

William Morford Investment Grade Collectibles

Sign, Monarch Paints, early double-sided wooden painted wall-mount with display pedestal coming from hand area made for holding/displaying gallon-sized paint bucket, excellent condition, 18-1/4"l. x 14-3/4" h. x 3/4" w. **$4,000**

William Morford Investment Grade Collectibles

Letter opener, Planters Peanuts Co., early, metal with heavy detailed inlaid cloisonné enameled images of Mr. Peanut on both sides, excellent condition, 9 l. x 1-3/8" w. **$300**

William Morford Investment Grade Collectibles

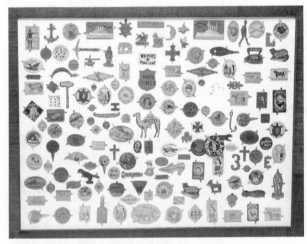

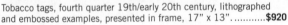

Tobacco tags, fourth quarter 19th/early 20th century, lithographed and embossed examples, presented in frame, 17" x 13". **$920**

Jeffrey S. Evans

Black Cat Cigarettes early, heavy enameled porcelain over metal advertising ashtray with glass-covered metal revolving dice gambling mechanism at top, likely Canadian or British, excellent condition, 6" dia.................... **$325**

William Morford Investment Grade Collectibles

Brotherhood brand overalls early celluloid pocket mirror with image of topless girl putting on coveralls, excellent condition, 2-1/8" dia. **$275**

William Morford Investment Grade Collectibles

Asian Art & Artifacts

ASIAN ART (AKA EASTERN ART) is highly prized by collectors attracted to its fine workmanship and exquisite attention to detail, plus the undeniable lure of the exotic.

Often lumped under the generic header "Oriental," Asian art actually embraces a wide variety of cultures. Among the many countries falling under the Asian/Eastern art umbrella: Bali, Bhutan, Cambodia, China, India, Indonesia, Japan, Korea, Laos, Thailand, Tibet, Vietnam, and the Pacific Islands. Also in the mix: art forms indigenous to the native cultures of Australia and New Zealand, and works of art celebrating the traditions of such Eastern-based religions as Buddhism and Hinduism.

The influence of Eastern art on Western art is strong. As Western artisans absorbed the cultural traditions of the East, stylistic similarities crept into their work, whether subconsciously or deliberately. (The soft matte glazes popularized by Van Briggle Pottery, for example, resulted from founder Artus Van Briggle's ongoing quest to replicate the "dead" glazes of the Chinese Ming Dynasty.)

Chinese porcelain was one of the first representations of Asian art to entice buyers in the United States; export of the ware began in the 1780s. Japanese porcelain, originally billed as "Nippon," began to make its way to U.S. shores near the end of the 19th century. Early Chinese porcelain was often distinguished by a liberal use of blue and white; Japanese porcelain, by a similar reliance on floral and landscape motifs. Consumers found the products of both countries desirable, not only because of their delicacy, but also because pieces of comparable quality were not yet available domestically.

Chinese famille rose porcelain footed bowl, 18th century, 5" h. x 11-1/8" dia...........................$3,250
Heritage Auctions

Porcelain was not the only outlet for Eastern creativity. Among the many other materials utilized: ivory, jade, bone, hardstone, marble, bronze, brass, gold, silver, wood, and fabric (primarily silk). Decorative treatments ranged from cloisonné (enamel sections in a pattern of metal strips) to intricate hand carving to the elaborate use of embroidery, gilt, and lacquer.

Asian art in any form offers a unique blend of the decorative and the functional. The richness of the materials and treatments utilized transforms even everyday objects into dazzling works of art. Among myriad items receiving this Cinderella treatment: bowls, vases, planters, chess sets, snuff bottles, rugs, robes, tapestries, tables, trays, jars, screens, incense burners, cabinets, and tea caddies. Even a simple item such as an oil lamp could be reborn through imaginative artistry: A Chinese version from the 1920s, its exterior worked in cloisonné, emerged as a colorful, ferocious dragon.

This multitude of products makes Asian art an ideal cross-collectible. Some may be interested only in the output of a specific country or region.

Carved ivory ball, Japan, 19th/20th century, decorated in relief with three Daoist Sennin, including Koreijin with tiger and Juronjin with deer, in natural scene with mountain, bird, waterfall, bamboo, and rocks, stained in brown, with carved wood stand, ball 2-1/4" dia., stand 2-1/4" h.... **$900**

Skinner, Inc., www.skinnerinc.com

Others may be drawn to a specific type of collectible (kimonos, snuff boxes, depictions of Buddha). There will even be those attracted solely to pieces created from a specific material, such as jade, ivory, or porcelain. Aficionados of any of these categories have a lifetime of collecting pleasure in store.

The timeline of Asian art is a long one, with value often determined by antiquity. Due to age and rarity, minor flaws (jade nicks, porcelain cracks, and chips) are not generally a detriment to purchase. Any restoration should only be done by a professional, and only after careful analysis as to whether or not restoration will affect value.

Asian art continues to be produced and imported today at an overwhelming rate (and often of "souvenir-only" quality). Collectors seeking museum-quality pieces are strongly advised to purchase only from reputable dealers, and to insist on proof of provenance. A Chinese gilt bronze figure of Vajrasattva, with an incised "Xuande" mark, sold for more than $1.5 million at auction. Modern replicas fetch considerably less.

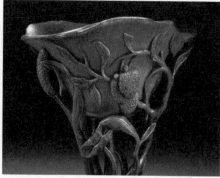

TOP LOT!

Important rhinoceros horn "Magnolia" cup, China, 17th/18th century, tapered ovoid form depicting hollowed magnolia, exterior sides carved with branching magnolia blossoms intertwined with branches of lychee, branches forming reticulated handle are tied at base with magnolia branch, horn of rich caramel color deepening to darker brown at center of cup and ends of exterior bound branches, with stand, 7" h. The combination of magnolia and lychee symbolizes wishes for a rich and noble home with many sons. Provenance: Small New England museum. $122,400

Skinner, Inc., www.skinnerinc.com

Chinese calligraphy with signature, 19th century, 25" w. x 19-1/2". Provenance: American Asian Art Gallery...$2,800

Capitoline Auction Gallery

Chinese Dehua Guanyin figurine with deer and flowers, 19th century, 25-1/2" h. Provenance: American Asian Art Gallery **$1,100**

Capitoline Auction Gallery

Pair of Chinese ivory figurines, 19th century, 19" h. Provenance: American Asian Art Gallery.... **$2,100**

Capitoline Auction Gallery

Kodai-ji lacquer letter box, Japan, late 17th century, lid and box decorated with gold and silver foil in hiramaki-e and takamaki-e on sprinkled gold ground with flowering paulownia branches on diagonal ground of fine branches, diagonal design extends onto interior of lid and box, lid also depicting courtier playing flute seated on horse, silk tassels mounted with shakudo metal baskets, 8-1/2" l. **$1,800**

Skinner, Inc., www.skinnerinc.com

$

Japanese painted porcelain charger on wood stand, early 20th century, 16" dia................... **$406**

Heritage Auctions

Bronze bust of Buddha, Thailand, possibly Ayutthaya period, face cast in serene expression, with elongated ear lobes, hair in tight curls, ushnisha topped by flaming finial, robe draped over left shoulder, mounted on wood stand, overall 18" h. **$1,560**

Skinner, Inc., www.skinnerinc.com

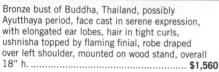

TOP LOT!

Jade censer, China, 19th/20th century, small globular shape incised in low relief with scrolling lotus and tendrils, reverse-scroll handles rise from base of body supported by three lion-mask feet, pierced lid with scrolling lotus and tendrils, finial in form of flower, pale celadon stone, 6" dia............................ **$2,160**

Skinner, Inc., www.skinnerinc.com

Cloisonné and Zitan armchair, China, back and arms set with cloisonné plaques of figures in landscapes with rivers, mountains, pine trees, and pavilions, seat with cloisonné plaque with five vignettes of figures in landscapes against blossom-patterned ground with lotus and ruyi border, exterior of arms and apron carved with stylized lotus blossoms and ruyi-scrolls, supported on four legs set into base stretcher, 40" x 42" x 27"...**$11,880**

Skinner, Inc., www.skinnerinc.com

Portrait painting, China, in manner of Jin Shangyi (b. 1934), depicting Western man in three-quarter right side view, white ground, signed, oil on canvas, framed, 17" x 14-3/4". Provenance: From former New England Center for Contemporary Art (NECCA) in Brooklyn, Connecticut **$5,100**

Skinner, Inc., www.skinnerinc.com

Gourd cricket cage with ivory cover, China, 19th/20th century, domed, reticulated ivory cover pierced with bats amidst clouds, waisted body carved in low relief with pair of mandarin ducks in lotus pond with flourishing lotus plants, fitted with wide ivory rim, four-character Daoguang mark on base, 8-1/2" h................ **$4,500**

Skinner, Inc., www.skinnerinc.com

Pair of painted porcelain and gilt bronze mounted foo dog table lamps, 20th century, 19" h **$1,875**

Heritage Auctions

Southeast Asian carved and painted panel, 37" x 17" **$148**

Pook & Pook, Inc.

Cloisonné jardiniere, China, 19th century, decorated with dragons chasing flaming pearls among clouds, band of lotus leaves encircles top, band of waves at bottom, brass rim and bottom, 21" h. x 22-1/2" dia.................................... **$1,800**

Skinner, Inc., www.skinnerinc.com

Unfinished blue dragon robe, China, 19th/20th century, with alterations, eight gold couched dragons amidst clouds and auspicious emblems, with bats, dragon-fish, and peonies floating in rolling waves above lishui border at hem, 48-1/2" h **$5,228**

Skinner, Inc., www.skinnerinc.com

Painting depicting Heavenly Peach Banquet, China, 20th century, with angry monkey under peach trees with seven worried fairies watching, from Chinese opera, "Monkey: Journey to the West," based on a novel, *Journey to the West*, signed with a seal, color on cotton or flax, hanging scroll, 40" x 33-3/8" **$1,353**

Skinner, Inc., www.skinnerinc.com

Set of four embroidered panels (two shown), China, 19th/early 20th century, Suzhou-style, depicting birds amidst bamboo and trees with peonies, chrysanthemums, and plum blossoms, with inscriptions above, brocade border added, 46" x 12"... **$2,760**

Skinner, Inc., www.skinnerinc.com

Two Japanese cloisonné enamel footed plates and stands, late 19th century, 12" dia **$563**

Heritage Auctions

Huge Chinese Famille Rose vase, 19th century, 24" h. Provenance: American Asian Art Gallery **$2,300**

Capitoline Auction Gallery

Jade brush washer with cover and stand, China, 19th/20th century, four-lobed lozenge-shape, two carved chilong at rim, exterior decorated with horizontal bar of incised swirl design in center, white-green jade with white and russet markings, cover in shape of matching lobed lozenge, domed top carved with cloud motifs, stand decorated with openwork cloud and scroll designs, 3-3/4" h. (jade, 2-1/8"), 4-3/4" w. **$10,200**

Skinner, Inc., www.skinnerinc.com

Famille Rose pink-ground vase, China, 19th/20th century, bottle shape, bats interspersed with leafy stalks of lotus, iris, peony flowers on pink sgraffito ground incised with scrolling tendrils, with turquoise enameled base and interior, six-character Qianlong mark on base, 11-1/4" h **$2,160**

Skinner, Inc., www.skinnerinc.com

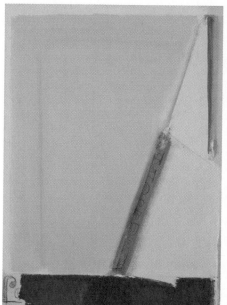

Abstract painting with blue, orange, and green, Japan, Minoru Kawabata (1911-2001), acrylic on canvas, signed on verso "M. Kawabata," 39" x 52"... **$3,360**

Skinner, Inc., www.skinnerinc.com

Framed Famille Rose painted porcelain plaque, China, early 20th century, with woman seated beneath willow tree in fenced garden, surrounded by children, with inscription regarding motherhood on left side, 20-3/4" x 13", wood frame 28-1/2" x 20-1/4".. **$2,040**

Skinner, Inc., www.skinnerinc.com

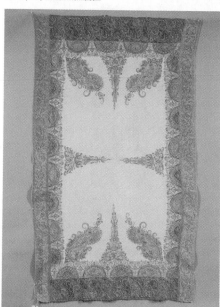

Kashmir Jamawar-type shawl, India, 19th century, rectangular, with polychrome woven border of palmettes, floral mosaic boteh, and scrolling foliage, with eight tendrils of similar design extending into quilted cream-colored center, 72" x 44"... **$1,200**

Skinner, Inc., www.skinnerinc.com

Woodblock, "Woman with Hawk," Japan, Munakata Shiko (1903-1975), with hand-applied color, dated "1956.9.25," signed in pencil Munakata, sealed, nampo no in, 18-1/8" x 14-1/8". **$10,200**

Skinner, Inc., www.skinnerinc.com

Monumental Japanese porcelain vase on stand, 19th century, marks to underside: (script), 31" h. with stand... **$6,250**

Heritage Auctions

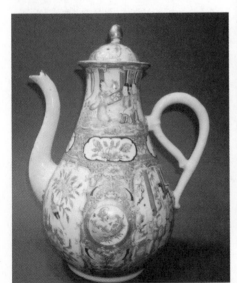

Large Chinese Rose Medallion teapot, 19th century, 10" h. Provenance: American Asian Art Gallery. **$300**

Capitoline Auction Gallery

Ivory and wood tea tasting cane, circa 1900, system cane has ivory handle etched with Chinese characters and outdoor scene, ivory collar and malacca wood shaft with metal ferrule and tip, handle twists from shaft to reveal compartment with removable brass tea straw, 36-1/4" l. overall. **$1,375**

Heritage Auctions

Painting of birds of various kinds flying in and out of trees, China, in manner of Lin Liang (1424-1500), depicted in boneless style, with numerous seals including Qianlong, Jiaqing, and Xuantong, accompanied by calligraphic works including four-character calligraphy at front and four at end, all signed with two to three seals, ink on paper, hand scroll, 13" h. x approximately 500" w., with nine 49-3/4" w. papers joined together for painting with seal on each join. **$6,000**

Skinner, Inc., www.skinnerinc.com

Ivory netsuke of face, Japan, 19th century, carved in flattened oval shape with loose eyes popping from eye sockets, incised, colored, and stained, ivory with distinctive grain, signed "Hiroyuki," 2-1/8" h **$420**

Skinner, Inc., www.skinnerinc.com

Ivory netsuke of rodent, Japan, 18th/19th century, sitting with its tail in its mouth, ivory with stained and incised details, signed "Okatori" to base, 2" l. **$615**

Skinner, Inc., www.skinnerinc.com

Ivory netsuke of basket, Japan, 19th/20th century, with fish inside, incised details lightly stained with fish eyes in black, patina along one side, signed "Gyokuseki" to side, 1-1/8" h. **$420**

Skinner, Inc., www.skinnerinc.com

Ivory netsuke of dog, Japan, 19th/20th century, sitting, ear incised with fine lines and stained in black, face with big eyes and tongue out, four paws carved in bas-relief on base, ivory glazed and with unique grain, signed "Tomoichi" to base, 1-1/2" h. **$780**

Skinner, Inc., www.skinnerinc.com

ASIAN ART & ARTIFACTS

Two ivory netsuke creatures, Japan, 19th/20th century: octopus coming out of jar, stained in red-brown tones, signed "Tomomitsu" to base, 1-7/8" h.; carving of snake and two frogs in hibernating underground, with incised and stained details, fine patina, signed "Tomoyuki" to base, 1-7/8" h.. **$431**

Skinner, Inc., www.skinnerinc.com

Ivory netsuke of Yokai Monster, Japan, 19th/20th century, carving of Nure-onna, snake-like creature with head of woman, intertwined with monkey on her back, with stained and incised details, ivory with fine patina, 1-3/4" w **$200**

Skinner, Inc., www.skinnerinc.com

Three ivory netsuke figures, Japan, 19th/20th century: seated man with mask, signed "Koushin," 1-5/8" h.; smiling man holding fish on string with both hands, unsigned, 2" h.; and old man with cane carrying boy on his back, signed "Chutomo," 2" h **$660**

Skinner, Inc., www.skinnerinc.com

AUTOGRAPHS

Autographs

IN *THE MEANING AND BEAUTY OF AUTOGRAPHS,* first published in 1935 and translated from the German by David H. Lowenherz of Lion Heart Autographs, Inc. in 1995, Stefan Zweig explained that to love a manuscript, we must first love the human being "whose characteristics are immortalized in them." When we do, then "a single page with a few lines can contain the highest expression of human happiness, and... the expression of deepest human sadness. To those who have eyes to look at such pages correctly, eyes not only in the head, but also in the soul, they will not receive less of an impression from these plain signs than from the obvious beauty of pictures and books."

Alfred Hitchcock signature beneath self-portrait sketch **$1,250**

Nate D. Sanders

John M. Reznikoff, founder and president of University Archives, has been a leading dealer and authority on historical letters and artifacts for 32 years. He described the current market for autographs as "very, very strong on many fronts. Possibly because of people being afraid to invest in the market and in real estate, we are seeing investment in autographs that seems to parallel gold and silver."

Reznikoff suspects that Civil War items peaked after Ken Burns' series but that Revolutionary War documents, included those by signers of the Declaration of Independence and the Constitution, are still undervalued and can be purchased for under $500.

Currently, space is in high demand, especially Apollo 11. Pop culture, previously looked at as secondary by people who dealt in Washingtons and Lincolns, has come into its own. Reznikoff anticipates continued growth in memorabilia that includes music, television, movies, and sports. Babe Ruth, Lou Gehrig, Ty Cobb, and Tiger Woods are still good investments, but Reznikoff warns that authentication is much more of a concern in sports than in any other field.

The Internet allows for a lot of disinformation and this is a significant issue with autographs. There are two widely accepted authentication services: Professional Sports Authenticator (PSA/DNA) and James Spence Authentication (JSA). A dealer's reliability can be evaluated by seeing whether he is a member of one or more of the major organizations in the field: the Antique Booksellers Association of America, UACC Registered Dealers Program, and the National Professional Autograph Dealers Association (NPADA), which Reznikoff founded.

There is an additional caveat to remember and it is true for all collectibles: rarity. The value of an autograph is often determined less by the prominence of the signer than by the number of autographs he signed.

—Zac Bissonnette

AUTOGRAPHS

Apollo 11 crew photo signed by Neil Armstrong, Buzz Aldrin and Michael Collins, 8" x 10"..............**$7,200**

Collect Auctions

Photo of Rosa Parks while sitting on the bus in 1955, 8" x 10".. **$180**

Collect Auctions

Photo of Teddy Roosevelt with signature, dated "Jan 17th 1908," while he was president of the United States, matted to 6" x 9-1/2" **$1,130**

Collect Auctions

NASA National Aeronautics and
Space Administration

Crew of Space Shuttle
Mission 51-L

Color NASA photo of crew of Challenger Mission 51-L in blue flight suits holding helmets, signed in black felt tip by all seven crew members: Ellison Onizuka, S. Christa McAuliffe, Greg Jarvis, Judy Resnik, Mike Smith, Dick Scobee, and Ronald E. McNair, 8" x 10" **$4,640**

Collect Auctions

First Day Cover of Orville and Wilbur Wright, signed by Orville in black ink, postmark dated May 14, 1938 .... **$468**

Collect Auctions

Peter Yarrow, Paul Stookey, and Mary Travers, known as Peter, Paul and Mary singing group, signed black and white photo, 8" x 10" **$173**

Goldin Auctions

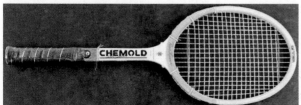

Arthur Ashe signed Chemold pro model tennis racquet **$437**

Iconic Auctions

One-page handwritten letter dated Oct. 4, 1828, in the hand of Noah Webster, who published the first edition of *American Dictionary of the English Language* the same year this letter was written.
.... **$1,850**

Collect Auctions

Typed letter dated "August 11, 1936," signed by Henry Ford in black ink **$700**

Collect Auctions

Jesse Owens signed photo, inscribed in black felt tip pen "36 Olympics," 8" x 10" **$260**

Collect Auctions

EMCE Toys, The Twilight Zone doll signed by Richard Kiel in black Sharpie, "Kanamit" under signature **$83**

Collect Auctions

Charlie Sheen signed OML Selig baseball, inscribed "#99," number he wore in "Major League" movies. **$465**

Goldin Auctions

Photo of Jim Parsons from "The Big Bang Theory," signed in blue Sharpie, 8" x 10" **$137**

Collect Auctions

Langston Hughes signed album page with inscription, "Dayton, March 19, 1940." Hughes (d. 1967) was an American poet, social activist, novelist, playwright, and columnist, best known as a leader of the Harlem Renaissance. **$323**

Goldin Auctions

George "Buddy" Guy signed black Fender Squire six-string electric guitar, black ink on white front panel **$565**

Goldin Auctions

AUTOGRAPHS

Bill Clinton signed
hardback book, *Giving
– How Each of Us Can
Change the World* ...**$259**

Goldin Auctions

Mick Jagger signed British Airways boarding pass for
Goldberg R Concorde flight from London's Heathrow
Airport to JFK airport in New York, approximately
5-1/2" x 3" **$525**

Goldin Auctions

Famed comedic troupe Marx Brothers signed MGM
contract, dated Dec. 2, 1937, signed on signature
lines, "Chico Marx," "Harpo Marx," and "Groucho
Marx" in black ink. Contract delineates payments to
each of the Marx brothers for $3,450 .... **$2,500**

Nate D. Sanders

Albert Einstein's signature, "A. Einstein / 1946" on slip of paper **$2,063**

Nate D. Sanders

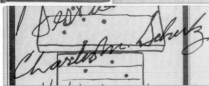

Charles Schulz signed *Snoopy and the Red Baron* book, published by Holt, Rinehart & Winston, New York, 1966; Schulz inscribed pictorial flyleaf, "Best wishes - / Charles M. Schulz." **$375**

Nate D. Sanders

Norman Rockwell signed print of painting he composed for *Ladies Home Journal* in 1972 of presidential candidate Richard Nixon and his wife, Pat, signed at bottom in black felt tip pen, 10-1/2" x 13-3/4" **$625**

Nate D. Sanders

Three-time World Champion and 1968 Olympic gold medalist figure skater Peggy Fleming signed ice skate. **$625**

Nate D. Sanders

Truman Capote glossy photo, signed and inscribed by author in black ink at top left, 8" x 9" **$625**

Nate D. Sanders

Ernest Hemingway signed check, filled out entirely in his hand and dated Oct. 15, 1952, just weeks after publishing his Pulitzer-prize winning novel, *The Old Man and the Sea*.. **$1,250**

Nate D. Sanders

"Desert Fox" Erwin Rommel signed postcard, in heavy pencil on edge **$1,250**

Nate D. Sanders

Dale Earnhardt, Jr. worn and signed racing suit, signed in metallic color pen to left of Budweiser brand name on front. **$9,375**

Nate D. Sanders

Harry Houdini signed studio photograph dated 1914, 4-7/8" x 6-7/8" **$2,271**

Legendary Auctions

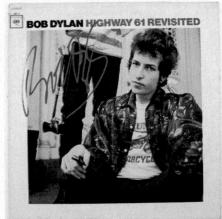

Bob Dylan signed "Highway 61 Revisited" record album, signature obtained in early 1990s by employee of famed Bleeker Bob's record store in New York City.. **$5,020**

Iconic Auctions

Margaret Hamilton signed photo; Hamilton played the Wicked Witch in "Wizard of Oz."................ **$956**

Legendary Auctions

Millard Fillmore free frank signed "M. Fillmore" as president-elect of United States, envelope postmarked "Washington D.C. Oct 15," no year, but styling of postmark dates to 1850 .... **$500**

Nate D. Sanders

Jimmie Foxx signed guest member card for The Denver Press Club, 1950s.............................. **$515**

SCP Auctions

Marilyn Monroe scarce, handwritten, and signed early bank check from 1953 .... **$3,257**

Iconic Auctions

AUTOGRAPHS

$

Martin Luther King, Jr. signed letter with March On Washington and "I Have a Dream" references, only known letter with direct "Dream" reference.
....**$27,456**

Iconic Auctions

Beatles signed 1963 "The Beatles & Roy Orbison" concert program, Paul and Ringo in black, John and George in blue, 10-1/2" x 7-3/4".........**$23,271**

Iconic Auctions

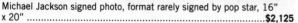

Michael Jackson signed photo, format rarely signed by pop star, 16" x 20" **$2,125**

Iconic Auctions

Adolf Hitler signed document, dated on his 47th birthday, April 20, 1936, 8-1/4" x 11"... **$3,185**

Iconic Auctions

Banks

MOST COLLECTIBLE BANKS are designed for one purpose: to encourage children to save money. How well the bank accomplished this task makes all the difference in making it collectible by later generations.

Manufactured from the late 1800s to the mid-1900s, mechanical, still, and register banks (which indicate the value of the coins deposited) are marvels of ingenuity made of tin, lead or cast iron. Although banks come in all makes and functions, the most desirable banks employ a novelty or mechanical action when a coin is placed inside. Banks are sought after because they so efficiently represent the popular culture at the time they were made. This is evident in the wartime registering banks sporting tin lithographic decorations of superheroes or animation characters or the cast iron figures that propagated racial stereotypes common from 1880 to 1930. Many early cast iron bank models have been reproduced during the years, especially in the 1950s and 1960s. A key indicator of a reproduction is fresh, glossy paint or dull details in the casting.

According to 10 years of sales data on LiveAuctioneers.com, most mechanical banks sell at auction for between $500 and $1,000. Morphy Auctions is the world leader in selling mechanical banks, offering more than 5,800 at auction during the last 11 years alone. The

Six lithographed tin banks: mechanical house bank, West Germany, with child at counter accepting money, insert coin, push tray, and money disappears into bank, with original trap and key; copyright 1905 register coin bank by Shonk, Chicago, deposit coin, swing lever down to tally total amount of coins deposited; growing bank, England, black man with exaggerated facial features strumming banjo, remove hat, deposit coins, and bank grows in height with weight of money; circus dog tin bank originally containing Mallow Puff candy; German tin coin register bank, tin litho of children at play, insert coin, slide lever, and bank tallies deposited amount, retains trap; and Uncle Sam's Budget Bank in original box by Durable Toy Co., New York, facade of bank shows four different windows for keeping tally on accumulated coins, each compartment designated for different budget; very good+ condition, all mechanical functions working, largest 7". **$365**

James D. Julia, Inc.

most important collection sold at auction so far is the Stephen and Marilyn Steckbeck Collection offered in October 2007. The top lot of the collection was an exceptional "Jonah and the Whale" mechanical bank, which realized $414,000. The $7.7 million collection still holds records for the most valuable banks ever sold, and they continue to dominate headlines whenever a piece from the Steckbeck collection is resold. In September 2012, Morphy's auctioned an early Freedman's mechanical bank of a seated figure, measuring 10-1/2" high, with Steckbeck provenance, for $117,500.

A collection as fine and complete as the Steckbeck Collection hasn't come to auction since, but that doesn't mean fine examples are not coming to market. "There are a dozen

Jonah and the Whale mechanical bank attributed
to Shepard Hardware, deep red base with gold
lettering and yellow supports and moldings,
top is simulated ocean in sea green with white
highlights, multicolored boat, gray whale with
painted eyes and teeth, very good original
condition with scattered paint chips and general
wear, lacking trap, 10-1/4" l. x 3-1/2" w. x 5" h.
Based on biblical story in which Jonah, who is
holding coin, is being fed to whale; when bank
is activated, whale's bottom jaw flaps open and
closed. **$1,185**

James D. Julia, Inc.

Cast iron "Calamity Bank," J. & E. Stevens Co.,
Cromwell, Connecticut, circa 1905, depicting
collegiate football at beginning of 20th century,
two defense tacklers from Harvard (crimson
details) and fullback from Yale (blue details).
Wearing only nominal protective gear, many
football players sustained serious injuries.
President Teddy Roosevelt viewed this situation
as very dangerous. He planned to incorporate
abolition of collegiate football as part of his
platform for re-election in 1904.............**$37,650**

RSL Auction Co.

or so collections that I know of that would bring over $1 million," said Dan Morphy, owner and founder of Morphy Auctions. "There are dozens of other bank collections that would fall in the six figure ranges."

However, it is apparent that collectors are holding out for those special examples. The number of fine banks offered at auction does not appear to be increasing. In fact, many auctioneers have taken to grouping banks together in order to push lot values over several hundred dollars, although this is only true with lesser quality or common banks.

Morphy says condition – like all other categories of collecting – is king. "Banks in top condition seem to be the trend these days," he said.

So, on the basis of affordability, now is the time to start a collection. "I always tell new collectors that they should buy what they like," Morphy said. "Even if you pay a little more than you should for a bank, the value in the enjoyment of owning it will more than offset the high price one may pay."

A top on Morphy's list to offer at auction is a "Darkey & the Watermelon" mechanical bank. Otherwise known as the Football Bank, it was designed and patented by Charles A. Bailey, June 26, 1888. Known as the leader in mechanical bank design, Bailey's "Darkey & the Watermelon" bank incorporated all of his imagination and design talents: When the right leg of a figure is pulled back into position, a coin is then placed in a small football; a lever in the figure's coattails is pressed and the football with coin is kicked over into a large watermelon. Only one or two of these banks are known to exist.

"That would be my dream bank," Morphy said, "in that I would also want to buy it!"

Like their predecessors crafted nearly 150 years ago, contemporary banks blur the line between tool and toy. Some modern banks that may make interesting collectibles in the future include digital registering banks that tabulate coin and paper money deposits or those licensed by famous designers. But beware, antique banks are still being reproduced and can be found very cheaply at lesser-quality flea markets or sold online.

For more information on banks, see *The Official Price Guide to Mechanical Banks* by Dan Morphy, 2007, morphyauction.com.

TOP LOT!

Cast iron palace bank, Ives Blakeslee Co., Bridgeport, Connecticut, circa 1885, deluxe polychromed version, original owner's name and address on back, "Horace Marion Fulton 1211 Vt. Ave.," factory crack in finial.........................**$40,787**

RSL Auction Co.

Ten cast iron mechanical and still banks: Kyser & Rex apple; gold sitting rabbit; small double-faced black boy with gold highlights; standing rooster; playing cat with gold ball; mechanical rabbit (flip ears to deposit coin) with trap; sitting dog on platform; standing black farmer; mechanical Santa at chimney; and standing gold cow; fair to good paint, standing rooster with excellent paint, Santa mechanical with poor paint, tallest 6". **$1,823**

James D. Julia, Inc.

Sixteen metal building banks: Four 3" cast iron banks, one house, three bank buildings; two 5-1/2" cast iron buildings, both marked "BANK"; three 4-1/4" cast iron banks, two marked "STATE BANK"; four bank buildings, 6", one with mechanical locked front door, another reads "HOME SAVINGS BANK"; silver-plated tin bank marked "Denmark," depicts Hansel and Gretel's candy house; cast iron barn bank with very good original paint in red and white; and largest building bank, 7", marked "STATE BANK"; no breaks, chips, or cracks, finishes in good to very good condition with largest building bank in near excellent condition, tallest 7"....................................... **$1,541**

James D. Julia, Inc.

Cast iron frog and bicycle bank, J & E Stevens Co., Cromwell, Connecticut, circa 1886, white blanket with red lettering, coin is placed on top of rear wheel, frog does somersaults when lever is pressed...**$34,787**

RSL Auction Co.

Seven still banks and one novelty mechanical bank: Five various safe-type banks in original finish from good to very good condition; painted bank building; die-cast Boston Federal Savings bank; and original novelty bank with no apparent cracks or damage to iron castings; good to very good condition, novelty bank with replaced spring lever cover on underside, 3" to 7".................... **$948**

James D. Julia, Inc.

Left to right: Cast iron J. M. Harper, Chicago Illinois, circa 1907. Provenance: Andy & Susan Moore Collection...... **$5,800; $5,400; $7,100; $6,200**

RSL Auction Co.

Dog and hoop bank, Hubley Manufacturing Co., circa 1896, coin is placed in dog's mouth, touching lever causes dog to jump through hoop and deposit coin in barrel, excellent plus condition, 9" l........................$720
Morphy Auctions

Hand-painted bank, wooden back, winds up and tin figures dance, very good condition, 5-1/2" h. $1,140
Morphy Auctions

Cast iron dog bank, J & E Stevens Co., circa 1880, coin is placed on dog's nose and is swallowed when tail is pulled...............$13,282
RSL Auction Co.

Dog and hoop bank, Hubley Manufacturing Co., circa 1920, mint plus condition, 8-1/2" l..............$1,920
Morphy Auctions

Cast iron political satire bank, John Harper, Ltd., England, circa 1885, probably depicts Paul Kruger of Boer War era, includes original pipe. Provenance: Andy and Susan Moore collection. $6,500
RSL Auction Co.

Cast iron bust of Abraham Lincoln bank, J.M. Harper, Chicago, circa 1907, one of two known. $8,157
RSL Auction Co.

Cast iron building bank, unknown maker, circa 1890, marked "Oakes Pat. Appld. For" on base plate. Provenance: From the Robert Peirce collection..........$11,922
RSL Auction Co.

Cashier and vault bank, J & E Stevens Co., designer C.C. Johnson, patented Oct. 28, 1879, white, after cashier receives coin, slight touch causes door to close and coin is deposited in vault, excellent condition, 6-1/2" h. $450
Morphy Auctions

Cast iron bank, J & E Stevens Co., circa 1915, when coin placed in slot at top of head, figure sticks out his tongue and rolls his eyes..................$24,035
RSL Auction Co.

Cast iron bank, Kenton Hardware, Kenton, Ohio, circa 1915, painted silver and gold, tiny casting flaw at top.........$11,922
RSL Auction Co.

Frog bank, Kilgore Manufacturing Co., Westerville, Ohio, designer Elizabeth Cook, circa 1920s, push lever and frog opens mouth, insert coin in mouth and release lever, mint plus condition, 3-1/2" l. $1,020
Morphy Auctions

Sewing machine bank, "American Bank" in raised letters, turn crank and sewing machine wheel and needle go up and down, near mint condition, 5-1/2". Provenance: Bob McCumber collection. $28,800
Morphy Auctions

Cast iron horse bank, unknown maker, circa 1890, one of two known, horse rocks when coin is placed in slot in mane. **$16,700**

RSL Auction Co.

Lithographed tin fortune-telling bank, unknown maker, London, circa 1920s, when coin is placed in slot, dial spins and lands on fortune. **$4,100**

RSL Auction Co.

Horse bank, J & E Stevens Co., all original, original box with complete label, box lid missing one small section, near mint condition, 6-1/2" l. **$52,800**

Morphy Auctions

Cast iron hen and chicks bank, J & E Stevens Co., circa 1901, coin is placed in slot in front of hen, chicks appear when lever is raised and coin is deposited................ **$5,060**

RSL Auction Co.

Native American and bear cast iron mechanical bank with nodding head native firing coin into moving mouth of standing bear, J & E Stevens Co., patented 1888, missing coin trap, heavy patina over all original paint, chipping to chin area of Indian and paint loss to feather area, mechanism working, 10-1/2" l. **$1,823**

James D. Julia, Inc.

Cast iron girl skipping rope bank, J & E Stevens Co., circa 1890, wind up and girl skips 12-15 times, exceptional condition. **$22,500**

RSL Auctions Co.

German spelter and tin Mickey Mouse bank, circa 1930. . **$2,866**

RSL Auction Co.

Cast iron Uncle Sam Bank, Shepard Hardware Co., Buffalo, New York, circa 1886, coin is placed in Uncle Sam's hand and drops into satchel when lever depressed......................**$27,830**

RSL Auction Co.

Cast iron bull and bear bank, J.M. Harper, Chicago, circa 1905, one of three known, bull and bear fight over bag of grain. Provenance: From the former Bert Whitings collection. .**$26,000**

RSL Auction Co.

Barbie

AT THE TIME of the Barbie doll's introduction in 1959, no one could have guessed that this statuesque doll would become a national phenomenon and eventually the most famous girl's plaything ever produced.

Over the years, Barbie and her growing range of family and friends have evolved with the times, serving as an excellent mirror of the fashion and social changes taking place in American society. Today, after 55 years of continuous production, Barbie's popularity remains unabated among both young girls and older collectors. Early and rare Barbie dolls can sell for remarkable prices, and it is every collector's hope to find a mint condition #1 Barbie.

Brunette Barbie #1 in box, hair topknot in original set but missing rubber band, end of ponytail reset, fingernails repainted, little or no paint remains on toenails, some discoloration on feet where tops of shoes rest, original black-and-white striped swimsuit, black slide-style, high-heeled shoes, blue-lensed and white-framed sunglasses and booklet, box discolored, splits at three corners, original Gimbels price tag, reproduction earrings and stand. **$2,300**

McMasters Harris Apple Tree Doll Auctions

Blonde Ponytail Barbie #1 in original box, 1959, with Ruth Handler signature, doll autographed on back torso by Handler, original swimsuit, earrings and sunglasses, stand and shoes not original, doll and box in near mint condition. **$2,900**

Theriault's Antique Doll Auctions

Blonde Barbie #1 in box, probably professional restoration to hair and facial paint, touch-up to nails, black and white strapless swimsuit, original earrings, sunglasses and mule-style black heels with holes, original box worn but intact and includes original liner. **$2,200**

McMasters Harris Apple Tree Doll Auctions

◄ Brunette Ponytail Barbie #1, 1958-1959, in "Evening Splendour" (No. 961) dress and coat ensemble, V-shaped brows, original hoop earrings and mule-style shoes, doll and stand in excellent condition. **$3,100**

Theriault's Antique Doll Auctions

► Blonde Ponytail Barbie #1 dressed in "Wedding Day" ensemble (No. 972), 1958-1959, strapless satin gown with full lace overlay, pearl necklace, shoes, wrist-length gloves, bouquet, pearl earrings and pearl-trimmed headpiece with veil, tops of toes of left foot missing, one shoe split. **$1,300**

Theriault's Antique Doll Auctions

Brunette Barbie #2, 1959, in original black and white striped strapless swimsuit, sunglasses and black mule-style heels, V-shaped brows, red lips and solid feet, first-year "Gay Parisienne" ensemble (No. 964) with blue and white polka dot dress, fur trim and blue hat, missing coordinating clutch purse, excellent condition **$2,100**

Theriault's Antique Doll Auctions

Blonde Ponytail Barbie #2 in original box labeled "Dressed Doll" and "Golden Elegance," 1958/1959, in ensemble with all accessories, original stand, box slightly worn, doll in near mint to mint condition..... **$1,700**

Theriault's Antique Doll Auctions

TOP LOT!

Barbie #2 "Wedding Day" set in box (No. 872), blonde hair reset, end of ponytail fuzzy, minor loss to eyelashes, tagged costume in good condition, gold-beaded headpiece, white satin dress with sweetheart neckline and long-sleeved lace overlay, wrist-length gloves, lace-wrapped bouquet of pink and white flowers, pedestal stand and replaced earrings, missing pearl necklace, box with original liner, lid splits at corners with tape residue ... **$5,000**

McMasters Harris Apple Tree Doll Auctions

Brunette Ponytail Barbie #3, circa 1960, in "Sweater Girl" ensemble (No. 976) in original Dressed Display Box with original stand, two-piece coral sweater set, pearls, gray pencil skirt and black mule-style heels, basket with yarn, knitting needles and scissors, instruction booklet, excellent condition. **$1,400**

Theriault's Antique Doll Auctions

Brunette Ponytail Barbie #3, 1960, in original black and white striped strapless swimsuit, earrings, black mule-style heels and sunglasses, with original box autographed by Ruth Handler on lid, doll and box in near mint condition. **$1,300**

Theriault's Antique Doll Auctions

Brunette Barbie #3 in tagged dress, ponytail reset and makeup retouched, wear and possible touch-up to nails, doll's skin retains some original pink skin tone, apple print sheath dress with TM tag, open-toe shoes. **$400**

McMasters Harris Apple Tree Doll Auctions

Brunette Ponytail Barbie #5, 1961, in red swimsuit with original stand, booklet, wrist tag and red shoes (in cellophane pack), in original box autographed by Ruth Handler, near mint condition. **$500**

Theriault's Antique Doll Auctions

Three different vintages of Ponytail Barbies (two blonde, one brunette), 1960-1962, each with curled bangs, black and white swimsuit and sunglasses, brunette with mule-style shoes, dolls in very good to excellent condition. **$900**
Five-piece 1950s-era "Mattel Modern" Danish-style furniture set, circa 1960, sofa with four original cushions, arm chair with two original cushions, coffee table in original box, and table lamp, excellent condition. **$200**

Theriault's Antique Doll Auctions

Platinum-haired Bubblecut Barbie with side part in original box, hard-to-find hairstyle, replaced earrings, repainted nails, box in good condition, wire stand and booklet, replaced liner. $500

McMasters Harris Apple Tree Doll Auctions

Brunette Bubblecut Barbie in red swimsuit, 1961, with wrist tag, cellophane packaging containing booklet and red shoes, in original box autographed by Ruth Handler, excellent condition. $400

Theriault's Antique Doll Auctions

Titian Bubblecut Barbie, 1961, in "Orange Blossom" ensemble of pale gold sleeveless yellow dress with white lace overdress, floral corsage, wrist-length gloves and open-toed white shoes (No. 987, 1962), missing hat. $200

Brunette Bubble Cut Barbie, 1961, with original earrings and pearl necklace, in "Country Club Dance" ensemble (No. 1627, 1965), white and gold dress with gold and white striped bodice, white skirt and white and gold trim, open-toed white shoes, gold clutch and elbow-length white gloves. $200

Theriault's Antique Doll Auctions

Brunette Bubblecut Barbie in box, in "Career Girl" ensemble of black and white patterned short-sleeve skirt suit with matching rose-decorated hat, red shell and black elbow-length gloves and black mule-style heels, red swimsuit and red mule-style heels, box in good condition with missing paper on left side and upper front cover, doll stand and booklet included.....$175

McMasters Harris Apple Tree Doll Auctions

Barbie Sparkling Pink gift set in original box, 1963 set, Bubblecut Barbie with five-piece pink satin and glitter dots bolero, blouse, coat and wrap skirt, excellent condition, some wear to box, doll's wrist tag torn $550

McMasters Harris Apple Tree Doll Auctions

BARBIE

American Girl Barbie with bendable knees and brunette bobbed hair with bangs in original box, 1965, original swimsuit with turquoise bottom and multicolored striped top on pink background, wrist tag, cellophane package with turquoise shoes, excellent condition. **$500**

Theriault's Antique Doll Auctions

Color Magic Barbie in original sealed box, Mattel No. 1150, 1966, excellent condition, bendable knees, red hair, blue eyeliner and coral lips, in original multicolored, harlequin-patterned one-piece swimsuit and head-band, with wrist tag, original hair coloring and accessories, remnants of Two Guys sticker on front cellophane. **$1,000**

Theriault's Antique Doll Auctions

Color Magic Barbie in original box, Mattel No. 1150, 1966, excellent condition, bendable knees, blonde hair, blue eyeliner, in original multicolored, harlequin-patterned one-piece swimsuit and headband, with wrist tag, cellophane wrap intact around doll's head, in original box with all accessories (including color magic changers A and B) and booklet. **$850**

Theriault's Antique Doll Auctions

Barbie Swirl Ponytail doll, titian-haired with fuzziness at end of ponytail, some paint loss to lips, faint polish on toes and repainted fingernails, discoloration at earring holes, wearing Country Club Dance ensemble. **$225**

McMasters Harris Apple Tree Doll Auctions

Fashion Queen Barbie set in original box, unplayed-with condition, gold and white striped swimsuit and hair wrap, blonde, brunette and red-headed wigs in cellophane wraps, doll's original wrist label intact, cellophane off box with minor staining at bottom..... **$375**

McMasters Harris Apple Tree Doll Auctions

BARBIE

Blonde Talking Barbie with bendable legs, Mattel No. 1115, 1969-1970, rooted eyelashes, blue eyes, coral lips and pull-string ring for talking, talking mechanism does not work, original coral-colored swimsuit and gold and coral sleeveless cover-up, in original box with wrist tag and original stand, excellent condition, box worn and bears marks. **$500**

Theriault's Antique Doll Auctions

Standard Brunette Barbie, Mattel No. 1190, 1969-1970, with straight hair, bangs, large blue eyes and pink lips, in original two-piece pink swimsuit and matching pink headband, in original box with booklet, excellent condition. **$500**

Theriault's Antique Doll Auctions

Brunette Barbie American Girl doll, center-part, bob-style hair in good condition, small paint voids on eyelashes, faint lip color, fingernail paint in good condition, knees work well, "Golden Elegance" ensemble with orange and gold brocade dress, coordinating coat with orange satin lining and fur trim on cuffs, fur headpiece, white wrist-length gloves, white hankie and brown mule-style heels, original one-piece swimsuit with blue bottom and multicolored tank-style top. . **$200**

McMasters Harris Apple Tree Doll Auctions

Mattel FAO Schwarz No. 91 Bob Mackie Le Papillion Barbie with artist-signed lithograph of doll in pink and black costume, never removed from box, doll in original unopened shipping box. **$100**

McMasters Harris Apple Tree Doll Auctions

BARBIE

BARBIE'S FRIENDS

Blonde Francie "Hair Happenin's" doll, Mattel No. 1122, 1970, with Twist 'n Turn waist and bendable knees, turquoise and white mini dress with crocheted sleeves and turquoise pumps, four interchangeable hair pieces, sealed in original box, excellent condition. **$500**

Theriault's Antique Doll Auctions

Black Francie with Twist 'n Turn waist and bendable knees, Mattel No. 1100, 1967, brown complexion, dark-brown hair with bangs, inset eyelashes, brown eyes and coral lips, in original multicolored and mesh swimsuit, in original box with plexiglass stand, no cellophane lid, excellent condition. **$650**

Theriault's Antique Doll Auctions

Twist 'n Turn Francie and Casey dolls with excellent condition hair and facial paint, Casey's face with slight yellow cast, knee joints hold pose, Casey in sleeveless dress with gold lamé bodice and peach skirt with gold lamé fishnet overlay, gold envelope-style clutch and peach flats; Francie in sleeveless pink dress with silver fishnet overlay, pink fishnet tights and pink flats, silver envelope-style purse..........**$200**

McMasters Harris Apple Tree Doll Auctions

Brunette Sunset Malibu Skipper doll with tanned skin and inset eyelashes, waist and knees work well, two-piece orange swimsuit with orange and yellow cover-up and pink sunglasses. **$1,600**

McMasters Harris Apple Tree Doll Auctions

Midge in original box, all original and near mint condition, dark blonde hair in original flip-style set, cellophane still around head, accessories and booklet in original cellophane, original wrist tag, two-piece suit, box clean with minor wear to corners and original liner, original store price tag on lid. **$125**

McMasters Harris Apple Tree Doll Auctions

Tiff and Twist 'n Turn Skipper, both wearing original outfits, Tiff in excellent condition with original wrist tag, sneakers and red skateboard, Skipper with original hair in pink and orange patterned swimsuit set. **$275**

McMasters Harris Apple Tree Doll Auctions

Blonde Ken doll with painted blonde hair and bendable legs, 1964, red trunks and blue and red short-sleeved jacket, excellent condition, with original box with cellophane pack containing booklet and sandals. **$400**

Theriault's Antique Doll Auctions

Platinum-haired Twist 'n Turn Stacey doll with bendable knees, Mattel No. 1165, 1967, coral lips and rooted lashes, original one-piece swimsuit with three buttons and cutout on front torso, plexiglass stand, wrist tag and booklet in sealed cellophane package and original sealed box, excellent condition... **$450**

Theriault's Antique Doll Auctions

Twist 'n Turn Julia doll based on Dihann Carroll character from same-named TV show, Mattel No. 1127, 1968, brown complexion and dark brown hair, rooted eyelashes, brown eyes, pink lips and bendable legs, in original nurse's uniform with coordinating cap and shoes, wrist tag and booklet, in original sealed box, cellophane punctured, excellent condition. **$358**

Theriault's Antique Doll Auctions

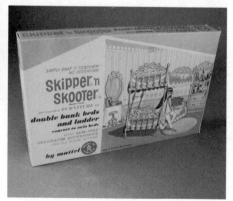

Skipper 'n Skooter Go-Together Furniture Kit with snap-together bunk bed set (converts to twin beds) with ladder, "Sew-Free Decorator Accessories" and "3-D Room Setting," still in plastic with unassembled pieces. **$200**

McMasters Harris Apple Tree Doll Auctions

MISCELLANEOUS

Katherine Baumann full-bead, multicolor crystal and pearl Barbie minaudiere evening bag with push-lock top closure and gold metallic leather interior, gold chain shoulder strap, excellent condition, minimal signs of use to interior, dust bag and extra crystals included, 3.5" w. x 6" h. x 4" d. **$1,375**

Heritage Auctions

Ken's Sports Plane with box, made by Irwin and licensed by Mattel, ivory-colored wings and cockpit seating, red instrument panel console and nose cone, silver-tone propeller and controls, and turquoise fuselage, identification letters and numbers in cream, plane detaches from wings to fit into box, all components intact, original box with normal wear with some crimping at corners, original assembly instructions tattered. **$1,400**

McMasters Harris Apple Tree Doll Auctions

Official Barbie speedboat by Irwin, plastic with wheels, made under license by Mattel for Barbie and Friends (Ken, Midge, Allan, and Skipper), piece broken off rear of boat but included, box in good condition with bend at rear. **$350**

McMasters Harris Apple Tree Doll Auctions

Nine-piece Barbie Dream Kitchen plastic play set by Deluxe Reading Corp., teal refrigerator, white sink, yellow stove with silver-tone range, brown dishwasher, various colored cabinets, white rectangular table and four chairs, cooking pans, Brillo pad box, Soap & Suds detergent box, milk bottle, towels, three plates, fruit, two cups and saucers, and boxes of Kellogg's Corn Flakes, Rice Krispies, and Nabisco Honey Grahams, played-with condition. **$150**

McMasters Harris Apple Tree Doll Auctions

ENSEMBLES

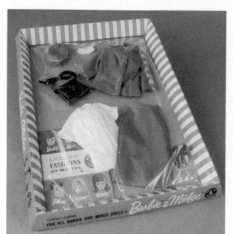

Barbie "Pan American Airways Stewardess" ensemble (No. 1678), hard-to-find set with original cellophane intact, box with minor wear to corners and crimping to bottom left corner and top edge, "299" stamped on bottom inner part of box, blue pencil skirt and matching six-button coat, short-sleeved shawl-collared white blouse, blue pillbox hat with white piping, white wrist-length gloves, black pumps and black flap-style purse with shoulder strap. **$1,900**

McMasters Harris Apple Tree Doll Auctions

Barbie "Poodle Parade" ensemble (No. 1643), never removed from box, cellophane intact, box wear and damage to side and bottom corner, creasing to upper corner, green and white harlequin-print coat with pink piping, green handbag with white handles and poodle graphic, pink scarf, pink dickie, green sheath-style dress, green pumps, sunglasses and trophy cup. **$425**

McMasters Harris Apple Tree Doll Auctions

"Sophisticated Lady" ensemble (No. 993), circa 1963, pink dress, elbow-length white gloves, pearls, tiara, shoes and dark pink wrap, sealed in original box, with original paper label sticker on side, mint condition. **$300**

Theriault's Antique Doll Auctions

"Solo in the Spotlight" ensemble (No. 982), circa 1960, black strapless mermaid-style evening gown with tulle bottom skirt, pink scarf, black elbow-length gloves and black shoes, sealed, in original box and with original paper label sticker on side, mint condition. **$350**

Theriault's Antique Doll Auctions

BASKETS

Baskets

THE AMERICAN INDIANS were the first basket weavers on this continent and, of necessity, the early Colonial settlers and their descendants pursued this artistic handicraft to provide essential containers for berries, eggs, and endless other items to be carried or stored.

Rye straw, split willow and reeds are but a few of the wide variety of materials used. Nantucket baskets, plainly and sturdily constructed, along with those made by specialized groups, seem to draw the greatest attention to this area of collecting.

Virginia tooled leather key basket, shaped rim and oblong form with "shark skin" sides and red-lined interior, probably made by S.S. Cottrell & Co., Richmond, Virginia........... **$1,680**

Jeffrey S. Evans & Associates

Pima basket with deep bowl form, circa 1900, tuning fork geometrics decorate upper third of basket, 7-1/2" h. x 18-1/4" dia. **$500**

Cowan's Auctions

Apache figural basket, circa 1925-1950, designed with central flower and eight dogs, outlined diamonds and banded rim, 3-1/4" h. x 12" dia.. **$850**

Cowan's Auctions

Yokuts basket, early 20th century, slightly flared walls and double zigzag band around midsection, three tick marks incorporated into basket wall, 9-3/4" h. x 21-1/2" dia............................... **$1,353**

Cowan's Auctions

California Mission figural basket, circa 1925-1950, decorated with three bees, cowboy, duck and flowers, bottom of basket detailed with four-pointed star, 3-3/4" h. x 6-1/2" dia................. **$615**

Cowan's Auctions

Reticulated gilt sterling basket with swing handle, 5" dia. Provenance: Property of Oprah Winfrey.. **$923**

Kaminski Auctions

Pima Olla basket with gila monsters and figures, 8" h. x 10-1/2" dia.. **$590**

California Auctioneers

Hupa basket, early 1900s, finer weave polychrome acorn basket with crisp geometric design, 5" x 5-3/4". **$660**

Allard Auctions, Inc.

Klickitat round lidded basket, circa 1900, very fine condition with fully imbricated exterior (may be Yakima), 8" x 9-1/2"... **$1,920**

Allard Auctions, Inc.

Large Japanese bamboo basket, late 19th century, pounded bamboo with insertions forming self-rim and twisted bamboo rope handle, with black stand, 24" x 22"......................... **$976**

Clars Auction Gallery

Navajo basket, 1930s, buffalo nickel button applied to center, 3" h. x 13-1/4" l.. **$738**

Kaminski Auctions

Abe Sanchez Mission 20th century basket, squat globular form woven with stair-stepped bands around body, flat shoulder and short neck, bottom of basket embellished with six paired birds and two single birds, 7" h............. **$1,845**

Cowan's Auctions

Pennsylvania rye straw basket, 19th century, bentwood handles, 6-1/2" x 18"......... **$972**

Pook & Pook, Inc.

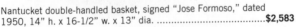

Nantucket double-handled basket, signed "Jose Formoso," dated 1950, 14" h. x 16-1/2" w. x 13" dia. **$2,583**

Kaminski Auctions

Ken Ferguson glazed stoneware Chief's basket, 1995, 13" x 13" x 12", signed and dated on underside.......................**$1,845**

Concept Art Gallery

Eskimo basket, 1950s, baleen basket with scrimshaw polar bear of walrus ivory on lid and ivory disk woven into bottom, 2-1/2" x 3-1/2"..................**$840**

Allard Auctions, Inc.

Southwest-style lidded woven basket. **$30**

EJ's Auction & Consignment

Miwok Burden basket, 24" x 21" **$1,416**

California Auctioneers

Tobacco picking basket, 20" x 15" x 18"............................**$68**

Gallery 95 Auction

Nantucket basket purse, stamped Boyer, carved ivory whale on lid, 6-1/2" h. x 8" w. **$1,336**

Pook & Pook, Inc.

Hickory rinsing basket, 19th century, footed stretcher base, 20" x 30"........................**$1,094**

Pook & Pook, Inc.

Apache Burden basket, Arizona, with tinkler drops, 12-1/2" x 9-1/4".................................**$395**

Old Barn Auctions

Painted split oak basket, 19th century, retaining old blue/gray surface, 11-1/2" h. x 10-1/2" w.......................................**$790**

Pook & Pook, Inc.

BASKETS

Lehigh County melon basket, painted red, 10"... **$295**

Hartzell's Auction Gallery

Irish silver basket, 18th century, with handle, 5" dia. x 6-1/2" h. to top of handle...................... **$984**

Grogan & Co.

Rye bee skep basket, 19th century, Pennsylvania, original sticks, 15". **$796**

Hartzell's Auction Gallery

Pennsylvania painted sewing basket with diminutive drawer in base, inscribed "J.J.F. no. 26 1838," 4-1/2" h. **$2,066**

Pook & Pook, Inc.

Hawkeye basket outdoor "refrigerator" used by actor Clark Gable, circa 1950s, with removable hinged top, initials C.G. stenciled on cover, interior lined with stainless steel, 15" x 19" **$840**

Hampton Estate Auction

Bookends

ONCE A STAPLE in many homes, bookends serve both functional and decorative purposes. They not only keep a person's books in order, they look good while they're doing it.

Bookends are commonly made of a variety of metals – bronze, brass, pewter, or silver plate – as well as marble, wood, ceramic, and other natural or manmade materials. The art they feature represents many subjects, with wildlife, domesticated animals and pets, sports figures or items, nautical themes, and fantasy themes as favorites.

The value of an antique bookend is determined by its age, the material it is made from, what it represents, the company that created it, and how scarce it is.

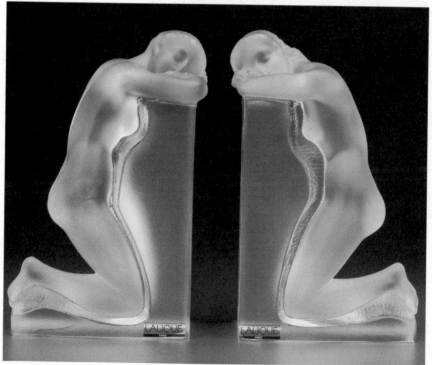

Lalique glass Reverie bookends, late 20th century, marks: Lalique, France, good condition in original box, 8-3/4" h. **$1,625**

Heritage Auctions

Owl bookends, bronze, each cast as owl standing on rocky outcropping, incised "Heinrich W. Hirschler" and impressed "MADE IN AUSTRIA," on verde marble plinths, 5" h **$600**

Skinner, Inc., www.skinnerinc.com

Bronze bookends, Newark, New Jersey, early 20th century, cast by Griffoul Foundry, chocolate brown patina, each with depiction of worker, 5-3/4" h **$180**

Skinner, Inc., www.skinnerinc.com

Kathodian Artbronz figural bookends of Native Americans, signed on verso KBW, 7-3/4" h **$385**

Pook & Pook, Inc.

Tiffany Studios bronze Zodiac
bookends, marked on base
"TIFFANY STUDIOS NEW
YORK 1091," 5-7/8" h **$350**

Case Antiques Auctions & Appraisals

French figural Faience
bookends, 6" h. x 4" w **$50**

Bill Hood & Sons Art & Antique Auctions

Jenfredware bookends, marked,
5-3/4" h. x 5-1/4" w. x 3" d.**$100**

Uniques & Antiques, Inc.

Rare cast iron cottage-form
bookends, circa 1920, original
paint, 5-1/4" h. x 4-1/2" w ... **$95**

Marion Antique Auctions

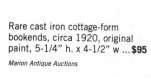

BOOKENDS

Roseville Magnolia bookends, No. 13, blue **$145**

Heritage Antiques & Auction

Plaster bookends of seated female nudes, both signed "C. Horsman" in plaster on top of bases, cast plaster with bronze-colored patina, with self bases, scattered chips and wear to surfaces, sizes to 10-1/2" x 4" x 8-1/4" **$70**

Skinner, Inc., www.skinnerinc.com

Nude bookends, bronze finish on base metal with faux marble bases, 7-1/2" h. x 6" w **$75**

Kraft Auction Service

Lalique figural crystal bookends, 5" x 8" x 6" .. **$550**

Lewis & Maese Auction Co.

Harriett Wallace bookends, circa early to mid-20th century, two bronze sculptures, one of soldier and other of sailor, both signed Harriet Wallace on back of base, 9" and 5-1/2"... **$650**

Akiba Antiques

Modernist wood slab
bookends, unmarked,
7-3/4" h. x 5-1/2" w.............**$40**

Uniques & Antiques, Inc.

Bronze polychrome cardinal
bookends, marble bases, 6-1/4"
h. x 3-1/2" w......................**$150**

Bill Hood & Sons Art & Antique Auctions

New Bedford Whaler bookends,
signed J.B., good condition, 7"
h. x 5" w. x 5-3/4" d...........**$140**

Marion Antique Auctions

Bronze pushing men bookends, 1911, natural dark patina, not a matched pair, signed Conti, 6-1/2" h **$1,400**

Marion Antique Auctions

Bronze elephant bookends on marble bases, 12" h **$200**

Bill Hood & Sons Art & Antique Auctions

Bronze and marble bookends, Octave Georges Lelievre (1869-?), signed, 6-1/8" h. overall x 3-1/2" w. x 2-11/16" d., figures 4-1/8" h **$450**

Antiques Supermarket Auctions

Art Deco ceramic bookends, each depicting busts of blonde-haired woman, very good condition with minor wear, 8" h **$30**

Morphy Auctions

Solid brass with enamel bookends, stamped "Terra Sancta Guild 1969," original felt bottoms, very good condition, 5-1/2" h. x 3-3/4" w **$53**

Heritage Auctions

Rookwood green rook bookends (one shown), dated 1953, shape #2275, designed by William McDonald, excellent condition, 5-1/4" h. x 5-1/4" w **$180**

Morphy Auctions

Rare Harriet Whitney Frishmuth bronze bookends of beautiful women in flowing dresses, signed Harriet W. Frishmuth and dated 1910 on base, excellent condition with original green felt backing and old patina, 9-1/2" h. x 5-1/2" w. x 3-1/2" d **$3,800**

Marion Antique Auctions

Egyptian bookends finished in gold foil, original felt bottoms, very good condition, approximately 7" h. x 8" w. x 3-1/2" d **$163**

Heritage Auctions

BOOKS

Books

WITH IN EXCESS of 100 million books in existence, there are plenty of opportunities and avenues for bibliophiles to feed their enthusiasm and build a satisfying collection of noteworthy tomes without taking out a second mortgage or sacrificing their children's college funds. With so many to choose from, the true challenge is limiting a collection to a manageable size and scale, adding only volumes that meet the requirements of bringing the collector pleasure and holding their values.

What collectors are really searching for when they refer to "first editions" are the first printings of first editions. Every book has a first edition, each of which is special in its own right. As Matthew Budman points out in *Collecting Books* (House of Collectibles, 2004), "A first represents the launching of a work into the world, with or without fanfare, to have a great impact, or no impact, immediately or decades later.Holding a first edition puts you directly in contact with that moment of impact."

Devon Gray, director of Fine Books and Manuscripts at Skinner, Inc., www. skinnerinc.com, explains the fascination with collectible books: "Collectors are always interested in landmarks of human thought and culture, and important moments in the history of printing."

What makes a first edition special enough to be considered collectible is rarity and demand; the number of people who want a book has to be greater than the number of books available. So, even if there are relatively few in existence, there has to be a demand for any particular first edition to be monetarily valuable.

Author Richard Russell has been collecting and selling books since 1973; in his book, *Antique Trader Book Collector's Price Guide*, he explains that innovative (or perhaps even unpopular) books that are initially released in small printings "will eventually become some of the most sought after and expensive books in the collector's market." He gives as an example John Grisham's *A Time To Kill* (Wynwood Press, 1989), which had an initial print run of just 5,000 hardcover copies. The author bought 1,000 himself at wholesale with the plan to sell at retail and turn a bit of profit. When Grisham couldn't sell them at $10 apiece, he was giving them away out of his law office.[1] The book is valued at about $4,000 today.

Learning how to recognize first editions is a key to protecting yourself as a collector; you can't take it for granted that the person you are buying from (especially if he or she is not a professional bookseller) has identified the book properly. Entire volumes have been written on identifying first editions; different publishing houses use different means of identification, many utilizing differing methods and codes. However, according to *Antique Trader Book Collector's Price Guide*, there are several details that will identify a first edition:

- The date on the title page matches the copyright date with no other printings listed on the copyright page (verso).
- "First Edition," "First Printing," "First Issue" or something similar is listed on the copyright page.

BOOKS

- A publisher's seal or logo (colophon) is printed on the title page, copyright page, or at the end of the text block.
- The printer's code on the copyright page shows a "1" or an "A" at one end or the other (example: "9 8 7 6 5 4 3 2 1" indicates first edition; "9 8 7 6 5 4 3 2" indicates second edition).

As is the case with so many collectibles, condition is paramount. If a book was published with a dust jacket, it must be present and in great condition to attain the book's maximum value. Gray uses an example to illustrate the importance of condition.

"A book with a very large value basically has farther to fall before it loses it all," she says. "A great example is the first edition of the printed account of the Lewis and Clarke expedition. In bad condition its value is in the four-figure range; in better condition, it gets up to five figures; and in excellent condition, six figures.

"Another example: The 1920 first American edition of T.S. Eliot's *Poems* sells for around $300 in poor condition with no dust jacket; and $1,200 to $1,500 in good condition in a good dust jacket; the copy that Eliot gave to Virginia Woolf sold for 90,000 British pounds [approximately $136,000]; all the same edition."

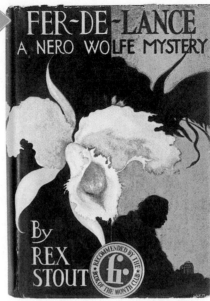

TOP LOT!

Rex Stout, *Fer-de-Lance*, New York: Farrar & Rinehart, 1934. First edition of author's first detective novel in unrestored, rare original dust jacket and first appearance of detective genius Nero Wolfe; 8vo, publisher's gilt-stamped black cloth, top edges stained red with one small blemish; pictorial dust jacket, 1" closed tears at bottom of front flap fold and spine panel front, small chip to top of rear panel, head of spine panel with small chip with tiny loss of top of "R" in title, mild finger-soiling, spine panel faded slightly but colors bright on front panel, unclipped with $2 price intact; interior clean and unmarked.
....**$21,250**

Swann Auction Galleries

A signature enhances a book's value because it often places the book in the author's hands. Cut signatures add slightly to a book's value because the author didn't actually sign the book – he or she may have never even held the book with the added cut signature. When the book itself is signed, even if with a brief inscription, it holds a slightly higher value. If the author is known for making regular appearances and accommodating all signature requests, the signature adds little to the value of the book because the supply for signed examples is plentiful.

"Real value potential comes into play with association material," Gray explains. "For example, a famous novelist's Nobel-winning story is based on a tumultuous affair he had with a famous starlet under his heiress-wife's nose, and you have the copy he presented to his wife, with her 'notes.'"

Even a title that has been labeled as "great," "important," or "essential" doesn't mean a particular edition — even a first edition — is collectible or monetarily valuable. After all, if a much-anticipated book is released with an initial print run of 350,000, chances

BOOKS

are there will be hundreds of thousands of "firsts" to choose from – even decades after publication. Supply far outweighs demand, diminishing value.

The overly abundant supply of book club editions (which can be reprinted indefinitely) is just one of the reasons they're not valued by collectors. Some vintage book club editions were also made from inferior materials, such as high-acid paper using lower quality manufacturing processes.

Determining if a book is a book club edition is easier than determining if it is a first edition. Some of the giveaways that Matthew Budman lists in *Collecting Books* include:

- No price on dust jacket
- Blind stamp on back cover (small impression on the back board under the dust jacket); can be as small as a pinprick hole
- "Book Club Edition" (or similar notation) on dust jacket
- Books published by the Literary Guild after World War II are smaller format, thinner and printed on cheap paper.

Fledgling book collectors should also be aware of companies that built a burgeoning business of publishing a copious number of "classic" and best-seller reprints; just a few of the long list are Grosset & Dunlap, Reader's Digest, Modern Library, A.L. Burt, Collier, Tower and Triangle. Many of these companies' editions are valued only as reading copies, not as collectibles worthy of investment.

Jane Austen, *Mansfield Park*, Philadelphia: Carey & Lea, 1832. First American edition, extremely rare in original binding, one of 1,250 copies printed, two volumes, four-page publisher's catalog inserted at front of volume 1, 8vo, original publisher's 1/4 cloth-backed drab boards, lettering labels on spines **$5,376**

Swann Auction Galleries

Proper care should be implemented early on when building a collection to assure the books retain their condition and value. Books should be stored upright on shelves in a climate-controlled environment out of direct (or even bright indirect) sunlight. Too much humidity will warp covers; high temperatures will break down glues. Arrange them so similar-sized books are side-by-side for maximum support, and use bookends so the books don't lean, which will eventually cause the spines to shift and cause permanent damage.

A bookplate usually will reduce a book's value, so keep that in mind when you're thinking of adding a book with a bookplate to your collection, and avoid adding bookplates to your own volumes. Also, don't pack your volumes with high-acid paper such as newspaper clippings, and always be careful when placing or removing them from the shelf so you don't tear the spine.

Building a book collection — or any collection, for that matter — on a budget involves knowing more about the subject than the seller. Learning everything possible about proper identification of coveted books and significant authors involves diligence and dedication, but the reward is maximum enjoyment of collecting at any level.

—*Karen Knapstein, Print Editor,* Antique Trader *magazine*

[1]John Grisham's Favorite Mistake: Giving Away First Editions, http:// www.thedailybeast.com/newsweek/2012/04/01/john-grisham-s-favorite- mistake-giving-away-first-editions.html

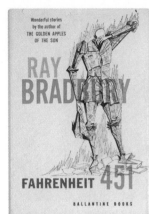

Jacques-Charles Bar (1740-1811), *Collection of Thirty Aquatints, Nuns, Priests, and other Religious* from *Recueil de Tous les Costumes des Ordres Religieux et Militaires,* Paris: Chez l'Auteur, 1778-1789. Folio, 30 hand-colored engraved plates with no text, slim volume, green half parchment and corners and mottled paper boards, with manuscript table inserted in front, very clean, 16-1/4" x 10-1/4" **$510**

Skinner, Inc., www.skinnerinc.com

Ray Bradbury, *Fahrenheit 451*, New York: Ballantine, 1953. First edition, 8vo, red boards lettered in yellow, covers bright and clean with minor rubbing to spine tips and corners; dust jacket, spine panel faded slightly, small nicks at corners, few minor short tears, unclipped; collector's custom cloth drop-back box **$1,375**

Swann Auction Galleries

Fredric Brown (1906-1972), *The Dead Ringer*, New York: Dutton, 1948. Stated first edition, red cloth publisher's binding, good dust jacket, spine slightly sunned, back panel with minor foxing, 8" x 5-1/4". Brown was an important and influential science fiction and mystery writer who gained the favorable attention of fellow writers from Ayn Rand to Philip K. Dick.............................. **$480**

Skinner, Inc., www.skinnerinc.com

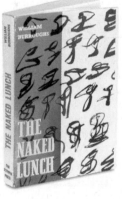

Charles Bukowski, *Hot Water Music*, Santa Barbara: Black Sparrow Press, 1983. 8vo, publisher's 1/4 striped cloth over printed paper boards, paper spine label, acetate jacket as issued, few light spots to top edges, clean and bright **$2,048**

Swann Auction Galleries

Edgar Rice Burroughs, *Thuvia, Maid of Mars*, Chicago: A.C. McClurg, 1920. First edition, first printing, publisher's green cloth, later Grosset & Dunlap dust jacket, rubbing to cloth extremities, jacket severely worn with wrinkles, tears, and tape repairs to verso, good condition **$100**

Heritage Auctions

William Burroughs, *The Naked Lunch*, Paris: The Olympia Press, 1959. First issue, inscribed by Burroughs on title page to fellow writer John Seelye, true first editions of *Naked Lunch* infrequently found inscribed, this is one of 5,000 copies; 8vo, original green wrappers, trace of rubbing to spine foot, originally priced wrappers and dust jacket, title-page with green typographic border. **$2,250**

Swann Auction Galleries

BOOKS

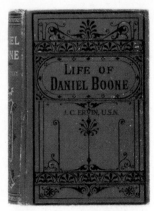

Thomas Godfrey, editor, *Murder for Christmas*, illustrated by Gahan Wilson, New York: Mysterious Press, 1982. First edition, limited to 250 copies, signed by editor and illustrator on limitation page, collection of "yuletide malfeasance" featuring works by Sir Arthur Conan Doyle, Charles Dickens, Robert Louis Stevenson, Agatha Christie, et al, publisher's red cloth and original dust jacket, fine condition, in slipcase......**$36**

Heritage Auctions

Cecil B. Hartley, *Life of Daniel Boone*, Philadelphia: Porter & Coates, 1865. Ownership stamps on boards and flyleaves, publisher's maroon cloth stamped in black with gilt titles, rubbing to extremities, some scratches to boards, hinges cracked, good condition **$81**

Heritage Auctions

Ernest Hemingway, *The Torrents of Spring*, London: Jonathan Cape, 1933. First edition, facsimile jacket, spurious author's signature to half-title page, publisher's yellow cloth over boards, boards severely rubbed with some foxing to fore-edge **$94**

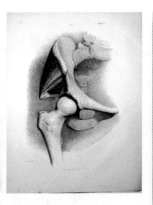

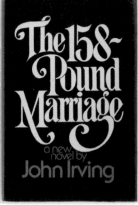

George William Hind, *Fractures of the Extremities*, London: Taylor and Walton, 1836. Series of 20 lithographed plates illustrating causes of displacement in various fractures of bones of extremities, second edition, corrected, folio, original cloth, backstrip chipped and repaired, missing portion at top, varying foxing, damp stain on last few plates **$500**

Swann Auction Galleries

John Irving, *The 158-Pound Marriage*, New York: Random House, 1974. First edition, publisher's binding in dust jacket, sticker remnants on front pastedown, jacket lightly rubbed with creases, very good condition **$65**

Heritage Auctions

William Shakespeare, *Twelfth Night*, wood-engraved title, borders and illustrations by Eric Ravilious printed in brown and grey-green, Golden Cockerel Press, 1932. 4to, original 1/2 morocco over pictorial cloth by Sangorski & Sutcliffe, mild edgewear, few scuffs and two small puncture holes to front cover; top edges trimmed and gilt, others uncut, number 274 from an edition of 275. Chanticleer 82. GG. Waltham St. Lawrence, 1932......... **$2,250**

Swann Auction Galleries

Harriet Beecher Stowe, *Uncle Tom's Cabin*, Boston: Houghton, Osgood and Co., 1879. New edition with illustrations and bibliography of work, octavo, 529 pages, illustrations throughout, publisher's cloth with gilt decorations and titles stamped in black, all edges gilt, edgeworn, very good condition...............**$59**

Heritage Auctions

The Book of Common Prayer, Oxford: T. Wright & W. Gill, 1773. 8vo, contemporary red Morocco gilt with English royal arms on covers and royal monogram in spine compartments, early 19th-century manuscript register of Scafe family on verso of front free endpaper, Althorp book label, two armorial bookplates of Charles Robert Spencer, sixth Earl Spencer (1857-1922), his initialed inscription on title: "C.R.S. given me by Margaret."............. **$1,875**

Swann Auction Galleries

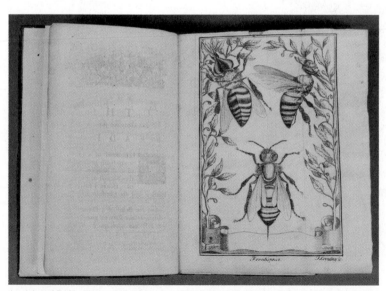

John Thorley (circa 1740), *Melisselogia* [Greek], or *The Female Monarchy. Being an Enquiry into the Nature, Order, and Government of Bees.* London: for the author, sold by N. Thorley and J. Advidson, 1744. First edition, octavo, illustrated by Loveday with folding frontispiece and four additional folding plates, as called for in explanation at end of text, in contemporary speckled sheepskin boards, rebacked, new end leaves, 7-1/2" x 4-1/2". **$431**

Skinner, Inc., www.skinnerinc.com

BOOKS

CHILDREN'S BOOKS

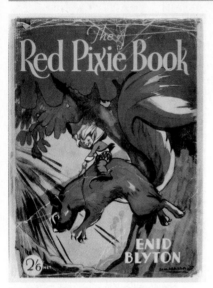

Enid Blyton, *The Red Pixie Book*, George Newnes Limited, circa 1934. First edition, illustrated by Katherine Nixon, publisher's original cloth and dust jacket...................**$138**

Heritage Auctions

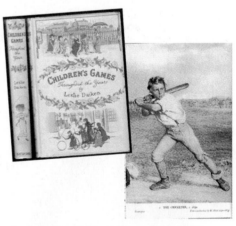

Jean De Brunhoff, group of four Babar books, Paris: Éditions du Jardin des Modes of New York, vd. illustrated by de Brunoff, folio, cloth-backed boards, condition varies but with usual edgewear, covers scuffed **$288**

Swann Auction Galleries

Leslie Daiken, *Children's Games Throughout the Year*, London: Batsford, 1949. ....**$16**

Laguna Book Auctions

Ingri and Edgar Parin d'Aulaire, *Abraham Lincoln*, Doubleday: Doran & Co., 1940. First edition, stone lithograph illustrations, publisher's original pictorial boards and dust jacket, very good condition **$138**

Heritage Auctions

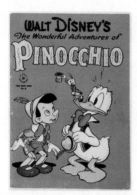

Walt Disney, Chase Craig and Walt Kelly, *The Wonderful Adventures of Pinocchio*, No. 92, Dell, 1946. Publisher's wrappers, near fine condition **$40**

Heritage Auctions

Walt Disney, *Stories from Walt Disney's Fantasia*, Random House, 1940. First edition, publisher's cloth/pictorial boards and dust jacket **$34**

Heritage Auctions

Zane Grey, Big Little Book, *King of the Royal Mounted and the Northern Treasure*, Whitman Publishing, 1937. Illustrated, small format, pictorial boards, very good condition **$16**

Heritage Auctions

Helena Maguire, Walter Paget, Lizzie Mack, et al, *Blue Eyes and Cherry Pies*, Ernest Nister and E.P. Dutton, circa 1900. First edition, illustrated, publisher's original pictorial boards, fair condition **$15**

Heritage Auctions

Olive Beaupre Miller, *Little Pictures of Japan*, Chicago: Katharine Sturges, 1925 .... **$14**

Laguna Book Auctions

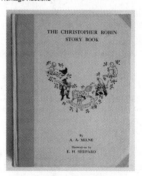

A.A. Milne, *The Christopher Robin Story Book*, New York, 1929. Illustrated throughout by Ernest H. Shepard, 8vo, publisher's 1/2 green cloth and pictorial salmon paper-covered boards, spine label (chipped), scattered spotting and light rubbing along edges, scattered soiling and splits between signatures, first limited edition, number 189 of 300 copies signed by Milne and Shepard............................. **$688**

Swann Auction Galleries

Dean O'Day, editor; *Shirley Temple Pastime Book*, The Saalfield Publishing Co., 1935. Authorized edition, dust jacket **$20**

Heritage Auctions

Dr. Seuss, *Horton Hears a Who!*, New York: Random House, 1954. First edition, publisher's binding and original pictorial dust jacket, jacket spine sunned, rubbing to panels, very good condition .. **$375**

Heritage Auctions

COOKBOOKS

The Lady's Companion. Containing Upwards of Three Thousand Different Receipts in Every Kind of Cookery, and those the Best and Most Fashionable; Being Four Times the Quantity of any Book of this Sort. London: J. Hodges and R. Baldwin, 1753. Engraved frontispiece depicting kitchen scene, eight engraved plates on four folding leaves, two volumes $1,375

Swann Auction Galleries

Souvenir Cook Book, compiled by the Women of Hadassah, New York: Business and Professional Group, Woodmere-Hewlett Chapter of Hadassah, 1951. Original handwritten recipes of Hadassah Jewish Women Organization **$300**

Kedem Auctions

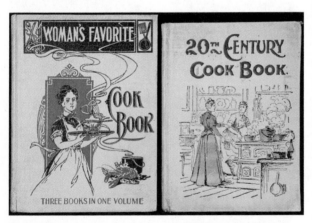

Two salesman's dummies for popular turn-of-the-century cookbooks: Annie R. Gregory, *Woman's Favorite Cook Book*, Philadelphia: American Book and Bible House, circa 1900, pictorial white cloth; Maud C. Cooke, *20th Century Cook Book*, Philadelphia: L.F. Elliott Co., circa 1900, pictorial white cloth. Each book has a selection of text and illustration pages, scarce sample copies for popular cookbooks sold by subscription **$100**

PBA Galleries

The New American Cook Book, Springfield: The Crowell & Kirkpatrick Co., 1899. Eight volumes, numerous illustrations in text, original pictorial paper wrappers. Early cookbook providing recipes for popular 19th century dishes and including bills of fare, glossary of terms................................ **$40**

Gray's Auctioneers

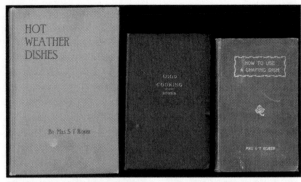

Mrs. S. T. Rorer, *Hot Weather Dishes*, brown cloth, 1888; *Good Cooking*, green cloth, 1898; *How to Use a Chafing Dish*, green cloth, new edition, 1894. Sarah Tyson Rorer was an instructor at the Philadelphia Cooking School and culinary editor of *Ladies Home Journal* **$70**

PBA Galleries

Sara Bosse and Onoto Watanna, *Chinese-Japanese Cook Book*, Chicago: Rand McNally, 1914. First Chinese and Japanese cookbook in America, original red cloth with color pictorial cover label, first edition, nearly 200 recipes **$250**

PBA Galleries

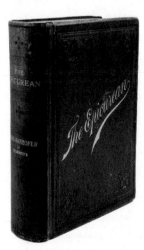

Mary and Vincent Price, *A Treasury of Great Recipes*, 1965. Rare first edition.........**$50**

Stover's Auctions

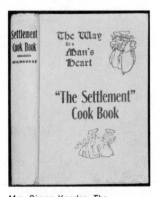

Mrs. Simon Kander, *The Way to a Man's Heart: The "Settlement" Cook Book*, Milwaukee: The Settlement, 1912. Fifth edition, original white cloth. One of the most celebrated charitable fund-raising cookbook ever published, the first edition was published in 1901 in an issue of only 1,000 copies and later editions followed rapidly. The book, with its common sense approach to food preparation and appetizing recipes for hearty Jewish Eastern European fare, is one of the most influential and financially successful American cookbooks of all time, having gone through 40 or more editions. All early editions are scarce, especially pre-World War I. **$180**

PBA Galleries

Southern Cook Book, Culinary Arts Press of Reading, Pennsylvania, 1939, contains 322 Old Dixie recipes. **$35**

Estate Auction Co.

Chas Ranhofer, *The Epicurean: A Complete Treatise of Analytical and Practical Studies on the Culinary Art Including Table and Wine Service*, New York: Charles Ranhofer, 1894. First edition, hundreds of woodcut illustrations within text, also additional illustrated title page, original blind-stamped cloth lettered in gilt **$200**

PBA Galleries

Harriet A. De Salis, *Oysters a la Mode; Or, The Oyster and Over 100 Ways of Cooking It*, London: Longmans, Green and Co., 1888. First edition, original cloth-backed boards. De Salis was the author of several similarly titled late 19th-century English cookbooks... **$250**

PBA Galleries

Abby C. Fisher, *What Mrs. Fisher Knows About Old Southern Cooking, Soups, Pickles, Preserves, Etc.*, San Francisco: Women's Co-operative Printing Office, 1881. First edition of second cookbook authored by an African American, original cloth, lettered in gilt on front, covers bordered with blind rules.. **$5,000**

PBA Galleries

Texas Cook Book, A Thorough Treatise on the Art of Cookery, edited by the Ladies Association of the First Presbyterian Church, Houston, 1883. First edition of first cookbook published in Texas, original dark green blind-embossed cloth, lettered in gilt on upper cover, with recipes for standard and regional cuisine. **$1,200**

Dorothy Sloan Rare Books

Mary Mason Campbell, *The New England Butt'ry Shelf Cookbook: Receipts for Very Special Occasions*, Cleveland and New York: World Publishing Co., 1968. First edition with approximately 200 recipes, eight full-page color Tasha Tudor illustrations and numerous ones in black and white, rust cloth **$90**

Quinn's Auction Galleries

Barbara and George Reiger, *The Zane Grey Cookbook*, Prentice-Hall, Inc., 1976. First edition, from library of Zane Grey, publisher's cloth and dust jacket. **$36**

Heritage Auctions

Cow Brand Soda Cook Book and Facts Worth Knowing, Church & Dwight, 1900, original printed wraps **$32**

Heritage Auctions

Bottles

INTEREST IN BOTTLE COLLECTING, and high interest in extremely rare bottles, continues to grow, with new bottle clubs forming throughout the United States and Europe. More collectors are spending their free time digging through old dumps and foraging through ghost towns, digging out old outhouses (that's right), exploring abandoned mine shafts, and searching their favorite bottle or antique shows, swap meets, flea markets, and garage sales. In addition, the Internet has greatly expanded, offering collectors numerous opportunities and resources to buy and sell bottles with many new auction websites, without even leaving the house. Many bottle clubs now have websites providing even more information for the collector. These new technologies and resources have helped bottle collecting continue to grow and gain interest.

Most collectors, however, still look beyond the type and value of a bottle to its origin and history. Researching the history of a bottle is almost as interesting as finding the bottle itself.

"The knowledge and experience of collectors in the hobby today is at a record pace," according to Jeff Wichmann, president of American Bottle Auctions. "It has not only brought a keener appreciation for the hobby, but apparently a bag full of money with it. Prices for the best of the best [have] never been greater, and as we continue to gain more experienced collectors, I see no limit in sight. It's still a very affordable hobby to pursue, but if the Tiffany of antique bottles is what you're looking for, you'd be advised to bring your checkbook and have a load of cash to cover it.

Rib pattern chestnut flask, medium yellow amber, 5-1/8", 24-rib pattern swirled to left, American, 1815-1835. ....**$225-$250**

"It's not the addition of new offerings to the market as much as the limited availability of pieces that fit into that world of the very best," Wichmann said. "When a piece comes up, unlike even five years ago, it's now every [person] for himself. There has always been the average example and there always will be, but it's the one known bitters or odd-colored historical flask that is finally getting its due respect."

For more information on bottles, see *Antique Trader Bottles: Identification & Price Guide*, 7th edition, by Michael Polak.

Barber bottle, 6-7/8", fiery opalescent turquoise blue, Spanish lace pattern, smooth base, rolled lip, American, 1885-1920 ....**$100-$125**

Charles Cordial London Gin, brilliant turquoise, 8", applied top, American, 1860-1870 .... **$200-225**

Ale/gin bottle, A.M. Binninger & Co. – No. 19 Broad St. N.Y. – Old London Dock Gin, medium dark amber, 10", applied top, American, 1865-1875.. **$275-300**

Beer bottle, American Brewing Co. – West Berkley Cal. – This Bottle Not To Be Sold, medium amber, one-half pint (split), tooled top, 1890-1910. ....**$180-$200**

Barber bottle, 10-1/2", turquoise blue with gold and white enamel, pontil base, tooled lip with original glass stopper, American, 1885-1910.............**$100-$125**

Barber bottle, 7-1/2", medium pink over white with fancy enameled decoration, pontiled base, tooled lip, American, 1885-1920 ....**$100-$125**

BOTTLES

Bitters bottle, A.M.S.2 – 1864
– Constitution Bitters – A.M.S.2
– 1864 – Seward & Bentley
– Buffalo, N.Y., medium olive
amber, 9", smooth base,
applied tapered collar top,
1865-1875. ....**$650-$700**

Beer bottle, Golden Gate
Bottling Works – Chas.
Roschmann – San Francisco
– This Bottle Never Sold,
light amber, one-half pint
(split), tooled top, 1890-
1910.............**$300-$325**

Beer bottle, Bay View – Brewing
Co. – Seattle, Wash, mint
green, quart, applied top,
1890-1905 ....**$200-$250**

Blown bottle, early two-chamber
freeblown cruet, blue turquoise,
6", pontil base, applied top,
1815-1835. ....**$100-$130**

Bitters bottle, Reed's Bitters
– Reed's Bitters, golden
yellow amber, 12-1/2",
lady's leg shape, smooth
base, applied top, 1870-
1880.............**$250-$270**

Black glass onion, deep yellow green, 7-1/8" x 5-3/8" dia., Dutch, 1820-1840 ...**$150-$200**

Master ink, dark amber, drippy applied top, 7-3/4", American, 1850-1870 ...... **$40-$50**

Figural bottle, apple, bright yellow green, 3-1/8", 5/8" dia. hole with ground rim on one side, American, 20th century ..... **$40-$50**

Cobalt blue medicine bottle, D.D.D., 7-1/4", tooled top, 1885-1900.............. **$90-$100**

Medicine bottle, M.B. Robert's Vegetable Embrocation, medium teal blue, 5-1/4", open pontil, American, 1840-1860 ...**$300-$325**

Hutchinson bottle, Benicia – Steam-Soda Works – Custav Gnauch, medium green, 7", American, 1901-1915 (rare).
.....................$125-$150

Mineral water bottle, Bakers Mineral Water – Louisville – B, medium blue green, 7-3/8", iron pontil, American, 1840-1860.............$200-$225

Black glass seal bottle (motif of crown above shield with hounds on either side), olive amber, 9-3/4", English 1850-1870 ...$100-$130

Mineral water bottle, Kissingen Water – T.H.D. – The Spa Phila, medium olive yellow, half-pint, smooth base, American, 1870-1880.............$250-$275

Freeblown decanter bottle, light teal, 8-1/4", flared lip, pontil base, English, 1783-1820. ....**$200-$225**

Cobalt blue medicine bottle, Dickey – Pioneer 1850 – Chemist, 6", tooled top, 1880-1900. ..... **$70-$80**

Blown three-mold decanter, olive yellow with amber tone, 7-1/8", open pontil, sheared and tooled top, 1815-1835..........**$300-$350**

Medicine bottle, Thomson's Compound Syrup Of Tar For Consumption – Philada, deep blue aqua, 5-3/4", open pontil, American, 1840-1860. **$125-$150**

Hair restorer bottle, Shaker – Hair Restorer, medium amber, tooled top, 1890-1900............**$140-$160**

Fire grenade, "Star (inside a star) – Harden Hand Grenade – Fire Extinguisher," clear glass, 6-1/2", original neck label, sheared and ground lip, French, 1875-1895. ....**$150-$175**

Teakettle ink, emerald green, 2-1/2", American, 1840-1860. ....**$350-$400**

Pair of Owl Drug poison bottles, medium amber, 3-1/4" and 4-1/2", American, 1890-1920 ....**$125-$150**

Fire grenade, "Grenade Labbe-Grenade-Labbe-L'Incombustibilite 139 Rue La Fayette-Paris," orange amber, 5-1/2", sheared and ground lip, French, 1880-1900...............................**$125-$150**

Fire grenade, "Hayward's Hand Fire Grenade – S.F. Hayward – 407 Broadway- N.Y. – Patented Aug. – 8 –1871," medium lime green, 6-1/8", sheared and tooled lip, American, 1872-1895. ....**$200-$250**

Umbrella ink, emerald green, 2-1/2", open pontil, rolled lip, American, 1840-1860. ....**$400-$425**

BOTTLES

Pattern molded bottle, Midwestern chestnut flask, yellow amber, 4-1/2", 24-vertical rib pattern, American, 1820-1835...........................**$250-$300**

Pattern molded flask, medium green, 7", 18-horizontal-rib pattern, American, 1815-1835...........................**$200-$225**

Sarsaparilla bottle, Bristol's Genuine – Sarsaparilla – New York, aqua, 8", applied top, American, 1885-1895.... **$50-$75**

Labeled three-sided poison bottle, cobalt blue, 5-1/4', tooled top, American, 1890-1910..........................**$125-$150**

Mineral water bottle, Teller's Mineral Water – Detroit – The Bottle Must Be Returned, deep cobalt blue, 10-pin shape, 8-3/8", smooth base, American, 1855-1865. ....**$200-$250**

Soda bottle, Brutche & Tuchshmit – Newport, KY, deep blue aqua, 7-1/2", American, 1840-1860 .... **$90-$100**

BOTTLES

Black glass snuff jar, yellow amber, 4-3/4", English, 1800-1830.............................$100-$125

Soda bottle, W. Ryer – R (in script) – Union Glass Works – Philada, deep cobalt blue, 7-3/8", American, 1840-1860 ...$250-$300

Whiskey bottle, Golden Rule – XXXX – Whiskey – Braunschweiger & Co. Inc. – S.F. Cal., medium amber, 11-5/8", American, 1895-1905 ...$200-$225

Target ball (motif of man shooting on two sides), medium amethyst, 2-5/8" dia., English, 1877-1895 ....$200-$250

Whiskey bottle, Remington Liquor Co. – Distilled Just Right – 101 Third St. – Portland Ore., medium amber, 12", American, 1900-1910.............$175-$200

Whiskey bottle, Turkish Wine – Goodwin & Edgerly – New York, medium yellow green, 9-7/8", American, 1865-1875.............$750-$800

Boxes

BOXES COME IN ALL SHAPES, sizes, and degree of antiquity—good news for the collector seeking a lifelong passion. Once early mankind reached the point where accumulation began, the next step was the introduction of containers designed especially to preserve those treasures.

Boxes have been created from every source material imaginable: wood, stone, precious metals, papier maché, porcelain, horn, and even shell. Among the most collectible:

Snuff boxes. These small, lidded boxes first came to favor in the 1700s. Although originally intended as "for use" items, snuff boxes are now prized for the elegant miniatures often painted on both the box exterior and interior.

Pillboxes. Like the snuffbox, these tiny boxes were as much in demand for their design as for their usefulness. Among the most desirable are 18th century pillboxes with enameled or repoussé (metal relief) decoration.

Match safes. In the days before safety matches, metal boxes with a striker on the base kept matches from inadvertently bursting into flame. Match safe material ranged from base metal to sterling silver. Although flat, hinged safes were the most common, novelty shapes, such as animal heads, also proved popular.

Lacquered boxes. Often classified as "Oriental" due to the 19th century fondness for decorating them with Asian motifs, lacquered boxes are actually found in almost every culture. Ranging anywhere from trinket- to trunk-sized, the common denominator is a highly polished, lacquered surface.

Chinese smoothly polished hardwood scholar box of dark wood, handle decorated with geometric openwork design, 11"... **$550**

Altair Auctions

Folk art boxes. The diversity of available folk art boxes accounts for their modern collectibility. Folk art boxes were often the work of untrained artisans, created solely for their own needs from materials readily at hand. Among the many choices: wallpaper boxes, decoupage boxes, and tramp art boxes. Fueled by the imagination and ingenuity of their makers, the selection is both fascinating and limitless.

Chinese lacquer box with dense overall pattern of scrolling lotus flowers and vines in black, Qianlong mark, minor repair inside, 4-1/2" h. x 10-3/4" w. **$275**

Altair Auctions

Chinese rectangular bamboo box displaying natural joints and waves of bamboo, polished to feature natural grain of wood 7" l. x 4" w......... **$350**

Altair Auctions

Chinese antique metal box in form of lotus, blue paint with gold relief floral bands on body, scalloped band on base, mythical creatures and floral design on surface with scalloped edge, 4-1/4" h. **$700**

Altair Auctions

Chinese 19th century wooden box with stone inlays of birds and lotus flowers, decorated hinge, 10" h. x 19" w. x 8-1/2" l. **$525**

Altair Auctions

Chinese Huanghuali wooden box with brass handles and closings, interior in two sections, auspicious symbols carved into top of lid, 6" h. x 10" w. **$165**

Altair Auctions

Chinese 19th century scholar box with metal detailing and colorful stone inlays carved into floral and bird forms, 15-1/2" l. x 4-1/2" h. x 6" w... **$315**

Altair Auctions

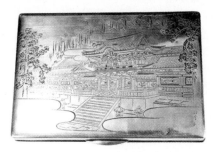

Japanese silver jewelry box, minor dents and scratches, 8-1/2" l. x 5-3/4" w. x 2-3/4" h., 1,058 g. **$1,722**

Antique Reader

Chinese sterling silver box with figure, very good condition, 2-3/4" h. x 3-1/2" w., 236 g. **$369**

Antique Reader

Continental 14k gold snuff box, etched floral and foliate design to all sides, ribbed sides to lid and hinge, maker unidentified, circa 1900, marks: (CK), (arrow-CCS-in diamond), 2-1/2" h., 2.46 troy oz. **$2,500**

Heritage Auctions

Silver gilt woven lidded box, Tiffany & Co., New York, circa 1970, hinged lid opening to void interior, monogrammed JSD to underside, marks: TIFFANY & CO., STERLING SILVER, MAKERS, 25367, 2" x 7-3/4" x 5-1/8", 38.3 oz.......... **$1,875**

Heritage Auctions

Silver lidded box, hinged lid, engraved decoration of scrolls and flowers throughout linear grid ground, Shreve & Co., San Francisco, circa 1910, monogrammed LMB to lid cartouche, marks: (S-bell-S), SHREVE & CO, STERLING, SAN FRANCISCO, 4001, 1-1/2" x 5-1/4" x 3-1/4", 6.5 oz. **$331**

Heritage Auctions

Italian gilt snuff box retailed by Bergdorf Goodman, early 20th century, hinged lidded box with strap-work decoration throughout, oval inset of mother and child to center, marks: MADE IN ITALY, BERGDORF GOODMAN, 5/8" x 3" x 2-1/4".. **$300**

Heritage Auctions

Continental brass mounted mahogany lock box, rectangular hinged lid over conforming case, fitted with bail handles, 25-1/2" w. **$500**

Leslie Hindman Auctioneers

Chinese lacquer and hardstone mounted octagonal box, 17-3/4" dia.. **$250**

Leslie Hindman Auctioneers

Chinese cinnabar lacquer box, rectangular form, lid with finial decoration, signed in Chinese characters, 5-3/4" w. **$406**

Leslie Hindman Auctioneers

Victorian lacquered sewing box of rectangular form, lid decorated with figures playing chess, opening to fitted interior comprising partial set of sewing implements, case further decorated with gilt foliate motifs throughout, 11-1/4" w. **$688**

Leslie Hindman Auctioneers

Two Continental steel, brass, and ivory inlaid boxes, one of rectangular form with hinged lid inscribed Gants, other of three-part form, decorated in playing card motif, 9-5/8" w. **$875**

Leslie Hindman Auctioneers

TOP LOT!

Napoleon III burl wood and fruitwood box with mother-of-pearl and brass inlaid lozenge to hinged lid, brass mounts to banded rim, opening to tufted aqua silk interior, 3-1/2" h. x 8-1/2" w. x 6-1/4" d. Provenance: From personal collection of famed artist Aline Renoir...................................... **$5,000**

Heritage Auctions

Persian lacquered box, oval form, lid with figural decoration, base with band of animals, some minor areas of scuffing, tight split through base running from left to right, likely mid-20th century, 12-3/4" w. **$1,000**

Leslie Hindman Auctioneers

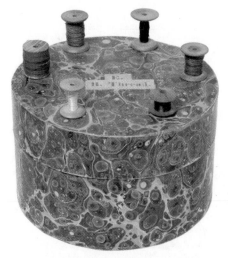

Two oval boxes, top box of maple and pine, early Shaker green over original gray painted finish, three fingers right to left, copper tacks, held cloves, in-use wear with good patina, 2-1/8" h. x 6-1/8" l.; bottom box of maple and pine, original putty red/pink painted finish with patina, copper tacks, four fingers right to left, carved initials on bottom "E F," Sabbathday Lake or Alfred, Maine, circa 1850, 4" h. x 10" l. **$1,180**

Willis-Henry Auctions

Round cardboard box with green and white papered exterior, white interior with light blue paper-covered bottom inside and out, Canterbury, New Hampshire, circa 1840, printed labels on top of lid say "E." and "B. Thread.," with six small Shaker turned spools on lid, each with silk and cotton threads, 1/2" to 1" h., box 3" h. x 5-1/4" dia................................. **$1,416**

Willis-Henry Auctions

Pair of Huanghuali boxes, each of honeyed hue and rectangular lidded form, 10" w...........................**$1,250**
Leslie Hindman Auctioneers

Rectangular work box, tiger maple, original varnish finish with oxidation and patina, dovetailed construction, rectangular bone escutcheon plate, original cast steel lock and brass hinges, tiger maple sectioned interior, circa 1850-1860, possibly used as a Shaker gift shop money box as sections appear fashioned for coins and bills, penciled numbers in added columns on inside of lid, 3-3/4" h. x 11-3/4" w. x 7-7/8" d...**$2,478**

Willis-Henry Auctions

Seed box, pine, original natural finish, leather hinged lid with leather handle, left hinge is split, lid with two brass hook-and-eye closures, original paper label on front says "Shakers' Garden Seeds, Raised at New Lebanon, N.Y.," 6" h. x 14-3/4" w. x 7-1/4" d. **$2,478**

Willis-Henry Auctions

Seed box and stencil plate, pine, original red paint, original paper front label says "Shakers Genuine Garden Seeds, Mount Lebanon, N.Y.," "74 papers" in black paint on lid, "Smith & Laniton, Smithville" on bottom, six-section interior later lined with red felt, 3-1/4" h. x 23-1/2" l.; brass stencil plate, "Shaker Seeds 10 Doz." thumbtacked to small pine board on red, with hole for peg, 2-1/2" x 6-3/4"...**$1,888**

Willis-Henry Auctions

BOXES

Two boxes, smaller box of maple and pine, original natural finish, three fingers, copper tacks and points, part of envelope inside with Dr. McCue's handwritten pencil notation "Bought in Chatham, N.Y. auction of Nora Mallory Estate, May 1967, $20," 3" h. x 7" l.; larger box with four fingers, copper tacks and steel points, tag attached to lid says "Old – $3.00," marked on reverse in chalk "Cole. P.," 4-3/8" h. x 11-1/2" l **$826**

Willis-Henry Auctions

Japanese lacquer box with multiple tiers, decorated with folding fans, with extra lid, 13" h **$469**

Leslie Hindman Auctioneers

Five oval boxes, maple and pine, smallest box with birch top and base, three fingers, 1-1/2" h. x 4-1/4" l.; second smallest box with decoupage lid with 19th century lithograph of two women skating, three fingers, 2-1/8" h. x 5-1/8" l.; third box, #1203, "Oval Box given by ECB on Xmas 1960," three fingers, 3" h. x 7-1/8" l.; fourth box, #502, "SDL, $3.50," three fingers, 3-1/8" h. x 7-3/4" l.; bottom box, originally gray/blue painted finish, initialed "J C" on bottom, three fingers, 3-1/4" h. x 8-3/4" l. **$1,416**

Willis-Henry Auctions

Two Japanese lacquer boxes, each with multiple tiers, decorated with cranes and trees, taller box 10-3/4" h **$594**

Leslie Hindman Auctioneers

Spit box, pine and maple, original mustard patina, round head copper tacks, three fingers, oil cloth-covered interior decorated with purple and white stars and geometric designs, printed paper label on side says "3," signed in pencil on bottom "Anna Lane," 3-1/8" h. x 8-3/4" dia. **$1,652**

Willis-Henry Auctions

Work box, pine, original bittersweet red thin painted finish, hinged lid with one-quarter round molding, interior black fabric lid catch, dovetailed construction, possibly had lid catch on front, 5" h. x 12" w. x 8-1/4" d. **$2,950**

Willis-Henry Auctions

Rare round box, figured maple, pine bottom and fruitwood top, original light varnish finish with darkened patina, small round and flathead copper tacks, copper points, "5" in pencil under lid, three fingers, 2-1/4" h. x 4" dia. **$944**

Willis-Henry Auctions

Oval box, pine and maple, original heavy brick red painted finish, three fingers, copper tacks and points, painted bottom and under lid, small imperfection, "Oval Box, Sabbathday Lake, $4.00," includes business card that says "The Shaker Store, handmade Gifts and Candy," "Knitting box belonging to Sister Ada Cummings, Sabbathday Lake, Me" written in pencil on back, 2-3/4" h. x 7-1/2" l. **$1,180**

Willis-Henry Auctions

Three Tibetan lidded boxes, each of circular form with metal mounts depicting Buddhist emblems with turquoise and coral inlaid decoration throughout, overall fair condition, wear throughout, small flake losses and small veneer losses to lacquered wood, scattered lost inset stones, light oxidation and pitting to metal mounts, minor compressions and dents, bowls stable, traces of old glue repairs, largest 6-7/8" dia. **$2,000**

Leslie Hindman Auctioneers

Ceramics

BELLEEK

THE NAME BELLEEK refers to an industrious village in County Fermanagh, Northern Ireland, on the banks of the River Erne, and to the lustrous porcelain wares produced there.

In 1849, John Caldwell Bloomfield inherited a large estate near Belleek. Interested in ceramics and having discovered rich deposits of feldspar and kaolin (china clay) on his lands, he soon envisioned a pottery that would make use of these materials, local craftspeople, and water power of the River Erne. He was also anxious to enhance Ireland's prestige with superior porcelain products.

Bloomfield had a chance meeting with Robert Williams Armstrong who had established a substantial architectural business building potteries. Keenly interested in the manufacturing process, he agreed to design, build, and manage the new factory for Bloomfield. The factory was to be located on Rose Isle on a bend in the River Erne.

Bloomfield and Armstrong then approached David McBirney, a highly successful merchant and director of railway companies, and enticed him to provide financing. Impressed by the plans, he agreed to raise funds for the enterprise. As agreed, the factory was named McBirney and Armstrong, then later D. McBirney and Co.

Although 1857 is given as the founding date of the pottery, it is recorded that the pottery's foundation stone was laid by Mrs. J.C. Bloomfield on Nov. 18, 1858. Although not completed until 1860, the pottery was producing earthenware from its inception.

With the arrival of ceramic experts from the (William Henry) Goss Pottery in England, principally William Bromley, Sr. and William Wood Gallimore, Parian ware was perfected and, by 1863, the wares we associate with Belleek today were in production.

With Belleek Pottery workers and others emigrating to the United States in the late 1800s and early 1900s, Belleek-style china manufacture, known as American Belleek, commenced at several American firms, including Ceramic Art Co., Colombian Art Pottery, Lenox Inc., Ott & Brewer, and Willets Manufacturing Co.

Throughout its Parian production, Belleek Pottery marked its items with an Irish harp and wolfhound and the Devenish Tower. Its second period began with the advent of the McKinley Tariff Act of 1891 and the (revised) British Merchandise Act as Belleek

Willets vase decorated by Florence McLee-Sentacy with male peacocks and flowers placed over gold design, black and gold accents, signature of artist and Willets Belleek green logo beneath, excellent condition, 10" h.................**$550**

Mark Mussio, Humler & Nolan

CERAMICS

added the ribbon "Co. FERMANAGH IRELAND" beneath its mark in 1891. Both the first and second period marks were black, although they occasionally appeared in burnt orange, green, blue or brown, especially on earthenware items. Its third period begin in 1926, when it added a Celtic emblem under the second period mark as well as the government trademark "Reg No 0857," which was granted in 1884. The Celtic emblem was registered by the Irish Industrial Development Association in 1906 and reads "Deanta in Eirinn," and means "Made in Ireland." The pottery is now utilizing its 13th mark, following a succession of three black marks, three green marks, a gold mark, two blue marks and three green. The final green mark was used only a single year, in 2007, to commemorate its 150th anniversary. In 2008, Belleek changed its mark to brown. Early earthenware was often marked in the same color as the majority of its surface decoration. Early basketware has Parian strips applied to its base with the impressed verbiage "BELLEEK" and later on, additionally "Co FERMANAGH" with or without "IRELAND." Current basketware carries the same mark as its Parian counterpart.

The item identification scheme that follows is in the works by Richard K. Degenhardt: *Belleek The Complete Collector's Guide and Illustrated Reference* (both first and second editions). Additional information, as well as a thorough discussion of the early marks is located in these works as well as on Del E. Domke's website: http://home.comcast. net/~belleek_website.

Willets vase decorated and signed by artist Jeannette Boyd Negley, 1909, male peacock on tree stump with white flower, appearing two more times around circumference, Willets Belleek logo and artist name and date beneath, Oriental style design, excellent condition, 10" h. x 5" w. $600

Mark Mussio, Humler & Nolan

Ceramic Art Co. vase with blue irises and gold trim inside throat, marked with CAC Belleek green palette, excellent original condition, 10-7/8" h. $350

Mark Mussio, Humler & Nolan

Marks:

American Art China Works – R&E, 1891-1895
AAC (superimposed), 1891-1895
American Belleek Co. – Company name, banner and globe
Ceramic Art Co. – CAC palette, 1889-1906
Colombian Art Pottery – CAP, 1893-1902
Cook Pottery – Three feathers with "CHC," 1894-1904
Coxon Belleek Pottery – "Coxon Belleek" in shield, 1926-1930
Gordon Belleek – "Gordon Belleek," 1920-1928
Knowles, Taylor & Knowles – "Lotusware" in circle with crown, 1891-1896
Lenox China – Palette mark, 1906-1924
Ott & Brewer – Crown and shield, 1883-1893
Perlee – "P" in wreath, 1925-1930
Willets Manufacturing Co. – Serpent mark, 1880-1909

Lenox tyg with luster decoration of irises in blue with gold clouds, marked with Lenox Belleek palette logo in green and "Heyt. Bellevue Pa.," excellent original condition, wear to gold handles, 7-5/8" h. **$150**

Mark Mussio, Humler & Nolan

Porcelain handled basket with lid, three-strand basket with applied flowers, thistles, shamrocks, and vine form handles, first period impressed mark on underside, minor chips to foliate décor, light splits throughout from firing, bubbles in glaze in cervices on edge, light yellow discoloration, 5-1/2" x 8-1/2". **$768**

Susanin's Auctioneers & Appraisers

Lenox American cylinder vase with scene of sailing vessels moored side by side silhouetted by light of full moon, repeated in triplet around form, artist monogram "EEL" beneath with Lenox green brush and palette logo, excellent condition, 11-1/8" h. **$650**

Mark Mussio, Humler & Nolan

Tall Willets vase with blue and yellow irises silhouetted on black ground with band on shoulder, marked "Willets Belleek" on bottom, minor wear to gold on rim and foot ring, 17" h. **$160**

Mark Mussio, Humler & Nolan

Willets porcelain tankard pitcher and two matching mugs, late 19th/early 20th century, each with dragon-form handle, hand-painted with grapes on vines, green marks, undamaged, 15-1/2" and 5-3/4" h. **$230**

Jeffrey S. Evans & Associates

Round porcelain basket with lid, three-strand basket with vine form scrolled handles, applied flowers and leaves on lid, Belleek first period impressed mark on underside, light ash from firing in clay scattered throughout, small chips to foliate décor, glued crack in middle of one handle, some glue buildup where handle connects to base, 6" x 8".... **$704**

Susanin's Auctioneers & Appraisers

American Lenox vase enamel-decorated with repeat design of geisha with umbrella beneath wisteria vine, gold band on base, Lenox palette logo beneath, excellent condition. **$250**

Mark Mussio, Humler & Nolan

CERAMICS

BENNINGTON POTTERY

BENNINGTON WARES, which ranged from stoneware to parian and porcelain, were made in Bennington, Vermont, primarily in two potteries, one in which Captain John Norton and his descendants were principals, and the other in which Christopher Webber Fenton (also once associated with the Nortons) was a principal. Various marks are found on the wares made in the two major potteries, including J. & E. Norton, E. & L. P. Norton, L. Norton & Co., Norton & Fenton, Edward Norton, Lyman Fenton & Co., Fenton's Works, United States Pottery Co., U.S.P., and others.

The popular pottery with the mottled brown on yellowware glaze was also produced in Bennington, but such wares should be referred to as "Rockingham" or "Bennington-type" unless they can be specifically attributed to a Bennington, Vermont, factory.

Three-gallon stoneware jug, 19th century, impressed J Norton & Co. Bennington VT, with cobalt floral decoration, very good condition, 15-1/2" h. **$450**

Pook & Pook, Inc.

Two-gallon stoneware jug, 19th century, impressed Norton & Fenton East Bennington VT, with cobalt rabbit jumping over bush, very good condition, 13" h. **$840**

Pook & Pook, Inc.

New York stoneware jug, 19th century, impressed J. & F. Norton Bennington, VT, with cobalt bird on stump, large repair around base rim, 9" hairline to right of decoration, 17" h. ...**$450**

Pook & Pook, Inc.

Four-gallon stoneware crock, 19th century, impressed J. & E. Norton Bennington VT, with cobalt basket of flowers, very good condition, 11-1/4" h. $1,007

Pook & Pook, Inc.

Flint enamel pitcher and basin, 19th century, impressed Lyman Fenton & Co., bowl with 6" hairline, handle on pitcher restored, large repaired break to rim behind handle, both with impressed stamp on bottom, pitcher 12-1/2" h., basin 4-1/2" h. x 13-3/4" dia....... **$304**

Pook & Pook, Inc.

Flint enamel Rockingham glaze pottery tobacco jar, mottled brown, Alternate Rib pattern, faint impressed Type A mark, 1849-1858, excellent overall condition, glaze flakes to cover flange, probably as made, shallow flake/glaze loss to one handle, 7" h. overall, 5-1/2" d. overall. **$288**

Jeffrey S. Evans & Associates

American yellowware spaniel figure, running Rockingham glaze, seated on oblong base molded with rocks along front edge, open front legs, firing vent hole under base, second half 19th century, excellent undamaged condition, small manufacturing chip to foot rim as made, 10" h., 7-1/2" x 4-3/4" base. **$345**

Jeffrey S. Evans & Associates

Toby pitcher by Lyman Fenton & Co., cow creamer, and figure of squat man, mid-19th century, repair to spout of pitcher, others in good condition, tallest 5-3/4"............................... **$356**

Pook & Pook, Inc.

Pair of flint enamel candlesticks, circa 1850, very good condition, 9-1/4" h. **$668**

Pook & Pook, Inc.

Two flint enamel coachman bottles, mid-19th century, by Lyman Fenton & Co., feet reattached to one, other in good condition, 10-1/2" h. **$182**

Pook & Pook, Inc.

Pistol-form ceramic bottle flask with Bennington-type glaze, 6-1/4" l., with ceramic hammer-form flask, 11-1/4" l. **$267**

Pook & Pook, Inc.

CERAMICS

BUFFALO POTTERY

INCORPORATED IN 1901 as a wholly owned subsidiary of the Larkin Soap Co. founded by John D. Larkin of Buffalo, New York, in 1875, the Buffalo Pottery was a manufactory built to produce premium wares included with purchases of Larkin's chief product: soap.

In October 1903, the first kiln was fired and Buffalo Pottery became the only pottery in the world run entirely by electricity. In 1904 Larkin offered its first premium produced by the pottery. This concept of using premiums caused sales to skyrocket and, in 1905, the first Blue Willow pattern pottery made in the United States was introduced as a premium.

The Buffalo Pottery administrative building, built in 1904 to house 1,800 clerical workers, was the creation of a 32-year-old architect, Frank Lloyd Wright. The building was demolished in 1953.

By 1910 annual soap production peaked and the number of premiums offered in the catalogs exceeded 600. By 1915 this number had grown to 1,500. The first catalog of premiums was issued in 1893 and continued to appear through the late 1930s.

John D. Larkin died in 1926, and during the Great Depression the firm suffered severe losses, going into bankruptcy in 1940. After World War II, the pottery resumed production under new management, but its vitreous wares were generally limited to mass-produced china for the institutional market.

Among the pottery lines produced during Buffalo's heyday were Blue Willow (1905-1916), Gaudy Willow (1905-1916), Deldare Ware (1908-1909, 1923-1925), Abino Ware (1911-1913), historical and commemorative plates, and unique hand-painted jugs and pitchers. In the 1920s and 1930s the firm concentrated on personalized wares for commercial clients including hotels, clubs, railroads, and restaurants.

For more information on Buffalo Pottery, see *Antique Trader Pottery & Porcelain Ceramics Price Guide*, 6th edition.

—*Phillip M. Sullivan*

Pug with fisherman and lighthouse, 1-1/2 liter, glued chip on pouring spout. ....**$100-$200**

Fox Auctions

Gloriana pitcher of standing and kneeling fairies in woods, 9" h. **$115**

Vero Beach Auction

Deldare Ware

In the mid-1960s, my wife, Brenda, and I attended a large outdoor antique flea market in Hartville, Ohio. The Hartville markets were held monthly during the warm weather months, and we almost always found something to add to our glassware collection, which consisted of Chocolate glass. We knew little about the attractive Deldare ware from Buffalo Pottery, but that was about to change.

As we browsed, Brenda was attracted to an interesting brown teapot, hexagonal in shape, which featured an elaborate decoration of a scene going around all six sides. The foreground of the decoration depicted men and women in what appeared to be fashionable clothing from 18th or 19th century England, and the background had various homes and other buildings. Lettering read, "Scenes of village life in ye olden days."

The dealer saw us admiring the teapot and told us it was Deldare ware, made at the Buffalo Pottery in New York State. We left the teapot behind, but later that evening, Brenda said, "I wish we'd got the teapot," and I agreed, hoping that it would turn up at Hartville in another month or so. I found the same dealer sometime later, but the Deldare teapot was gone.

On a trip to an antique show in Pittsburgh a year or so later, we came upon a booth that had Deldare ware everywhere—mugs, plates, cups and saucers, pitchers in various sizes, relish dishes, platters, cream and sugar sets, candlesticks, vases, etc. The dealers, Seymour and Violet Altman, were natives of Buffalo, New York, and collecting Buffalo Pottery products, especially Deldare ware, was their passion. "Si and Vi," as they liked to be known, were in the process of writing a book devoted to Buffalo Pottery products, especially Deldare. Published by Bonanza Books in 1969, their *Book of Buffalo Pottery* remains a valuable source today.

The Buffalo Pottery was a subsidiary of the Larkin Co., which began in Buffalo about 1875. Over the subsequent quarter century, it grew exponentially to become one of America's largest manufacturers of soap, toiletries and related products. Much of Larkin's marketing was based on premiums, useful or decorative items that came with the soap or could be acquired by redeeming coupons packaged with the Larkin products. The Buffalo Pottery operation was founded by Larkin interests in 1901, and the pottery produced both premiums for Larkin marketing as well as ceramic items for general sale.

As the Altmans reported, the distinctive greenish brown color used for Deldare ware was a mixture of different clays and was in production as early as 1906-1907, but the origin of the term "Deldare" is itself quite a mystery. The Altmans mention several theories regarding the Deldare appellation, and one of the most logical of these indicates that the term is likely derived from "Delaware."

The applied decorations on Deldare ware were accomplished by a transfer process followed by incredibly meticulous hand-painting using a wide variety of realistic colors to complete the elaborate English scenes. The origins of many of the scenes on Deldare ware were revealed by the Altmans' research. A sequence of events in a foxhunt called "The Fallowfield Hunt" are derived from the work of English artist Cecil Alden (1870-1935). Produced only in 1908-1909, the Fallowfield Hunt series consists of nine different scenes, ranging from the hunters at their early morning meal ("Breakfast at the Three Pigeons") to the hunt itself (for example, "The Dash," "Breaking Cover," and "The Death"). Other scenes depicted on Deldare ware come from Oliver Goldsmith's *Vicar of Wakefield* (1766) or Elizabeth Gaskell's 19th-century work, *Cranford*. There are many more English scenes on Deldare ware, and the Altmans' book illustrates dozens of different Deldare ware items, including some in color.

Deldare ware was produced in two distinctive periods at the Buffalo Pottery, 1908-1909 and 1923-1925. Deldare articles are dated within the distinctive trademark, an English tavern sign depicting a buffalo in silhouette with "MADE AT YE BUFFALO POTTERY" and "DELDARE WARE UNDERGLAZE" in small capital letters. In addition, Deldare items bear the initials or name of the employee who decorated the individual piece. The Altmans provide a listing of more than 60 men and women decorators, and their research included interviews with some of them. The initials or name on a Deldare item are rendered in very small letters, sometimes requiring a magnifying glass to read them.

— *James Measell*

Altman , Seymour and Violet. *The Book of Buffalo Pottery.* New York: Bonanza Books, 1969 (a recent reprint of this volume is available from Schiffer Publishing, but you can find earlier editions on www.abebooks.com).

Emerald Deldare ware vase with Art Nouveau design of white daisies, lacy and craquelle patterns and other designs, stencil mark "1911 Buffalo Pottery Emerald Deldare Ware Underglaze," artist cipher S.R. and number 134 beneath, 3" line extends from rim, 6-3/4" h.. **$400**

Mark Mussio, Humler & Nolan

Deldare pitcher and tray, each with figural decoration, pitcher 9-3/4" h. **$150**

Leslie Hindman Auctioneers

Emerald ware plate, early 20th century, transfer decorated with scene from *Dr. Syntax* by John Alden, fine condition........... **$180**

Stefek's Auctioneers & Appraisers

Deldare tankard painted by artist T or L Ball, Bell or Bill, scene titled "The Great Controversy" depicting discussion about claim "All you have to do is teach Dutchman English," marked on base with Deldare logo and date, titled and signed by artist on surface, excellent original condition, 12-3/4" h........... **$200**

Mark Mussio, Humler & Nolan

Deldare charger with professional repair, 12", and celery tray, 12" **$148**

Woody Auction

Deldare pitcher and tray, each with figural decoration, pitcher 9-3/4" h. **$150**

Leslie Hindman Auctioneers

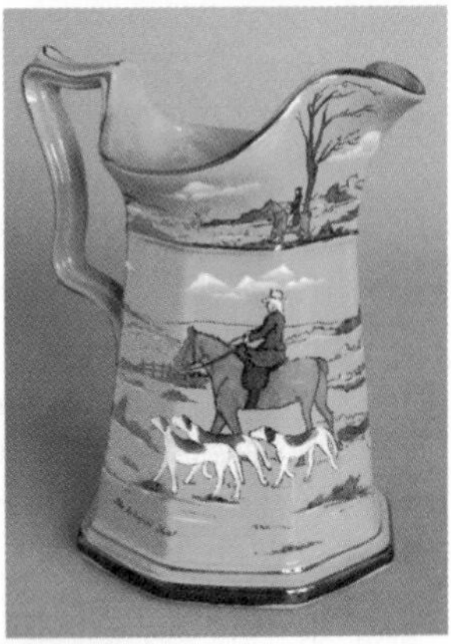

Deldare water pitcher, hexagonal shape, decorated with hunting scene, marked on bottom, 8" h. **$118**

Rachel Davis Fine Arts, Cleveland, Ohio

Deldare ware advertising plate, painted design of three buildings, marked, initials M.H., mint condition with scratches consistent with age and handling, stamped logo and painted initials on base, overall very good condition, 6-1/2" dia. **$438**

Treadway Gallery

Emerald Deldare ale bowl on plateau, both pieces marked with 1911 Buffalo logo reading "Buffalo Pottery Emerald Deldare Ware Underglaze," decorator monogram M.G., possibly for M. Gerhardt, beneath bowl, excellent original condition, bowl 5-1/4" x 10-1/4", plateau 12-3/4" x 10-1/2". **$600**

Mark Mussio, Humler & Nolan

COWAN

R. GUY COWAN opened his first pottery studio in 1912 in Lakewood, Ohio. The pottery operated almost continuously, with the exception of a break during World War I, at various locations in the Cleveland area until it was forced to close in 1931 due to financial difficulties.

Many of the 20th century's finest artists began with Cowan and its associate, the Cleveland School of Art. This fine art pottery, particularly the designer pieces, is highly sought after by collectors.

Many people are unaware that it was due to R. Guy Cowan's perseverance and tireless work that art pottery is today considered an art form and found in many art museums.

For more information on Cowan pottery, see *Antique Trader Pottery & Porcelain Ceramics Price Guide,* 7th edition.

Viktor Schreckengost's "Danse Moderne" plate, also known as "Jazz" plate, created in 1931 while at Cowan Pottery, depicts couple dancing with stars and cocktails surrounding them, dry point decoration in Egyptian Blue and black engobe, excellent original condition, impressed on back with circular Cowan logo and Cowan in block letters, 11-1/4" dia. **$14,500**

Mark Mussio, Humler & Nolan

Octagonal wall plaque, Thelma Frazier design, depicting trio of nudes with several birds in Cerise glaze, diagonal and back has impressed Cowan logo, light surface scratches, 14-3/8" h. **$1,000**

Mark Mussio, Humler & Nolan

Elephant paperweight, Margaret Postgate design, mat black glaze, impressed "Cowan" with Cowan logo on back of plinth, excellent original condition, 3-5/8" h. **$400**

Mark Mussio, Humler & Nolan

"Mayflower Stag" flower holder, Waylande Gregory design, with bowl and stand in Caramel glaze, all three pieces impressed with circular Cowan logo, stag 8-1/4" h., bowl 2-1/2" h. x 11-1/2" w. and marked B-2 in pencil, stand 1-3/4" h. x 12" w. and marked X-1 in pencil on bottom with light surface scratches................ **$300**

Mark Mussio, Humler & Nolan

CERAMICS

"Mary" statue, Margaret Postgate design, in flowing drape, kneeling on stepped base, impressed on back of base with circular Cowan logo covered by Terra Cotta glaze, fine overall crazing, statue 10" h., base 14-1/2" x 5-1/4"............... **$2,500**

Mark Mussio, Humler & Nolan

Large floor vase in Arabian Night high glaze (deep blue with aquamarine overspray), impressed with circular Cowan logo and Cowan in block letters on bottom, excellent original condition, 19-1/2" h. **$950**

Mark Mussio, Humler & Nolan

"Young Fawn" statue, Waylande Gregory design created in 1930, black mat glaze, artist's name molded into plinth, no Cowan markings, excellent original condition, 13-1/4" h.**$900**

Mark Mussio, Humler & Nolan

Pair of bookends featuring baby elephants poised on staircase in Egyptian Blue glaze, impressed with circular Cowan logo on back covered with glaze, excellent original condition, 7-1/2" h. **$700**

Mark Mussio, Humler & Nolan

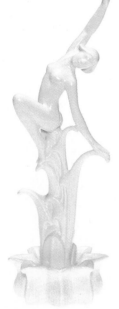

Lamp base with doe feeding fawn in Caramel glaze, marked on bottom with impressed circular Cowan logo and shape number 942 written in pencil, excellent original condition, 9-1/4" h...**$200**

Mark Mussio, Humler & Nolan

Pair of "Kicking Horse" bookends in black glaze, marked with circular Cowan logo on plinth covered with thick black glaze, excellent original condition, 9-1/4" h. **$750**

Mark Mussio, Humler & Nolan

Large "Debutante" flower holder in Special Ivory glaze, impressed Cowan logo and shape number 812 in pencil, fine overall crazing, 14-1/2" h.........................**$1,100**

Mark Mussio, Humler & Nolan

"Aztec Man" lamp base in Antique Green crystalline glaze, impressed Cowan logo and shape number 843 written on bottom, professional repairs to some areas of base, 13-1/4" h. **$950**

Mark Mussio, Humler & Nolan

Pair of elephant bookends, Copper glazed luster ceramic, 5" h. x 5-3/4" w. x 3-3/4" d..............**$308**

Cowan's Auctions, Inc.

DEDHAM

THIS POTTERY WAS ORGANIZED in 1866 by Alexander W. Robertson in Chelsea, Massachusetts, and became A.W. & H. Roberson in 1868. In 1872, the name was changed to Chelsea Keramic Art Works and in 1891 to Chelsea Pottery, U.S.A. About 1895, the pottery was moved to Dedham, Massachusetts, and was renamed Dedham Pottery. Production ceased in 1943. High-fired colored wares and crackle ware were specialties. The rabbit is said to have been the most popular decoration on crackle ware in blue.

Five plates, pitcher, and covered bowl, glazed earthenware, early 20th century, all in blue and white crackle ware; Maude Davenport footed plate decorated with flowering tree branch, artist's cipher, and initials HR in decoration, Dedham blue stamp and foreshortened rabbit mark; Chestnut, Iris, Magnolia, and Azalea plates, each with foreshortened rabbit stamp, 8-1/2" dia.; pitcher and covered bowl in Rabbit pattern, both with Dedham blue stamp and foreshortened rabbit, bowl marked 22 and with illegible pencil marks, 3-1/2" h. x 4-3/4".............................. **$3,600**

Skinner, Inc.; www.skinnerinc.com

CERAMICS

Experimental stoneware vase, gray, cream, and brown drip glaze, 1896-1908, signed, Hugh C. Robertson (1845-1908), 10" x 5".............. **$1,125**

Rago Arts

Tall experimental stoneware vase, mahogany and green drip glaze, 1896-1908, signed, Hugh C. Robertson (1845-1908), 13-1/2" x 6-1/2".. **$3,750**

Rago Arts

Experimental cabinet vase, dripping oxblood glaze, 1896-1908, signed Dedham Pottery HR, Hugh C. Robertson (1845-1908), 2-1/2" x 3-1/4".... **$2,375**

Rago Arts

Experimental stoneware vase, mottled iridescent oxblood, green, and blue glazes, 1896-1908, incised Dedham Pottery / HR, DP75D in ink, Hugh C. Robertson (1845-1908), 8-1/2" x 5"..................... **$2,625**

Rago Arts

Pottery plate with blue and white rabbit decoration encircling rim, signed on underside with rabbit stamp "Dedham Pottery," very good to excellent condition, 6" dia. ...**$59**

James D. Julia, Inc.

Day and Night pitcher, glazed earthenware, 1929-1943, blue and white crackle ware, relief decorated with roosters and owl, blue registered Dedham mark on base, 4-7/8" h. **$369**

Skinner, Inc.; www.skinnerinc.com

Lobster and Crab plates, glazed earthenware, 1896-1928, blue and white crackle ware, each with blue Dedham stamp and foreshortened rabbit on base, Lobster 8-3/4" dia., Crab 6-1/4" dia...........................**$615**

Skinner, Inc.; www.skinnerinc.com

Large experimental stoneware vase, brown, green, and lapis drip glaze, 1896-1908, signed, Hugh C. Robertson (1845-1908), 9-3/4" x 7-1/2".... **$1,875**

Rago Arts

Seven glazed earthenware rabbit pieces, 1897-1943, blue and white crackle ware, pitcher, creamer, dish, saucer, cup and saucer, and large bowl, each with blue Dedham stamp on base, pitcher with registered mark, bowl stamped twice and with handwritten price "2.50" in pencil, bowl and cup out of round, bowl with glaze imperfections, 1" to 6-3/4" h., up to 9" dia. **$584**

Skinner, Inc.; www.skinnerinc.com

Seven glazed earthenware plates, 1896-1943, blue and white crackle ware, Turkey, Iris, Chestnut, and Magnolia patterns decorated by Maude Davenport, and Moth, Rabbit, and Grapes patterns, each with blue Dedham stamp and foreshortened rabbit on base, Grape with registered mark, all approximately 10" dia. **$554**

Skinner, Inc.; www.skinnerinc.com

Four stoneware plates with crackle glaze and cobalt borders, late 19th-early 20th century, two with magnolias, one with birds, and one with chestnuts, marked on bottom with underglazed crouching rabbit and Dedham Pottery in blue square, some manufacturing glaze misses and chips, largest 8-1/2" dia. **$600**

Cowan's Auctions, Inc.

Three crackle ware plates, Magnolia plate, 8-3/8"dia., Rabbit plate, 8-1/2" dia., and bird in potted orange tree plate, 9-7/8" dia., all signed, all in excellent original condition..................... **$225**

Mark Mussio, Humler & Nolan

Four glazed earthenware rabbit tableware pieces, 1896-1928, blue and white crackle ware plate, bowl, charger, and tray with raised rim, each with blue Dedham stamp, plate and server registered and with foreshortened rabbits, bowl and tray incised DP and Dedham Pottery, respectively, bowl also with pencil marks, charger crudely repaired, bowl out of round, highest 4-1/8" h., 8-1/2" to 13-3/4" dia. **$615**

Skinner, Inc.; www.skinnerinc.com

DELFT

IN THE EARLY 17TH CENTURY, Italian potters settled in Holland and began producing tin-glazed earthenwares, often decorated with pseudo-Oriental designs based on Chinese porcelain wares. The city of Delft became the center of this pottery production and several firms produced the wares throughout the 17th and early 18th century. A majority of the pieces featured blue on white designs, but polychrome wares were also made. The Dutch Delftwares were also shipped to England, where eventually the English copied them at potteries in such cities as Bristol, Lambeth, and Liverpool. Although still produced today, Delft peaked in popularity by the mid-18th century.

For more information on Delft pottery, see *Antique Trader Porcelain & Pottery Ceramics Price Guide,* 7th edition.

Delft (de Porceleyne Fles) vase, circa 1920, decorated with trio of fish in reddish brown on off-white crackle ware ground, marked Delft on bottom with what is likely artist's signature, excellent original condition, 4-1/4" h. **$200**

Mark Mussio, Humler & Nolan

Blue and white Delft-style mantel clock with Dutch scenes, including windmills and sailboats, Continental, early 20th century, case raised on animal paw feet, 12" h. x 8" w. x 4" d.................... **$92**

Cowan's Auctions, Inc.

Shield-shaped plaque, circa 1890, lakeside farm after painting by Fredricus Jacobus van Rossum du Chattel (1856-1917), backstamped Joost Thoovt & Labouchere, fine craquelure, 21" x 14-3/4". **$805**

Thomaston Place Auction Galleries

Blue and white eight-sided, ribbed covered urn with flared rim lid, 19th century, seated foo lion finial, chinoiserie decoration of floral urns alternating with floral panels, marked with entwined TYB monogram, 109-G and 64 on underside, fine condition, original glaze occlusions at neck under lid, 16-1/2" h. x 7-3/4" w. **$978**

Thomaston Place Auction Galleries

Four polychrome bowls, English, early 19th century, decorated with groups of flower sprays on interior and stylized band around rim, unmarked, some paint loss and small chips around rims, kiln marks on undersides, 9" dia. **$185**

Cowan's Auctions, Inc.

Tin-glazed Dutch charger in Chinese manner, 18th century, rim chips, 12" dia............... **$288**

Thomaston Place Auction Galleries

Pair of polychrome decorated covered vases, Dutch or English, baluster form, each with molded bird finial and central molded floral and foliate-framed cartouche with bird set within landscape, marked K on underside, each 14-1/4" h .. **$660**

Cowan's Auctions, Inc.

Blue and white Dutch charger, 18th century, with wide border of alternating floral panels and lattice designs, centered with basket of flowers, rim chips, 11-3/4" dia........................**$308**

Skinner, Inc.; www.skinnerinc.com

Framed Dutch ceramic portrait plaque based on Franz Hals' "The Lute Player," made by Joost Thoovt & Lebouchere, circa 1880s, impressed mark and artist's marks, square oak frame, round spandrel, 24-1/2" sq., 17" dia. **$518**

Thomaston Place Auction Galleries

Blue and white Dutch charger, Peacock pattern, 18th century, tin-glazed earthenware decorated with central urn of flowers and feathers and butterfly rim, yellow edge, rim chips, 2-3/8" d. x 14-1/8" dia. **$748**

Thomaston Place Auction Galleries

Twelve-tile panel wall hanging in blue and white, 18th-19th century, swan within ornate frame, scrollwork at top, in white painted slat frame, minor chips, 20" x 17". **$489**

Thomaston Place Auction Galleries

Dutch tobacco jar, circa 1780, ovoid form with blue decoration depicting Indians smoking pipes flanking label inscription "RAPPE DE DUINKERQUE," slightly domed brass cover, repairs, chips, glaze losses, 12" h. **$1,353**

Skinner, Inc.; www.skinnerinc.com

Royal Bonn medium-sized ceramic charger with portrait of gentleman after Rembrandt, circa 1920, scrolled shaped edge, trefoil piercing at top, good condition, 12-3/4" x 12"....................**$173**

Thomaston Place Auction Galleries

Pair of blue and white pottery jars, 18th century, baluster bodies decorated with chinoiserie landscapes, mounted as kerosene lamps with 19th century bronze collars, burners and bases, burners marked "Williams & Bach / 92 New Bond St. London," jars 15" h., 25-1/2" overall. **$4,375**

Neal Auction Co.

Decorative bowl with country girl holding posy, late 19th century, floral border, tin glaze over redware, flakes to glaze on edges, 1-3/4" x 9" dia. **$69**

Thomaston Place Auction Galleries

CERAMICS

DOULTON AND ROYAL DOULTON

DOULTON & COMPANY, LTD., was founded in Lambeth, London, in about 1858. It operated there until 1956 and often incorporated the words "Doulton" and "Lambeth" in its marks. Pinder, Bourne & Co. Burslem was purchased by the Doultons in 1878 and in 1882 became Doulton & Co., Ltd. It added porcelain to its earthenware production in 1884. The "Royal Doulton" mark has been used since 1902 by this factory, which is still in operation.

John Doulton, the founder, was born in 1793. He became an apprentice at the age of 12 to a potter in south London. Five years later he was employed in another small pottery near Lambeth. His two sons, John and Henry, subsequently joined their father in 1830 in a partnership he had formed with the name of Doulton & Watts. Watts retired in 1864 and the partnership was dissolved. Henry formed a new company that traded as Doulton and Co.

In the early 1870s the proprietor of the Pinder Bourne Co., located in Burslem, Staffordshire, offered Henry a partnership. The Pinder Bourne Co. was purchased by Henry in 1878 and became part of Doulton & Co. in 1882.

With the passage of time, the demand for the Lambeth industrial and decorative stoneware declined whereas demand for the Burslem manufactured and decorated bone china wares increased.

Doulton & Co. was incorporated as a limited liability company in 1899. In 1901 the company was allowed to use the word "Royal" on its trademarks by Royal Charter. The well-known "lion on crown" logo came into use in 1902. In 2000 the logo was changed on the company's advertising literature to one showing a more stylized lion's head in profile.

Today Royal Doulton is one of the world's leading manufacturers and distributors of premium grade ceramic tabletop wares and collectibles. The Doulton Group comprises Minton, Royal Albert, Caithness Glass, Holland Studio Craft, and Royal Doulton. Royal Crown Derby was part of the group from 1971 until 2000, when it became an independent company. These companies market collectibles using their own brand names.

For more information on Royal Doulton, see *Antique Trader Porcelain & Pottery Ceramics Price Guide*, 7th edition, or *Antique Trader Royal Doulton Price Guide* by Kyle Husfloen.

Humidor, covered, thin foot ring on slightly swelled cylindrical body with wide flat rim, inset metal-fitted patented cover, continuous stylized landscape scene, impressed mark, early 20th century, 5-3/4" h **$207**

Jar, covered, Silicon Ware, stylized model of bulbous owl, domed head forming cover, head with incised and enameled light blue and white feathers around dark blue-ringed white eyes, body with stylized blossom-like designs across breast in dark and light blue, white and cream, further blue and white scaled feathers across back, dark buff ground, Doulton Lambeth – Silicon logo, minor nicks, 7-5/8" h **$1,093**

Vase, Titanian Ware, footed ovoid body with short flaring neck, overall glossy shaded dark to teal blue crystalline glaze, Titanian logo mark on base, early 20th century, 5-7/8" h. **$230**

Jardiniere and pedestal, heavy pottery, large hexagonal urn-form jardiniere with side panels molded in relief with classical designs of white putti playing musical instruments among leafy scrolls against blue ground, dark brown borders and pale yellow rim, conforming paneled pedestal with matching decoration, top of jardiniere stamped "Doulton – Lambeth," restoration around rim of jardiniere, small chips on pedestal, late 19th century, jardiniere 18-1/4" w. x 15-1/2" h., pedestal 13" w. x 20-1/2" h...................................... **$2,530**

Pitcher, Series Ware, Old English Coaching Scenes, yellow ground with figure of elderly man in long overcoat, stagecoach design rim band, inside of rim printed in black "Old Bob Ye Guard," circa 1953-1967, 7-3/4" h **$173**

Model of salmon, Rouge Flambé, leaping fish glazed in dark red shading to black, Model No. 666, early 20th century, 12-1/2" h **$1,440**

Baby feeding plate, Dickens Ware, pale yellow rim and interior color scene of "Shylock," brown printed backstamp, early 20th century, 8-1/2" dia..................... **$75-100**

CERAMICS

Compote, covered, Sung Ware, flaring octagonal low pedestal base supporting wide rounded octagonal bowl with conforming fitted domed cover, mottled Flambé glaze in shades of dark and light blue and deep red, Flambé and Sung marks, decorated by Noke & Moore, early 20th century, 2-3/4" h $690

Charger, central scene of lady riding horse sidesaddle with hound racing alongside, in yellow, brown, green, black and white, border band of dark green stylized grapevine, marked "George Morland #1784," 14" dia $125

Tea set: covered teapot, open sugar and creamer, Cockerel pattern, teapot modeled as rooster, sugar bowl as hen, creamer as chick, introduced circa 1935 .... $2,500

CERAMICS

Tea tile, oval, Under the Greenwood Tree Series, color scene of Robin Hood seated under a tree watching archers in distance, "Lincoln the Forest of Sherwood" around rim, introduced in 1914. .... **$250**

Doulton Lambethware pitcher, Hannah Barlow, design of hounds chasing fox, 1875, vertical hairline crack, 11" h........ **$1,250**

Hunting Ware tea set: large covered teapot, small covered teapot, covered sugar bowl and creamer, dark brown shaded to tan ground decorated with applied relief-molded English hunting scenes, Doulton-Lambeth marks, circa 1905 .... **$600**

Teapot, covered, bone china, hand-painted with images of exotic birds and heavy gilt scroll trim, painted by Joseph Birbeck, circa 1910......... **$2,000**

Kingsware tea set: covered teapot, open sugar, and creamer, each piece with different embossed figural scene, introduced in 1902. ....**$750**

CERAMICS

Plate, Robin Hood Series,"Friar Tuck Joins Robin Hood," natural-colored scene of Robin Hood and Friar Tuck standing and talking under large tree, 7-1/2" sq.. **$85**

Plate, Sayings Ware Series, "The Cup That Cheers," center bust portrait of elderly woman drinking tea, band of teacups around rim, circa 1907, 9" dia.. **$300**

Sugar bowl, covered, Welsh Ladies Series, long straight-sided oval body with angled end handles and flattened shoulder centering flat covers with peaked finial, scenes of Welsh ladies around sides, introduced in 1906 .... **$300**

Charger, Dickens Ware, round, color scene of Tony Weller, early 20th century, 13-1/2" dia......**$200-300**

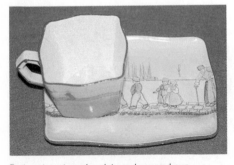

Party set, rectangular plate and squared cup, Dutch Series, scenes of Dutch people at waterfront around sides, circa 1920 .... **$200**

Soap dish, stoneware, oblong with large brown and lavender flying insect molded along one side of dark blue glazed dish, impressed markings on base for Wright's Coal Tar Soap, 4-1/4" x 5-3/4", 1-1/2" h **$150**

CERAMICS

Teapot, covered, bone china, wide squatty bulbous body with long angled spout, forked C-form handle and low domed cover with button finial, overall floral gilding, circa 1923. .... **$500**

Urn, covered, tall slender ovoid body raised on ribbed and gadrooned gold and green pedestal base with square foot and flanked by long gold full-length handles, tapering to ringed and ribbed cylindrical neck with flaring rim fitted with high Gothic spire-form cover, hand painted with scene of highland cattle against purplish mountain backdrop, glossy glaze, artist-signed by S. Kelsall, small professional repair to handle and pedestal, circa 1910, 32" h. **$2,500**

Teapot, covered, Bunnykins Series, model of large rabbit, designed by Charles Noke, introduced in 1939. ....**$3,000**

Teapot, covered, stoneware, tapering cylindrical body with flaring rim, angled spout, large rectangular panel with scene of Bladud, founder of city of Bath, made for R.S. Carey, Bath, Doulton-Lambeth, circa 1894. .... **$750**

Teapot, covered, figural, crouching camel with heavy load, Arab driver pulling from behind and forming handle, ruby glaze, designed by Moore Brothers, apparently made by Doulton, Doulton-Lambeth, circa 1877...**$5,000**

CERAMICS

FIESTA

THE HOMER LAUGHLIN CHINA CO. originated with a two-kiln pottery on the banks of the Ohio River in East Liverpool, Ohio. Built in 1873-'74 by Homer Laughlin and his brother, Shakespeare, the firm was first known as the Ohio Valley Pottery, and later Laughlin Bros. Pottery. It was one of the first white-ware plants in the country.

After a tentative beginning, the company was awarded a prize for having the best white-ware at the 1876 Centennial Exposition in Philadelphia.

Three years later, Shakespeare sold his interest in the business to Homer, who continued on until 1897. At that time, Homer sold his interest in the newly incorporated firm to a group of investors, including Charles, Louis, and Marcus Aaron and the company bookkeeper, William E. Wells.

Under new ownership in 1907, the headquarters and a new 30-kiln plant were built across the Ohio River in Newell, West Virginia, the present manufacturing and headquarters location.

In the 1920s, two additions to the Homer Laughlin staff set the stage for the company's greatest success: the Fiesta line. Dr. Albert V. Bleininger was hired in 1920. A scientist, author, and educator, he oversaw the conversion from bottle kilns to the more efficient tunnel kilns. In 1927, the company hired designer Frederick Hurten Rhead, a member of a distinguished family of English ceramists. Having previously worked at Weller Pottery and Roseville Pottery, Rhead began to develop the artistic quality of the company's wares, and to experiment with shapes and glazes. In 1935, this work culminated in his designs for the Fiesta line.

For more information on Fiesta, see *Warman's Fiesta Identification and Price Guide* by Glen Victorey.

Fiesta Colors

From 1936 to 1972, Fiesta was produced in 14 colors (other than special promotions). These colors are usually divided into the "original colors" of cobalt blue, light green, ivory, red, turquoise, and yellow; the "1950s colors" of chartreuse, forest green, gray, and rose (introduced in 1951); medium green (introduced in 1959); plus the later additions of Casuals, Amberstone, Fiesta Ironstone, and Casualstone ("Coventry") in antique gold, mango red, and turf green; and the striped, decal, and Lustre pieces. No Fiesta was produced from 1973 to 1985. The colors that make up the "original" and "1950s" groups are sometimes referred to as "the standard 11."

In many pieces, medium green is the hardest to find and the most expensive Fiesta color.

Fiesta Colors and Years of Production to 1972

Antique Gold	1969-1972	Ivory	1936-1951
Chartreuse	1951-1959	Mango Red (same as original red)	1970-1972
Cobalt Blue	1936-1951	Medium Green	1959-1969
Forest Green	1951-1959	Red	1936-1944 and 1959-1972
Gray	1951-1959	Rose	1951-1959
Green	1936-1951	Turf Green	1969-1972
(often called light green when comparing it to		Turquoise	1937-1969
other green glazes; also called "original" green)		Yellow	1936-1969

Red covered onion soup bowl............................ **$303**
Strawser Auctions

Green World's Fair Four Seasons bowl.............. **$121**
Strawser Auctions

Medium green dessert bowl. **$303**
Strawser Auctions

Ivory covered onion soup bowl......................... **$424**
Strawser Auctions

Red footed salad bowl. **$85**
Strawser Auctions

Green covered onion soup bowl. **$575**
Strawser Auctions

Turquoise demitasse coffee pot. **$424**
Strawser Auctions

Yellow demitasse coffee pot. **$169**
Strawser Auctions

Forest green two-pint jug. **$72**
Strawser Auctions

Turquoise World's Fair Four Seasons bowl. **$121**
Strawser Auctions

Medium green fruit bowl. **$205**
Strawser Auctions

Medium green casserole. **$414**
Strawser Auctions

Green cake plate.. $847
Strawser Auctions

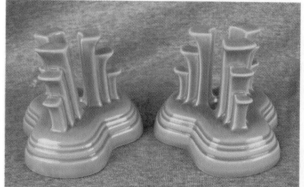

Green tripod candleholders... $242
Strawser Auctions

Yellow French casserole... $103
Strawser Auctions

Yellow water carafe $115
Strawser Auctions

Green water carafe.............. $121
Strawser Auctions

Gray coffee pot. $145
Strawser Auctions

CERAMICS

Red creamer and yellow sugar on turquoise tray............................ $484
Strawser Auctions

Red stick-handle creamer and sugar. $79
Strawser Auctions

Green #1 mixing bowl lid $333
Strawser Auctions

Pair of medium green 6" plates. $48
Strawser Auctions

Rose coffee pot. $121
Strawser Auctions

Forest green eggcup.............. $67
Strawser Auctions

Chartreuse eggcup. $91
Strawser Auctions

Rose eggcup. $42
Strawser Auctions

CERAMICS

Green marmalade. **$145**
Strawser Auctions

Cobalt marmalade.. **$133**
Strawser Auctions

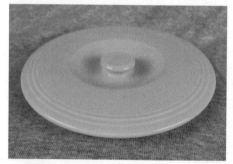

Yellow #3 mixing bowl lid. **$454**
Strawser Auctions

Cobalt #2 mixing bowl. **$182**
Strawser Auctions

Red two-pint jug. **$79**
Strawser Auctions

Medium green disk pitcher **$545**
Strawser Auctions

CERAMICS

Turquoise chop plate with handle. **$72**
Strawser Auctions

Red ice lip pitcher. **$85**
Strawser Auctions

Medium green platter. **$193**
Strawser Auctions

Turquoise compartment plate. **$30**
Strawser Auctions

Red chop plate. **$42**
Strawser Auctions

Green compartment plate. **$6**
Strawser Auctions

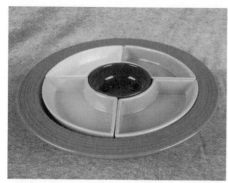

Relish tray with red base, all six colors............. **$182**

Strawser Auctions

Relish tray with cobalt base, all six colors. **$303**

Strawser Auctions

Red sauceboat.. **$42**

Strawser Auctions

Red platter... **$30**

Strawser Auctions

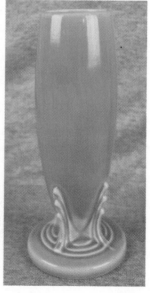

Cobalt 12" vase.................. **$908**

Strawser Auctions

Red 10" vase. **$787**

Strawser Auctions

Green bud vase..................... **$36**

Strawser Auctions

CERAMICS

FRANKOMA

JOHN FRANK STARTED HIS POTTERY COMPANY in 1933 in Norman, Oklahoma. However, when he moved the business to Sapulpa, Oklahoma, in 1938, he felt he was home. Frank could not know the horrendous storms and trials that would follow him. Just after his move, on Nov. 11, 1938, a fire destroyed the entire operation, which included the "pot and leopard" mark he had created in 1935. Then, in 1942, the war effort needed men and materials, so Frankoma could not survive. In 1943, John and Grace Lee Frank bought the plant as junk salvage and began again.

The time in Norman had produced some of the finest art ware that John would ever create and most of the items were marked either "Frank Potteries," "Frank Pottery," or to a lesser degree, the "pot and leopard" mark. Today these marks are avidly and enthusiastically sought by collectors. Another elusive mark wanted by collectors shows "Firsts Kiln Sapulpa 6-7-38." The mark was used for one day only and denotes the first firing in Sapulpa. It has been estimated that perhaps 50 to 75 pieces were fired on that day.

The clay Frankoma used is helpful to collectors in determining when an item was made. Creamy beige clay known as "Ada" clay was in use until 1953. Then a red brick shale was found in Sapulpa and used until about 1985 when, with the addition of an additive, the clay became a reddish pink.

Rutile glazes were used early in Frankoma's history. Glazes with rutile have caused more confusion among collectors than any other glazes. For example, a Prairie Green piece shows a lot of green but it also has some brown. The same is true for the Desert Gold glaze; the piece shows a sandy-beige glaze with some brown. Generally speaking, Prairie Green, Desert Gold, White Sand, and Woodland Moss are the most puzzling to collectors.

In 1970 the government closed the rutile mines in America, and Frankoma had to buy it from Australia. It was not the same, so the results were different. Values are higher for the glazes with rutile. Also, the pre-Australian Woodland Moss glaze is more desirable than that created after 1970.

After John Frank died in 1973, his daughter Joniece Frank, a ceramic designer at the pottery, became president of the company. In 1983 another fire destroyed everything Frankoma had worked so hard to create. They rebuilt, but in 1990, after the IRS shut the doors for nonpayment, Joniece, true to the Frank legacy, filed for Chapter 11 (instead of bankruptcy) so she could reopen and continue the work she loved.

In 1991 Richard Bernstein purchased the pottery, and the name was changed to Frankoma Industries. The company was sold again in 2005 to Det and Crystal Merryman. Yet another owner, Joe Ragosta, purchased the pottery in 2008.

Frankoma Pottery was closed for good in 2010 with a factory closeout auction in Oklahoma in 2011.

CERAMICS

Two early vases, Desert Gold glaze over Ada clay vase with stylized landscape of clouds and trees, marked with impressed Pacing Leopard Frankoma logo, glaze flake off base, 4-3/4" h.; Prairie Green glaze over Ada clay vase, marked "Frank Potteries Norman, Oklahoma" in black, excellent original condition, 4-5/8" h. **$300**

Mark Mussio, Humler & Nolan

Ponytail woman figure, marked Frankoma 106, mint condition, 9-3/4" h. **$90**

Belhorn Auction Services, LLC

Two black panthers, both marked, mint condition, 7" h. and 9-1/4" l.........................**$41**

Belhorn Auction Services, LLC

Cups from 1980 for GOP and Democratic parties, both marked, mint condition, 3-7/8" h..**$6**

Belhorn Auction Services, LLC

Cabinet pitcher marked 553 and Frankoma, mint condition, 2-5/8" h. **$8**

Belhorn Auction Services, LLC

Centerpiece bowl marked Frankoma 214, mint condition, 11-3/4" l. **$5**

Belhorn Auction Services, LLC

Nude dancer candelabra, marked Frankoma GS 51, mint condition, 11-1/2" h...........**$150**

Belhorn Auction Services, LLC

Pair of candelabras in white with nudes holding flowing drapery, marked Frankoma GS51, mint condition, 11-1/2" h...........**$275**

Belhorn Auction Services, LLC

Circular vase with desert scene, marked Frankoma 4, mint condition, 7" h.....................**$29**

Belhorn Auction Services, LLC

Nude figure with cheetah, marked Frankoma GS 52 and 176, mint condition, 11-3/8" h..**$120**

Belhorn Auction Services, LLC

CERAMICS

FULPER POTTERY

FROM THE "GERM-PROOF FILTER" to enduring Arts & Crafts acclaim – that's the unlikely journey of Fulper Pottery, maker of the early 20th-century uniquely glazed artware that's become a favorite with today's collectors.

Fulper began life in 1814 as the Samuel Hill Pottery, named after its founder, a New Jersey potter. In its early years, the pottery specialized in useful items such as storage crocks and drainpipes fashioned from the area's red clay. Abraham Fulper, a worker at the pottery, eventually became Hill's partner, purchasing the company in 1860. Renamed after its new owner, Fulper Pottery continued to produce a variety of utilitarian tile and crockery. By the turn of the 20th century, the firm, now led by Abraham's sons, introduced a line of fire-proof cookware and the hugely successful "Germ-Proof Filter." An ancestor of today's water cooler, the filter provided sanitary drinking water in less-than-sanitary public places, such as offices and railway stations.

In the early 1900s, Fulper's master potter, John Kunsman, began creating various solid-glaze vessels, such as jugs and vases, which were offered for sale outside the pottery. On a whim, William H. Fulper II (Abraham's grandson, who'd become the company's secretary/treasurer) took an assortment of these items for exhibit at the 1904 Louisiana Purchase Exposition—along with, of course, the Germ-Proof Filter. Kunsman's artware took home an honorable mention.

Since Chinese art pottery was then attracting national attention, Fulper saw an opening to produce similarly styled modern ware. Dr. Cullen Parmelee, who headed the ceramics department at Rutgers, was recruited to create a contemporary series of glazes patterned after those of ancient China. The Fulper Vasekraft line of art pottery incorporating these glazes made its debut in 1909. Unfortunately, Parmelee's glazes did not lend themselves well to mass production; they did not result in reliable coloration. Even more to their detriment, they were expensive to produce.

In 1910, most of Parmelee's glazes disappeared from the line. A new ceramic engineer, Martin Stangl, was given the assignment of revitalizing Vasekraft. His most notable innovation: steering designs and glazes away from reinterpretations of ornate Chinese classics and toward the simplicity of the burgeoning Arts & Crafts movement. Among his many Vasekraft successes: candleholders, bookends, perfume lamps, desk accessories, tobacco jars, and even

Fine, rare Vasekraft lamp, Cafe au Lait and Cucumber Green glaze, circa 1908, glazed ceramic, leaded glass, two sockets, vertical rectangular stamp, PATENT PENDING US AND CANADA, 22-1/2" x 16" dia.
.... **$11,250**

Rago Arts

Vasekraft lamps. Here, both the lamp base and shade were of pottery; stained glass inserts in the shades allowed light to shine through.

Always attuned to the mood of the times, William Fulper realized that by World War I the heavy Vasekraft stylings were fading in popularity. A new and lighter line of Fulper Pottery Artware, featuring Spanish Revival and English themes, was introduced. Among the most admired Fulper releases following the war were Fulper Porcelaines: dresser boxes, powder jars, ashtrays, lamps, and other accessories designed to complement the fashionable boudoir.

Fayence, the popular line of solid-color, open-stock dinnerware eventually known as Stangl Pottery, was introduced in the 1920s. In 1928, following William Fulper's death, Martin Stangl was named company president. The artware that continued into the 1930s embraced Art Deco as well as Classical and Primitive stylistic themes. From 1935 onward, Stangl Pottery became the sole Fulper output. In 1978, the Stangl assets came under the ownership of Pfaltzgraff.

Unlike wheel-thrown pottery, Fulper was made in molds; the true artistry came in the use of exceptionally rich, color-blended glazes. Each Fulper piece is one-of-a-kind. Because of glaze divergence, two Fulper objects from the same mold can show a great variance. While once a drawback for retailers seeking consistency, that uniqueness is now a boon to collectors: Each Fulper piece possesses its own singular visual appeal.

Urn, blue crystalline glaze, 1910-1916, incised racetrack mark, 12" x 8-1/2" h. **$2,000**

Rago Arts

Rare buttress vase, largest of three sizes Fulper made, in Flemington Green glaze over which Mirror Black glaze has been dripped from rim, marked with early non-serifed rectangular ink stamp, tiny grinding chips at base and areas of light glaze scratches not uncommon with forms this large, 13-1/2" h. **$1,600**

Mark Mussio, Humler & Nolan

Hooded candleholder with handle in blue flambé glaze, impressed oval mark, small grinding chip on base, 7-1/4" h........**$225**

Mark Mussio, Humler & Nolan

CERAMICS

Twin-handled vase in Copper Dust crystalline glaze over mirrored green, raised oval racetrack logo, minor grinding chips on base, 9-1/2" h **$325**

Mark Mussio, Humler & Nolan

Vase in Chinese Blue flambé glaze over which tan glaze has been dripped, marked on bottom with die-stamped "incised" Fulper mark, majority of original "Panama-Pacific International Exposition San Francisco 1915 Highest Award to Fulper Pottery" paper label on side, uncrazed, 7" h **$200**

Mark Mussio, Humler & Nolan

Bud vase in Cucumber crystalline glaze, marked on bottom with die-stamped "incised" Fulper mark, minor crazing, 8-7/8" h **$100**

Mark Mussio, Humler & Nolan

Single peacock book block in blue mat glaze over which green high glaze was applied, marked on bottom with vertical ink-stamped racetrack mark, paper label attached to back of piece, 1/4" x 1/2" glaze skip on bottom right corner, 5-7/8" h **$160**

Mark Mussio, Humler & Nolan

Vase in blue mat glaze to which Copper Dust crystalline flambé has been dripped from rim, bottom marked with larger rectangular Fulper ink stamp, excellent original condition, 8" h. **$120**

Mark Mussio, Humler & Nolan

Twin-handled vase in Leopard Skin crystalline glaze, marked on bottom with ink-stamped vertical racetrack mark, 1/4" grinding chip at base, 6-1/4" h **$150**

Mark Mussio, Humler & Nolan

Buttress vase, rarest of three sizes of buttress vases by Fulper, in Mirror Black over cream glazes, marked on bottom with die-stamped, incised mark, 3/4" firing separation at rim and grinding chips at base, crazing towards bottom of piece, 10-1/2" h.. **$450**

Mark Mussio, Humler & Nolan

"Woman in Canoe" flower frog in olive green mat glaze, marked on bottom with larger rectangular ink mark, 1/4" chip at base, 3-3/4" h. x 7-1/2" l.. **$70**

Mark Mussio, Humler & Nolan

Buttress vase in tan flambé glaze over which Mirror Black glaze has been dripped from rim, marked on bottom with Fulper racetrack ink stamp, minor crazing toward bottom of piece, minor grinding chips at base, 8-1/4" h.................... **$200**

Mark Mussio, Humler & Nolan

Vase in Mirror Black flambé glaze layered over brown, green over blue, ink stamp racetrack mark, small burst glaze bubble, excellent original condition, 11-3/4" h **$325**

Mark Mussio, Humler & Nolan

Vase in Elephant's Breath glaze, marked on bottom with raised vertical oval Fulper mark obscured by glaze, excellent original condition, 9-1/8" h .. **$325**

Mark Mussio, Humler & Nolan

Vase in Butterscotch flambé glaze, marked on bottom with die stamped "incised" mark mostly obliterated by drill hole through center, grinding chips at base, thick glaze, 11-1/2" h. **$170**

Mark Mussio, Humler & Nolan

Three-handled vase in green mat glaze, marked with Fulper racetrack ink stamp, excellent original condition, 4-1/8" h ... **$275**

Mark Mussio, Humler & Nolan

Cat doorstop in rose flambé glaze with spots of blue and green crystalline glazes, marked on bottom FULPER in block letters, 1/4" chip to left ear, 6-7/8" h. **$500**

Mark Mussio, Humler & Nolan

CERAMICS

Early Arts & Crafts-style hooded candle shield in deep blue crystalline glaze with all three original glass inserts, two triangular white and one rectangular blue, marked on bottom with die-stamped "incised" mark with small remnant of original paper label, minor grinding chip on foot ring, 10-5/8" h................ **$1,300**

Mark Mussio, Humler & Nolan

Vase with slender body and flaring bulbous shoulder and two square applied handles, mauve striated and speckled glaze, marked on underside with original Fulper paper label, nick to underside of foot, very good condition, 8" h............. **$89**

James D. Julia, Inc.

Rare twin-handled vase in blue, green, and cream flambé glazes, 1/2" glaze scratch on one handle, open glaze bubbles, bottom marked with raised, vertical oval Fulper mark, 14-1/2" h............. **$1,000**

Mark Mussio, Humler & Nolan

Vase in tan flambé glaze over which Mirror Black glaze has been dripped from rim resulting in blue- and copper-colored highlights, marked on base with Fulper racetrack ink stamp, excellent original condition, 7-1/4" h............. **$150**

Mark Mussio, Humler & Nolan

Vase with two squared-off handles in glossy green and blue flambé glazes, handles and area near bottom in mat colors, marked with original Fulper square label that reads "480 Vase Blue Wisteria Green $10," excellent original condition with some bubbles in glaze, 9-3/8" h............. **$400**

Mark Mussio, Humler & Nolan

Rare Vasekraft three-handled vase in Mission Matte brown glaze, three molded 5-1/4" recessed areas with strap handles, marked on bottom with early Fulper rectangular ink mark, small grinding chips on foot ring, open glaze bubbles, 9-1/4" h. x 11" dia. **$6,750**

Mark Mussio, Humler & Nolan

Artichoke bowl in ivory glaze at rim shading to Flemington Green flambé, impressed with Fulper middle-period racetrack mark, small burst glaze bubbles, 5-1/2" h. x 8-1/2" w...................... **$700**

Mark Mussio, Humler & Nolan

Shell bowl in Copper Dust crystalline glaze on interior and Mirror Black glaze on exterior, excellent original condition, marked with die-stamped "incised" mark, 3-3/4" h. x 11-3/4" w. **$200**

Mark Mussio, Humler & Nolan

Bulldog doorstop in mustard mat glaze over which blue flambé glaze has been dripped, marked on bottom with Fulper racetrack ink stamp, some tight firing separations on bottom, professional repair to right ear, 8-3/8" h. **$425**

Mark Mussio, Humler & Nolan

Vase in blue over cream flambé glazes, marked on bottom with early rectangular Fulper ink stamp, original Fulper Pottery Panama-Pacific International Exposition label affixed to side of vase, slight crazing at shoulder and minor grinding chips at base, 10-1/8" h. **$225**

Mark Mussio, Humler & Nolan

Twin-handled vase with Leopard Skin glaze, marked on bottom with Fulper racetrack ink stamp, excellent original condition, 8" h. **$225**

Mark Mussio, Humler & Nolan

Vase in Mirror Black glaze over navy blue glaze over rose glaze, marked on bottom with Fulper die-stamped "incised" mark, bruise and small chip at base, fine crazing and open glaze bubbles, 7-1/2" h. **$150**

Mark Mussio, Humler & Nolan

Vase in Cucumber crystalline glaze, marked on bottom with die-stamped "incised" Fulper mark, excellent original condition, 6-3/4" h. x 8-3/8" dia. **$400**

Mark Mussio, Humler & Nolan

Chinese form vase in blue flambé glaze over Elephant's Breath glaze, marked on bottom with raised vertical oval Fulper mark, tight firing separations from base, 11-1/2" h. **$200**

Mark Mussio, Humler & Nolan

Four-footed urn, Cafe au Lait glaze, 1916-1922, racetrack stamp, 16-1/2" x 5-3/4" h ... **$563**

Rago Arts

CERAMICS

Three-horned vase in cream over blue flambé glazes, marked on bottom with Fulper die-stamped "incised" mark, small open glaze bubbles, 6-1/4" h. **$400**

Mark Mussio, Humler & Nolan

Twin-handled vase in Cucumber crystalline glaze, open glaze bubbles, marked on bottom with raised Fulper vertical oval mark, 8-3/8" h **$900**

Mark Mussio, Humler & Nolan

Early square tapering vase in black over crystalline blue over Wisteria glazes, marked with early rectangular Fulper ink stamp logo and letter "D," 8" h. **$550**

Mark Mussio, Humler & Nolan

Tall baluster vase in Cat's Eye flambé glaze, 1910-1920, ink racetrack stamp, 14" x 6-1/2" h. **$1,875**

Rago Arts

Vase in tan glaze shading to brown striated glaze at shoulder and neck, signed on bottom with black oval stamped signature "Fulper" and incised "DS8," very good to excellent condition, 9-1/2" h............. **$237**

James D. Julia, Inc.

Vase in Cucumber crystalline glaze, marked on bottom with small Fulper racetrack ink stamp and original paper label, excellent condition, 11-1/2" h. **$700**

Mark Mussio, Humler & Nolan

Tall vase in Venetian Blue glaze, 1916-1922, raised racetrack mark, 17" x 9" h.. **$688**

Rago Arts

Crescent moon flower holder in green crystalline glaze, no crazing, marked on bottom with rectangular Fulper ink stamp, 8-1/4" h. **$150**

Mark Mussio, Humler & Nolan

Large vase with bulbous body and squared handles in light brown glaze with dark brown interior, marked on bottom with stamped oval signature "Fulper," very good to excellent condition, 7-1/2" h. x 8-1/2" dia. **$415**

James D. Julia, Inc.

Vase in maroon glaze and double handles, signed on underside "Fulper"; vase in maroon glaze shading to green at top, four raised ribs extending vertically up sides, signed on underside "Fulper"; and pitcher in maroon glaze shading to mottled blue and green at top, signed on underside with impressed signature "Fulper 830L"; very good to excellent condition, pitcher with firing crack in bottom interior, tallest 8-1/2" h. **$296**

James D. Julia, Inc.

Tall vase in Mirror Black glaze, 1916-1922, incised racetrack mark, 17" x 7" h............. **$2,875**

Rago Arts

Standing duck figural with glass eyes in green flambé glaze, impressed on bottom "Fulper" in block letters and 875, minor chips at duck's beak, 7-1/8"; bird wall pocket in white, yellow, green and black glazes, marked on back with racetrack ink stamp and shape number 369, remnants of Fulper paper label, bottom two feathers have been over sprayed, indicating restoration, 9" h... **$375**

Mark Mussio, Humler & Nolan

Three vases with light bluish-green bodies with blue and gold striations and gold striated glaze at top, two larger vases signed on bottom with incised signature "Fulper," smallest vase signed with stamped oval signature "Fulper," all very good to excellent condition, tallest 9" h. **$415**

James D. Julia, Inc.

Bottle vase in green crystalline glaze over brown flambé, marked on bottom with early Fulper larger rectangular ink stamp, excellent original condition, 7-3/4" h............. **$350**

Mark Mussio, Humler & Nolan

Porcelain novelty dish of female bather by Anne Fish, who signed piece in black slip on blue water, marked on bottom with Fulper racetrack ink stamp and stamped 567, professional repair to rim, 2-3/4" h. x 5" dia. **$160**

Mark Mussio, Humler & Nolan

Temple jar in Flemington Blue flambé glaze, 1916-1922, raised racetrack mark, 11-3/4" x 8-1/2" h.......................... **$813**

Rago Arts

CERAMICS

GOUDA

GOUDA IS ONE of the decorative art world's strong and silent types, notwithstanding its beautifully bright colors and rich floral and abstract designs – considered by many to be its calling card. While its place in today's market is less robust than some of its contemporaries, such as Weller and Rookwood, its pairing of subtle strength of identity and eye-catching design is what attracts people to it and makes it a collecting category to watch.

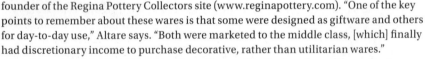

It was 1898 when Plateelbakkerij Zuid-Holland, often referred to as PZH or Zuid-Holland, produced its first piece of Gouda pottery. Named for the region in the Netherlands, Gouda encompasses the pottery produced by several factories located there. While the earliest examples of Gouda were not the same as the brightly colored, mat glaze pieces collected today, they were often sought after for the same reason as today: décor for the home.

However, like many types of pottery, it didn't necessarily start out that way, according to Joe Altare, founder of the Regina Pottery Collectors site (www.reginapottery.com). "One of the key points to remember about these wares is that some were designed as giftware and others for day-to-day use," Altare says. "Both were marketed to the middle class, [which] finally had discretionary income to purchase decorative, rather than utilitarian wares."

Looking at the history of Gouda pottery, it's possible the founders of the earliest factories would be surprised to see what has become of their pottery — especially since many of the first companies to produce Gouda pottery did so to diversify their primary operation of clay pipe production. With an abundance of clay in the Gouda region of the Netherlands, it made good sense for the companies to expand into pottery; and the public demand confirmed it, according to information on the Museumgouda website, www.museumgouda.nl.

People, then and now, are drawn in by the remarkable colors and designs.

"I stumbled across my first piece, a Regina compote, on eBay about 10 years ago. I knew nothing about Gouda pottery or the Regina factory, but the design captivated me and I had to have it," Altare says. "The design, variety and quality of execution captured my attention, and the many untold secrets of the [Regina] factory have fueled my passion these many years."

Although many of the companies that produced Gouda pottery remained in operation through the mid-1960s and 1970s, many consider the heyday of Gouda to have lasted through the first three decades of the 20th century. In fact, in the 1920s, a quarter of the workforce in the Gouda region was employed in the pottery industry, according to Museumgouda.

As with many situations, there are exceptions to the status quo, and that's also true in today's Gouda pottery market. While the most common Gouda pieces are seen in mat finishes, which are more modern and also more plentiful, early pieces, especially those with birds or butterflies under their gloss finishes, may be somewhat hard to find and tend to be more interesting, according to Riley Humler, auction director and art pottery expert at Humler & Nolan.

While Gouda pieces may not be setting high-profile auction records today, it remains a strong and serious representative of the ingenuity of decorative pottery. Plus, as more people are shopping at places like IKEA and Crate & Barrel for modern décor and furnishings, decorative pottery like Gouda lends itself nicely to that scene.

Art Nouveau glazed ceramic wall-hanging charger, Netherlands, circa 1900, signed MADE IN ZUID HOLLAND/F with house cipher, impressed 8DUW with shield, 16" dia. **$813**

Rago Arts

In addition to fitting into society's modern décor and design interests, another advantage for Gouda is that it is more affordable, according to Humler. "Even the best pieces are in most people's price range," he says.

Higher-end pieces continue to attract attention, not unlike many other categories of antiques today. "There appears to be a line in the sand with Gouda right now," says Stuart Slavid, vice president and director of Fine Ceramics, Fine Silver, European Furniture & Decorative Arts at Skinner, Inc. "Spectacular pieces are still doing very well, but there is very little or no movement at all for lower-end pieces."

The reasons for that vary, but some contributing factors appear to be advanced collectors looking for advanced pieces rather than more basic items; and the way in which people collect overall has changed some, Slavid explains.

"It used to be more people would start with good pieces, move to better pieces and then to great. Now more people with available discretionary income are starting with the very best pieces," he says.

Humler echoes Slavid's sentiments, adding that high-end pieces in every collecting arena are doing far better than the rest.

"I think the reason is serious collectors are looking for better pieces and avoiding lesser items," Humler says. "Quality has finally taken over for quantity. Part of that may be that serious collectors are generally older and have money."

With a history steeped in innovation primed by practicality and fans across the globe, a renewal and widespread rediscovery of Gouda pottery isn't out of the question.

—Antoinette Rahn, editor, Antique Trader *magazine*

CERAMICS

Gouda PZH Mat Bloemen vase with exotic bird and flowers, marked "Zuid Holland 137 35" along with small house, incised artist marks, uncrazed, 10-5/8" h. **$275**

Mark Mussio, Humler & Nolan

Arnhem Gouda mat glaze handled vase decorated with large bird perched in clematis vine, faint painted factory mark, good color and design, excellent condition, 13" h. **$250**

Mark Mussio, Humler & Nolan

Five Gouda Regina items: three vases, covered box, and pitcher, all decorated with flowers and ornate designs, all marked with Crown WB logo and Gouda Holland with numbers, some have artist's name, one vase also marked "Special Made for Woodward L. Lothrop," all in excellent condition, tallest vase 11", box 3-1/4" x 4-1/2", pitcher 5-1/4"..**$400**

Mark Mussio, Humler & Nolan

CERAMICS

Five assorted Gouda vases: turquoise blue Flora Fhenza, 7-1/4"; C.M. Bergen handled vase, 4-3/4"; Nadro handled vase, 4"; Logari ewer, 7-1/2"; Metz Royal ewer, 6-1/2"; all have maker's marks and logos painted on bottom, all in excellent condition. **$140**

Mark Mussio, Humler & Nolan

Gouda pottery vase and candlestick, Dutch, early 20th century, decorated with stylized floral motifs in shades of green, yellow, blue, and orange, candlestick with incised 0124/2 / D and Camdia(?) / Holland / 0.124/2 / F in blue, vase marked Suley(?) / 951 / Holland / Gouda / 2 in black with house and branch logo; holes drilled on one side of foot and under base to accommodate electric cord, some pitting to glaze primarily around bobeche, vase with crazing, repair to lip with two hairlines running from lip to shoulder, small chip to underside of foot, candlestick 16-3/4" h. **$90**

Cowan's Auctions, Inc.

Five PZH Gouda items: Roma candleholder with attached tray, 6"; pair of Rhodian vases, 7-1/2"; Gold eté "bird" vase, 6"; and Beek stick vase, 10"; all marked "Gouda Holland" with house logo, all in excellent condition. **$400**

Mark Mussio, Humler & Nolan

CERAMICS

Five PZH Gouda pieces: three vases, Emma, 4-1/2", Corona (glaze nick to rim), 4-3/8"; and Lunette, 6"; two boxes, Roba, 3-1/4" x 5-1/4", and Coes, 1-1/2" x 4"; all hand-painted Gouda Holland with house marks, excellent condition.. **$350**

Mark Mussio, Humler & Nolan

Distel Art Nouveau floral vase in high glaze, circa 1900, exotic flowers cover six-sided form, marked in black slip "Distel T.V.V. 62/dec. III." on bottom, 8-1/2" tall. **$375**

Mark Mussio, Humler & Nolan

Four Gouda high glaze floral vases; poppies, unknown maker, marked with wooden shoe and several obscure words, 7-3/4" h.; ivory vase with exotic flowers, marked Ivory Holland, 8-1/4" h.; covered jar marked Gouda, 4-3/4" h.; two-handled vase marked Talos Gouda Holland, 3" h.; all in excellent condition except vase with poppies, which has restoration to rim and base... **$325**

Mark Mussio, Humler & Nolan

Regina windmill ashtray in Rosario pattern, sails of windmill turn on tiny spindle, marked "Regina Rosario Gouda Holland 923 M" on bottom, excellent original condition, 4-1/4" h. **$130**

Mark Mussio, Humler & Nolan

Three miniature Zuide Gouda high glaze vases showing artistic floral design, all hand-marked Zuide Holland along with other marks, faint crazing, tallest 6-3/8". **$180**

Mark Mussio, Humler & Nolan

PZH Gouda Jella high glaze pitcher, circa 1918, decoration of leaves and flowers over entire surface, marked "Jella Holland Gouda" along with image of small house, also artist's marks and codes, light crazing, 10-1/2" h. **$200**

Mark Mussio, Humler & Nolan

Two small PZH Gouda high glaze vases with Art Nouveau floral decoration, both marked with PZH logo and small house design, excellent original condition, 2-3/4" and 3-5/8" h......................... **$150**

Gouda Regina advertising sign in Rosario pattern, "Regina Gouda plateel," no other marks, excellent original condition, 3-7/8" h. x 6-1/8" w. **$140**

Mark Mussio, Humler & Nolan

Arnhem Gouda high glaze vase with clematis decoration, marked Arnhem Holland with rooster symbol and signed H.S. Gelri 254, fine overall crazing, 11-1/8" h. **$325**

Mark Mussio, Humler & Nolan

CERAMICS

$

GRUEBY

SOME FINE ART POTTERY was produced by the Grueby
Faience and Tile Co., established in Boston in 1891. Choice
pieces were created with molded designs on a semi-porcelain
body. The ware is marked and often bears the initials of the
decorators. The pottery closed in 1907.

GRUEBY

TOP LOT!

Vase with tooled leaves by Wilhelmine
Post, in signature green mat glaze,
impressed Grueby logo, shape number 75
and incised initials of Post, nicks to high
points, 7-3/4" h. **$2,400**

Mark Mussio, Humler & Nolan

Large vase carved with leaves in curdled brown
over green glaze, Boston, circa 1905, circular
Grueby Pottery stamp and remnants of paper
label, 14-1/2" x 9"............................. **$12,500**

Rago Arts

CERAMICS

Large low bowl carved with leaves, Boston, circa 1905, circular Grueby Pottery stamp, artist's cipher, 4" x 10" sq......................**$1,625**
Rago Arts

Vase with five hand-tooled buttresses in feathery green mat glaze, impressed Grueby circular logo, excellent original condition, 7" h................ **$1,400**

Mark Mussio, Humler & Nolan

Scarab paperweight in blue over green mat glazes, impressed with circular Grueby Faience logo on base, one glaze nick near base, 1-1/4" h. x 3-1/4" l. **$350**

Mark Mussio, Humler & Nolan

Tall vase with overlapping leaves, Boston, circa 1905, circular Grueby Pottery stamp, triangle with key, 13" x 8". **$4,375**
Rago Arts

Cabinet vase with ribs in mat brown glaze, Boston, circa 1905, circular Grueby Pottery stamp, 5" x 3". **$1,750**
Rago Arts

Small lime green vase with tooled spiky leaves in mottled glaze, impressed but faint Grueby circular logo, excellent original condition, 2-7/8" h. **$500**

Mark Mussio, Humler & Nolan

Rare high glaze vase, Boston, circa 1905, circular Grueby Pottery stamp, 10" x 9". .. **$1,875**
Rago Arts

Cabinet vase in curdled light blue glaze, Boston, circa 1905, circular Grueby Pottery stamp, 5" x 3-1/2"........................**$531**
Rago Arts

CERAMICS

Low bowl with carved leaf design in blue mat glaze, no crazing, thin glaze in some areas, marks include impressed circular Grueby logo, incised ER and 2/28, 2" h. x 6" dia. **$750**

Mark Mussio, Humler & Nolan

Squat vase with three rings at shoulder in yellow mat glaze, impressed with circular Grueby mark and incised 958, single open glaze bubble on side, 3-1/4" h. x 5-1/4" dia. **$500**

Mark Mussio, Humler & Nolan

Tall gourd-shaped vase in curdled indigo glaze, Boston, circa 1905, circular Grueby Pottery stamp, remnants of paper label, 15-3/4" x 9-1/4".... **$3,750**

Rago Arts

Tile with tulip, Boston, circa 1907, artist's initials, 6" sq. **$2,375**

Rago Arts

Six rare Alice in Wonderland tiles, Boston, 1920s, all stamped C. PARDEE WORKS with decorator's initials, each 4" sq. **$5,625**

Rago Arts

"Clipper Ship" tile in five matte colors on red clay with detail, unmarked, normal crazing, small glaze nick in lower left corner, 8" x 8". **$600**

Mark Mussio, Humler & Nolan

Large bulbous vase with irises, buds, and leaves, Boston, circa 1905, circular Grueby Faience stamp/20, 14" x 8". **$8,125**

Rago Arts

Pear-shaped vase with stacked leaves, Boston, circa 1905, circular Grueby Pottery stamp, 9" x 5". **$2,750**

Rago Arts

Vase with three tooled and applied leaves in green leathery mat glaze, impressed on bottom with circular Grueby Faience logo and 136, excellent original condition, 7-7/8". **$2,300**

Mark Mussio, Humler & Nolan

Large barrel-shaped vase carved with leaves, Boston, circa 1905, circular Grueby Faience stamp, 12" x 8". **$4,375**

Rago Arts

HAEGER

SLEEK. SINUOUS. COLORFUL AND CUTTING EDGE. Timeless, trim of line, and, above all, thoroughly modern. That's the hallmark of Haeger Potteries. Since its 1871 founding in Dundee, Illinois, the firm has successfully moved from the utilitarian to the decorative. Whether freshly minted or vintage, Haeger creations continue to provide what ads called "a galaxy of exquisite designs...visual achievements symbolizing expert craftsmanship and pottery-making knowledge."

Today's collectors are particularly captivated by the modernistic Haeger output of the 1940s and '50s – from "panther" TV lamps and figurines of exotic Oriental maidens to chomping-at-the-bit statuary of rearing wild horses and snorting bulls. But the Haeger story began long before then, with the Great Chicago Fire of 1871.

Founder David Haeger had recently purchased a budding brickyard on the banks of

Two large vases, good condition, 12" h., 9" dia. **$60/pair**
Royka's

Dundee's Fox River. Following the fire, his firm produced bricks to replace decimated Chicagoland structures. For the next 30 years, industrial production remained the primary emphasis of the Haeger Brick and Tile Co. It wasn't until 1914 that the company, now under the guidance of Edmund Haeger, noted the growing popularity of the Arts & Crafts movement and turned its attention to artware.

From the very beginning, Haeger was distinguished by its star roster of designers. The first: J. Martin Stangl, former glaze wizard for Fulper. The design emphasis of Stangl and his early Haeger successors was on classically simple, uncluttered Arts & Crafts stylings. Haeger's roster of pots, jugs, vases, bowls, and candleholders all proved big hits with buyers.

An early zenith was reached with a pavilion at the 1934 Chicago World's Fair. In addition to home environment settings accented with Haeger, there was an actual working factory. Once fair-goers had viewed the step-by-step pottery production process, they could purchase a piece of Haeger on the way out. The World's Fair brought Haeger to America's attention – but its grandest days of glory were still ahead.

The year 1938 saw the promotion of Edmund Haeger's forward-thinking son-in-law, Joseph Estes, to general manager, the arrival of equally forward-thinking designer Royal Arden Hickman, and the introduction of the popular "Royal Haeger" line.

The multi-talented Hickman, snapped up by Haeger after stays at J.H Vernon, Kosta Crystal, and his own Ra Art, quickly made his mark. Earlier Haeger figurals were generally of animals and humans at rest. Under the guidance of Hickman, and the

Royal Haeger elongated cat figure, seated, glass eyes inset into head, blue highlights on light brown body, imprinted marks, mid-20th century, 19-7/8" h. $92

Jeffrey S. Evans & Associates

soon-to-follow Eric Olsen, *motion* was key: leaping fish, birds taking wing, and a ubiquitous snarling black panther. The energetic air of underlying excitement in these designs was ideally suited to the action-packed atmosphere of World War II, and the postwar new day that followed.

In 1944, Hickman left Haeger following a dispute over lamp production, returning only for occasional free-lance assignments. The 1947 arrival of his successor, Eric Olsen, coincided with the official celebration of Haeger's "Diamond Jubilee"; that's when much of the Olsen line made its debut. From towering abstract figural lamps to long-legged colts, self-absorbed stalking lions, and mystic pre-Columbian priests, his designs were ideal for the soon-to-be-ultra-current "1950s modern" décor.

"A work of art," Olsen stated, "is not only based on the 'beautiful', but also on such ingredients as interest, character, craftsmanship, and imagination."

Today, "The Haeger Potteries" continues as a family affair under the leadership of Joseph Estes' daughter, Alexandra Haeger Estes. And whether collectors favor the early Arts & Crafts pieces, the modernistic designs of the 1940s and '50s, or examples of today's output, one constant remains: This is artware collectors are eager to own. Retailer Marshall Field & Co. said it best in 1929: "Haeger Pottery will become an indispensible charm in your home!"

Royal Haeger vase with multicolor high glaze over black matte, marked Royal Haeger, 493, USA, mint condition, 16-3/4" h. $95

Belhorn Auction Services, LLC

Royal Haeger bottle vase with multicolor high glaze over black matte, marked Royal Haeger, R191S, USA, mint condition, 15-1/4" h. $25

Belhorn Auction Services, LLC

Royal Haeger bottle vase with multicolor high glaze over black matte, marked Royal Haeger, 493, USA, mint condition, 16-3/4" h. $80

Belhorn Auction Services, LLC

CERAMICS

HAMPSHIRE POTTERY

HAMPSHIRE POTTERY was made in Keene, New Hampshire, where several potteries operated as far back as the late 18th century. The pottery now known as Hampshire Pottery was established by J.S. Taft shortly after 1870. Various types of wares, including art pottery, were produced through the years. Taft's brother-in-law, Cadmon Robertson, joined the firm in 1904 and was responsible for developing more than 900 glaze formulas while in charge of all manufacturing. His death in 1914 created problems for the firm, and Taft sold out to George Morton in 1916. Closed during part of World War I, the pottery was later reopened by Morton for a short time and manufactured white hotel china. From 1919 to 1921, mosaic floor tiles became the main production. All production ceased in 1923.

For more information on Hampshire Pottery, see *Antique Trader Pottery & Porcelain Ceramics Price Guide,* 6th Edition.

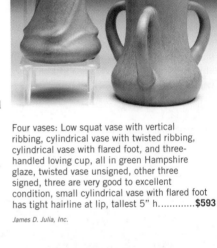

Four vases: Low squat vase with vertical ribbing, cylindrical vase with twisted ribbing, cylindrical vase with flared foot, and three-handled loving cup, all in green Hampshire glaze, twisted vase unsigned, other three signed, three are very good to excellent condition, small cylindrical vase with flared foot has tight hairline at lip, tallest 5" h............**$593**

James D. Julia, Inc.

Vase with raised floral design and split handle, marked Hampshire Pottery, excellent condition, 8-1/2" h. **$600**

Dan Morphy Auctions

Vase in matte blue glaze with mottling at shoulder, marked Hampshire Pottery, "Emoretta" mark and shape number 33, no crazing, 6-5/8"....**$275**

Mark Mussio, Humler & Nolan

Lotus bowl in brown matte glaze, marked on bottom Hampshire Pottery with encircled M of designer Cadmon Robertson, numbers 356 in blue slip, patches of tiny burst glaze bubbles near base and some crazing, 2" h. x 5-3/4" dia. ..**$225**

Mark Mussio, Humler & Nolan

HAVILAND

Over 60,000 chinaware patterns: Since its founding in 1840, that's the number totaled by the Haviland China Co.

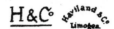

The company's story is a unique one. Although based in the United States, Haviland China produced its wares in the French porcelain capital of Limoges, exporting those products for sale domestically. Over the years, Haviland has become so closely identified with Limoges that many have used the terms interchangeably, or assumed Haviland was yet another of the numerous French firms that made Limoges its manufacturing base.

The Haviland company was actually the result of its founder's quest for the "ideal" china. New York importer David Haviland was dissatisfied with the china then available for his clientele. Its varying coloration (never consistently white) and grainy, porous texture made it not only visually unappealing, but also unsuitable for long-term use.

Haviland's search led him to Limoges, already a busy hub of porcelain production and home to more than 40 manufacturing firms because of the 1765 discovery of rare kaolin deposits there, a necessary component of fine, hard paste porcelain. Blessed with abundant supplies of other necessities for porcelain manufacture (wood, water, and a willing work force), Limoges quickly gained renown for its superb product.

Impressed by the area's output—the porcelain had a pristine whiteness as well as a smooth, non-porous finish—Haviland set up shop. The firm's dinnerware exports found immediate success, thanks to the delicate translucence of the ware and its exquisitely detailed decoration.

In the mid-19th century, at Haviland's peak of popularity, "fine dining" was a term taken seriously. Specific foods required specific serving dishes, and each course of a meal mandated its own type of tableware. China cabinets in affluent homes were filled to overflowing, and much of that overflow was thanks to Haviland. Imagine any conceivable fine dining need, and Haviland dinnerware was there to meet it.

Although dinnerware was its mainstay, Haviland also produced a multitude of other decorative yet useful porcelain housewares. Among them were dresser trays, hair receivers, ashtrays, and decorative baskets. A limited line of art pottery was also released from 1885 into the 1890s, utilizing the underglaze slip decoration technique known as "Barbotine." Developer Ernest Chaplet supervised this series for Haviland, in

Set of 20 Limoges bouillon cups and saucers, nine 2" bouillon cups and 11 5-1/2" saucers, each marked "Haviland France" and "Haviland & Co Limoges," small chip and touch-up to one bouillon cup, light overall wear. **$805**

Cordier Auctions

CERAMICS

which pigments were combined with heavy white clay slip. The mixture, applied to the clay body of a piece, had the consistency of oil paint; the resulting finish had the texture of an oil painting.

Because various Haviland family members eventually branched out on their own, the porcelain markings are many. "H & Co." was the earliest, succeeded by such variations as "Haviland, France" and "Decorated by Haviland & Co." Theodore Haviland achieved much acclaim after forming his own firm in 1892, and those pieces are often marked "Theodore Haviland" or other variants of his name. (In 1941, the Theodore Haviland facility relocated to the United States.)

Haviland's overwhelming variety of available product, a necessity when first introduced, is a boon to today's avid porcelain collectors. Hunting down and accumulating a complete set of Haviland—even in a single dinnerware pattern—can (quite enjoyably) occupy a lifetime.

Six Limoges five-well turkey oyster plates, 7-1/2" dia. **$696**

Tory Hill Auction Co.

Limoges Drop Rose porcelain plates, late 19th/early 20th century, 10 assorted with pink rose transfer and gilt decoration: eight 7-1/2" dessert/salad plates, 9-5/8" dinner plate, and saucer, each with maker's red stamp mark and various other marks including four with "Made expressly for BAILEY BANKS & BIDDLE CO," undamaged, some minute wear to gilt decoration. **$690**

Jeffrey S. Evans & Associates

Early Limoges-style canteen vase with image of white duck in swampy setting, fired on gold, impressed "Haviland Limoges" on bottom and possibly incised with letter H on top of shoulder, restoration to small rim chip, 6-1/4" h. **$400**

Mark Mussio, Humler & Nolan

Limoges Mozart Chantoung porcelain tablewares, French, 20th century, 12 five-piece place settings and three serving dishes: 12 dinner plates, 12 salad plates, 12 dessert plates, 12 cups and saucers, one serving bowl, one serving platter, and one sauce bowl with attached tray, all with CH Field Haviland Limoges circular mark in red above "Limoges / France," all plates and serving dishes with additional markings including Label De Qualité crown and shield mark in red with Mozart "Chantoung" in gray, platter 14-1/2" l., dinner plate 10" dia. **$600**

Cowan's Auctions, Inc.

Limoges hand-painted porcelain fish service, early 20th century, 11 plates and platter, platter 23-1/2" l. **$375**

Doyle New York

HULL POTTERY

THE A.E. HULL POTTERY CO. grew from the clay soil of Perry County, Ohio, in 1905. By the 1930s, its unpretentious line of wares could be found in shops and, more importantly, homes from coast to coast, making it one of the nation's largest potteries. Leveled by flood and ensuing fire in 1950, like a phoenix, Hull rose from the ashes and reestablished its position in the marketplace. Less than four decades later, however, the firm succumbed after eight bitter strikes by workers, leaving behind empty buildings, memories and the pottery shown here.

Addis Emmet Hull founded A.E. Hull Pottery in July 1905. By the time the company was formed, the Crooksville/Roseville/Zanesville area was already well established as a pottery center. Hull constructed an all-new pottery, featuring six kilns, four of them large natural gas-fired beehive kilns.

The early years were good to Hull. In fact, after only two years of operation, Hull augmented the new plant by taking over the former facilities of the Acme pottery. By 1910, Hull was claiming to be the largest manufacturer of blue-banded kitchenware in the United States. By 1925 production reached three million pieces annually.

This early ware included spice and cereal jars and salt boxes. Some of these items were lavishly decorated with decals, high-gloss glazes, or bands. This evolved into some early artware pieces including vases and flowerpots. However, Hull could

Blossom Flite cornucopia, marked Hull USA T6 © '55, mint condition, 10-1/2" l...........................$19
Belhorn Auctions, LLC

not keep up with the demand, especially the growing demand for artwares, which could be sold in five-and-dime stores. Hence, Addis Hull visited Europe and made arrangements to import decorative items from Czechoslovakia, England, France, Germany, and Italy. To accommodate the influx of these items, Hull opened a facility in Jersey City, New Jersey. This arrangement continued until 1929, when import operations were discontinued.

In 1926 Plant 1 was converted to manufacture decorative floor and wall tiles, which were popular at the time. But by the time of Addis Hull's death in 1930, the company bearing his name was exiting the tile business. Plant 1, Hull's original, which had been converted to the now-discontinued line of tile production, as well as being elderly, was closed in 1933.

When Addis Hull, Sr. died in 1930, management of the works was passed to his son, Addis Hull, Jr., who was involved in the formation of the Shawnee Pottery Co. By the late 1930s, Addis, Jr. left the family business and assumed the presidency of Shawnee.

World War II affected the entire nation, and Hull was no exception. This period saw the production of some of Hull's most famous lines, including Orchid, Iris, Tulip, and Poppy. Airbrushed matte hues of pink, blue, green, and yellow became synonymous with the Hull name. Sales of such wares through chain and dime stores soared.

The close of the decade saw the emergence of high-gloss glazed art pottery as the growing trend in decorative ceramics. Hull responded initially by merely changing the glaze applied to some of its earlier lines. Another significant development of the time was the growing influence of designer Louise Bauer on Hull's lines. First and most notable was her 1943 Red Riding Hood design, but also significant were her Bow-Knot and Woodland lines.

While the late 1940s and early 1950s saw the demise of longtime rivals Weller and Roseville, business at Hull flourished. This is particularly surprising given that on June 16, 1950, the pottery was completely destroyed by a flood, which in turn caused the kiln to explode, and the ensuing fire finished off the venerable plant.

A new plant officially opened on Jan. 1, 1952. With the new plant came a new company name – Hull Pottery Co.

Hull entered into dinnerware manufacture in the early 1960s at the behest of one of its largest customers, the J.C. Penney Co. Penney, whose offers to purchase Pfaltzgraff dinnerware were declined by the manufacturer, turned to Hull to create a competitive line. Hull's response to this was the new House 'n Garden line, which would remain in production until 1967 and would grow to 100 items.

During the 1970s and 1980s, the pottery was closed by no fewer than eight strikes, one of which lasted for seven weeks. The eighth and final strike by workers sounded the death knell for the pottery. In 1986, the Hull Pottery Co. ceased business operations.

For more information on Hull pottery, see *Warman's Hull Pottery Identification and Price Guide* by David Doyle.

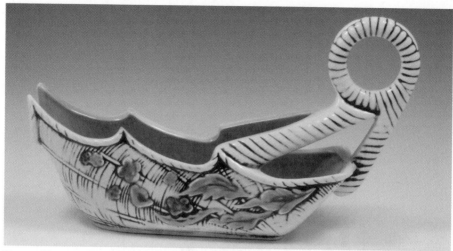

Blossom Flite boat, marked Hull USA T12 © '55, hairline to rim, 12-1/2" l..$15

Belhorn Auctions, LLC

Blossom Flite T9 basket, marked Hull USA T9 © '55, mint condition, 11-1/2" w...$22

Belhorn Auctions, LLC

Blossom Flite pitcher, marked Hull USA T3 © '55, mint condition, 8-3/4" h...............$19

Belhorn Auctions, LLC

Blossom Flite teapot and creamer, both marked, chip to teapot lid, 8-1/8" and 4-1/2" h..$14

Belhorn Auctions, LLC

Bow-Knot flowerpot in blue and turquoise, marked Hull Art USA B-6-6-1/2", excellent condition with factory glazed-over chip to rim of attached saucer, 5-3/4" h...................$16

Belhorn Auctions, LLC

CERAMICS

Ebb Tide fish vase, marked Hull USA E-6, small nicks to fins, 9-1/2" h..**$13**

Belhorn Auctions, LLC

Ebb Tide vase, marked Hull USA E-1, mint condition, 7" h......................................**$21**

Belhorn Auctions, LLC

Ebb Tide fish vase, unmarked, tip of one fin broken and repaired, small glaze nicks, 7" h...**$14**

Belhorn Auctions, LLC

Ebb Tide basket, unmarked, mint condition, 6-3/4" h **$22**

Belhorn Auctions, LLC

Magnolia cornucopia in dusty rose, marked with original label and Hull Art USA 19-8-1/2, small chip to underside of base foot, 8-3/4" h........................**$12**

Belhorn Auctions, LLC

Two Parchment & Pine vases, unmarked, one in mint condition, other had top segment broken and glued, 6-3/4" h **$11**

Belhorn Auctions, LLC

Parchment & Pine vase, marked Hull USA S-4, small chip to tip, 10-3/4" h **$8.50**

Parchment & Pine basket, unmarked, mint condition, 8-1/4" w **$15**

Belhorn Auctions, LLC

Parchment & Pine cornucopia, marked Hull USA S-2, mint condition, 7-3/4" h **$18**

Belhorn Auctions, LLC

Parchment & Pine bowl, unmarked, mint condition, 15-3/4" l **$19**

Belhorn Auctions, LLC

Parchment & Pine vase, marked Hull USA S-4, small chip to tip, 10-3/4" h **$7.50**

Belhorn Auctions, LLC

CERAMICS

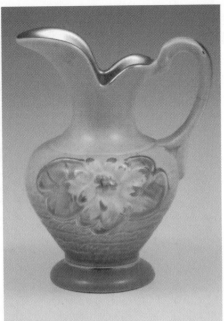

Tropicana basket, marked Hull USA 55, professionally restored, 12-1/2" h **$21**

Belhorn Auctions, LLC

Water Lily ewer in dusty rose with gold trim, marked Hull Art USA L-3-5-1/2", hairline to handle, flake to base foot, 5-3/4" h **$5.50**

Belhorn Auctions, LLC

Wildflower bowl in dusty rose, marked Hull Art USA W-21-12", excellent condition, 12-5/8" w............... **$14**

Belhorn Auctions, LLC

Wildflower vase in dusty rose, marked Hull Art USA W-3-5-1/2", excellent condition, 5-5/8" h .. **$15**

Belhorn Auctions, LLC

Wildflower cornucopia in pink and blue, marked Hull Art USA W-10-8-1/2", segment of rim broken and glued back in place, 9-1/8" h.......................**$5**

Belhorn Auctions, LLC

Wildflower candleholder in dusty rose, unmarked, mint condition, 2-3/4" h... **$5**

Belhorn Auctions, LLC

CERAMICS

Woodland Gloss double cornucopia, marked Hull USA W15-8-1/2", mint condition, 9" h **$23**

Belhorn Auctions, LLC

Woodland Gloss vase, marked Hull USA W16-8-1/2", mint condition, 9" h **$14**

Belhorn Auctions, LLC

Woodland Gloss pitcher, marked Hull USA W6-6-1/2", mint condition, 6-3/4" h **$12**

Belhorn Auctions, LLC

Woodland Gloss vase, marked Hull USA W18-10-1/2", mint condition, 11" h **$14**

Belhorn Auctions, LLC

Woodland Gloss cornucopia, marked Hull USA W10-11", mint condition, 11-1/2" l. **$14**
Belhorn Auctions, LLC

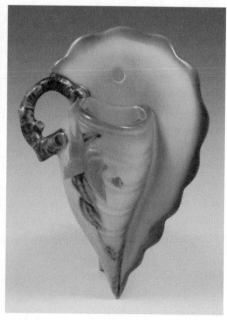

Woodland Gloss wall pocket, marked Hull USA
W13-7-1/2", mint condition, 7-3/4" h...............**$17**
Belhorn Auctions, LLC

Woodland Gloss cornucopia, marked Hull USA W2-
5-1/2", mint condition, 5-7/8" h.......................**$10**

Belhorn Auctions, LLC

Little Red Riding Hood (LRRH) cookie jar, marked Little Red Riding Hood Pat. Des. No. 135889 USA, restoration to lid, 12-3/4" h...**$21**

Belhorn Auctions, LLC

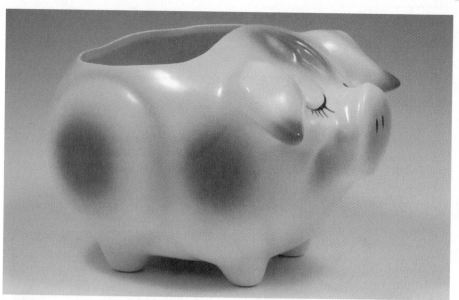

Hull Pottery Association commemorative Corky Pig planter from 2007, marked and dated, mint condition, 7-3/4" l. **$21**

Belhorn Auctions, LLC

Corky Pig bank in brown with blue highlights, fully marked and dated 1957, nicks around snout, 7" l. **$10**

Belhorn Auctions, LLC

Corky Pig bank in brown with pink highlights, fully marked and dated 1957, restoration to tip of one ear, 7" l. **$5.50**

Belhorn Auctions, LLC

Corky Pig bank in blue, pink and white, fully marked and dated 1957, small nicks to one ear, 7" l. **$11**

Belhorn Auctions, LLC

Razorback pig bank in brown with blue highlights, marked Hull USA, roughness to coin opening has been colored over, 10" l. **$17**

Belhorn Auctions, LLC

CERAMICS

IRONSTONE

Durability: When introduced in the early 1800s, that was ironstone china's major selling point. Durability also accounts for the still-ready availability of vintage ironstone china, literally centuries after it first captivated consumers. Unlike its fragile porcelain contemporaries, this utilitarian earthenware was intended to withstand the ravages of time—and it did.

Ironstone owes its innate sturdiness to a formula incorporating iron slag with the clay. Cobalt, added to the mix, eliminated the yellowish tinge that plagued earlier attempts at white china. The earliest form of this opaque dinnerware made its debut in 1800 England, patented by potters William and John Turner. However, by 1806 the Turner firm was bankrupt.

Ironstone achieved its first real popularity in 1813, when Charles Mason first offered for sale his "Patent Ironstone China." Mason's white ironstone was an immediate hit, offering vessels for a wide variety of household uses, from teapots and tureens to washbowls and pitchers.

Royal ironstone commemorative transferware lemonade pitcher with portrait of assassinated American President McKinley, pale blue glaze, star hairline in bottom and side just below McK, two hairlines at spout, 9-1/4" h. ... **$115**

Thomaston Place Auction Galleries

Although the inexpensive simplicity of white ironstone proved popular with frugal householders, by the 1830s in-mold and transfer patterns were providing a dose of visual variety. Among the decorative favorites: Oriental motifs and homey images such as grains, fruits, and flowers.

Mason's patented formula for white ironstone lasted for 14 years. Upon its expiration, numerous other potteries jumped into the fray. By the 1840s, white ironstone found its way across the ocean, enjoying the same success in the United States and Canada as it had in England. By the 1880s, however, the appeal of white ware began to fade. Its successor, soon overtaking the original, was ironstone's most enduring incarnation, Tea Leaf.

First marketed as Lustre Band and Sprig, the Tea Leaf Lustreware motif is attributed to Anthony Shaw of Burslem; his ironstone pieces of the 1880s featured hand-painted copper lustre bands and leaves. Tea Leaf was, however, a decorative *style* rather than a specific product line. Since the design was not patented, potteries throughout England and the United States soon introduced their own versions. Design modifications were minor; today, collectors can assemble entire sets of ironstone in the Tea Leaf pattern from the output of different manufacturers. Although independently produced, the pieces easily complement each other.

During the late 1800s, ironstone tea sets were so ubiquitous that ornamenting them with a tea leaf was a logical choice. Buyers were intrigued with this simple, nature-themed visual on a field of white. Their interest quickly translated into a bumper crop of tea leaf-themed ironstone pieces. Soon, the tea leaf adorned objects with absolutely no relation whatsoever to tea. Among them: gravy boats, salt and peppers shakers, ladles, and even toothbrush holders and soap dishes.

There were, of course, more romantic rationales given for the introduction of the tea leaf motif. One holds that this decoration was the modern manifestation of an ancient legend. Finding an open tea leaf at the bottom of a teacup would bring good luck to the fortunate tea drinker. In this scenario, the tea leaf motif becomes a harbinger of happy times ahead, whether emblazoned on a cake plate, a candlestick, or a chamber pot.

For makers of Tea Leaf, the good fortune continued into the early 1900s. Eventually, however, Tea Leaf pieces became so prevalent that the novelty wore off. By mid-century, the pattern had drifted into obscurity; its appeal was briefly resuscitated with lesser-quality reproductions, in vogue from 1950 to 1980. Marked "Red Cliff" (the name of the Chicago-based distributor), these reproductions generally used blanks supplied by Hall China.

For today's collectors, the most desirable Tea Leaf pieces are those created during the pattern's late-Victorian heyday. Like ironstone itself, the Tea Leaf pattern remains remarkably durable.

State in Schuylkill centerpiece bowl, with transfer fish decoration, very good condition, 5-1/2" h. x 11-3/4" dia.... **$4,800**

Pook & Pook, Inc.

Set of five English ironstone dishes, Black Staffordshire Nanking pattern by E. Challinor, chip to rim of one, 9-1/2" dia.......................... **$173**

Thomaston Place Auction Galleries

Set of 12 ironstone dinner plates in Gaudy Dutch pattern, for Higgenbotham & Son, Blackville Street, Dublin, circa 1840, good condition, 10" dia. **$431**

Thomaston Place Auction Galleries

Blue and white transferware ironstone footbath, English, 20th century, oval form with two handles, decorated with figures in landscape, marked Victoria Ware / Ironstone on bottom, 7-3/4" h. x 19" l. **$215**

Cowan's Auctions, Inc.

Set of Imari palette tureens, second quarter 19th century, soup tureen on stand and pair of sauce tureens on stands, each with domed lid surmounted by floral knop above conforming bowl, on hexagonal foot, soup tureen impressed Mason's Ironstone China, wear, cracks, and chips throughout, some paint loss and discoloration, soup tureen 13" h. **$1,500**

Doyle New York

Rum barrel, English, late 19th century, lid by association, chips to inner rim of lid, 13" h. **$360**

Pook & Pook, Inc.

Floral pitcher with serpent handle, marked with Mason's crown ink stamp, excellent condition, 8-1/4" h. **$130**

Belhorn Auction Services LLC

Spatterware coffeepot, 19th century, with bird form finial, one firing bubble to glazing on lid, 10" h. **$277**

Weiderseim Associates, Inc.

Six Tea Leaf items, English, fourth quarter 19th/early 20th century, Wedgwood & Co. and Mellor, Taylor & Co. teapots, Alfred Meakin sugar bowl, and creamers by Wedgwood & Co., A.J. Wilkinson and R. Burgess, each with copper-luster decoration and printed marks, minor imperfections, square pot with mismatched cover, 5" to 8-1/2" h. overall. **$240**

Jeffrey S. Evans & Associates

Three-piece ironstone tea service in Grapevine pattern, teapot, covered sugar and creamer, 19th century, white glaze, all marked "B&C Challinor," good condition, teapot 11", sugar 8", creamer 6". **$115**

Thomaston Place Auction Galleries

CERAMICS

KPM

KPM PLAQUES ARE HIGHLY GLAZED, enamel paintings on porcelain bases that were produced by Konigliche Porzellan Manufaktur (KPM), the King's Porcelain Factory, in Berlin, Germany, between 1880 and 1901.

Their secret, according to Afshine Emrani, dealer and appraiser at www.some-of-my-favorite-things.com, is KPM's highly superior, smooth, hard paste porcelain, which could be fired at very high temperatures.

"The magic of a KPM plaque is that it will look as crisp and beautiful 100 years from now as it does today," he says. Even when they were introduced, these plaques proved highly collectible, with art lovers, collectors, tourists, and the wealthy acquiring them for extravagant sums.

KPM rarely marketed painted porcelain plaques itself, however. Instead, it usually supplied white, undecorated ones to independent artists who specialized in this genre. Not all artists signed their KPM paintings, however.

While most KPM plaques were copies of famous paintings, some, commissioned by wealthy Americans and Europeans in the 1920s, bear images of actual people in contemporary clothing. These least collectible of KPM plaques command between $500 and $1,500 each, depending on the attractiveness of their subjects.

Gilded, hand-painted plaques featuring Middle Eastern or female Gypsy subjects and bearing round red "Made in Germany" stamps were produced just before and after World War I for export. They command between $500 and $2,000 each. Plaques portraying religious subjects, such as the Virgin Mary or the Flight into Egypt, command higher prices but are less popular.

Popular scenes of hunters, merrymakers, musicians, etc., generally fetch less than $10,000 apiece because they have been reproduced time and again. Rarer, more elaborate scenes, however, like "The Dance Lesson" and "Turkish Card Players" may be worth many times more.

Highly stylized portraits copied from famous paintings – especially those of attractive children or décolleté women – allowed art lovers to own their own "masterpieces." These are currently worth between $2,000 and $20,000 each. Romanticized portrayals of cupids and women in the nude, the most desirable KPMs subjects of all, currently sell for up to $40,000 each. Portraits of men, it must be noted, are not only less popular, but also less expensive.

Size also matters. A 4" x 6" inch plaque, whose subject has

Porcelain commemorative presentation vase and cover, Germany, circa 1901, cobalt ground with gold trim and raised gold scrolled foliage, polychrome enamel decorated cartouche to either side, one with depiction of statue of officer on horseback, reverse with official building, banded inscription below, underglaze blue scepter and red print "KPM" mark, 19-3/4" h... **$1,200**

Skinner, Inc.; www.skinnerinc.com

Painted porcelain plaque of children, Berlin, late 19th century, after artist's sons by Christian Leberecht Vogel (German, 1759-1816), book in elder child's hands, in gilded and ebonized frame carved with flowers and leaves, visible impressed mark to reverse, sight 10" l. **$2,400**

Skinner, Inc.; www.skinnerinc.com

CERAMICS

Porcelain plaque depicting Saint Jerome, Berlin, late 19th century, after Koninck, shown with his head resting on his hand reading book, against naturalistic background, impressed marks, 7-3/8" x 6-1/4". **$960**

Skinner, Inc.; www.skinnerinc.com

Hand-painted rectangular porcelain plaque depicting young woman by Conrad Kiesel (German, 1846-1921), 19th century, in gilt frame, signed on front Nach C. Kiesel, signed on verso Nach C. Kiesel / L. Schinzel, impressed KPM and "255_195," sight 10" x 7-1/2". **$4,200**

Cowan's Auctions, Inc.

Porcelain rumtopf (rum pot), 19th century, with transfer scenes of aristocratic garden feasting and overall floral decoration over basketweave textured border, gilt edged, cover surmounted by putti holding flask and hoisting cup, wearing grapevine crown, fine condition, 12-1/2" h. x 10" dia. **$1,380**

Thomaston Place Auction Galleries

been repeatedly reproduced, may sell for a few thousand dollars. Larger ones that portray the same subject will fetch proportionately more. A "Sistine Madonna" plaque, fashioned after the original work by Rafael and measuring 10" x 7-1/2", might cost $4,200. One featuring the identical subject, but measuring 15" x 11", might cost $7,800. A larger plaque, measuring 22" x 16", might command twice that price.

The largest KPM plaques, measuring 22" x 26", for example, often burst during production. Although no formula exists for determining prices of those that have survived, Afshine Emrani says that each may sell for as much as $250,000. Rare plaques like these are often found in museums.

The condition of a KPM plaque also affects its price. Most, since they were highly glazed and customarily hung instead of handled, have survived in perfect condition. Thus those that have sustained even minor damage, like scratches, cracks, or chips, fetch considerably lower prices. Those suffering major damage are worthless.

KPM painted plaques arouse so much interest and command such high prices that, over the last couple of years, unscrupulous dealers have entered the market. According to dealer Balazs Benedek, KPM plaques are "the mother of all fakes. About 90 percent of KPM plaques are mid- to late-20th century reproductions. And about 70 percent are not hand painted."

Collectors should be aware that genuine KPM paintings always boast rich, shiny glazes that preserve their colors, and though subject matter may vary, they typically feature nude scenes, indoor portraits of women, or group gatherings in lush settings. Anything wildly different should raise suspicion.

Genuine KPMs, on their backs or edges, feature small icons of scepters deeply set in the porcelain, over the letters KPM. These marks are sometimes accompanied by an "H" or some other letter, which may indicate their production date or size. Some are imprinted with the size of the plaque as well, which facilitated sorting or shipping. Shallow or crooked imprints may reveal a fake.

—*Melody Amsel-Arieli*

TOP LOT!

Rectangular plaque of smiling Bacchante in bower of fruiting grapevines, holding goblet of wine, late 19th century, later wooden frame, signed lower right "Bauer," impressed K.P.M. and scepter mark verso, also impressed "H," plaque 15-1/2" h. x 13-1/4" w., 23" h. x 20-3/4" w. x 1-1/4" d. overall........**$11,295**

John Moran Auctioneers

Porcelain plaque titled "Woodcutter Defforge," depicting young man toting axes and smoking pipe while conversing with young woman seated peeling vegetables, dog at her knee, three men seated to side smoking pipes, "KPM" impression with scepter, incised 12-9-3/4, aged paper label on back reads, "Woodcutter Defforge," partial label also, each placed over handwritten notations in pencil, excellent original condition, 10" x 12-1/2", ornate wood frame 18" x 14-3/4"... **$4,300**

Mark Mussio, Humler & Nolan

Rectangular plaque of blonde woman in profile, hands folded beneath chin, in carved, pierced giltwood frame, late 19th/early 20th century, signed illegibly lower right, impressed KPM monogram and scepter mark, also impressed "S," "255," "195," and with cipher, plaque 9-3/4" h. x 7-1/4" w.; 21" h. x 18-1/2" w. overall........ **$2,385**

John Moran Auctioneers

Porcelain plaque of Abraham sending Hagar and Ishmael away while Sarah and Isaac look on, marked KPM, good condition, 11" x 9", gilt wooden frame 17" x 14".............................. **$4,250**

Woody Auction

CERAMICS

LIMOGES

"LIMOGES" HAS BECOME the generic identifier for porcelain produced in Limoges, France, and the surrounding vicinity. Over 40 manufacturers in the area have, at some point, used the term as a descriptor of their work, and there are at least 400 different Limoges identification marks. The common denominator is the product itself: fine hard paste porcelain created from the necessary components found in abundance in the Limoges region: kaolin and feldspar.

Until the 1700s, porcelain was exclusively a product of China, introduced to the Western world by Marco Polo and imported at great expense. In 1765, the discovery of kaolin in St. Yrieixin, a small town near Limoges, made French production of porcelain possible.

Limoges entrepreneurs quickly capitalized on the find. Adding to the area's allure: expansive forests, providing fuel for wood-burning kilns; the nearby Vienne River, with water for working clay; and a workforce eager to trade farming for a more lucrative pursuit. Additionally, as the companies would be operating outside metropolitan Paris, labor and production costs would be significantly less.

By the early 1770s, numerous porcelain manufacturers were at work in Limoges and its environs. Demand for the porcelain was high because it was both useful and decorative. To meet that demand, firms employed trained, as well as untrained, artisans for the detailed hand painting required. At its industrial peak in 1900, Limoges factories employed over 8,000 workers in some aspect of porcelain production.

Seven-piece beverage set, Tressemanes & Vogt (T&V), France, late 19th/early 20th century, ivory between gold and green bands with overall hand-painted vintage decoration, hexagonal form, tankard pitcher with bulge-form base and tapered foot, six tumblers, five with artist initials "F. E. W.," each with green stamp mark, tankard with "T&V / Limoges / Depose" and tumblers with "Limoges / France," excellent condition, tankard with shallow flake to edge of foot, tumblers undamaged, tankard 16-1/2" h. overall, tumblers 4-3/8" h. **$207**

Jeffrey S. Evans & Associates

Myriad products classified as Limoges flooded the marketplace from the late 1700s onward. Among them were tableware pieces, such as tea and punch sets, trays, pitchers, compotes, bowls, and plates. Also popular were vases and flower baskets, dresser sets, trinket boxes, ash receivers, figural busts, and decorative plaques.

Although produced in France, Limoges porcelain was destined for export overseas. The United States proved a reliable customer. Notable among the importers was the Haviland China Co.; until the 1940s, its superior decorated china was produced in Limoges and distributed in the United States.

By the early 20th century, many exporters in the United States were purchasing porcelain blanks from the Limoges factories for decoration stateside. The base product was authentically made in France, but production costs were significantly lower: Thousands of untrained porcelain painters put their skills to work for a minimal wage. Domestic decoration of the blanks also meant that importers could select designs suited to the specific tastes of target audiences.

Because Limoges was a regional designation, rather than the identifier of a specific manufacturer, imported pieces were often marked with the name of the exporting firm, followed by the word "Limoges." Beginning in 1891, "France" was added. Some confusion has arisen from products marked "Limoges China Co." (aka "American Limoges"). This Ohio-based firm, in business from 1902-1955, has no connection to the porcelain produced in France.

The heyday of quality French Limoges lasted roughly into the 1930s. Production continues today, but after World War II, designs and painting techniques became much more standardized.

Vintage Limoges is highly sought-after by today's collectors. They're drawn to the delicacy of the porcelain as well as the colors and skill of decoration. Valuation is based on age, decorative execution, and individual visual appeal.

For more information on Limoges, see *Antique Trader Pottery and Porcelain Ceramics Price Guide*, 7th edition.

Porcelain mantel clock in Rococo style, France, 19th century, polychrome enamel and gilt decorated with heavily applied flowers, backplate and face marked "Henry Marc of Paris," on matching base, small chips on flower petals, gilding worn on base, 13" h. overall. **$461**

Skinner, Inc.; www.skinnerinc.com

Porcelain game bird plate, Coronet, France, first quarter 20th century, hand-painted in earth tones with gilded scalloped rim, depicting bird in flight, artist signed "LiHc" in lower left, undamaged, minor expected wear to decoration, 10-3/8" dia. **$92**

Jeffrey S. Evans & Associates

Large footed punch bowl on separate stand, decorated with grapevine, leaves and bunches of grapes, over salmon to pale yellow to crimson ombre, three-footed base in crimson with gilt feet, gilt rimmed bowl, inscribed in gold on underside of both pieces "Mrs. W. Glendinning," bowl marked "Jan 1913," bowl in fine condition, small losses to glaze on stand, 9-3/4" h. x 15-3/8" dia. overall. **$374**

Thomaston Place Auction Galleries

Three hand-painted porcelain items, pastel floral and gilt decoration, France, late 19th/early 20th century: covered vegetable bowl marked for Elite Works in red stamp, ovoid form vase marked for William Guerin & Co. in green stamp, and figural sleigh-form basket marked for Jean Pougat with handwritten gift note; each with normal wear to gilt decoration, covered bowl with high-point wear; covered bowl 5" h. x 10-1/4" dia. overall, vase 4-3/4" h. x 6" x 8-1/2", basket 5-3/4" h. x 7-1/2" l..**$184**

Jeffrey S. Evans & Associates

Covered round enamel box, 19th century, 8" dia. x 3" h. **$720**

Don Presley Auctions

CERAMICS

MAJOLICA

IN 1851, AN ENGLISH POTTER was hoping that his new interpretation of a centuries-old style of ceramics would be well received at the "Great Exhibition of the Industries of All Nations" set to open May 1 in London's Hyde Park.

Potter Herbert Minton had high hopes for his display. His father, Thomas Minton, founded a pottery works in the mid-1790s in Stoke-on-Trent, Staffordshire. Herbert Minton had designed a "new" line of pottery, and his chemist, Leon Arnoux, had developed a process that resulted in vibrant, colorful glazes that came to be called "majolica."

Trained as an engineer, Arnoux also studied the making of encaustic tiles, and had been appointed art director at Minton's works in 1848. His job was to introduce and promote new products. Victorian fascination with the natural world prompted Arnoux to reintroduce the work of Bernard Palissy, whose naturalistic, bright-colored "maiolica" wares had been created in the 16th century. But Arnoux used a thicker body to make pieces sturdier. This body was given a coating of opaque white glaze, which provided a surface for decoration.

Pieces were modeled in high relief, featuring butterflies and other insects, flowers and leaves, fruit, shells, animals and fish. Queen Victoria's endorsement of the new pottery prompted its acceptance by the general public.

When Minton introduced his wares at Philadelphia's 1876 Centennial Exhibition, American potters also began to produce majolica.

For more information on majolica, see *Warman's Majolica Identification and Price Guide* by Mark F. Moran.

Footed planter with bird decoration, glazed earthenware, 20th century, illegible marking, 7-1/2" x 17-3/4" x 8-1/2"..**$188**

Rago Arts

Austrian portrait of seated African-American banjo player in top hat, waistcoat, vest and cravat, breeches and leggings, pink shoes, with original bamboo chair, 19th century, impressed 4907-51 on underside, fine condition, 12" h. **$805**

Thomaston Place Auction Galleries

Jardinière and pedestal, Continental, late 19th-early 20th century, jardinière with circular flared rim and tapering body in black, pedestal with raised shoulder and circular flared foot in blue, each molded in relief with flowers and acanthus leaves, marked on bottom of jardinière RP and incised ROL(?) on bottom of pedestal, some crazing, jardinière with light scratches on side of foot and nicks to glaze on underside of foot, top of pedestal with scratches and surface wear, pedestal foot with wear on bottom, jardinière 18" dia. x 16" h., pedestal 29" h................................... **$270**

Cowan's Auctions, Inc.

Pair of large English mantel cobalt-covered urns by Thomas C. Brown, Westhead Moore & Co., Cladon Place, Stoke-on-Trent (old Ridgway works), marked on underside, with trellis trim, fine condition, 22" h. **$2,415**

Thomaston Place Auction Galleries

Pair of bird-form planters, 19th century, European parrots on tree branches, 6051-51 impressed on interior, fine condition, 10-1/2" h **$748**

Thomaston Place Auction Galleries

CERAMICS

Asparagus jar in form of bundled stems, unmarked, probably Italian, circa 1890, 8-1/2" h. x 6-1/2" dia......... **$144**

Thomaston Place Auction Galleries

Eight Minton oyster plates, one pair with nine pockets and six plates with six pockets, pair in moss green with aubergine center, shell decoration, one with flake to base rim, 10" dia.; pair in black marbled seafoam green, seashells, registry mark, stamped 1323 and N, fine condition, 9-1/4" dia.; pair in yellow with green underside, seashells, registry mark, stamped 1323 and C, fine condition, 9-1/4" dia.; two in pale lavender with sky blue center and pale green with dark green center, green underside, seashells, registry mark, stamped 1323 and C, edge chip to green plate, 9-1/4" dia......................**$3,795**

Thomaston Place Auction Galleries

Art Nouveau Continental pitcher with plant-form handle and twisted stem, no maker's mark, fine condition, 15" h. **$403**

Thomaston Place Auction Galleries

Six-sided footed pottery garden seat in green glaze with russet top, faux tassels, lift-hole top center, 19th century, losses to glaze on high points of top, one area of edge, 20" h................**$75**

Thomaston Place Auction Galleries

Rare American blue glaze milk pitcher depicting boys playing baseball and soccer, unmarked, fine condition, original glaze flaw at top of handle, 7-1/2" h ...**$345**

Thomaston Place Auction Galleries

Figural smoking stand, American advertising piece with black dandy sitting by bundles of cigars that hold cheroots and matches, striker on right edge, legs crossed in tray marked Colorado Pina, old repair to head, 7" h. **$115**

Thomaston Place Auction Galleries

Three 19th century Continental leaf pattern compotes or footed tazzas in tin glazes, yellow, brown, and green, minor imperfections, 4-1/2" to 5-1/2" h., 9" to 10" dia................................. **$259**

Thomaston Place Auction Galleries

Round footed jardiniere in bright blue with pink interior, decorated with dogwood blossoms, four branches form feet, fine condition, 4" x 9" dia .. **$115**

Thomaston Place Auction Galleries

Rustic bark-form ewer with grapevine and lizard, in brown and green glaze, unmarked, loss to leaves, 15" h., 8-1/2" handle to spout. **$115**

Thomaston Place Auction Galleries

Figural smoking stand, Continental porcelain in form of castle ruins, turrets holding cigars and matches, pool as ashtray, unmarked, one small chip to rim of match holder, 6" h. **$144**

Thomaston Place Auction Galleries

Six pieces of Minton Pottery green-glazed majolica with latticework border, tazza and five matching plates, all marked, good condition, 2" x 9-1/4" and 9"... **$345**

Thomaston Place Auction Galleries

Covered cheese dish by J. Holdcraft with flowering blackberry and dogwood branches over rustic plank fence, blue top, branch form handle, moss green platform top, stamped on underside, minor roughness to handle, 10-1/2" x 10" dia........... **$575**

Thomaston Place Auction Galleries

Unmarked bread tray in Sunflower and Basketweave pattern, fine condition, 13" x 11-1/2".. **$259**

Thomaston Place Auction Galleries

Seven Minton basketweave-edged plates with fan-shaped centers, registry marks, good condition, 9" dia. **$489**

Thomaston Place Auction Galleries

Ten pieces of majolica pottery in Etruscan Seashell pattern by Griffin, Smith & Hill, teapot, two pitchers, covered sugar, two plates, large bowl, small plate, teacup and saucer, 6-1/2" h. to 8" dia. **$460**

Thomaston Place Auction Galleries

English fruit compote with apple branch decoration over basketweave, teal key border, stamped 30, marked with black A, very good condition, 4-1/2" x 9" dia... **$115**

Thomaston Place Auction Galleries

Wedgwood shell form dish in green and brown modulated glazes, stamped on underside, fine condition, 12-3/4" x 7" x 1-3/4" dia. . **$115**

Thomaston Place Auction Galleries

English milk pitcher in form of Prime Minister Gladstone, circa 1880, unmarked, good condition, 11-1/2" h...........**$115**

Thomaston Place Auction Galleries

Set of eight tobacco leaf plates in yellow, green, and brown glazes, marked 33, probably American, 8-1/2" dia. **$259**

Thomaston Place Auction Galleries

Figural pitcher of spaniel dog in barrel, grass along bottom, marked H2 on underside, probably American, good condition, 10" h.................**$201**

Thomaston Place Auction Galleries

"Swallow on Nest" pitcher with British Registry mark for George Jones, circa 1847, bird as handle, sky blue interior, one flaw in original glaze on side, 7-3/4" h. x 5" dia...............**$920**

Thomaston Place Auction Galleries

Plant pot decorated with morning glories on plank fence, pink and yellow rim, aqua interior, unmarked, good condition, 6" x 6-1/2" dia...**$144**

Thomaston Place Auction Galleries

CERAMICS

Continental two-compartment serving dish in form of cabbage leaves with stem-form central handle, artist's mark on underside, good condition, 17-1/2" x 8-1/2" x 5".. **$173**

Thomaston Place Auction Galleries

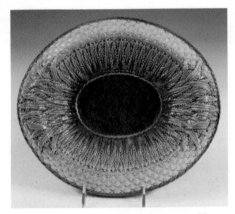

English oval bread tray in yellow basketweave with fern leaf center, fine condition, 12-1/2" x 11"... **$201**

Thomaston Place Auction Galleries

English serving tray with leaves over faux napkin decoration, branch form handle, marked Stoke-on-Trent within raised artist's palette on underside, minor abrasions, 12" x 10". **$201**

Thomaston Place Auction Galleries

Continental deep oval server in wood grain with raspberry and wheat decoration, unmarked, good condition, 13-1/2" x 11-1/2" x 2" d................ **$144**

Thomaston Place Auction Galleries

Unmarked late 19th century covered butter dish in Sunflower pattern with bird form knop, integral underplate, pink interior, chip to bird's beak, hairline to lid, 4-1/2" x 5-3/4" dia. **$104**

Thomaston Place Auction Galleries

Sardine dish, covered, in green and yellow glazed Basketweave and Leaf pattern, with sardine form handle, hairlines and discoloration to interior, 4" x 8-1/4" x 7"... **$345**

Thomaston Place Auction Galleries

MARBLEHEAD

MARBLEHEAD POTTERY was organized in 1904 by Dr. Herbert J. Hall as a therapeutic aid to patients in a sanitarium he ran in Marblehead, Massachusetts. It was later separated from the sanitarium and directed by Arthur E. Baggs, a fine artist and designer, who bought out the factory in 1916 and operated it until its closing in 1936. Most wares were hand-thrown and decorated and carry the company mark of a stylized sailing vessel flanked by the letters "M" and "P."

Hand-decorated vase encircled with repeating pattern of brown branches with green leaves and green and orange berries set against tan matte glaze, inside greenish-blue crystalline glaze, impressed on bottom with Marblehead ship logo, area of rim roughness, 4-1/8" h..............**$1,800**

Mark Mussio, Humler & Nolan

Rare vase decorated with parrots, circa 1905, stamped ship mark MP with B in circle, Arthur Baggs (1886-1947), 7" x 5"..............**$4,063**

Rago Arts

Vase decorated with cranes, 1910s, stamped ship mark MP, incised MT, 5-3/4" x 5"....................**$1,063**

Rago Arts

Circular trivet with brown rooster with red comb and tan feet and feathers against gray ground, marked with impressed Marblehead ship logo, nicks on surface and along bottom edge, professional restoration to rooster's head, 5-1/4". ..**$400**

Mark Mussio, Humler & Nolan

Vase with stylized trees, 1910s, stamped ship mark MP, painted HT, Arthur Hennessey (b. 1882), Sarah Tutt (1859-1947), 4-3/4" x 4-1/4"..........................**$3,250**

Rago Arts

Tile decorated with house in landscape, 1910s, stamped ship mark MP, 6" sq. x 1". **$2,750**

Rago Arts

CERAMICS

$

Small vase decorated with stylized flowering branches, 1920s, stamped ship mark MP, incised HT, Arthur Hennessey (b. 1882), Sarah Tutt (1859-1947), 4-1/2" x 3-1/2".... **$1,750**

Rago Arts

Bud vase with stylized blossoms, circa 1905, incised ship mark MP and HT, Arthur Hennessey (b. 1882), Sarah Tutt (1859-1947), 4-1/2" x 2-3/4".......................... **$2,500**

Rago Arts

Bud vase with stylized trees, circa 1910, stamped ship mark MP, incised HT, Arthur Hennessey (b. 1882), Sarah Tutt (1859-1947), 4-1/2" x 2-1/2".......................... **$3,750**

Rago Arts

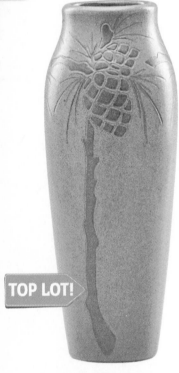

TOP LOT!

Large vase decorated with pinecones, circa 1905, stamped ship mark MP, incised AB and T, Arthur Baggs (1886-1947), Sarah Tutt (1859-1947), 12" x 4-1/2".......**$16,250**

Rago Arts

Tall vase decorated with stylized trees, 1910s, stamped ship mark MP, incised MT, Maude Milner, Sarah Tutt (1859-1947), 11" x 4-1/2"........ **$3,375**

Rago Arts

Vase with geometric design, 1910s, stamped ship mark MP with artist's cipher AB, Arthur Baggs (1886-1947), 5-3/4" x 3-1/2"..........................**$11,250**

Rago Arts

CERAMICS

Vase decorated with holly boughs, 1920s, stamped ship mark MP, 4" x 5". **$1,500**

Rago Arts

Rare, large vase, curdled blue glaze, circa 1905, incised ship mark MP, 11-1/2" x 11-1/2".........................**$8,125**

Rago Arts

Small tapering vase decorated with stylized blossoms, 1920s, stamped ship mark MP, incised MT, Maude Milner, Sarah Tutt (1859-1947), 3-1/2" x 4-1/4".......**$875**

Rago Arts

Decorated vase with repeating pattern of holly branches with reddish-colored berries set against light blue ground, impressed on bottom with Marblehead ship logo, excellent original condition, 7-1/8" h. **$2,200**

Mark Mussio, Humler & Nolan

Plate in green with dark green lined edge and low powder blue vase with raised rim opening, both with MP mark, good condition, plate 9-1/2" dia., vase 5-1/4" dia. **$374**

Thomaston Place Auction Galleries

Wedge-shaped doorstops in deep blue mat glaze with bas relief decorations of galleon and Viking ship, latter with original paper label, very good condition, 5-1/4" and 5-1/2" h. **$403**

Thomaston Place Auction Galleries

CERAMICS

MCCOY POTTERY

THE FIRST MCCOY with clay under his fingernails was W. Nelson McCoy. With his uncle, W.F. McCoy, he founded a pottery works in Putnam, Ohio, in 1848, making stoneware crocks and jugs.

That same year, W. Nelson's son, James W., was born in Zanesville, Ohio. James established the J.W. McCoy Pottery Co. in Roseville, Ohio, in the fall of 1899. The J.W. McCoy plant was destroyed by fire in 1903 and was rebuilt two years later.

It was at this time that the first examples of Loy-Nel-Art wares were produced. The line's distinctive title came from the names of James McCoy's three sons, Lloyd, Nelson, and Arthur. Like other "standard" glazed pieces produced at this time by several Ohio potteries, Loy-Nel-Art has a glossy finish on a dark brown-black body, but Loy-Nel-Art featured a splash of green color on the front and a burnt-orange splash on the back.

George Brush became general manager of J.W. McCoy Pottery Co. in 1909. The company became Brush-McCoy Pottery Co. in 1911, and in 1925 the name was shortened to Brush Pottery Co. This firm remained in business until 1982.

Separately, in 1910, Nelson McCoy, Sr. founded the Nelson McCoy Sanitary and Stoneware Co., also in Roseville. By the early 1930s, production had shifted from utilitarian wares to art pottery, and the company name was changed to Nelson McCoy Pottery.

Designer Sydney Cope was hired in 1934, and was joined by his son, Leslie, in 1936. The Copes' influence on McCoy wares continued until Sydney's death in 1966. That same year, Leslie opened a gallery devoted to his family's design heritage and featuring his own original art.

Brush-McCoy Jewel experimental jardiniere with blue ground, unmarked, small beads of glaze missing, otherwise in excellent original condition, 9-3/8" h. x 11-3/4" w.......................................$200

Mark Mussio, Humler & Nolan

Nelson McCoy, Sr. died in 1945, and was succeeded as company president by his nephew, Nelson McCoy Melick.

A fire destroyed the plant in 1950, but company officials – including Nelson McCoy, Jr., then 29 – decided to rebuild, and the new Nelson McCoy Pottery Co. was up and running in just six months.

Nelson Melick died in 1954. Nelson, Jr. became company president, and oversaw the company's continued growth. In 1967, the operation was sold to entrepreneur David Chase. At this time, the words "Mt. Clemens Pottery" were added to the company marks. In 1974, Chase sold the company to Lancaster Colony Corp., and the company marks included a stylized "LCC" logo. Nelson Jr. and his wife, Billie, who had served as a products supervisor, left the company in 1981.

In 1985, the company was sold again, this time to Designer Accents. The McCoy pottery factory closed in 1990.

For more information on McCoy pottery, see *Warman's McCoy Pottery Identification and Price Guide*, 2nd edition, by Mark F. Moran.

Brush-McCoy
Rosewood vase,
unmarked, excellent
condition, 5-7/8" h...**$11**

Belhorn Auction Services, LLC

Vase marked McCoy,
excellent condition,
6-1/4" h. **$5**

Belhorn Auction Services, LLC

Mammy cookie jar, marked on underside, some
loss to paint, 11" h...**$58**

Thomaston Place Auction Galleries

Brush-McCoy
Rosewood vase,
unmarked, excellent
condition, 6-3/4" h...**$22**

Belhorn Auction Services, LLC

Liberty Bell umbrella
stand, unmarked,
excellent condition,
21-1/2" h. **$90**

Belhorn Auction Services, LLC

Two blended glaze jardinières, unmarked, small
nicks, otherwise excellent condition, 8" w. x
6-1/2" h. **$15**

Belhorn Auction Services, LLC

Olympia vase,
unmarked, excellent
condition, 9" h.........**$70**

Belhorn Auction Services, LLC

Blended glaze
jardiniere and pedestal
with Greek key design,
unmarked, pedestal in
very good condition,
jardiniere with large
bruise to rim and dry
crazing, 29-1/2" h....**$25**

Belhorn Auction Services, LLC

Stoneware hanging basket and jardiniere,
unmarked, excellent condition, 6-1/2" w. and
4-1/2" w. **$5**

Belhorn Auction Services, LLC

CERAMICS

Slender Brush-McCoy Jetwood vase with landscape of foliaged trees, conifers and hills at dusk, unmarked, excellent condition, 10" h. **$650**

Mark Mussio, Humler & Nolan

Brush-McCoy brown onyx vase fitted with ormolu-style holder encircled with five classical maidens, holder in excellent condition and marked on bottom with number 6113 and inverted triangle with letters MWC with O to left of it and CO beneath, some burst glaze bubbles, no crazing, 9-3/4" h....**$475**

Mark Mussio, Humler & Nolan

Brush-McCoy piggy bank, unmarked, chips to edges of coin slot, 5-3/4" l. **$18**

Belhorn Auction Services, LLC

Antique silver-colored basket marked McCoy, excellent condition, 7-3/4" l. **$10**

Belhorn Auction Services, LLC

Double Tulip vase, marked McCoy, mint condition, 8" h. ..**$20**

Belhorn Auction Services, LLC

MEISSEN

KNOWN FOR ITS FINELY DETAILED FIGURINES and exceptional tableware, Meissen is recognized as the first European maker of fine porcelain.

The company owes its beginnings to Johann Friedrich Bottger's 1708 discovery of the process necessary for the manufacture of porcelain. "Rediscovery" might be a better term, since the secret of producing hard paste porcelain had been known to the Chinese for centuries. However, Bottger, a goldsmith and alchemist, was the first to successfully replicate the formula in Europe. Soon after, The Royal Saxon Porcelain Works set up shop in Dresden. Because Bottger's formula was highly sought after by would-be competitors, in 1710 the firm moved its base of operations to Albrechtburg Castle in Meissen, Saxony. There, in fortress-like surroundings, prying eyes could be successfully obstructed. And, because of that move, the company name eventually became one with its locale: Meissen.

Rare Art Nouveau pate-sur-pate vase decorated with Three Graces, Germany, circa 1900, crossed swords mark, stamped 133/I/116, 9" x 3-1/2"............. **$16,250**

Rago Arts

The earliest Meissen pieces were red stoneware, reminiscent of Chinese work, and incised with Chinese characters. Porcelain became the Meissen focus in 1713; early releases included figurines and tea sets, the decorations reminiscent of baroque metal. In 1719, after Bottger's death, artist J.J. Horoldt took over the firm's direction. His Chinese-influenced designs, which employed a lavish use of color and decoration, are categorized as chinoiserie.

By the 1730s, Meissen employed nearly 100 workers, among them renowned modelers J.G. Kirchner and J.J. Kandler. The firm became known for its porcelain sculptures; subjects included birds, animals, and familiar figures from commedia dell'arte. Meissen dinnerware also won acclaim; in earlier attempts, the company's white porcelain had only managed to achieve off-white. Now, at last, there were dazzling white porcelain surfaces that proved ideal for the exquisite, richly colored decoration that became a Meissen trademark.

Following Horoldt's retirement in the mid-1700s, Victor Acier became Meissen's master modeler. Under Acier, the design focus relied heavily on mythological themes. By the early 1800s, however, Meissen's popularity began to wane. With production costs mounting and quality inconsistent, changes were instituted, especially technical improvements in production that allowed Meissen to operate more efficiently and profitably. More importantly, the Meissen designs, which had remained relatively stagnant for nearly a century, were refurbished. The goal: to connect with current popular culture. Meissen's artists (and its porcelain) proved perfectly capable of adapting to the prevailing tastes of the times. The range was wide: the ornate fussiness of the Rococo period; the more subdued Neoclassicism of the late 1700s; the nature-tinged voluptuousness of early 20th century Art Nouveau; and today's Meissen, which

CERAMICS

$

reinterprets, and builds on, all of these design eras.

Despite diligent efforts, Meissen eventually found its work widely copied. A crossed-swords trademark, applied to Meissen pieces from 1731 onward, is a good indicator of authenticity. However, even the markings had their imitators. Because Meissen originals, particularly those from the 18th and 19th centuries, are both rare and costly, the most reliable guarantee that a piece is authentic is to purchase from a reputable source.

Meissen porcelain is an acquired taste. Its gilded glory, lavish use of color, and almost overwhelmingly intricate detailing require just the right setting for effective display. Meissen pieces also often tell a story: a cherub and a woman in 18th century dress read a book, surrounded by a bevy of shepherdesses; the goddess Diana perches on a clock above a winged head of Father Time; the painted inset on a cobalt teacup depicts an ancient Dresden cathedral approached by devout churchgoers. Unforgettable images all, and all part of the miracle that is Meissen.

Flower-encrusted basket, 19th century, first quality, crossed swords mark and incised number...................**$2,040**

Don Presley Auctions

Forty-two-piece porcelain dessert set (part shown), 19th century, teapot, coffee pot, sugar bowl, milk jug, two 12" round chargers, 12 8" dessert plates, 12 cups and saucers, repaired lid on teapot. **$2,875**

Thomaston Place Auction Galleries

"L" series cherub making heart, 19th century, 7-1/2" h.**$960**

Don Presley Auctions

TOP LOT!

Elemental series museum-quality set of four pedestal handled ewers, approximately 25" h., featuring earth, wind, fire, and water, with traditional blue crossed swords marks; earth represented by Diana the Huntress and Pan with hounds chasing various game animals, wheat stalk handle; wind represented by cherubs playing bagpipes and angel expelling gust of wind, storks and eagles in flight, woman astride cloud; fire represented by woman kindling fire and man perched with hammer, figural dragon handle, volcano motif; water represented by Neptune, four seahorses and mermaid with galleon ships on sea; Diana's bow needs repair, old hairline running behind Diana, Pan with horn repair, cherub at top with complete arm restoration; wind ewer woman reattached, angel wing reattached, top cherub with leg repair, body of ewer restored; fire ewer with one wing of dragon with partial restoration; water ewer with tail of mermaid restored, two of eight horse legs partially missing...**$57,500**

Woody Auction

Porcelain figure, Allegory of Harvest, semi-nude woman holding sheaf of wheat, marked on underside, good condition, 5-1/2" h................**$431**

Thomaston Place Auction Galleries

Porcelain figural group of Mary and cherub, German, Mary gazing down to warm left hand over open flame, cherub stands at her waist supporting fiery urn with both arms extended, Mary holds bundle of kindling in her right hand, firewood covers ground near her feet, marked with blue underglaze Meissen crossed swords and impressed 1717 next to cursive L, chip near bottom edge of base, fire lines scattered throughout, 12-1/2" h...............**$615**

Cowan's Auctions, Inc.

Figural dress cane handle, German, late 19th century, three-quarter-length depiction of woman, body of handle decorated with gilt accents and pink, purple, orange, and blue flowers, marked on inside of shaft with underglaze blue crossed swords, 4-3/4" l. **$800**

Cowan's Auctions, Inc.

New gold porcelain deep dish, Germany, 20th century, floriform shape with raised foliate border surrounding vinework, crossed swords mark, second quality mark, very good condition, 11" dia..................**$185**

Skinner, Inc.; www.skinnerinc.com

Figure of napping lady, circa 1870, crossed swords mark and incised numbers, 7-1/2" h.
..........................**$1,200**

Don Presley Auctions

Porcelain figural mantel clock, German, late 19th century, gilt and polychrome enameled case with applied flowers, dial flanked by putti, rectangular plinth with painted bird reserves centering trophy, back with floral reserves, underglaze blue crossed swords mark, clock manufactured by Japy Frères, chips and losses to applied elements, missing part of applied trophy, clockworks currently not running, key not included, pendulum missing, 19-1/2" h. **$4,200**

Cowan's Auctions, Inc.

Porcelain platter in Red Dragon pattern, German, 20th century, shaped gilt rim, marked with underglaze blue double crossed swords, minor loss to gilding on rim, 19-3/4" l. **$180**

Cowan's Auctions, Inc.

Figural group, Dutch farmer with two oxen hitched to plow, horn of one ox has possible restoration, blue crossed swords mark, 11" x 16-1/2".....**$1,000**

Woody Auction

Portrait plaque of woman with long hair and blue wrap with eyes looking upward, signed on back with blue crossed sword mark and inscribed 118 and G-lt, contemporary gold frame, very good to excellent condition, frame with minor wear, 16-1/2" x 19-3/4" overall, plaque 12" x 15-1/2".
.............**$9,000-$12,000**

James D. Julia, Inc.

Porcelain plaque of man with earring and white shirt handing coin to Jesus, marked on back with blue crossed swords mark, contemporary gilded frame with leaf design, very good to excellent condition with some wear to edges of frame, 12" x 15-1/2" overall, sight 7-3/8" x 10-3/4"...**$6,000-$8,000**

James D. Julia, Inc.

CERAMICS

METTLACH

CERAMICS WITH THE NAME METTLACH were produced by Villeroy & Boch and other potteries in the Mettlach area of Germany. Villeroy & Boch's finest years of production are thought to be from about 1890-1910.

Two relief-molded steins with hinged lids, German, late 19th century, half-liter stein with figural decorations, 3/10th-liter stein with crests, architectural elements, and small mold imperfections to lid, marked Mettlach / VB / 2182 / 1 / 96 and Villeroy & Boch / Mettlach / 2077 / 19 / II / 93, respectively, larger stein 7-1/2" h............**$154**

Cowan's Auctions, Inc.

Villeroy and Boch stein, #1336, 7" h. **$120**

Hartzell's Auction Gallery, Inc.

Three decorative plates, two portraits of German luthier, one of servant pouring wine, all stamped, first pattern 2625, second 2621, circa 1920s, fine condition, 7-3/4" dia. **$230**

Thomaston Place Auction Galleries

Villeroy and Boch stein, #1397, 5-1/2" h.**$266**

Hartzell's Auction Gallery, Inc.

Figural paperweight, dwarf lying in grass, mint condition, 6" x 3-1/4". **$197**

Fox Auctions

Etched plaque, #3162, cavaliers, mint condition, 17".....................**$492**

Fox Auctions

Bulbous pottery stein, #2099, 4-1/2" h. **$142**

Hartzell's Auction Gallery, Inc.

Etched plate, #2960, Art Nouveau design, mint condition, 12"........**$172**

Fox Auctions

Half-liter stein with inlaid lid, #2627, mint cameo decoration with safety riders, winged wheel and eagle thumb lift, good condition **$468**

Copake Auction, Inc.

Pug coaster, #1032, drinking dwarfs, mint condition. **$62**

Fox Auctions

Etched half-liter stein, #3087, woman with stein of beer, mint condition. **$246**

Fox Auctions

Cameo plaque, 1885-1930, #2443, with scene of woman and attendants in classical style, blue-green ground, signed "Stahl," very good condition throughout, 18-1/8" dia............**$738**

Skinner, Inc.; www.skinnerinc.com

Half-liter stein, #1566, 19th century, high wheel ordinary rider, lid with high wheel with uniformed rider, good condition. **$614**

Copake Auction, Inc.

Three-handled loving cup with courting scenes in white on pale blue, representing poetry, art, and music, tan baroque frame, very good condition, 6-1/4" h.................**$115**

Thomaston Place Auction Galleries

Book stein, #2001A, lawyer profession, inlay lid, mint condition. .**$400**

Fox Auctions

Pug four-liter vessel, #5003/5192, cavaliers in blue coloring, mint condition. **$400**

Fox Auctions

Etched half-liter stein, #2093, suites of playing cards, inlay lid, base rim chip. **$369**

Fox Auctions

MINTON

THOMAS MINTON ESTABLISHED the Minton factory in England in 1793. The factory made earthenware, especially the blue-printed variety, and Thomas Minton is sometimes credited with the invention of the blue "Willow" pattern. For a time, majolica and tiles were also important parts of production, but bone china soon became the principal ware.

For more information on Minton, see *Antique Trader Pottery & Porcelain Ceramics*, 6th edition, or *Warman's Antiques & Collectibles*, 2015 edition.

Two-handled vase with hand-painted floral design with light blue background, gilt and cobalt trimming, 19th century, 7-1/2" h. **$333**

Elite Decorative Arts

Set of 12 enameled and partial gilt porcelain plates for W. H. Plummer & Co., New York, late 19th century, each border with floral cartouche connected by turquoise bands and floral swags, overall good condition, faint scratches, 10-1/4" dia. **$1,063**

Doyle New York

Two majolica pitchers, larger carved with Daphne, smaller with frog on eggplant, England, 1851/1874, larger stamped MINTON / 1420 / D / artist's cipher / date code, smaller stamped with numbers / MINTON / date code, larger 8-1/2" x 7"... **$2,000**

Rago Arts

Pair of majolica jardinières with underplates en suite, third quarter 19th century, each in urn form, decorated with ram's head masks and garlands on turquoise ground, minor chips and losses, hairline, areas of restoration, 14-3/4" h. x 17-1/4" dia... **$1,875**

Doyle New York

Two reticulated bird plates with 24kt gold painted leaves and birds, imported to New York to Davis Collamore & Co. stores, early 20th century, 9" dia. **$150**

Elite Decorative Arts

MOCHAWARE

MOCHA DECORATION IS FOUND on utilitarian creamware or yellowware articles and is achieved by a simple chemical reaction. A color pigment of brown, blue, green, or black is given an acid nature by infusion of tobacco or hops. When this acid nature colorant is applied in blobs to an alkaline ground color, it reacts by spreading in feathery seaweed designs. This type of decoration is usually accompanied by horizontal bands of light color slip.

Produced in many Staffordshire potteries from the late 18th until the late 19th centuries, its name is derived from the similar markings found on mocha quartz. In addition to the Seaweed decoration, mocha wares are also seen with Earthworm and Cat's-Eye patterns or a marbleized effect.

Pottery beaker, Britain, early 19th century, rouletted diamond band on rim and lower reeded band flanking wide brown band with Seaweed motifs, minor chips, 3-1/2" h. ..**$308**

Skinner, Inc.; www.skinnerinc.com

Three pieces of marbled pottery, England, 19th century, small cream jug, tumbler, and small footed bowl, imperfections, creamer with tight hairline on spout, repair on rim, minute rim chip, tumbler in good condition, footed bowl with crazing and brownish staining to bowl interior, base edge chip, 3-1/2" to 4" h. **$677**

Skinner, Inc.; www.skinnerinc.com

Mochaware pitcher, Britain, early 19th century, barrel-form, ornamented with wide band of inlaid patterned rouletting on shoulder, bands of rust and blue, and thin black bands, restoration, 8" h. ..**$554**

Skinner, Inc.; www.skinnerinc.com

Silver-mounted mustard pot, England, early 19th century, baluster-form, with marbled brown mocha exterior and applied silver hinged cover, unmarked, 3-1/2" h. **$180**

Skinner, Inc.; www.skinnerinc.com

Three pepper pots, Britain, early 19th century, baluster-form, one with bands of light blue, rust, and brown and beaded band on neck, one with bands of blue and black and black patterned, inlaid, rouletted bands, and one with wide Seaweed-decorated blue band flanked by rust and green shoulder band, 4-1/2" to 4-5/8" h.. **$1,140**

Skinner, Inc.; www.skinnerinc.com

Pitcher with Earthworm decoration, Britain, 19th century, barrel-form with three reeded bands flanked by two bands with looping Earthworm designs and thin brown bands, chips to spout, restoration, 7-1/2" h. **$600**

Skinner, Inc.; www.skinnerinc.com

Yellowware coaster with Earthworm decoration, North America or England, circa 1870, straight-sided dish with molded base, decorated with intersecting undulating Earthworm bands, flanked by blue bands, minor rim chips, crazing, 2-3/4" h. x 4-5/8" dia. **$420**

Skinner, Inc.; www.skinnerinc.com

Marbleized half-pint mug, Britain, 19th century, molded base, and inlaid rouletted rim band over field of blue, brown, rust, and white marbleized slip, minor rim chip and hairline, 3-1/4" h. **$900**

Skinner, Inc.; www.skinnerinc.com

Engine-turned frog mug, Britain, late 18th century, pearlware pint mug with olive and blue bands flanking dark brown slip-filled engine-turned field, extruded handle with rust-painted outline with foliate terminals, interior bottom with applied frog figure, imperfections, glaze wear on rim and handle edges, small rim and base chip, three vertical lines from rim, horizontal hairline on top of rim, 4-5/8" h. **$461**

Skinner, Inc.; www.skinnerinc.com

Seaweed-decorated pitcher, Britain, early 19th century, baluster-shaped jug with rouletted diamond-patterned rim band over striped body in olive, blue, and rust, with two bands with blue and black Seaweed decoration, repairs, 7-3/8" h. **$677**

Skinner, Inc.; www.skinnerinc.com

Small marbleized half-pint mug with sprig-mold portrait medallion, Britain, early 19th century, with rust, brown, and white marbling with applied white shield-shaped sprig-molded bust-length profile portrait, imperfections, 3-3/8" h....... **$677**

Skinner, Inc.; www.skinnerinc.com

Pearlware quart mug with molded base, Britain, early 19th century, two wide tan-colored bands with Seaweed decoration flanked by black and blue bands, and two green-glazed chevron rouletted bands, minor rim repair and base chip, 5-7/8" h. **$523**

Skinner, Inc.; www.skinnerinc.com

Striped pitcher with Cat's-Eye decoration, Britain, early 19th century, baluster-form pitcher with applied handle with leaf terminals with bands of light blue, rust, and black, and medial rust band dotted with blue, black, and white slip cat's-eyes, restoration, 7-1/8" h. **$738**

Skinner, Inc.; www.skinnerinc.com

Small bowl, Britain, 19th century, hemispherical-shaped pearlware bowl with brown slip-filled Greek key engine-turned rim band over brown, white, blue, and rust slip-marbled field, minor base chip, 2-5/8" h. x 5-1/4" dia. **$510**

Skinner, Inc.; www.skinnerinc.com

Striped pottery bowl, Britain, early 19th century, blue, rust, and black stripes with wide engine-turned band, two hairlines, 3" h. x 6-1/4" dia........................... **$492**

Skinner, Inc.; www.skinnerinc.com

Chamber crockery pot with blue on white feather decorated band, small rim chip, 4-3/4" x 9" dia **$115**

Thomaston Place Auction Galleries

MOORCROFT

WILLIAM MOORCROFT WAS FIRST EMPLOYED as
a potter by James Macintyre & Co., Ltd. of Burslem,
Staffordshire, England, in 1897. He established the
Moorcroft pottery in 1913. Walter Moorcroft, William's
son, continued the business upon his father's death
and made wares in the same style. The majority of the
art pottery wares were hand thrown, resulting in a great variation among similarly
styled pieces. Colors and marks are keys to determining age. The company initially
used an impressed mark, "Moorcroft, Burslem"; a signature mark, "W. Moorcroft,"
followed. Modern pieces are marked simply "Moorcroft," with export pieces also
marked "Made in England."

Florian low bowl with daisy-like flowers in green and blue,
marked "W. Moorcroft des." in green slip with Registry
Number 360370 in red, faint crazing, excellent original
condition, 2-3/8" h. x 7-3/4" w.. **$500**

Mark Mussio, Humler & Nolan

MacIntyre Florian vase with tulip
decoration in blue, gold, and rose,
signed with "MacIntyre Burslem
England" circular ink stamp logo and
notation "M+1832 W" in red, excellent
original condition with no crazing,
small rub to extensive gold surfaces,
5-1/8" h. **$400**

Mark Mussio, Humler & Nolan

Compote in Wisteria pattern fitted with hammered
Tudric pewter base, made for Liberty, marked "Made in
England Tudric Moorcroft Q 1514," excellent original
condition with faint crazing to bowl, 2-5/8" h. x 5-1/4"
bowl dia.. **$160**

Mark Mussio, Humler & Nolan

CERAMICS

Early Pomegranate vase with green ground, signed W. Moorcroft on bottom and impressed 1075, fine overall crazing, glaze chips at rim, 4-5/8" h. **$750**

Mark Mussio, Humler & Nolan

MacIntyre Brown Chrysanthemum vase, circa 1913, made for John Walsh, Ltd., Sheffield, marked with circular "MacIntyre Burslem England" ink stamp logo, impressed shape number 98 A, W. Moorcroft signature in green slip and ink stamp notation about retailer John Walsh, excellent original condition with faint crazing, 8-5/8" h. **$2,700**

Mark Mussio, Humler & Nolan

MacIntyre Aurelian vase designed by William Moorcroft in transfer designs, marked with circular "MacIntyre Burslem England" ink stamp logo and Registry Number 314901, excellent original condition with minor wear to gold trim, 8" h. **$190**

Mark Mussio, Humler & Nolan

MacIntyre Florian Ware vase with decoration of forget-me-nots, marked on bottom with Florian Ware stamp and painted W. Moorcroft signature, fine overall crazing, 6-1/2" h. **$400**

Mark Mussio, Humler & Nolan

Pair of MacIntyre Florian vases in Honesty pattern, each marked with winged "Florian Ware Jas. MacIntyre Burslem England" ink stamp logo and each signed "W. Moorcroft Des." in green slip, excellent original condition with no crazing, each 3-7/8" h. **$1,100**

Mark Mussio, Humler & Nolan

Wisteria vase on cobalt ground, impressed factory mark, painted Walter Moorcroft initials and shape number 1265, some crazing, excellent condition, 5-1/8 h". **$275**

Mark Mussio, Humler & Nolan

Large Florian oil lamp vase with floral decoration in blue and green, body made with a dozen cast holes where it rolls under toward foot, marked "W. Moorcroft Des." in green slip on bottom, short tight line at rim, minor nicks to thin tube lines, comes with font and burner, 8-3/8" h. **$2,500**

Mark Mussio, Humler & Nolan

Pomegranate vase with deep blue ground, impressed Cobridge mark, impressed Made in England, painted signature, excellent original condition, 9-1/8" h. **$550**

Mark Mussio, Humler & Nolan

MacIntyre Aurelian ware chalice with lid designed by William Moorcroft with floral and flow blue designs, marked with circular "MacIntyre Burslem England" ink stamp logo and impressed number 143.9, excellent original condition, some wear to fired-on gold, 8-3/4" h. **$500**

Mark Mussio, Humler & Nolan

Early "Spanish" vase with inverted rim, marked "W Moorcroft" in green slip and impressed with number 26, faint overall crazing, excellent original condition, 5-3/4" h. **$2,300**

Mark Mussio, Humler & Nolan

Early Claremont jar with threaded lid, signed W. Moorcroft in green slip and impressed 853, marked "Rd No 420061," minor restoration to threads of body and jar, two glaze flakes at shoulder, 5-1/4" h. **$1,300**

Mark Mussio, Humler & Nolan

Eventide vase, 1928-1949, stamped Moorcroft Made in England, script signature, 8-1/4" x 5". **$2,625**

Rago Arts

Ashtray with metal rim and revolving ash dumper attached, impressed "Moorcroft Burslem 1010," metal mounts impressed "English Made," peeling chrome plating on ash dumper, 2-7/8" h. **$100**

Mark Mussio, Humler & Nolan

Miniature Florian Ware vase decorated with poppies, 1902-1913, MacIntyre stamp, Burslem, England, script signature, 2-1/4" x 2"...... **$2,750**

Rago Arts

Ombréd pale yellow vase with sparrows among fruit, stamped on underside, with monogram of William John Moorcroft plus secondary mark, fine condition, 12-3/8" h. **$518**

Thomaston Place Auction Galleries

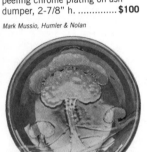

Eventide shallow bowl, 1928-1949, stamped MOORCROFT MADE IN ENGLAND, blue script signature, 1-1/4" x 7-1/2". **$1,500**

Rago Arts

Deep blue plate with sparrows among fruit, stamped on underside, with monogram of William John Moorcroft plus secondary mark, fine condition, 10-1/4" dia........................ **$230**

Thomaston Place Auction Galleries

TOP LOT!

Massive landscape vase, red flambé glaze, 1928-1949, original label "BY APPOINTMENT W. Moorcroft POTTER TO H.M. QUEEN," 15" x 10-1/2". **$16,250**

Rago Arts

Large ginger jar-form vase decorated with flowers on deep blue ground, stamped on underside, with monogram of William John Moorcroft plus secondary mark, fine condition, 11-1/2" h. x 9-1/2" dia....... **$863**

Thomaston Place Auction Galleries

Tall Claremont vase, 1920s, script signature, green stamp MADE FOR SPAULDING & CO. No. 420081, 10-1/4" x 5".................... **$1,188**

Rago Arts

NEWCOMB COLLEGE

THIS POTTERY WAS ESTABLISHED in the art department of Newcomb College in New Orleans in 1897. Each piece was hand-thrown and bore the potter's mark and decorator's monogram on the base. It was always a studio business and never operated as a factory. Its pieces are, therefore, scarce, with the early wares eagerly sought. The pottery closed in 1940.

Early vase decorated with geraniums, 1906, by artist Mary Williams Butler, signed BB30 / NC / M.W.B., stamped JM / Q, 6" x 8-1/2". **$10,000**

Rago Arts

CERAMICS

$

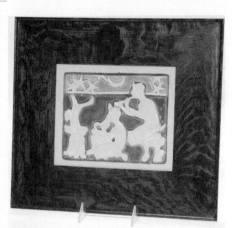

Rare high glaze plaque carved and painted by artist Leona Nicholson, circa 1900, two satyrs playing musical instruments under exaggerated moon and stars, slight luster to blue and green background color, incised marks include Newcomb College logo with letters H and B on either side indicating hand-built, artist's initials, letter M, two firing cracks extend from bottom edge to middle of plaque, edge chips covered by oak frame, glaze chips to horns of one satyr, 7 x 8-1/2".......... **$1,500**

Mark Mussio, Humler & Nolan

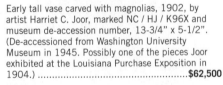

TOP LOT!

Early vase with freesia, 1911, by artist Mazie T. Ryan, signed NC / M.T.R. / EE67, 9-1/2" x 5-1/2"..**$17,500**

Rago Arts

Early tall vase carved with magnolias, 1902, by artist Harriet C. Joor, marked NC / HJ / K96X and museum de-accession number, 13-3/4" x 5-1/2". (De-accessioned from Washington University Museum in 1945. Possibly one of the pieces Joor exhibited at the Louisiana Purchase Exposition in 1904.) **$62,500**

Rago Arts

Vase thrown by Joseph Meyer, decorated with jonquils and covered with mat glazes by artist Cynthia Pugh Littlejohn in 1916, marks on bottom include Newcomb College logo, date code IC86, shape 195, and potter's and decorator's monograms, professional repair of drill hole through center of bottom and inside of rim, tight line extending 3/4" from rim, 8-1/2" h **$1,100**

Mark Mussio, Humler & Nolan

Vase thrown by Jonathan Browne Hunt and decorated by artist Sadie Irvine, palm trees covered in dark blue/purple mat glaze set against lighter purple/pink sky, marked on bottom with Newcomb College logo, date code RT53, and incised monogram of potter and decorator, excellent condition, 5-1/4". **$3,500**

Mark Mussio, Humler & Nolan

Transitional bud vase with forsythia, 1910, by artist Henrietta Bailey, marked NC / DN95 / K / JM, artist's cipher, 4-3/4" x 2-3/4". **$875**

Rago Arts

Carved and painted vase with repeating floral pattern decorated in mat glazes by artist Corinne Marie Chalaron, marked on bottom with Newcomb logo, JM for potter Joseph Meyer, 33, date code MG96 for 1922 and artist's incised initials, excellent original condition, 5-3/4" .. **$1,600**

Mark Mussio, Humler & Nolan

Vase with incised and painted vinca decoration done in 1905 by artist Maria de Hoa Le Blanc, band of stylized flowers around shoulder in periwinkle with green vines and blue trim, marks include Newcomb logo, date code for 1905 (AL 6) in blue slip, JM for potter Joseph Meyer, Q for type of clay body and artist's initials in blue slip, faint crazing, excellent original condition, 5-5/8" h. **$4,200**

Mark Mussio, Humler & Nolan

Hand-thrown vase with ashes of roses glaze, most likely done by Joseph Meyer, marked with Newcomb logo and JM for Meyer, glaze with horizontal and vertical firing cracks in lower half of body where clay is thickest, thumbnail-size chip at base, 8-3/8" h. **$350**

Mark Mussio, Humler & Nolan

CERAMICS

Small vase decorated with live oaks and Spanish moss, 1929, by artist Anna Frances Simpson, marked NC/RQ58/4/artist's cipher, 5-1/2" x 3"...........**$3,375**

Rago Arts

Large vase with live oaks, Spanish moss, full moon, and cabin, 1929, by artist Sadie Irvine, marked NC/JH/211/RV63/artist's initials, 11" x 6"... **$5,313**

Rago Arts

Vase with variegated green glaze with brown highlights, possibly work of Paul Cox, vase appears to be thrown and collar is marked with parallel concentric rings over which glaze flows and separates, marked with Newcomb logo and impressed letter "F," excellent condition with no crazing, 6-3/8" h. **$400**

Mark Mussio, Humler & Nolan

Tall vase decorated with live oaks, Spanish moss, and full moon, 1927, by artist Anna Frances Simpson, marked NC / QC85 / 150 / artist's cipher, 10-3/4" x 4-1/2"...........**$12,500**

Rago Arts

Mat glaze vase with wild rose decoration done in 1922 by artist Sadie Irvine, band of red roses with yellow centers encircle collar of vase, marks include Newcomb College logo, date code for 1922 (MI 95), shape number 92, impressed monogram for potter Joseph Meyer and incised initials of artist, excellent original condition, 8-1/8" h..........**$2,000**

Mark Mussio, Humler & Nolan

Tall transitional vase with irises, 1915, by artist Cynthia Littlejohn, marked NC / HT13 / artist's cipher, 12" x 5-1/4" .. **$5,313**

Rago Arts

Transitional six-piece chocolate set decorated with spiderwort, 1915, by artist Sadie Irvine, pot signed NC / SI / HI / 18 / 76, cups marked HI / 18, pot 10" x 6"..... **$10,625**

Rago Arts

Tall vase decorated with live oaks, Spanish moss, and full moon, 1922, by artist Anna Frances Simpson, marked NC / MK21 / 161 / JM / artist's cipher, 8-1/2" x 5"......... **$6,875**

Rago Arts

Vase decorated with live oaks and Spanish moss, 1928, by artist Anna Frances Simpson, marked NC / RB83 / 35 / artist's cipher, 4-3/4" x 3-1/2". **$3,375**

Large vase decorated with pink irises, 1928, by artist Sadie Irvine, signed NC / SI / 157 / RI36 with paper label, 10" x 7"....... **$4,375**

Rago Arts

Early vase with loblolly pines and vines, circa 1903, by artist Leona Nicholson, signed NC / LN / G (illegible letter) 59, 9" x 4-1/2"........................... **$2,625**

Rago Arts

CERAMICS

Short vase with live oaks and Spanish moss, 1930, by artist Anna Frances Simpson, marked NC SN78 8 AFS JH, 3-3/4" x 5" **$2,250**

Rago Arts

Trivet decorated with live oaks and Spanish moss, 1928, by artist Anna Frances Simpson, signed NC / AFS / QZ2, 5-1/2" dia............................... **$3,750**

Rago Arts

Vase decorated with live oaks and Spanish moss, 1930, by artist Anna Frances Simpson, marked NC / SB32 / 500 / AFS, 6-1/4" x 6-1/2"....... **$5,938**

Rago Arts

Squat vase with gladiolas, 1920, by artist Sadie Irvine, marked NC / KW45 / 271 / JM / artist's cipher, 4" x 4-3/4". **$1,500**

Rago Arts

Cabinet vase with spiderwort, 1917, by artist Sadie Irvine, marked NC / JE60 / artist's cipher, 2-1/2" x 3". **$1,250**

Rago Arts

Squat vase with nicotina, 1926, by artist Henrietta Bailey, marked NC / PM7 / 75 / artist's cipher, 4-1/4" x 5". **$1,125**

Rago Arts

Cylindrical vase decorated with live oaks, Spanish moss, and full moon, 1928, by artist Anna Frances Simpson, marked NC / QV76 / 32 / artist's cipher, 7" x 3"................................... **$3,500**

Rago Arts

Vase with live oaks, Spanish moss, and full moon, 1929, by artist Anna Frances Simpson, marked NC / RU2 / AFS / JH / 250, 7-3/4" x 3-1/2"....... **$3,750**

Rago Arts

Transitional vase with freesia, 1912, by artist Anna Frances Simpson, marked NC / AFS / FB35 / JM/B, 8-1/2" x 3-3/4". **$3,750**

Rago Arts

Early matching bowl and plate decorated with roosters and grape vines, 1907, by artist Maria de Hoa Le Blanc, bowl marked NC / BX83 / MHLB / JMQ, plate marked NC / BX70 / MHLB / JMQ, bowl 5-1/2" x 12", plate 10-3/4" dia..................**$15,000**

Rago Arts

CERAMICS

$

TOP LOT!

Rare and important oil lamp, 1907, by artist Mary Sheerer, glazed ceramic, leaded glass, metal, glass, inscribed, "Live and Love Till Life and Love Are One," base signed NC JM Q BQ13 M.S., with paper label, 18" x 14" to top of shade, base 8-1/2" x 8"..**$93,750**

Rago Arts

Low vase with carved and painted dandelions by artist Anna Frances Simpson in 1926, band of flowers and leaves encircle shoulder, marks include Newcomb College logo, date code for 1926 (PJ 7), shape number 66, impressed monogram for potter Joseph Meyer and incised monogram for artist, excellent original condition with no crazing, strong color, 4-1/2" h. x 7-3/4" dia.. **$2,000**

Mark Mussio, Humler & Nolan

Early vase with stylized flower buds, 1904, by unidentified artist, marked NC / AE27 / JM / 1904 / artist's cipher with remnants of paper label, 4-3/4" x 6".. **$2,875**

Rago Arts

Large vase with New Orleans skyline with St. Louis Cathedral, windmill palms, and crescent moon, 1916, by artist Sadie Irvine, marked NC / SI / 138 / IK74 / 404, 10" x 7-3/4". (New Orleans is also known as the Crescent City, referenced by moon sliver.) **$15,000**

Rago Arts

Squat transitional vase with daffodils, 1914, by unidentified artist, marked NC JM256 / GY66 / indecipherable artist signature, possibly AM, 3-1/2" x 6".. **$1,125**

Rago Arts

NILOAK

THE YEAR 2010 MARKED THE 100TH ANNIVERSARY of Niloak pottery, famous for its marbleized swirls of red, blue, gray, white, and other clay colors.

Niloak, once produced in Benton, Arkansas, has achieved center stage in national auctions. Rago Arts' auctions in recent years have seen the values paid for Niloak demonstrate a pottery that holds its value, commanding prices that would have been impressive before the recession. The Belhorn Auction Service American Art Pottery Auction held in 2009 also witnessed increases in what collectors were willing to pay for Niloak and other older brands.

It's no surprise to Arlene Hyten Rainey that Niloak has an appeal that has become worldwide. Rainey's family founded the pottery a century ago.

"I think the appeal of it is that, from the ground to the finished product, it's home done. A man put his hands on this clay that came from this earth," says Rainey, now 93. "It's never been made anyplace else."

Niloak derived its name from the backwards spelling of the clay type known as kaolin. In regular production from 1910 to 1934, Niloak was produced as vases, penholders, kitchenware, ewers, creamers, sand jars to douse cigarettes, umbrella jars, and even limited special-order production as tile. The family pottery produced housewares with the name "Hyten Brothers" and "Eagle Pottery" on it.

Rainey's father, Charles "Bullet" Hyten, was born in Benton in 1877. His father died while he was a child. Hyten learned the pottery trade from his stepfather, Frank Woosley. Woosley worked for the elder Hyten and cared for him until his death, also keeping the family business going. Woosley married Bullet's mother, Harriet, in 1882.

In 1895, Woosley sold the family business to Bullet, who was 18. Soon after, a fire consumed one of the kilns. Bullet almost lost the business.

In time, he and other potters in the area noticed the amazing colors of clay in the local ground. He had a business connection with a potter in Hot Springs. Together, they discovered that kiln heat burned out the unique colors of Saline County clays. They found a way to add chemicals and colors that

Rare Mission ware bowl in swirl design in metal mount with cattail designs, marked, minor wear to metal holder, impressed logo on base, overall good condition, 8" w. x 4" h.
.... **$281**

Treadway Gallery

duplicated the color of what was in the ground.

Hyten started to experiment seriously in 1909. To Rainey's best recollection, 1910 was the year they perfected the Niloak process. Confident of success, Bullet Hyten sought financing for his company in 1911. Then fire destroyed the pottery a year later. Undaunted, Bullet built a brick factory alongside the railroad tracks, capitalizing on the rail line for shipping and tourist traffic.

At full strength, about 35 people worked at Niloak full-time, including four to five potters. According to Rainey, workers brought clay into the pottery and separated it by color. The process was long and resulted in four to five potters shaping the clay forms. They then placed the clay items in a kiln and fired the pottery.

The Niloak pottery manufactured Eagle brand pottery and red clay flowerpots, thriving during World War I and the early 1920s recession years. But the company

Two vases, both signed Niloak, no chips, cracks or repairs, 36-1/4" x 3-1/2" and 5-1/2" x 2-3/4". **$127**

Dirk Soulis Auctions

couldn't survive the Great Depression. Her father lost the pottery in 1934. Official Niloak production ceased that year, too.

Some Little Rock businessmen bought the business and Hyten worked for them. The new pottery sold Hywood, which was a glazed cast ware, and produced Niloak in limited quantities. In time, the factory sold all pottery under the Niloak name because the brand was very marketable. Wartime limits on materials in the 1940s hurt the quality of production, and the factory closed in the 1950s.

—John J. Archibald

Vase in marbleized blue, brown, and tan, signed on underside with impressed signature "Niloak," very good to excellent condition, 9-1/2" h. **$122**

James D. Julia, Inc.

Mission swirl vase in green, tan, and light and dark brown, impressed Niloak on bottom with paper label of Original Manitou Curio Shop, which is unusual since it specialized in Van Briggle, excellent original condition, 6-1/8" h. **$110**

Mark Mussio, Humler & Nolan

Mission swirl vase in blue, gray, white, and reddish brown, impressed Niloak on bottom, excellent original condition, 8-1/2" h. **$80**

Mark Mussio, Humler & Nolan

Large Mission ware vase with swirling pattern, signed, very good condition, 9" dia. x 18-1/2" h **$1,063**

Treadway Gallery

CERAMICS

NIPPON

"NIPPON" IS A TERM USED to describe a wide range of porcelain wares produced in Japan from the late 19th century until about 1921. It was in 1891 that the United States implemented the McKinley Tariff Act, which required that all wares exported to the United States carry a marking indicating their country of origin. The Japanese chose to use "Nippon," their name for Japan. In 1921 the import laws were revised and the words "Made in" had to be added to the markings. Japan was also required to replace the "Nippon" with the English name "Japan" on all wares sent to the United States.

Many Japanese factories produced Nippon porcelain, much of it hand-painted with ornate floral or landscape decoration and heavy gold decoration, applied beading and slip-trailed designs referred to as moriage. Be aware that a number of Nippon markings have been reproduced and used on new porcelain wares.

Six porcelain vases, all ovoid and two-handled, three floral, three with landscapes, one footed, one with elephant head handles, one with large ring handles, some gilt moriage, some wear to gilding, 6" to 9" h. **$546**

Thomaston Place Auction Galleries

Six pieces, four two-handled vases, baluster vase, and covered jar with hand-painted landscapes, some with gilt moriage, one with relief decoration of dogs harrying deer, wear to gilding, 6-1/2" to 8-1/2" h. **$633**

Thomaston Place Auction Galleries

CERAMICS

Coralene porcelain melon-form biscuit jar with three stem feet, shaped edge opening, domed lid, flower blossoms over wetlands, and Art Nouveau stem vase with landscape, repair to lid, some wear to gilding, 7-3/4" and 9-1/4" h. **$748**

Thomaston Place Auction Galleries

Pair of classical Greek-form two-handled vases decorated with climbing roses, geometric gilt moriage trim, minor difference to gilding of handles, very good condition, 8" h. **$201**

Thomaston Place Auction Galleries

Pair of small two-handled ovoid vases with nearly identical landscapes (one with clouds), gilt moriage decoration, light rubs in lower portions, 7-3/4" h. **$230**

Thomaston Place Auction Galleries

Moriage Arts & Crafts-style vase with scroll handles decorated with pinecones, pine needles and reflective gold, green leaf Nippon hand-painted logo on bottom, excellent condition, 8" h.......**$275**

Mark Mussio, Humler & Nolan

Japanese Coraline handled vase with irises and foliage on front, bud and foliage on back, textured gold handles and rim, three-column Asian character marks beneath, Coraline missing on front bud and area on leaf, color skip on shoulder, 12-1/2" h. **$1,500**

Mark Mussio, Humler & Nolan

Two similar porcelain four-handled vases in same shape, ovoid with square mouths, shaped feet and wave-form handles, with different decoration, one floral, one landscape, with gilt moriage, some wear to gilding, 8" h... **$403**

Thomaston Place Auction Galleries

Four-handled vase in black with gold, four contiguous landscape panels depicting lakeside European village, fine condition, 12-3/4" h. x 7-1/2" dia.............. **$403**

Thomaston Place Auction Galleries

NORITAKE

ALTHOUGH NORITAKE is the long-recognized identifier for a particular brand of fine china, the firm began life in 1904 as Nippon Gomei Kaisha. The "Noritake" moniker came from the company's location in the village of Noritake, Japan. Because it was a geographic designation, the firm had to wait until the 1980s before receiving permission to officially register "Noritake" as a trade name.

Noritake was developed by Morimura Brothers, a distributorship founded in 1876. In its earliest years, Morimura operated as an exporter, bringing traditional Japanese giftware to buyers in America. The company eventually produced a line of fine china dinnerware that proved irresistible in styling and execution to Western consumers.

Noritake dinnerware debuted in 1904. In 1914 exports began. The first Noritake pieces were hand-painted with gold trim, both costly and time-consuming to produce. Much of the decorative work was farmed out to independent artisans throughout the region. Quality varied due to the varying skills of individual freelancers. With the onset of mass production in the 1920s, Noritake achieved consistency in its output, expanded productivity, lowered costs, and increased brand name recognition. From the 1920s until World War II, Noritake achieved its greatest prominence.

Hand-painted Art Deco porcelain covered dresser box depicting young woman with hand mirror, early 20th century, marked with green M-in-wreath backstamp, 3-3/4" dia..........................**$210**

Jackson's International

The inventory fell into two categories: dinnerware and fancy ware. Dinnerware included plates, bowls, tea sets, condiment holders, etc. Fancy ware included wall pockets and vases to elaborately decorated display platters.

The onset of World War II meant that, overnight, Noritake china was no longer available or even welcome in American homes. The company continued to produce china on a limited basis during the war, but only for domestic buyers.

During the American occupation of Japan from 1945-1952, Noritake china became popular with servicemen stationed there; the company's increased production was one factor in assisting Japan along the road to economic recovery. The "Noritake China" name was, for a time, replaced with a more indeterminate "Rose China." The company indicated this was because the china was not yet at its pre-war level of quality; concerns about identifying the product too closely with a recent adversary may also have been a contributing factor.

In the years following the war, Noritake regained its previous worldwide reputation for quality.

CERAMICS

GEORGE OHR

GEORGE OHR, eccentric potter of Biloxi, Mississippi, worked from about 1883 to 1906. Some think him to be one of the most expert throwers the craft will ever see. The majority of his works were hand-thrown, exceedingly thin-walled items, some of which have a crushed or folded appearance. He considered himself the foremost potter in the world and declined to sell much of his production, instead accumulating a great horde to leave as a legacy to his children. In 1972 this collection was purchased for resale by an antiques dealer.

Bowl with torn and folded rim, dark green, black, and gunmetal speckled glaze, 1897-1900, stamped G.E. OHR, Biloxi, Miss., 3-1/2" x 5-3/4". **$2,875**

Rago Arts

Chamberstick with in-body twist, pink and teal glaze, circa 1900, incised GE OHR, 3-1/4" x 4".
.... **$1,250**
Rago Arts

Chamberstick, ochre, raspberry, and purple sponged-on glaze, 1898-1910, script signature, 4" x 4-1/4". **$1,750**

Rago Arts

Three puzzle mugs, 1898-1910, all with script signatures, 3-1/2" x 4-1/2" ea...**$1,875**

Rago Arts

Mug with mottled brown high glaze, incised on bottom GE Ohr in script, small chip on foot and kiln kiss on side of rim, small open glaze bubbles, 3-7/8". **$600**

Mark Mussio, Humler & Nolan

Small folded and crimped coupe with melt fissures, green and gunmetal glaze, 1897-1900, stamped G.E. Ohr, Biloxi, Miss., 3" x 4" x 3-1/2" **$3,125**

Rago Arts

CERAMICS

$

TOP LOT!

Pitcher with ribbon handle, blue, raspberry, and ochre mottled glaze, 1897-1900, stamped G.E. OHR, Biloxi, Miss., 7-1/2" x 5"....... **$10,000**

Rago Arts

Tapered vase with maroon high glaze over which black glaze has been dripped, impressed G.E. Ohr Biloxi on bottom, repair to rim and tight horizontal hairline at waist, 3-1/2" h...**$475**

Mark Mussio, Humler & Nolan

Vase with twisted body with faces on opposing sides and green and black splotches on orange clay body, clear high glaze, impressed G.E. Ohr Biloxi on bottom, excellent original condition, 5-1/4" h.......................**$5,500**

Mark Mussio, Humler & Nolan

Large bisque vase with in-body twist and folded rim, 1898-1910, script signature, 6" x 5". **$2,375**

Rago Arts

Large quatrefoil vase, ochre and brown speckled glaze, 1897-1900, stamped G.E. OHR, Biloxi, Miss., 7-1/2" x 4-1/4" **$8,125**

Rago Arts

Tall baluster vase with clear overglaze, 1880-1910, incised OHR BILOXI, 7" x 4"........ **$1,000**

Rago Arts

Large bulbous vase, ochre, green, and gunmetal sponged-on glaze, 1897-1900, stamped G.E. OHR, Biloxi, Miss., 5-1/2" x 5". **$1,250**

Rago Arts

Tall baluster vase with in-body twist, blistered gunmetal glaze, 1898-1910, script signature, 8" x 4-1/2"..... **$5,313**

Rago Arts

Small thin vase with brown to black glaze, impressed G.E. Ohr Biloxi, Miss. twice on bottom, excellent original condition with visible craze lines showing up lighter on surface, 4-5/8" h .. **$900**

Mark Mussio, Humler & Nolan

Vase with in-body folds, ochre and mossy green speckled glaze, 1897-1900, stamped twice G.E. OHR, Biloxi Miss., 4-1/4" x 3-1/2".............. **$5,625**

Rago Arts

CERAMICS

Large baluster vase, ochre
and brown glaze, 1897-1900,
G.E. OHR, 9-1/2" x 4" **$1,750**

Rago Arts

Large bulbous vase with folded
rim, gunmetal glaze, 1897-
1900, stamped G.E. OHR,
Biloxi, Miss, 8" x 5-1/4" .. **$5,000**

Rago Arts

Baluster vase with in-body
twist, gunmetal and green
glaze, 1898-1910, script
signature, 6-3/4" x 4-1/4" **$5,000**

Rago Arts

Small vase with in-body twist,
mahogany and gunmetal glaze,
1897-1900, stamped G.E. OHR,
Biloxi Miss., 4" x 3" **$6,875**

Rago Arts

Vase with green and orange
glaze, 1895-1896, stamped
GEO E OHR/Biloxi, Miss,
4-1/2" x 3-1/4" **$3,250**

Rago Arts

Large flared vessel, green,
ochre, and gunmetal
sponged-on glaze, 1897-1900,
stamped G.E. OHR, Biloxi,
Miss., 6" x 5" **$1,750**

Rago Arts

Two small vessels, speckled green and gunmetal glaze, 1892-1910,
smaller vessel stamped GEO. E. OHR BILOXI, script signature to
larger, larger vessel 3" x 4". **$2,875**

Rago Arts

Boat-shaped vessel with folded and pinched rim, ochre and gunmetal glaze, 1895-1896, stamped G.E. OHR, BILOXI, 1-3/4" x 3-1/4" x 3-1/4". **$2,500**

Rago Arts

Large dimpled vessel with folded rim, tricolor glaze, 1897-1900, stamped G.E. OHR, Biloxi, Miss., 6-1/4" x 7" **$7,500**

Rago Arts

Vessel with folded and crimped rim, ochre, green and gunmetal glaze, 1897-1900, stamped G.E. OHR, Biloxi Miss., 2-3/4" x 5". **$4,375**

Rago Arts

Pinched vessel, raspberry and multicolor sponged-on glaze, 1895-1896, stamped G.E. OHR, BILOXI, 3" x 4-1/2"........................... **$8,750**

Rago Arts

Small folded vessel, mossy green glaze with speckles, 1895-1896, stamped G.E. OHR, BILOXI, MISS, 3" x 4" x 3-1/4".................... **$3,125**

Rago Arts

Folded vessel, mottled brown, green, and light blue sponged-on glaze, 1897-1900, stamped G.E. OHR, Biloxi, Miss., 4" x 5". **$1,625**

Rago Arts

CERAMICS

OVERBECK

THE OVERBECK STUDIO POTTERY
was founded by four sisters, Hannah,
Mary Francis, Elizabeth, and Harriet,
in the Overbeck family home in
Cambridge City, Indiana, in 1911. A
fifth sister, Margaret, who worked
as a decorator at Zanesville Art
Pottery in 1910, was the catalyst for
establishing the pottery, but died the
same year. Launching at the tail end
of the Arts and Crafts movement,
and believing "borrowed art is bad
art," the sister potters dedicated
themselves to producing unique,
quality pieces with original design
elements, which often were inspired
by the natural world. Pieces can also
be found worked in the Art Nouveau
and Art Deco styles, as well as unique
figurines and grotesques. The studio
used several marks through the years,
including an incised "O" and incised
"OBK," often accompanied by the
artist's initials. The pottery ceased
production in 1955.

Glazed ceramic footed
coupe with stylized
figures and trees, circa
1920, incised OBK/E/F,
Elizabeth Overbeck
(1875-1936) and
Mary Frances Overbeck
(1878-1955), 7" x
5-1/2"............**$6,875**

Rago Arts

Cabinet vase incised
with birds, circa 1920,
incised OBK/E/F,
Elizabeth Overbeck
(1875-1936) and
Mary Frances Overbeck
(1878-1955), 3-1/2"
x 4". **$4,063**

Rago Arts

Figures of ladies and gentlemen, 1911-1955, Southern belle and gentleman, lady with ermine
muff in winter garb, and another lady and gentleman, all in 19th century dress, all with impressed
Overbeck logo on bases, largest 5" h., others 4-1/2" and 4-1/4" h. **$1,320**

Cowan's Auctions, Inc.

OWENS

OWENS POTTERY was the product of J.B. Owens Pottery Co., which operated in Ohio from 1890 to 1929. In 1891 it was located in Zanesville and produced art pottery from 1896, introducing Utopian wares as its first art pottery. The company switched to tile after 1907. Efforts to rebuild after the factory burned in 1928 failed, and the company closed in 1929.

Lightweight vase with fish by artist Harry Larzelere, artist cipher etched in bottom with other obscure marks, vase oversprayed with repair to base and rim, 8-3/4" h. **$350**

Mark Mussio, Humler & Nolan

Arts & Crafts vase with green mat glaze covering large dandelion foliage carved about circumference with hand-tool sculpting in backdrop, impressed "Owens 222," excellent original condition, 9-7/8" h...............**$750**

Mark Mussio, Humler & Nolan

Opalesce inlaid vase with Art Nouveau poppy decoration outlined with gold, marked with paper label with notation "Inlaid" faintly visible, minor rubs and missing beads, 10-1/8" h.........................**$250**

Mark Mussio, Humler & Nolan

Henri Deux handled vase of nude seated among large lotus blossoms on either side and finished with four-color glazing, outlined by gold with gold sponged on lower section, excellent condition, 14" h. **$600**

Mark Mussio, Humler & Nolan

Opalesce inlaid malachite Arts & Crafts porcelain cider jug painted with leaves and flowers of arrowhead plant in gold, unmarked, minor surface scuffs, excellent condition, 6-3/4" h. **$180**

Mark Mussio, Humler & Nolan

Lightweight pillow vase painted by artist Frank Ferrell, baby chick scratching in straw pile, marked with Ferrell's monogram, faint crazing and tiny nick on one foot, 4-1/4" h.**$550**

Mark Mussio, Humler & Nolan

Venetian handled vase in gold luster finish with reflections of rainbow highlights, faint oval mark beneath, 10-1/4" h **$180**

Mark Mussio, Humler & Nolan

Aqua Verde basket molded with arrowhead shape pendants, two-tone glaze, excellent original condition, 5" h. **$275**

Mark Mussio, Humler & Nolan

CERAMICS

Henry Deux vase incised with stand of irises and foliage painted and highlighted with bright gold, small open glaze bubble on shoulder, otherwise excellent condition, 10-3/4".............. **$450**

Mark Mussio, Humler & Nolan

Lotus vase with large peony blossoms painted by artist Charles Chilcote, signature on front, impressed Torch mark and "1243," glaze runs on body and glaze skips on base, excellent original condition, 10-1/8" h. **$350**

Mark Mussio, Humler & Nolan

Large Utopian vase in standard glaze with floral decoration by artist Albert Haubrich, late 19th-early 20th century, underside marked "Utopian, 787, J.B. Owens," even crazing throughout, 13" h. **$360**

Cowan's Auctions, Inc.

Utopian handled vase with flower and scroll design, impressed "Utopian 279 J.B. Owens," crazed, surface scratches to wide area, 6-1/4" h. **$170**

Mark Mussio, Humler & Nolan

Large Opalesce Utopian vase painted with nasturtium and leaf among surround of oyster white coraline-like beading spattered with painted-on amoeba designs, impressed Owens 1068, small dark spots at wide area, possibly factory, excellent original condition, 13-1/4" h. **$200**

Mark Mussio, Humler & Nolan

Vase with curling ocean waves and sprays of bubbles applied by squeeze bag technique, white over gray-green, by artist Frank Ferrell, monogrammed with F in circle on side, impressed "Owens," minor nicks to high points, otherwise excellent condition, 8-1/4" h. **$600**

Mark Mussio, Humler & Nolan

Henri Deux vase with poppy decoration, unmarked, restoration to rim chip, 6-1/2" h. **$110**

Mark Mussio, Humler & Nolan

Vase with molded dragonflies in light green over yellow mat glazes, marked "OWENS" and shape "201" on bottom, fine overall crazing and small grinding chip on bottom, 4" h. **$550**

Mark Mussio, Humler & Nolan

REDWARE

RED EARTHENWARE POTTERY was made in the American colonies from the late 1600s. Bowls, crocks, and all types of utilitarian wares were turned out in great abundance to supplement the pewter and hand-made treenware. The ready availability of the clay, the same used in making bricks and roof tiles, accounted for the vast production. The lead-glazed redware retained its reddish color, although a variety of colors could be obtained by adding various metals to the glaze. Interesting effects occurred accidentally through unsuspected impurities in the clay or uneven temperatures in the firing kiln, which sometimes resulted in streaks or mottled splotches. Redware pottery was seldom marked by the maker.

Mold, unglazed, depicting bird on branch with sprig, circa 1851, incised "15 / G S / 1851" on verso, John George Schweinfurt, New Market, Shenandoah Valley of Virginia, undamaged, 1-3/4" x 1-3/4". **$690**

Jeffrey S. Evans & Associates

Startled cat figure, standing, with inset glass eyes and streaked brown glossy glaze, late 19th/early 20th century, glaze chip on one ear, 9-1/4" h. x 9-1/2" l. **$400**

Skinner, Inc.; www.skinnerinc.com

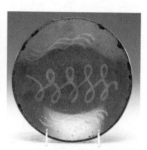

Plate with yellow slip decoration and coggled edge, Pennsylvania, 19th century, 11-1/4" dia. **$400**

Cowan's Auctions, Inc.

Slip-decorated dish, lead glazed, inscribed "Cheap Dish" flanking central corkscrew design, coggled rim, mid-19th century, Pennsylvania or New England, Y-shape crack from rim into center, 11" dia. **$1,265**

Jeffrey S. Evans & Associates

Puzzle jug, neck pierced with small holes, circa 1818, impressed "SARH BURTON / 1818" on shoulder, five spots around rim from old losses, minor small base edge chips, 6" h. **$400**

Skinner, Inc.; www.skinnerinc.com

Hollow-modeled rooster figure with incised detailed features, circular base with crimped edges, early 19th century, repairs to beak, comb, and tail, 14" h. **$861**

Skinner, Inc.; www.skinnerinc.com

CERAMICS

$

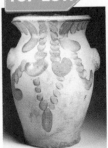

TOP LOT!

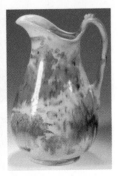

Crock, double lead glazed with iron-oxide spotting, with "1/4" and "1/2" gallon capacity marks, wide-mouth form with two incised rings below broad squared rim, bevel-edge base, circa 1870-1890, Emanuel Suter's New Erection Pottery, Rockingham Co., Shenandoah Valley of Virginia, excellent condition with small shallow chip to top of rim and two flakes to outer rim, 6-1/4" h., 5-1/2" dia. rim. **$431**

Jeffrey S. Evans & Associates

Decorated flower urn, slip washed, baluster form with four incised shoulder rings, coggled piecrust rim and molded bird-wing grape handles, brushed manganese hanging necklace and feather decoration on each side, second half 19th century, stamped "J. Eberly & Bro / Strasburg Va.," original drain hole in base, excellent as-found condition with no restoration and with handles intact, light chipping to foot, minor spots of exfoliation, one to decoration, expected wear to rim, 14-1/2" h. rim, 9" dia. rim. ..**$9,200**

Jeffrey S. Evans & Associates

Polychrome-glazed vase, lead, copper and manganese glazes over slip wash, baluster form with incised shoulder rings, plain rim and pronounced foot, fourth quarter 19th century, attributed to J. Eberly & Co., Strasburg, Shenandoah Valley of Virginia, excellent overall condition, rim interior with shallow chip, outer rim and foot with minor glaze flakes, 10-3/8" h. x 4-1/4" dia. rim.... **$3,450**

Jeffrey S. Evans & Associates

Polychrome-glazed wash pitcher, lead, copper and manganese glazes over slip wash, tall low-belly form with molded tied bow under upper handle and applied thumbrest to top of handle, raised on slight foot, fourth quarter 19th century, attributed to J. Eberly & Co., Strasburg, Shenandoah Valley of Virginia, minor flake to foot, no wear of glaze loss, small firing separation to edge of handle, as made, 11-1/4" h. x 4-1/2" dia. rim, 4-1/4" dia. foot. **$4,313**

Jeffrey S. Evans & Associates

Pitcher, lead glazed with iron-oxide spotting, approximately half-gallon capacity, ovoid body with cylindrical neck, double-ring rim and plain handle, circa 1866-1890, probably Joseph Silber at Emanuel Suter's New Erection Pottery, Rockingham Co., or possibly John George Schweinfurt, New Market, Shenandoah Co., Virginia, excellent condition with slight glaze wear to rim and chip and flake to base, 8-1/4" h. x 4" dia. rim. **$374**

Jeffrey S. Evans & Associates

Miniature crock, double lead glazed, wide-mouth form with incised band below slightly flared rim, circa 1840-1880, probably Rockingham or Shenandoah Co., Virginia, excellent condition, light V-shape hairline off rim and minor chip to foot, 4" h. x 3-3/8" dia. rim. **$403**

Jeffrey S. Evans & Associates

Bavarian basket, three-glazed pottery with pretzel-braided handle, shallow bowl within floral reticulated stand, rare form, Kroning, circa 1880, fine condition, 8" h. **$201**

Thomaston Place Auction Galleries

Vase, lead glazed with manganese splashed decoration, baluster urn form with coggled shoulder ring and rim, open reeded strap handles, pronounced foot, late 19th/early 20th century, Jacob Medinger, Montgomery Co., Pennsylvania, undamaged with some minor wear and crazing, short exterior-only firing under base, 11" h. x 5-3/4" dia. rim. **$489**

Jeffrey S. Evans & Associates

RED WING POTTERY

VARIOUS POTTERIES OPERATED in Red Wing, Minnesota, starting in 1868, the most successful being the Red Wing Stoneware Co., organized in 1877. Merged with other local potteries through the years, it became known as Red Wing Union Stoneware Co. in 1906 and was one of the largest producers of utilitarian stoneware items in the United States.

After a decline in the popularity of stoneware products, an art pottery line was introduced to compensate for the loss. This was reflected in a new name for the company, Red Wing Potteries, Inc., in 1936. Stoneware production ceased entirely in 1947, but vases, planters, cookie jars, and dinnerware of art pottery quality continued in production until 1967, when the pottery ceased operation altogether.

For more information on Red Wing pottery, see *Warman's Red Wing Pottery Identification and Price Guide* by Mark F. Moran.

Stoneware crocks with birch leaf design, six-gallon crock with Union Stoneware oval, black lettering and tab handles, excellent condition, 15" h. x 12" dia.; two-gallon crock with Red Wing Union Stoneware oval and blue lettering, excellent condition, 10" h. x 10" dia...........**$108**

Rich Penn Auctions

Five-gallon stoneware crock and jug with large wings and Red Wing Union Stoneware ovals, jug with small chip on lip, otherwise both in excellent condition, 13" and 18" h. **$120**

Rich Penn Auctions

Art Deco nude holding lyre, Charles Murphy design from 1942, coffee brown matte finish with drape in blue-green glossy finish, impressed Red Wing USA along with shape number 1144, excellent original condition, 10" h. **$1,000**

Mark Mussio, Humler & Nolan

CERAMICS

Nokomis vase in brown, tan, and green matte glazes, marked on bottom in blue with Red Wing Art Pottery ink stamp and incised with numbers 208, excellent original condition, 10-3/8" h. **$225**

Mark Mussio, Humler & Nolan

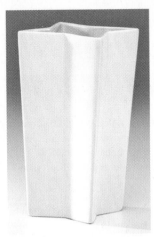

Tall geometric vase with apple green interior, marked Red Wing / USA / 412, 9-1/2" h. x 5" w. **$31**

Cowan's Auctions, Inc.

Water pitcher, circa 1900, cream-colored quart-size stoneware stenciled "COMPLIMENTS OF JOHNSON MERC. CO. / BONESTEEL, SO. DAK.," stamped on bottom "MADE IN RED WING," 8" x 6". **$269**

Holabird-Kagin Americana

Wall-hung stoneware salt box with original cover and advertisement, "Compliments of J. J. Wolfram, 1934, Hart, Minn.," good condition, 7-1/2" h. with lid x 5-1/2" w. **$1,413**

Cedarburg Auction Co., Inc.

Deer in the Woods sand jar, circa 1930s, six-gallon size, in brushed ware line with brushed light blue glaze over tan bisque with bas relief forest scene of deer in woods, 15" h. x 12" dia. **$123**

Cowan's Auctions, Inc.

Eight-gallon stoneware water cooler, Red Wing Union Stoneware oval, original spigot, no lid, no chips or cracks. ...**$270**

Showtime Auction Services

Bowl marked with circular Red Wing Union Stoneware ink stamp, small flake to body, 6-1/2" w. **$5**

Belhorn Auction Services, LLC

Fruit bowl marked Red Wing USA, small nicks to rim, 12-1/4" w. **$6**

Belhorn Auction Services, LLC

Gray line sponge-banded stoneware mug in good condition, 4" h. x 4-1/4" w. to handle. **$452**

Cedarburg Auction Co., Inc.

ROOKWOOD

Maria Longworth Nichols founded Rookwood Pottery in Cincinnati, Ohio in 1880. The name, she later reported, paid homage to the many crows (rooks) on her father's estate and was also designed to remind customers of Wedgwood. Production began on Thanksgiving Day 1880 when the first kiln was drawn.

Rookwood's earliest productions demonstrated a continued reliance on European precedents and the Japanese aesthetic. Although the firm offered a variety of wares (Dull Glaze, Cameo, and Limoges, for example), it lacked a clearly defined artistic identity. With the introduction of what became known as its "standard glaze" in 1884, Rookwood inaugurated a period in which the company won consistent recognition for its artistic merit and technical innovation.

Rookwood's first decade ended on a high note when the company was awarded two gold medals: one at the Exhibition of American Art Industry in Philadelphia and another later in the year at the Exposition Universelle in Paris. Significant, too, was Maria Longworth Nichols' decision to transfer her interest in the company to William W. Taylor, who had been the firm's manager since 1883. In May 1890, the board of a newly reorganized Rookwood Pottery Co. purchased "the real estate, personal property, goodwill, patents, trade-marks... now the sole property of William W. Taylor" for $40,000.

Under Taylor's leadership, Rookwood was transformed from a fledgling startup to successful business that expanded throughout the following decades to meet rising demand.

Throughout the 1890s, Rookwood continued to attract critical notice as it kept the tradition of innovation alive. Taylor rolled out three new glaze lines—Iris, Sea Green, and Aerial Blue—from late 1894 into early 1895.

At the Paris Exposition in 1900, Rookwood cemented its reputation by winning the Grand Prix, a feat largely due to the favorable reception of the new Iris glaze and its variants.

Over the next several years, Rookwood's record of achievement at domestic and international exhibitions remained unmatched.

Throughout the 1910s, Rookwood continued in a similar vein and began to more thoroughly embrace the simplified aesthetic promoted by many Arts & Crafts figures. Production of the Iris line, which had been instrumental in the firm's success at the Paris Exposition in 1900, ceased around 1912. Not only did the company abandon its older, fussier underglaze wares, but the newer lines the pottery introduced also trended toward simplicity.

Unfortunately, the collapse of the stock market in October 1929 and ensuing economic hard times dealt Rookwood a blow from which it did not recover. The Great Depression took a toll on the company and eventually led to bankruptcy in April 1941.

Rookwood's history might have ended there were it not for the purchase of the firm by a group of investors led by automobile dealer Walter E. Schott and his wife, Margaret. Production started once again. In the years that followed, Rookwood changed hands a number of times before being moved to Starkville, Mississippi, in 1960. It finally closed its doors there in 1967.

Standard Glaze vase decorated with pinecones and needles by Katherine Van Horne in 1908, marks: Rookwood logo, date, shape 952E and artist's incised initials, fine overall crazing and glaze flake at rim, 7-1/4" h. **$400**

Mark Mussio, Humler & Nolan

Some Lines of Note

AERIAL BLUE: Commercially, this line was among the least successful. As a result, there are a limited number of pieces, and this scarcity has increased their values relative to other wares.

BLACK IRIS: This line is among the most sought after by collectors, commanding significantly more than examples of similar size and design in virtually any other glaze. In fact, the current auction record for Rookwood – over $350,000 – was set in 2004 for a Black Iris vase decorated by Kitaro Shirayamadani in 1900.

IRIS: Uncrazed examples are exceptionally rare, with large pieces featuring conventional designs commanding the highest prices. Smaller, naturalistically painted examples, though still desirable, are gradually becoming more affordable for the less advanced collector.

PRODUCTION WARE: This commercial and mass-produced artware is significantly less expensive than pieces in most other lines.

STANDARD GLAZE: These wares peaked in the 1970s-1980s, and the market has remained thin in recent years, but regardless of the state of the market, examples of superlative quality, including those with silver overlay, have found their places in the finest of collections.

WAX MAT: This is among the most affordable of the hand-decorated lines.

Vellum Glaze vase decorated with violets against light blue ground by Ed Diers in 1922, marks: Rookwood logo, date, shape 63, impressed V for vellum and artist's initials, fine overall crazing and wheel ground X due to glaze skip at rim, tight hairline at rim, 4-3/8" h. **$180**

Mark Mussio, Humler & Nolan

Iris Glaze vase decorated with Snowdrops by Sara Sax in 1902, marks: Rookwood logo, date, shape 937, w for Iris glaze, and Sax's impressed cipher, fine overall crazing, professional repair near base, 8-7/8" h. **$425**

Mark Mussio, Humler & Nolan

Lidded cigarette holder with mottled gray high glaze on exterior and turquoise high glaze on interior, 1950s, marks: Rookwood logo and shape 7002, no date indicated, small frog perched atop matching lid, which is unmarked, small glaze chips to base, 5" h..............**$130**

Mark Mussio, Humler & Nolan

Mat Glaze vase decorated with wisteria by Margaret McDonald in 1937, marks: Rookwood logo, date, shape 2032E and artist's initials in green slip, excellent original condition, 7-3/8" h...**$450**

Mark Mussio, Humler & Nolan

Vellum Glaze vase decorated with cornflowers and roses by Fred Rothenbusch in 1924, marks: Rookwood logo, date, shape 1369F, V for vellum and artist's monogram, no crazing, 6-1/4" h. **$500**

Mark Mussio, Humler & Nolan

Iris Glaze vase decorated with violets by Irene Bishop in 1904, marks: Rookwood logo, date, shape 943F and artist's initials, overall crazing, 4-5/8" h. **$550**

Mark Mussio, Humler & Nolan

Letter holder depicting first United States postage stamp cast in 1956 and covered with blue high glaze, impressed on base with Rookwood logo, date and "Rookwood Cinti, O.," no crazing, unevenness in glaze application, 3" h. x 4-1/4" w. **$180**

Mark Mussio, Humler & Nolan

Nautilus shell vase, cast in 1940, exterior of piece not glazed, light blue high glaze on interior, marks: Rookwood logo, date and shape 6657, excellent original condition, 6" h.......**$150**

Mark Mussio, Humler & Nolan

Five-sided rook pencil holder, cast in 1948, in wine madder glaze with brown high glaze at top and blue high glaze on rooks at bottom, marks: Rookwood logo, date and shape 1795, light crazing, 4-3/4" h. **$325**

Mark Mussio, Humler & Nolan

Flower holder topped by two dancing female nudes, cast in 1923, blue high glaze, marks: Rookwood logo, date and shape 2536, tight firing separation and some roughness at base, 5-1/2" h. **$250**

Mark Mussio, Humler & Nolan

Commercial ware ashtray made for Baldwin Piano Co., upright piano in bowl of elaborate tray in dark green mat glaze, produced in 1914, base marked with Rookwood logo, date and logo of company, Baldwin name molded into bowl, professional repair to upper portion of piano, 1-7/8" h **$120**

Mark Mussio, Humler & Nolan

Seated elephant with candleholder atop head, cast in 1929, Shirayamadani design, medium mat green glaze with pink accents near candle aperture, marks: Rookwood logo, date and shape 6059, uncrazed, 4" h. **$100**

Mark Mussio, Humler & Nolan

Paperweight in shape of rectangle with molded flowers and leaves, cast in 1904, mat green glaze, marks: Rookwood logo, date and shape 696 Z, excellent original condition, 2-5/8" x 4-3/4" h. **$475**

Mark Mussio, Humler & Nolan

CERAMICS

ROSEVILLE POTTERY

ROSEVILLE IS ONE OF THE MOST widely recognizable of potteries across the United States. Having been sold in flower shops and drug stores around the country, its art and production wares became a staple in American homes through the time Roseville closed in the 1950s.

Rare Art Deco Roseville Pottery dealer sign with teal-colored matte glaze, professional repair to small corner chips, 4" x 9-1/2"....................**$700**

Mark Mussio, Humler & Nolan

The Roseville Pottery Co., located in Roseville, Ohio, was incorporated on Jan. 4, 1892, with George F. Young as general manager. The company had been producing stoneware since 1890, when it purchased the J. B. Owens Pottery, also of Roseville.

The popularity of Roseville Pottery's original lines of stoneware continued to grow. The company acquired new plants in 1892 and 1898, and production started to shift to Zanesville, just a few miles away. By about 1910, all of the work was centered in Zanesville, but the company name was unchanged.

Young hired Ross C. Purdy as artistic designer in 1900, and Purdy created Rozane—a contraction of the words "Roseville" and "Zanesville." The first Roseville artwork pieces were marked either Rozane or RPCO, both impressed or ink-stamped on the bottom.

In 1902, a line was developed called Azurean. Some pieces were marked Azurean, but often RPCO. In 1904 at the St. Louis Exposition, Roseville's Rozane Mongol, a high-gloss oxblood red line, captured first prize, gaining recognition for the firm and its creator, John Herold.

Many Roseville lines were a response to the innovations of Weller Pottery, and in 1904 Frederick Rhead was hired away from Weller as artistic director. He created the Olympic and Della Robbia lines for Roseville. His brother Harry took over as artistic director in 1908, and in 1915 he introduced the popular Donatello line.

By 1908, all handcrafting ended except for Rozane Royal. Roseville was the first pottery in Ohio to install a tunnel kiln, which increased its production capacity.

Frank Ferrell, who was a top decorator at the Weller Pottery by 1904, was Roseville's artistic director from 1917 until 1954. This Zanesville native created many of the most popular lines, including Pine Cone, which had scores of individual pieces.

Many collectors believe Roseville's circa 1925 glazes were the best of any Zanesville pottery. George Krause, who in 1915 became Roseville's technical supervisor responsible for glaze, remained with Roseville until the 1950s.

Company sales declined after World War II, especially in the early 1950s when cheap Japanese imports began to replace American wares, and a simpler, more modern style made many of Roseville's elaborate floral designs seem old-fashioned.

In the late 1940s, Roseville began to issue lines with glossy glazes. Roseville tried to offset its flagging artware sales by launching a dinnerware line—Raymor—in 1953. The line was a commercial failure.

Roseville issued its last new designs in 1953. On Nov. 29, 1954, the facilities of Roseville were sold to the Mosaic Tile Company.

For more information on Roseville, see *Warman's Roseville Pottery Identification and Price Guide*, 2nd edition, by Denise Rago.

CERAMICS

Bottom Marks

There is no consistency to Roseville bottom marks. Even within a single popular pattern like Pine Cone, the marks vary.

Several shape-numbering systems were implemented during the company's almost 70-year history, with some denoting a vessel style and some applied to separate lines. Though many pieces are unmarked, from 1900 until the late teens or early 1920s, Roseville used a variety of marks including "RPCo," "Roseville Pottery Company," and the word "Rozane," the last often with a line name, i.e., "Egypt."

The underglaze ink script "Rv" mark was used on lines introduced from the mid-to-late teens through the mid-1920s. Around 1926 or 1927, Roseville began to use a small, triangular black paper label on lines such as Futura and Imperial II. Silver or gold foil labels began to appear around 1930, continuing for several years on lines such as Blackberry and Tourmaline, and on some early Pine Cone.

From 1932 to 1937, an impressed script mark was added to the molds used on new lines, and around 1937 the raised script mark was added to the molds of new lines. The relief mark includes "U.S.A."

All of the following bottom mark images appear courtesy of Adamstown Antique Gallery, Adamstown, Pennsylvania.

Impressed mark on Azurean vase, 8" h.

Raised mark on a Bushberry vase.

Ink stamp on a Cherry Blossom pink vase, 10" h.

Wafer mark on a Della Robbia vase, 10-1/2" h.

Gold foil label and grease pencil marks on an Imperial II vase, 10" h.

Impressed mark on an Iris vase.

Ink stamps on a Wisteria bowl, 5" h.

Impressed marks on a Rozane portrait vase, 13" h.

Azetc vase decorated with four stylized blue flowers with yellow seeds alternating with buds on green stems applied over black-green glaze, artist "CS" cipher on side, Rozane Ware wafer seal, excellent condition, 6-5/8" h. **$650**

Mark Mussio, Humler & Nolan

Tall green Baneda vase, shape 598 with handles, marked with shape number in red crayon and firm's triangular sticker beneath, repair to base and lower section of each handle, 12-1/4". **$300**

Mark Mussio, Humler & Nolan

Aztec vase with tall stalks of cream and yellow flowers above blue scrolled foliage over blue glaze done by artist who placed an "E" on base, professional repair to base, 11-1/8" h. **$120**

Mark Mussio, Humler & Nolan

Baneda vase with foot and handles in rose pink glaze, shape 606, excellent condition, 7" h. **$275**

Mark Mussio, Humler & Nolan

Baneda vase in green, shape number 595-8, marked with number 595 in orange grease pencil, excellent glaze, mold and color, 8-1/8" h. **$475**

Mark Mussio, Humler & Nolan

Blackberry vase, shape 569, with closed handles, company black triangular sticker beneath, excellent condition, 5-1/8" h. **$275**

Mark Mussio, Humler & Nolan

Large Carnelian II vase with scroll handles and mingle of glazes, turquoise and maroon, combination producing some gray qualities, marked "318" in red crayon and "R" in black, excellent condition, 8" h. x 9-1/2" w. **$250**

Mark Mussio, Humler & Nolan

Cherry Blossom vase with rose pink and aqua glaze in shape 624, marked "3" in blue crayon under glaze, flat glaze chip on base, 8" h. **$225**

Mark Mussio, Humler & Nolan

TOP LOT!

Della Robbia vase hand-carved with 12 fish shoaling over hand-chiseled watery-looking backdrop, green glaze, chevrons carved into base where two artists incised initials "DB" and possibly "GB," line mid-body, rim and base with professional repair, 10-3/8" h. **$3,100**

Mark Mussio, Humler & Nolan

Della Robbia vase with arrowhead leaves and pink fruit on tan vines carved by artisan with initial "E" using six colors, listed as shape 54 in Della Robbia listings, professional restoration to minor nicks on foot and rim, 6-1/2" h. **$4,700**

Mark Mussio, Humler & Nolan

Rare Donatello incense burner, unmarked, tiny chips to both rims and staining in bowl from use, 3-5/8" h...................................... **$225**

Mark Mussio, Humler & Nolan

Rozane Egypto molded leaf design in green matte glaze, marked with raised Rozane Ware Egypto wafer, excellent original condition, 5-3/8" h **$600**

Mark Mussio, Humler & Nolan

Falline round vase, shape 644, green to blue glaze, marked with shape number in red crayon with firm's silver triangular foil sticker, professional repair to handles, 6-1/8" h. **$225**

Mark Mussio, Humler & Nolan

Freesia jardiniere on pedestal with stalks of cream and yellow flowers set against tangerine and chocolate backdrop, jardiniere bears company's raised marks and shape number 669-8" beneath, pedestal marked USA on top, 25" h. combined........................... **$400**

Mark Mussio, Humler & Nolan

Fudji vase with Japanese design applied in jade green and indigo blue enamel, repeated throughout grayish matte body, professional repair to drill hole on bottom, 10" h............. **$3,500**

Mark Mussio, Humler & Nolan

Ferella vase, shape 500, in dark rose mottled glaze, excellent original condition, 5-1/4" h. **$425**

Mark Mussio, Humler & Nolan

Furtura handled jardiniere, shape 616, gray-green with pink and blue foliage, unmarked, glaze miss to base rim, 7" x 10". **$200**

Mark Mussio, Humler & Nolan

Futura footed vase, shape 427, with teasel pattern under lilac and pink glazes, excellent condition, 8" h. **$550**

Mark Mussio, Humler & Nolan

Imperial II vase with ridges and lilac glaze drizzled over turquoise, shape 468, excellent original condition, 5" h. **$180**

Mark Mussio, Humler & Nolan

Imperial II vase, shape 471, mottled red glaze combined with turquoise and cream on ridged neck, excellent condition, 7" h. **$350**

Mark Mussio, Humler & Nolan

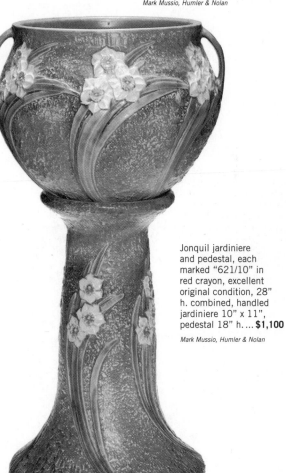

Jonquil jardiniere and pedestal, each marked "621/10" in red crayon, excellent original condition, 28" h. combined, handled jardiniere 10" x 11", pedestal 18" h. **$1,100**

Mark Mussio, Humler & Nolan

Large Iris vase in pink with handles in shape 929-15" incised on bottom, overall crazing, otherwise excellent condition, 12-1/4" h. **$150**

Mark Mussio, Humler & Nolan

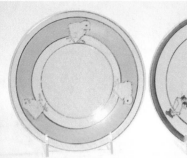

Two Juvenile plates, one decorated with yellow chicks, other with rainy day ducks, both with Rv stamped beneath, excellent condition, 8" dia. **$120**

Mark Mussio, Humler & Nolan

Montacello handled vase mottled with tan and turquoise glaze, shape 561, excellent condition, 7-1/8" h. **$50**

Mark Mussio, Humler & Nolan

Montacello handled vase, shape 556, in aqua green, shape number written in red crayon beneath, excellent condition, 5-1/4" h. **$190**

Mark Mussio, Humler & Nolan

Mara slender bud vase with copper luster glaze that is reflective and drippy textured, excellent condition, 8-7/8" h. **$1,500**

Mark Mussio, Humler & Nolan

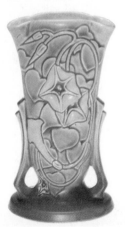

Fan-shaped Morning Glory vase in green with handles, shape 725, excellent original condition, 7-3/8" h. **$250**

Mark Mussio, Humler & Nolan

Panel vase in green with scarf-dancing nudes in various poses in each of four windows, blue Rv factory stamp logo, crack at rim descends into body with repairs to rim chips in same area, 10-1/4" h. **$225**

Mark Mussio, Humler & Nolan

Rosecraft Panel vase with nudes posed in four panels, glaze separation on rim and small clay bumps on one nude, stamped Rv on bottom, 10-1/4" h. **$350**

Mark Mussio, Humler & Nolan

Rozane Pattern figure of fish peeking from curved seaweed, aqua blue glaze with tan accents, raised factory marks with number 1 on bottom, excellent condition, 5" h. **$275**

Mark Mussio, Humler & Nolan

Rozane Royal vase decorated with portrait of Native American chief in full headdress by artist Anthony Dunlavy, impressed on bottom "ROZANE," "RPco," 861, 4 and letter B, chips at rim and shoulder, fine overall crazing and several patches of dry crazing, 15-1/2" h. **$1,000**

Mark Mussio, Humler & Nolan

Tall Rozane Royal Light vase decorated by artist Elizabeth Ayers, two yellow roses on leaf stems over complementary green, Rozane Ware Royal wafer beneath, artist signature below painted design, excellent original condition, 14-3/4" h.**$300**

Mark Mussio, Humler & Nolan

Rozane Royal "twist" vase with jonquils hand-decorated by artist Virginia Adams, raised wafer logo beneath, artist signature on side, excellent condition, 10" h.................**$170**

Mark Mussio, Humler & Nolan

Large Rozane Royal Light vase with woodbine decoration by artist Mae Timberlake, signed by artist on top edge of foot ring, fine overall crazing and some small open glaze bubbles, 17-5/8" h. **$700**

Mark Mussio, Humler & Nolan

Silhouette vase glazed in red showing kneeling nude in two panels, raised marks with shape number 787-10" and large incised X and painted X beneath, flat chip on bottom corner of base, 10-1/4" h....**$100**

Mark Mussio, Humler & Nolan

CERAMICS

R.S. PRUSSIA

ORNATELY DECORATED CHINA marked "R.S. Prussia" and "R.S. Germany" continues to grow in popularity. According to the Third Series of Mary Frank Gaston's *Encyclopedia of R.S. Prussia* (Collector Books, Paducah, Kentucky), these marks were used by the Reinhold Schlegelmilch porcelain factories located in Suhl in the Germanic regions known as "Prussia" prior to World War I, and in Tillowitz, Silesia, which became part of Poland after World War II. Other marks sought by collectors include "R.S. Suhl," "R.S." steeple or church marks, and "R.S. Poland."

The Suhl factory was founded by Reinhold Schlegelmilch in 1869 and closed in 1917. The Tillowitz factory was established in 1895 by Erhard Schlegelmilch, Reinhold's son. This china customarily bears the phrase "R.S. Germany" and "R.S. Tillowitz." The Tillowitz factory closed in 1945, but it was reopened for a few years under Polish administration.

Prices are high and collectors should beware of the forgeries that sometimes find their way onto the market. Mold names and numbers are taken from Mary Frank Gaston's books on R.S. Prussia.

The "Prussia" and "R.S. Suhl" marks have been reproduced, so buy with care. Later copies of these marks are well done, but the quality of porcelain is inferior to the production in the 1890-1920 era.

Decorated portrait "Madame Recamier" china tankard pitcher, mold 29/Lily, scalloped base, portrait transfer between bands of lavender iridescent "Tiffany" finish, gilt decoration, circa 1904, unmarked, undamaged, expected minor wear to decoration, 15" h. overall. **$1,150**

Jeffrey S. Evans & Associates

Collectors are also interested in the porcelain products made by the Erdmann Schlegelmilch factory. This factory was founded by three brothers in Suhl in 1861. They named the factory in honor of their father, Erdmann Schlegelmilch. A variety of marks incorporating the "E.S." initials were used. The factory closed circa 1935. The Erdmann Schlegelmilch factory was an earlier and entirely separate business from the Reinhold Schlegelmilch factory. The two were not related to each other.

CERAMICS

Decorated china bowl, mold 211 with two open-work hearts, green to yellow ground with pink poppy transfer in center, satin finish, early 20th century, red RSP with green wreath mark, undamaged, minute wear to gilt decoration on rim and two small losses to yellow ground, 2" h. x 10-3/4" dia. **$127**

Jeffrey S. Evans & Associates

Decorated china bowl, mold 28 with polychrome pink poppies transfer in center, satin finish, early 20th century, red RSP with green wreath mark, excellent condition, rim with two minor flakes to flower petals touched-up with gold, remaining rim with expected wear to gilt decoration, 3" h. x 10-1/2" dia............. **$115**

Jeffrey S. Evans & Associates

Decorated china bowl, mold 16, green to yellow ground with still life "Reflecting Water Lily" in center, glossy finish, early 20th century, red RSP with green wreath mark, excellent condition, interior rim with small shallow chip, 3-1/4" h. x 10-3/4" dia........................**$115**

Jeffrey S. Evans & Associates

Decorated china seven-piece berry set, master bowl and six individual bows, scalloped rim, polychrome yellow and pink tulip decoration, glossy finish, early 20th century, red RSP with green wreath mark, master bowl impressed "GERMANY," undamaged, expected minor wear to gilt decoration on rims, master bowl 2-1/2" h. x 10" dia.; individual bowls 1" h. x 5-1/4" dia.. **$127**

Jeffrey S. Evans & Associates

Decorated china bowl, mold 211a with polychrome poppies transfer in center, satin finish, early 20th century, red RSP with green wreath mark, undamaged, expected wear to gilt decoration on rim, 3-1/2" h. x 10-1/2" dia. **$150**

Jeffrey S. Evans & Associates

Decorated china shaving mugs, one with lavender shading and basket of flowers transfer and the other with yellow and green shading and rose transfer, early 20th century, each with red RSP and green wreath mark, undamaged, 3-1/2" h. overall. **$69**

Jeffrey S. Evans & Associates

CERAMICS

SATURDAY EVENING GIRLS

SATURDAY EVENING GIRLS (Paul Revere) pottery was established in Boston, Massachusetts, in 1906, by a group of philanthropists seeking to establish better conditions for underprivileged young girls of the area. Edith Brown served as supervisor of the small "Saturday Evening Girls Club" pottery operation, which was moved, in 1912, to a house close to the Old North Church where Paul Revere's signal lanterns had been placed. The wares were mostly hand-decorated in mineral colors, and both sgraffito and molded decorations were employed. Although it became popular, it was never a profitable operation and always depended on financial contributions to operate. After the death of Edith Brown in 1932, the pottery foundered and finally closed in 1942.

S.E.G.

Large four-color bowl decorated in cuerda seca with nasturtiums, circa 1910, artist Sara Galner, signed SG / SEG / illegible numbers, 4-3/4" x 11-3/4"...**$32,500**

Rago Arts

Glazed ceramic breakfast set, 1940, decorated by Lili Shapiro, plate, bowl and cup, each in pink with blue band reading "Janice, Her Plate," central medallion of chicks, bunny, and duck with black outlining, each marked P.R.P, dated 7-40, signed LS on base, bowl with rim hairline, 1/2" to 3/4" h., plate 7-1/2" dia. Provenance: Given to consignor by Fannie Levine.................... **$570**

Skinner, Inc.; www.skinnerinc.com

Circular trivet with hand-decorated scene in blue, green, yellow, brown, and white mat glazes, impressed with circular Paul Revere Pottery logo on bottom and V in dark slip, no crazing, 5-1/2".................**$325**

Mark Mussio, Humler & Nolan

Early pitcher with three sets of three rabbits racing around shoulder, design by Rose Bacchini in 1910, hand-marked S.E.G., 288 5/10, RB in black glaze on bottom, small bruise on rim with short lines, 4-1/2" h.......................................**$850**

Mark Mussio, Humler & Nolan

Bowl decorated at shoulder with floral design in black, white, and green mat glazes against light blue ground, marked in slip on bottom S.E.G., 5-22, 015 underlined and artist's initials, which appear to be ECT, excellent original condition, 2-3/4" h. x 6-1/4" dia. **$500**

Mark Mussio, Humler & Nolan

Octagonal paperweight decorated with image of ship, original Paul Revere Pottery paper label affixed to bottom, small burst glaze bubbles in "sea" area of decoration, 1" h. x 2-5/8" w. **$170**

Mark Mussio, Humler & Nolan

Teal mat glaze vase by Eva Geneco in 1920, signed "S.E.G. 6-20" with monogram of artist, all in black slip, excellent original condition, small area of silvery glaze on foot ring, 7" h. **$150**

Mark Mussio, Humler & Nolan

Glazed ceramic vase, baluster form in mottled glossy moss green glaze, 1916, artist Lili Shapiro, base marked S.E.G., 6-16, LS, and another illegible set of initials, imperfection to rim in making, 10-3/4" h. ...**$270**

Skinner, Inc.; www.skinnerinc.com

Pitcher with repeating pattern, initials AR under spout, impressed on bottom with company logo and November 1925 date marked in black slip, minor glaze nicks at rim, 4-1/4" h. **$200**

Mark Mussio, Humler & Nolan

Trivet decorated with lake and trees in cuerda seca, 1913, artist Fannie Levine, signed FL/S.E.G./12.13, 5-1/2" dia.......................**$1,875**

Rago Arts

Pitcher with band of irises outlined in black on cream ground, work of artist with initials J.G., marked on base in black slip S.E.G. 4-6-14 JG, excellent original condition, no crazing, 7-3/8" h. **$1,000**

Mark Mussio, Humler & Nolan

CERAMICS

$

Child's matching bowl and plate, both decorated with white rabbit at center with "Dorothy Her Plate" in white ring against yellow ground, both pieces marked on bottom with Paul Revere logo, overall crazing and toning due to age, bruise on rim of bowl, plate 7-5/8" dia., bowl 2-1/4" h. x 5-1/2" dia.. **$375**

Mark Mussio, Humler & Nolan

Pitcher and two trivets decorated in cuerda seca with geese and ship, all signed and dated, pitcher 5-1/2" x 5-3/4", trivets 5-1/2" dia.............. **$1,625**

Rago Arts

TOP LOT!

Important glazed ceramic fireplace surround decorated in cuerda seca, depicting wooded landscape with river, circa 1915, artists Fannie Levine, Albina Mangini, and Edith Brown, signed FL / AM / PAUL REVERE POTTERY and Edith Brown's cipher, surround approximately 38" x 52", hearth approximately 21" x 60". **$219,750**

Rago Arts

Fruit bowl and plate, bowl with impressed stamp, small foot, flared rim, marked A3-2b, plate hand-marked P-R-P, 12-37 with artist's initials LS, good condition, 9" and 8-1/2" dia. **$173**

Thomaston Place Auction Galleries

Bowl decorated in cuerda seca with trees, 1912, artist Fannie Levine, marked S.E.G. / 3.12 / FL, 2-1/2" x 8-1/2"..**$1,250**

Rago Arts

Arts & Crafts pottery berry set, large bowl with seven matching bowls by artist Sarah Galner, dated 2-12 and 8-14, in blue with black and white band of cuerda seca decoration, two smaller bowls of later date have different glaze, small chip to rim of one small bowl, 2-1/2" x 8-1/2" and 1-1/2" x 4-3/4"..**$2,300**

Thomaston Place Auction Galleries

Low bowl decorated in cuerda seca with white blossoms, 1917, artist Albina Mangini, marked AM / S.E.G. / 1-17, 2-1/2" x 9"...........**$800-$1,200**

Rago Arts

CERAMICS

SÈVRES PORCELAIN

SÈVRES PORCELAIN, the grandest of ultimate luxury, artistic ceramics, was favored by European royalty, the aristocracy of the 19th century, and 20th century collectors. Its story begins in 1708, when German alchemist Johann Bottger discovered the formula for strong, delicate, translucent hard-paste porcelain. Unlike imported white "chinaware," Bottger's porcelain could also be painted and gilded. Soon potteries across Europe were producing decorative items with fashionable gilt and flowers.

French potters lacked an ample source of kaolin, a requisite for hard-paste porcelain, however, so they developed a soft-paste formula from clay and powdered glass. Soft-paste, though fragile, could be fired at a lower temperature than hard-paste. This allowed a wider variety of colors and glazes.

The Sèvres porcelain factory was originally founded at Chateau de Vincennes in 1738. Its soft-paste porcelain was prized for its characteristic whiteness and purity. By the time this workshop relocated to Sèvres in 1756, its craftsmen were creating small porcelain birds, figurals of children in white or delicate hues, and innovative pieces with characteristic rosy-hued backgrounds. They also produced detailed allegorical and thematic pieces with transparent, colorless glazes.

Pair of gilt bronze-mounted porcelain urns and covers, France, circa 1900, each with multicolored luster borders and central cartouches of allegorical subjects with landscapes on reverse, nymph handles, signed under covers, hairline crack to one cover, each vase with scattered gilt wear to trim lines along top rim of socle, 17-1/4" h., body 5-1/2" w., 8-3/4" handle to handle. **$5,228**

Skinner, Inc.; www.skinnerinc.com

The introduction of unglazed, natural-toned "biscuit" porcelain, a favorite of Madame de Pompadour, the mistress of Louis XV, followed. Biscuit porcelain is extremely fragile. Madame de Pompadour also adored Sèvres' porcelain flowers.

When Louis XV assumed full control of Sèvres porcelain in 1759, he insisted on flawless, extravagant creations, many of which he commissioned for his personal collection. The Sèvres mark, blue interlaced Ls, was born of his royal patronage and helps determine dates of production. Other marks, either painted or incised, indicate specific Sevres painters, gilders, sculptors, and potters by name. Louis XV's successor, Louis XVI, continued to support the royal Sèvres tradition.

Although kaolin deposits were discovered near Limoges in 1768, Sèvres began producing hard-paste porcelain commercially only from 1773. During this period, they continued to produce soft-paste items as well.

After suffering financial ruin during the French Revolution, Sèvres began producing simpler, less expensive items. During this period its craftsmen also abandoned their old-fashioned soft-paste formula for hard-paste porcelain. Sèvres porcelain regained its former glory under Napoleon Bonaparte, who assumed power in 1804. He promoted ornamented pieces in the classical style.

The range of Sèvres creations is extensive, varying in shape, historical styles, motifs, and ornamentation. Vases typically feature double round, oval, or elliptical finely painted scenes edged in white against pastel backgrounds. One side portrays figures, while the other features flower bouquets. Their lavish gilding is often embellished with engraved detail, like flowers or geometric motifs.

Simple plates and tea wares can be found for a few hundred dollars. Because large numbers were made to accompany dessert services, quite a few Sèvres biscuit porcelains have also survived. These fragile pieces command between $3,000 to as much as $70,000 apiece.

According to Errol Manners, author, lecturer, and proprietor of London's H & E Manners: Ceramics and Works of Art, the Sèvres market has strengthened considerably in recent years. "Pieces linked directly to the Court and very early experimental wares... command the highest prices of all," he explains. "Major pieces can command a few hundred thousand dollars. A set of Sèvres vases can command over $1 million."

Collecting Sèvres porcelain is, in his experience, "a minefield for the unwary, since many fakes and pastiches – showy, decorative 'Sèvres-style' imitations – abound. These were produced during the 19th century in the style of the 18th century, but not by Sèvres," he says.

"While Sèvres-style pieces are not authentic Sèvres, they may be authentic antiques," counters Edan Sassoon, representing the Artes Antiques and Fine Art Gallery in Beverly Hills, Calif. "If they faithfully imitate Sèvres pieces in quality, style, and opulence, they may not only have decorative value, but may also be quite expensive. In today's market, a piece of Sèvres-style porcelain, depending on its color, condition, size, and quality, may command hundreds of thousands of dollars."

— *Melody Amsel-Arieli*

Rare stoneware vide-poche decorated with cherubs and chestnuts, Joseph Cheret (1838-1894), crystalline glaze, France, 1898, stamped Sevres/1898, 2-1/2" x 10-1/2" x 8-1/2" **$6,250**

Rago Arts

Hinged dresser box, cobalt blue border with gold enamel highlights surrounding elaborate palace scenes, white interior with scattered floral decorative décor, marked Sevres French, good condition, 4-1/2" x 8". **$1,500**

Woody Auction

Fruitwood planter, mounted with ormolu and Sevres plaque, 19th century, 15-1/2" l.... **$1,200**

Don Presley Auctions

CERAMICS

$

Glazed porcelain cabinet vase, Taxile Doat (1851-1939), France, 1920s, signed TD, 3-1/2" x 2-1/4"............... **$1,000**

Rago Arts

TOP LOT!

Porcelain gourd-shaped vase, copper red and blue glaze, Taxile Doat (1851-1939), France, circa 1900, signed T. DOAT Sevres, 4-1/4" x 3-1/2".............**$15,000**

Rago Arts

Gourd-shaped porcelain cabinet vase, Taxile Doat (1851-1939), France, 1927, signed T. DOAT 1927 Sevres, 4" x 3"....... **$1,000**

Rago Arts

Plate dated 1831, Chateau des Tuillerie, 19th century, 9-1/2" dia. **$540**

Don Presley Auctions

Plate with true Sevres marks, circa 1876, 9-1/2" dia........ **$480**

Don Presley Auctions

Vase with ormolu mounts, French, 19th/early 20th century, painted with idealized classical figures, obverse with gilt floral ribbons, raised on stepped base, marked with "S" set within blue interlaced Ls, signed Lheri to front, 16" h......................... **$431**

Cowan's Auctions, Inc.

Chateau des Tuileries dresser box, hand-painted and bronze-mounted with gilt highlights, putti presenting flowers on lid, signed Rene, floral interior, landscapes on side cartouches, Tuileries red mark, Sevres crown mark, circa 1870s, good condition, 4-1/2" x 7" x 4-1/2". **$690**

Thomaston Place Auction Galleries

SPATTERWARE

SPATTERWARE TAKES ITS NAME from the "spattered" decoration, in various colors, used to trim pieces hand painted with rustic center designs of flowers, birds, houses, etc. Popular in the early 19th century, most was imported from England.

Related wares, called "stick spatter," had freehand designs applied with pieces of cut sponge attached to sticks, hence the name. Examples date from the 19th and early 20th century and were produced in England, Europe, and America.

Some early spatter-decorated wares were marked by the manufacturers, but not many. Twentieth century reproductions are also sometimes marked, including those produced by Boleslaw Cybis.

Five pieces of rainbow spatterware, 19th century, soft paste, octagonal platter with rose, two different plates, saucer, and teapot with peafowl decoration, in various colors, good condition, 7-1/2" dia., platter 13-1/2" x 10". **$805**

Thomaston Place Auction Galleries

Spatterware saucer with central multicolored peafowl and green background, American, 19th century, pit to glaze on underside, 4-3/4" dia. **$215**

Cowan's Auctions, Inc.

Three pieces of spatterware, plate with peacock, plate with basket of flowers marked "Saint Clement," and creamer with flowers, all with crazing, creamer handle with crack, plates 8-1/4" to 8-1/2" dia., creamer 5-3/4" h... **$230**

Cordier Auctions

Ironstone Rabbitware spatterware plate with red, blue, and green floral border and transfer design of rabbits in center, English, 19th century, chip to edge of rim on underside, 9-1/4" dia. **$60**

Cowan's Auctions, Inc.

Two spatterware items in Wigwam pattern, plate 8-1/2" dia., sugar 4-1/2" h. **$708**

Hartzell's Auction Gallery, Inc.

Set of six spatterware soup plates, 19th century, 9-1/4" dia. **$215**

Weiderseim Associates, Inc.

Large Spatterware platter, American, 19th century, blue and purple, well-worn foot, crazing and chip to one side, 15-3/4" l. **$246**

Cowan's Auctions, Inc.

Miniature blue spatterware Adam's Rose tea service, 19th century, teapot, sugar, creamer, plate, and two cups and saucers.......... **$780**

Pook & Pook, Inc.

CERAMICS

SPONGEWARE

SPONGEWARE: THE NAME SAYS IT ALL. A sponge dipped in colored pigment is daubed onto a piece of earthenware pottery of a contrasting color, creating an overall mottled, "sponged" pattern. A clear glaze is applied, and the piece fired. The final product, with its seemingly random, somewhat smudged coloration, conveys an overall impression of handmade folk art.

Most spongeware, however, was factory-made from the mid-1800s well into the 1930s. Any folk art appeal was secondary, the result of design simplicity intended to facilitate maximum production at minimum cost. Although mass-manufacturing produced most spongeware, it did in fact originate in the work of independent potters. Glasgow, Scotland, circa 1835, is recognized as the birthplace of spongeware. The goal: the production of utilitarian everyday pottery with appeal to the budget-conscious. Sponged surface decorations were a means of adding visual interest both easily and inexpensively.

Since early spongeware was quickly made, usually by amateur artisans, the base pottery was often insubstantial and the sponging perfunctory. However, due to its general usefulness, and especially because of its low cost, spongeware quickly found an audience. Production spread across Great Britain and Europe, finally reaching the United States. Eventually, quality improved, as even frugal buyers demanded more for their money.

The terms "spongeware" and "spatterware" are often used interchangeably. Spatterware took its name from the initial means of application: A pipe was used to blow colored pigment onto a piece of pottery, creating a spattered coloration. Since the process was tedious, sponging soon became the preferred means of color application, although the "spatterware" designation remained in use. Specific patterns were achieved by means of sponge printing (aka "stick spatter"): A small piece of sponge was cut in the pattern shape desired, attached to a stick, then dipped in color. The stick served as a more precise means of application, giving the decorator more control, creating designs with greater border definition. Applied colors varied, with blue (on white) proving most popular. Other colors included red, black, green, pink, yellow, brown, tan, and purple.

Because of the overlap in style, there really is no "right or wrong" in classifying a

Blue whiskey jug, one gallon capacity, yellow ground, first quarter 20th century, undamaged, 10-1/2" h. ...**$104**

Jeffrey S. Evans & Associates

Salt-glazed blue and white water cooler with cover, four-gallon capacity, original metal spigot, first quarter 20th century, cover with two chips to finial edge, 15" h. overall, 11" dia............................**$196**

Jeffrey S. Evans & Associates

CERAMICS

Six lemonade pitchers in tapered cylindrical form with scrolled handles, some raised decoration, in various finishes, 19th century, minor rim and spout flakes, spider hairline to bottom of one, all roughly 9" h., 8" handle to spout................ **$2,070**

Thomaston Place Auction Galleries

Oatmeal barrel, sugar barrel, four butter crocks (one with lid), wall-hanging salter, and bean pot with lid, mid- to late-19th century, minor chips, hairline to bottom of covered butter crock, small chip to bean pot lid, hairline to side of sugar barrel, 4" h. x 6" dia. to 10" h. x 8" dia.......... **$920**

Thomaston Place Auction Galleries

Two salt-glazed blue and white pitchers, each of slightly differing form and without pattern, first quarter 20th century, one undamaged, other with minor rim flake and firing pop/hole to exterior glaze, 9" h... **$161**

Jeffrey S. Evans & Associates

Chamber set, pitcher and bowl, soap holder with lid, small pitcher, cup and toothbrush holder, chamber pot with lid, slop pot with lid, and water carrier, 19th century, minor chips to several pieces, hairline to chamber pot, chip and crack to spout of large pitcher, 4" x 3-1/2" dia. to 12" x 10" dia... **$748**

Thomaston Place Auction Galleries

particular object as "spongeware" or "spatterware"; often the manufacturer's advertising designation is the one used. Spatterware, however, has become more closely identified with pottery in which the mottled color pattern (whether spattered or sponged) surrounds a central image, either stamped or painted free-hand. Spongeware usually has no central image; the entire visual consists of the applied "splotching." Any break in that pattern comes in the form of contrasting bands, either in a solid color matching the mottling, or in a portion of the base earthenware kept free of applied color. Some spongeware pieces also carry stampings indicating the name of an advertiser, or the use intent of a specific object ("Butter," "Coffee," "1 Qt.").

    Much of what is classified as spatterware has a certain delicacy of purpose: tea sets, cups and saucers, sugar bowls, and the like. Spongeware is more down-to-earth, both in intended usage and sturdiness. Among the many examples of no-nonsense spongeware: crocks, washbowl and pitcher sets, jugs, jars, canisters, soap dishes, shaving mugs, spittoons, umbrella stands, washboards, and even chamber pots. These are pottery pieces that mean business; their shapes, stylings, and simple decoration are devoid of fussiness.

    Spongeware was usually a secondary operation for the many companies that produced it and was marketed as bargain-priced service ware; it's seldom marked. Today, spongeware is an ideal collectible for those whose taste in 19th century pottery veers away from the overly detailed and ornate. Spongeware's major appeal is due in large part to the minimalism it represents.

CERAMICS

STAFFORDSHIRE

STAFFORDSHIRE FIGURES AND GROUPS made of pottery were produced by the majority of the Staffordshire, England, potters of the 19th century and were used as mantel decorations or "chimney ornaments," as they were sometimes called. Pairs of dogs were favorites and were turned out by the carload, and 19th century pieces are still readily available. Well-painted reproductions also abound, and collectors are urged to exercise caution before purchasing.

The process of transfer-printing designs on earthenwares developed in England in the late 18th century, and by the mid-19th century most common ceramic wares were decorated in this manner, most often with romantic European or Asian landscape scenes, animals or flowers. The earliest transferwares were printed in dark blue, but a little later light blue, pink, purple, red, black, green, and brown were used. A majority of these wares were produced at various English potteries right up until the turn of the 20th century, but French and other European firms also made similar pieces and all are quite collectible.

The best reference on this area is Petra Williams' *Staffordshire Romantic Transfer Patterns – Cup Plates and Early Victorian China* (Fountain House East, 1978).

Historic platter, "Landing of Gen. LaFayette – At Castle Garden New York 16th August 1824," English, early 19th century, pressed Clews Warranted Staffordshire mark on underside, 11-1/4" w. x 15-1/4" l...$554

Cowan's Auctions, Inc.

Polychrome porcelain portrait bust of Abraham Lincoln, English, 19th century, 8-3/4" h................**$185**

Cowan's Auctions, Inc.

Adams Staffordshire blue and white platter, Tixall pattern, early 19th century, stamped on underside, depicts seat of Aston family where Mary Queen of Scots was imprisoned, some discoloration, 14-1/2" x 19".. **$345**

Thomaston Place Auction Galleries

Portrait bust of George Washington, English, 19th century, subject wearing brownish-gray wig, blue waistcoat with orange buttons, yellow vest with purple flowers, and black cravat, presented on marbleized plinth, marked 354 in orange on bottom, retains old label "FROM / Mrs. M.A. Coolidge. / 164 Blossom St. / Fitchburg, Mass.," some crazing, glue repair to plinth with three chips around repair, small fleabite to left jawbone, 8" h. **$180**

Cowan's Auctions, Inc.

Unmarked blue and white platters, oval turkey well platter depicting Roman ruins, repaired, 18-1/2" x 15"; pastoral scene with mansion, edge losses, 19" x 15-1/2" **$863**

Thomaston Place Auction Galleries

CERAMICS

Eight figures: Double-sided gin/water standing figure, woman and dog, server, woman and bird, cricket player, man and woman holding doves, and man with basket of flowers, English, 19th century, each with varying degrees of crazing, largest 9" h............ **$185**

Cowan's Auctions, Inc.

Two painted porcelain stirrup cups in form of foxes, English, late 19th-early 20th century, one with leaves and grapes around neck, both unmarked, largest 4-3/4" l. **$277**

Cowan's Auctions, Inc.

Seven bud vases depicting Little Red Riding Hood, two girls and dog, two girls and rabbit, woman feeding donkey, fox and bird, and three seated children (pair), English, 19th century, each with chips, cracks, breaks, and crazing, largest 8-3/4" h... **$215**

Cowan's Auctions, Inc.

Six figures: Napoleon on horseback, pair of girls and rabbits, lighthouse, house, and seated couple, English, 19th century, lighthouse with broken pillars, Napoleon with repair, varying degrees of crazing on all, largest 7-3/4" h. **$123**

Cowan's Auctions, Inc.

Six figures: Large woman with rabbit in basket, French horn player, standing couple, seated woman, Napoleonic figure, and standing group of three, English, 19th century, each with varying degrees of crazing, largest 13-1/2" h.............. **$123**

Cowan's Auctions, Inc.

Six dogs, two being matched pair, two with cobalt bases, one brown, and one white with brown spots, British, late 19th-early 20th century, glue repairs, chips, and cracks to one large white dog and dog with brown spots, tallest 9-3/4" h. **$210**

Cowan's Auctions, Inc.

Child's cranberry transfer-printed teawares, English, 19th century, four cups and saucers in boy and dog pattern, sugar canister, and plate; two teacups and plate accompanying sugar canister with extensive repairs, one teacup with hairline crack extending from rim, two plates with hairlines extending from center of base, sugar canister 4-3/4" h. **$62**

Cowan's Auctions, Inc.

CERAMICS

Serving set, circa 1825, Riley "Gracefield, Queens County" set of four covered serving dishes in blue transfer, forming oval when assembled, with small Riley covered tureen at center, of different pattern, set into later custom wooden tray, covered dishes in fine condition, some discoloration to tureen, 26" x 21" overall..**$1,035**

Thomaston Place Auction Galleries

Three blue and white platters and one serving bowl: Roman ruins with Turks by Rogers, chafed, 14" x 11"; Gothic mansion with bridge, holly, discolored, 10" x 13"; Italian villa, same; unmarked floral bowl, good condition, 8-1/2" x 11-1/2" x 2-1/4" d...**$518**

Thomaston Place Auction Galleries

CERAMICS

Unmarked blue and white platter depicting fallow deer near couple on bridge with estate manse, light scratches, 17" x 21". **$690**

Thomaston Place Auction Galleries

Blue and white platter in Trophy pattern with impressed eagle, central motif of lyre, flower basket and torch, 19-1/2" x 15-3/4" **$173**

Thomaston Place Auction Galleries

Early 19th century Adams Staffordshire deep well oval platter depicting Regents Quadrant, London in deep blue, Providence Life Insurance & Annuity Office on right, light scratches and discoloration, 17" x 13-1/2". **$460**

Thomaston Place Auction Galleries

Unmarked early blue and white oval platter depicting boating scene, very good condition, 18-1/4" x 14-3/4". **$748**

Thomaston Place Auction Galleries

Transferware platters, brown and white Guy Mannering from Scott's Illustrations and blue and white Tuscan Rose, both 19th century, good condition, 12" x 15" and 16" x 20". **$345**

Thomaston Place Auction Galleries

Center or fruit bowl depicting castle and bridge, fruit and wheat on sides, 19th century, very good condition, 4-1/2" x 9-1/2" dia. **$115**

Thomaston Place Auction Galleries

Large late 19th century dogs in white with gilt detailing, painted faces, glass eyes, stained spot on paws of one, 13-1/2" h................................ **$259**

Thomaston Place Auction Galleries

Highland Scots couples in traditional costume, seated on faux clocks, good condition, 13" and 14-1/2" **$173**

Thomaston Place Auction Galleries

Clews dark blue platter depicting pagoda on river, with handles, stamped, repaired, 12" x 16"; unmarked platter of lakeside pagodas, cracked, 16" x 21"... **$403**

Thomaston Place Auction Galleries

Syrian pattern transferware vegetable dish in brown, marked G&RL, 3" x 12" x 10"; blue and white covered tureen with Persian cavalryman, old painted repair to edge, 6" x 11" x 9". **$58**

Thomaston Place Auction Galleries

Large eight-sided blue and white transferware ironstone platter depicting fishermen on river, bridge and village in background, knife marks, 18-3/4" x 14-1/2"... **$748**

Thomaston Place Auction Galleries

CERAMICS

SUMIDA GAWA POTTERY

SUMIDA GAWA WARES were made in Japan for Western export from the late 19th century through 1941. The pottery pieces, the popular forms of which include teapots, bowls, vases, jugs and tankards, are often heavy, brightly glazed and covered with figures in relief. Inscribed in kanji, more than 70 different marks are known, but not all pieces are marked. Pieces marked "Nippon" date to 1890-1921; pieces marked "Foreign" were made for export to England.

Two vases modeled with figures in high relief, sender vase with robed man keeping watch over pot, 9" h., and three-handled vase with two tigers, 6-1/4" h., both signed by same artist, signature on medallion, excellent condition. **$200**

Mark Mussio, Humler & Nolan

Slip glaze decorated figures of immortals or scholars, no apparent faults, all approximately 9" h. **$185**

Alex Cooper Auctioneers, Inc.

Vase with four partially glazed figures of children, beige and brown slip glaze, early 20th century, 12" h. **$400**

Alex Cooper Auctioneers, Inc.

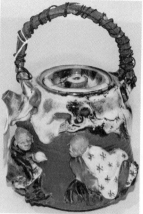

Teapot of slightly waisted handled form with applied molded figural decoration depicting two figures, one holding peach, 7-1/2" h. **$125**

Leslie Hindman Auctioneers

Porcelain vase of square form, late 19th century, 12" h. **$944**

Elegance Auction

Oriental mug, large red elephant with trunk as handle, small man and snail on side, 5" h...**$177**

Woody Auction

Covered jar or urn with applied porcelain imari miniature teapots, vases, chawan tea bowls, and various objects, signed in two places on sides, some applied pieces have controlled cracking, excellent condition, Meiji period, 19" x 12"................................. **$2,023**

Mroczek Brothers Seattle Auction House

Early 20th century baluster form vase with pinched polychrome glazed rim and neck, over body decorated with elephants in raised relief on gray ground, marked with porcelain seal on side, 31" h. x 18" w. **$2,420**

Great Gatsby's

Mug with partial slip glaze decoration with morning glory relief, early 20th century, two flake chips on rear of leaf, age wear, 5" h............................**$98**

Alex Cooper Auctioneers, Inc.

CERAMICS

TECO POTTERY

TECO POTTERY was a line of art pottery introduced by the American Terra Cotta and Ceramic Co. of Terra Cotta (Crystal Lake), Illinois, in 1902. Founded by William D. Gates in 1881, American Terra Cotta originally produced only bricks and drain tile. Because of superior facilities for experimentation, including a chemical laboratory, the company was able to develop an art pottery line, favoring a mat green glaze in the earlier years but eventually achieving a wide range of colors including a metallic luster glaze and a crystalline glaze. Although some hand-thrown pottery was made, Gates favored a molded ware because it was less expensive to produce. By 1923, Teco Pottery was no longer being made, and in 1930 American Terra Cotta and Ceramic Co. was sold. For more information on Teco Pottery, see *Teco: Art Pottery of the Prairie School* by Sharon S. Darling (Erie Art Museum, 1990).

Small pitcher with floral pattern in green mat over black glazes, impressed Teco logo on bottom, excellent original condition, 2" h. x 4-1/8" l. **$450**

Mark Mussio, Humler & Nolan

Ovoid bowl with outer ribs giving appearance of a thrown piece, rose mat glaze, impressed on bottom with Teco logo, excellent original condition, 2-3/4" h. x 4-3/4" w. **$225**

Mark Mussio, Humler & Nolan

Rare, tall four-buttressed vase, circa 1905, stamped TECO. **$13,750**

Rago Arts

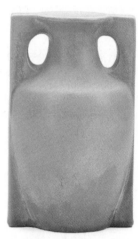

Carafe-form vase with closed buttress double handles in semi-mat green glaze, early 20th century, stamped Teco twice on base, 8-1/2" h.... **$1,020**

Skinner, Inc.; www.skinnerinc.com

Small buttress vase, circa 1905, stamped TECO, 7-1/2" x 4-1/4"............................. **$1,875**

Rago Arts

Buttressed vase, mat green glaze, circa 1905, stamped Teco twice, 7" x 4"......... **$1,188**

Rago Arts

Large buttressed vase, mat green glaze, circa 1905, stamped TECO, 8-1/4" x 6-1/2"............................ **$2,125**

Rago Arts

Tall ovoid vase, blue glaze, circa 1910, stamped TECO, 12" x 7".................................. **$1,250**

Rago Arts

Large four-handled vase, circa 1905, remnant of paper label, probable stamp under glaze, 14-1/2" x 8-1/2"......... **$5,000**

Rago Arts

CERAMICS

TEPLITZ (AMPHORA) POTTERY

ANTIQUE DEALERS AND COLLECTORS often refer to Art Nouveau-era art pottery produced in the kaolin-rich Turn-Teplitz region of Bohemia (today Teplice region, Czech Republic) collectively as Teplitz. Over the years, however, this area boasted many different potteries. To add to the confusion, they opened, closed, changed owners, merged, or shared common designers against a background of changing political borders.

Although all produced pottery, their techniques and products varied. Some ceramicists, like Josef Strnact and Julius Dressler, produced brightly glazed faience and majolica earthenware items. According to Elizabeth Dalton, Furniture and Decorative Arts Specialist at Michaan's Auctions, a strong earthenware body, rather than delicate, brittle porcelain, allowed more unusual manipulation of the ceramic surface of their vases, flowerpots, and tobacco jars.

Alfred Stellmacher, who founded the Imperial and Royal Porcelain Factory in 1859, produced fanciful, sculptural creations noted for their fine design and quality. Many feature applied natural motifs, Mucha and Klimt-like portraits, or simulated jewels.

A gilded, glossed, flowered Stellmacher ewer, for example, featuring a curvaceous mermaid handle, is currently offered for $4,000 on a popular Internet site.

A free-form, flowered Stellmacher pitcher featuring a ferocious, golden dragon handle commands nearly double.

"The most collectible Teplitz pieces of all, however," notes Stuart Slavid, vice president and director of European Furniture, Decorative Arts and Fine Ceramics at Skinner Auctions, "are those manufactured by the Riessner, Stellmacher and Kessel Amphora Porcelain Works (RStK), which was founded in 1892."

Archeology and history buffs may recognize amphoras as ceramic vessels used for storage and transport in the ancient world. Art collectors and dealers, however, know amphoras as RStK pieces that incorporate undulating, asymmetrical Art Nouveau interpretations of flora and fauna — both natural and fanciful — in their designs. Many RStK artists honed their skills at the Teplitz Imperial Technical School for

Large Amphora porcelain vase, maiden with calla lily, Riessner, Stellmacher & Kessel, circa 1900, by Ernst Wahliss, stamped MADE IN AUSTRIA with number, 24-1/2" x 24-1/2". **$3,125**

Rago Arts

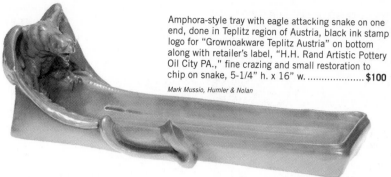

Amphora-style tray with eagle attacking snake on one end, done in Teplitz region of Austria, black ink stamp logo for "Grownoakware Teplitz Austria" on bottom along with retailer's label, "H.H. Rand Artistic Pottery Oil City PA.," fine crazing and small restoration to chip on snake, 5-1/4" h. x 16" w. **$100**

Mark Mussio, Humler & Nolan

Ceramics and Associated Applied Arts. Others drew on the fine ceramics manufacturing tradition of nearby Dresden.

Producing Amphora was time-consuming and prohibitively expensive. Each piece began with an artist's drawing, which would typically include lifelike images of snakes, sea creatures, dragons, maidens, flora or fauna. Once approved, each drawing was assigned a style number, which would subsequently appear on the bottom of identically shaped pieces, along with the word "Amphora."

Using these drawings as their guide, craftsmen carved and fired clay models, from which they created smooth plaster-of-Paris molds. These molds were then lined with thin layers of clay. Once the clay dried and the molds removed, the resulting Amphoras were fine-carved, hand-painted and glazed. Finally they were refired, sometimes as many as 10 times. Since each was decorated in a unique way, no two Amphoras were exactly alike. Since their manufacture was so complex, reproducing one is nearly impossible.

RStK's innovative pieces earned international acclaim almost immediately. After winning prizes at both the Chicago and St. Louis World's Fairs, exclusive establishments, including Tiffany & Co., marketed them in the United States.

Although many Amphoras retail for under $1,000, some are quite costly. Russell Colletti, dealer and owner of Colletti Gallery in Chicago, is currently offering an 8" marked, gilded vase featuring an applied fern design for $5,800.

Rare, larger pieces, probably commissioned or created expressly for exhibition, were far more prone to breakage in production and display, so they command far more. For example, Colletti's 29" "remarkable Stellmacher greenish metallic vase, featuring an applied, splay-footed Saurian (prehistoric lizard-like reptile) sidling up its delicate, furled lip – quite rare given its monumental size and excellent condition," goes for $68,000. (Colletti pieces are also available at 1stdibs.com.)

In addition to lavish Amphoras, Riessner, Stellmacher and Kessel also produced highly detailed, intricately

Rare Amphora porcelain bust with bat, Riessner, Stellmacher & Kessel, circa 1900, signed Ed. Stellmacher to side, base with red Stellmacher stamp, embossed ESC mark, stamped 503, 23" x 16". **$3,750**

Rago Arts

CERAMICS

Large Bohemian porcelain figure group, mother breastfeeding infant, small girl at her knee, large empty basket on her back (could be used as flower vase), mark of Amphora, Turn-Teplitz, in polychrome, 27" h. **$1,495**

Thomaston Place Auction Galleries

crafted female busts, both large and small. Beautiful virgins, nymphs and dancers, reflecting fashionable literary, religious and mythological motifs and themes of the day, were popular choices. Larger busts, because they were so complex and so rarely made, were expensive from the start. Today these 100-year-old beauties, especially those that escaped the ravages of time, are extremely desirable.

In 1894, leading Viennese porcelain retailer Ernst Wahliss purchased the RStK Amphora. Paul Dachsel, a company designer and Stellmacher's son-in-law, soon left to open his own pottery. Dachsel was known for adorning fairly simple forms with unique, intricate, stylized Art Nouveau embellishments, as well as modern-looking applied handles and rims. These, along with his Secessionist works — those influenced by Austrian exploration of innovative artistic forms outside academic and historical traditions — are highly collectible today.

The Jason Jacques Gallery, located in New York City, currently offers an iridized metallic cobalt earthenware cachepot, part of Dachsel's stylized "Elite Series," which features plant, animal and insect components, for $4,850. It also offers one of Dachsel's most startling and desirable designs, a "Grasshopper (or Praying Mantis) Vase," which features "cyclamen buds, each adorned with insect legs poised to spring," for $55,000.

After Wahliss' death, the Amphora Porcelain Works — now known as the Alexandra Porcelain Works Ernst Wahliss — became known for Serapis-Wahliss, its fine white earthenware line that features intricate, colorful, stylized natural forms. The Jason Jacques Gallery markets a Serapis-Wahliss covered dish whose lid boasts "a luscious pink flower, its stylized, gilded petals spreading with geometric precision toward its rim," for $20,000. (Jason Jacques pieces are also available at 1st.dibs.com.)

When Stellmacher established his own company in 1905, the firm continued operating as the Riessner and Kessel Amphora Works. After Kessel left five years later, Amphora Werke Riessner, as it became known, continued to produce Amphora pottery through the 1940s. In 1945, Amphora Werke Riessner was nationalized by the Czechoslovakian government.

Do Teplitz pieces make good investments? Though beginning collectors can find simpler pieces from $100 through $5,000 at auction, there has been a dip in the market since the downturn in the economy in 2008.

"Considering their rarity, quality, and decorative appeal, however," Slavid says, "there's still plenty of room for growth, especially at the higher end of the market. I personally think that higher-end Amphoras are exceptional. History says you can't go wrong buying the very best. There will always be collectors at that level."

– Melody Amsel-Arieli

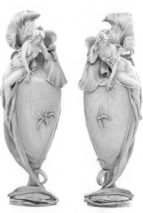

Large Gres-Bijou Amphora vase with pinecones, Riessner, Stellmacher & Kessel, circa 1900, by Eduard Stellmacher, stamped with crown AMPHORA AUSTRIA, illegible numbers, 17" x 7" x 5-1/2"............ **$3,375**

Rago Arts

Small Amphora "Allegory of Germany" vase, Nikolaus Kannhauser design, made at Riessner, Stellmacher and Kessel, marked with R.St.&K red ink stamp logo and initials of designer, excellent original condition, 4-3/8" h.......... **$1,000**

Mark Mussio, Humler & Nolan

Pair of Amphora porcelain vases, maidens with irises and dragonflies, Riessner, Stellmacher & Kessel, circa 1900, by Eduard Stellmacher, stamped Amphora with crown, 3 799 and 3 800, 17-3/4" x 6-1/2"............................. **$1,125**

Rago Arts

Two Amphora plaques with nude maidens, Riessner, Stellmacher & Kessel, circa 1900, by Ernst Wahliss, stamped MADE IN AUSTRIA ERNST WAHLISS TURN/WIEN 224 and 219, 14-1/2 h. x 15" dia...........**$1,250**

Rago Arts

Large Amphora sculptural porcelain bowl, maiden with poppy, Riessner, Stellmacher & Kessel, circa 1900, by Eduard Stellmacher, Amphora stamp, 774, 28" x 19"............... **$1,625**

Rago Arts

Two small Amphora Fates bowls, Riessner, Stellmacher & Kessel, circa 1900, by Eduard Stellmacher, raised "the Fates" seals and numbers, 4" x 7-1/2", 2" x 5-1/2"......... **$1,875**

Rago Arts

Amphora two-handled vase, Austrian, early 20th century, flared base and cylindrical tapering body, Art Nouveau style with raised organic-form decorations, painted in brown, green, and pink with gold accents, underside impressed with crown, circled Austria and Amphora marks, 0670, and 58, some crazing, one flower with chip on blossom, light cracking to raised decoration near top, 17-1/4" h. **$246**

Cowan's Auctions, Inc.

Amphora pitcher with lizard handle made by Reissner, Stellmacher and Kessel, body covered with grapes and grape leaves, handle, rim and base in fired-on gold, impressed "Amphora Austria" in thin ovals and marked with red ink stamp logo of Reissner, Stellmacher and Kessel. **$150**

Mark Mussio, Humler & Nolan

Amphora vase with leaves and three-dimensional fruit along with drip effect at rim, impressed "Amphora Austria" with glazed-over Edda wafer seal, break to one vine and one leaf, 6-1/2" h. **$100**

Mark Mussio, Humler & Nolan

Amphora twin-handled vase with four spouts, most likely a Paul Dachsel design, faintly impressed "Austria Amphora" logo in thin ovals, excellent original condition with slight iridescence to glaze, 13-1/2" h. **$225**

Mark Mussio, Humler & Nolan

Czech Amphora covered urn with lion heads at top of three legs, marked "Amphora Made in Czecho-Slovakia" oval ink stamp logo, excellent original condition, 8-3/4" h. **$80**

Mark Mussio, Humler & Nolan

Organic Amphora vase with leaves and tendrils at rim with thin gold outlining, marked "Austria Amphora" under crown on bottom, faint crazing, 10-1/8" h. ..**$250**

Mark Mussio, Humler & Nolan

Amphora porcelain center bowl, maiden with irises, Riessner, Stellmacher & Kessel, circa 1900, by Eduard Stellmacher, stamped Amphora 747 1, 17-3/4" x 19-1/2". **$813**

Rago Arts

VAN BRIGGLE POTTERY

THE VAN BRIGGLE POTTERY was established by Artus Van Briggle, who formerly worked for Rookwood Pottery in Colorado Springs, Colorado at the turn of the 20th century. He died in 1904, but the pottery was carried on by his widow and others. From 1900 until 1920, the pieces were dated. It remains in production today, specializing in art pottery.

Rare copper-clad vase produced between 1908 and 1911, marked on bottom AA VAN BRIGGLE COLO SPGS 654, tight line extends from rim to base, several spots of chipping in copper jacket, 3-3/4" h.....**$800**

Mark Mussio, Humler & Nolan

Pair of vases, both in mulberry glaze: Indian chief vase, marked on bottom with company logo, Van Briggle, and Colo. Spgs., no crazing, 11-1/4" h.; floral design vase, marked on bottom with company logo, Van Briggle, and U.S.A., some minor grinding chips, 9-7/8" h. **$650**

Mark Mussio, Humler & Nolan

Mug dated 1906 with blue mat glaze, marks include company logo, Van Briggle, Colo. Springs, 27B and 1906, no crazing, glaze skip on bottom of handle, 4-1/2" h. **$170**

Mark Mussio, Humler & Nolan

Plate with floral scene in brown mat glaze, bottom incised with company logo, Van Briggle Colo. Spgs., and 17, indicating date, uncrazed, excellent original condition, 8-1/4" dia.........**$400**

Mark Mussio, Humler & Nolan

CERAMICS

$

TOP LOT!

Vase with molded geometric design, 1906, green mat glaze, marks include company logo, Van Briggle, 1906 and shape number 347, excellent original condition, 6" h. **$600**

Mark Mussio, Humler & Nolan

Vase with molded leaf design in mulberry glaze, marked on bottom with company logo, Van Briggle and U.S.A., no crazing, 5-1/4" h. **$200**

Mark Mussio, Humler & Nolan

Fine, rare, and early vase with copper base, red and green glaze, 1903, signed AA VAN BRIGGLE / 1903 / III / 333, 11-1/2" x 4". **$27,500**

Rago Arts

Vase with repeating floral pattern, 1905, green mat glaze over which blue mat glaze has been dripped from rim, incised on bottom with company logo, Van Briggle, 1905 and VX, excellent original condition, 7-1/4" h. **$1,000**

Mark Mussio, Humler & Nolan

Twin-handled vase with embossed daisies, 1903, green over rose mat glazes, incised on bottom with company logo, Van Briggle, 1903 and Roman numeral III, glaze light in some areas, 9-3/4" h. **$1,700**

Mark Mussio, Humler & Nolan

Bud vase with molded floral design, 1905, purple mat glaze, marked on bottom with company logo, Van Briggle, 1905, 302 and what appears to be VX with line above and below, glaze skip near rim, 9-1/2" h. **$190**

Mark Mussio, Humler & Nolan

CERAMICS

Vase with tall tulips and foliage with three-color glaze, 1907-1912, incised Van Briggle Colo Spgs 653 with company logo, restoration to X crack on bottom, stilt pull at base edge, 10-1/2" h. **$700**

Mark Mussio, Humler & Nolan

Vase with cast poppy design with heavy green over rose mat glaze, restoration to rim, rose glaze with curdling, incised with company logo, Van Briggle Colo. Spgs and '16 and 7, appears to be much earlier piece than 1916, 7-7/8" h.**$1,600**

Mark Mussio, Humler & Nolan

Massive vase produced in 1907 with green mat glaze not typical of Van Briggle, marks include company logo, Van Briggle, Colo. Springs and 1907, chip at rim, blister in glaze and chip on bottom, 13" h. x 10" w. **$1,000**

Mark Mussio, Humler & Nolan

Newer calla lily vase with nude female clutching sides of form, incised AA along with Van Briggle Colo. Spgs Z on bottom, excellent original condition, 19-1/2" h. **$300**

Mark Mussio, Humler & Nolan

Newer "Despondency" vase in blue over mauve, incised AA along with Van Briggle Colo Spgs VI HVM on bottom, excellent original condition, 16-3/8" h. **$350**

Mark Mussio, Humler & Nolan

Post-1970 three-Indian head vase in blue and green mat glazes, marked on bottom with Van Briggle logo, Van Briggle Colo. Spgs and finisher's initials, HVM, uncrazed, excellent original condition, 12-1/8" h. **$375**

Mark Mussio, Humler & Nolan

Bowl with repeating leaf design at rim with dark blue over light green mat glazes, marks include company logo and Van Briggle, fine overall crazing, 5-1/2" h. x 11" dia..**$400**

Mark Mussio, Humler & Nolan

Substantial 1917 handled urn with turquoise over tan glaze and impressed with design of spear foliage on lengthy stems about circumference, incised 1917 with company logo below foot, excellent original condition, 10-1/2" x 12" handle to handle. **$1,200**

Mark Mussio, Humler & Nolan

Rare trivet with stylized roses, circa 1905, signed AA VAN BRIGGLE, 4-1/4". **$875**

Rago Arts

Early vase with peacock feathers and silver overlay, blue glaze, 1904, signed AA VAN BRIGGLE / 1904 / III / 231, 5-3/4" x 6-1/2".................**$10,000**

Rago Arts

Two glazed ceramic tiles with landscapes, circa 1905, one stamped, 6" sq.......................................**$2,625**

Rago Arts

Vase with peacock feathers, mottled teal/green glaze, 1908-1911, AA VAN BRIGGLE partially visible, 10-1/4" x 5-1/2". **$1,125**

Rago Arts

Tall early vase with leaves, mauve and green glaze, 1904, signed AA VAN BRIGGLE / 1904 / 241, 11" x 5". **$6,250**

Rago Arts

Tall early vase with stylized leaves, green glaze, 1906, marked AA VAN BRIGGLE 1906 / 106 / B, 15" x 5". **$2,000**

Rago Arts

Early and rare vase with poppies, olive and verdigris glaze, 1904, signed AA VAN BRIGGLE / 1904 / V / 143, 9-3/4" x 8-1/2". **$8,125**

Rago Arts

Vase with molded flower design at neck with green over blue mat glazes, 1907 to 1912 era, incised on bottom with company logo, Van Briggle, Colo. Spgs. and 696, excellent original condition, 4-7/8" h. **$450**

Mark Mussio, Humler & Nolan

Early vase with poppy pods, celadon and mauve glaze, 1902, AA VAN BRIGGLE / 1902 / III, 3-3/4" x 3-3/4". **$1,750**

Rago Arts

Vase in two-tone blue mat glaze with embossed leaves, 1907-1912, incised AA Van Briggle 9 on bottom, faint overall crazing, 5-1/8" h. **$400**

Mark Mussio, Humler & Nolan

Early bulbous vase with Virginia creepers, pink and green glaze, 1904, signed AA VAN BRIGGLE / 1904 / V / 164, 8" x 7". **$1,500**

Rago Arts

Iris design vase, marked Van Briggle, Colo Spgs, 14" h. **$308**

Cowan's Auctions, Inc.

Vase with molded floral design, cast in 1920, Persian rose glaze, incised on bottom with company logo, Van Briggle and 20, excellent original condition, 8-3/4" h. x 10" dia **$425**

Mark Mussio, Humler & Nolan

Tall early vase with leaves, blue and green glaze, 1904, signed AA VAN BRIGGLE / 1904 / V / 241, 11" x 5". **$1,875**

Rago Arts

Tall and early vase with tulips, purple and maroon glaze, 1904, incised AA VAN BRIGGLE 1904, 12" x 4". **$6,250**

Rago Arts

WEDGWOOD

THE NAME "WEDGWOOD" has, over the years, become nearly synonymous with "Jasperware," a specific pottery line produced by this British firm. But while Jasperware may be Wedgwood's most enduring contribution to the world of pottery, it is by no means the only one.

Wedgwood was founded in 1759 by Josiah Wedgwood in Burslem, England. The earliest Wedgwood efforts were focused on utilitarian earthenware. Ornamental pottery made its debut in 1770, with the opening of new production facilities in Etruria. Jasperware became the company's first artware success.

WEDGWOOD

Fairyland Lustre lily tray, England, circa 1920, pattern Z4968 Garden of Paradise to daylight sky, exterior with gilded flying geese to mottled green ground, printed mark, very good condition, 11" dia.............. **$7,800**

Skinner, Inc.; www.skinnerinc.com

Wedgwood's Jasperware has been so often imitated that a brief description immediately conjures up its basics: solid-color, unglazed stoneware, the decoration consisting of white, bas-relief "classic" figures encircling the object. The most common Jasperware color is blue, although other shades have included black, white, yellow, green, and even lilac. Most pieces are single-color, but some of the most striking examples of Jasperware use three or more alternating colors.

Once established, the Jasperware format remained quite consistent. The reason was simple: It filled a niche for the sort of elegant yet relatively inexpensive décor pieces that buyers craved. The Jasperware appeal was particularly understandable during the Victorian era, as adventurers unearthed the wonders of ancient Greece and Rome. Jasperware's images of toga-clad warriors and water-bearing maidens effectively romanticized a theme occupying the public interest, presenting civilizations of the past at their most civilized.

As noted, Jasperware was just one of the Wedgwood successes. Among the others:

• **Creamware.** Of a lighter weight than traditional china, this Wedgwood line proved less expensive both to produce and transport. Creamware was so acclaimed that Queen Charlotte of England eventually permitted it to be marketed as "Queen's Ware."

• **Moonlight Lustre.** Produced from 1805-1815, the "moonlight" decorative effect was achieved by varied colors (pink, gray, brown, and sometimes yellow) intermingled and "splashed" across the ware.

• **Varied lustrewares.** In the early 20th century, Wedgwood produced an in-demand line of pottery in assorted lustre finishes, their names and multicolored hues once again stressing the romantic: Butterfly, Dragon, and Fairyland. Within each series, designs held true to the theme: Fairyland, for example, featured such pattern images as Woodland Elves, Fairy in a Cage, and Toad and Dwarf. The overall, dreamlike effect was often enhanced by the use of mottled colors and hypnotically repeating borders. Decades later, similarities to the Fairyland decorative technique could be found in the psychedelic stylings of the 1960s.

During its long history, Wedgwood also experimented, to alternating effect, with other processes and treatments. These included fine porcelain, bone china, stone china, majolica, and Pearlware.

Fortunately for collectors, most Wedgwood pieces carry the marking "Wedgwood." In 1891, the additional identifier "England" was added (later pieces are marked "Made In England"). A limited line of artware, produced from 1769 to 1780, carries the marking "Wedgwood & Bentley"; during that time Josiah Wedgwood was in partnership with Thomas Bentley.

Pottery marked "Wedgwood & Co." and "Wedgeood" (note the additional "e") was the work of competitors, hoping to capitalize on Josiah Wedgwood's fame. They have no relation to the Wedgwood firm; the only advantage of owning one of these pieces would be for its curiosity value.

Wedgwood has certainly set the record for endurance: Jasperware has remained in continuous production since first being introduced in the 1700s. Collectors remain drawn to this line, thanks to its eye-catching juxtaposition of vivid base colors with the stark-white relief images. And, while many are first exposed to the Wedgwood legacy through Jasperware, a significant number delight in exploring the numerous other directions in pottery the company has taken during its 250-year history.

TOP LOT!

Fairyland Lustre vase, England, circa 1920, pattern Z5244 with Imps on Bridge pattern to flame sky, printed factory mark, very good condition, 11-3/4" h. **$20,400**

Skinner, Inc.; www.skinnerinc.com

Light blue Jasper dip Michelangelo potpourri vase and cover, England, early 19th century, pierced cover with cherub finial, bowl with applied white floral festoons and arabesque floral motif and mounted atop back of three classical figures set atop triangular base, impressed mark, cover heavily restored, bowl with firing lines and chip to collar rim underneath, one figure on base broken through at neck and repaired, 13-5/8" h. **$8,610**

Skinner, Inc.; www.skinnerinc.com

Black Jasper dip canopic jar and cover, England, 19th century, applied white Jasper relief bands with hieroglyphs and zodiac motifs, impressed mark; cover: restored hairline to one side of headdress and with associated chip repair to inner collar; jar: inner rim with chips; 10" h **$10,200**

Skinner, Inc.; www.skinnerinc.com

CERAMICS

Black basalt bust of Venus, England, 19th century, mounted atop waisted circular socle, impressed title and mark, very good condition, 13-3/4" h. **$1,353**

Skinner, Inc.; www.skinnerinc.com

Black basalt bust of Shakespeare, England, circa 1864, mounted atop waisted circular socle, impressed mark, very good condition, 12-3/8" h. **$1,140**

Skinner, Inc.; www.skinnerinc.com

Black basalt teakettle and cover, England, early 19th century, cover with lemon finial centering engine-turned and foliate borders, kettle with Dancing Hours centering engine-turned borders, impressed mark, finial likely replacement, one side of lower body with puncture repair, 9-3/4" h............................**$330**

Skinner, Inc.; www.skinnerinc.com

Black basalt tripod base vase and cover, England, 19th century, engine-turned cover and bowl, cover set with three Sybil finials, bowl supported atop backs of three winged lions with single pawed leg, all set atop raised triangular base, impressed mark, cover with all three finials broken off and reglued, no other evidence of any cracks, chips or restorations, 11-7/8" h. **$9,000**

Skinner, Inc.; www.skinnerinc.com

Black basalt vase and cover, England, late 18th century, Bacchus head mask and horn handles, raised classical medallion to either side, impressed circular mark, cover with replaced finial, vase with restored handles and chips on frame of one medallion, 10" h. **$720**

Skinner, Inc.; www.skinnerinc.com

Auro black basalt vase, England, circa 1885, gilded and enameled slip decorated with leaves and berries, impressed mark, very good condition, 6-3/8" h. **$2,040**

Skinner, Inc.; www.skinnerinc.com

Coronation pattern dinnerware, English, early 20th century, 119-piece set with 12 dinner plates, 11 luncheon plates, 11 salad plates, 13 bread and butter plates, nine soup bowls, nine fruit bowls, 10 teacups and 13 saucers, 10 coffee cups and 11 saucers, six eggcups, two serving dishes, one covered tureen, and one platter, all marked Wedgwood / Etruria / England in black or red transfer print with impressed Wedgwood and date mark, some with pattern number A5710 in green, others with A5410, some marked Gilman Collamore & Co. / Fifth Avenue & 30th St. / New York, some crazing, light paint wear, toning, small chips and cracks, two teacups with glue repairs to handles, platter 12-3/4" l. ...**$185**

Cowan's Auctions, Inc.

Majolica angel plate and bowl, English, late 19th century, in Argenta color palette, each decorated with four standing spread-winged angels and four reserves of dancing children, plate with impressed Wedgwood / M / M / WGH marks and M / 2829 / l. in blue, bowl with impressed Wedgwood / MBH / TW marks and M / 2829 / l.; some crazing and light wear to paint on raised decorations, plate with small chip to arm of one child, tip of angel wing, and on foot, glaze bubbles to underside, bowl with some chips around rim, plate 9" dia..................**$123**

Cowan's Auctions, Inc.

Emile Lessore-decorated potpourri and cover, England, circa 1861, pierced cover, polychrome enamel-decorated with male and female figure in landscape setting bordered by foliate vines, artist signed, impressed mark, very good condition, 8-5/8" h......... **$900**

Skinner, Inc.; www.skinnerinc.com

Porcelain bust of Egyptian head on pedestal, England, 1928, stamped WEDGWOOD, 8" x 2-1/2" x 3-1/2"... **$3,125**

Rago Arts

Pair of early maple leaf plates, English, set of two, underside with impressed Wedgwood mark, 8" dia... **$31**

Cowan's Auctions, Inc.

Pair of early maple leaf plates, English, set of two, underside with impressed Wedgwood mark, 8" dia... **$31**

Cowan's Auctions, Inc.

Five-piece Drabware tea service, England, 19th century, each with applied blue fruiting grapevine band, covers with Sybil finials, including two teapots, 5-7/8" and 7-1/4"; sugar bowl, 5"; waste bowl, 4-3/4" dia.; and creamer, 4-1/4"; impressed marks, scattered staining to interior of waste bowl, no other evidence of any cracks, chips or restorations... **$480**

Skinner, Inc.; www.skinnerinc.com

Rosso Antico wine cooler, England, early 19th century, barrel shape with bearded mask handles, black ground surface incised with striping, impressed mark, smalls chips to each handle, 9-1/4" h .. **$3,480**

Skinner, Inc.; www.skinnerinc.com

Encaustic decorated sugar bowl and cover, England, early 19th century, iron red and white enamel decorated with meander and beadwork banding, upturned loop handles, impressed mark, cover with slight rim chip repair, 4-1/2" dia. **$1,230**

Skinner, Inc.; www.skinnerinc.com

Queen's Ware Emile Lessore-decorated shell dish, England, circa 1860, polychrome enamel decorated landscape with Bacchanalian boys and goat, artist signed, Wedgwood marked removed from back, surface hairline to center, 10-1/8" l............... **$510**

Skinner, Inc.; www.skinnerinc.com

WELLER POTTERY

WELLER POTTERY WAS MADE from 1872 to 1945 at a pottery established originally by Samuel A. Weller at Fultonham, Ohio, and moved in 1882 to Zanesville, Ohio.

Weller's famous pottery slugged it out with several other important Zanesville potteries for decades. Cross-town rivals such as Roseville, Owens, La Moro, and McCoy were all serious fish in a fairly small and well-stocked lake. While Weller occasionally landed some solid body punches with many of his better art lines, the prevailing thought was that his later production ware just wasn't up to snuff.

Samuel Weller was a notorious copier and, it is said, a bit of a scallywag. He paid designers like William Long to bring their famous discoveries to Zanesville. He then attempted to steal their secrets, and, when successful, renamed them and made them his own.

After World War I, when the cost of materials became less expensive than the cost of labor, many

Ardsley flower frog with fish, green and purple mat glazes, Weller full kiln ink stamp and number 2 in black slip on bottom, minor crazing, 6-1/4" h. **$475**

Mark Mussio, Humler & Nolan

companies, including the famous Rookwood Pottery, increased their output of less expensive production ware. Weller Pottery followed along in the trend of production ware by introducing scores of interesting and unique lines, the likes of which have never been created anywhere else, before or since.

In addition to a number of noteworthy production lines, Weller continued in the creation of hand-painted ware long after Roseville abandoned them. Some of the more interesting Hudson pieces, for example, are post-World War I pieces. Even later lines, such as Bonito, were hand painted and often signed by important artists such as Hester Pillsbury. The closer you look at Weller's output after 1920, the more obvious the fact that it was the only Zanesville company still producing both quality art ware and quality production ware.

For more information on Weller pottery, see *Warman's Weller Pottery Identification and Price Guide* by Denise Rago and David Rago.

Aurelian vase with blackberries lighted by sunbeam, painted and initialed under berries by Eugene Roberts, marked with "Aurelian" inscribed and "Weller" and numbers impressed, glaze burst in sunbeam, excellent condition, 8-5/8" h. **$325**

Mark Mussio, Humler & Nolan

CERAMICS

Besline "basket" vase, marigold body acid-decorated with berried vine of Virginia creeper, unmarked, fine overall crazing, some white patches in orange luster glaze, 7-3/4" h.......... **$150**

Mark Mussio, Humler & Nolan

Brighton kingfisher flower holder with high glazes, impressed WELLER on bottom, minor crazing and professional repair to bird's crest, 8-1/2" h.................**$90**

Mark Mussio, Humler & Nolan

Dickensware vase incised with young woman swinging on crescent moon while playing stringed instrument, impressed "Weller Dickensware, 314" on bottom, 8-3/4" h................**$275**

Mark Mussio, Humler & Nolan

Cameo Jewel vase with embossed profile of Pope Pius X with jewels in form of rosary, marked with circular Weller Ware mark, light crazing, 10-5/8" h. **$150**

Mark Mussio, Humler & Nolan

Hudson vase with clump of stemmed trillium to one side, by artist Hester Pillsbury, artist signature near base, scalloped Weller Ware ink stamp on bottom, interior ink marks, excellent condition, 8-1/8" h.............**$300**

Mark Mussio, Humler & Nolan

Cloudburst vase with maroon luster glaze, several short lines at rim, 10-3/4" h................**$160**

Mark Mussio, Humler & Nolan

Muskota "Leda and Swan" flower frog, Weller mark not visible on bottom, most likely obscured by glaze, light crazing, swan's left wing broken off and repaired, 6-3/4" h. x 7-1/2" l. $110

Mark Mussio, Humler & Nolan

Coppertone flower frog with frog in lotus pod, unmarked, minor crazing, 4-3/8" h. x 5" dia.... $300

Mark Mussio, Humler & Nolan

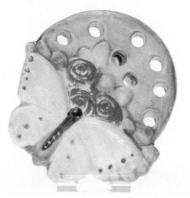

Muskota flower frog with yellow butterfly and purple flowers, unmarked, "12X" in black slip, minor crazing, 1-1/2" h. x 4" w........................$160

Mark Mussio, Humler & Nolan

Geode vase decorated with white stars and comets by Hester Pillsbury, artist signed at base with script "Weller Pottery" on bottom, fine overall crazing, 5-1/8" h. $500

Mark Mussio, Humler & Nolan

Muskota pagoda flower frog with green and brown mat glazes, impressed on bottom with WELLER in block letters, minor crazing and overspray at top of pagoda indicating professional repair, 6-1/8" h... $90

Mark Mussio, Humler & Nolan

Unusual Coppertone bowl with latticework rim, marked with full-kiln Weller Ware ink stamp logo and signed F.E.W. on bottom, excellent original condition, 3-1/4" h. x 11-1/4" dia.. ....$190

Mark Mussio, Humler & Nolan

CERAMICS

Eocean vase with spray of blue forget-me-nots, marked on bottom with WELLER in raised block letters, incised "Eocean" and impressed "9058," fine overall crazing, 5-7/8" h......**$180**

Mark Mussio, Humler & Nolan

Late Eocean vase in gray with bouquet of pink hawthorn blossoms over rim band, impressed "Weller" beneath, small burst glaze bubble at base edge, 11" h........................**$120**

Mark Mussio, Humler & Nolan

Rare Forest lamp vase with attached ceramic base and factory cast hole in side for wiring, unmarked, rewired, light crazing, excellent original condition, dark gray foot is part of piece but glazed different color, ceramic portion 11-1/8" h..**$375**

Mark Mussio, Humler & Nolan

Eocean vase with grouping of flowers by unknown artist, marked on bottom "Weller" in block letters, incised "Eocean" with impressed X and numbers 649, no artist's signature, light crazing, 12-3/4" h..............**$170**

Mark Mussio, Humler & Nolan

Tall Etna vase with embossed roses, impressed Weller on side and "Etna Weller" on bottom, fine overall crazing, 14" h ...**$170**

Mark Mussio, Humler & Nolan

Forest umbrella stand, two base chips, unmarked, 19-3/4" h...**$400**

Mark Mussio, Humler & Nolan

CERAMICS

Eocean gourd vase with red currents with leaves and branches front and back, dark green backdrop, hand-incised "Eocean Weller" beneath, excellent condition, 6-1/2" h............ **$275**

Mark Mussio, Humler & Nolan

Hobart flower frog bowl, cover with kneeling nude figure under aqua glaze, crazing, otherwise excellent condition, combined 7" bowl, 5-1/4" dia. **$90**

Mark Mussio, Humler & Nolan

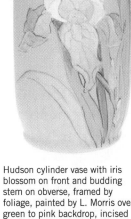

Frosted Matt lamp vase textured and covered with purple blue glaze, unmarked, not drilled, base has indent for electric cord, excellent original condition, 11-3/4" h.......... **$325**

Mark Mussio, Humler & Nolan

L'Art Nouveau vase with poppies on three sides and young woman in diaphanous dress on fourth side, impressed circular "Weller L'Art Nouveau" logo, small chip on underside of rim on back side, 11-1/8" h....................................... **$150**

Mark Mussio, Humler & Nolan

Hudson cylinder vase with iris blossom on front and budding stem on obverse, framed by foliage, painted by L. Morris over green to pink backdrop, incised Weller Pottery beneath, artist signature near base, excellent condition, 9-3/8" h. **$425**

Mark Mussio, Humler & Nolan

Hudson vase painted by Ruth Axeline, red and pink nasturtiums and green leaves about rim, stamped with half circle mark, painted signature of Ms. Ruth on side with "A" on bottom, fine crazing, excellent condition, 6-5/8" h. **$300**

Mark Mussio, Humler & Nolan

Hudson gray vase decorated with water lilies, impressed Weller on bottom, fine overall crazing, 8-1/4" h. **$300**

Mark Mussio, Humler & Nolan

LaSa vase with palm trees, mountain range beyond lake and clouds in sky, vase left factory with tiny areas where luster did not adhere, leaving white showing through, otherwise excellent condition, 6" h. **$100**

Mark Mussio, Humler & Nolan

Knifewood vase with repeating scene of swans on lake, viewed through trees, impressed Weller in block letters, minor crazing, 4-7/8" h. **$300**

Mark Mussio, Humler & Nolan

Louwelsa tankard decorated with two ears of corn, impressed on bottom with "WELLER LOUWELSA," "436," "K," and "8," artist's initials "LS" to lower right of decoration, fine overall crazing, tight firing line on bottom and overspray indicating repair at rim, 16-3/4" h. **$100**

Mark Mussio, Humler & Nolan

LaSa scenic vase with red skies above mountains in background and pair of green trees in foreground, some minor crazing in green glaze that encircles lower half of piece, bottom not ground flat, 6" h. **$275**

Mark Mussio, Humler & Nolan

LaSa scenic vase with lone tree in foreground against backdrop of lake with hills and clouds against gold and red sky, signed LaSa beneath tree, some minor rubs in glaze, 5-3/8" h. **$200**

Mark Mussio, Humler & Nolan

Muskota "Fisher Boy" flower frog, unmarked, fine crazing, missing fishing pole, otherwise in excellent original condition, is 6-1/2" h........................ **$100**

Mark Mussio, Humler & Nolan

Rochelle vase with two roses, pink and white, on prickly stems with foliage over brown to yellow shaded backdrop, by artist Hester Pillsbury, incised Weller, poor repair to chip inside rim, 10-1/2" h......... **$140**

Mark Mussio, Humler & Nolan

Patra vase formed with large textured foliage and small flowers tucked in between and covered with thick trial glazes, excellent condition, 7-7/8" h. **$325**

Mark Mussio, Humler & Nolan

Raceme bi-color vase with decorative blue and white floral bouquets in slip, signed by artist with initials "IF" near base, inscribed "Weller Pottery" beneath, excellent condition, 6" h. **$150**

Mark Mussio, Humler & Nolan

Roma jardinière and pedestal displaying pink flowers and arched leafy stems, unmarked, excellent condition, combined height 32" **$475**

Mark Mussio, Humler & Nolan

Experimental Rosemont Second Line vase with three-dimensional flowers, incised "Weller Pottery" and signed "F.B." on bottom, restoration to small chip on large dimensional flower, 11-1/8" h................ **$200**

Mark Mussio, Humler & Nolan

Selma bowl with two pairs of swans, cattails, and greenery in high glaze cream, green, and brown, unmarked, light overall crazing, 3-1/4".h................ **$120**

Mark Mussio, Humler & Nolan

CERAMICS

Sicard vase with honeysuckle flowers on vine and turquoise at rim, one area undecorated where outer glaze did not reach base, excellent original condition, 5-7/8" h............. **$325**

Mark Mussio, Humler & Nolan

Sicard vase with leaf and berry design, signed Weller Sicard on side, slightly overfired on one side, 7" h. **$375**

Mark Mussio, Humler & Nolan

Sicard triangular-shaped vase with teazel decoration, signed Weller on bottom and Sicard on side, restoration to small rim chips, 6-7/8" h. **$300**

Mark Mussio, Humler & Nolan

Woodcraft flower frog with kingfisher perched on branch, ink-stamped Weller on bottom, minor crazing and roughness toward tip of beak, 6-1/4" h................ **$250**

Mark Mussio, Humler & Nolan

Sicard vase with irises, signed Weller Sicard on side, professional repair to significant break at rim, 8-3/4" h......... **$375**

Mark Mussio, Humler & Nolan

Xenia cylinder vase with lavender flowers on coiled green stems bordered by blackened net designs, impressed Weller, minor chips appearing factory related, dark crazing and gray cloudy areas in glaze, 10" h........... **$200**

Mark Mussio, Humler & Nolan

Woodcraft jardinière with repeating pattern of cat stalking bird, unmarked with fine overall crazing and three tight lines at rim, 7-3/4" h. x 9-1/4" dia.. **$250**

Mark Mussio, Humler & Nolan

Selma or glossy Knifewood hanging basket with band of hunting dogs around border, unmarked, faint crazing, excellent condition, 4-1/4" h. x 9-3/8" dia... **$300**

Mark Mussio, Humler & Nolan

Sicard star-shaped covered box scattered with four-leaf clover designs and lid arrayed with stars, unmarked, overspray to cover and box indicating repair, 2-1/2" h. x 4-5/8"............................... **$275**

Mark Mussio, Humler & Nolan

Stellar vase with blue stars against white mat background, marked on base with script Weller Pottery, fine overall crazing, 5-3/8" h............... **$225**

Mark Mussio, Humler & Nolan

Large doorstop in form of basket overflowing with fruit and flowers, impressed Weller on bottom, excellent original condition, 8 lbs., 9-3/4" h. ... **$200**

Mark Mussio, Humler & Nolan

Stellar vase with white stars set against deep blue field, marked on bottom with Weller Pottery in script and T and O, glaze skip at rim, minor crazing towards bottom of piece, 6-1/4" h........ **$225**

Mark Mussio, Humler & Nolan

Xenia vase with stylized flowers on blue ground, impressed Weller in medium-sized block letters, excellent original condition, 5-1/2" h **$500**

Mark Mussio, Humler & Nolan

CERAMICS

ZSOLNAY

ZSOLNAY POTTERY was made in Pecs, Hungary, in a factory founded in 1862 by Vilmos Zsolnay. Utilitarian earthenware was originally produced with an increase in art pottery production from as early as 1870. The highest level of production employed more than 1,000 workers.

The Art Nouveau era produced the most collectible and valuable pieces in today's marketplace. Examples are displayed in major art museums worldwide. Zsolnay is always well marked and easy to identify. One specialty was the metallic eosin glaze.

With more than 10,000 different forms created over the years, and dozens of glaze variations for each form, there is always something new being discovered in Zsolnay. Today the original factory size has been significantly reduced with pieces being made in a new factory.

Two-handled vase decorated with etched peacock feathers, eosin glaze, circa 1900, five churches medallion, 7076/23, 9-1/4" x 3-1/2"......$12,500

Rago Arts

Vase with open twisted base and decorated with bell flowers, eosin glaze, circa 1900, by artist Jozsef Rippl-Ronai, five churches medallion, M23/6181, 9" x 3-3/4".........$5,313

Rago Arts

CERAMICS

$

Cabinet vase, eosin glaze, circa 1900, five churches medallion, 5303 2 M22, 3-1/4" x 2-3/4". **$1,875**
Rago Arts

Rare bowl with stylized landscape, eosin glaze, circa 1900, five churches medallion, 644 00 16 11, 5" x 6-1/2".............**$9,375**
Rago Arts

TOP LOT!

Coupe with dimples, eosin glaze, circa 1900, ghost of medallion, marked 5412, 7-1/4" x 3-1/4"..**$15,000**
Rago Arts

Bowl with blossoms, eosin glaze, circa 1900, five churches medallion / 36 / 22 / glazed over numbers, 4" x 6". **$1,750**
Rago Arts

CERAMICS

Three-footed "giraffe" vase, eosin glaze, circa 1900, stamped PECS 5879 / 1003, 9-1/4" x 5-1/2"............... **$7,500**

Rago Arts

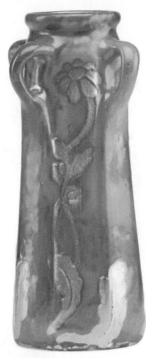

Four-handled bud vase, eosin glaze, circa 1900, five churches medallion, 6012 M 22, 6-1/4" x 2-1/2" **$2,500**

Rago Arts

Rare howling otter pitcher, circa 1900, raised five churches mark / 6349M / original Korona paper label, 15-1/2" x 6". **$2,625**

Rago Arts

Vase modeled with angel figure, eosin glaze, circa 1915-1920, five churches medallion, stamped 01636, 10-1/2" x 6"....... **$3,125**

Rago Arts

Early Hungarian faience vase, 1878-1890, give churches medallion, stamped 669, 12" x 7-3/4"................................$625

Rago Arts

Vase with ostriches and cacti, eosin glaze, circa 1900, five churches medallion, illegible numbers, 5-3/4" x 4-1/2".. **$2,750**

Rago Arts

Chalkware

CHALKWARE FIGURES are made of sculpted gypsum or cast from plaster molds and painted with watercolors. Portraying everything from whimsical animals to historical characters, chalkware was made from the late 18th century through the beginning of the 20th century, and again during the Great Depression. Early chalkware was often hollow and can be difficult to find unblemished.

Lighthouse light-up painted lamp display, 16" h. **$36**

Victorian Casino Antiques

Cat by David Guilmet, 15-1/2" h. **$92**

Pook & Pook, Inc.

Hiawatha Native American bust, 19-1/2" h. **$360**

Showtime Auction Services

Cigar store Lady Liberty figure with wood base, 1920s, 80" h. overall on 22" sq. base..........**$1,920**

Showtime Auction Services

Figure of parrot perched on top of orb, original paint, 8-1/4" h. **$1,020**

Hyde Park Country Auctions

Oriental gentleman figure, glazed, 13-1/2" h. **$20**

Marian Aubry Appraisals

Figure of rabbit hatching from egg, original paint, 6-1/4" h. **$540**

Hyde Park Country Auctions

CHALKWARE

$

Pair of Pennsylvania chalkware spaniels, 19th century, 7" h. each. **$338**

Pook & Pook, Inc.

Indian Chief bust, cigar store display, early 20th century, painted, 22" h. **$173**

Cordier Auctions & Appraisals

Santa Claus Pennsylvania chalkware figure, 19th century, original paint, 14" h. **$1,215**

Pook & Pook, Inc.

Woman statue, 19th century, 39" h. **$170**

Kimballs Auction and Estate Service

Fruit garniture Pennsylvania chalkware piece, 19th century, 10" h. **$1,094**

Pook & Pook, Inc.

Louis Armstrong bust, 16" h. **$61**

Saco River Auction Co.

Owl figure on two books, glass eyes, early 20th century, painted, 16" h. **$46**

Cordier Auctions & Appraisals

TOP LOT!

Fireman Pennsylvania chalkware figure, 19th century, holding trumpet, original surface, 14" h. **$3,888**

Pook & Pook, Inc.

Christmas light, 19th century, in form of Belsnickle standing atop church, 19" h. **$2,340**

Pook & Pook, Inc.

"Billie Can Billie Can't" ashtray, Billiekins sitting on chamber pots, 3-3/4" x 5" x 4". **$21**

Pioneer Auction Gallery

Rare hollow-cast seated cat, 19th century, original smoke decoration, 13" h. **$3,075**

Wiederseim Associates, Inc.

Compote with lovebirds, squirrel and rabbit, 19th century, 11-1/2"............................. **$1,215**

Pook & Pook, Inc.

Pennsylvania chalkware watch hutch, 19th century, 12-1/2" h. **$213**

Pook & Pook, Inc.

Goebel back bar display, Goebel Brewing Co. of Detroit and Muskegon, Michigan, 10" x 8" x 4". **$120**

Showtime Auction Services

Pair of Pennsylvania chalkware figures of praying girls, 19th century, 15" h.................... **$243**

Pook & Pook, Inc.

Pig with wooden cart, American, early 20th century, hollow-bodied, glass eyes and polychrome painted details, 14-3/4" h. **$60**

Cowan's Auctions

Watta-A-Pup store display, 5-1/2" x 7-1/4" x 6-3/4"..... **$180**

Showtime Auction Services

Boy and girl string holders, 9" h. each. **$92**

Hewlett's Auctions

Decorative pillars, cherubs on front, 45" h. **$295**

Fusco Auctions

Modern table lamps, winged women with toadstools, original matching shades, 36" h. **$183**

Uniques & Antiques, Inc.

Pennsylvania chalkware goat, 19th century, 7-3/4" h........ **$365**

Pook & Pook, Inc.

Statue of African man on elephant with attacking tigers, 1950s, 16" x 22". **$272**

Kimball's Auction

Native American Indian display,
Ohio Match Co., 25" l...... **$2,160**

Showtime Auction Services

Popeye vintage figure,
King Featured Syndicate,
Inc., Popeye's leg
embossed 1933 K.F.S.,
Inc., 10" h. x 7" w. at
base x 3-1/2" d. **$228**

Stout Auctions

Amos 'n Andy ashtray,
10-1/4" h. x 7" w. ... **$270**

Rich Penn Auctions

OTC store display
for trusses, 22" x 25" x
5". **$180**

Showtime Auction Services

Carnival animals, horse and piggy bank, hollow-
body form, 1950s, pig with old label inscribed
"Skyline Drive-1/28/46," horse 17-1/2" h., pig
9-1/4" h. **$144**

Jeffrey S. Evans & Associates

Boy with schoolbook,
Pennsylvania chalkware
figure, 19th century,
17". **$1,944**

Pook & Pook, Inc.

Admiration Cigars
sign, 11" x 15" x
2-1/2". **$660**

Showtime Auction Services

Standing foxhunter and
hound marked "Trade
Mark Reg. US Pat. Off.,"
14-1/4" h. x 7" w. ... **$123**

Wiederseim Associates, Inc.

Happy Hooligan figure
based on cartoon
running in *New York
Journal* from 1900-
1932, 11-1/2" h. **$120**

Showtime Auction Services

Bust of Abraham Lincoln,
13-1/2" h. **$120**

Showtime Auction Services

Chief Watta Pop
store display, original
condition, 8" x 9-1/2" x
5". **$960**

Showtime Auction Services

Circus Collectibles

THE 200TH ANNIVERSARY of Phineas Taylor Barnum's birth in 2010 triggered a renewed interest in collecting circus memorabilia. Collectibles range from broadsides announcing the circus is coming to town, to banners with brightly embellished visages of freakish sideshow acts, to windup tin toys depicting the lions, tigers, elephants, and clowns that no circus or sideshow would be complete without.

1910 Ringling Bros. circus clown original photograph, 11" x 14"...............**$70**

Alexander Historical Auctions

Circus Bank by Shepard Hardware Co., Buffalo, New York, cast iron, circa 1888. ....**$32,500**

The RSL Auction Co.

Counter display box of Circus Pals drinking straws consisting of 12 boxes of straws, each box containing two Circus Pal cut-outs...................**$80**

Philip Weiss Auctions

1923 portrait button of P.T. Barnum that reads "Fifth Annual Convention / New England Inter-Grotto Assn. / Bridgeport. Conn. Aug. 24-25-1923," includes lettering "M.O.V.P.E.R. Obeh," referring to Freemasonry group Mystic Order of Veiled Prophets of the Enchanted Realm, 2-1/16"...................**$86**

Hake's Americana

Jack Hoxie Circus poster of clowns and equestrian performers, printed by Donaldson Litho Co., circa 1937, 27" x 41"................ **$139**

Hake's Americana

Al G. Barnes Wild Animal Circus one-sheet poster, Erie Litho, 28" x 40"................. **$210**

Potter & Potter Auctions

Tiffany & Co. silver and enamel circus bear on roller skates, designed by Gene Moore, circa 1990, 4-5/8" h., 10.8 oz... **$1,250**

Heritage Auctions

Mickey Mouse Circus Game, Marks Bros. Co., circa 1934, with Mickey Mouse as ringmaster, Pluto as clown, Minnie Mouse balancing on back of Horace Horsecollar, and Clarabelle Cow on trapeze.... **$285**

Hake's Americana

Circa 1956 Emmett Kelly single-signed baseball, James Spence Authentication, PSA/DNA (autograph authentication arm of Professional Sports Authenticators). Kelly was famous as Weary Willie, a hobo clown who was the most recognizable figure in the Ringling Bros. and Barnum & Bailey Circus. **$448**

Heritage Auctions

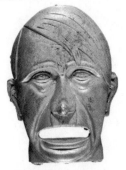

Carnival attraction, World War II anti-Hitler face, circa 1940s, hollow and heavy cast aluminum, 15-1/2" h.......... **$325**

Hake's Americana

P.T. Barnum-signed Barnum Bridgeport Circus Pass, circa 1880, free pass to Barnum's Circus on editor of *The Bridgeport [Connecticut] Daily and Weekly Standard* calling card, bearing A.D.S. ca. 1880, by Barnum, signed twice, in full: "Pass Mr. Candee & friends. P.T. Barnum" and beneath, "Paid for all...P.T. Barnum," with 1892 letter of condolence to Mrs. Candee after her husband's death. **$250**

Raynors' Historical Collectible Auctions

Kenton Overland Circus Bandwagon, cast iron, with driver, six band members, and two-horse team with riders. **$390**

Jeffery S. Evans & Associates

Kenton Overland Circus Wagon, mid-1920s, painted disc wheels, 9" l. Provenance: From the Don Kaufman Collection. **$675**

Bertoia Auctions

The Circus Kings of All Time Ringling Bros. and Barnum & Bailey circus poster, printed by Erie Litho Co., circa 1936, 26-1/2" x 39-1/4" **$230**

Hake's Americana

German Dresden circus bear with trainer, 2-3/4" l. **$1,475**

Bertoia Auctions

Large archive of Bozo the Clown memorabilia, merchandise, original artwork, and related material including 10 original black and white 8" x 10" photographs of Bozo (television), group of seven "How To Make-Up as Bozo (The Capitol Clown)" instruction pamphlets, and Bozo poster titled "The Circus Is Here." **$800**

Julien's Auctions

Captain Paul Boyton's Marvelous Aquatic Exhibition, P.T. Barnum & the Great London Circus poster by Strobridge Litho. Co., one of two surviving examples, 30" x 40". **$2,640**

Cowan's Auctions

Hubley Royal Circus Bandwagon, cast iron, with driver, six band members, and four-horse team, 23" l. **$960**

Jeffrey S. Evans & Associates

Cole Bros. Circus poster featuring Betty Lou, who starred in "Tarzan" pictures, 40" h. x 28" w. **$150**

1930s circus sideshow banner promoting the "World's Strangest Girls," 9' 8" x 11' 5". **$1,000**

JMW Auction Gallery

Bachmann Emmett Kelly, Jr. The Ringmaster Circus Train electronic set, #90020, with four train cars, Emmett Kelly, Jr. figure, and track... **$325**

Austin Auction Gallery

Magic Circus-Roll tin litho target game by American Toys..........**$25**

Philip Weiss Auctions

Revell Circus boxed play set, Marx, 1950s. **$55**

Philip Weiss Auctions

Early wooden circus trunk, 32" x 25" x 15"....... **$30**

Philip Weiss Auctions

Mallet with large burl head with wooden handle, possibly used for circus or carnival activities, 38" l. and 1" w.. **$60**

Midwest Auction Galleries

Big Noise! punchboard with clown and majorette, circa 1940s, more than 1,200 unpunched holes, with key, 13" x 14-1/2". **$158**

Hake's Americana

Figurines of Alexander the Elephant and Poppy the Performing Pony from Cybis Circus Collection, Poppy limited edition figurine numbered 88/1,000... **$180**

S&S Auction Inc.

"Circus Clown" serigraph, Wayland Moore, signed, limited edition of 300, 31" x 29-1/4". **$50**

Wittlin & Serfer Auctioneers

1935 Little Orphan Annie's Circus by American Advertising & Research Corp., Chicago............. **$170**

Philip Weiss Auctions

Civil War Collectibles

THE CIVIL WAR began on April 12, 1861, at Fort Sumter, the Confederates surrendered at Appomattox Courthouse on April 9, 1865, and all official fighting ceased on May 26, 1865.

Between the beginning and end of the Civil War, the way wars were fought and the tools soldiers used changed irrevocably. When troops first formed battle lines to face each other near Bull Run Creek in Virginia on June 21, 1861, they were dressed in a widely disparate assemblage of uniforms. They carried state-issued, federally supplied, or brought-from-home weapons, some of which dated back to the Revolutionary War, and marched to the orders and rhythms of tactics that had served land forces for at least the previous 100 years. Four short years later, the generals and soldiers had made major leaps in the art of warfare on the North American continent, having developed the repeating rifle, the movement of siege artillery by rail, the extensive employment of trenches and field fortifications, the use of ironclad ships for naval combat, the widespread use of portable telegraph units on the battlefield, the draft, the organized use of African-American troops in combat, and even the levying of an income tax to finance the war.

Nine Civil War-era state buttons, circa 1860s, three Wisconsin, one Kentucky, two Pennsylvania, one Michigan, one Missouri, and one Maryland, 23 mm dia... **$780**

Skinner, Inc., www.skinnerinc.com

For some Civil War enthusiasts, collecting war relics is the best way to understand the heritage and role of thousands who served. Collecting mementos and artifacts from the Civil War is not a new hobby. Even before the war ended, people were gathering remembrances. As with any period of warfare, the first collectors were the participants themselves. Soldiers sent home scraps of flags, collected minie-ball shattered logs, purchased privately marketed unit insignias, or obtained a musket or carbine for their own use after the war. Civilians wrote to prominent officers asking for autographs, exchanged photographs (carte-de-visites) with soldiers, or kept scrapbooks of items that represented the progress of the conflict.

After the war, the passion for owning a piece of it did not subside. Early collectors gathered representative weapons, collected battlefield-found relics, and created personal or public memorials to the veterans. Simultaneously, surplus sales emerged on a grand scale. This was the heyday of Civil War collecting. Dealers such as Francis Bannerman made hundreds of Civil War relics available to the general public.

Following World War II, a new wave of collecting emerged. Reveling in the victories in Japan and in Europe, Americans were charged with a renewed sense of patriotism and heritage. At the same time, newspapers started to track the passing of the last few veterans of the Civil War. As the nation paid tribute to the few survivors of the Rebellion, it also acknowledged that the 100-year anniversary of the war was fast upon them. In an effort to capture a sense of the heritage, Civil War buffs began collecting in earnest.

During the Civil War Centennial in the 1960s, thousands of outstanding relics emerged from closets, attics, and long-forgotten chests, while collectors eagerly bought and sold firearms, swords, and uniforms. It was during this time that metal detectors first played a large role in Civil War collecting, as hundreds donned headphones and swept battlefields and campsites, uncovering thousands of spent bullets, buttons, belt plates, and artillery projectiles.

By the 1970s, as this first wave of prominent and easily recognized collectibles disappeared into collections, Civil War buffs discovered carte-de-visites, tintypes, and ambrotypes. Accoutrements reached prices that far outstretched what surplus dealers could have only hoped for just a few years prior. The demand for soldiers' letters and diaries prompted people to open boxes and drawers to rediscover long-forgotten manuscript records of battles and campaigns.

By the end of the 20th century, collectors who had once provided good homes for the objects began to disperse their collections, and Civil War relics reemerged on the market. It is this era of Civil War relic reemergence in which we currently live. The fabulous collections assembled in the late 1940s and early 1950s are reappearing.

It has become commonplace to have major sales of Civil War artifacts by a few major auction houses, in addition to the private trading, local auctions and Internet sales of these items. These auction houses handle the majority of significant Civil War items coming to the marketplace.

The majority of these valuable items are in repositories of museums, universities, and colleges, but many items were also traded between private citizens. Items that are being released by museums and from private collections make up the base of items currently being traded and sold to collectors of Civil War material culture. In addition, many family collections collected over the years have been recently coming to the marketplace as new generations have decided to liquidate some of them.

Civil War items are now acquired by collectors in the same fashion as any material cultural item. Individuals interested in antiques and collectibles find items at farm auction sales, yard sales, estate sales, specialized auctions, private collectors trading or selling items, and the Internet and online auction sales.

Provenance is important in Civil War collectibles – maybe even more important than with most other collectibles. Also, many Civil War items have well-documented provenances as they come from family collections or their authenticity has been previously documented by auction houses, museums, or other experts in the field.

For more information on Civil War memorabilia, see *Warman's Civil War Collectibles Identification and Price Guide*, 3rd edition, by Russell L. Lewis.

CIVIL WAR COLLECTIBLES

$

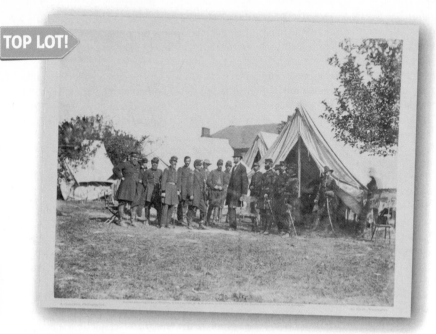

TOP LOT!

Photographic sketchbooks of Civil War by Alexander Gardner (1821-1882). Washington, D.C.: Philip & Solomons [1866]. Two oblong folio volumes, first edition, first issue, with phrase "Incidents of the War" printed on every page below mounted photograph; both volumes with lithographic title pages after drawings by Alfred A. Waud (1828-1891), single-page preface in volume one, contents page (present in both volumes), and 100 albumen photographs (50 in each volume), each photograph covered with light overleaf printed with subject and description of circumstances of photograph; photograph itself mounted on heavy sheet printed within tinted frame containing photo credits, title, date, etc.; bound in uniform publisher's full green morocco, tooled in gold, stamped with title on front boards, inner gilt dentelles, a.e.g. Gardner put himself directly into conflict. He set out with equipment, materials, and a skilled crew, working under crude conditions. With glass plate negatives, necessary chemical solutions, and traveling darkroom wagon, he was able to bring the war home to Americans..$192,000

Skinner, Inc., www.skinnerinc.com

Flag of The First Brigade, Third Division, Twenty-first Army Corps, circa 1863, three stripes of red, white, and some remaining blue wool bunting, two soiled white stars with a 1 in each star, also included is a note written by color bearer, John Webb, which states, "Battle Flag of Gen' Sam'l Beatty 1st Brig 3d Div 21st Army Corps Carried by John Webb Co A 19th O From Stone River to Last day of Atlanta Campaign" with passes dated 1863 and 1864, and a few other military documents, also includes documents relating to Webb's post-Civil War employment as a member of the Secret Service, including his identification as Special Operative, flag hoist 70" l. x 48" w.................$6,765

Skinner, Inc., www.skinnerinc.com

Civil War 1861-1865 Battles for the Union and the Union Forces Engaged Therein Together With a Record of Casualties. Illinois Central Railroad Co., 1887, produced for the 21st Annual Encampment of the Grand Army of the Republic; folding map, handbook size with illustrations of Corps insignia wrappers scuffed and soiled, otherwise good condition. **$81**

Heritage Auctions

Union Model 1859 forage cap with chinstrap, federal eagle side buttons, visor, and complete lining and sweatband, burlap reinforcing under 1-3/4" brown leather sweatband, brown polished cotton liner, including original "Size No 2 / 7 / U.S. Army / F.G & Co" paper label, reproduction cavalry insignia to crown **$2,750**

Heritage Auctions

Rare Civil War-period rotary valve, E flat circular helicon cornet, marked on bell by desirable Civil War maker "Firth Pond & Co./New York," overall about perfect untouched condition, rotary valves work perfectly, silvered finish overall with 3/4" silvered floating rim, 12" w. x 10-1/2" h..... **$8,750**

Heritage Auctions

Civil War brass eagle sword belt buckle with silver wreath, 2" x 3-1/4" **$210**

Pook & Pook, Inc.

Civil War painted regimental drum, labeled A. Rogers, Flushing Long Island, with original eagle decoration, inscribed Regt. US Infantry, 13-1/2" h. x 16-1/2" w **$4,029**

Pook & Pook, Inc.

Pair of Civil War officer's square-toe boots, heavy leather square-pegged soles and heels, both marked size 7, no obvious right or left foot, soft brown leather lining with cloth tabs/loops for pulling boots on, exterior leather and method of construction exhibit fine quality commensurate with ownership/use by officer, 14-1/2" h. from bottom of heel.................... **$313**

Heritage Auctions

Civil War U.S. lieutenant of artillery officer's uniform set with sash and sword belt, nine-button front with all original eagle A buttons with period Horstmann backmarks, non-functional cuffs, left with three eagle A buttons and right with two period General Service buttons and one eagle A button, stand-up collar 1-1/2" high at back, double gold bullion 2d lieutenant of artillery shoulder straps with gold bullion bars on heavily worn red velvet background. Black polished cotton lining with quilted breast and one breast pocket, white cotton sleeve lining, tail pockets lined with brown polished cotton. Double-thickness red silk sash is 4" wide with some small, scattered snags/holes but generally excellent condition; 9" tassels with wooden cores show wear but also excellent and sound. Sword belt with fine quality M1851 rectangular officer's eagle plate with medium-width tongue and matching numbers on plate and keeper. Black patent leather belt with sword slings and brass sword suspension hook. $4,688

Heritage Auctions

Nineteen Civil War carte-de-visites and two cabinet cards, circa late 19th century, carte-de-visite images include Abraham Lincoln, James Garfield, General Sherman, General Grant, General Custer, a Brady of General Winfield Scott Hancock, and Ohio officers and enlisted men.
.... **$3,480**

Skinner, Inc., www.skinnerinc.com

CIVIL WAR COLLECTIBLES

U.S. Cavalry officer's vest, dark blue wool front with two pockets lined with brown polished cotton, nine-button front with all original eagle A buttons with period Scovill back mark, interesting detail with back of vest along bottom edge lined with leather and light brown polished cotton lining with two large inside pockets, exterior of belted back with darker polished cotton and gilt brass buckle dated 1860, standup collar 1-1/8".......**$1,063**

Heritage Auctions

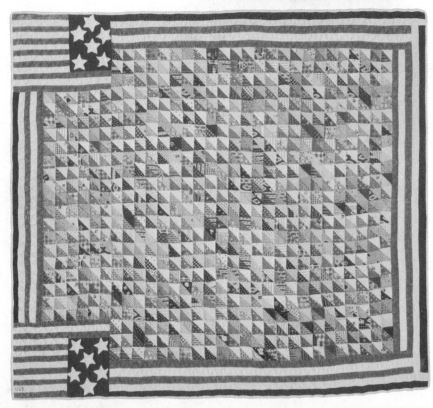

Rare Civil War flag crib quilt, dated 1862, composed of tiny triangles hand-pieced together, six white stars appliquéd on each of two flags, stripes form border, mounted on stretcher, 38-1/4" x 32-1/4"............**$5,938**

Sotheby's

Quarter-plate ambrotype of Civil War corporal, circa late 19th century, bearded soldier standing in frock coat with corporal stripes, with forage cap, musket, bayonet, accoutrements, 3-3/4" w. x 4-3/4" h. **$300**

Skinner, Inc., www.skinnerinc.com

Eight carte-de-visites and 12 cabinet cards, all Civil War-related, circa late 19th century, carte-de-visites of various officers, including General Buell, a New Hampshire militia officer, a Brady of Lt. R.H. Lamson, U.S.N., General Ambrose Burnside, General J.N. Bethune, and others, cabinet cards of unidentified naval officer, post-war images of General Butler, his wife, daughter, and son-in-law Adelbert Ames, some by Brady, four W. Tipton Gettysburg-related images, and Lookout Mountain, Tennessee, battlefield scene. **$1,560**

Skinner, Inc., www.skinnerinc.com

Civil War U.S. regulation eagle snare drum, retains about 95 percent of original painted decoration, brass tack design around air hole perfect, original interior paper label from "Ernest Vogt / Manufacturer of / Drums, Banjos, Tamborines / No 225 Beaver Street / Philadelphia / Contract Dec 29 1864," both heads, ropes and leather tighteners are correct restorations, 16-1/2" dia., 15-1/2" h. including hoops **$6,875**

Heritage Auctions

Oil on board portrait of Civil War officer, 19th century, 9" x 7" **$213**

Pook & Pook, Inc.

Large tintype of Civil War soldier, circa late 19th century, hand-colored copy on tin of seated soldier in overcoat, back of image has paper label marked "NORTH AMERICAN PHOTO-COPYING CO., JAMESTOWN, N.Y.," 9-3/4" h. x 8" w. **$98**

Skinner, Inc., www.skinnerinc.com

Carved burl pipe bowl, circa 1861-1865, in shape of bearded head, with Federal shield on top and bottom of neck, sword on each side, 2-1/4" h. x 3-1/4" l **$240**

Skinner, Inc., www.skinnerinc.com

Thirteen Civil War Naval letters, maps, and engravings, circa early to late 19th century, 1807 ship's manifest of the James Adams, maps of Boston Harbor, Portsmouth, letters from various naval officers including a surgeon's commission signed by Gideon Welles, and engravings of naval officers. **$390**

Skinner, Inc., www.skinnerinc.com

Two framed Civil War discharges and American flag, circa 1863-1870, discharge papers of Horace F. Davis, 30th Massachusetts Regiment, wool bunting flag marked "PATENTED APR. 26TH 1870 AMERICAN ENSIGN 20-FT." **$120**

Skinner, Inc., www.skinnerinc.com

Packet of Civil War-era letters, circa 1861-1917, group of letters and documents pertaining to the Woodbury family of Beverly, Massachusetts, letters home during the Civil War from various ships including the U.S.S. St. Louis, the Ohio, and others, including July 10, 1863, draft notice for John Woodbury, two carte-de-visites, George Washington and family, Abraham Lincoln and family, and two discharge documents for Thomas Woodbury, one with a carte-de-visite of Lt. Woodbury. **$2,280**

Skinner, Inc., www.skinnerinc.com

Smith breech-loading saddle ring Civil War carbine, serial no. 10340, .50 caliber, blued finish with case-hardened breech and hammer, iron mountings, left side of frame marked "Smith's Patent and Address / POULTNEY & TRIMBLE / BALTIMORE USA," barrel on left side marked "L.F.R." No cartouche marks present on wood, retaining approximately 75-80 percent finish on barrel, 20-25 percent case-hardened finish remaining on breech and hammer, moderate to heavy pitting on lower tang, frame, mountings, trigger guard and buttplate, fore-end appears original and in good condition, buttstock appears to be a replacement and in fair condition with some stress cracks, some replaced screws, 21-1/2" part round barrel with front and rear folding sight. **$1,554**

Heritage Auctions

CIVIL WAR COLLECTIBLES

Correspondence of Louis West Froelick, including 25 autograph letters signed "Louis West Froelick" or "Louis," 92-1/2 pages (4to and 8vo), aboard steamers Bugler, Baltimore, and Philadelphia moored in and around Washington, D.C. or Fort Monroe, Virginia, April 24-July 30, 1861, and at Camp Martin near Tennallytown (near Georgetown) June 20-Aug. 26, 1862, to his friend and colleague at the *New York Sun*, Albert Wiggers, and two written to his aunt; with oval portrait photograph of his squad, 6" x 8", taken in 1861, plus an autograph letter by his employer James G. Cooper to him, and an unrelated letter from 1866...**$5,000**

Sotheby's

Rare Confederate Selma arsenal small iron hand grenade, much of its original paint remaining and only light pitting in the body, fuse hole has two small chips in the edge, 2-1/2". **$531**

Heritage Auctions

Non-regulation staff officer's sword carried by Brigadier General Nathan Goff, 37th Regiment Colored Troops, slightly curved blade with center floral and scroll etched panels, obverse with "US" motif and reverse with spread wing eagle, obverse ricasso stamped "W. Clauberg Solingen," reverse with inset disc bearing word "Prooved" surrounded by faintly etched name "Hostmann & Sons Philadelphia." Blade is smooth, steel guard pierced with spread wing eagle over letters "US," steel is smooth and gray with minor dark staining, 32-12". **$1,563**

Heritage Auctions

Model 1854 Austrian Lorenz rifle musket, circa 1861, beech stock with cheek rest, steel fittings, lockplate marked 861 with faint Austrian eagle, 52-1/2"............................ **$720**

Skinner, Inc., www.skinnerinc.com

Confederate read bolt, fired specimen as evidenced by rifling marks on upper bourrelet, iron body mostly smooth with small scattered amounts of pitting, sabot appears to have blown off bolt when fired, meant for use in 3" Confederate rifle, 3" h **$238**

Heritage Auctions

Three small Civil War patches, one monogram and two embroidered feathers. **$49**

Skinner, Inc., www.skinnerinc.com

Confederate marked/imported Enfield .577 caliber percussion rifled musket, metal with overall attractive smooth dark patina, crisp markings, "Tower 1862," with appropriate barrel proofs, complete and original in every respect including rear sight, nipple protector and ramrod, stock bears stamped mark "(crown) / SH / C" behind rear trigger guard tang and also bears mark of crown with some illegible figures and mark of W. & C. Scott in oval on right side of buttstock..................... **$2,151**

Heritage Auctions

Clocks

THE MEASUREMENT AND RECORDING of time has been a vital part of human civilization for thousands of years, and the clock, an instrument that measures and shows time, is one of the oldest human inventions.

Mechanical, weight-driven clocks were first developed and came into use in the Middle Ages. Since the 16th century, Western societies have become more concerned with keeping accurate time and developing timekeeping devices that were available to a wider public. By the mid-1600s, spring-driven clocks were keeping much more accurate time using minute and seconds hands. The clock became a common object in most households in the early 19th century.

Clocks are a prime example of form following function. In its earliest incarnations, the functionality of a timepiece was of paramount importance. Was it telling the time? More importantly, was it telling the correct time? Once those basic questions had been answered, designers could experiment with form. With the introduction of electronics in the 20th century, almost all traditional clockwork parts were eliminated, allowing clocks to become much more compact and stylistically adaptable.

In lavish Art Deco styles of the 1920s and 1930s, clocks featured the same attention to exterior detail as a painting or sculpture. Fashioned of materials ranging from exotic woods to marble, bronze, and even wedges of Bakelite, Art Deco clocks were so lovely that it was actually an unexpected bonus if they kept perfect time.

Inlaid Baltimore Standard tall clock, American, circa 1800-1816, mahogany case clock by Baltimore clock maker Charles Tinges (1765-1816), dial with moon phase disk in lunette and hand-painted allegorical figures of four continents in spandrels, fitted with sweep hand and corresponding ring of date numbers, dial signed with maker's name and location, Charles Tinges / Baltimore, case of figured mahogany veneers with eagle inlays in spandrels and line inlays on hood edges, waist door and on face of base; 89-1/2" h **$15,000**

Cowan's Auctions

The Parisian firm, Leon Hatot, for instance, offered a clear glass stunner with hands and numerals of silver.

For the budget-conscious, particularly during the 1930s Depression years, inexpensive novelty clocks found favor. Prominent among these were molded-wood clocks by Syroco (Syracuse Ornamental Co.). Offering the look of hand-carving at a fraction of the cost, Syroco clocks featured an interior mechanism by Lux.

Also popular: affordable clocks ideally suited for a specific room in the home, such as the Seth Thomas line of kitchen-ready Red Apple clocks. Other companies specialized in attractively priced clocks with added whimsy. Haddon's Ship Ahoy clock lamp had a sailboat rocking on its painted waves, while MasterCrafters ceramic clocks replicated a pendulum effect with moving figures, such as children on swings or old folks in rocking chairs. Another best-seller, still in production today, is the Kit-Cat Clock with pendulum tail and hypnotic moving eyes.

And possessing an irresistible kitschy charm: "souvenir" clocks from locales as diverse as New York and Las Vegas. What better way to travel back in time than with a Statue of Liberty clock (complete with glowing torch) or a sparkly Vegas version with casino dice marking the hours?

After the production restraints of World War II, postwar clock designers found inspiration in fresh shapes and materials. Among the most unusual: clock lamps by San Francisco's Moss Manufacturing. These Plexiglas eye-poppers exhibit a mastery of multi-purposing. They tell time. They light up. They hold flowers. Many even include a rotating platform: flick the switch, and a ceramic figurine (often by a prominent design name, such as deLee, Hedi Schoop, or Lefton) begins to twirl.

Equally modern yet less over-the-top were fused glass clocks by Higgins Glass Studio of Chicago. Although artisans such as Georges Briard also designed glass clocks, those by Michael and Frances Higgins are among the mid-century's most innovative. Clocks were a natural outgrowth for these pioneers of practical design, whose decorative housewares ran the gamut from cigarette boxes to candleholders.

According to Michael Higgins, "We try to make things [that] may be thought beautiful. But we are not ashamed if our pieces are useful. It makes them easier to sell."

A 1954 Higgins clock for GE, featuring ball-tipped rays radiating outward on the glass face, is as unexpectedly glorious as an alien sun. A later line of glass-on-glass clocks was created for Haddon during the Higgins' stay at Dearborn Glass Co. The hours are indicated by colorful glass chunks fused to a vibrantly patterned glass slab. While from the mid-century, a Higgins clock is not of the mid-century. Simplicity and clarity of line, coupled with a bold use of color, make Higgins clocks right at home in any age.

There's no time like the present to explore the limitless treasure trove of mid-20th century clocks. Which will be your favorite? Only time will tell.

Gilt bronze mantel clock with decorative floral ormolu mounts and Corinthian columns, French, 19th century, 21" h..............$799

Cowan's Auctions

Antique Sitzendorf German porcelain figural mantel clock with standing woman and man on each side of movement, circa 1865, overall flowers in relief, Lenzkirch movement, serial number 335760, 13-1/2" h. x 12-3/8" w. x 6" d............$3,100

Elite Decorative Arts

Monumental Tiffany-retailed Belle Epoque bronze mantel clock, fourth quarter 19th century, Louis XIV style, paw feet flanking masque ornament crowned with pierced shell, seated griffins atop feet flanking pierced pendulum, decorated with sphinxes and scrollwork, dial with enamel numeral chapter ring and enamel Tiffany & Co. plate, works stamped "Tiffany & Co., New York," 37-3/4" h x 21-3/4" w. x 11-3/4" d. $13,000

New Orleans Auction Galleries

Louis-Philippe bronze-mounted mahogany mantel clock, casket form in Restauration style, set with silk string suspension movement, second quarter 19th century, 19" h. x 14-1/2" w. x 6-3/4" dia $760

New Orleans Auction Galleries

Small Germanic brass "zappler" timepiece with alarm, unsigned, late 18th century, short duration four-pillar movement with standing barrels for both going and alarm trains, latter striking on bell mounted above plates, verge escapement and short bob pendulum swinging in front of dial, 3-3/4" brass break-arch dial plate engraved with alternating plain and scroll-hatched vertical bands incorporating ribbon-tied floral panel flanked by husk swags to arch and rosette engraved ovoid feet, center with alarm disc and applied Roman numeral chapter ring with Arabic five minutes and arcaded minute ring, rear with rectangular brass cover for movement, side doors (one missing) and back foot, 6" h..$831

Dreweatts & Bloomsbury

French Louis XV-style bois d'Urci fronted mantel clock, unsigned, mid-19th century, eight-day countwheel bell striking movement stamped CJ & Co. above number 01266 to backplate, with circular white enamel Roman numeral dial with Arabic five minutes to outer track and fine scroll pierced brass hands set within milled brass glazed bezel, in waisted case molded with fine rococo scrolls around oval musical trophy panel to front, on scroll cast brass feet, 11-1/4" h. $199

Dreweatts & Bloomsbury

CLOCKS

Tiffany & Co. mahogany Horner grandfather clock, silvered chapter ring with applied brass Arabic hour numbers, sub seconds dial and moon phase dial, fancy pierced swirling leaf decoration in center of dial and spandrels, fancy pierced black hour and minute hands, sub seconds dial, chime/silent lever, signed Tiffany & Co. on silvered plaque, quality brass movement strikes on five silvered tubes signed "Walter H. Durfee," three quality brass weights and pulleys, brass pendulum bob with steel stick, carved mahogany case Attr: R. J. Horner, serpentine form with broken arch crest, winged griffins and swirling leaves on bonnet, carved lion heads on corners of body, figural putti on base and claw feet, good running condition, 105" h. **$20,000**

Fontaine's Auction Gallery

Inlaid rosewood Vienna Regulator, 9-1/2" inset porcelain dial with black Roman hour numerals on chapter ring, sub seconds dial in inset center, pierced and blued hands, brass bezel and dial signed "Jacob Weber, In Wein," brass, eight-day time, weight-driven movement with dead-beat escapement, maintaining power, long pendulum with ebonized wood stick, large brass-covered bob and quality weight and pulley, rosewood case with pierced carved floral and filigree crest and corner finials, brass and mother-of-pearl inlays on frieze and door columns with standing figural armored soldiers at tops of columns, backboard of case inlaid with figures, fruit, branches, filigree and borders using brass, mother-of-pearl, select woods and ivory, excellent condition and original finish, 73" h. x 21" w. x 10" d........**$21,500**

Fontaine's Auction Gallery

R.J. Horner carved oak nine-tube grandfather clock, circa 1890............................**$21,850**

Stevens Auctions

Antique French bronze and marble clock with large bronze cup on top, circa 1880 .... **$7,475**

Stevens Auctions

Gothic triple fusee Whittington chime eight-bell skeleton clock, two large pierced brass cathedral-shaped plates, silvered 8" chapter ring with black incised Roman numerals, good original fusee chains, recoil escapement, drop hammer strike on nest of eight bells with quarter-hour progressive Whittington strike, signed "Bennett, London" on metal tag, stands on white marble base, 23" h. x 15" w. x 9-1/2" d. **$14,000**

Fontaine's Auction Gallery

Shelf clock by Robert Swannell, London, circa 18th century .... **$2,000-$4,000**

Louis Dianni

1934 Ingersoll Disney Three Little Pigs alarm clock with the Wolf, his arms as clock's hands, surrounded by three little pigs with phrase, "Who's Afraid of the Big Bad Wolf?" printed on dial face, 4-1/2" h. **$250**

Case Antiques, Inc.

Victor Vasarely (French/Hungarian, 1906-1997) alpha clock, numbered 21/500, 12-1/2" x 7-1/4" **$300**

Sloan & Kenyon

French-Style polychromed bombe-form grandmother clock, early 20th century, movement signed "Marti," 68-1/4" x 17" x 8"............. **$615**

New Orleans Auction Galleries

Courvoisier Freres gilt-bronze Swiss presentation clock, 20th century, Louis XVI-style case, gilt-stamped leather presentation box with easel-back, 7-3/4" x 5-1/2" x 1-1/4".................. **$525**

New Orleans Auction Galleries

William IV brass inlaid mahogany octagonal fusee dial timepiece, dial signed for Rieder, London, circa 1830, four-pillar single fusee movement with anchor escapement, shouldered plates and 12" cream-painted Roman numeral convex dial with inscription RIEDER, LONDON, pierced blued steel hands within convex glazed cast bezel, octagonal case with side door and pendulum access flap to base, front inlaid with repeating scroll motifs within gadroon molded border, 18-3/4" w.. **$432**

Dreweatts & Bloomsbury

Nine-tube tall case clock, late 19th century, dial signed Tiffany & Co., oak case carved with full figure musicians on hood and tavern scene on base, side columns with lions' heads and putti, door with scrollwork, fruit and satyr head, silvered chapter ring over ornate face, moon phase, subsidiary seconds, Westminster eight-bell chime, nine tubes marked "Walter Durfee," running, recently serviced, small chip out of filigree on door, 28" x 17-1/2" x 102". Provenance: Purchased by consignor's grandfather at Tiffany's in New York.......**$17,000**

Cordier Auctions

CLOCKS

Pedro Friedeberg (Mexican, b. 1936), "Double Time," painted and gilded carved wood sculpture with inset clock and compass, double-headed, four-handed, and four-footed figure in seated position, signed at bottom of one foot, 14-3/4" h. x 6-3/4" w. x 4-1/2" d........ **$2,100**

New Orleans Auction Galleries

Silver-mounted gilt brass petit sonnerie carriage clock with perpetual calendar, moon phase, alarm and push-button quarter repeat, Le Roy and Fils, Paris, circa 1885, eight-day two-train movement, silvered platform lever escapement, enamel alarm setting dial positioned within coil of gongs to backplate and unusual engraved signature LE ROY & FILS PALAIS-ROYAL 13-15 PARIS, 9928 to right-hand edge of backplate itself, circular white enamel Roman numeral dial with repeat signature above rolling moon phase aperture with engraved gilt lunar disc to center and blued steel moon hands set within rectangular frosted silvered mask, bevel glazed gilt brass case with hinged silver handle, guilloche-scroll bordered escapement aperture and repeat button to top above conforming guilloche-bordered front door with female mask crest flanked by canted angles, standing putti, sides with conforming glazed apertures and rear matching front with further figures to rear angles, on molded skirt base, squat turned tapered feet, 7" high excluding handle, original tooled leather outer traveling case........**$43,200**

Dreweatts & Bloomsbury

Early grandfather clock made by David Elias Bangor, 97" h.. **$2,875**

Stevens Auctions

German gilt copper and brass crucifix clock, attributed to Hans Schlottheim, Augsburg, circa 1600 and later, movement mounted onto hinged cover with herringbone engraved inner border, exterior fitted with later silver-colored metal cylindrical section crucifix surmount with cast Corpus Christi beneath cream-painted rotating sphere with Roman numeral annular chapters, circular gilt copper base with engraved decoration and ogee-shaped border to platform cover above arcade-pierced frieze enclosing bell, flanked by pair of gilt finials and open scroll cast mounts applied to broad ogee-outline foot engraved with foliage and scrolling strapwork on matted ground within leafy outer ring molding, on three small brass bun feet, 13" h., 2-1/4" dia. movement........................ **$8,310**

Dreweatts & Bloomsbury

CLOCKS

$

TOP LOT!

Charles II small ebonized architectural eight-day long case clock, Joseph Knibb, Oxford, circa 1665-1667, six knopped, finned and latched pillar movement with tall bottle-shaped plates, 8-1/2" square latched brass dial centered with five-petal rose engraved motif to matted center with ring-turned decoration to shuttered winding holes within 1" w. silvered Roman numeral chapter ring with stylized trident half-hour markers, fine pierced sculpted steel Oxford hands and spandrel areas engraved with symmetrical foliate decoration, lower two flanking signature Joseph Knibb of Oxford, ebonized case with rising hood constructed of pine with ebonized fruitwood veneers and moldings, triangular tympanum above plain lintel and square glazed dial aperture flanked by rectangular side windows with raised aperture moldings, trunk with convex throat molding over full-width door veneered in ebonized fruitwood onto oak with central short between two long narrow vertical raised panels, sides of plain ebonized pine, on conforming broken-ogee molded plinth base with bun feet, 6' 3" h.....**$399,000**

Dreweatts & Bloomsbury

Victorian gilt brass-mounted ebonized giant carriage clock with push-button hour repeat, Dent, London, circa 1857-1858, 3-1/2" circular white enamel Roman numeral dial with seconds dial above signature DENT, 33 COCKSPUR ST., LONDON, 22594 to center and blued steel spade hands set within arched gilt mask, case with cast gilt brass handle over bevel-glazed panel, bevel-glazed panels to sides, right-hand side with trip-hour repeat button, rear with rectangular door, on molded skirt base with shallow squab feet, 9-1/2" h. excluding handle **$36,500**

Dreweatts & Bloomsbury

William IV Gothic revival carved oak library timepiece, Frodsham, London, circa 1830, four-pillar single chain fusee movement with shouldered plates, anchor escapement, Vulliamy-type wide jaw pendulum suspension, pendulum holdfast bracket and stamped FRODSHAM, GRACECHURCH STREET, LONDON to backplate, 4" w. ogee Gothic arch-shaped single sheet silvered brass Roman numeral dial with steel moon hands and foliate scroll-engraved infill incorporating cartouche with repeat signature to apron, triangular gabled case with Gothic leafy trail carved decoration to pediment, spire finials above glazed front door with shaped silvered brass canted insert and applied fleur-de-lys motif above dial, angles with opposing spiral twist columns, sides with rectangular bevel glazed apertures, on molded skirt base with squab feet, 13" h...................... **$1,080**

Dreweatts & Bloomsbury

Rare diamond-shaped small weight-driven wall timepiece, dial signed for John Knibb, Oxford, circa 1685, dial signed John Knibb, Oxon to tulip and leafy trail engraved center with single pierced iron hand within 4-1/2" Roman numeral chapter ring with inner track divided for quarters and Knibb stylized trident half-hour markers, dial secured via pinned lugs passing through apertures in four integral shaped spandrel extensions to chapter ring to 7" square red velvet covered iron plate, in a case with figured walnut veneered cavetto frame incorporating broken-ogee slip insert, rear with box enclosing movement, sliding pendulum access panel and keyhole hanging aperture to backboard, 18" h., 13" sq **$13,300**

Dreweatts & Bloomsbury

French Louis XV-style gilt brass-mounted tortoishell bracket clock, unsigned, circa 1900, rectangular eight-day gong striking movement, 25-piece circular Roman numeral cartouche dial with Arabic five minute panels to outer track within scallop shell and rococo scroll cast borders, blued steel trident-shaped hands within cast brass bevel glazed hinged bezel, waisted case veneered in mottled red shell and applied with naturalistic floral spray cast surmount to asymetric upstand fronted by conforming spray above dial flanked by foliate cast shoulder mounts to front and rear angles, back with circular pierced patinated brass door within ebonized surround, scroll feet with applied leafy apron mount between, 27" h **$1,330**

Dreweatts & Bloomsbury

French ormolu and white marble figural timepiece, unsigned, circa 1900, circular eight-day movement with platform cylinder escapement and numbered 378 to backplate, set into dark blue japanned orb applied with gilt Roman numerals to form chapter ring and series of five-pointed stars, mounted on cloud next to figure of seated cherub, on stepped white marble oval base with toupe feet, 5-3/4" h......................**$698**

Dreweatts & Bloomsbury

Victorian brass fusee skeleton timepiece, William Frederick Evans and Sons, Birmingham, mid-19th century, single chain fusee movement with anchor escapement set between three tier scroll pierced brass plates united by six column-turned pillars, stamped W.F. EVANS & SONS. to rear of frontplate, pierced silvered chapter ring with shield-shaped cartouche Roman numerals and blued steel Breguet-style moon hands, four turned brass feet, 12-1/4" h., ebonised wood stand with compressed bun feet 14" h. overall **$631**

Dreweatts & Bloomsbury

Swiss Renaissance iron chamber clock, unsigned, circa 1600, iron box-form case with single lugged bell supported within domed bearer decorated with forged iron flower buds, front with hour wheel and gilt painted arrow-shaped hand against cream-painted chapter ring with Gothic Roman numerals, polychrome painted with symmetrical bird-inhabited foliate scrolls on chocolate brown ground beneath molded gilt band and panel painted with owl, sides with hinged doors secured by sprung clasps and painted with large floral sprays, rear with forged hanging hoop and spurs, escapement restored, case decoration refreshed, 10-1/2" h **$6,980**

Dreweatts & Bloomsbury

French Belge noir marble perpetual calendar mantel clock with moonphase, unsigned, late 19th century, eight-day bell striking movement with visible Brocot escapement to recessed center of two-piece white enamel Roman numeral dial with blued steel moon hands behind bevel glazed bezel, cavetto molded break-arch case fitted with secondary enamel dial for perpetual calendar featuring subsidiary day-of-the-week and date-of-the-month dials beneath moonphase aperture, within outer ring annotated for month-of-the-year with signs of zodiac behind similar glazed bezel, within mottled red marble banded borders and flanked by carved side scrolls, on cavetto molded cushion-shaped base inset with lozenge-shaped band to front, squat bracket feet with pendant apron between, 16" h.............. **$1,330**

Dreweatts & Bloomsbury

French Egyptian-style bronze mounted Belge noir and Breccia marble mantel clock garniture, A. Ecalt, Paris, late 19th century, eight-day gong striking movement with circular mottled panel, centered black Roman numeral dial inscribed A. ECALT, Horloger de la Marine, PARIS, ... Royal 94 to chapter ring, gilt spade hands within two-tone gilded stylized lotus leaf cast bevel glazed bezel, tapered case with patinated bronze reclining winged female sphinx surmount above canted cornice and pseudo Egyptian deity incised spandrel decoration around dial, flanked by mottled marble battered side sections with inscribed faux hieroglyph decoration to fascia, on canted skirt base with scarab beetle decoration to front and gilt brass fillet-edged bottom edge, 17-1/4" h **$1,250**

Dreweatts & Bloomsbury

CLOCKS

Continental porcelain figural timepiece, unsigned, late 19th century, Swiss five-bar watch type movement with cylinder escapement regulated by sprung monometallic balance, circular white enamel Roman numeral dial with red Arabic five minutes to outer track and fine pierced gilt hands within convex glazed milled brass bezel, set in polychrome-painted porcelain case modeled as a globe on stack of books draped with map beside figure of standing cherub holding sprays of flowers, on square plinth base with canted angles and repeating gilt panel decoration, underside bears underglaze blue mark, 7-1/4" h.................... **$299**

Dreweatts & Bloomsbury

William III walnut and floral marquetry eight-day long case clock, John Greenhill, Maidstone, circa 1695, five finned pillar (one removed) inside countwheel bell striking movement with 11" square rosette-centered brass dial with subsidiary seconds dial, scroll engraved shaped calendar aperture and ringed winding holes to matted center within silvered Roman numeral chapter ring with fleur-de-lys half-hour markers, signed John Greenhill, Maidston fecit to lower edge, angles with applied winged cherub head and foliate cast spandrels, case with ogee molded cornice and brass repoussé fret to frieze above dial surround, trunk with 42" door centered with lenticle and with three shaped marquetry panels decorated with birds and foliage on ebonized ground within walnut field, base with conforming rectangular marquetry panel within crossbanded borders, 79" h..................................... **$9,970**

Dreweatts & Bloomsbury

Queen Anne japanned eight-day longcase clock, Joshua Hutchin, London, early 18th century, five finned pillar inside countwheel bell striking movement with 11" square rosette-centered brass dial, ringed winding holes, applied silvered Roman numeral chapter ring with sword hilt half-hour markers, signed Joshua Hutchin, London to lower margin, angles applied with winged cherub head and foliate scroll cast spandrels, in cream and polychrome japanned case with Ho-Ho bird decorated caddy, molded cornice and shaped panel over three-quarter columns applied to lattice painted hood door, 41" rectangular door centered with lenticle in polychrome and gilt with figures in Oriental garden landscape within trellis-painted surround, sides with foliage and game birds, plinth with shaped panel painted with figural landscape over molded double skirt, 93" h. **$2,990**

Dreweatts & Bloomsbury

Coca-Cola & Other Soda Pop Collectibles

COLLECTIBLES PROVIDE a nostalgic look at our youth and a time when things were simpler and easier to understand. Through collecting, many adults try to recapture this time loaded with fond memories.

The American soft drink industry has always been part of this collectible nostalgia phenomenon. It fits all the criteria associated with the good times, fond memories, and fun. The world of soda pop collecting has been one of the mainstays of modern collectibles since the start of the genre.

Can soda pop advertising be considered true art? Without a doubt! The very best artists in America were an integral part of that honorary place in art history. Renowned artists like Rockwell, Sundbloom, Elvgren, and Wyeth helped take a quality product and advance it to the status of an American icon and all that exemplifies the very best about America.

Coca-Cola tin serving tray, American Art Works, boy and his dog, 10-1/2" x 13-1/4" **$600**
Showtime Auctions

This beautiful advertising directly reflects the history of our country: its styles and fashion, patriotism, family life, the best of times, and the worst of times. Nearly everything this country has gone through can be seen in these wonderful images.

Organized Coca-Cola collecting began in the early 1970s. The Coca-Cola Co., since its conception in 1886, has taken advertising to a whole new level. This advertising art, which used to be thought of as a simple area of collecting, has reached a whole new level of appreciation. So much so, that it has been studied and dissected by scholars as to why it has proved to be so successful for more than 120 years.

For more information on Coca-Cola collectibles, see *Petretti's Coca-Cola Collectibles Price Guide*, 12th edition, by Allan Petretti.

Box of unused Coca-Cola Sweetheart straws, 1950s, 8-1/2" h.......**$60**

Morphy Auctions

1960s Coca-Cola salesman book, 7-1/2" l....................**$36**

Morphy Auctions

Coca-Cola soda fountain advertisement, "Meet Me at the Soda Fountain," 1920s, framed display 13" x 18"...**$300**

Morphy Auctions

1957 Coca-Cola square dance festoon, 33" l ... **$270**

Morphy Auctions

Coca-Cola sheet music, "The Coca-Cola Girl," 1927, framed 13-1/2" x 19-1/2".....................**$210**

Morphy Auctions

Coca-Cola paper sign, 1939, framed 28-1/4" x 19-3/4"..**$84**

Morphy Auctions

Coca-Cola toy shopping cart, 1950s, miniature display boxes on side, 20" h...........................**$360**

Morphy Auctions

Coca-Cola belt buckle, "15 Years Safe Driving," 1960s-1970s..**$72**

Morphy Auctions

COCA-COLA AND OTHER SODA POP

1960 Coca-Cola merchandising book filled with machines pictured and priced, includes signs, carriers, matches, display racks and more.................**$270**

Morphy Auctions

Coca-Cola life-size cutout, 1940s, 65" h.....................**$210**

Morphy Auctions

Coca-Cola vendor's apron, 1950s. **$270**

Morphy Auction

Coca-Cola light-up clock, 1960, 16" x 14-1/4"....................**$270**

Morphy Auctions

Coca-Cola bottle vending machine, endo Model #56A. **$2,185**

Matthews Auctions

1928 Coca-Cola calendar, framed, 13" x 26"..............**$120**

Morphy Auctions

Coca-Cola syrup tip, one gallon size, "Delicious and Refreshing.".......................**$390**

Showtime Auctions

Coca-Cola baseball counter, 3-1/2" l. **$108**

Morphy Auctions

1960s VW Coca-Cola bus, 8-3/4" l. **$360**

Morphy Auctions

Coca-Cola delivery truck, Marx, 1950s,
16-3/4" l. **$300**

Morphy Auctions

"Drink Coca-Cola Ice Cold" sign with soda fountain
dispenser graphics, DSP sign, 28" x 27". **$1,840**

Matthews Auctions

1930s Coca-Cola cardboard sign, "Ice Cold Coca-
Cola As Always Five 5 Cents," 12" x 15". **$180**

Morphy Auctions

Coca-Cola Silent
Policeman "Slow
School Zone,"
2-SST die-cut sign,
62" h. with original
cast-iron base......... **$891**

Matthews Auctions

Early Coca-Cola six-
pack store display,
61-1/2" h. **$510**

Showtime Auctions

Coca-Cola cooler radio, 12" x 9" x 7"............. **$180**

Showtime Auctions

Coca-Cola salesman's sample Coke cooler with original opener, cap catcher and sample cases of bottles, 10-1/2" x 13" x 7-1/2"..................**$18,000**

Showtime Auctions

Rare Coca-Cola nude tin serving tray, Western Coca-Cola Bottling Co., Chicago, "Wherever Ginger Ale, Seltzer or Soda is Good Coca-Cola is Better – Try It," 12" dia.. **$2,700**

Showtime Auctions

Coca-Cola Kay-Display menu board with wood product price inserts, 38" x 20". **$945**

Showtime Auctions

Coca-Cola sandwich plate, "Drink Coca-Cola Refresh Yourself" with bottle and glass in center, E.M. Knowles China Co., 1931, 7-1/2" dia. **$420**

Rich Penn Auctions

Coca-Cola soda fountain globe, 1930s, Coca-Cola mark on metal fixture and original hardware, 13-1/2" x 18"... **$1,955**

Showtime Auctions

Coca-Cola green glass bowl, "Drink Coca-Cola / Ice Cold," for iced bottles, Vernonware, 1930s, 4-1/4" x 10"... **$780**

Rich Penn Auctions

White Rock Club Soda advertising sign, die-cut cardboard standup with easel back, 30" h. x 21-1/4" w.. **$420**

Rich Penn Auctions

Canada Dry soda fountain cooler, rare model C2P, Heintz, 1940s, professionally restored, 38-1/2" h. x 33-1/2" w. x 30" d................................... **$3,120**

Rich Penn Auctions

Whistle Soda advertising clock, No. WC6-92, Phelps Mfg. Co., Terre Haute, Indiana, 24" x 24" x 2-1/2" **$1,320**

Showtime Auctions

Vintage Pepsi-Cola swirl bottle store countertop cardboard easel-back advertisement display sign with Pepsi swirl bottle, approximately 14" x 15".... **$3,000**

Victorian Casino Antiques

Pepsin Punch A. Asti advertisement sign in ornate frame, Star Mfg. Co., Dallas, 22" x 28"...........................$510

Victorian Casino Antiques

Orange Crush soda advertising sign, 1939, embossed tin-litho $151

Lloyd Ralston Gallery

Original artwork by F. Sands Brunner, for Ketterliuns Litho Company in Philadelphia, executed for soda pop company (probably R.C. Cola or Dr. Pepper). $1,140

Morphy Auctions

NuGrape Soda tin thermometer advertisement sign, "Everybody likes a change," U.S., 7" x 16"....................................$450

Victorian Casino Antiques

Pepsi-Cola transistor radio, "Say Pepsi Please," dispenser shape with plastic glass and three dials, 9-1/2" h. x 6" w.................$120

Rich Penn Auctions

Vintage Pepsi-Cola light-up bubble face advertisement clock, 15" dia....................$540

Victorian Casino Antiques

7Up soda shop syrup dispenser with original paper label, 16" h. x 10" w $157

Pioneer Auction Gallery

Nichol Kola advertising sign, embossed tin-litho, 14-1/2" x 14"....................................$23

Lloyd Ralston Gallery

Veep soda advertising sign, tin-litho, 12" x 32".. **$81**

Lloyd Ralston Gallery

Vintage Bowser gas station pump, restored in Pepsi-Cola motif with Pepsi-Cola double glass lens top globe with key. **$1,140**

Victorian Casino Antiques

Early Pepsi-Cola thick embossed Hutchinson glass bottle "ESCAMBIA Pepsi-Cola Bottling Co. Pensacola, Fla.".................... **$600**

Victorian Casino Antiques

Oversized display bottle for Smile soda pop, embossed glass with original paint, "Pat'd July 11, 1922, Contents 1 Gallon," 18-1/2" h.......................... **$900**

Rich Penn Auctions

Fruit Bowl Soda embossed tin advertisement sign, "Nectar For a Nickel," Stout Sign Co., 7" x 20" **$330**

Victorian Casino Antiques

Early tin Pepsi-Cola can with original lid and paint, 17" h. x 15" dia..................... **$77**

Burnt Chimney Auction

Green Spot soda pop, "Thirsty?" easel-back sign, 1937, 33" x 23"......**$70**

Rich Penn Auctions

Squirt Soda figural advertising stand, terra cotta, 1947, 13" h. x 8" w. x 5" d...........**$303**

Fontaine's Auction Gallery

Coin-Ops

DID YOU KNOW coin-operated dispensers date back to ancient times when they were used in houses of worship to deliver holy water? You'd be hard-pressed to find one of those offered at auction today, but many other types of coin-operated gadget-like gizmos certainly come up for sale, and there are always eager buyers lining up to add them to collections.

Coin-ops, as they're often referenced by both marketers and aficionados, come in all shapes and sizes and fall into three main categories: gambling, including slot machines and trade stimulators; vending machines with service devices like scales and shoe shiners as a subcategory; and arcade machines. From simple post-World War II gumball and peanut machines that can usually be found for under $100, to rare antique arcade machines that bring to mind the fortune teller amusement working magic in the popular movie "Big" starring Tom Hanks, these are all considered collectible.

Today one of those talking fortune-teller machines can easily bring five figures at auction. Other interesting models without talking features can be purchased more reasonably, in the $1,000-$5,000 range, but none of them come cheap when they're in good working order.

Amusements such as these originated in penny arcades of the late 1800s. There were machines allowing patrons to demonstrate their skill at bowling, shooting or golf, among other pastimes, along with the familiar strength testers that sprang to life at a

Batmobile coin-operated ride, circa 1960s, heavy-duty Batmobile-replica ride, 25¢ for 30 seconds, black, yellow, aqua, and red painted car, 44" h. x 65" l. **$2,270**

Heritage Auctions

Zeno Chewing Gum coin-op, small crack in front below Zeno sign, coin entry chipped, no key to wind the mechanism, excellent condition, 16-1/2" h. .... **$800-$1,000**

penny a pop. Some machines known as "shockers" were marketed as medical devices. In fact, one made by Mills, a huge manufacturer of coin-ops, was actually named Electricity is Life, and it would supposedly cure what ails you, according to Bill Petrochuk, an avid collector actively involved with the Coin Operated Collectors Association (http://coinopclub.org). Another lung tester, which operated by blowing into a mouthpiece attached to a hose causing water to rise in the device as a measurement tool, was eventually banned, ironically, due to the spread of tuberculosis.

There are also those aforementioned trade stimulators, some of which skirted gambling laws, according to Larry DeBaugh, a frequent consultant for Morphy Auctions (www.morphyauctions.com), who knows his stuff when it comes to devices powered by pocket change. These machines stimulated the trade of businesses like tobacco stores and bars by offering patrons a chance to win products, many times by spinning reels or playing a game. Later machines dispensed gum on the side for each coin spent. Customers received something for their money, and presto, law enforcement couldn't technically deem it gambling.

The earliest trade stimulators were cigar machines with no gambling involved, however. They were truly cigar dispensers, and for a nickel a customer would get a cigar. What made it different from buying from the guy down the block is that you might get two or three for the same nickel using the machine. Petrochuk adds that these were used to free up some of the tobacco shop clerk's time as well. When taxes were imposed on cigars, requiring that they be sold from original boxes, these machines were no longer serviceable. They're now considered rare collectibles and sell for $10,000 and up in most instances, when you can find them.

There were also slot machines designed for use outside casinos that would vend a pack of mints, or do a bit of fortune telling, in the same way as later trade stimulators. These machines were fought by authorities for decades, according to DeBaugh. Finally, in the 1950s and 1960s, vending-style gambling machines of this sort were outlawed, and their makers concentrated their marketing efforts on Las Vegas going forward.

Traditional slot machines are quite popular today as well, and collectors like DeBaugh, who've studied, bought and sold these types of items for 35-40 years, have seen a bit of everything including those in pretty rough shape.

"An average machine, one that's seen a lot of play from the '40s or late '30s and is basically worn out, will run about $1,000. But they won't be worth anything unless they are restored. After they're running, you might have a $3,000 machine."

Petrochuk notes that collectors of coin-ops in general look for "nice, clean, original machines," but a very small percentage fall into that category. He likes to use the term "preservation" when referring to giving old coin-ops new life, as in keeping things as original as possible. He sees restoration as more of a redo that might require totally new paint or extensive replating. "These old machines took a real beating. A few battle scars are acceptable," he adds.

Preserving coin-ops means using as many original parts as possible to replace those that are worn, and fabricating new ones out of appropriate materials when needed. DeBaugh actually supplies Rick Dale of the History Channel's hit television series

Wrigley rotating gum dispenser, metal and glass, professionally restored, excellent condition, 14-1/2" h. .....**$400-$800**

Coin-operated Indian Motorcycle ride, 53" x 28" x 54"......... **$7,500**

Heritage Auctions

"American Restoration" with many parts salvaged from old slot machines that can't be repaired. He also notes that it's tough to find older slots from the early 1900s in anything but poor condition. The wood usually needs work, and sometimes the nickel or copper finishes will need to be replated as well.

Other unusual coin-ops beyond the familiar "one-armed bandits" include devices that sold match books, collar buttons, and sprays of perfume. Going even further into the unimaginable zone are machines that actually dispensed live lobsters via a game of sorts. Others even provided live bait for fishing excursions. Or, maybe a machine that dispensed gold bars in airports might pique your curiosity? These oddball items made the list of "10 Things You Didn't Know About Coin-Op Antiques" published in the 2014 edition of *Antique Trader Antiques & Collectibles Price Guide*.

Nut and gum dispensers are the most common vending models, but unusual brands in this category most definitely appeal to advertising collectors in addition to coin-op enthusiasts. In fact, many coin-ops are direct extensions of advertising collectibles since vending machines made in the 1920s and '30s, unlike those that dispense multiple types of snacks today, usually focused on a single brand. Hershey's machines dispensed chocolate bars. Wrigley's dispensers rotated to deliver packs of gum. There were even coin-operated dispensers for Dixie Cups. Add an unusual shape or size to the equation and advanced collectors will pay big bucks to own them.

Even those old-fashioned red, white, and blue stamp dispensers used in post offices 30-40 years ago appeal to collectors of newer machines, and those can be found for less than $100. If you want a slot machine for use in a "man cave" or game room, DeBaugh suggests looking at a Mills machine from the 1940s or '50s. Both high top and half top models can be found for around $1,000 in good working order. What's even better, they're dependable and reliable for home use for hours of coin-op fun.

—*Pamela Y. Wiggins*

COIN-OPS

Pinball machine, Williams Fairway, wooden rail, manufactured by Williams Manufacturing Co., Chicago, circa 1949, 24-1/2" w. x 64-1/2" h. x 53" d. Williams Fairway is purported to be one of the earliest golf-related upright pinball machines ever made............................. **$1,434**

Heritage Auctions

Gumball machine, Leaf Play Ball, 1960, likely restored, 14" h. **$383**

Heritage Auctions

Master 1¢/5¢ vending machine, five turns for a nickel and one turn for a penny, original condition, box and keys present, excellent condition, 16" h. **$408**

Miniature Baseball World Champion coin-operated game, 1931, all original, accepts pennies and flips steel balls in spiral to obtain hits or outs, 16-1/2" x 10-1/4" x 8-1/2"... **$1,340**

Heritage Auctions

Advanced 1¢ Climax 10 vendor, circa 1915, with extended gooseneck coin entry, excellent condition, 20-1/2".
.... **$1,000-$1,600**

Morphy Auctions

Glenn Ford's *Ocean's Eleven* slot machine, gift from Frank Sinatra, from fabled Sands Casino, *Ocean's Eleven* hotel-casino; one of several machines seen in the movie and later obtained by Sinatra, who gave them as gifts. **$6,572**

Heritage Auctions

Standard Gum Co. 1¢ aluminum gumball dispenser, original condition with marquee, working condition, padlock but no key, wall mounting bracket, very good condition, 17-1/2" h...........**$336**

Vintage coffee vending machine, 64" x 21-1/2" x 19-1/4." **$750**

Heritage Auctions

Baseball-themed gumball machine, 1958, fully functional, free standing, spring-operated "bat" hurls ball toward pockets representing hits and outs, 45" h. on heavy iron base.............................**$650**

Heritage Auctions

Mutoscope Skyscraper traveling crane digger machine, 1920s, sold by Mills Sales Co. of Oakland, California, front compartment facades of Empire State Building, 42" h. x 23" w. x 20" d...........................**$1,093**

One-cent Pocket Lighter Fuel coin-op, missing piece of metal below cash door, otherwise good condition, 16"....**$400-$600**

Morphy Auctions

Pole Vault 1-cent skill game gum trade stimulator, as-found good condition, no key, not working, 14-1/2" h. ....**$300-$500**

Morphy Auctions

COIN-OPS

Chicago Club House 1¢ trade stimulator gum vendor in fair, as-found condition, 15-1/2" h. ....$300-$500

Morphy Auctions

Beatles pinball machine, Williams, 1966, reconditioned. $4,182

Heritage Auctions

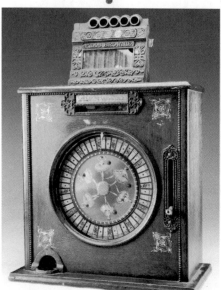

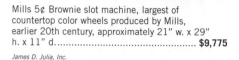

Mills 5¢ Brownie slot machine, largest of countertop color wheels produced by Mills, earlier 20th century, approximately 21" w. x 29" h. x 11" d.. $9,775

James D. Julia, Inc.

Gottlieb Frontiersman pinball machine, 5¢ play, one leg with vertical stress split, some replaced bumpers with celluloid bumper tops showing distress, lacking key but unlocked, 54" l. x 66" h. x 25" w.. $374

James D. Julia, Inc.

COIN-OPS

Rare 5¢ Blackhawk Brand Aspirin coin-operated dispenser, original excellent condition, 12" h.
..................................$500-$800

Morphy Auctions

Caille Upright Slot Machine, 25¢ play, restored, antique copper finish, oak case, missing pay out pointer and cover for center of wheel, excellent condition, 69" h. ....$16,000-$24,000

Morphy Auctions

Jennings coin-drop trade stimulator, horse race theme on aluminum castings, very fine condition, 12-1/2" d. x 14" w. x 20" h. Depending upon where penny landed, player received 0 to 25 points, plus a gumball.
....$2,300

5¢ Real Moving Pictures arcade machine on original stand, excellent condition, 75" h.
.... $1,200-$1,400

Morphy Auctions

Price 10¢ Collar Button Machine Co. vending machine full of collar buttons, excellent condition, 11-1/2" h.............. $1,000-$1,200

Morphy Auctions

Coins & Currency

COIN COLLECTING and the study of numismatics has long been one of the most respected and honored aspects of the collecting world. Today it still holds fascination as new collectors come onto the scene every day. The 50 State Quarters series, issued from 1999 to 2008, spurred many to save quarters again and encouraged all types of coin collecting.

The United States has a rich history of coinage. Many of the early states created their own coins until April 1792, when Congress passed an act establishing the U.S. Mint. By 1796, in addition to half cents and cents, the Mint was producing silver half dimes, dimes, quarters, half dollars, and dollars, and gold $2.50, $5, and $10 coins. By the mid-1800s, the Mint was producing about 17 million coins annually in 12 denominations.

The Coinage Act of 1873 brought sweeping changes to the U.S. monetary and coinage systems, and to the Mint's governing structure. The act established the main mint at Philadelphia. President Theodore Roosevelt is credited with encouraging Congress to pass legislation for providing new coin designs. Designs on coins continue to change to reflect events.

Over the years, the Mint has made various adjustments and revisions to U.S. coinage in response to economic conditions prevailing at the time and the cost and supply of the metals from which the coins are produced.

1882 bronze Indian head cent .... **$5-$20**

A coin collection can be whatever an individual wants it to be. Collect the kind of coins and paper money you like and what brings you pleasure as a leisure-time hobby. It's also good to have a strategy and a road map to your collecting pursuits. Here are some tips and comments on traditional collecting strategies.

BY SERIES. The traditional coin-collecting pursuit of acquiring one example of each date and mint mark within a particular series may seem daunting at first considering the long runs of some U.S. coin series. To get started, a collector can break down a series into smaller parts. For example, a collector interested in Lincoln cents can start with those depicting the Lincoln Memorial on the reverse, which began in 1959. A collector can also get started by collecting simply one date of each Lincoln Memorial cent rather than seeking an example of every mint mark of a particular date.

BY TYPE. Rather than seeking an example of every date and mint mark within a series, many collectors seek just one example of each type of coin within a particular focus. For example, a collector assembling a 20th century type set of U.S. 5-cent coins would seek one Liberty nickel, one Buffalo nickel, and one Jefferson nickel. The representative coins could be of any date and mint mark within each series, thus accommodating any collecting budget.

BY THEME. The proliferation of modern commemorative and circulating commemorative coins gave rise to collecting coins with a common theme. Examples include coins that depict animals or ships, coins that commemorate a certain event, or coins of a certain date, such as 2000.

COINS & CURRENCY

BY COLLECTOR'S CHOICE. Various aspects of the listed strategies overlap and can be combined and mixed to form a goal that interests an individual collector. The result should be a coin collection that is affordable and attainable for the collector, and a collection that brings enjoyment and satisfaction.

The first paper money to circulate in the United States was issued during the Colonial era. During the Revolutionary War, the states and Continental Congress continued to issue paper money, but its backing in hard currency was spotty at best.

Demand notes of 1861 were the first paper money issued by the U.S. government, as an emergency measure during the Civil War. The nickname "greenback" for paper money began with these notes, which have a distinctive green back.

The Federal Reserve System was created in 1913. It consists of 12 Federal Reserve banks governed in part by the U.S. government through the Federal Reserve Board. The paper money used today in the United States is issued by the Federal Reserve banks. Federal Reserve notes are produced at the Bureau of Engraving and Printing's main facility in Washington, D.C., and at its Western Currency Facility in Fort Worth, Texas.

For more information on U.S. coins and currency, see *Warman's U.S. Coins & Currency Field Guide*, 5th edition, by Arlyn G. Sieber.

1825 half cent with classic head .... **$75-$110**

1828 large cent with coronet.................. **$35-$80**

1840 large cent with braided hair .... **$30-$35**

1902 Indian head cent .... **$2.50-$10**

1943-S Lincoln cents were produced in zinc-coated steel during World War II ....**65¢-$3**

1964-D Lincoln cent with Lincoln Memorial reverse... **$7**

1863 silver three-cent piece with double border around star .... **$450-$520**

1865 nickel three-cent piece.............. **$17.50-$35**

1896 Liberty nickel. .... **$40-$100**

1913-D Buffalo nickel, buffalo standing on line. .... **$180-$285**

1939 Jefferson nickel .... **25¢-$1.75**

2005-D Jefferson nickel with bison reverse ...**$1.50**

1863 Seated Liberty half dime. .... **$300-$485**

1877 Seated Liberty dime........................**$20-$30**

1898-S Barber dime...............................**$35-$80**

1916-D Mercury dime..................**$3,950-$13,950**

1964 Roosevelt dime........................ **$2.50-$7.50**

1873 Seated Liberty quarter, open 3...... **$45-$130**

1903 Barber quarter... ....**$20-$70**

1916 Standing Liberty quarter, type 1.
.... **$6,900-$9,500**

1945 Washington quarter.. .... **$5-$6**

1966 Washington quarter. **$7.50**

1999-P Delaware State Quarter **$8**

1858-S Seated Liberty half dollar .... **$65-$140**

1921-D Walking Liberty half dollar.... **$575-$2,700**

1976-D Kennedy half dollar with Bicentennial
reverse... **$9**

1871 Seated Liberty dollar with motto above
eagle .... **$330-$545**

1974-D Eisenhower dollar **$7.50**

2007-P George Washington Presidential dollar .. **$3**

1911-D Indian Head gold $2.50.....**$1,150-$2,850**

1850 Liberty gold $20...................**$2,295-$2,475**

1892-S Morgan dollar.....................**$135-$44,500**

1903 Liberty gold $20..................**$1,470-$1,500**

1992-S Olympics commemorative half dollar.... . **$9**

Philadelphia $5 demand note, Series 1861 .... **$3,300-$11,750**

$50 national bank note, Third Charter .... **$2,000-$2,400**

$10 large-size United States note, Series 1901 .... **$800-$2,900**

$10 small-size gold certificate, Series 1928 .... **$90-$250**

$2 large-size silver certificate, Series 1896 .... **$850-$3,000**

$10 small-size silver certificate, special yellow seal, Series 1934A .... **$60-$300**

$10 large-size Federal Reserve note, red seal, Series 1914 ....**$750-$1,500**

$10 large-size Federal Reserve note, blue seal, Series 1914...**$100-$225**

$5 small-size Federal Reserve note, green seal, Series 1928A .... **$25-$100**

$10 small-size Federal Reserve note, Series 2003...**$15**

$50 small-size Federal Reserve note, Series 1969A..**$150**

Comic Books

BACK IN 1993, Sotheby's auctioned a copy of *Fantastic Four #1* (1961) that was said to be the finest copy known to exist. It sold for $27,600, which at the time was considered an unheard-of price for a 1960s comic. Last year, Heritage Auctions sold that same copy for $203,000 ... and it's not even the finest known copy anymore.

It used to be that only comics from the 1930s or 1940s could be worth thousands of dollars. Now, truly high-grade copies of comics from the Silver Age (1956-1969 by most people's reckoning) can sell for four, five, or even six figures. Note I said truly high-grade. Long gone are the days when a near mint condition copy was only worth triple the price of a good condition copy. Now near mint is more like 10-20 times good, and sometimes it's as much as a factor of 1,000.

A trend of the last couple of years has been that the "key" issues have separated even further from the pack, value-wise. Note that not every key is a "#1" issue – if you have *Amazing Fantasy #15, Tales of Suspense #39,* and *Journey into Mystery #83,* you've got the first appearances of Spider-Man, Iron Man, and Thor. (Beware of reprints and replica editions, however.)

The most expensive comics of all remain the Golden Age (1938-1949) first appearances, like Superman's 1938 debut in Action Comics #1, several copies of which have sold for $1 million or more.

Action Comics #1 (1938), CGC-graded 3.0 (good/very good), Billy Wright Collection .. **$298,750**

However, not every single comic from the old days is going up in value. Take western-themed comics. Values are actually going down in this genre as the generation that grew up watching westerns is at the age where they're looking to sell, and there are more sellers than potential buyers.

Comics from the 1970s and later, while increasing in value, rarely reach anywhere near the same value as 1960s issues, primarily because in the 1970s, the general public began to look at comics as a potentially valuable collectible. People took better care of them, and in many cases hoarded multiple copies.

What about 1980s favorites like *The Dark Knight Returns* and *Watchmen*? Here the demand is high, but the supply is really high. These series were heavily hyped at the time and were done by well-known creators, so copies were socked away in great quantities. We've come across more than one dealer who has 20-30 mint copies of every single 1980s

The Amazing Spider-Man #1 (Marvel 1963), CGC-graded 9.0 (very fine/near mint); one of the most sought-after comic books; first issue of most-collected comic book series features first appearances of John Jameson, J. Jonah Jameson, and Chameleon; Jack Kirby and Steve Ditko cover art....... **$47,800**

comic socked away in a warehouse, waiting for the day when they're worth selling.

I should mention one surprise hit of the last couple of years. When Image Comics published *The Walking Dead #1* in 2003, it had a low print run and made no particular splash in the comics world. Once AMC made it into a television series, however, it was a whole different story. High-grade copies of #1 have been fetching $1,000 and up lately.

If you've bought comics at an auction house or on eBay, you might have seen some in CGC holders. Certified Guaranty Co., or CGC, is a third-party grading service that grades a comic book on a scale from 0.5 to 10. These numbers correspond with traditional descriptive grades of good, very fine, near mint and mint, with the higher numbers indicating a better grade. Once graded, CGC encapsulates the comic book in plastic. The grade remains valid as long as the plastic holder is not broken open. CGC has been a boon to the hobby, allowing people to buy comics with more confidence and with the subjectivity of grading taken out of the equation. Unless extremely rare, it's usually only high-grade comics that are worth certifying.

One aspect of collecting that has absolutely exploded in the last 20 years has been original comic art, and not just art for the vintage stuff. In fact, the most expensive piece Heritage Auctions has ever sold was from 1990: Todd McFarlane's cover art for *Amazing Spider-Man #328*, which sold for more than $650,000. It's not unusual for a page that was bought for $20 in the 1980s to be worth $5,000 now.

If you want to get into collecting original comic art, McFarlane would not be the place to start unless you've got a really fat wallet. I suggest picking a current comic artist you like who isn't yet a major "name." Chances are his originals will be a lot more affordable. Another idea is to collect the original art for comic strips. You can find originals for as little as $20, as long as you're not expecting a Peanuts or a Prince Valiant. Heritage Auctions (HA.com) maintains a free online archive of every piece of art they've sold and it is an excellent research tool.

As expensive as both comic books and comic art can be at the high-end of the spectrum, in many ways this is a buyer's market. In the old days you might search for years to find a given issue of a comic; now you can often search eBay and see 10 different copies for sale. Also, comic conventions seem to be thriving in almost every major city – and while the people in crazy costumes get all the publicity, you can also find plenty of vintage comic dealers at these shows. From that point of view, it's a great time to be a comic collector.

—*Barry Sandoval*

Barry Sandoval is Director of Operations for Comics and Comic Art, Heritage Auctions. In addition to managing Heritage's Comics division, which sells some $20 million worth of comics and original comic art each year, Sandoval is a noted comic book evaluator and serves as an advisor to the Overstreet Comic Book Price Guide.

The Amazing Spider-Man #50 (1967), CGC-graded 9.8 (near mint/mint). **$26,290**

All Star Comics #3 (DC, 1940), CGC-graded 9.6 (near mint+), Mile High pedigree. One of the most influential books published during the Golden Age, All Star #3 introduced the team concept to comics.. **$126,500**

Police Comics #1 (Quality, 1941), CGC-graded 9.2 (near mint); book introduces Plastic Man and Phantom Lady and contains first appearances of several other mainstays in Quality lineup, including The Human Bomb and Firebrand; inside art by Will Eisner, Jack Cole, and Reed Crandall.......... **$19,550**

Marvel Comics #1 (Timely, 1939) CGC-graded 8.5 (very fine+), Denver pedigree **$172,500**

The Avengers #4 (1964), CGC-graded 9.6 (near mint)..**$31,070**

The Avengers #1 (Marvel, 1963) CGC-graded 9.4 (near mint)...**$16,900**

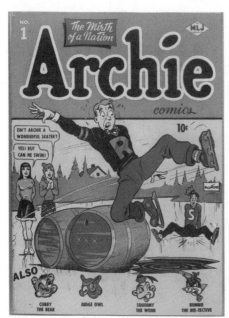

Archie Comics #1 (1942), CGC-graded 8.5 (very fine+). **$167,300**

Vault of Horror #12 (1950), CGC-graded 9.2, Gaines File pedigree. **$29,900**

Daredevil Comics #1 (Lev Gleason, 1941) CGC-
graded 9.6 (near mint)................................**$11,500**

Batman #1 (1940), CGC-graded 8.5 (very fine+),
Billy Wright Collection.............................**$274,850**

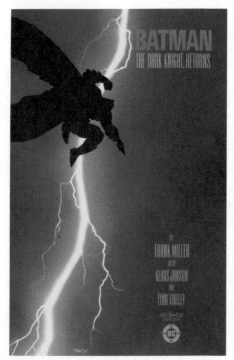

The Brave and the Bold #29 (1960), CGC-graded
8.0 (very fine). **$5,975**

Batman: The Dark Knight Returns #1 (1986),
CGC-graded 9.6 (near mint+)..........................**$143**

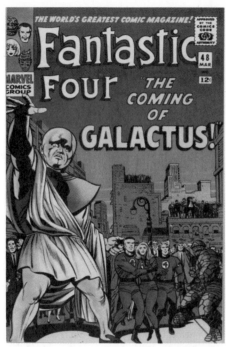

Fantastic Four #48 (1966), CGC-graded 9.8 (near mint/mint). **$13,145**

Conan the Barbarian #1 (1970), CGC-graded 9.8 (near mint/mint), Empire Comics Collection .. **$3,884**

Captain America Comics #1 (1941), CGC-rated 9.0 (very fine/near mint).............................**$96,686**

Flash Comics #1 (1940), CGC-rated 9.6 (near mint)...**$273,125**

Four Color #9 (1942), CGC-graded 8.5 (very fine+). **$7,768**

Green Hornet Comics #1 (1940), CGC-graded 8.5 (very fine). **$14,375**

Green Lantern #76 (1970), CGC-rated 9.8 (near mint/mint). **$37,343**

The Incredible Hulk #1 (1962), CGC-graded 9.2 (near mint)..**$125,475**

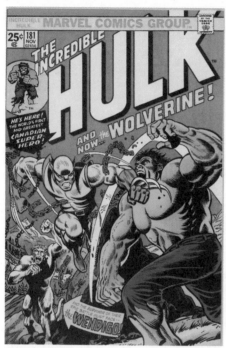

The Incredible Hulk #181 (1974), CGC-graded 9.8 (near mint/mint). **$9,560**

Iron Man #1 (1968), CGC-graded 9.8 (near mint/mint). **$7,468**

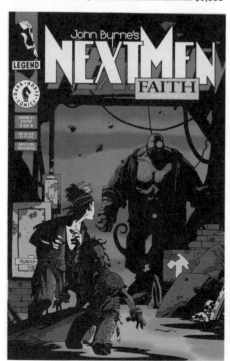

John Byrne's Next Men #21 (1993), second appearance of Hellboy, CGC-graded 9.6 (near mint). **$62**

Journey into Mystery #83 (1962), introduction of Thor, CGC-graded 9.0 (very fine/near mint)...**$13,225**

Justice League of America #28 (1964), CGC-graded 9.6 (near mint). **$1,610**

Marvel Feature #1 Red Sonja (1975), CGC-graded 9.8 (near mint/mint). **$430**

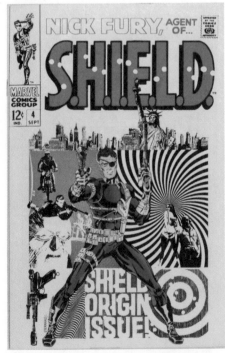

Nick Fury, Agent of S.H.I.E.L.D. #4 (1968), CGC-graded 9.8 (near mint/mint). **$1,135**

Mystery in Space #90 (1964) CGC-graded 9.6 (near mint).. **$1,150**

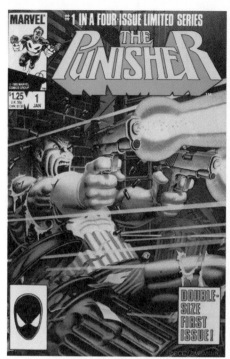

The Punisher #1 (1986), CGC-graded 9.8 (near mint/mint). **$286**

Spawn #1 (1992), CGC-graded 9.8 (near mint/mint). **$42**

The Savage She-Hulk #1 (1980), CGC-graded 9.8 (near mint/mint). **$131**

The Silver Surfer #1 (1968), CGC-graded 9.8 (near mint/mint). **$11,950**

Star Wars #1 (1977), CGC-graded 9.2
(near mint)... **$508**

Tales of Suspense #59 (1964), CGC-graded 9.4
(near mint)... **$1,912**

Superman vs. the Amazing Spider-Man #1 (1976),
very fine/near mint. **$180**

Superman #24 (1943), CGC-graded 9.4 (near
mint)...**$41,825**

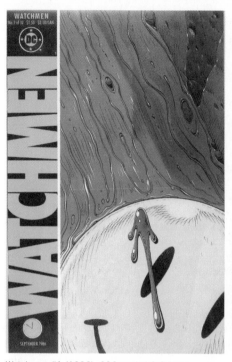

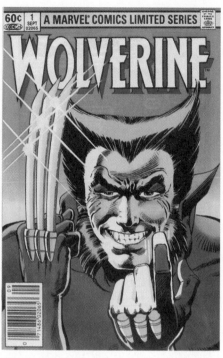

Watchmen #1 (1986), CGC-graded 9.8 (near mint/mint). **$478**

Wolverine (Limited Series) #1 (1982), CGC-graded 10 (mint)..**$15,535**

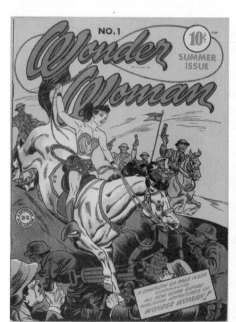

Wonder Woman #1 (1942), CGC-graded 8.5 (very fine+). **$53,775**

X-Men #3 (1964), CGC-graded 9.8 (near mint/mint)..**$16,730**

Cookie Jars

COOKIE JARS EVOLVED from the elegant British biscuit jars found on Victorian-era tables. These 19th century containers featured bail handles, and were often made of sterling silver and cut crystal.

As the biscuit jar was adapted for use in America, it migrated from the dining table to the kitchen and, by the late 1920s, it was common to find a green-glass jar (or pink or clear), often with an applied label and a screw-top lid, on kitchen counters in the typical American home.

Deforest of California Halo Boy/Holy Devil, marked "DeForest of California Copyright 1956" on bottom, crazing, good condition. **$92**

Victorian Casino Antiques

During the Great Depression – when stoneware was still popular, but before the arrival of widespread electric refrigeration – cookie jars in round and barrel shapes arrived. These heavy-bodied jars could be hand-painted after firing. This decoration was easily worn away by eager hands reaching for Mom's bakery. The lids of many stoneware jars typically had small tapering finials or knobs that also contributed to cracks and chips.

The golden age of cookie jars began in the 1940s and lasted for less than three decades, but the examples that survive represent an exuberance and style that have captivated collectors.

It wasn't until the 1970s that many collectors decided – instead of hiding their money in cookie jars – to invest their money in cookie jars. It was also at this time that cookie jars ceased to be simply storage vessels for bakery and evolved into a contemporary art form. And it's because of this evolution from utility to art that, with some exceptions, we have limited the scope of this section to jars made from the 1930s to the early 1970s.

The Brush Pottery Co. of Zanesville, Ohio, produced one of the first ceramic cookie jars in about 1929, and Red Wing's spongeware line from the late 1920s also included a ridged, barrel-shaped jar. Many established potteries began adding a selection of cookie jars in the 1930s.

The 1940s saw the arrival of two of the most famous cookie jars: Shawnee's Smiley and Winnie, two portly, bashful little pigs who stand with eyes closed and heads cocked, he in overalls and bandana, she in flowered hat and long coat. And a host of Disney characters also made their way into American kitchens.

In the 1950s, the first television-influenced jars appeared, including images of Davy Crockett and Popeye. This decade also saw the end of several prominent American potteries (including Roseville) and the continued rise of imported ceramics.

A new collection of cartoon-inspired jars was popular in the 1960s, featuring characters drawn from the Flintstones, Yogi Bear, Woody Woodpecker, and Casper the Friendly Ghost. Jars reflecting the race for space included examples from McCoy and American Bisque. This decade also marked the peak production era for a host of West Coast manufacturers, led by the twin brothers Don and Ross Winton.

For more information on cookie jars, see *Warman's Cookie Jars Identification and Price Guide* by Mark F. Moran.

American Bisque Bear with Beehive flasher, marked "Corner Cookie Jar" on side and "804 USA" near back bottom, eyes look different ways and tongue sticks out, good condition with crazing. **$69**

Victorian Casino Antiques

American Bisque Cheerleaders flasher with "HAVE A COOKIE" and "COOKIE TIME" lettering, marked "802 USA" near bottom, cheerleaders' expressions change. **$84**

Victorian Casino Antiques

American Bisque Clown on Stage flasher, marked "805 USA" near bottom, blue curtains version, "Cookies" embossed at top, flasher eye opens and closes, good condition with some crazing. **$46**

Victorian Casino Antiques

American Bisque Cookies Out of This World Spaceship, marked "USA" near bottom, small chip near front bottom.................. **$84**

Victorian Casino Antiques

American Bisque Fred and Dino, marked "USA" near bottom and "FLINTSTONES" on front, first in Flintstones series, minor crazing. **$115**

Victorian Casino Antiques

American Bisque The Rubbles House, marked "USA" near bottom, very nice condition.. **$108**

Victorian Casino Antiques

American Bisque Sandman Cookies flasher, marked "801 USA" near bottom, "Sandman Cookies" embossed on front, clown on TV flasher version, clown juggles balls, good condition.. **$96**

Victorian Casino Antiques

Victorian Casino Antiques American Bisque Sweet Pea/Swee'pea, unmarked, excellent condition with minor crazing. **$109**

Victorian Casino Antiques

American Bisque Tortoise and the Hare flasher, marked "803 USA" near bottom, hare face changes expression, small hairline crack on bottom part of lid, hard to find jar................ **$75**

Victorian Casino Antiques

COOKIE JARS

American Bisque Umbrella Kids, marked "USA 739" near bottom, raised "COOKIES" lettering on front, good condition with some crazing. **$109**

Victorian Casino Antiques

Brush Pottery Clown with Brown Pants, marked "W22 Brush USA" on bottom, Winton designed, two hairline cracks in back on left side of pants, small chip at top of hat, some crazing. **$60**

Victorian Casino Antiques

Brush Pottery Formal Pig with green coat, marked "W7 USA" on bottom, Winton designed, some crazing. **$84**

Victorian Casino Antiques

Brush Pottery Hillbilly Frog, marked "43D" on bottom, circa 1969, rare and sought after, some crazing, good condition. **$108**

Victorian Casino Antiques

Brush Pottery Humpty Dumpty with yellow beanie, marked "Brush W18 USA" on bottom, Winton designed, circa 1956-1961, good condition with small blemish on left side of beanie, some crazing. **$108**

Victorian Casino Antiques

Brush Pottery Peter Pan, marked "K23 Brush USA" on bottom, circa 1956, smaller size version, good condition.................... **$108**

Victorian Casino Antiques

Brush Pottery Squirrel with Top Hat, marked "W15 USA" on bottom, made in early 1950s, Winton designed, good condition with some crazing... **$58**

Victorian Casino Antiques

Cardinal China Co. Soldier, marked "312 USA Cardinal Copyright" on back near bottom, very good condition. **$108**

Victorian Casino Antiques

McCoy Pottery Green Leprechaun, No. 169, unmarked, limited production, never appeared in McCoy catalogs, excellent condition, exceptionally rare..................**$96**

Victorian Casino Antiques

McCoy Pottery Touring Car, marked "McCoy USA" on bottom, No. 139, good condition. **$36**

Victorian Casino Antiques

National Potteries Corp. Spaceship, marked "NAPCO 1961 Bedford Ohio K5324" on bottom with NAPCO Ceramics paper label, yellow version, "COOKIES OUT OF THIS WORLD!" on front, small paint chipping around jar..............**$96**

Victorian Casino Antiques

Shawnee Pottery Jo Jo the Clown, marked "Shawnee USA 12" on bottom, no gold trim, designed by Robert Heckman, small chip near bottom of lid and on bottom side of clown's collar, good condition..........**$108**

Victorian Casino Antiques

Shawnee Pottery Puss-N-Boots, marked "Patented Puss n Boots USA" on bottom, short tail and maroon bow version, good condition. **$48**

Victorian Casino Antiques

Shawnee Pottery Smiley Pig, marked "USA" on bottom, "1949 W.C." written on bottom, green bandana with shamrocks version, no gold trim, 6" hairline crack on front left side, good condition, no crazing.....**$84**

Victorian Casino Antiques

Sierra Vista Family Circus Billy, unmarked but believed to be Starnes, smiling with teeth version, some crazing, good condition, under-the-paint factory chip near bottom. **$115**

Victorian Casino Antiques

Sierra Vista Stagecoach, marked "Sierra Vista Ceramics Pasadena Calif. USA Copyright 1956" on bottom, glass windows, small chip near bottom and small blemish on lid. **$84**

Victorian Casino Antiques

Weller Mammy, unmarked, circa 1935, crazing, hard-to-find jar. **$48**

Victorian Casino Antiques

Country Store

FEW CATEGORIES OF FINE COLLECTIBLES are as fun and colorful as country store memorabilia. The staple of quality antiques shows and shops nationwide, the phrase often refers to such an expansive field of items that it's often difficult to decide where "country store collectibles" begin and "advertising collectibles" end. However, that's one of the very reasons why the category remains so popular and is growing in value and appeal.

Country store collectibles are associated with items in use in general or frontier retail establishments dating from the mid-1800s and well into the 1940s. The country store was a natural evolution of the pioneer trading post as the more affordable source of day-to-day living items, baking and cooking supplies, or goods for general household and home garden use. Country store furniture is rare, but larger pieces usually include retail countertops and dry goods bins.

The appeal of country store memorabilia has never really waned during the last 40 years; however, the emergence of online trading in the late 1990s redefined items dealers once described as rare. Much like how mid-20th century rock 'n roll and entertainment memorabilia is used to decorate Applebee's restaurants, so have country store collectibles been used to line the walls of Cracker Barrel Restaurant and Old Country Store establishments to evoke big appetites for comfort food.

Kendall's Spavin Cure chromolithograph store poster with metal strips at top and bottom and suspension loop on verso, issued by "d.r. B. J. Kendall Company, Enosburg Falls, VT. U.S.A.," scene of people preparing for hunt with array of Kendall veterinary products placed on steps, girl holding book titled *The Horse*, excellent condition, 22" x 28.5". Posters like this one were displayed in drug stores and general stores throughout the country............**$812**

Heritage Auctions

Among items in high demand are original and complete store displays in top condition. These displays were originally intended to hold the product sold to customers and were not generally available for private ownership. Those that survive are highly sought after by collectors for their graphic appeal and their rarity. Until recently, restoration of these items would negatively impact auction prices. However, recent auction results show strong prices for these items if they are rare and retain most of the original graphics.

A great deal of time, talent and production value was invested in these store displays. Think of them as the Super Bowl commercials of their day. With limited counter space and a captive audience, marketers used every technique and theme available to catch

Paper on board with no glass, unusual piece rarely seen for sale, 1890s, cotton plantation with product being harvested, produced by Johnson & Johnson to go in drug stores to advertise its product. **$840**

Morphy Auctions

customers' eyes. And here is where the appeal of country store collectibles crosses over so many different categories of collectibles. A store display of a fine paper poster advertising DeLaval Cream Separators may appeal to those who collect farming items, cows, and country maidens in addition to country store items. The same principal applies to store displays. Are they collected as country store items or as well-preserved examples of vintage advertising, or both? The definition takes shape when the items are added to a well-curated collection, like the one Bill and Kathie Gasperino amassed over the last 35 years.

The couple sold the collection in April 2013 with Showtime Auction Services, as part of a massive collectibles event that realized more than $2.2 million. The couple happily traveled across the Pacific Northwest and beyond cultivating a collection of obscure and unusual items. It was a true team effort. "Kathie and I drove all over – Montana, Idaho and Oregon," Bill says. "Half the fun was finding the stuff. We loved crawling around attics and basements of old stores finding things."

The Gasperino collection was displayed next to the couple's Washington State home in a large building designed to look like a circa 1880s country store. "We had dry goods on one side, and on the other was a combination of things you'd find in a store of that period," Bill says. As they encountered more items, the two began branching out to larger and larger items, such as country spool cabinets and eventually back bars, a bank teller booth, and even a 19th century soda fountain.

When it came time to downsize, the Gasperino collection hit the hobby like a comet. It remains one of the most important collections offered in recent years. Even the Gasperinos were surprised at the prices collectors were willing to pay for especially rare items in top condition.

"People called us and let us know how much they appreciated the collection and the quality," says Bill, a retired police officer. "We knew it was special to us, but it was interesting to hear from collectors who said they hadn't seen some of these items."

The Gasperino Collection is a good example of why the country store collectibles category continues to hold its own. The category was extremely popular between the late 1970s and the mid-1990s. It appears the hobby is reaching a point at which longtime collectors are ready to begin a new phase of their lives – one that requires fewer items and less space – and are offering these collections for the first time in decades.

So if the old adage, "The best time to buy an antique is when you see it" is true, the country store collectibles category stands to grow as these large collections come to market, and the crossover appeal catches the attention of a wide variety of collectors.

COUNTRY STORE

Bottle with label from Peoples Service Drug Store in Harrisburg, Pennsylvania, bottle has no wear, near mint condition, 5" h...... **$240**

Morphy Auctions

Knight's Castile Toilet Soap counter display, wood with slanted glass bottom, late 19th century, soapwork company based in London, three columns for red, purple, and gold brands, very good/excellent condition, 21" h. x 13" w. x 11" d. **$300**

Rich Penn Auctions

Art Deco toilet paper die-cut cardboard sign, A.P.W. Paper Co., Albany, New York, dated 1926, "Four rolls are one year's supply," shows young girl on giant roll, old bend on girl's foot, otherwise excellent condition, matted and framed, 25" h. x 21" w. **$300**

Rich Penn Auctions

Diamond Dye cabinet, fairy with wand front panel, lithograph on embossed metal by Wells and Richardson Co., oak/ash case, advertising panel, late 19th century, fair/good condition, case very good condition, 30" h. x 23" w. x 10" d. **$480**

Rich Penn Auctions

Red Rose Tea embossed metal sign, good/very good condition with additional mounting holes, 19-1/2" h. x 29" w. **$900**

Rich Penn Auctions

Advertising signs: Old Reliable Coffee lithograph on paper, Yeast Foam lithograph on paper with metal top and bottom edges, and Farmers Pride embossed metal by Geo Ackermann and Sons, Cincinnati, Ohio, all excellent condition, 6" h. to 21" h....... **$36**

Rich Penn Auctions

Advertising wrapping paper holder with cutter, "Chew Spear-Head" embossed on cutoff blade, in wood shipping frame, circa 1895, original paper reads, "From E.B. Weston and Co., makers of Climax Roll Paper Holders and Cutters-Dayton, OH," rare find in excellent condition, 21" h. x 18" w. x 7-1/2" d. **$210**

Rich Penn Auctions

Curtiss Candies 5¢ candy bars display, lithograph on metal multi-shelf with graphics, manufactured by Advertising Metal Display Co., New York and Chicago, some paint loss and wear, otherwise very good+ condition, 20" h. x 9-1/2" w. x 21-3/4" d. **$900**

Rich Penn Auctions

COUNTRY STORE

Seed counter, oak flat front, 10 windows and 10 drawers with iron pulls, early 20th century, excellent refinished condition, 34" h. x 90" w. x 28" d. **$1,440**

Rich Penn Auctions

Sunbeam Bread advertising sign, Little Miss Sunbeam lithograph on self-framed embossed metal by Stout Sign Co., circa 1960s, good+ condition, 12" h. x 30" w.................................**$330**

Rich Penn Auctions

Coffee bean dispenser, King Bee Coffee, reverse-painted glass advertising on three sides, metal base, lid and frame, lights up with bulb inside lid, corner crack in back glass panel, excellent condition, 27-1/2" h. x 14" w. x 16" d. **$780**

Rich Penn Auctions

Red Goose Shoes display, figural papier-mâché goose in pressed cardboard base that lays golden eggs full of surprises, electric, very good working condition, 32-1/2" h. x 26" l. ..**$600**

Rich Penn Auctions

Seed counter, Sherer, mid-20th century, oak with 10 front display windows on angled front and 10 drawers at back with iron pulls, metal "Sherer" maker's tag at bottom, paneled sides, excellent refinished condition, 34" h. x 90" w............................**$1,440**

Rich Penn Auctions

Advertising display rack, Wear-Ever advertising on all sides, triangular-shaped cast iron with graduated display shelves, excellent condition, 53" h. x 20-1/2" w...............**$210**

Rich Penn Auctions

Peanut dispenser, circa 1920s, cast aluminum base with tall glass cylinder and domed metal lid, door at bottom to dispense product, very good/excellent original condition, 33" h. x 13" sq. **$300**

Rich Penn Auctions

Boye Curtain Fixture and Dress Fasteners counter displays, metal and wood, one dated 1920, one very good condition, other excellent condition, larger 8" h. x 18" sq. **$150**

Rich Penn Auctions

K&W Fancy Print Butter carrier, wood with iron handle, latch and corner straps, excellent condition, 8-1/2" h. x 17" w.**$180**

Rich Penn Auctions

Tins for potato chips, cream mints, marshmallows, pretzel sticks and tea, 20th century, all very good and excellent condition, up to 11-1/2" h. . **$420**

Rich Penn Auctions

Counter display case, Sauer's Flavoring Extracts, wood with etched front panel and reverse gold leaf, early 1900s, old crack in one side of glass, desirable case in very good condition with old surface, 21" h. x 15" w. X 11" d. **$1,020**

Rich Penn Auctions

Collar case, oak with original Illinois Showcase Works decal, late 19th century, very good condition with no bottom, 25-1/2" h. x 20-1/2" w. x 8-1/2" d. **$480**

Rich Penn Auctions

Diamond Dyes cabinet, "May Pole" embossed lithograph on metal, circa 1900, very good condition with some paint loss and minor rust, 30" h. x 23-1/4" w. x 10" d. **$780**

Rich Penn Auctions

Uncle Sam Peanut Warmer, circa 1900, lithograph on metal counter display from U.S. Baking Co., Fort Wayne, Indiana, rare, some roughness on top panel, otherwise very good condition, 22" h. **$2,640**

Rich Penn Auctions

Oversized pair of Fitz overalls display, circa 1930s, denim, name across front and on each suspender, very good+ condition with minor wear, 120" h. x 40" w. **$1,200**

Rich Penn Auctions

Nuts and bolts cabinet, octagon shape on revolving base, 72 drawers with pressed fronts and porcelain knobs, painted wood, very good condition, 29-3/4" h. x 20-3/4" dia. **$1,320**

Rich Penn Auctions

Display figure for Chi-namel Paint, papier-mâché "Coolie" with detachable hand, made by Old King Cole, circa 1910, very good condition with some repair, 30" h. **$960**

Rich Penn Auctions

DECOYS

Decoys

THE ORIGIN OF THE DECOY in America lies in early American history, pre-dating the American pioneer by at least 1,000, perhaps 2,000 years. In 1924, at an archeological site in Nevada, the Lovelock Cave excavations yielded a group of 11 decoys preserved in protective containers. The careful manner of their storage preserved them for us to enjoy an estimated 1,000 to 2,000 years later.

When the first settlers came to North America, their survival was just as dependent upon hunting wild game for food as it was for the Indians. They began to fashion likenesses of their prey out of different materials, ultimately finding that wood was an ideal raw material. Thus, the carving of wildfowl decoys was born out of necessity for food.

Historical records indicate wooden decoys were in general use as early as the 1770s, but it seems likely that they would have been widely used before then.

Carved and painted swan decoy, 20th century, 35" l. **$1,020**

Pook & Pook, Inc.

Until the middle of the 1800s, there was not sufficient commercial demand for decoys to enable carvers to make a living selling them, so most decoys were made for themselves and friends. Then the middle of the 19th century saw the birth of the market gunners. During the market-gunning period, many carvers began making a living with their decoys, and the first factory-made decoys came into existence. The huge numbers of decoys needed to supply the market hunters and the rising numbers of hunters for sport or sustenance made commercial decoy carving possible.

The market hunters and other hunters killed anything that flew. This indiscriminate destruction of wildfowl was the coup de grace for many bird species, rendering them extinct.

The United States Congress, with the passage of the Migratory Bird Treaty Act in 1918, outlawed the killing of waterfowl for sale. Following the passage of the 1918 act came the demise of the factory decoys of the day.

Today a few contemporary carvers carry on their tradition. They produce incredibly intricate, lifelike birds. Decoy carving is one of the few early American folk arts that has survived into our modern times and is still being pursued.

For more information on decoys, see *Warman's Duck Decoys* by Russell E. Lewis.

DECOYS

$

Life-size decorative carved robin with glass eyes, circa 1930, by A. Elmer Crowell of East Harwich, Massachusetts, exceptional painted feather detail, rectangular stamp...................................... **$5,500**

Life-size decorative carved kingfisher with glass eyes, holding carved fish in its bill, mounted on oval painted wooden base, circa 1930, by A. Elmer Crowell of East Harwich, Massachusetts, rectangular stamp......................................**$16,000**

Eldred's

Pair of carved and painted hollow body red head duck decoys, mid-20th century, 14-1/2" l........ **$660**

Pook & Pook, Inc.

Two carved and painted duck decoys, both signed and dated R. Madison Mitchell 1972, 15" l. and 15-1/2" l., together with carved and painted widgeon, signed and dated 1973, 14" l........... **$510**

Pook & Pook, Inc.

Two life-size shorebird decoys, greater yellowlegs and lesser yellowlegs, mounted together on driftwood base, 20th century, both by Alvin A. White of Sandwich, Massachusetts, both signed "White" under tails.. **$265**
Life-size yellowlegs in running form, mounted on driftwood base, 20th century, by Alvin A. White of Sandwich, Massachusetts, some paint loss, signed "White" under tail. **$185**

Eldred's

Canadian carved and painted eider decoy, circa 1930, attributed to Jesse Obed, Nova Scotia, 14-1/4" l. **$2,280**

Pook & Pook, Inc.

Carved and painted preening swan decoy, 20th century, 28" l. **$450**

Pook & Pook, Inc.

Carved and painted Cobb Island-style Brandt decoy, signed M. S. McNair, mid-20th century, 24" l. **$660**

Pook & Pook, Inc.

Carved and painted Cobb Island-style swimming Canada goose decoy, mid-20th century, signed M. S. McNair, 28-1/4" l. **$2,880**

Pook & Pook, Inc.

Pair of carved and painted fish decoys, mid-20th century, 13" l. and 13-1/2" l., together with another decoy, 13" l. **$2,400**

Pook & Pook, Inc.

Eight duck hunting decoys, including one signed on underside "Red Breasted Merganser / by my hand / Joe Anderlik / Jan. 1983 / For Jonathan Winters"; common goldeneye engraved on underside "W. Wandelt - L.I. N.Y."; and large waterfowl stamped JP on underside; largest 21-1/4" x 9-1/2" x 8". Provenance: From the Estate of Jonathan Winters. .... **$400-$600**

Julien's Auctions

Vintage pintail drake duck hunting decoy, inscribed in ink to underside "The Ward Bros. / Crisfield, MD. / 1936 / REJ" along with small sticker that reads, "Pintail Dr." **$125**

Julien's Auctions

Finely carved redhead drake, retains original paint, early Canadian, circa 1900, 16" l. ....**$200-$300**

Midwest Auction Galleries

Miniature barn owl, maker unknown, some damage to legs, mounted on driftwood base. ....**$200-$300**

Eldred's

Quarter-size redhead drake decoy and near life-size cardinal, both by Peter Peltz of East Sandwich, Massachusetts, both signed and identified on underside of driftwood bases..**$330**

Eldred's

DECOYS

Miniature horned grebe with chick on its back, mounted on driftwood base, 20th century, by Stan Sparre of Hingham, Massachusetts.................. **$285**

Eldred's

Miniature pair of sanderlings, 20th century, mounted on driftwood base, by Stan Sparre of Hingham, Massachusetts, signed on base "Stan Sparre, Hingham Mass." **$205**

Massachusetts carved and painted yellowlegs shorebird decoy, circa 1900, 9-1/2" l. **$780**

Pook & Pook, Inc.

A. Elmer Crowell-style black-bellied plover decoy by Jerome Howes of Putney, Vermont, turned head with glass eyes, carved wings. **$185**

Eldred's

Fifty-piece collection of A. Elmer Crowell-style miniature bird carvings, 23 ducks or geese, four shorebirds, two upland birds, and 21 assorted songbirds, most mounted on circular wooden bases, all stamped on underside "Elmer Crowell by Jerome Howes" with rubber stamp. **$4,600**

Eldred's

DECOYS

Life-size robin snipe decoy with glass eyes, 20th century, by Alvin A. White of Sandwich, Massachusetts, bill reglued, signed "White" under tail. **$230**

Life-size piping plover decoy with glass eyes, 20th century, by Alvin A. White of Sandwich, Massachusetts, mounted on driftwood base, signed "White" under tail. **$265**

Life-size black-bellied plover decoy with glass eyes, 20th century, by Alvin A. White of Sandwich, Massachusetts, mounted on driftwood base, signed "White" under tail. **$205**

Two life-size decoys, curlew and sanderling, 20th century, both with glass eyes and mounted on driftwood bases, both by Alvin A. White of Sandwich, Massachusetts, curlew with minor paint flaking. **$310**

Eldred's

Miniature goldeneye drake, head turned slightly right, raised wingtips, by James Lapham of Dennisport, Massachusetts, signed on underside of round wooden base. **$420**

Miniature green-winged teal drake in unusual tucked head position, by James Lapham of Dennisport, Massachusetts, signed on underside of round wooden base. **$380**

Miniature wood duck drake by James Lapham of Dennisport, Massachusetts, signed on underside of round wooden base. **$350**

Eldred's

Pair of wood duck decoys by George Strunk of Glendora, New Jersey, glass eyes, carved wings and tail feathers, drake with head turned slightly to right, hen in resting position with head turned to left, branded on bottom "G. Strunk." **$1,100**

Eldred's

DECOYS

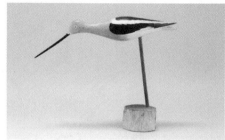

Life-size carving of a common tern by Robert Innis (1893-1983) of South Dennis, Massachusetts, green patinated finish, damage to bill and wing tip, mounted on carved rockery wooden base, signed on base "Robert Innis, South Dennis Massachusetts 1967." **$440**

Eldred's

Life-size avocet decoy in running form with iron bill, 20th century, by Alvin A. White of Sandwich, Massachusetts, hairline crack at area of bill, mounted on a cedar post base. **$245**

Eldred's

Brant decoy, original paint, rough carved finish, discovered in Whiting barn in Chilmark, Martha's Vineyard. **$764**

Life-size carving of a black-footed penguin by Daniel Bruffee of Plymouth, Massachusetts, glass eyes, carved bill and wings, chip-carved base, stamped in black ink on bottom "Daniel L. Bruffee Decoys Plymouth, MA," signed in pencil below stamp.. **$965**

Eldred's

Two contemporary eider drake decoys from Tenant's Harbor, Maine, carved and painted eyes, inletted heads. **$535**

Eldred's

Canvas-covered Canada goose decoy, circa 1940s, original paint with gunning wear, from Orleans, Massachusetts, maker unknown. **$295**

Eldred's

Life-size Atlantic brant decoy in flying form, glass eyes, carved bill, tail and feet, by Mike Borrett of Madison, Wisconsin. **$1,750**

Eldred's

Life-size great horned owl decoy, glass eyes, mechanized wings, mounted on rockery-style base, by Mike Borrett of Madison, Wisconsin, branded Borrett on base, 25.5" h. **$2,100**

Eldred's

Life-size decorative carved blue jay with glass eyes, carved tail feathers, circa 1930, by A. Elmer Crowell of East Harwich, Massachusetts, mounted on oval base with oval brand **$7,500**

Life-size decorative carved towhee with painted tack eyes, circa 1930, by A. Elmer Crowell of East Harwich, Massachusetts, mounted on oval painted base, no stamp **$3,500**

Eldred's

DECOYS

Pair of mallard duck plaques, glass eyes, by Mike Borrett of Madison, Wisconsin, drake carved on reverse "Borrett 02". **$560**

Eldred's

Life-sized carving of a hooded merganser hen, in flying form, glass eyes, ornate carved and painted feather detail, maker unknown, right wing with restoration, branded on reverse "Ferreira." **$285**

Eldred's

Folk art carving of life-size great blue heron, mid-20th century, painted shades of gray, blue, black and white, tack eyes, rectangular wooden base, discovered in Westport, Massachusetts home, 46" h. x 41" l. **$385**

Eldred's

Full-size competition goose by Jim Denison of Rockford, Michigan, 1983, hollow carved, finished in acrylics, entered in woodcarving contests, which explains its lifelike realism, 10-3/4" h. x 21" l.; Denison won international acclaim for his decoys................. **$250**

Cowan's Auctions

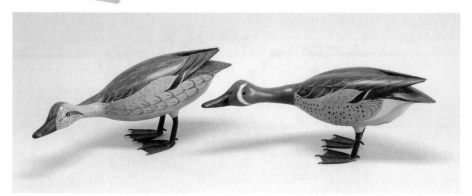

Pair of blue-winged teal carvings in standing form by Charles Moore and Virgil Hodge. **$510**

Eldred's

Mason Decoy Co. carved and painted premier grade mallard duck, circa 1910, minor paint wear, age crack to body, 17-1/2" l. .... **$1,500-$2,500**

Pook & Pook, Inc.

Male and female pintails, American, third quarter 20th century, attributed to James Mossmeier (1897-1969) of New Orleans, minor paint loss, drake's beak repaired, left side of hen's body has sustained shots, areas cracked, male duck 17-1/2" l. **$600**

Cowan's Auctions

Swimming canvasback branded White (probably S.R. White), American, 20th century, working decoy with lead pad weight and anchor line wrapped around chest, 5-1/2" h. x 17" l. **$125**

Cowan's Auctions

Carved and painted wood mallard drake, American, attributed to Louisiana tradition, 15" l. **$275**

Cowan's Auctions

Carved and hand-painted shorebird with painted eyes by Lou Barkelow, Forked River, New Jersey, circa 1880-1890, stamped S.G.H. and B.P. on bottom, on driftwood stand, 10-1/2" l. **$500**

Cowan's Auctions

Five repainted shaped wood Downeast black ducks with wing detail and glass eyes, American (Maine), 19" l. **$500**

Cowan's Auctions

10 **Things** You Didn't Know About **Wildfowl Decoys**

1 Today decoy carving is considered one of the earliest forms of American folk art.

2 An early bufflehead drake decoy, circa 1910, made by renowned carver A. E. Crowell, fetched $207,000 during Decoys Unlimited's 2013 Summer Decoy Auction. This drake decoy is believed to be one of only two in such pristine grade to exist, and it was built to be a working decoy but was never rigged.

During Guyette, Schmidt & Deeter's Summer Decoy Auction in August 2013, a near mint "dust jacket" black bellied plover sold for $190,000.

3 Every April thousands of people gather for the Midwest Decoy Collector's Show. Regularly held in Chicago, the number of decoys on display at the show routinely tops 20,000. In 2013, the show marked its 47th anniversary.

4 Initially decoys were created to draw birds in closer to the shore, and awaiting hunters. Archeological research has shown early decoys made by Native Americans were made of grass and mud as well as skin and feathers of other birds. European settlers brought the idea of carving decoys from wood, and by the mid-19th century the practice was widespread.

5 Two magazines popular with decoy carvers and collectors are Decoy Magazine and Wildfowl Carving Magazine.

6 During Guyette, Schmidt & Deeter's Summer Decoy Auction on Aug. 1-2, 2013, a near mint "dust jacket" black bellied plover carved in the late 1800s by A.E. Crowell earned top lot fame, ahead of all 627 duck decoy lots, when it sold for $190,000.

7 The waterfowl market hunting business of the late 1800s and 1900s brought "factory decoys" into the mainstream, putting decoy companies like Dodge, Peterson, and Mason on the map. In 1918 things changed with the approval of the Migratory Bird Treaty Act, which outlawed the hunting of waterfowl for sale.

8 While various museums across the country feature decoys among their exhibits, two of the most popular destinations for decoy lovers is the Havre de Grace Decoy Museum in Havre de Grace, Maryland (www.decoymuseum.com) and The Ward Museum of Wildfowl Art at Salisbury University, Maryland (www.wardmuseum.org).

9 In addition to the "traditional" criteria that factor into determining the value of most antiques (condition, rarity, and grade), when assessing duck decoys, species and sex matter because the majority of decoys made were drakes versus hens. A decoy in an uncommon position, such as sleeping, swimming, preening, etc., has added value.

10 While factory-made decoys are often identified by brand, traditional hand-carved decoys are categorized by schools, which are based largely on geographic region. For instance, the Maine School and Canadian Maritime Provinces, among others.

— *Compiled by Antoinette Rahn*

WILDFOWL DECOYS

10 THINGS

Sources: Thousand Island Museum (www.timuseum.org), Decoy Magazine (www.decoymag.com), Warman's Duck Decoys, Guyette, Schmidt & Deeter (www.guyetteandschmidt.com), Decoys Unlimited (www.decoysunlimitedinc.net)

Disney

COLLECTIBLES THAT FEATURE Mickey Mouse, Donald Duck, and other famous characters of cartoon icon Walt Disney are everywhere. They can be found with little effort at flea markets, garage sales, local antiques and toys shows, and online as well as through auction houses and specialty catalogs.

Of Disney toys, comics, posters, and other items produced from 1930s through 1960s, prewar Disney material is by far the most desirable.

Part of seven 11" x 14" lobby cards for "Snow White and the Seven Dwarfs" issued in 1937. Provenance: From Don Maris Collection............................ **$2,783**

Hake's Americana

Full-figure production drawing of Mickey Mouse as Steamboat Willie credited to Ub Iwerks, from 1928 animation short known as first Mickey Mouse cartoon, 4-5/8" h. lead pencil image on 9-1/2" x 12" animation sheet....................................... **$4,668**

Hake's Americana

Mickey the Musical Mouse tin litho toy, 1930, Germany, 4-5/8" x 9-3/4"..**$13,891**

Hake's Americana

DISNEY

"Mickey Mouse" 1962 daily comic strip original art with Mickey Mouse and Morty, India ink image area with three panels, 5" x 17-3/4"... **$417**

Hake's Americana

Mickey Mouse Mouscar Award presented to legendary Big Band leader Benny Goodman in 1961 after first Disneyland Big Band Festival at Plaza Garden, Disneyland, 8-1/2" h. award on 2-1/2" h. plastic base. **$2,783**

Hake's Americana

Mickey Mouse Magazine, Vol. 1, No. 7, April 1936, published by Hal Horne, Inc., 8-1/4" x 11-1/2", 36 pages.............. **$256**

Hake's Americana

Mickey Mouse Soap button, 1930s, with "You're Telling Me!" tagline, backstamp reads "The Leo Hart Co., Rochester, N.Y.," 1-1/4". Provenance: From Maurice Sendak Collection. **$1,771**

Hake's Americana

Mickey Mouse cowboy doll, Knickerbocker Toy Co., 1936, 9" h. **$1,202**

Hake's Americana

Mickey Mouse Walker celluloid toy with original box, 1934, George Borgfeldt Corp., made in Japan...**$6,092**

Hake's Americana

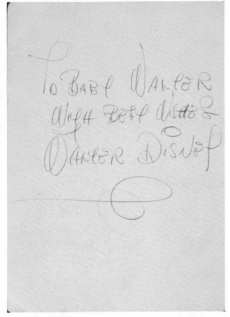

Walt Disney signed London chop menu, signed in rare "Walter" version, PSA/DNA. **$1,110**

Collect Auctions

Large theater cartoon display standee advertising 1937 Mickey Mouse cartoon "The Whalers," 1936, 35-1/2" x 59-1/2".................................... **$6,199**

Hake's Americana

Walt Disney signed check display, dated May 11, 1960, PSA/DNA. **$1,434**

Legendary Auctions

Mickey Mouse and Clarabelle Cow Bavarian china alphabet bowl, Schumann, 1932, 8" dia. x 1-3/4" d... **$209**

Hake's Americana

1965 Donruss "Disneyland" unopened five-cent wax box with 24 packs. **$1,126**

Legendary Auctions

DISNEY

Mickey Mouse metal cigarette and matchbox holder, German, 1930s. **$863**

Hake's Americana

Donald Duck waddling wind-up celluloid toy, 1930s, made in Japan, 8" h....................**$13,017**

Hake's Americana

Mickey Mouse Jack-in-the-Box, Marks Bros. Co., 1930s.... **$1,518**

Hake's Americana

Alice in Wonderland Walrus decanter set, Goebel, eight pieces, 1951. .... **$1,025**

Hake's Americana

Mickey Mouse Dutch chocolate tin, "Simon DeWit's Gestampte Muisjes," each of 14 windows with different image of Mickey or Minnie Mouse, 4-3/4" h .. **$230**

Hake's Americana

Walt Disney's Donald Duck comic, No. 4, CGC FN-5.5, Dell, 1940. .... **$6,573**

Heritage Auctions

Mickey Mouse and Pluto bisque toothbrush holder, 1930s, made in Japan, 4-3/4" h. **$171**

Hake's Americana

Three Little Pigs watch, Ingersoll, 1934, with original box, 4-1/2" l. **$630**

Hake's Americana

Charles Fazzino 3-D limited edition artwork, "Disney at Drive In." **$1,093**

Wickliff Auctioneers

Mickey Mouse wind-up clock, Ingersoll, 1933, metal case with paper strip across top and down each side showing images of Mickey and Minnie Mouse, Pluto, Horace Horsecollar and Clarabelle Cow, 4-1/2" sq. x 2-1/2" d. **$782**

Hake's Americana

1958 Topps Zorro five-cent bubble gum display box, empty. **$533**

Legendary Auctions

Original Walt Disney photo, March 6, 1934.......**$119**

Legendary Auctions

Mickey Mouse celluloid inkwell set, 1930s, Japan. **$173**

Hake's Americana

Mickey Mouse enamel and silvered metal figure on celluloid bookmark, 1930s, likely made in Great Britain. **$474**

Hake's Americana

DISNEY

$

TOP LOT!

Mickey Mouse With the Movie Stars complete set, 24 cards in all, all SGC-graded, 1930s. Provenance: From Maurice Sendak Collection. **$14,438**

Hake's Americana

Early Mickey Mouse pencil sharpener by Catalin Plastic, 1930s, 1" l............**$421**

Hake's Americana

"Steamboat Willie" animation cel, 9-1/2" x 11-3/4". **$633**

Burns White Galleries

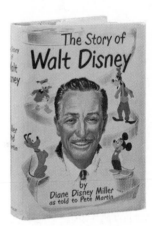

The Story of Walt Disney signed by Disney and 38 members of his staff, 1956, first edition book. **$5,535**

Profiles in History

Donald Duck Bread promotional countertop standee, 1950s, cardboard display with easel back, 8" x 10". **$224**

Hake's Americana

Fantasia Pegasus ceramic vase by Vernon Kilns, solid light blue, 1940, 4-3/4" x 11-1/2" x 8" h. **$348**

Hake's Americana

DISNEY

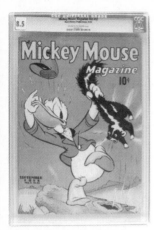

Mickey Mouse Magazine, Vol. 3, No. 12, CGC VF+ 8.5, K/K Publications/Western Publishing Co., 1938. .... **$359**

Heritage Auctions

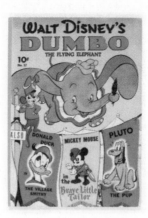

Dumbo the Flying Elephant, No. 17, Dell, 1941, FR condition. **$102**

Heritage Auctions

1938 R45 Yankee Doodle Gum Co. "Dopey's Dominoes" display box with 85 unopened packs. **$1,554**

Legendary Auctions

1956 Davy Crockett coonskin cap in original box. **$598**

Legendary Auctions

"Dude Duck" original movie poster, 1951, 39" x 25". . **$1,323**

DuMouchelles

1956 Topps Davy Crockett salesman's sample three-card advertising panel, 7-7/8" x 3-3/4". **$837**

Legendary Auctions

Mickey Mouse tin litho sand pail, Ohio Art Co. **$900**

Morphy Auctions

Arnold Palmer signed Mickey Mouse animation cel, "A Swell Day for Golf," 9-1/2". **$923**

DuMouchelles

Mickey Mouse Express with original box, Marx Toys, 9" dia **$680**

Bertoia Auctions

Dolls

TODAY AS WE SHOP FOR DOLLS, the label "Made in China" is ever present, but the Asian influence in the doll world was seen much earlier.

In 1851, Edmund Lindner, a prominent doll merchant from Sonneberg, Germany, visited the London World Exhibition. One of the doll displays that caught his eye was a group of dolls from the Orient. These dolls, unlike any others seen by Linder, were different. Most of the dolls previously produced in Germany and in France represented ladies. These Oriental dolls had youthful faces and represented young children and infants.

Oriental taufling dolls were first seen in London in 1851.

Sherry Minton

Dressed very simply, the Oriental dolls had moveable hands and feet. The lower arms and legs were hollow cylinders made of stiffened paper or papier maché. The hip was also papier maché as was the head and shoulder plate. The torso area was made of paper. This paper connected the shoulder plate to the hips. Within this paper cylinder, a round crier was placed. When the body was squeezed together, a sound was made. Rice paper also connected the lower arm to the shoulder and the lower leg to the hip. This type of jointing is referred to as a "floating joint" because of its ease of movement.

When Lindner saw these unique dolls, he purchased one and took it back to one of the doll manufacturers in Sonneberg. He asked that the manufacturer produce a similar doll.

The doll was an instant success and the manufacturer could not keep up with the orders. The first dolls produced were of papier maché; the next were wax or wax over papier maché. The dolls were dressed simply in a shift and a bonnet and were referred to as "tauflings," meaning baby or young child.

These round-faced, short-necked dolls became an instant hit with children. Many doll firms in both Germany and France produced examples. The paper joints were eventually replaced by fine kid leather or linen, and along with the wax and papier maché heads, china and bisque heads were added. The very round face and short neck remained fashionable for about 30 years.

Along with the taufling body with its many floating joints, round-faced heads were also placed on the more familiar cloth and kid bodies. The round head with little or no hair, very popular in the 1850s, was modified and heads with molded hairstyles became very desirable. Even with molded hair, including curls and molded decorations, the round face and short neck remained popular, especially in Germany and therefore in America because Americans were their major customers.

The "covered wagon" china head doll epitomizes the simple hairstyle we think of when we imagine women in wagon trains headed to the American West in the 1800s.

Sherry Minton

The Frozen Charlotte, also known as a "pillar" or "bathing doll," is immobile and composed entirely of china. Also shown: A bald china head that would have sported a wig of hair.

Sherry Minton

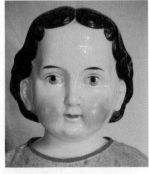

Modified flat top china head doll features hair that is parted in the middle and flat on top with short curls around the base.

Sherry Minton

One of the most beautiful dolls from this period is the "covered wagon" hairstyle. While very simple in design, a covered wagon china is the picture of what a china should be. Her hair is parted in the middle, falls smoothly down to her ears and is in vertical curls around her head. Hers is the face we visualize when we picture covered wagons traveling West with strong women in bonnets protecting themselves from the weather. While much different from the earlier tauflings, this doll still retains the round face and short neck that Lindner found so appealing.

During the period from 1850 through 1880, hairstyles of chinas varied. Some were bald and had hair wigs. Some had elaborate molded decorations in their hair. Some were simple and elegant.

The doll business in Germany was very competitive, and manufacturers were always in search of the next "look" to grab the market. One new look was the Frozen Charlotte doll. This immobile doll, entirely made of china, came in sizes from less than an inch to at least 16 inches. More correctly called a pillar doll or a bathing doll, this doll still retained the very round face and short neck of the taufling.

By the 1880s, the popularity of china heads was beginning to wane. Bisque dolls with open and close eyes and realistic ball joint bodies were pushing chinas aside. Many chinas of the 1880s have variations of the popular flat top hairstyle—parted in the middle and flat on top with short curls around the base. This face still retained the short neck and round face of the Oriental tauflings first seen in London in 1851.

The Doll Market

We know the current economy is still recovering and that all markets have suffered, including the doll market. But there is light at the end of the tunnel.

There is plenty of supply on the market right now, allowing collectors to pick and choose. Perfect examples are still bringing top dollar while mediocre examples stay on the table.

Attendance at doll shows is improving. Auction prices at the last three major doll auctions have exceeded presale estimates for the rare and unusual.

Now is the time to buy. If you are trying to sell your dolls, it will depend on what you have. If you have collected wisely and have dolls in excellent condition, you should do well.

—Sherry Minton

Kestner 162 bisque socket head lady doll, glass sleep eyes, open mouth, antique, possibly original human hair wig, slender composition lady body with straight wrists, original finish, stamped Germany on rear of torso, cheek rubs, detailed finger and toe paint, 16".....**$700**

McMasters Harris Auction Co.

ABG 1322 character baby doll, German bisque socket head, fully incised, made by Alt, Beck & Gottschalck, wig pulls, black specks, multi-stroked eyebrows, side-glancing flirty eyes with tin eyelids, open mouth with upper teeth, original human hair wig, chubby composition baby body with original finish, some soil, crocheted dress and sweater, booties, hat and extra white lace-trimmed baby dress, 23".....**$480**

Morphy Auctions

French Tete Jumeau bisque musical automaton doll, late 19th century, inscribed, "Depose Tete Jumeau 3te S.G.D.G. 4," 18" h..........**$2,160**

Pook & Pook, Inc.

French composition doll, 19th century, glass eyes, painted mouth, kid leather body, period glass dome (not shown), 21-1/2" h..........**$492**

Pook & Pook, Inc.

Gebruder Heubach 7759 pouty baby doll, solid dome bisque socket head with molded and painted hair and facial features, chipped bisque at neck well, five-piece composition baby body, arms repainted, with cradle and bedding, 11".....................................**$100**

McMasters Harris Auction Co.

DOLLS

Schoenhut character girl doll, painted features, intaglio eyes, replaced human hair wig, spring-jointed body with label, minor touch-ups on face, tight joints, 14-1/2" **$160**

McMasters Harris Auction Co.

Chase boy doll, oil painted stockinet head and limbs on sateen covered body, jointed at shoulders, elbows, hips and knees, painted hair with some paint voids, wool suit, knickers, hat, and antique shoes, 24" .. **$200**

McMasters Harris Auction Co.

Bisque head doll, 19th century, French body and German head, fixed eyes, closed mouth, jointed composition body, inscribed on head "32_33," shoes marked "Depose," 27-1/2" h **$1,320**

Pook & Pook, Inc.

Poured wax shoulder head lady, inset glass eyes, human hair wig, cloth body with composition lower arms and legs, original costume and necklace, 13". **$160**

McMasters Harris Auction Co.

Large Chase stockinet heavily weighted doll with fully oil-painted head and body, jointed limbs, wear at joints, heavily painted blonde hair, minor paint loss, blue painted eyes with upper eyelashes, rosy cheeks, open/closed mouth, vintage cotton dress, onesie and booties, 22"..................................... **$210**

Morphy Auctions

Sonneberg Belton-type bisque socket head doll, solid dome head with flattened crown and two stringing holes, glass paperweight eyes, closed mouth, pierced-in ears, human hair wig, fully jointed composition body, some repaint to body and uneven tint to bisque at forehead, covered by wig, 14-1/2". **$450**

McMasters Harris Auction Co.

Kestner J.D.K. Hilda baby doll, black bisque socket head with glass set eyes, open/closed mouth, mohair wig (has not been removed), five-piece black composition baby body, long L-shaped crack from rim to below ear to back of head, bisque color uneven with chip on left side below ear, small composition chip on right toe, 15" ... **$375**

McMasters Harris Auction Co.

Swiss all-wood articulated girl doll and small German wood dolly, hand-carved and fully articulated Swiss Miss with original costume, all-wood dolly, 10" **$275**

McMasters Harris Auction Co.

Bruckner cloth mask face Topsy Turvy two-sided doll with white girl at one end and black girl at other, all original with some wear and staining to aprons, dress is tagged, overall excellent condition, 12" **$140**

McMasters Harris Auction Co.

Vogue Ginny baby doll, hard plastic Crib Crowd Baby with platinum caracul wig, eyes stuck open, rosy cheeks, organdy dress (no tag), diaper, shoes, and stockings, excellent condition, 7" **$480**

Morphy Auctions

Rare Lenci pouty 300 Series Model "L" doll, circa 1931, pressed and oil-painted felt swivel head, short plump face with side-glancing painted blue eyes, painted lashes, eye shadow and feathered brows, closed mouth, blonde mohair wig in braids, five-piece felt body with separated fingers, original multicolor felt dress in diamond pattern with crisscross felt decoration, organdy pantaloons, yellow felt bonnet, black felt shoes, cotton socks, yellow mohair duck, 17-1/2" **$2,000**

Frasher's Doll Auction

Large German china doll, porcelain shoulder and head with sculpted black hair in short style with waved bangs, painted features, large shaded blue eyes, red and black eyelid lines, accented pink lips, replacement cloth body with porcelain lower arms and black boots, cotton and lace dress, 27".....**$225**

Frasher's Doll Auction

German china doll with head band and snood, circa 1870s, porcelain shoulder and head with black hair drawn away from face with brush-marked detail, pageboy-style hair covered with molded snood, painted features, shaded blue eyes, red and black lid lines, tapered brows, closed mouth with hint of smile, replacement cloth body with porcelain hands, floral gown with velvet trim, 23" **$350**

Frasher's Doll Auction

Kammer & Reinhardt mold 117/A doll of character known as "Mein Liebling," marks: K * R Simon & Halbig 117/A, bisque socket head, blue sleep eyes, painted lashes, feathered brows, closed mouth, shaded and accented lips, original light brown mohair wig, composition ball-jointed body, white pinafore over blue and white plaid cotton dress, straw bonnet, old white leather shoes, 19".... **$3,600**

Frasher's Doll Auction

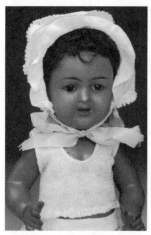

K & R 126 black character baby doll, German bisque socket head incised "K [star] R Simon & Halbig 126 28," nose rub, light red line by eyebrow, multi-stroked eyebrows, sleeping eyes, painted eyelashes, open mouth with two upper teeth and tongue, curly black wig glued down and not removed, original brown composition baby body with original finish, antique white cotton baby gown, hat and underwear, excellent condition, 11"................................... **$480**

Morphy Auctions

Rare Effanbee Skippy aviator composition doll, 1929, marks: Effanbee Skippy © P. L. Cosby, composition socket head on five-piece jointed composition body, molded and painted hair, painted features, side-glancing blue eyes, pointed brows, long upper eyelashes, closed mouth, plump cheeks, original brown leatherette jacket with fur collar, side-snap leatherette leggings, hat with earflaps, goggles, black leatherette shoes, 14"......................... **$350**

Frasher's Doll Auction

French bisque Rabery & Delphieu bebe doll, marks: R.D. 3, bisque socket head, brown paperweight eyes, painted lashes, rose-blushed eyelids, eyeliner, feathered brows, pierced ears, closed mouth with shaded and accented lips, dark blonde human hair wig over cork pate, French wood and composition jointed body, antique white cotton frock, straw bonnet, dark leather French-style shoes, 27". **$700**

Frasher's Doll Auction

Ideal Shirley Temple composition doll, nice hair, head is slightly loose, original pin, cowboy costume including gun with holster, hat is replaced, leather on costume in very good condition, some stains to neck scarf, 12" **$425**

McMasters Harris Auction Co.

Lenci all-felt girl doll, molded and painted facial features, mohair wig, jointed felt body, original costume, 10-1/2" ... **$225**

McMasters Harris Auction Co.

Miniature German all-bisque googly-eye doll, marks: 330, jointed at shoulders and hips, inset side-glancing blue glass eyes, painted lashes, single-stroke brows, open/closed mouth, mohair wig, painted blue socks and brown shoes, original gauze body suit under newer lace dress, unusual tiny size, excellent condition, 4"...................... **$325**

Frasher's Doll Auction

Kestner all-bisque child doll, incised 208 with swivel neck, loop strung arms and legs, glass eyes, painted lashes, tapered eyebrows, closed mouth, molded and painted yellow boots with black heels, all parts original, excellent condition, 3-1/2".... **$300**

Morphy Auctions

Armand Marseille 310/N Just Me doll, painted bisque socket head, curly wig, glass sleep eyes, closed mouth, five-piece painted bisque body, two original outfits and coat and hat in cardboard trunk, bunny has been added, wig has come apart at back, 7-1/2" **$500**

McMasters Harris Auction Co.

Two Effanbee composition Skippy dolls, marks: Effanbee Skippy © P. L. Cosby, composition socket head on five-piece jointed composition body, molded and painted hair, painted features, side-glancing blue eyes, pointed brows, long upper eyelashes, closed mouth, plump cheeks, one doll in original brown cotton shorts and white shirt, black leatherette shoes; other doll redressed in gray wool suit, molded and painted black knee socks and shoes, 14"..................................... **$275**

Frasher's Doll Auction

Georgene Raggedy Ann and Andy dolls, glued-on wigs, flat tin eyes, 1947 labels, both dolls in played-with condition, Andy has stains on both arms, Ann missing apron and bloomers, 22". ... **$100**

McMasters Harris Auction Co.

Four Alexander-kins dolls, each all-hard plastic, bend-knee walker with blue sleep eyes, molded lashes, and painted features, wig in original set. Includes: doll in tagged white polished cotton sleeveless dress and panties, black and white checked coat, white straw hat, black suede boots; doll in untagged pink cotton dress, taffeta pantaloons, straw hat, suede shoes; doll in pink and white cotton checked and tagged Alexander-kins dress, tulle petticoat, taffeta panties, black suede side-snap shoes; doll in untagged white organdy dress, tulle petticoat, cotton panties, white leatherette tie shoes, all very good condition. **$400**

Frasher's Doll Auction

Kestner J.D.K. Hilda baby doll, solid dome bisque socket head, hairline from right eye to temple (not visible), glass sleep eyes, open mouth, painted hair, five-piece composition baby body, typical wear and surface dirt to composition, 16".......**$300**

McMasters Harris Auction Co.

Jumeau E. J. French bisque bebe doll, marks: Depose E 8 J, bisque socket head, blue paperweight eyes, painted lashes, rose-blushed eyelids, feathered and brush-stroked brow, separately modeled and applied pierced ears, closed mouth, thin white space between lips, brown human hair wig over cork pate, Jumeau Medialle D'or Paris marked eight-ball-jointed composition body with straight wrists, French-style patterned silk frock of antique fabrics, matching bonnet, newer black leather boots, 19". **$3,500**

Frasher's Doll Auction

Simon & Halbig 550 doll, bisque socket head, sleep eyes, open mouth with four teeth, antique wig and pate, fully jointed composition body with original finish, antique outfit with wear and age spots, 22". **$475**

McMasters Harris Auction Co.

DOLLHOUSES & FURNITURE

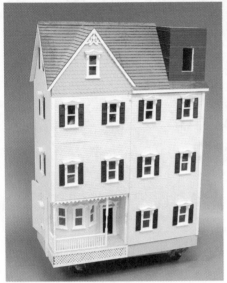

Schoenhut dollhouse, all original, roof is separate, side opens to reveal single room with original wallpaper and flooring, label on side of porch, 19" x 15" x 14" h.. **$325**

McMasters Harris Auction Co.

Large three-story Victorian-style dollhouse with furnishings, painted wood and plywood with front porch and hinged doors on front opening to eight rooms with planked wood flooring and wallpapered walls, furnishings for dining room, living room/ parlor, bedroom, bathroom, sewing/playroom, kitchen hall, and entryway, with 12 dolls, electrically lit from within, 52" h. x 38" w. x 19" d.. **$100**

Skinner, Inc., www.skinnerinc.com

Schoenhut dollhouse piano and table with chairs, upright wooden piano with rosewood finish, hinged top, gold painted metal candelabras and curved front legs, 15 wooden keys, Schoenhut lithographed trademark on front, wooden table and two chairs with rosewood finish and gilt-painted accents, piano 16" w. x 13" h., table 6-1/2" h .. **$300**

Frasher's Doll Auction

Three-story open-front dollhouse with small group of furnishings, white-painted scratch-built house with four rooms and porches, nine pieces of painted cast metal furniture and accoutrements, two tables marked "Tootsietoy," house 28-1/2" h. x 26" w. x 8-3/4" d... **$510**

Skinner, Inc., www.skinnerinc.com

Schoenhut two-story wooden dollhouse with furnishings, all original, circa 1920s, colonial style, removable front, four interior rooms, hinged roof lifts to reveal two attic rooms, windows front and sides with divided upper panes, paneled green shutters, window boxes, steeled painted green pressed shingle roof, eave above front door, original window curtains, wooden room furnishings, well-preserved condition, 21" h. x 22" w. x 17" d...**$400**

Frasher's Doll Auction

Antique dollhouse laundry items: wooden folding ironing board with cloth cover, sad iron and electric iron, large painted red wooden washtub, wooden clothes wringer with metal handle, wooden clothesline with slated wooden base, fitted wooden pegs and twine clotheslines, "Merry Monday" wood and metal washboard, tall folding wooden clothes drying rack, slatted wooden folding wash tub table.. **$150**

Frasher's Doll Auction

Hand-crafted wooden dollhouse furniture for Bleuette, bed with linens, mirrored wardrobe (needs new hinge pins) with drawer, bed 14", wardrobe 14"... **$100**

McMasters Harris Auction Co.

German bentwood dollhouse furniture set, two armchairs, settee, and mirrored hall table, circa 1890, all in classic Thonet style with painted ebony and white finish, red velvet upholstered seats, all original excellent condition, 6" l **$250**

Frasher's Doll Auction

Furnished wooden two-story dollhouse with period-style furniture and accessories..... **$304**

Pook & Pook, Inc.

Figurines

HUMMEL FIGURINES & COLLECTIBLES

THE GOEBEL CO. of Oeslau, Germany, first produced M.I. Hummel porcelain figurines in 1934, having obtained the rights to adapt the beautiful pastel sketches of children by Sister Maria Innocentia (Berta) Hummel. Every design by the Goebel artisans was approved by the nun until her death in 1946. Goebel produced these charming collectibles until Sept. 30, 2008. Manufaktur Rödental GmbH resumed production in 2009.

For more information on M.I. Hummel collectibles, see *The Official M.I. Hummel Price Guide*, 2nd Edition, by Heidi Ann von Recklinghausen.

Hummel Trademarks

Since 1935, there have been several changes in the trademarks on M.I. Hummel items. In later years of production, each new trademark design merely replaced the old one, but in the earlier years, frequently the new design trademark would be placed on a figurine that already bore the older style trademark.

The Crown Mark (TMK-1): 1934-1950

The Crown Mark (TMK-1 or CM), sometimes referred to as the "Crown-WG," was used by Goebel on all of its products in 1935, when M.I. Hummel figurines were first made commercially available. The letters WG below the crown in the mark are the initials of William Goebel, one of the founders of the company. The crown signifies his loyalty to the imperial family of Germany at the time of the mark's design, around 1900. The mark is sometimes found in an incised circle.

Another Crown-type mark is sometimes confusing to collectors; some refer to it as the "Narrow Crown" and others the "Wide Ducal Crown." This mark was introduced by Goebel in 1937 and used on many of its products.

Often, the Crown Mark will appear twice on the same piece, more often one mark incised and the other stamped. This is, as we know, the "Double Crown."

When World War II ended and the United States Occupation Forces allowed Goebel to begin exporting, the pieces were marked as having been made in the occupied zone.

These marks were applied to the bases of the figurines, along with the other markings, from 1946 through 1948. They were sometimes applied under the glaze and often over the glaze. Between 1948 and 1949, the U.S. Zone mark requirement was dropped, and the word "Germany" took its place. With the partitioning of Germany into East and West, "W. Germany," "West Germany," or "Western Germany" began to appear most of the time instead.

Incised
Crown Mark

Stamped
Crown Mark

Wide Ducal
Crown Mark

FIGURINES

Incised Full Bee

High Bee

Small Bee.
*Note that the bee's wingtips
are level with the top of the V.*

Stamped Full Bee

Baby Bee

Vee Bee

The Full Bee Mark (TMK-2): 1940-1959

In 1950, Goebel made a major change in its trademark. The company incorporated a bee in a V. It is thought that the bumblebee part of the mark was derived from a childhood nickname of Sister Maria Innocentia Hummel, meaning bumblebee. The bee flies within a V, which is the first letter of the German word for distributing company, Verkaufsgesellschaft.

There are actually 12 variations of the Bee marks to be found on Goebel-produced M.I. Hummel items.

The Full Bee mark, also referred to as TMK-2 or abbreviated FB, is the first of the Bee marks to appear. The mark evolved over nearly 20 years until the company began to modernize it. It is sometimes found in an incised circle.

The very large bee flying in the V remained until around 1956, when the bee was reduced in size and lowered into the V. It can be found incised, stamped in black, or stamped in blue, in that order, through its evolution.

The Stylized Bee (TMK-3): 1958-1972

A major change in the way the bee is rendered in the trademark made its appearance in 1960. The Stylized Bee (TMK-3), sometimes abbreviated as Sty-Bee, as the major component of the trademark appeared in three basic forms through 1972. The first two are both classified as the Stylized Bee (TMK-3), but the third is considered a fourth step in the evolution, the Three Line Mark (TMK-4).

THE LARGE STYLIZED BEE: This trademark was used primarily from 1960 through 1963. The color of the mark will be black or blue. It is sometimes found inside an incised circle. When you find the Large Stylized Bee mark, you will normally find a stamped "West" or "Western Germany" in black elsewhere on the base, but not always.

Large Stylized Bee

THE SMALL STYLIZED BEE: This mark is also considered to be TMK-3. It was used concurrently with the Large Stylized Bee from about 1960 and continued in this use until about 1972. The mark is usually rendered in blue, and it too is often accompanied by a stamped black "West" or "Western Germany." Collectors and dealers sometimes refer to the mark as the One Line Mark.

Small Stylized Bee

FIGURINES

The Three Line Mark (TMK-4): 1964-1972

This trademark is sometimes abbreviated 3-line or 3L1 same stylized V and bee as the others, but also included major change appeared in blue.

Three Line Mark

The Last Bee Mark (TMK-5): 1972-1979

Developed and occasionally used as early as 1970, this major change was known by some collectors as the Last Bee Mark because the next change in the trademark no longer incorporated any form of the V and the bee. However, with the reinstatement of a bee in TMK-8 with the turn of the century, TMK-5 is not technically the "Last Bee" any longer. The mark was used until about mid-1979. There are three minor variations in the mark shown in the illustration. Generally, the mark was placed under the glaze from 1972 through 1976 and is found placed over the glaze from 1976 through 1979.

Last Bee Mark

The Missing Bee Mark (TMK 6): 1979-1991

The transition to this trademark began in 1979 and was complete by mid-1980. Goebel removed the V and bee from the mark altogether, calling it the Missing Bee. In conjunction with this change, the company instituted the practice of adding to the traditional artist's mark the date the artist finished painting the piece.

Missing Bee Mark

The Hummel Mark (TMK-7): 1991-1999

In 1991, Goebel changed the trademark once again. This time, the change was not only symbolic of the reunification of the two Germanys by removal of the "West" from the mark, but very significant in another way. Until then, Goebel used the same trademark on virtually all of its products. The mark illustrated here was for exclusive use on Goebel products made from the paintings and drawings of M.I. Hummel.

Hummel Mark

The Millennium Bee (TMK-8): 2000-2008

Goebel decided to celebrate the beginning of a new century with a revival in a bee-adorned trademark. Seeking once again to honor the memory of Sister Maria Innocentia Hummel, a bumblebee, this time flying solo without the V, was reinstated into the mark in 2000 and ended in 2008. Goebel stopped production of the M.I. Hummel figurines on Sept. 30, 2008.

Millennium Bee Mark

The Manufaktur Rödental Mark (TKM-9): 2009-Present

Manufaktur Rödental purchased the rights to produce M.I. Hummel figurines from Goebel in 2009. This trademark signified a new era for Hummel figurines while maintaining the same quality and workmanship from the master sculptors and master painters at the Rödental factory. This trademark has a full bee using yellow and black for the bumblebee, which circles around the words "Original M.I. Hummel Germany" with the copyright sign next to M.I. Hummel. Manufaktur Rödental is underneath the circle with a copyright sign.

Manufaktur Rödental Mark

For purposes of simplification, the various trademarks have been abbreviated in the list below.

Generally speaking, earlier trademarks are worth more than later trademarks.

TRADEMARK	ABBREVIATIONS	DATES
Crown	TMK-1	1934-1950
Full Bee	TMK-2	1940-1959
Stylized Bee	TMK-3	1958-1972
Three Line Mark	TMK-4	1964-1972
Last Bee	TMK-5	1972-1979
Missing Bee	TMK-6	1979-1991
Hummel Mark	TMK-7	1991-1999
Millennium Bee/Goebel Bee	TMK-8	2000-2008
Manufaktur Rödental Mark	TMK-9	2009-present

FIGURINES

Hum 60/A: Farm Boy bookend, trademarks 1-6. ....$250-$760

Hum 10: Flower Madonna, trademarks 1-7. .... $225-$800 (open halo)

Hum 24: Lullaby candleholder, trademarks 1-7..........$150-$900

Hum 83: Angel Serenade With Lamb, trademarks 1-7......$165-$450

FIGURINES

Hum 14/A and 14/B: Book Worm bookends, trademarks 1-8......................................**$350-$800**

Hum 11: Merry Wanderer, trademarks 1-8..**$100-$625**

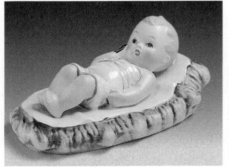

Hum 18: Christ Child, trademarks 1-7.....**$125-$250**

Hum 25: Angelic Sleep candleholder, trademarks 1-6. ....**$150-$450**

Hum 22: Angel With Bird holy water font, trademarks 1-8.......................................**$50-$300**

Hum 31: Advent Group, trademark 1...........**$12,000**

Hum 110: Let's Sing, trademarks 1-8...........**$110-$360**

Hum 143: Boots, trademarks 1-7 ....**$140-$630**

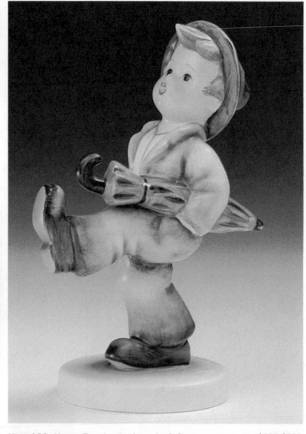

Hum 109: Happy Traveler, trademarks 1-8..........................**$105-$900**

Hum 56/A: Culprits, trademarks 2-8. ....**$210-$400**

Hum 56/B: Out of Danger, trademarks 2-8...........**$210-$360**

Hum 133: Mother's Helper, trademarks 1-8...........**$135-$420**

Hum 200: Little Goat Herder, trademarks
1-9. ....$140-$2,200

Hum 195: Barnyard Hero, trademarks 1-8..$130-$720

Hum 307: Good Hunting, trademarks
2-8 ....$170-$3,000

Hum 176: Happy Birthday, trademarks
1-8 ....$165-$690

Hum 196: Telling Her Secret, trademarks
1-8 ....$180-$900

Hum 300: Bird Watcher, trademarks 2-8........**$150-$3,000**

Hum 153: Auf Wiedersehen, trademarks 1-8........**$170-$2,400**

Hum 204: Weary Wanderer, trademarks 1-7 and 9...**$170-$540**

Hum 339: Behave!, trademarks 2, 3, 7, and 8. ....**$270-$6,000**

Hum 240: Little Drummer, trademarks 2-8...........**$105-$225**

Hum 220: We Congratulate, trademarks 2-8...........**$110-$345**

Hum 105: Adoration With Bird, trademark 1 .... **$4,200-$4,800**

Hum 54: Silent Night candleholder, trademarks 1-7 ....**$220-$9,000**

FIGURINES

Hum 118: Little Thrifty, trademarks 1-9..........**$110-$450**

Hum 119: Postman, trademarks 1-8.............**$99-$450**

Hum 26: Child Jesus holy water font, trademarks 1-7 .....**$40-$450**

Hum 123: Max and Moritz, trademarks 1-8...........**$155-$480**

Hum 112: Just Resting, trademarks 1-8...........**$105-$510**

Hum 111: Wayside Harmony, trademarks 1-8...........**$110-$510**

Hum 415: Thoughtful, trademarks 5-8. ....**$165-$2,400**

Hum 136: Friends, trademarks 1-8. ....**$150-$9,000**

Hum 184: Latest News, trademarks 1-8........**$205-$1,200**

Hum 304: The Artist, trademarks 2-8... **$175-$3,000**

Hum 171: Little Sweeper,
trademarks 1-8.............**$70-$300**

Hum 152/A: Umbrella Boy,
trademarks 1-8........ **$279-$4,200**

Hum 152/B: Umbrella Girl, trademarks
1-8 .... **$329-$4,200**

Hum 319: Doll Bath,
trademarks 2-8........**$200-$3,000**

Hum 311: Kiss Me, trademarks
2-8. ....**$200-$3,000**

Hum 257: For Mother,
trademarks 3-8.............**$55-$525**

Hum 327: The
Run-a-way, trademarks
2-8 ....**$175-$3,000**

Hum 261: Angel Duet,
trademarks 4-8...........**$165-$510**

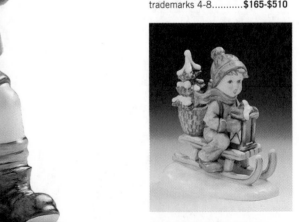

Hum 396: Ride Into Christmas,
trademarks 4-8........**$165-$1,550**

FIGURINES

LLADRÓ

LLADRÓ FIGURINES – distinctive, elegant creations often glazed in the trademark colors of blue and white – hail from a Spanish company founded by three brothers nearly

ptures in their parents'
stablished their own
they moved to a factory

ent, the Lladró company
for a new factory
of Porcelain, was

can market. In 1974,
bol – appeared on the

dró Collectors Society
eral awards for their
world, and the company
way to Lladró

ploys 2,000 people and
.

'M" refers to a mat

Listen to Don Quixote"
1520, limited edition of
50, issued in 1987 and
tired in 1995, good
ondition, approximately
21" h. **$950**

Bunte Auction Services, Inc.

umbrella with small chips to lace, approximately 12" h................. **$900**

Bunte Auction Services, Inc.

FIGURINES

"Gemini" #6219,
issued in 1995 and
retired in 1998,
good condition,
approximately
9-3/4" h. **$110**

Bunte Auction Services, Inc.

"Scorpio" #6225,
issued in 1995 and
retired in 1998,
good condition,
approximately 11" h. .. **$90**

Bunte Auction Services, Inc.

"Aquarius" #6216,
issued in 1995 and
retired in 1998,
good condition,
approximately
10-1/2" h. **$90**

Bunte Auction Services, Inc.

"Cancer" #6224,
issued in 1995 and
retired in 1998,
good condition,
approximately
9-1/2" h. **$120**

Bunte Auction Services, Inc.

"Little Jester"
#5203, issued
in 1984, good
condition,
approximately
7-3/4" h. **$50**

Bunte Auction Services, Inc.

"Curious Girl With
Straw Hat" #5009,
issued in 1978,
good condition,
approximately 9-3/4"
h. **$30**

Bunte Auction Services, Inc.

"Hats Off to Fun"
#5765, issued
in 1991 and
retired in 1995,
good condition,
approximately
16-1/2" h. **$300**

Bunte Auction Services, Inc.

"The Aviator" #5891,
issued in 1992 and
retired in 1997, good
condition, approximately
16-1/4" h. **$160**

Bunte Auction Services, Inc.

FIGURINES

"Small Bust with Veil" #1539, issued in 1988 and retired in 2002, good condition, approximately 9-1/2" h. **$60**

Bunte Auction Services, Inc.

"A Christmas Wish" #5711, issued in 1990 and retired in 1998, good condition, approximately 7-1/2" h. **$170**

Bunte Auction Services, Inc.

"Boy with Concertina" #1179, issued in 1971 and retired in 1986, good condition, approximately 5" h. ..**$70**

Bunte Auction Services, Inc.

"Peace Offering" #3559, issued in 1985, good condition, approximately 22" h. **$450**

Bunte Auction Services, Inc.

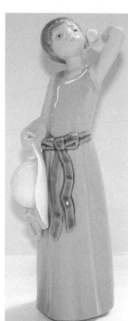

"Just One More" #5899, issued in 1992 and retired in 1998, good condition, approximately 8-1/2" h. **$250**

Bunte Auction Services, Inc.

"Naughty Girl" #5006, issued in 1978 and retired in 1998, firing flaw, approximately 9-1/2" h.; "Prissy" #5010, issued in 1978 and retired in 1998, repaired chip to hat, 9-1/2" h. ....**$70 pr.**

Bunte Auction Services, Inc.

"Onward!" #1742, limited edition of 1,000, issued in 1991 and retired in 1994, glue marks on dog's tail, approximately 9-1/2" h. x 25" l. **$1,200**

Bunte Auction Services, Inc.

FIGURINES

"Don Quixote" #1030, issued in 1970, good condition, approximately 15-3/4" h. **$700**

Bunte Auction Services, Inc.

"Angel Tree Topper" #5719, issued and retired in 1990, good condition, approximately 7" h. **$60**

Bunte Auction Services, Inc.

"My Chores" #5782, issued in 1991 and retired in 1995, good condition, approximately 6-1/4" h. **$170**

Bunte Auction Services, Inc.

"Seesaw" #1255, issued in 1974 and retired in 1991, good condition, approximately 9-1/2" h. **$170**

Bunte Auction Services, Inc.

"All Aboard" #7619, issued in 1992 and retired in 1995, good condition, approximately 5" h **$100**

Bunte Auction Services, Inc.

"Checking the Time" #5762, issued in 1991 and retired in 1995, good condition, approximately 9-1/2" h. **$300**

Bunte Auction Services, Inc.

"Couple of Doves" #1169, issued in 1971, good condition, approximately 5" h. **$45**

"Clown with Saxophone" #5059, issued in 1980 and retired in 1985, good condition, approximately 10" h. **$160**

Bunte Auction Services, Inc.

"The Snowman" #5713, issued in 1990, good condition, approximately 8" h. **$140**

Bunte Auction Services, Inc.

"Rubber Duckie" #6300, issued in 1996 and retired in 2001, good condition, approximately 7" h. **90**

Bunte Auction Services, Inc.

"Little Bear" #6299, issued in 1996 and retired in 2000, good condition, approximately 7" h. ..**$80**

Bunte Auction Services, Inc.

"Football Player" #6107, issued in 1994 and retired in 1998, good condition, approximately 7-1/2" h. **$90**

Bunte Auction Services, Inc.

"Young Harlequin" #1229, issued in 1972 and retired in 1999, good condition, approximately 10" h. **$90**

Bunte Auction Services, Inc.

"On the Move" #5838, issued in 1991 and retired in 1998, good condition, approximately 11" h...........................**$225**

Bunte Auction Services, Inc.

"Circus Sam" #5472, issued in 1988, good condition, approximately 8-1/2" h...........................**$100**

Bunte Auction Services, Inc.

"Sad Sax" #5471, issued in 1988, good condition, approximately 9-1/2" h. **$120**

Bunte Auction Services, Inc.

"The Wanderer" #2271, issued in 1994 and retired in 1998, good condition, approximately 8-3/4" h. **$100**

Bunte Auction Services, Inc.

FIGURINES

"Sea of Love" #6432, issued in 1997 and retired in 2001, good condition, approximately 13-1/2" h. **$375**

Bunte Auction Services, Inc.

"A New Doll House" #5139, issued in 1982 and retired in 1985, good condition, approximately 7" h. **$190**

Bunte Auction Services, Inc.

"The Desert People" #3555, limited edition of 750, issued in 1982 and retired in 1992, good condition, approximately 21" h. **$750**

Bunte Auction Services, Inc.

"The Gossips" #4984, issued in 1978 and retired in 1985, good condition, approximately 12" h. **$120**

Bunte Auction Services, Inc.

"Carnival Couple" #4882, issued in 1974, top pink mask needs to be reglued to hand, approximately 10-3/8" h. **$80**

Bunte Auction Services, Inc.

"Circus Time" #1758, limited edition of 2,500, issued in 1992 and retired in 2013, good condition, approximately 23" h. x 29" l. with wooden stand............................... **$1,800**

Bunte Auction Services, Inc.

"Winter Wonderland" #1429, issued in 1982 and retired in 2002, good condition, approximately 17" h. x 20" l. **$650**

Bunte Auction Services, Inc.

"Up and Away" #5975, issued in 1993 and retired in 1996, good condition, approximately 13-5/16" h. x 20" l. **$650**

Bunte Auction Services, Inc.

"Trimming the Tree" #5897, issued in 1992, good condition, approximately 13" h. **$275**

Bunte Auction Services, Inc.

FIGURINES

"Over the Clouds" #5697, issued in 1990 and retired in 2005, good condition, approximately 5-1/2" h. **$100**

Bunte Auction Services, Inc.

"Don't Look Down" #5698, issued in 1990 and retired in 2005, good condition, approximately 6-1/2" h. **$160**

Bunte Auction Services, Inc.

"Circus Train" #1517, issued in 1987 and retired in 1994, needs cleaning, approximately 10" h. x 24-1/2" l. **$1,000**

Bunte Auction Services, Inc.

"Sleigh Ride" #5037, issued in 1980 and retired in 1996, good condition, approximately 10" h. x 16-1/2" l. **$400**

Bunte Auction Services, Inc.

"Rock A Bye Baby" #5717, issued in 1990 and retired in 2000, good condition, 4-3/4" h. **$90**

Bunte Auction Services, Inc.

"Little Dreamers" #5772, issued in 1991 and retired in 2007, good condition, approximately 3-1/2" h. **$100**

Bunte Auction Services, Inc.

"Circus Parade" #1609, limited edition of 1,000, issued in 1989 and retired in 1998, saxophone repaired, approximately 14" h. x 28" l.......... **$1,200**

Bunte Auction Services, Inc.

ROYAL DOULTON FIGURINES

DOULTON & CO., LTD., was founded in Lambeth, London, in about 1858. It operated there until 1956 and often incorporated the words "Doulton" and "Lambeth" in its marks. Pinder, Bourne & Co., Burslem, was purchased by the Doultons in 1878 and in 1882 became Doulton & Co., Ltd. It added porcelain to its earthenware production in 1884. The "Royal Doulton" mark has been used since 1902 by this factory, which is still in operation.

John Doulton, the founder, was born in 1793. He became an apprentice at the age of 12 to a potter in south London. Five years later he was employed in another small pottery near Lambeth. His two sons, John and Henry, subsequently joined their father in 1830 in a partnership he had formed with the name of Doulton & Watts. Watts retired in 1864 and the partnership was dissolved. Henry formed a new company that traded as Doulton and Co.

In the early 1870s the proprietor of the Pinder Bourne Co., located in Burslem, Staffordshire, offered Henry a partnership. The Pinder Bourne Co. was purchased by Henry in 1878 and became part of Doulton & Co. in 1882.

With the passage of time, the demand for the Lambeth industrial and decorative stoneware declined whereas demand for the Burslem manufactured and decorated bone china wares increased.

Doulton & Co. was incorporated as a limited liability company in 1899. In 1901 the company was allowed to use the word "Royal" on its trademarks by Royal Charter. The well-known lion-on-crown logo came into use in 1902. In 2000 the logo was changed on the company's advertising literature to one showing a more stylized lion's head in profile.

Today Royal Doulton is one of the world's leading manufacturers and distributors of premium grade ceramic tabletop wares and collectibles. The Doulton Group comprises Minton, Royal Albert, Caithness Glass, Holland Studio Craft and Royal Doulton. Royal Crown Derby was part of the group from 1971 until 2000 when it became an independent company. These companies market collectibles using their own brand names.

"Pointer With Pheasant," HN 2829, large size. **$90**

Michael Spooner Auctions, Inc.

"Flower Seller's Children," HN 1342, issued 1929-1993, 8" h.. **$100**

Michael Spooner Auctions, Inc.

"First Waltz," HN 2862, issued 1979-1983, 7-1/4" h. **$26**

Michael Spooner Auctions, Inc.

"Springtime," HN 3033, issued 1983, "The Seasons" series, signed Adrienne Hughes........**$26**

Michael Spooner Auctions, Inc.

"Pollyanna," HN 2965, issued 1982-1985, "Characters from Children's Literature" series, 6-1/2" h. **$26**

Michael Spooner Auctions, Inc.

"The Doctor," HN 2858, issued 1979-1992, 7-1/2" h. **$26**

Michael Spooner Auctions, Inc.

"All Aboard," HN 2940, issued 1982-1986, 23-1/2" h. **$31**

Michael Spooner Auctions, Inc.

"Santa Claus," HN 2725, issued 1982-1993. ....**$50**

Michael Spooner Auctions, Inc.

"Fiona," HN 2694, issued 1974-1981, 7" h. **$26**

Michael Spooner Auctions, Inc.

"Fair Lady," HN 2193, 1962, 7-1/2" h. **$31**

Michael Spooner Auctions, Inc.

"Schoolmarm," HN 2223, issued 1958-1991, 6-3/4" h. **$26**

Michael Spooner Auctions, Inc.

"Old Lavender Seller," HN 1492, issued 1932-1949, 6" h. **$51**

Michael Spooner Auctions, Inc.

"Grace," HN 2318, issued
1966-1981, 7-3/4" h. **$26**

Michael Spooner Auctions, Inc.

"Cup of Tea," HN 2322, 7" h. **$26**

Michael Spooner Auctions, Inc.

"Fair Lady," HN 2835, "Pretty
Ladies" series, coral pink, 7-1/4"
h. **$26**

Michael Spooner Auctions, Inc.

"The Old King," HN 2134, issued
1954-1992, 10-3/4" h. **$120**

Michael Spooner Auctions, Inc.

"Christmas Parcels," HN 2851. **$26**

Michael Spooner Auctions, Inc.

"Delight," #814285. .... **$26**

Michael Spooner Auctions, Inc.

"A Stitch in Time," HN 2352,
issued 1966-1981, 6-1/4" h. **$31**

Michael Spooner Auctions, Inc.

"The Mask Seller," HN 2103,
issued 1953-1995, 8-1/2" h.. **$26**

Michael Spooner Auctions, Inc.

"Officer of the Line," HN 2733,
issued 1982-1986, 9" h. **$50**

Michael Spooner Auctions, Inc.

FIGURINES

"Queen Elizabeth II," HN 2878, 1983, limited edition of 2,500, issued in celebration of 30th anniversary of her coronation.**$100**

Michael Spooner Auctions, Inc.

"HRH The Princess of Wales," HN 2887, issued 1982, limited edition of 1,500, #1156, with case, base and certificate of authenticity, 7-3/4" h. **$240**

Michael Spooner Auctions, Inc.

"Yum Yum," HN 2899, signed by Doulton, issued 1980-1985, 10-3/4" h. **$90**

Michael Spooner Auctions, Inc.

"New Companions," HN 2770, 7-1/4" h. **$41**

Michael Spooner Auctions, Inc.

"Carpet Seller," HN 1464, issued until 1969, 9" h. **$41**

Michael Spooner Auctions, Inc.

"Pied Piper," HN 2907, issued 1980-1992, 8" h. **$31**

Michael Spooner Auctions, Inc.

"Regency Beau," HN 1972. ...**$90**

Michael Spooner Auctions, Inc.

"The Judge," HN 2443, 7" h.**$41**

Michael Spooner Auctions, Inc.

"The Favorite," HN 2249, issued 1960-1990, 7-3/4" h. **$36**

Michael Spooner Auctions, Inc.

"The Skater," HN 2117, issued
1953-1971, 7-1/4" h. **$80**

Michael Spooner Auctions, Inc.

"Sailor's Holiday," HN 2442,
issued 1972-1979, 6-1/4" h. **$90**

Michael Spooner Auctions, Inc.

"The Laird," HN 2361, issued
beginning in 1969, 8" h. **$50**

Michael Spooner Auctions, Inc.

"Cavalier," HN 2716, issued
1976-1982, 9-3/4" h. **$51**

Michael Spooner Auctions, Inc.

"Blue Beard," HN 2105, issued
1953-1992, 11" h. **$80**

Michael Spooner Auctions, Inc.

"St. George," HN 2051, issued
1950-1985, 7-1/2" h.**$80**

Michael Spooner Auctions, Inc.

"The Auctioneer," HN 2988,
issued 1986, 8-1/2" h. **$51**

Michael Spooner Auctions, Inc.

"Captain Cook," HN 2889,
issued 1980-1984, 8" h. **$140**

Michael Spooner Auctions, Inc.

"The Pirate King," HN 2901,
issued 1981-1985, "Gilbert and
Sullivan" series, 10" h. **$46**

Michael Spooner Auctions, Inc.

"Sir Walter Raleigh,"
HN 2015, issued 1948-
1955, 11-1/2" h. ...**$120**

Michael Spooner Auctions, Inc.

"Drummer Boy," HN
2679, issued 1976-
1981, 8-1/2" h. **$60**

Michael Spooner Auctions, Inc.

"Elizabeth," HN 2946,
issued 1982-1986,
"Pretty Ladies" series,
8" h. **$60**

Michael Spooner Auctions, Inc.

"Sweet Anne," HN 1330,
signed MT, rare and early
model, issued 1929-
1949, 7-1/4" h. **$51**

Michael Spooner Auctions, Inc.

"Jack Point," HN 2080,
marked 13.10.10 to
base, issued 1952-
2009, approximately
16-1/2" h. **$280**

Michael Spooner Auctions, Inc.

"King Charles," no HN
number, marked 25.6.80
to base, issued 1992,
limited edition of 350,
approximately 17" h.
.............................**$300**

Michael Spooner Auctions, Inc.

"The Detective," HN
2359, issued 1977-
1983, 9-1/4" h. **$51**

Michael Spooner Auctions, Inc.

"At Ease," HN 2473,
issued 1973-1979,
"Pretty Ladies" series,
6" h. **$46**

Michael Spooner Auctions, Inc.

"Dalmatian," HN 1113
DB. **$26**

Michael Spooner Auctions, Inc.

"Solitude," HN 2810, 5-1/2" h. **$36**

Michael Spooner Auctions, Inc.

"Reverie," HN 2306, 6-1/2" h. **$26**

Michael Spooner Auctions, Inc.

Fine Art

DESPITE A FLUCTUATING GLOBAL ECONOMY, the art market continues to see an expansion of its buyer pool and growth of some genres, with modern art commanding attention in the leader spot in terms of popularity and prices paid, especially among the world's wealthiest buyers.

Western art—paintings and sculpture that celebrate the history, lifestyles, cultures and artists living in the American West—remains a bright spot in the global market.

Fine art continues to offer some ground for diversifying investments; however, as with any collectible item, the purpose should be steeped more in enjoyment and appreciation than profit.

Woman in market, oil on canvas, 19th century, signed, 34" x 24".......................................$3,250
Fine Arts Auctions, LLC

"Two Women on an Alley Along the Zuiderzee: Study for the Oil 'Kirchgang in Laren,'" Max Liebermann (1847-1935), black chalk heightened with white on brown paper, signed "M. Liebermann" lower left, 6-3/8" x 9-3/4" **$5,000**

Sotheby's

"Indian Paint Brush," Dawson Watson (American, 1864-1939), 1930, oil on canvas, signed "Dawson-Watson" lower right, 21" x 16" **$28,000**

David Dike Fine Art

"Rabbi," Giovanella aka Joan Markson (American, b. 1935), oil on canvas, signature upper right, framed, 52" x 35"... **$200**

Clark's Fine Art & Auctioneers, Inc.

FINE ART

"Portrait of a lady," said to be Lady Wood, oil on canvas, English School, circa 1810, 30" x 25".. **$375**

Sotheby's

"Kikoo Le Pony," Nicola Simbari (1927-2012), 1977, oil on canvas, signed Simbari lower right, 43-3/8" x 39-1/2"...................................... **$4,600**

Sotheby's

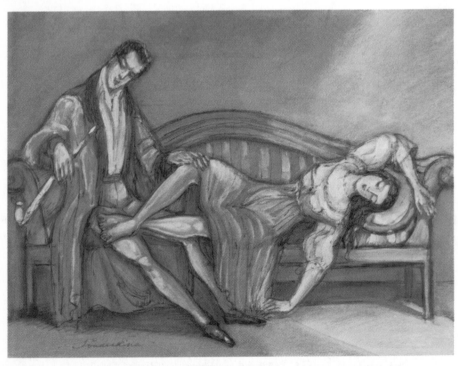

"Lovers," Sergei Soudeikine (1883-1946), pen and ink and gouache on brown paper mounted on paperboard, signed "Soudeikine" lower left, 9" x 12" **$5,625**

Sotheby's

"Refracting Light," Leonardo Nierman (Mexican, b. 1932), oil on Masonite, signed lower left, framed, 31" x 23".. **$900**

Clark's Fine Art & Auctioneers, Inc.

"Portrait of the Courtship," Thomas Heaphy, oil on canvas, signed, painting 26" h. x 20" w., frame 37" h. x 30" w... **$600**

Kaminski Auctions

"Gholla Bristha in the Rosses," James Humbert Craig (Irish, 1877-1944), oil on canvas, signed "J.H. CRAIG" lower left, identified on label from Combridge's Fine Art Galleries in Dublin, Ireland, and with labels from Museum of Fine Arts, Boston, and John Magee, Belfast, Ireland, affixed to stretchers, 18" x 24"... **$8,400**

Skinner, Inc., www.skinnerinc.com

"Fowl," primitive oil on canvas, unsigned, unframed, 15" x 12" **$250**

Kaminski Auctions

Oil on canvas board composition, Agnes Weinrich (American, 1873-1946), circa 1935, signed "A. Weinrich" lower right, 24" x 20" **$9,225**

Skinner, Inc., www.skinnerinc.com

"Lake George," A.L.P. Skilling (American, 19th century), oil on canvas, signed, titled, and dated 1869 verso, painting 20" h. x 30" w., frame 29" h. x 39" w **$500**

Kaminski Auctions

"Twilight," Harry Willson Watrous (1857-1940), oil on panel, signed "Watrous" lower right, 25-1/4" x 30" .. **$5,000**

Sotheby's

"Interior – Brittany," Martha Walter (1875-1976), oil on canvasboard, signed "Martha" lower left, signed "Martha Walter" and "Interior – Brittany" on reverse, 11" x 9" **$6,250**

Sotheby's

"Ceramic Vase on Table," Hubert Vos (American, 1855-1935), oil on canvas, signed and dated "Hubert Vos / 195430" lower right, 24" **$5,313**

Heritage Auctions

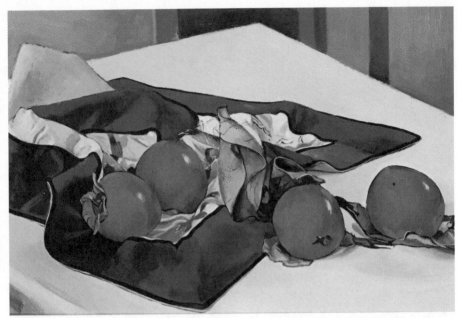

"Persimmons," Stanton MacDonald-Wright (1890-1973), oil on Masonite, signed "S. Macdonald-Wright," 13-1/4" x 19-1/2" **$5,625**

Sotheby's

"Study for the Nursemaid," Milton Avery (1885-1965), circa 1934, watercolor with traces of pencil on paper, signed "Milton Avery" lower right, 22-1/4" x 15-1/4" **$5,000**

Sotheby's

"The White Cockade," Robert Hope (British, 1869-1936), oil on canvas, signed and dated "R. Hope" lower left, 36-1/4" x 28-1/4" **$5,000**

Heritage Auctions

"Winter Landscape," Robert Emmett Owen (1878-1957), oil on canvas, signed "R. Emmet Owen" lower right, 22" x 42" **$6,250**

Sotheby's

"Port of Call," Robert Watson (American, 1923-2004), 1971, oil on canvas, signed and dated lower right, 14" x 10" **$400**

Clark's Fine Art & Auctioneers, Inc.

"Mosque de Sidi Abdel Rahman," Marcus Waterman (American, 1834-1914), oil on canvas, signed "Waterman" lower left, artist's label with title verso, 16" x 12" **$1,250**

Heritage Auctions

"Circus Performers on Trial Before Three Judges," Jack Levitz (American, 20th century), oil on canvas, signed "Levitz" lower right, 32" x 36" **$1,750**

Heritage Auctions

"Equilibrium," Charles Green Shaw (1892-1974), 1959, oil on canvas, signed "Shaw" lower right, 32" x 39-1/4" **$10,625**

Sotheby's

"Roof Top View From Chartres Cathedral," Jacques Lagrange (1917-1995), watercolor on paper, signed "Lagrange" and dated indistinctly lower center, 19-1/2" x 25-1/4" **$625**

Sotheby's

WESTERN ART

"Two Indians in a Canoe, Forest Interior," Gilbert Gaul (American, 1855-1919), oil on canvas, signed "Gilbert Gaul" at lower left, identified on labels from Dartmouth College, Hanover, New Hampshire, and M.R. Schweitzer Gallery, New York, affixed to stretchers, framed, 30" x 40"... **$16,200**

Skinner, Inc., www.skinnerinc.com

"Full View of Yosemite Valley," Manuel Valencia (American, 1856-1935), oil on canvas, signed M. Valencia lower right, titled and signed verso "Full View Yosemite Valley / M. Valencia," 30" x 60"...... **$4,687**

Heritage Auctions

Group of four American Indian prints, Thomas L. McKenney and James Hall, four hand-colored lithographs, from *History of the Indian Tribes of North America*, on wove paper, Tulcee-Mathla with publication line, Ma-Ka-Tai-Me-She-Kia-Kiah partially trimmed, sheets 20" x 13-3/4" **$1,250**

Sotheby's

"Grand Canyon," Gunnar Mauritz Widforss (Swedish, 1879-1934), oil on canvas, inscribed verso: "This is a genuine Gunnar Widforss left unsigned by him / Daniel McDade / administrator of the estate / Subscribed and sworn to Daniel McDade before me this 7th day of August 1937 / Coconino Co. State of Arizona / SG Stephens Notary Public," 30" x 24"..........................**$32,500**

Heritage Auctions

"Short Bull Sioux," Leonard Baskin (American, 1922-2000), 1972-1973, color lithograph on cream Arches paper with watermark, edition of 85 (Fern & O'Sullivan, 623), signed "Baskin" in pencil at lower right, signed, titled, and dated within matrix, numbered "39/85" in pencil at lower left, dry stamp lower left, 23" x 21" **$450**

Skinner, Inc., www.skinnerinc.com

"Indian on Horseback," Charles Craig (American, 1846-1931), oil on canvas, signed "Chas Craig" lower right, 16" x 12"................................. **$2,750**

Heritage Auctions

"Ranch Hands Get the Word," Donald Teague (American, 1897-1991), 1941, gouache on paper, signed and dated "Donald Teague 1941" lower right, 13-1/2" x 26-1/2" **$3,750**

Heritage Auctions

"Indian Buffalo Hunt with Spear," M. Lone Wolf (American, 1882-1970), circa 1919, oil on canvas, signed "Lone Wolf" (with artist's cipher) lower left, 24" x 34".**$2,000**

Heritage Auctions

"Riders in the Landscape," Carl (Karl) Everton Moon (American, 1879-1948), oil on canvas, dedicated, signed, and dated "To my good friend / Mr. GEORGE HAZEN. / CARL MOON.- / 1924" at lower right, 16" x 20"...... **$1,353**

Skinner, Inc., www. skinnerinc.com

"Ropin' Steer," Edward Borein (American, 1873-1945), watercolor on paper, signed "Edward Borein" lower right, 7-1/2" x 11-1/2".. **$18,750**

Heritage Auctions

"Sierra Sunrise," Robert William Wood (American, 1889-1979), 1962, oil on canvas, signed and dated "Robert Wood / Oct 62" lower left, inscribed and titled verso: "View From Our Window / NR Bishop / Sierra Sunrise," artist's stamp verso, 24" x 36"... **$6,250**

Heritage Auctions

SCULPTURES

"Le Rieur Napolitain (Laughing Neapolitan Boy)," Jean-Baptiste Carpeaux (French, 1827-1875), bronze, dark brown patina, signed "Jbte Carpeaux," 20-1/2". **$6,215**

Sotheby's

Bronze with greenish-brown patina, Harriet Whitney Frishmuh (American, 1880-1980), Desha, modeled 1927, cast 1927-65, inscribed along base "HARRIET W FRISHMUTH 1927 ©," stamped with foundry mark along base "GORHAM CO FOUNDERS / QFSK," bronze 14-1/2" h., marble base 1/2" h. **$15,000**

Heritage Auctions

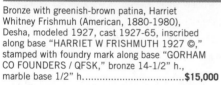

"Petit Taureau," Antoine-Louis Barye (French, 1796-1875), bronze, green patina, signed "BARYE" and inscribed "Susse Fres. Edrs. Paris," 3-3/4" h. x 5-3/4" w. **$2,250**

Sotheby's

Bronze figurine of recumbent lion with prey, 20th century, marked FRATIN, 2-1/8" x 5-1/2" x 2-3/4". **$300**

Heritage Auctions

Grand Tour bronze of Marcus Aurelius, Rome, 19th century, after Roman antique currently in Palazzo dei Conservatori, cast on his horse with one hand stretched in front of him and other at his side with palm turned up, rectangular pedestal with dedication inscriptions on either side, raised on shaped wood plinth, bronze incised "W. HOPFGARTEN ROMA," 23-1/2" h. **$6,000**

Skinner, Inc., www.skinnerinc.com

Bronze of Kannon, Japan, 19th/20th century, standing on downturned double lotus pedestal with right hand raised to her chest and left hand at hip, eyes half-closed, robe decorated with cast details, 18-1/8" h. **$2,160**

Skinner, Inc., www.skinnerinc.com

"Untitled," Day Schnabel (American, 1905-1991), 1955, bronze, date and initials incised at bottom, 9-1/2" x 6" x 5-1/2". **$5,313**

Heritage Auctions

"Goat," Jeanne Marie Van Rozen (active 20th century), bronze, dark brown patina, stamped "CIRE PERDUE / SIOT" and with three paper labels numbered 2.277 and 277 in ink and one printed No 139 to underside, signed "VAN. ROZEN," 7-7/8".................**$121**

Sotheby's

"Last One In," Mark Hopkins (American, 20th/21st century), 1989, bronze with brown patina, inscribed on base "Mark Hopkins 89," 13" x 10" x 6"...**$2,250**

Heritage Auctions

FIREARMS

Firearms

GUN COLLECTING has been going on since the first chunks of lead were fired out of old muskets, but it wasn't until the Industrial Revolution that things got interesting. Early manufacturers and inventors changed the way firearms were produced and conceived and, as a result, hundreds of makes and models of handguns, shotguns, and rifles have been produced. Some of these guns have changed the world through their use in wars, exploration, and hunting.

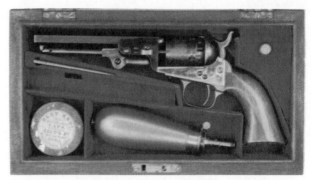

London Colt Model 1849 pocket revolver, SN 8364, .31 caliber, blue and color case hardened with 5" octagon barrel. More Model 1849 revolvers were produced than any other Colt percussion firearm. Production began in 1850 and continued through 1873. The total of the Hartford-made series was about 340,000. The London Model 1849 totaled about 11,000 from 1853-1857, during the height of British colonialism throughout Asia, Africa, and the Middle East.**$8,050**

James D. Julia, Inc.

Collectible guns receiving the most attention are ones used by both famous and infamous people alike. In the last decade, the guns of Theodore Roosevelt, Ernest Hemingway, and baseball great Ted Williams have sold for staggering amounts of money. Roosevelt's specially made double-barreled shotgun set a world record when it sold for $862,500 at a James D. Julia auction in 2010, while a Hemingway-owned Westley Richards side-by-side safari rifle sold for $340,000 at auction in 2011. Two pistols found on the bodies of famed Depression-era outlaws Bonnie Parker and Clyde Barrow, after they were killed in 1934, sold for $504,000 at an RR Auction sale in 2012. The Colt .45 used by James Arness in his iconic role as Sheriff Matt Dillon on TV's "Gunsmoke" sold for $59,000, over five times its high estimate, at High Noon's Western Americana auction in Mesa, Arizona, in January 2014.

In these rare cases provenance is everything, according to Wes Dillon, head of James D. Julia Rare Firearm & Military Division. "The results (from the Roosevelt sale) were a direct reflection of the significance and importance of the man and his gun," Dillon said.

Keep in mind, however, that these are exceptional, historical finds in the gun-collecting world and command extraordinary prices befitting the historical figure associated with the weapon. Some of these high prices are certainly driven by vanity – the desire to own a one-of-a-kind gun – while others are seen as investments. Either way, the right gun with the right history can realize staggering results at auction.

—James Card, Editor,
Gun Digest the Magazine

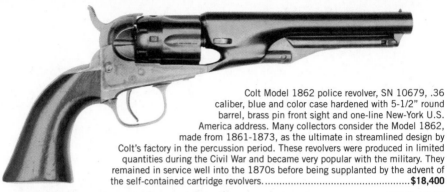

Colt Model 1862 police revolver, SN 10679, .36 caliber, blue and color case hardened with 5-1/2" round barrel, brass pin front sight and one-line New-York U.S. America address. Many collectors consider the Model 1862, made from 1861-1873, as the ultimate in streamlined design by Colt's factory in the percussion period. These revolvers were produced in limited quantities during the Civil War and became very popular with the military. They remained in service well into the 1870s before being supplanted by the advent of the self-contained cartridge revolvers...**$18,400**

James D. Julia, Inc.

Understanding Value

Like any collectible item, it is important to understand that the value of a used firearm greatly depends on its condition. There are six grades of gun conditions, and how a gun is graded is key to its value:

NEW IN BOX: The gun is in its original box with the papers that came with it. But this grade also means that the gun has never been fired, and there is no sign whatsoever that the gun has been handled or used. This is the highest grade for a used gun.

EXCELLENT: The gun may have been used but so gently and lightly that 98 percent of its finish remains as if it were brand new. All of its parts are still original and have not been swapped out with foreign ones. That includes no repairs or alternations.

VERY GOOD: The gun is in good working order and 100 percent original but may have had some minor repair work or alterations. Finish should be around 92 percent.

GOOD: The gun must have 80 percent of its original finish remaining. Alterations, repairs, or additions are acceptable as long as they are not major ones. Must be safe to fire and in decent working condition.

FAIR: The gun is safe and in working order but only about 30 percent of its original finish remains. May have had a major overhaul in a refinishing process or some other kind of alteration.

POOR: Gun is piece of junk and unsafe to fire – rusty, cracked wood. Unless the gun has some incredible historical significance, it is not worth your time or money to mess around with other than hanging it above a fireplace as a conversation piece.

It is important not to deceive yourself about a gun's value. Professional gun appraisers will notice small details that were missed in your amateur inspection. If you think you have an old gun of value, or you are contemplating buying one, please do your homework. The landscape is pockmarked with unscrupulous people more than happy to separate you from your hard-earned money for something of dubious value. As always, knowledge is power. An excellent reference for antique American arms is *Flayderman's Guide to Antique American Firearms...and Their Values*. Norm Flayderman is arguably the world's best-known antique arms dealer and authority. Gun collectors and historians have long considered his book an indispensable tool. Other excellent resources are the *Standard Catalog of Firearms* and *The Blue Book of Gun Values*. Both offer an impressive depth and breadth of knowledge to the gun-collecting hobby.

Even with the help of a dependable reference such as *Flayderman's*, you may be well served getting the advice of a professional gun appraiser, especially if you think there is something unique or special about the gun you have or are considering buying. Armed with that knowledge, you can make an intelligent buying or selling decision.

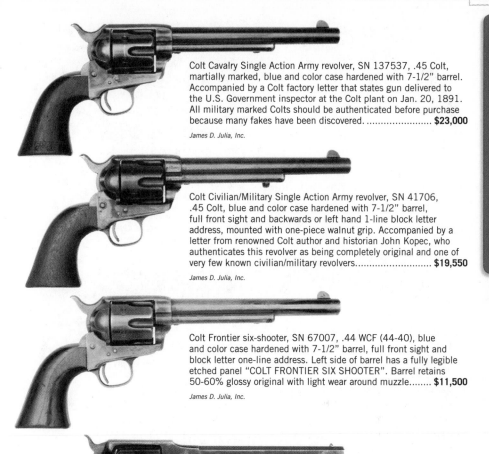

Colt Cavalry Single Action Army revolver, SN 137537, .45 Colt, martially marked, blue and color case hardened with 7-1/2" barrel. Accompanied by a Colt factory letter that states gun delivered to the U.S. Government inspector at the Colt plant on Jan. 20, 1891. All military marked Colts should be authenticated before purchase because many fakes have been discovered. **$23,000**

James D. Julia, Inc.

Colt Civilian/Military Single Action Army revolver, SN 41706, .45 Colt, blue and color case hardened with 7-1/2" barrel, full front sight and backwards or left hand 1-line block letter address, mounted with one-piece walnut grip. Accompanied by a letter from renowned Colt author and historian John Kopec, who authenticates this revolver as being completely original and one of very few known civilian/military revolvers........................... **$19,550**

James D. Julia, Inc.

Colt Frontier six-shooter, SN 67007, .44 WCF (44-40), blue and color case hardened with 7-1/2" barrel, full front sight and block letter one-line address. Left side of barrel has a fully legible etched panel "COLT FRONTIER SIX SHOOTER". Barrel retains 50-60% glossy original with light wear around muzzle........ **$11,500**

James D. Julia, Inc.

Remington Beals Army Percussion revolver, SN 1173, .44 caliber, 8" octagon barrel, dovetailed German silver cone front sight with grooved top strap rear sight. Few Beals Army revolvers remain today with only about 1,900 produced from 1861-1862. They were all issued to Union troops and saw continuous service throughout the Civil War and later on the American frontier, usually under harsh and adverse conditions with limited or no maintenance. **$20,700**

James D. Julia, Inc.

Collectible Guns as an Investment

On Internet message boards, there is considerable debate about collectible guns as an investment. There are arguments for and against the idea that acquiring guns could enhance your financial portfolio. It's true that certain collectible firearms have realized substantial return on investment. As with any investment, however, there is risk.

Here are some points to consider before you decide to include collectible firearms in your investment portfolio:

- Don't venture into gun collecting as an investment unless you know what you're doing.
- To get to the point of knowing could take years of study of both guns and the marketplace.
- If you decide to invest in firearms, it's often wise to choose a specialty, preferably with a type of gun that you are personally interested in. There are numerous manufacturer-specific gun collector associations and they are a great place to start your research.
- Investing in anything entails risk.

FIREARMS

Colt Sheriff's Model D.A. revolver, SN 1389, .38 Colt, nickel finish with 3-1/2" barrel, full front sight and 2-line address with etched panel on left side "COLT D.A. 38," mounted with one-piece checkered walnut grip. Colt factory letter states revolver shipped to George E. Pond, address unknown, on June 14, 1877.........................$11,500

James D. Julia, Inc.

Boxed pair Colt Third Model "Thuer" Deringer, SN 4563 and 12739, .41 RF, nickel finish, 2-1/2" barrels, tiny half moon front sights, marked "COLT" on tops. Made from 1870-1912, the Third Model, or Thuer Deringer, outsold by nearly three times its No. 1 and No. 2 companions. Both mounted with two-piece, smooth, birdhead pearl grips. Accompanied by rare two-piece dark burgundy cardboard box with pink top label...............$11,500

James D. Julia, Inc.

Remington Model 1875 Single Action Army revolver, SN 1296, .44 WCF (44-40), nickel finished with 7-1/2" barrel. Only about 25,000-30,000 Model 1875s were produced from 1875-1889. Remington revolvers were popular with their users but they arrived late on the market. Given Colt's head start with their Model 1873 and government contracts, along with Colt's advanced distribution system, Remingtons were never plentiful on the frontier. Mounted with smooth two-piece ivory grips. $17,250

James D. Julia, Inc.

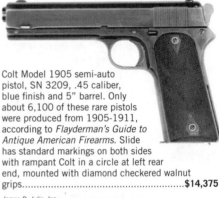

Colt Model 1905 semi-auto pistol, SN 3209, .45 caliber, blue finish and 5" barrel. Only about 6,100 of these rare pistols were produced from 1905-1911, according to *Flayderman's Guide to Antique American Firearms*. Slide has standard markings on both sides with rampant Colt in a circle at left rear end, mounted with diamond checkered walnut grips...$14,375

James D. Julia, Inc.

Smith & Wesson No. 3 Second Model American Single Action revolver (dubbed the "American"), .44 revolver with 8" barrel, first such gun adopted by U.S. military. About 20,700 guns were made from 1872-1874. The interlocking hammer and latch and a bump in the bottom of the frame just above the trigger identify it. $23,000

Rock Island Auction Co.

One of an estimated 2,000 Remington Model 1890 Single Action Army revolvers manufactured from 1891-1896. This scarce model revolver is one of the most sought after of all Remington produced handguns. Top of the barrel is marked "REMINGTON ARMS CO. ILION, N.Y." and "44 C.F.W." on the left side of the frame just below the cylinder. $25,875

Rock Island Auction Co.

Rifles

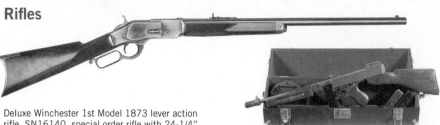

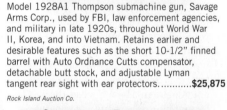

Deluxe Winchester 1st Model 1873 lever action rifle, SN16140, special order rifle with 24-1/4" round barrel. Winchester Museum factory records are virtually complete for the rifle, making it a model collectors can specialize in. This rifle was received in the warehouse April 19, 1876....**$57,500**

James D. Julia, Inc.

Model 1928A1 Thompson submachine gun, Savage Arms Corp., used by FBI, law enforcement agencies, and military in late 1920s, throughout World War II, Korea, and into Vietnam. Retains earlier and desirable features such as the short 10-1/2" finned barrel with Auto Ordnance Cutts compensator, detachable butt stock, and adjustable Lyman tangent rear sight with ear protectors............**$25,875**

Rock Island Auction Co.

Rare U.S. Department of Indian Affairs Saddle Ring carbine, SN 16214, .45-70 caliber, Winchester-Hotchkiss Second Model Bolt Action with 24" barrel with standard sights, single barrel band and marked near breech: Co. D. Varnished walnut stock, left side marked: USDIA [U.S. Department of Indian Affairs]. One of 4396 manufactured... **$2,760**

Heritage Auctions, Inc.

Winchester Model 20 Junior Trap Shooting Outfit, SN 9945, .410 with 26" barrel with full choke, small bore shotgun offered 1920-1924. Black leatherette case (30"x 8-3/4" x 6") contains a Winchester midget hand trap and steel two-piece cleaning rod; two ounce tube of Winchester gun grease in green box; Winchester gun oil; Winchester rust remover; and a case of 100 midget-sized clay targets. **$12,075**

James D. Julia, Inc.

Browning Superposed Grade IV-W.410, SN P83RN1064, 26-1/2" barrels with raised, ventilated rib, choked IC and modified. Pheasants and quail engraved on left sideplate; four ducks in marsh on right; flying quail on bottom of action; and dog's head on trigger guard bow. Each sideplate is signed by engraver, "J. Lewanczyk," 6 lbs., 9 oz. **$29,900**

James D. Julia, Inc.

Folk Art/Americana

FOR A COUNTRY that takes deep pride in calling itself a nation of immigrants, American folk art and Americana is like the ribbon tying our collective heritage together. Rich with evidence of German woodworking, Scottish ship-carving, or perhaps African tribal motifs, each work is one-of-a-kind and stands on its own, backed by good ol' American individuality. The fact that most works were completed by self-taught artists who had little to no formal training enhances the appeal to the collectors of American folk art and Americana. In one sense, the vernacular charm symbolizes the country's reputation for ambition, ingenuity, and imagination. There's little wonder why American folk art and Americana are more popular than ever.

The last few years saw several large folk art and Americana collections come to market with spectacular results. It also saw preservationists and scholars take major steps to ensure folk art remains an important art form in our national heritage.

Sotheby's presentation of the Ralph Esmerian collection of American folk art in early 2014 generated the highest proceeds ever for an American folk art collection. The 228-lot selection from the former chairman emeritus of the American Folk Art Museum was as noteworthy as its owner was notorious. Esmerian is serving a six-year federal sentence for fraud associated with the sale of jewelry and collectibles worth millions. The collection was ordered to be sold to provide restitution to victims and generated more than $10.5 million.

The collection held true American treasures. The top lot was a carved figure of Santa Claus by master carver Samuel Robb — the last figure he ever carved, in fact. Famous for his cigar store American Indian figures, Robb completed the 38" Santa in 1923 as a Christmas present to his daughter, Elizabeth. The figure more than doubled its pre-auction estimate to hammer for $875,000.

The sale meant that two Samuel Robb-carved figures achieved world records within just months of each other. The Maryland-based auction firm of Guyette, Schmidt and Deeter sold a rare Robb cigar store American Indian princess, circa 1880, in late 2013 for a record $747,000.

Another sign of this category's growing interest with collectors and the general public is the popularity of the only museum dedicated to the scholarly study and exhibition of the country's self-taught artisans. In 2013, the American Folk Art Museum had record attendance with over 100,000 visitors. The museum's more than 5,000 items were collected almost entirely through gifts. Collectors cheered in December 2013 when the museum digitized and gave away free 118 issues of *Folk Art* magazine (formerly *The Clarion*), originally published between winter 1971 and fall 2008. The trove may be accessed online (as of 2015) at issuu.com/american_folk_art_museum.

– Eric Bradley

Fish spearing decoy, 20th century, Chautauqua Lake, New York type with "through body" line tie, brass tack eyes, painted leather tail, and classic carved gills and mouth, 6-7/8" l..............................**$2,800**

Conestoga Auction Co.

Desk accessories, circa 1840-1850, letter holders, hand painted, likely manufactured in England, made specifically for export to America where abolition movement was active, base rests on four bun feet, bottom stamped "Ennens & Bettridge Makers to the Queen," 8" l. x 8" h. x 2-1/2" d.. **$500**

Heritage Auctions

Americana cigar store Indian featured in *Treasury of American Design* by Clarence P. Hornung, 19th century. ...**$37,000**

Cottone Auctions

Col. Harlan Sanders trademark white suit and string bow-tie, jacket with label from tailor Merton Chesher of Toronto, slacks with label from tailor Warren K. Cook with name of client, Col. H. Sanders, framed 16" x 20" Similart photograph of Sanders, vinyl album containing 16 8" x 10" black and white and color photos of Sanders, booklet issued in conjunction with Sanders' 80th birthday, reel of color 16mm film, and other personal items................**$21,510**

Heritage Auctions

Whirlygig, man with top hat, carved and painted, 19th century, missing flags, chips to hat and coattails, original paint, 18" h. **$6,600**

Cottone Auctions

Lamp commemorating Philadelphia Sesquicentennial, 1926, glass lamp in shape of Liberty Bell, mounted on swinging yoke, base reads: "Souvenir The Sesqui-Centennial International Exposition 1776 Philadelphia 1926 150 Years of American Independence," 7" h. **$593**

Heritage Auctions

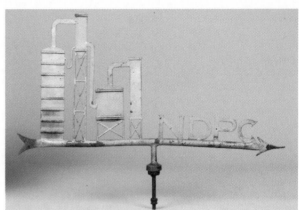

Weathervane, early 20th century, sheet metal in form of liquor distillery, old surface, unusual, 17" h. x 36" w. **$1,400**

Cottone Auctions

Civil War-period carvings by Private John A. Bair, Co. B, 45th Pennsylvania Volunteer Infantry: four wooden carved chains, two sections about 5" and two about 12" with words "Lincoln," "Dead," "Gone," and "April" on edge of links, longer section features battle or engagement Bair participated in on edge of each link including "Wilderness," "Annapolis," "Hanover," "James River" and several others, also two wooden whimsies and Victorian sewing box with inscription inside lid: "John Bair / 45th Co. B / Pennsylvania." **$597**

Heritage Auctions

TOP LOT!

Santa Claus figure by Samuel Robb, circa 1923, New York, paint on wood with mica flakes, inscribed underside of base, THIS IS THE / LAST FIGURE / MADE BY SAMUEL A. ROBB / ABOUT 1923 / Elizabeth W. Robb / MAY 16, 1966, 38-3/4" x 16" x 15-7/8" **$875,000**

Heritage Auctions

Cast iron coal chute cover, "J.W. FISKE, N.Y.," disk with cast knob in diamond pattern design with manufactory name in relief, custom stand, 17-3/4" h. x 15-1/2" dia. **$461**

Skinner, Inc. www.skinnerinc.com

U.S. Civil War soldier's bawdy song, "Miss Tickletoe air Bow Wow Wow," unsigned eight-verse poem with single stanza, handwritten on vintage paper, U.S. capitol embossing in corner, two sheets, 8" l. x 5" w. **$200**

Thomaston Place Auctions

Carving, pine panel, early 20th century, marked "St. Joe Arkansas R.P. Kreider," (Rupert, 1897-1983), carved with image of drunk man snoozing by tree next to outhouse, dead bird draped over branch above, wife sawing wood, 9-1/2" w. x 12" h. **$1,500**

Thomaston Place Auctions

Mirror frame, late 19th century, with fully dimensional fruit and foliage made from leather, gilt edge of what is probably walnut frame exposed, 24" x 28"...**$275**

Thomaston Place Auctions

Masonic folk art carved horn dipper or ladle, 1790s, with design elements that include arch and keystone, all-seeing eye, beehive, hand-colored American flags (one with 14 stars), mallet, pick, quarter moon, birds, Masonic lodge, rooster on roof, keys, hand-colored thistles, scrolls or book with Masonic tools and symbols, hand-colored vine-covered column and full moon, brass, 5" h......................**$1,673**

Heritage Auctions

Sculpture, stone, circa 19th century, New England, "Portrait of a Sea Faring Gentleman" with moustache, arms crossed, in turtleneck and jacket, 20" h. **$6,500**

Thomaston Place Auctions

Folk art carved cane by artist Bill Pollard (Virginia, 1929-2005), circa 1990-1995, original polychrome-painted surface, unidentified hardwood, pierced and spiral-carved example with contrasting color snakes and stylized African American head at handle, inscriptions include "For JOHN / PALMER / by POLLARD" and "MONEY AIN'T EVERYTHING - / JUST WAY AHEAD OF / WHAT IS 2nd," 36-1/4" l...........**$3,335**

Jeffrey S. Evans & Associates

FOLK ART/AMERICANA

Large burl bowl, possibly Native American, early 19th century, elliptical form with pierced integral handles, shrinkage cracks, 9-1/2" h. x 22-1/2" w. x 28" l.. **$7,995**

Skinner, Inc. www.skinnerinc.com

New England hooked rug, circa 1900, with three cow heads on plum field, gray trim, inscribed at bottom "Feb 1900 Alice," twill tape-bound edge, 20" h. x 40" w. **$950**

Thomaston Place Auctions

Needlework memorial, circa 1869, with angels and weeping willow trees, period bird's-eye maple frame, 26" x 17".. **$125**

Cottone Auctions

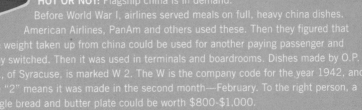

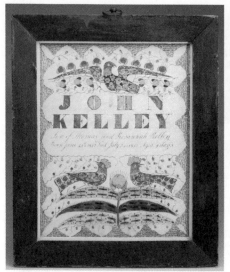

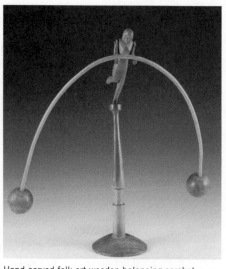

Fraktur, unidentified artist, circa 1846, Hampshire County, Virginia (now West Virginia), watercolor, ink, and gold leaf on paper, birth and death record made for John Kelley with spread-wing eagle perched on flowering vine above "JOHN / KELLEY / Son of Thomas and Rosannah Kelley / Born June 25th 1847 Died July 3rd 1847 Aged 9 Days," lower section with birds perched on elongated leaves of flowering plant surrounded by flowering vine, whole within drape-like border, period green-painted frame with brass hanger; work attributed to Shenandoah Valley Illuminated Artist, Winchester, Virginia area, one of only six known examples by this unidentified artist working in Frederick and Hampshire Counties in 1840s and 1850s, rare, 10" x 8" sight. **$32,200**

Jeffrey S. Evans & Associates

Hand-carved folk art wooden balancing acrobat toy, early 20th century, New Haven, Connecticut, 15" h. x 14" w. **$550**

Thomaston Place Auctions

Baseball painted by folk artist George Sosnak, 1969, produced in honor of St. Louis Cardinals player Stan Musial, applied clear coat, signed "By Geo. H. Sosnak 1969." Sosnak was a former umpire who produced many of these painted balls over his lifetime **$15,535**

Heritage Auctions

Spool holder, circa 1900, with carved deer, missing two deer and row of spool holders, 28" h. x 15" w. **$250**

Cottone Auctions

FOLK ART/AMERICANA

$

Utility boxes, late 19th century, bentwood, three yellow-painted examples, two green-painted examples, and two red-painted examples, possibly Shaker, 6-1/2" l...$2,250

Doyle New York

TOP LOT!

Cigar store Indian princess, circa 1880, cigar bundle in left hand, tobacco leaves in right hand, attributed to New York workshop of Samuel Robb or Thomas Brooks, 83" h. World record sale in 2013. .....**$747,000**

Guyette, Schmidt and Deeter

Basket on stand, circa 1930s, yellow pine with pattern of applied used and unused bottle caps, bucket with scalloped rim and handles, stand with applied crimped tin molding, whole in fine original polychrome-painted surface as discovered in Colliersville, Rockbridge County, Virginia, 30" h. x 15" dia. **$2,990**

Jeffrey S. Evans & Associates

Stoneware jar, circa 1825, salt-glazed, James Miller (active 1797-1827), Alexandria, Virginia or Georgetown, D.C., reversed "3" gallon capacity mark, ovoid form with single incised ring below flanged flat-top rim, slightly arched tab-like handles, crudely beaded foot, brushed and slip-trailed cobalt spread-wing shield-breast Federal eagle decoration on one side, additional cobalt across top of handles, 12-1/4" h. x 7-1/4" dia. rim...............**$75,750**

Jeffrey S. Evans & Associates

Sternboard, eagle, circa 1960, softwood, by Harold B. Simmons of Rockland, Maine, gilt and black painted, signed with incised script on back, 77" w. **$12,000**

Thomaston Place Auctions

Relief-carved mahogany cake board, John Conger and James Y. Watkins, New York, circa 1850s, square board centered with circular carving of basket of flowers topped with bird with floral, foliate, and scalloped borders, impressed "J. CONGER" on two edges and "J.Y. WATKINS N.Y." twice on two corners on front, 10-1/2" x 10-3/4"........................... **$6,765**

Skinner, Inc. www.skinnerinc.com

Molded copper stag weathervane with stand, late 19th century, flattened full-body figure with molded sheet copper ears and antlers, mounted on tubular copper rod, weathered gilded surface, dents and seam separations, 31" h. x 21-1/2" l. **$19,680**

Skinner, Inc. www.skinnerinc.com

Betty lamp, circa 19th century, wrought iron with swivel cover and bird finial, hanging hook and wick pick, possibly Pennsylvania, 7" h. to top of arm. **$1,150**

Jeffrey S. Evans & Associates

Miniature blue-painted covered firkin, Edmund Hersey, Hingham, Massachusetts, 19th century, stave and lapped bentwood hoop-constructed container joined with copper tacks, conforming cover impressed with maker's initials "ELH," pegged swing handle, minor loss, 2-1/4" h., 3-1/4" h. to top of handle. **$8,610**

Skinner, Inc. www.skinnerinc.com

Hourglass, Shamokin Lodge #664, 19th century, turned maple, original finish and gilded decoration, 12" h. x 7" dia............................ **$1,750**

Cottone Auctions

Folk art carving of Boston sperm whale, circa 1890, fully dimensional, black enameled hardwood, later screw-eyes for hanging, 23" l... **$2,000**

Thomaston Place Auctions

John James Trumbull Arnold (Pennsylvania, Maryland, Virginia, 1812-1865), oil on canvas, circa 1850, depicting four-year-old Mary Mattingly of Mount Savage, Maryland, holding rose in one hand, signed, inscribed, and dated "Portrait of Mary Mattingly / Drawn by John Arnold / On the 26th of October / 1850" in Arnold's calligraphic script verso, 32" x 25" sight........................**$33,350**

Jeffrey S. Evans & Associates

Picture, folk art cut paper pin-prick image, circa 1840-1860, watercolor and ink on paper, polychrome decoration depicting swans, urns, and hunt scene framing central mariner's compass with portrait of ship at center, 16-3/4" w. x 11-1/2" h. **$2,530**

Jeffrey S. Evans & Associates

Figural folk art carved and painted maple pipe, late 19th/early 20th century, pipe bowl depicting head of man smoking large cigar, stem with brass band connector, on custom-made stand, 6-1/2" h. overall, pipe 6-5/8" l. **$2,337**

Skinner, Inc. www.skinnerinc.com

Display of carved and painted songbirds, contemporary, Rochester, New York, 30" h. x 24" w. **$6,700**

Cottone Auctions

10 **Things** You Didn't Know About
Presidents and Presidential Collectibles

1 Five days after the assassination of President John F. Kennedy, the American flag and the presidential flag that stood in the White House Oval Office during his term were given by First Lady Jackie Kennedy to the president's personal secretary, Evelyn Lincoln. The pair of flags sold for $350,000, nearly three times the presale estimate, during Heritage Auctions' Political & Americana Auction in November 2013.

2 Good friends and equally good rivals, John Adams and Thomas Jefferson, second and third U.S. presidents, respectively, both passed away on the same day, July 4, 1826.

3 John Tyler, the 10th president of the United States, married twice and fathered 15 children – more than any other president in history.

Cox and Roosevelt jugate pinback from the 1920 presidential election sold for $26,000 in November 2011.

4 In July 2010 the black silk shawl, folding parasol, and folding fan belonging to President Abraham Lincoln's widow, Mary Todd Lincoln, sold for $16,500 during a sale at Cowan's Auctions. The final sale price was more than three times the presale estimate.

5 The 18th U.S. president, Ulysses S. Grant, was a cigar aficionado. It's reported Grant routinely smoked at least 20 a day, and ultimately it was part of his demise. He died of throat cancer at the age of 63.

6 Dwight Eisenhower, 34th U.S. president, enjoyed golf so much he ordered a putting green be installed at the White House. It's reported he played more than 800 rounds during his time in office. A fraying, circa 1950s golf bag used by Eisenhower sold for $3,750 in May 2004 through Heritage Auctions.

7 Of the 43 individuals who have served as U.S. president, eight have died while in office, and four of those were assassinated.*

8 More than 2,000 people are members of the American Political Items Collectors group, www.apic.us. The organization was founded in 1945.

9 An uncommon red, white and blue "Cox Roosevelt Club" pinback jugate of the 1920 election, featuring Democratic running mates James Cox and Franklin D. Roosevelt, fetched $26,000 during a sale at Heritage Auctions in November 2011. The campaign didn't end well for Cox and Roosevelt, who lost the presidential election – the first election in which women were able to vote in all U.S. states, which numbered 48 at the time.

10 Jimmy Carter, the 39th U.S. president and a recipient of the Nobel Peace Prize, is on record as saying he witnessed an unidentified flying object in Georgia in the autumn of 1969.

— *Compiled by Antoinette Rahn*

---

*President Barack Obama is the 44th U.S. president, but there have been only 43 different individuals who have served the office. Grover Cleveland is counted twice because his two terms were non-consecutive.

Sources: www.pbs.org, www.sherwoodforest.org, www.history.com, www.liveauctioneers.com, Golf Week, www.apic.us, New York Times Learning Network, and *White House Confidential: The Little Book of Weird Presidential History*.

Furniture

ANTIQUE FURNITURE

FURNITURE COLLECTING has been a major part of the world of collecting for more than 100 years. It is interesting to note how this marketplace has evolved.

In past decades, 18th century and early 19th century furniture was the mainstay of the American furniture market, but in recent years there has been a growing demand for furniture manufactured since the 1920s. Factory-made furniture from the 1920s and 1930s, often featuring Colonial Revival style, has seen a growing appreciation among collectors. It is well made and features solid wood and fine veneers rather than the cheap compressed wood materials often used since the 1960s. Also much in demand in recent ears is furniture in the Modernistic and Mid-Century taste, ranging from Art Deco through quality designer furniture of the 1950s through the1970s (see "Modern Furniture" later in this section).

These latest trends have offered even the less well-heeled buyer the opportunity to purchase fine furniture at often reasonable prices. Buying antique and collectible furniture is no longer the domain of millionaires and museums.

Today more furniture is showing up on Internet sites, and sometimes good buys can be made. However, it is important to deal with honest, well-informed sellers and have a good knowledge of what you want to purchase.

As in the past, it makes sense to purchase the best pieces you can find, whatever the style or era of production. Condition is still very important if you want your example to continue to appreciate in value in the coming years. For 18th century and early 19th century pieces, the original finish and hardware are especially important as it is with good furniture of the early 20th century Arts & Crafts era. These features are not quite as important for most manufactured furniture of the Victorian era and furniture from the 1920s and later. However, it is good to be aware that a good finish and original hardware will mean a stronger market when the pieces are resold. Of course, whatever style of furniture you buy, you are better off with examples that have not had major repair or replacements. On really early furniture, repairs and replacements will definitely have an impact on the sale value, but they will also be a factor on newer designs from the 20th century.

As with all types of antiques and collectibles, there is often a regional preference for certain furniture types. Although the American market is much more homogenous than it was in past decades, there still tends to be a preference for 18th century and early 19th century furniture along the Eastern Seaboard, whereas Victorian designs tend to have a larger market in the Midwest and South. In the West, country furniture and "western" designs definitely have the edge except in major cities along the West Coast.

Whatever your favorite furniture style, there are still fine examples to be found. Just study the history of your favorites and the important points of their construction before you invest heavily. A wise shopper will be a happy shopper and have a collection certain to continue to appreciate as time marches along.

For more information on furniture, see *Antique Trader Furniture Price Guide* by Kyle Husfloen.

FURNITURE

Miniature painted mammy's bench, late 19th century with decoupage decoration on red ground, 6-1/2" h. x 14-1/2" w. **$415**

Pook & Pook, Inc.

Philadelphia Federal mahogany bedstead, circa 1805, foot post with acanthus and swag carving, 95" h. x 59-1/2" w. x 87" l. **$4,029**

Pook & Pook, Inc.

Cast iron fern garden bench, 19th century, stamped James W. Carr Richmond, Virginia, 29-1/2" h. x 44-3/4" w. **$1,920**

Pook & Pook, Inc.

Pennsylvania walnut bucket bench, 19th century, 43-3/4" h. x 39-1/2" w. **$1,800**

Pook & Pook, Inc.

Pennsylvania painted bucket bench, 19th century, retaining old red stained surface, 49-1/2" h. x 41-3/4" w. **$1,320**

Pook & Pook, Inc.

George III-style mahogany and glass secretary bookcase, 19th century, in two parts, bookcase with latticework to glass paned doors, dentil border to upper rim, four shelves to interior with modern electrical wiring, secretary with two small drawers to upper corner of each side and four large drawers down center, fillet border to rims, 86-3/4" h. x 48" w. x 22-1/4" d. **$2,438**

Heritage Auctions

William IV rosewood bookcase, circa 1835, fitted with two shelves and mirror backsplash, 53-3/4" x 60" x 13". **$750**

Heritage Auctions

Red-painted candlestand, probably New England, late 18th century, circular top on vase- and ring-turned support ending hexagonal block and drop pendant on three shaped legs, old surface, imperfections, 25-1/2" h. x 15-1/2" d............. **$960**

Skinner, Inc., www.skinnerinc.com

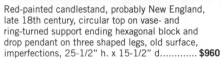

Walnut candlestand with game board-decorated top, probably New England, circa 1830, square top on vase- and ring-turned post and tripod base of shaped legs, top retains original decoration centering checkerboard, border with Union shields and geometric stars alternating with heart, spade, diamond, and club, 27" h. x 17" w. x 17" d... **$3,600**

Skinner, Inc., www.skinnerinc.com

Federal maple candlestand, New England, circa 1790, square top with ovolo corners on vase- and ring-turned support and tripod base of cabriole legs, remnants of old green paint, restoration, 27-1/2" h. x 16-1/2" w. x 16-1/4" d............. **$390**

Skinner, Inc., www.skinnerinc.com

Painted Windsor fan-back upholstered armchair, probably from shop of Joseph Henzey, Philadelphia, circa 1780-1790, with carved knuckle handholds and finely turned arm supports, legs, and stretchers, early green paint over earlier red, 41" h. x seat 15" h............................ **$4,800**

Skinner, Inc., www.skinnerinc.com

Queen Anne carved maple side chair, probably Boston, circa 1720-1740, with spooned scroll-carved cresting, valanced seat frame on block-, vase-, and ring-turned legs joined by bulbous turned front stretcher and square side stretchers, refinished, minor imperfections, 41-3/4" h., seat 17" h. **$960**

Skinner, Inc., www.skinnerinc.com

Pair of Queen Anne maple compass-seat side chairs, Massachusetts, circa 1740-1760, with spooned cresting, vasiform splats, and figured maple stretchers, refinished, minor imperfections, 38-1/4" h. x seat is 16-1/2" h...................... **$2,760**

Skinner, Inc., www.skinnerinc.com

Red-painted bamboo-turned birdcage Windsor armchair, New England, early 19th century, with upward-curving arms, old red paint with black striping over earlier gray-green, repair at crest, 32" h., seat 15-1/2" h. **$240**

Skinner, Inc., www.skinnerinc.com

Inlaid mahogany crewelwork-upholstered easy chair, New England, late 18th century, serpentine crest rail above shaped sides and scrolled arms, on square legs and stretchers, refinished, 46-1/4" h., seat 16-1/2" h. **$4,500**

Skinner, Inc., www.skinnerinc.com

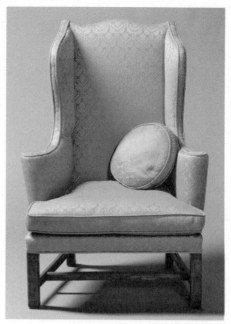

Chippendale upholstered easy chair, New England, late 18th century, serpentine crest rail above outward-scrolling arms and square beaded legs and stretchers, 45" h., seat 15-1/2" h. **$1,080**

Skinner, Inc., www.skinnerinc.com

Black-painted bannister-back armchair, New England, 18th century, shaped crest joining stiles topped with turned finials on five-baluster back, downward-sloping arms ending in scrolled handholds, and vase- and ring-turned supports continuing to ring-turned legs joined by double stretchers, later paint, restoration, 44-1/2" h., seat 17-1/4" h. **$480**

Skinner, Inc., www.skinnerinc.com

Comb-back maple and ash Windsor armed rocking chair, probably New England, early 19th century, with shaped comb and bamboo turnings, 38-1/2" h., seat 15-3/4" h. **$240**

Skinner, Inc., www.skinnerinc.com

Turned red-painted maple roundabout chair, New England, mid-18th century, with scrolled handholds, shaped splats, old splint seat, vase- and ring-turned posts, and turned double stretchers, old surface, imperfections, 29-1/2" h., seat 16" h. **$270**

Skinner, Inc., www.skinnerinc.com

Tall carved maple bannister-back side chair, probably Massachusetts, early 18th century, with Prince of Wales cresting joining block-, vase-, and ring-turned stiles topped with bulbous finials, on rush seat, bulbous-turned front stretcher, and turned double side stretchers joining block-, vase-, and ring-turned front legs to square rear legs with canted ends, old refinish, imperfections, 51-1/2" h., seat 18-1/2" h. **$1,080**

Skinner, Inc., www.skinnerinc.com

George II fruitwood wing chair, circa 1760....... **$608**

Pook & Pook, Inc.

Philadelphia Chippendale mahogany easy chair, circa 1780, with molded square legs. **$4,560**

Pook & Pook, Inc.

Pair of Philadelphia painted plank seat fancy chairs, early/mid 19th century, paper label of George Turner, retaining yellow surface with floral decoration... **$948**

Pook & Pook, Inc.

FURNITURE

Boston classical mahogany armchair, circa 1820. ...... **$2,160**

Pook & Pook, Inc.

George I oak wainscot armchair, circa 1700, with carved back and scrolled arms above plank seat supported by turned legs .. **$2,133**

Pook & Pook, Inc.

New York Chippendale mahogany armchair, circa 1775, with pierced splat and square legs **$180**

Pook & Pook, Inc.

Eleven Queen Anne rush seat dining chairs, probably Massachusetts, circa 1740-1760, nine side chairs and two armchairs, all with spooned crest rails, vasiform splats, and block-, vase-, and ring-turnings, most with carved Spanish feet and old refinish, restoration to some, 44-3/4" h., seats to 17-3/4" h. **$1,680**

Skinner, Inc., www.skinnerinc.com

Eight Queen Anne-style maple and figured maple dining chairs, probably early 20th century, two armchairs and six side chairs, with beaded stiles and block-, vase-, and ring-turned legs ending in Spanish feet, minor imperfections, armchair 42" h., side chair 41" h., seat 18" h. **$1,020**

Skinner, Inc., www.skinnerinc.com

Mahogany and mahogany veneer bowfront chest of four drawers, Massachusetts, circa 1800, molded top above case of four cockbeaded graduated drawers, on molded ogee bracket base, refinished, imperfections, 34" h. x 38-3/4" w. x 23-1/4" d. **$923**

Skinner, Inc., www.skinnerinc.com

Pine chest of drawers, Massachusetts, circa 1700-1720, single arch-molded case of two half-drawers and three graduated long drawers, and applied molding, on turned turnip feet, replaced brass teardrop pulls, painted surface removed long ago, 36" h. x 36-1/2" w. x. 20-3/4" d. **$5,400**

Skinner, Inc., www.skinnerinc.com

Small painted blanket chest, probably Pennsylvania, early 19th century, lift top with molded edge opens to a well with till, on dovetail-constructed box and turned feet, lid in original red paint, box painted brown over earlier red, 21" h. x 29-1/4" w. x 16" d. **$390**

Skinner, Inc., www.skinnerinc.com

Paint-decorated poplar six-board chest, possibly New England, 19th century, lift-top opens to a well, on nail-constructed case with applied base molding, old sponge-applied surface of powder blue and dark blue swirls, paint wear, small molding loss on lid, 18-3/4" h. x 37" w. x 18-1/2" d. **$1,320**

Skinner, Inc., www.skinnerinc.com

Gray/blue-painted pine blanket chest, New England, late 18th century, molded top with cleated ends opens to a well, with applied front molding and cutout ends, original surface, imperfections, 24-1/2" h. x 43-1/4" w. x 17" d. **$450**

Skinner, Inc., www.skinnerinc.com

Small paint-decorated pine six-board chest, New England, late 18th century, molded lift-top opens to a well with till and drawer, on molded bracket base, later painted decoration of blue ground with black banding, yellow striping, and salmon swags with tassels, shrinkage crack on front left panel of box about midway down from top, scattered minor paint loss, 20-1/2" h. x 43" w. x 15" d. **$330**

Skinner, Inc., www.skinnerinc.com

Chippendale cherry chest of four drawers, probably Connecticut, late 18th century, molded top above case of four cockbeaded graduated drawers, all on ogee bracket base, original oval brass, refinished, minor restoration, 34-3/4" h. x 38-1/4" w. x 19" d... **$1,200**

Skinner, Inc., www.skinnerinc.com

Chippendale mahogany block-front chest of drawers, probably Boston, circa 1760-1780, molded overhanging top on cockbeaded case of four graduated drawers on conforming bracket feet, old replaced brasses, refinished, restoration, 31" h. x 29-1/4" w. x 19-3/4" d. **$4,000**

Skinner, Inc., www.skinnerinc.com

Diminutive Pennsylvania painted poplar blanket chest, 19th century, original ochre sponge decorated surface, 19" h. x 34" w................ **$2,133**

Pook & Pook, Inc.

Red-painted blanket chest, probably Massachusetts, early 18th century, molded lift-top opens to a well, cockbeaded case with two faux short drawers above faux long drawer and two working long drawers, with applied molded lower edge, all on turned feet, repainted red, 40-1/2" h. x 36-1/4" w. x 18" d.................................... **$1,920**

Skinner, Inc., www.skinnerinc.com

Pine chest over two drawers, probably Massachusetts, early 18th century, molded hinged top above double arch-molded case of four false drawers and two working drawers, on turned front feet and cutout rear brackets, brasses appear to be old, lacks paint, imperfections, 41" h. x 36-1/2" w. x 17-1/2" d... **$1,353**

Skinner, Inc., www.skinnerinc.com

Red-painted maple cupboard, probably New England, late 18th/early 19th century, hinged door with recessed panels opening to five shelves, on cutout base, original surface, paint wear, 78-1/4" h. x 36" w. x 12-1/2" d............................... **$1,200**

Skinner, Inc., www.skinnerinc.com

Cherry cupboard, New England, 19th century, molded cornice above paneled cupboard doors opening to four beaded shelves, above applied mid-molding and cupboard doors below opening to four red-painted drawers and shelf, all on tall cutout bracket base, 89" h. x 41-1/2" w. x 19-1/2" d. **$1,440**

Skinner, Inc., www.skinnerinc.com

Diminutive butternut two-part wall cupboard, circa 1800, 72" h. x 32-1/2" w. **$2,370**

Pook & Pook, Inc.

Red-painted eight-light hanging cupboard, New England, early 19th century, projecting frame surrounds glazed door opening to two shelves, case with paneled sides, imperfections, 32-1/2" h. x 27" w. x 15" d......................................**$780**

Skinner, Inc., www.skinnerinc.com

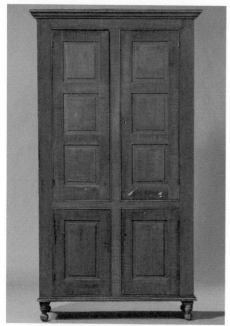

New England painted pine hanging teller's cupboard, circa 1800, with old red surface, 35-1/2" h. x 34" w. **$770**

Pook & Pook, Inc.

Large grain-painted paneled cupboard, New England, first half 19th century, molded cornice above case of tall paneled doors with short doors below opening to six shelves, applied molded lower edge, on removable turned feet, old paint resembling tiger maple, imperfections, 93" h. x 48" w. x 15-3/4" d. **$1,440**

Skinner, Inc., www.skinnerinc.com

Canadian painted pine stepback cupboard, early 19th century, with pierced cornice with hearts and lunettes, 90" h. x 53-1/2" w. **$1,304**

Pook & Pook, Inc.

Canadian painted pine cupboard, circa 1830, with original grained panels and yellow moldings, 46" h. x 58" w. **$2,015**

Pook & Pook, Inc.

Chippendale tiger maple slant-lid desk, probably Massachusetts, late 18th century, slant-lid opens to valanced interior of compartments and drawers centering fan-carved prospect door, on a case of four graduated thumb-molded drawers and ogee bracket feet, old refinish, imperfections, 41-1/2" h. x 37" w. x 18-1/2" d............................... **$1,920**

Skinner, Inc., www.skinnerinc.com

Federal carved and inlaid mahogany tambour writing desk on frame, possibly Thomas Seymour, Boston, while working for Isaac Vose, circa 1812-1825, hinged lid and tambour enclosure above frame with single drawer joining four fluted square tapering legs ending in herm feet, tambour enclosure retracts when drawer is opened, writing surface folds out to be supported by open drawer, refinished, imperfections, 34-1/2" h. x 30" w. x 18" d... **$2,760**

Skinner, Inc., www.skinnerinc.com

Chippendale carved walnut slant-lid desk, Pennsylvania, last half 18th century, lid opens to interior of four fan-carved valance drawers above eight divided compartments and eight drawers, all flanking the central prospect door opening to similarly arranged drawers and compartments, with case of four thumb-molded graduated drawers flanked by quarter-columns, all on ogee bracket feet, old surface, imperfections, 45" h. x 40" w. x 21-1/2" d.. **$1,800**

Skinner, Inc., www.skinnerinc.com

Queen Anne walnut-carved and inlaid fall-front desk, possibly New Hampshire, early 18th century, compass star-inlaid lid opens to interior of compartments and drawers and document drawers faced with pilaster fronts and flame finials, on a case of four thumb-molded, string-inlaid, graduated drawers on bracket feet, brasses replaced, restoration, 42-3/4" h. x 34-3/4" w. x 19-1/2" d.. **$1,400**

Skinner, Inc., www.skinnerinc.com

FURNITURE

New Hampshire Queen Anne tiger maple secretary desk, circa 1760, 80-1/2" h. x 36-1/2" w........................ **$5,925**

Pook & Pook, Inc.

New York Federal mahogany dressing table, circa 1825, with revolving mirror, two drawers, and square tapering legs, 58" h. x 37" w.......................... **$330**

Pook & Pook, Inc.

New York stained pine dressing stand, early 19th century, 56" h. x 23-1/2" w.................... **$330**

Pook & Pook, Inc.

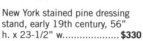

Federal carved and painted pine mantel, circa 1805, outside: 53-1/2" h. x 68-1/4" w; inside: 34-1/2" h. x 48-1/4" w........ **$504**

Pook & Pook, Inc.

New Jersey Chippendale gumwood linen press, late 18th century, 78-1/2" h. x 46" w..................................... **$2,916**

Pook & Pook, Inc.

Queen Anne mahogany dumbwaiter, circa 1760, retaining old dry surface, 47" h.. **$600**

Pook & Pook, Inc.

Pennsylvania walnut pie safe, mid-19th century, with philphlot punched tin panels, 52-3/4" h. x 38-1/4" w **$1,020**

Pook & Pook, Inc.

Carved cherry music stand, America, late 19th/ early 20th century, frame with scrolled top centering foliate cartouche, side rails with inside chamfer, and center with ivory boss and eight copper tacks affixing frame to turned post on cross base, refinished, 39" h **$549**

Skinner, Inc., www.skinnerinc.com

George III mahogany music stand, circa 1800, with adjustable brass candlearms, 44-1/4" h **$3,360**

Pook & Pook, Inc.

Victorian carved mahogany neoclassical pedestal, 20th century, 46" h **$375**

Heritage Auctions

Federal mahogany and mahogany veneer inlaid sideboard, Boston, circa 1800-1810, bowfront top with square corners and inlaid edge on conforming case of rosewood-crossbanded and ebony string-inlaid long drawer flanked by short drawers, above central cupboard flanked by bottle drawers and hinged doors, all vertically divided by bird's-eye maple panels continuing to double tapering legs inlaid with banded cuffs, replaced pulls, refinished, imperfections, 41-1/4" h. x 70" w. x 26-1/2" d **$3,690**

Skinner, Inc., www.skinnerinc.com

Lancaster, Pennsylvania Empire tiger maple sideboard, circa 1825, made by Andrew Snowberger for Snowhill Cloister in Greencastle, 49" x 86" **$6,600**

Pook & Pook, Inc.

China Trade gilt lacquer sewing stand, circa 1830, with carved ivory accoutrements, embroidery samples, etc., 29" h. x 24-1/2" w. x 16-1/2" d **$960**

Pook & Pook, Inc.

Child's painted Hitchcock settee, circa 1840, with original gold stencil decoration on black ground, 26-1/4" h. x 25-1/4" w **$1,422**

Pook & Pook, Inc.

Diminutive New England Sheraton two-seat settee, early 19th century, with overall floral stencil decoration on black ground, 31" h. x 38" w ... **$3,318**

Pook & Pook, Inc.

Chippendale upholstered camel-back sofa, probably England, late 18th century, serpentine crest rail joining outward scrolling arms, square front legs joined to raking rear legs by square stretchers, refinished, imperfections, 34-3/4" h., seat 16-3/4" h., overall length 75"............ **$1,920**

Skinner, Inc., www.skinnerinc.com

Victorian three-piece rosewood parlor suite with sofa and two chairs. **$577**

Pook & Pook

Pair of Queen Anne-style upholstered sofas (one shown)... **$480**

Pook & Pook, Inc.

Classical carved mahogany sofa, 19th century, 86" l. **$461**

Pook & Pook, Inc.

George III-style carved mahogany sofa, 40" h. x 74" w.. **$334**

Pook & Pook, Inc.

Painted pine hanging spoon rack, 19th century, with old red surface, 15-1/2" h. x 12-1/2" w.... **$830**

Pook & Pook, Inc.

Circular table with falling leaves, probably Massachusetts, early 18th century, on block-, vase-, and ring-turned legs joined by straight frame with drawer, old surface, imperfections, 26-3/4" **h.** x 42" **d.** **$1,200**

Skinner, Inc., www.skinnerinc.com

Queen Anne maple drop-leaf dining table, probably Massachusetts, circa 1740-1760, circular drop-leaf top on rolled shaped apron joining cabriole legs ending in pad feet on platforms, refinished, imperfections, 27-1/4" **h.** x 43-1/4" **w.** x 41-1/2" **d.** **$960**

Skinner, Inc., www.skinnerinc.com

Maple and pine drop-leaf table, Massachusetts, early 18th century, overhanging top with short drop leaves on block-, vase-, and ring-turned legs and straight skirt joining square stretchers on turned feet, old surface, alterations, 28" **h.** x 42" **w.** x 27" **d.** **$1,140**

Skinner, Inc., www.skinnerinc.com

Pine hutch table, New England, late 18th/early 19th century, circular top tilts on frame with drawer, sides with cutout ends and trestle feet, old surface, crack across drawer front, scattered stains/burns on top, chips to feet ends, 28-1/4" **h.** **$1,440**

Skinner, Inc., www.skinnerinc.com

Cherry, maple, and pine tavern table with drawer, New England, last half 18th century, rectangular overhanging top with breadboard ends, on block-, vase-, and ring-turned legs continuing to turned button feet, with straight skirt and box stretchers, old refinish, imperfections, 26-1/4" **h.** x top is 33" **w.** and 21-3/4" **d.** **$720**

Skinner, Inc., www.skinnerinc.com

Spanish-style painted iron tile-top side table, circa 1920, 22" x 19" x 12-1/2".............................. **$250**

Heritage Auctions

Pine and ash turned tavern table, New England, 18th century, top with breadboard ends on straight skirt and square stretchers joining four block- and ring-turned legs ending in turned feet, refinished, 26-1/4" h. x 28-1/2" w. x 21" d. **$570**

Skinner, Inc., www.skinnerinc.com

Classical tiger maple drop-leaf table, New England, early 19th century, rectangular top with two shaped leaves above straight skirt joining turned swelled legs ending in turned feet, old refinish, imperfections, 29" h. x 21" w. when closed, 44-1/2" w. open, 35-3/4" d. **$2,040**

Skinner, Inc., www.skinnerinc.com

Classical carved mahogany drop-leaf worktable, probably New England, circa 1810-1820, rectangular top with rounded drop leaves above two drawers, on carved post continuing to tripod base of shaped acanthus-carved legs on casters, old brass pulls, refinished, imperfections, 29" h. x 16" w. x 18" d. **$360**

Skinner, Inc., www.skinnerinc.com

Classical carved mahogany and mahogany veneer two-drawer work table, probably New England, circa 1815-1825, rectangular top with rounded drop leaves and molded edge on four turned and spiral-carved legs ending in tapering feet on brass casters, imperfections, 29-3/4" h. x 32-1/2" w. x 17-1/4" d. **$180**

Skinner, Inc., www.skinnerinc.com

New England Chippendale mahogany Pembroke table, circa 1790, probably Rhode Island, scalloped top with ovolo corners above frame supported by square tapering molded legs joined by serpentine cross stretchers, 28" h. x 19-1/2" w. x 30-1/2" d... **$2,133**

Pook & Pook, Inc.

Chinese gilt lacquer tea table, circa 1840, 30-1/2" h. x 35-1/2" w................................ **$1,200**

Pook & Pook, Inc.

New York classical mahogany washstand, circa 1835, 33" h. x 21-1/2" w............... **$570**

Pook & Pook, Inc.

Elaborate New England painted Sheraton washstand, circa 1825, with stencil and pinstripe decoration on faux rosewood reserve, 38" h. x 18" w............. **$889**

Pook & Pook, Inc.

Modern Furniture

MODERN DESIGN IS EVERYWHERE, evergreen and increasingly popular. Modernism has never gone out of style. Its reach into the present day is as deep as its roots in the past. Just as it can be seen and felt ubiquitously in the mass media of today – on film, television, in magazines and department stores – it can be traced to the mid-1800s post-Empire non-conformity of the Biedermeier Movement, the turn of the 20th century anti-Victorianism of the Vienna Secessionists, the radical reductionism of Frank Lloyd Wright and the revolutionary post-Depression thinking of Walter Gropius and the Bauhaus school in Germany.

"The Modernists really changed the way the world looked," said John Sollo, a partner in Sollo Rago Auction of Lambertville, New Jersey. Sollo's partner in business, and one of the most recognizable names in the field, David Rago, takes Sollo's idea a little further by saying that Modernism is actually more about the names behind the design than the design itself, at least as far as buying goes.

No discussion of Modern can be complete, however, without examining its genesis and enduring influence. Modernism is everywhere in today's pop culture. Austere Scandinavian furniture dominates the television commercials that hawk hotels and mutual funds. Post-war American design ranges across sitcom set dressings to movie sets patterned after Frank Lloyd Wright houses and Hollywood Modernist classics set high in the hills.

Set of four lounge chairs designed by Florence Knoll (American), 1954, upholstery, steel, wood frame, polished chrome finish, each 30-1/2" x 31-1/2" x 31-7/8". **$13,750**

You have to look at the dorm rooms of college students and the apartments of young people whose living spaces are packed with the undeniably Modern mass-produced products of IKEA, Target, Design Within Reach and the like.

There can be no denying that the post-World War II manufacturing techniques and subsequent boom led to the widespread acceptance of plastic and bent plywood chairs along with low-sitting coffee tables, couches and recliners.

"The modern aesthetic grew out of a perfect storm of post-war optimism, innovative materials and an incredible crop of designers," said Lisanne Dickson, director of 1950s/Modern Design at Treadway-Toomey.

Ball wall clock, brass and lacquered wood, designed by George Nelson (American), circa 1955, 13-1/2" x 13-1/2" x 3-1/2".................. **$875**

"I think that the people who designed the furniture were maybe ahead of society's ability to accept and understand what they were doing," Sollo said. "It's taken people another 30 to 40 years to catch up to it."

There are hundreds of great Modern designers, many who worked across categories – furniture, architecture, fine art, etc. – and many contributed to the work of other big names without ever seeking that glory for themselves.

For more information on Modernism, see *Warman's Modernism Furniture & Accessories Identification and Price Guide* by Noah Fleisher.

—Noah Fleisher

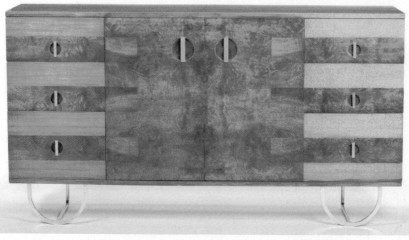

Buffet, walnut and burl walnut, designed by Gilbert Rohde (American), manufactured by Herman Miller, 1933, 35" x 66" x 17"..**$32,500**

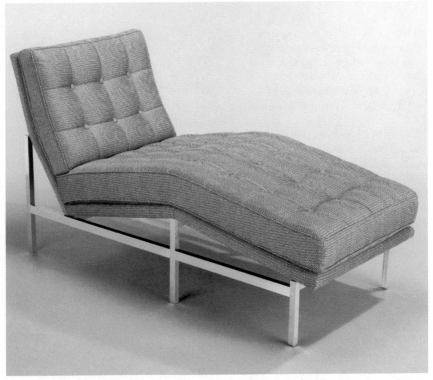

Chaise lounge, chrome-plated steel, upholstery, Knoll International, 29" x 53" x 24". **$7,500**

Set of eight side chairs (Model 149), aluminum, upholstery, designed by Richard Schultz, 1960, 32" x 20" x 22-1/2". **$3,750**

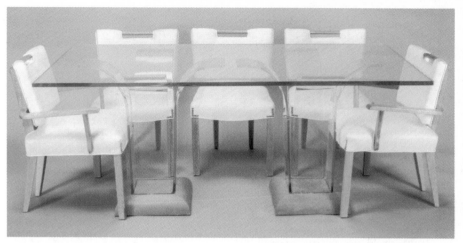

Bleached mahogany dining set, including glass-topped dining table with two four-piece glass pedestal legs and wooden bases and eight chairs, designed by Paul Laszlo (Hungary), 1953, table 30" x 72" x 40"; chairs 31" x 21" x 25" each. ....**$5,000-$7,000**

Four-door credenza designed by Florence Knoll (American), rosewood, marble, chrome-plated steel, 25-1/2" x 74-1/2" x 18". **$4,688**

Sofa, upholstery, steel, wood frame, polished chrome finish, designed by Florence Knoll (American), 1954, 30-1/2" x 89" x 32". **$2,500**

Pair of Danish black leather Egg Chairs designed by Arne Jacobsen (Denmark), 1958, manufactured by Fritz Hansen, metal foil label: MADE IN DENMARK BY FRITZ HANSEN, 0865, FH, FURNITURE MAKERS CONTROL DANISH, 41-3/4" x 34-1/8" x 30-1/2". The organically shaped chair was originally designed by Jacobsen for the lobby and reception areas of the SAS Royal Hotel in Copenhagen in 1958..............................**$10,157**

Leather upholstered aluminum Egg Chair (model no. 3316) with ottoman (model no. 3127) designed by Arne Jacobsen for Fritz Hansen, circa 1958, label on chair: Made in Denmark, 0867, FH by Fritz Hansen, Danish Furniture Makers Control, chair 41-1/2" x 32" x 31", ottoman 17" x 22" x 16". **$9,560**

Lounge chair, gray felt upholstery, steel, wood frame, polished chrome finish, designed by Florence Knoll (American), 1954, 31" x 32-1/2" x 32".. **$1,750**

Sycamore, acajou, and polished bronze center/dining table, circa 1950, 29" x 74" x 39".... **$6,572**

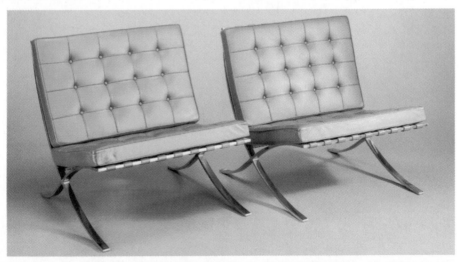

Pair of Barcelona chairs designed by Mies Van Der Rohe (German), Knoll International, circa 1960s, leather, chrome-plated steel, each 29-1/2" x 29" x 30"..**$5,625**

FURNITURE

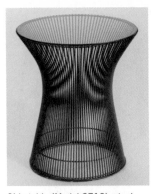

Side table (Model 3710), steel, smoked glass, plastic, designed by Warren Platner (American), 1966, 18" x 15-1/2" x 15-1/2".......................... **$1,188**

Pair of George Nakashima-designed walnut armless chairs with upholstered seat and back cushions, circa 1980, 30-1/2" x 23-1/2" x 34-1/2" each...**$5,676**

Seven-drawer walnut chest designed by George Nakashima, circa 1980, marks: Schure #1806 (in script), 54-3/4" x 36" x 21"........................ **$7,170**

Walnut desk designed by George Nakashima (American), circa 1970, 28" x 48" x 23-5/8"...**$16,730**

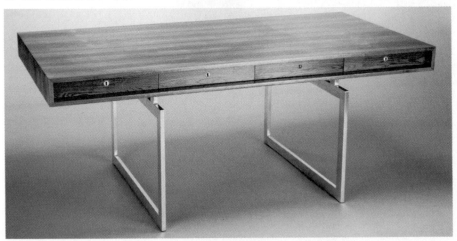

Rosewood veneer desk (Model 901) designed by Bodil Kjaer (Danish), 1959-1960, chrome-plated steel, chrome-plated brass, 28-1/2" x 72-1/2" x 36".. **$11,875**

FURNITURE

English walnut slab coffee table designed by George Nakashima, circa 1964, marks: Schure (in script), 13" x 42" x 31". **$11,352**

Pair of A-framed mahogany chairs (one shown) designed by Edward Wormley for Dunbar Furniture Co., Berne, Indiana, circa 1950, 27" x 25" x 19-1/2". **1,792**

Buffet with two sliding doors, glass shelves and two drawers (Model 1756), bleached mahogany, designed by Paul Laszlo (Hungary), circa 1950s, 38 x 60" x 18". **$625**

Occasional table, aluminum and Bakelite art moderne, designed by Walter Von Nessen, manufactured by Nessen Studio, Inc., United States, circa 1931, impressed on underside: NESSEN STUDIOS, NEW YORK, 451, 18" x 18-1/2" x 12". **$14,340**

Walnut single-pedestal desk designed by George Nakashima, circa 1960s, 28-3/4" x 63-1/4" x 25-1/8". **$9,560**

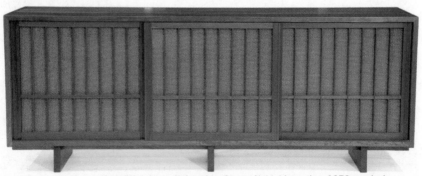

Cherry credenza with burlap cloth-lined doors designed by George Nakashima, circa 1970, marks in pencil to back: MCFADDEN, #3179, 32-1/8" x 84" x 20". **$11,353**

Lounge chair and ottoman designed by Charles Eames and Ray Kaiser Eames, manufactured by Herman Miller, 1956, rosewood veneer, plywood, leather, steel and aluminum; chair 32" x 32-3/4" x 32-3/4", ottoman 17-1/4" x 26" x 21-1/2". **$4,688**

Danish rosewood sideboard with tambour doors designed by Hans Wegner for Ry Mobler, Copenhagen, Denmark, circa 1960, marks: RY MOBLER, DEC 1965 (stamped), DANISH, FURNITURE MAKERS CONTROL (label), 31" x 78-3/4" x 19-1/4"....................................... **$1,792**

Two-piece china console (Model 1770), bleached mahogany and glass, designed by Paul Laszlo (Hungarian, 1900-1993), circa 1950s, 51-1/2" x 54" x 18"....................................... **$1,500-$2,500**

Small round dining table with tulip base (Model 172), marble, wood, enameled metal, designed by Eero Saarinen (American), 28-1/2" x 36" x 36" ... **$2,125**

Aluminum and marble table designed by Charles and Ray Eames for Herman Miller, circa 1958, 29-1/2" x 72" x 36".................................. **$1,493**

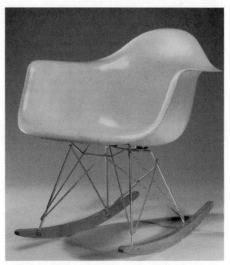

RAR rocker designed by Charles and Ray Eames for Herman Miller, circa 1950, Herman Miller patent label on underside, 26-3/4" x 24-3/4" x 27"... **$597**

FURNITURE

Coffee table designed by George Nakashima,
Persian walnut and rosewood, circa 1970,
13" x 65" x 20-1/2"......**$28,750**

Set of four vinyl upholstered side chairs designed by Russel Wright, circa 1950, stenciled on seat:
C2687A WALMA, 32" x 19-1/2" x 19" each **$2,500**

Set of six chromium-plated metal and leather upholstered chairs designed by Milo Baughman for Thayer
Coggin, circa 1960s, 28-1/4" x 23" x 29" each. **$3,465**

Glass

ART GLASS

ART GLASS IS ARTISTIC NOVELTY GLASSWARE created for decorative purposes. Types of art glass include leaded glass, molded glass, blown glass, and sandblasted glass. Tiffany, Lalique, and Steuben are some of the best-known makers of art glass. Daum Nancy, Baccarat, Gallé, Moser, Mt. Washington, Fenton, and Quezal are a few others.

Marked Stevens & Williams bulbous four-sided vase, clear cased interior with pink, silver, and blue textured exterior and green threaded overlay, factory burst bubbles, rare, 7-1/4". **$2,800**

Woody Auction

Stevens & Williams cameo glass vase, yellow satin background with pink satin overlay with blossom, branch, and butterfly, good condition, 5"......... **$1,000**

Woody Auction

Rare, signed Legras French cameo glass centerpiece compote, lavender cut to clear-center blossom with reeds radiating outward, clear pattern cut stem and base, good condition, 12" x 16". **$1,900**

Woody Auction

Wheel-carved and applied glass vase depicting dawn and dusk, Croismare, France, 1897-1914, Muller Fréres, incised Muller Croismare, 8-1/4" x 5-1/2".......... **$13,750**

Rago Arts

English cameo cabinet vase, white to medium blue, carved with flowering tree, factory polished table ring and concave base, probably Stevens & Williams, fourth quarter 19th century, undamaged, 4-1/4" h. **$575**

Jeffrey S. Evans & Associates

GLASS

$

Peloton-style footed vases, colorless with random applied green threads, polychrome enamel decorations of two birds on branch of flowering tree, additional decoration around rim and foot, probably English or Bohemian, fourth quarter 19th century, one with sliver chip to table ring, otherwise undamaged, 13-1/4" h. **$690**

Jeffrey S. Evans & Associates

Pate-de-verre pendant with ballerina on original silk cord with tassle, France, 1920s, Gabriel Argy-Rousseau (1885-1953), signed, 2" dia. **$1,875**

Rago Arts

Large cameo glass Chardons coupe, France, circa 1930, Charles Schneider (1881-1953), Le Verre Francais, signed Le Verre Francais, 9-1/4" x 8". **$2,000**

Rago Arts

Pilgrim Studio cameo glass fish whimsy, deep plum to green to white, flowering fuchsia and flying fairies, numbered, dated, and signed by Kelsey Murphy under base, 1994, undamaged, 6" h. x 13-1/2" l. **$431**

Jeffrey S. Evans & Associates

Large cameo glass vase in Necklace or Collier pattern, France, circa 1928, Charles Schneider (1881-1953), Le Verre Francais, signed Charder Le Verre Francais, 12" x 10-1/2". **$1,875**

Rago Arts

Verrerie d'Art French cameo glass vase, rare watermelon color background with carved cameo orchid, signed "Verrerie d'Art de Lorraine B & S Company" (Burgun & Schverer), good condition, 7". **$10,000**

Woody Auction

Verrerie Schneider glass compote, France, circa 1925, wide rim in mottled blue glass transitioning to pink raised on stem and circular foot of banded aubergine, foot inscribed Schneider, France, polished pontil, 6-3/4" h. x 12-1/2" dia. **$360**

Skinner, Inc.; www.skinnerinc.com

TOP LOT!

166

Rare French cameo ovoid handled bowl, dark red owl perched on tree branch, bat on reverse, applied figural "wolf's head" cabochon, signed "Muller Croismare" in cameo relief on base, good condition, some paint areas with small flecks, 4-1/2" x 11"......................**$26,000**

Woody Auction

English cameo glass vase, late 19th/early 20th century, inverted baluster form with cylindrical neck with white cameo bands and leaftip register, branch with two peaches on red ground, unmarked, top rim ground, 5-1/4" h. **$900**

Skinner, Inc.; www.skinnerinc.com

Dorflinger Honesdale cameo vase, green to colorless with gilt decoration, flowing leaf design on textured ground, gilt "Honesdale" script signature under base, C. Dorflinger & Sons, early 20th century, undamaged, light wear to gilding, 9-1/2" h. **$748**

Jeffrey S. Evans & Associates

Cameo glass Dahlias vase, France, circa 1930, Charles Schneider (1881-1953), Le Verre Francais, signed Le Verre Francais, 14-1/2" x 7"........ **$1,000**

Rago Arts

Rare, signed Devez French cameo glass vase, pink background with blue carved cameo Oriental dragon, good condition, 17". ... **$3,750**

Woody Auction

Verrerie Schneider vase, France, circa 1925, bulbous form of mottled pink and yellow shading to orange and rust at base, incised Schneider in script near base edge, base wear, 8" h.............**$246**

Skinner, Inc.; www.skinnerinc.com

Muller Fréres cameo vase, Luneville, France, early 20th century, footed baluster form with decoration of roses in pink cut to white glass mottled with yellow and green, marked Muller Fres Luneville in cameo, 5-1/4" h. **$660**

Skinner, Inc.; www.skinnerinc.com

Cameo glass Frenes vase, France, circa 1930, Charles Schneider (1881-1953), Le Verre Francais, signed Le Verre Francais, France, 13-3/4" x 4-3/4". **$1,875**

Rago Arts

Rindskopf vase, Austria, circa 1900, tri-pulled and scalloped rim on wide neck with dimpled accents to body in green striated iridescent glass, polished pontil, 14" h..........**$300**

Skinner, Inc.; www.skinnerinc.com

Monart tri-foil vase, circa 1920-1930s, orange mottled rim swirled with green mottled base, button pontil, good condition, 8". **$400**

Woody Auction

Signed Arsall French cameo glass vase, pink background with green cutback overlay of pyramids and oasis, signature, good condition, 8" x 8". **$950**

Woody Auction

GLASS

BACCARAT

BACCARAT GLASS has been made by Cristalleries de Baccarat, France, since 1765. The firm has produced various glassware of excellent quality as well as paperweights. Baccarat's Rose Tiente is often referred to as Baccarat's Amberina.

Goblet designed by Thomas Bastide, hexagonal stepped foot and stem leading to cobalt blue cup, signed on underside with acid etched Baccarat logo and signed on foot "Thomas Bastide," very good to excellent condition, 4-1/2" h. **$178**

James D. Julia, Inc.

Perfume and powder jars, amber cut to clear, original ostrich feather and ivory-handled puff, fine condition, 4-1/4" and 2-3/4" h. **$201**

Thomaston Place Auction Galleries

Crystal vase, abstract angular motif, signed at base, 9-1/2" h. **$677**

DuMouchelles

Glass sculpture, late 20th century, marks: BACCARAT, 20" h. x 10-3/4" w. **$2,250**

Heritage Auctions

GLASS

Crystal "swirl" lamp, 29-1/2" h. **$2,040**

A.B. Levy's

Cut glass twist vase, 20th century, marks: BACCARAT, FRANCE, 8-7/8" h. **$825**

Heritage Auctions

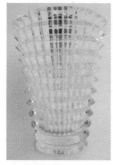

Crystal vase, signed, 9-3/8" h. **$210**

Don Presley Auctions

Pair of crystal decanters, stamped Baccarat France, 8" h. **$210**

A.B. Levy's

Painted opaline glass vase, circa 1900, marks: 8, wear to paint in interior of vase, wear to gold leaf, commensurate with age, 12-1/2" h. x 8" dia..... **$469**

Heritage Auctions

Castor and Pollux glass candlesticks designed by Salvador Dali, with original boxes, circa 1973, marks: DALI, POLLUX, 137/500; DALI, CASTOR, 137/500, BACCARAT, AUDOUIN, without bobeches, in good condition, with surface wear indicative of use and handling, 10-1/4" h. **$2,750**

Heritage Auctions

Cut crystal, thick-walled octagonal glass vase, etched with Baccarat trademark on base with original Baccarat sticker, 10" x 7" dia. **$738**

Kaminski Auctions

French cut glass and silver mounted decanters, Baccarat, France, circa 1900, two vertically faceted tapering decanters with silver cuff to rim, stoppers with tapered faceted finials, silver mounts: Bardies – Faure & Cie, Paris, France, marks: BACCARAT, FRANCE, (Minerva), B, F & C (surrounding fleur-de-lis), dent to lip of rim of one decanter, good condition with minor nicking to glass, light scratching to silver, 17" h. **$438**

Heritage Auctions

BRIDE'S BASKETS

THESE BERRY OR FRUIT BOWLS were popular late Victorian wedding gifts, hence the name. They were produced in a variety of quality art glass wares and sometimes were fitted in ornate silver plate holders.

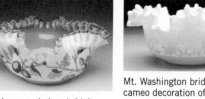

Mt. Washington bride's bowl, cameo decoration of blue cut to white in band surrounding sides, garlands of flowers along with gargoyles, bowl finished with heavily ruffled rim, very good to excellent condition with three spots on ruffled rim where ruffles have collapsed on themselves, 9-1/2" dia........................**$213**

James D. Julia, Inc.

Hobbs No. 323 Dew Drop/ Hobnail bride's basket, rubina verde (uranium) square bowl, ruffled rim and polished pontil mark, fitted in quadruple-plate stand marked for Pairpoint Mfg. Co. and numbered 2134, Hobbs, Brockunier & Co., introduced 1886, 8" h. overall, undamaged, bowl 3-1/4" h. x 7-1/2" sq..........................**$546**

Jeffrey S. Evans & Associates

Victorian cased glass bride's bowl, rose-cased opal with amber rim and gilt and polychrome decoration, each side depicting different fruit, late 19th/early 20th century, undamaged, interior with small open bubble, as made, 4-5/8" h. overall, 11-3/8" sq. **$138**

Jeffrey S. Evans & Associates

Victorian cased glass bride's basket, shaded blue to cream, crimped and ruffled rim, gilt-metal mounts including central slotted rack for fruit knives, late 19th/early 20th century, undamaged, 15-1/2" h. overall, 10" dia...........................**$138**

Jeffrey S. Evans & Associates

Bride's basket, pink satin herringbone mother-of-pearl melon ribbed bowl with enamel floral décor, pale green satin interior, set on ornate derby silverplate stand with three winged cherubs, silverplate base needs replating, one cherub wing missing, 12-1/2" x 10-1/2". **$2,000**

Woody Auction

Loetz-type Bohemian bride's/ centerpiece bowl, green iridescent, shallow rib-optic ruffled-rim form raised on brass and brass-plated high standard of mermaid resting on Art Nouveau base with four feet, circa 1900, undamaged, 15" h., 8-1/2" dia. rim. **$161**

Jeffrey S. Evans & Associates

GLASS

Victorian cased glass bride's basket, shaded butterscotch interior with enamel decoration, flared rim with fan and hobnail pattern, ground pontil mark with inscribed numbers, fitted in quadruple-plate stand marked for Eureka Silver Co. and numbered 298, fourth quarter 19th century, undamaged, wear to decoration, 11-5/8" h. overall, 12" dia. rim.................................**$184**

Jeffrey S. Evans & Associates

Victorian cased satin glass bride's basket, pale green interior, melon-rib body with crimped and ruffled rim, fitted in quadruple-plate stand marked for Webster & Son and numbered 102, fourth quarter 19th century, undamaged, some normal light scuffing in base of bowl, stand resilvered, 7-1/4" h. x 11-1/4" dia. rim. **$196**

Jeffrey S. Evans & Associates

Rindskopf Aurora Pearls bride's bowl, iridescent, ruffled and crimped rim, enameled vine and floral decoration, polished pontil mark, first quarter 20th century, undamaged, normal wear to decoration, 3-7/8" h. overall, 12" dia. **$92**

Jeffrey S. Evans & Associates

Moser-style decorated cased glass bride's basket, rose interior, deep bowl with crimped and fluted rim, base with peg extension, exterior enameled decoration of oak tree branches with applied molded-glass acorns, fitted in quadruple-plate stand marked for Meriden Britannia Co. and illegible number, bowl and stand together by association, fourth quarter 19th century, undamaged except for partial loss of one acorn, 11-1/2" h., 7-1/4" x 7-3/4" rim. **$518**

Jeffrey S. Evans & Associates

Victorian cased satin glass bride's basket, shaded rose interior with polychrome-enamel decoration, six-lobe body with crimped and ruffled rim, fitted in quadruple-plate stand marked for Meriden Britannia Co. and numbered 1685, fourth quarter 19th century, undamaged, some normal scuffing to exterior of bowl, 12-1/2" h. overall, 9-3/4" x 11-1/2" rim...................**$259**

Jeffrey S. Evans & Associates

Bride's basket, pink satin mother-of-pearl herringbone melon ribbed bowl with enamel floral decor and pale green satin interior, set on English silverplate stand, good condition, 13" x 10-1/2".**$1,800**

Woody Auction

Victorian cased glass bride's basket, shaded deep peach to butterscotch, crimped and ruffled rim, in EPNS stand with cherub stem, late 19th/early 20th century, undamaged, bowl slightly too small for stand, top of stand slightly bent, 12-1/2" h. overall, 11-3/4" dia. overall. **$230**

Jeffrey S. Evans & Associates

Lattice bride's bowl, opalescent cranberry in square-form with crimped rim, late 19th/early 20th century, undamaged, 4" h. overall. **$115**

Jeffrey S. Evans & Associates

BURMESE

BURMESE IS A SINGLE-LAYER GLASS that shades from pink to pale yellow. It was patented by Frederick S. Shirley and made by the Mt. Washington Glass Co. A license to produce the glass in England was granted to Thomas Webb & Sons, which called its articles Queen's Burmese. Gundersen Burmese was made briefly about the middle of the 20th century.

Epergne with 8" ruffled base with fairy lamp and five vases with bobeches surrounding fairy lamp, Mt. Washington Glass Co., good condition, 11-1/2" h. **$2,100**

Woody Auction

Tall pitcher, rose décor with four-line stanza by Thomas Hood, acid finish with applied glossy handle, Mt. Washington Glass Co., good condition, 7-3/4" h. **$5,000**

Woody Auction

Condiment set with pair of 4" salt and pepper shakers and 5-1/2" stoppered oil bottle, Mt. Washington Glass Co., Pairpoint silverplate holder, one shaker top with salt erosion on edge, otherwise excellent condition. **$275**

Mark Mussio, Humler & Nolan

Melon rib cruet set on Rockford silverplate frame, matching stopper, Mt. Washington Glass Co., good condition, 7-3/4" h. **$600**

Woody Auction

Five tumblers with plush finish and polished pontil marks, Mt. Washington Glass Co., circa 1885-1895, undamaged, 3-5/8" to 3-3/4" h. **$259**

Jeffrey S. Evans & Associates

GLASS

$

Four-footed bowl with applied leaf décor, Mt. Washington Glass Co., good condition, 6-3/4" x 8".. **$5,000**

Woody Auction

Pair of eggs flat-end salt and pepper shakers, opal with fired-on Burmese ground, plush/satin finish, polychrome floral decoration and matching, period lids, fitted in quadruple-plate stand marked for Pairpoint Manufacturing Co. and numbered 757, Mt. Washington Glass Co., fourth quarter 19th century, excellent overall condition, one shaker with flakes/roughness to rim, hidden by lid, other undamaged, shakers 2-1/4" h. overall, stand 4-3/8" h. overall... **$345**

Jeffrey S. Evans & Associates

Chinese-form vase, plush finish, undecorated, ground pontil mark, Mt. Washington Glass Co., circa 1885-1895, undamaged with normal scattered scuff marks, 9-1/2" h. **$219**

Jeffrey S. Evans & Associates

Vase with bulbous base, thin neck and tri-lip rim, Mt. Washington Glass Co., good condition, 9-3/4" h. **$150**

Woody Auction

Pillar-ribbed/ribbed salt and pepper shakers, plush/satin finish, each with matching period two-part lids, fitted in quadruple-plate stand marked for Middleton Plated Co. and numbered 32, Mt. Washington Glass Co., circa 1885-1895, undamaged, shakers 3-3/4" h. overall, stand 7-1/8" h. overall. **$161**

Jeffrey S. Evans & Associates

Albertine/Crown Milano cracker jar, custard with shaded Burmese ground, depicting flowering apple tree, glass not signed, quadruple-plate rim, bail handle, cover marked "MW / 4404/a" to underside, Mt. Washington Glass Co., circa 1890-1895, undamaged with normal light marking to surface, wear to plating on handle, 6" h. rim, 4-1/4" dia. rim. **$259**

Jeffrey S. Evans & Associates

Cider pitcher, acid finish, Mt. Washington Glass Co., good condition, 5-1/2" h. **$200**

Woody Auction

GLASS

Queen's Burmese two-handled bowl, floral décor, two applied frosted glass handles, applied frosted glass rim, Thomas Webb & Sons, signed, tip of one handle curls differently than other, 4" x 6". **$550**

Woody Auction

Miniature rose bowls, plush finish, crimped rims, polychrome Hawthorn and Leaf and Berry designs, polished pontil marks, Thomas Webb & Sons, circa 1886-1895, undamaged, 2-1/4" and 2-3/4" h. **$345**

Jeffrey S. Evans & Associates

Cabinet vases, plush finish, each with ruffled crimped rim and ruffled foot, one with polychrome decoration in Larch design and with rough pontil mark, Thomas Webb & Sons, circa 1886-1895, undamaged, 4" and 4-1/2" h.......................... **$207**

Jeffrey S. Evans & Associates

Cabinet vases, plush finish, each with crimped rim, polychrome decorations of Hawthorn and Grape designs, each with polished pontil mark, Grape example with "QUEEN'S BURMESEWARE" acid stamp in polished pontil mark, Thomas Webb & Sons, circa 1886-1895, undamaged, 2-3/4" and 3-1/2" h.. **$288**

Jeffrey S. Evans & Associates

Three-light centerpiece with four vases, original Clarke's frame, good condition, 7-1/2" h....... **$1,900**

Woody Auction

Monumental Victorian vase with gilded flowers, stems and leaves against Burmese colored shaded background with white cased interior, marked on underside "K. 126," very good to excellent condition, 18" h.. **$1,215**

James D. Julia, Inc.

Vase, probably American, early 20th century, ovoid form, green to pink, scalloped rim, unmarked, 10-3/4" h. **$62**

Cowan's Auctions, Inc.

CAMBRIDGE

THE CAMBRIDGE GLASS CO. was founded in Ohio in 1901. Numerous pieces are now sought, especially those designed by Arthur J. Bennett, including Crown Tuscan. Other productions included crystal animals, "Black Amethyst," "blanc opaque," and other types of colored glass. The company closed in 1954. It should not be confused with the New England Glass Co., Cambridge, Massachusetts.

Figured Lalique-style stemware glasses, 18 total, 1920s, tallest 6-1/2" h. **$369**

Kaminski Auctions

Millersburg/Cambridge Venetian carnival glass giant rose bowl/footed vase, green, serrated foot, first quarter 20th century, 9-1/4" h. x 5-1/2" dia. bowl. **$288**

Jeffrey S. Evans & Associates

No. 3011 statuesque nude-stem Crown Tuscan No. 60/Sea Shell candlesticks and No. 25/Ivy Ball, circa 1936, undamaged except for flake to rim of ivy ball, 8-1/2" h. and 9-1/2" h. **$288**

Jeffrey S. Evans & Associates

No. 3011 statuesque nude-stem cordials/brandies, yellow and green bowls, circa 1936, 6" h. **$127**

Jeffrey S. Evans & Associates

GLASS

CARNIVAL GLASS

CARNIVAL GLASS is what is fondly called mass-produced iridescent glassware. The term "carnival glass" has evolved through the years as glass collectors have responded to the idea that much of this beautiful glassware was made as give-away glass at local carnivals and fairs. However, more of it was made and sold through the same channels as pattern glass and Depression glass. Some patterns were indeed giveaways, and others were used as advertising premiums, souvenirs, etc. Whatever the origin, the term "carnival glass" today encompasses glassware that is usually pattern molded and treated with metallic salts, creating that unique coloration that is desirable to collectors.

Early names for iridescent glassware, which early 20th century consumers believed to have all come from foreign manufacturers, include Pompeiian Iridescent, Venetian Art, and Mexican Aurora. Another popular early name was "Nancy Glass," as some patterns were believed to have come from the Daum, Nancy, glassmaking area in France. This was at a time when the artistic cameo glass was enjoying great success. While the iridescent glassware being made by such European glassmakers as Loetz influenced the American marketplace, it was Louis Tiffany's Favrile glass that really caught the eye of glass consumers of the early 1900s. It seems an easy leap to transform Tiffany's shimmering glassware to something that could be mass produced, allowing what we call carnival glass today to become "poor man's Tiffany."

Carnival glass is iridized glassware that is created by pressing hot molten glass into molds, just as pattern glass had evolved. Some forms are hand finished, while others are completely formed by molds. To achieve the marvelous iridescent colors that carnival glass collectors seek, a process was developed where a liquid solution of metallic salts was put onto the still hot glass form after it was unmolded. As the liquid evaporated, a

Acorn Burrs assembled berry set, five pieces, amethyst master bowl and four green individual bowls, each with trademark, Northwood Glass Co., first quarter 20th century, undamaged, 9-1/4" and 4-3/4" dia...$161

Jeffrey S. Evans & Associates

fine metallic surface was left, which refracts light into wonderful colors. The name given to the iridescent spray by early glassmakers was "dope."

Many of the forms created by carnival glass manufacturers were accessories to the china American housewives loved. By the early 1900s, consumers could find carnival glassware at such popular stores as F. W. Woolworth and McCrory's. To capitalize on the popular fancy for these colored wares, some other industries bought large quantities of carnival glass and turned them into "packers." This term reflects the practice where baking powder, mustard, or other household products were packed into a special piece of glass that could take on another life after the original product was used. Lee Manufacturing Co. used iridized carnival glass as premiums for its baking powder and other products, causing some early carnival glass to be known by the generic term "baking powder glass."

Classic carnival glass production began in the early 1900s and continued about 20 years, but no one really documented or researched production until the first collecting wave struck in 1960.

It is important to remember that carnival glasswares were sold in department stores as well as mass merchants rather than through the general store often associated with a young America. Glassware by this time was mass-produced and sold in large quantities by such enterprising companies as Butler Brothers. When the economics of the country soured in the 1920s, those interested in purchasing iridized glassware were not spared. Many of the leftover inventories of glasshouses that hoped to sell this mass-produced glassware found their way to wholesalers who, in turn, sold the wares to those who offered the glittering glass as prizes at carnivals, fairs, circuses, etc. Possibly because this was the last venue people associated with iridized glassware, it became known as "carnival glass."

For more information on carnival glass, see *Warman's Carnival Glass Identification and Price Guide, 2nd edition*, by Ellen T. Schroy.

Carnival Glass Companies

Much of vintage American carnival glassware was created in the Ohio Valley in the glasshouse-rich areas of Pennsylvania, Ohio, and West Virginia. The abundance of natural materials, good transportation, and skilled craftsmen allowed many of the early American pattern glass manufacturing companies to add carnival glass to their production lines. They are:

Cambridge Glass Co. (Cambridge)
Diamond Glass Co. (Diamond)
Dugan Glass Co. (Dugan)
Fenton Art Glass Co. (Fenton)
Imperial Glass Co. (Imperial)
Millersburg Glass Co. (Millersburg)
Northwood Glass Co. (Northwood)
Westmoreland Glass Co. (Westmoreland)

— Ellen T. Schroy

GLASS

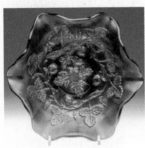

Blackberry Wreath bowl, blue, with ruffled rim, Millersburg Glass Co., first quarter 20th century, undamaged, 3-1/4" h., 8-3/4" x 10-1/4"................ **$518**

Jeffrey S. Evans & Associates

Corn salt and pepper shakers, marigold, with non-matching period and non-period two-part lids, fourth quarter 19th century, glass undamaged, one lid painted, other with wear, 4-3/4" and 4-5/8" h. overall. **$104**

Jeffrey S. Evans & Associates

Courthouse bowl, amethyst, embossed "MILLERSBURG SOUVENIR" with scalloped rim, Millersburg Glass Co., first quarter 20th century, undamaged, 6-1/4" x 7-1/2". **$345**

Jeffrey S. Evans & Associates

Diamonds water pitcher, amethyst, Millersburg Glass Co., first quarter 20th century, undamaged, 7-3/8" h. overall. **$150**

Jeffrey S. Evans & Associates

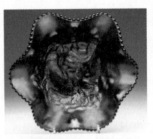

Farmyard bowl, purple, beaded rim with six ruffles, Jeweled Heart exterior, Dugan Glass Co., first quarter 20th century, undamaged, 3-5/8" h. overall, 10-1/2" dia. overall. **$2,990**

Jeffrey S. Evans & Associates

Good Luck bowl, blue/electric blue, piecrust rim, ribbed back, Northwood Glass Co., first quarter 20th century, excellent condition overall, shallow chip under edge of one rim point, 2" h. x 8-3/4" dia. **$230**

Jeffrey S. Evans & Associates

Grape and Cable 12-piece punch set, amethyst/purple, ruffled-rim bowl with stand and 11 cups, stand and cups signed, Northwood Glass Co., first quarter 20th century, undamaged, punch bowl 10-1/2" h. overall, 11" dia. overall. **$374**

Jeffrey S. Evans & Associates

Grape and Cable seven-piece water set, amethyst, pitcher and six tumblers, each signed, Northwood Glass Co., first quarter 20th century, undamaged, 8-1/2" and 4" h. **$207**

Jeffrey S. Evans & Associates

Two Grape and Cable covered compotes, amethyst, one signed, Northwood Glass Co., first quarter 20th century, undamaged, 8-3/4" h. overall, 6-3/4" h. rims, 6-1/2" dia. rims...................... **$219**

Jeffrey S. Evans & Associates

Assorted hatpin holders, green and amethyst Northwood Grape and Cable, both marked, and blue Fenton Orange Tree, each raised on three feet, first quarter 20th century, Grape and Cable examples undamaged, Orange Tree with minor flake to tip of two feet and some light polishing to underside of feet, possibly factory, 6-1/4" to 6-3/4" h. **$316**

Jeffrey S. Evans & Associates

Hanging Cherries water pitcher, green, Millersburg Glass Co., first quarter 20th century, undamaged, light wear to rim close to spout, 8" h. overall....................**$374**

Jeffrey S. Evans & Associates

Leaf and Little Flowers compote/sherbet, green, on octagonal foot, Millersburg Glass Co., first quarter 20th century, undamaged, 2-7/8" h. x 4-1/4" dia..............**$104**

Jeffrey S. Evans & Associates

Marilyn water pitcher, amethyst/purple, Millersburg Glass Co., first quarter 20th century, undamaged, 8" h. overall. **$316**

Jeffrey S. Evans & Associates

Multi-Fruits and Flowers sherbet, amethyst, on octagonal foot, Millersburg Glass Co., first quarter 20th century, excellent condition overall, scattered minute flakes, 3-1/4" h., 3-7/8" dia. **$345**

Jeffrey S. Evans & Associates

Nesting Swan bowl, green, with ruffled rim, Millersburg Glass Co., first quarter 20th century, undamaged, 2-7/8" h., 10" overall.............**$138**

Jeffrey S. Evans & Associates

Night Stars bonbon, green, double handles, Millersburg Glass Co., first quarter 20th century, undamaged, 3-1/8" h., 3-3/8" x 5-3/4"...................**$431**

Jeffrey S. Evans & Associates

Ohio Star vase, amethyst, Millersburg Glass Co., first quarter 20th century, undamaged, 10-1/4" h. **$920**

Jeffrey S. Evans & Associates

Peacock bowl, blue, with ruffled rim, Northwood Glass Co., first quarter 20th century, undamaged, 2" h. x 8-3/4" dia..............**$173**

Jeffrey S. Evans & Associates

GLASS

Primrose bowl, marigold, with scalloped rim, Millersburg Glass Co., first quarter 20th century, one tooth chipped off, otherwise undamaged, 2-3/8" h. x 9-1/4" dia................**$92**

Jeffrey S. Evans & Associates

Primrose bowls, amethyst and marigold, each with ruffled, serrated rims, Millersburg Glass Co., first quarter 20th century, amethyst example undamaged, marigold example with minor rim flakes, 9-1/4" and 9-5/8" overall. **$138**

Jeffrey S. Evans & Associates

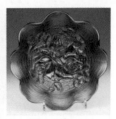

Rose Show bowl, blue, with ruffled rim, Northwood Glass Co., first quarter 20th century, undamaged, area of mold roughness approximately 3/4" long, as made, 2-5/8" h., 8-3/4" overall.........**$374**

Jeffrey S. Evans & Associates

Strawberry wreath compote, green, with ruffled rim, Millersburg Glass Co., first quarter 20th century, undamaged, 3-1/2" h., 6-3/4" overall. **$161**

Jeffrey S. Evans & Associates

Swirled Hobnail rose bowl, marigold, with scalloped rim, Millersburg Glass Co., first quarter 20th century, undamaged, 3-5/8" h. **$161**

Jeffrey S. Evans & Associates

Swirled Hobnail spittoon, amethyst, with scalloped rim, Millersburg Glass Co., first quarter 20th century, undamaged, 3" h. x 4-5/8" dia..........................**$374**

Jeffrey S. Evans & Associates

Tulip Scroll vase, marigold, Millersburg Glass Co., first quarter 20th century, undamaged with wear to finish, 6-3/4" h. overall. **$184**

Jeffrey S. Evans & Associates

Venetian giant rose bowl/footed vase, green, with serrated foot, Millersburg Glass Co. or Cambridge Glass Co., first quarter 20th century, undamaged, 9-1/4" h. x 5-1/2" dia..............**$288**

Jeffrey S. Evans & Associates

Wishbone epergne, amethyst, single lily, ruffled-rim bowl with basketweave pattern to exterior, Northwood Glass Co., first quarter 20th century, undamaged, 9-1/2" h. overall, bowl 3-7/8" h. overall x 8" dia. overall.............**$374**

Jeffrey S. Evans & Associates

Pillar-molded vase, marigold on light green, square form with protruding corners and four-fold rim, factory polished under base and large pontil mark, first quarter 20th century, undamaged, small pontil spall, 10" h. overall, 4-3/4" sq. base overall. **$115**

Jeffrey S. Evans & Associates

CENTRAL GLASS CO.

FROM THE 1890S until its closing in 1939, the Central Glass Co. of Wheeling, West Virginia, produced colorless and colored handmade glass in all the styles then popular. Decorations from etchings with acid to hand-painted enamels were used.

The popular "Depression" era colors of black, pink, green, light blue, ruby red and others were all produced. Two of its 1920s etchings are still familiar today, one named for the then-president of the United States and the other for the governor of West Virginia: Harding and Morgan patterns.

From high-end art glass to mass-produced plain barware tumblers, Central Glass Co. was a major glass producer throughout the period.

Central No. 140/Cabbage Rose colorless covered compote on high faceted octagonal standard with figural finial and one-quart milk pitcher with applied handle, 1870-1890, excellent condition with light scratches and flakes to inner rim of compote cover, otherwise undamaged, 7-7/8" h. overall, 5-1/2" dia. overall.......**$90**

Jeffrey S. Evans & Associates

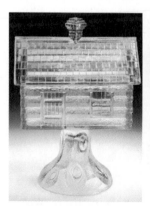

Log Cabin colorless covered compote, fourth quarter 19th century, cover with small chip under one corner, small finial flake and flange chip, base rim with small shallow chip, 9" h. overall, 4-1/8" x 6"..........**$425**

Jeffrey S. Evans & Associates

Log Cabin spooner, amber, fourth quarter 19th century, undamaged except for inner-rim roughness, 4-3/4" h., 2-5/8" x 3-1/4"................**$425**

Jeffrey S. Evans & Associates

Central No. 796/Rope and Thumbprint molasses pitcher, blue, hinged silverplate cover, fourth quarter 19th century, 7-1/2" h. overall, 7" h. spout.............................**$150**

Jeffrey S. Evans & Associates

GLASS

CONSOLIDATED GLASS

THE CONSOLIDATED LAMP & GLASS CO. of Coraopolis, Pennsylvania, was founded in 1894. For a number of years it was noted for its lighting wares but also produced popular lines of pressed and blown tableware. Highly collectible glass patterns of this early era include the Cone, Cosmos, Florette, and Guttate lines.

Lamps and shades continued to be good sellers, but in 1926 a new "art" line of molded decorative wares was introduced. This "Martelè" line was developed as a direct imitation of the fine glassware being produced by Renè Lalique of France, and many Consolidated patterns resembled their French counterparts. Other popular lines produced during the 1920s and 1930s were Dancing Nymph, the delightfully Art Deco Ruba Rombic introduced in 1928, and the Catalonian line, which debuted in 1927 and imitated 17th century Spanish glass.

Argus Swirl sugar shaker, cranberry, period lid, circa 1894-1898, undamaged, lid with light denting, 3-1/4" h. overall...................**$81**

Jeffrey S. Evans & Associates

Although the factory closed in 1933, it was reopened under new management in 1936 and prospered through the 1940s. It finally closed in 1967. Collectors should note that many later Consolidated patterns closely resemble wares of other competing firms, especially the Phoenix Glass Co. Careful study is needed to determine the maker of pieces from the 1920-1940 era.

A book that will be of help to collectors is *Phoenix & Consolidated Art Glass, 1926-1980*, by Jack D. Wilson (Antique Publications, 1989).

Cone squatty sugar shaker in cased yellow glossy finish, period lid, circa 1894, undamaged, 3-1/4" h. overall. ..**$92**

Jeffrey S. Evans & Associates

Criss Cross salt and pepper shakers, cranberry opalescent, near matching period lids, fourth quarter 19th century, glass with light wear to bodies and each with chipping/roughness to rim, hidden by lids, 3-1/4" and 3-1/8" h. overall. **$219**

Jeffrey S. Evans & Associates

Guttate syrup pitcher in cased pink with colorless applied handle, lid with patent date, fourth quarter 19th century, glass undamaged, cover together by association, 6-1/8" h. overall. **$115**

Jeffrey S. Evans & Associates

Cone syrup pitcher in cased mustard yellow, colorless applied handle and period lid, circa 1894, handle with horizontal crack to upper terminal, 6-1/4" h. overall... **$161**

Jeffrey S. Evans & Associates

Guttate syrup pitcher, cranberry, colorless applied handle, period lid marked with patent information, fourth quarter 19th century, undamaged, 6-5/8" h. overall. **$184**

Jeffrey S. Evans & Associates

Martelè center bowl with molded parakeets perched on branch entanglements with berries, birds tinted sky blue, recessed background in ruby purple, original paper sticker pasted near rim reads "Martelè Hand Wrought Art Glass," factory condition, 6" h. x 16" l. **$475**

Mark Mussio, Humler & Nolan

Three Cone sugar shakers in opaque blue and green and cased pink with period lids, circa 1894, undamaged, normal roughness to rims, as made, 5-1/8" to 5-1/4" h. overall. **$150**

Jeffrey S. Evans & Associates

Primrose parlor lamp, ruby with satin finish, matching patterned ball-form shade, embossed with stylized acanthus leaves under band of flowers pattern, brass base impressed "326" to underside, brass drop-in font with side refill feature, fitted with period Consolidated period burner, deflector embossed "CONSOLIDATED" and with patent dates, early 20th century, undamaged, shade fitter with normal flakes/roughness hidden by shade ring, font refill cap frozen, 22-3/4" h. overall, font 12-3/4" h., 8-1/4" sq. base. **$345**

Jeffrey S. Evans & Associates

GLASS

CRANBERRY GLASS

GOLD WAS ADDED to glass batches to give cranberry glass its color on reheating. It has been made by numerous glasshouses for years and is currently being reproduced. Both blown and molded articles were produced. A less expensive type of cranberry glass was made with the substitution of copper for gold.

Arabian Nights tumbler, cranberry opalescent, factory polished rim and molded base, possibly Beaumont Glass Co./ Northwood Glass Co., late 19th/ early 20th century, undamaged, 3-5/8" h. **$288**

Jeffrey S. Evans & Associates

Buttons and Braids tumbler, cranberry opalescent, tapered side with factory polished rim, Jefferson Glass Co., circa 1905, excellent condition overall, flake to exterior of rim, 4" h. **$92**

Jeffrey S. Evans & Associates

Christmas Snowflake water pitcher, cranberry opalescent, tapered bulbous form with five-part ruffled rim and twisted reed handle, Northwood Glass Co. and Dugan Glass Co., circa 1895, crack encircling third of foot, 9-1/4" h. overall. **$403**

Jeffrey S. Evans & Associates

Chrysanthemum Swirl covered butter dish, cranberry opalescent, circular form, cover with colorless applied ball-form finial, Northwood Glass Co., circa 1890, undamaged, 5-3/8" h. overall, 6" dia. overall base.........**$288**

Jeffrey S. Evans & Associates

Chrysanthemum Swirl mustard pot, cranberry opalescent, period screw-on hinged lid, Northwood Glass Co., circa 1890, undamaged, 3-1/2" h. overall.............**$161**

Jeffrey S. Evans & Associates

Coinspot square top water pitcher, cranberry opalescent, colorless applied handle with pressed fan design to upper terminal, Beaumont Glass Co., early 20th century, undamaged, 8-1/2" h. **$150**

Jeffrey S. Evans & Associates

GLASS

Curtain Optic Indiana mold cruet, cranberry opalescent, triangular and lightly crimped rim, colorless applied reeded handle, facet-cut stopper, late 19th or 20th century, undamaged, 7" h. overall. **$316**

Jeffrey S. Evans & Associates

Daisy in Criss-Cross tumbler, cranberry opalescent, factory polished rim, Beaumont Glass Co., circa 1897, undamaged. **$431**

Jeffrey S. Evans & Associates

Daisy and Fern-Northwood Swirl cruet, cranberry opalescent, bulbous form with colorless applied handle, colorless facet-cut stopper, Northwood Glass Co., circa 1894, undamaged cruet, stopper with flake and normal roughness to extension, as made, 6-1/2" h. overall. **$575**

Jeffrey S. Evans & Associates

Daisy and Fern-Northwood Swirl pickle caster, cranberry opalescent, fitted in Meriden quadruple-plate frame, marked "291," with cover and tongs, rim of jar polished during manufacturing process, Northwood Glass Co., circa 1894, undamaged, 8-3/4" h. overall, jar 3-1/2" h., 3-5/8" dia. overall. **$288**

Jeffrey S. Evans & Associates

Ellipse and Diamond creamer, cranberry opalescent, squat ball form with circular plain rim and colorless applied handle, polished pontil mark, circa 1890, excellent condition, body with high-point wear, 4-3/4" h. **$230**

Jeffrey S. Evans & Associates

Fern bitters/barber's bottle, cranberry opalescent, six-lobe melon rib form, polished pontil mark, probably Beaumont Glass Co., late 19th century, undamaged, light interior residue, 7" h. **$207**

Jeffrey S. Evans & Associates

Fern square-top water pitcher, cranberry opalescent, bulge form, colorless applied handle with pressed feather design to upper terminal, Beaumont Glass Co., circa 1894, undamaged, 8-5/8" h. **$748**

Jeffrey S. Evans & Associates

Fern West Virginia Optic mold toothpick holder, cranberry opalescent, factory polished rim, West Virginia Glass Co., circa 1894, undamaged, 2-3/8" h. **$1,035**

Jeffrey S. Evans & Associates

Fig/Beet salt and pepper shakers, cased cranberry, satin finish, with near-matching polychrome floral decoration, original lids, Mt. Washington Glass Co., fourth quarter 19th century, undamaged, 2-5/8" h. overall. **$288**

Jeffrey S. Evans & Associates

Fish Pond salt shaker, cased cranberry, with molded and polychrome enamel decorated fish, cattails, eel, and rayed shoulder, attributed to Moser Meierhofen Works, late 19th/ early 20th century, glass undamaged, less than expected wear to decoration, lid does not tighten, 4-1/2" h. overall. **$489**

Jeffrey S. Evans & Associates

GLASS

Herringbone tumbler, cranberry opalescent, factory polished rim, fourth quarter 19th century, excellent condition overall, small chip to interior of rim, 3-3/4" h. **$518**

Jeffrey S. Evans & Associates

Herringbone Variant celery vase, cranberry opalescent, without ribs, base with 11-petal daisy decoration, fourth quarter 19th century, undamaged, 6-3/4" h. **$403**

Jeffrey S. Evans & Associates

Hobbs No. 323 Dew Drop/Hobnail No. 2 jug/pitcher, ruby opalescent/cranberry opalescent, bulbous form, square rim, colorless applied reeded handle, polished pontil mark, Hobbs, Brockunier & Co., introduced 1886, undamaged, 4-7/8" h. **$184**

Jeffrey S. Evans & Associates

Hobbs No. 326/Windows Swirl syrup pitcher, ruby/cranberry opalescent, oval squatty form with colorless applied handle, period lid, Hobbs, Brockunier & Co., circa 1889, undamaged, 5-1/4" h. overall.....**$690**

Jeffrey S. Evans & Associates

Hobnail bottle vase, cranberry opalescent, three-section ruffled rim, neck interior not ground, fourth quarter 19th century, undamaged, 8-1/2" h. **$104**

Jeffrey S. Evans & Associates

Honeycomb/Big Windows cruet, cranberry opalescent, squat bulge form with triangular rim, colorless applied reeded handle and pressed-facet stopper, polished pontil mark, probably Phoenix Glass Co., fourth quarter 19th century, undamaged cruet, stopper with flakes/roughness to extension, 6" h. overall...........**$230**

Jeffrey S. Evans & Associates

LaBelle Opal toothpick holder, cranberry opalescent, scalloped rim and rough pontil mark, LaBelle Glass Co., circa 1886, undamaged, with open bubble to interior as made, which does not affect profile, 2-1/2" h...........................**$115**

Jeffrey S. Evans & Associates

Marbrie Loop decorated water pitcher, cranberry light opalescent, shouldered form, plain rim, colorless applied handle, polished pontil mark, fourth quarter 19th century, undamaged, light wear to body, 7-1/4" h. overall. **$403**

Jeffrey S. Evans & Associates

Opaline Brocade/Spanish Lace spooner, cranberry opalescent, gauffered rim, circa 1899, undamaged, 4-1/4" h. **$219**

Jeffrey S. Evans & Associates

Overlapping Drapery Columns tumbler, cranberry opalescent, factory polished rim, late 19th/early 20th century, undamaged, 3-3/4" h. **$489**

Jeffrey S. Evans & Associates

GLASS

Panel Optic celery vase and milk pitcher, cranberry opalescent, each with polished pontil mark, fourth quarter 19th century, pitcher undamaged, celery vase with light interior residue. **$69**

Jeffrey S. Evans & Associates

Poinsettia tumbler, cranberry opalescent, factory polished rim, Northwood Glass Co., circa 1903, undamaged with mold roughness, 4" h. overall. **$173**

Jeffrey S. Evans & Associates

Ribbed Rings tumbler, cranberry opalescent, Northwood Glass Co., fourth quarter 19th century, very good condition overall, post-production polishing to rim, 3-5/8" h. **$288**

Jeffrey S. Evans & Associates

Scottish Moor tumbler, cranberry opalescent, factory polished rim, late 19th/early 20th century, undamaged, 3-3/4" h. **$546**

Jeffrey S. Evans & Associates

Seaweed/Coral Reef toothpick holder, cranberry opalescent, Hobbs, Brockunier & Co. and Beaumont Glass Co., circa 1889, good condition overall, two chips off rim, one moderate, which does not affect profile, and one sizable, 2-1/2" h. ...**$431**

Jeffrey S. Evans & Associates

Swirling Maze water pitcher, cranberry opalescent, bulbous form with star-crimped rim, colorless, applied handle, Jefferson Glass Co., circa 1905, undamaged, 9-1/2" h.................**$690**

Jeffrey S. Evans & Associates

Unidentified floral pattern tumbler, shaded cranberry opalescent, with factory polished rim, late 19th/early 20th century, undamaged, 3-7/8" h. **$575**

Jeffrey S. Evans & Associates

Victorian glass epergne, cranberry opalescent to pale green, ruffle-edge bowl supporting central lily-form vase with applied rigaree, centering three twisted shepherd hooks each supporting basket, fourth quarter 19th century, undamaged, one basket mismatched, 20-1/2" h. overall, 9" dia. bowl..**$345**

Jeffrey S. Evans & Associates

Wave Optic bowl, cranberry opalescent, circular and wide-waisted form with plain rim, teardrops over diamonds pattern, base with graduated set of 12-point stars, factory polished rim, first quarter 20th century, undamaged, 3" h. x 6-3/8" dia. rim.**$115**

Jeffrey S. Evans & Associates

Wide Stripe and Horizontal Ribs creamer, cranberry opalescent, ball form, colorless applied reeded handle and polished pontil mark, late 19th/early 20th century, undamaged, with open bubble, 4-3/4" h. overall. **$138**

Jeffrey S. Evans & Associates

Windows water pitcher, shaded cranberry opalescent, shouldered form with short cylindrical neck, plain rim, colorless, applied handle, polished pontil mark, fourth quarter 19th century, undamaged, 8" h. x 3-3/4" dia. rim.**$259**

Jeffrey S. Evans & Associates

GLASS

CUSTARD GLASS

"CUSTARD GLASS," as collectors call it today, came on the American scene in the 1890s, more than a decade after similar colors were made in Europe and England. The Sowerby firm of Gateshead-on-Tyne, England had marketed its patented "Queen's Ivory Ware" quite successfully in the late 1870s and early 1880s.

There were many glass tableware factories operating in Pennsylvania and Ohio in the 1890s and early 1900s, and the competition among them was keen. Each company sought to capture the public's favor with distinctive colors and, often, hand-painted decoration. That is when "custard glass" appeared on the American scene.

Argonaut Shell pattern pitcher, Northwood Glass Co., circa 1900, bases decorated with green seaweed and gold shells, 8" h. **$90**

DuMouchelle's

The opaque yellow color of this glass varies from a rich, vivid yellow to a lustrous light yellow. Regardless of intensity, the hue was originally called "ivory" by several glass manufacturers who also used superlative sounding terms such as "Ivorina Verde" and "Carnelian." Most custard glass contains uranium, so it will "glow" under a black light.

The most important producer of custard glass was certainly Harry Northwood, who first made it at his plants in Indiana, Pennsylvania, in the late 1890s and, later, in his Wheeling, West Virginia, factory. Northwood marked some of his most famous patterns, but much early custard is unmarked. Other key manufacturers include the Heisey Glass Co., Newark, Ohio; Jefferson Glass Co., Steubenville, Ohio; Tarentum Glass Co., Tarentum, Pennsylvania; and Fenton Art Glass Co., Williamstown, West Virginia.

Custard glass fanciers are particular about condition and generally insist on pristine quality decorations free from fading or wear. Souvenir custard pieces with events, places, and dates on them usually bring the best prices in the areas commemorated on them rather than from the specialist collector. Also, collectors who specialize in pieces such as cruets, syrups, or salt and pepper shakers will often pay higher prices for these pieces than would a custard collector.

Key reference sources include William Heacock's *Custard Glass from A to Z*, published in 1976 but not out of print, and *Harry Northwood: The Early Years*, available from Glass Press. Heisey's custard glass is discussed in Shirley Dunbar's *Heisey Glass: The Early Years* (Krause Publications, 2000), and Coudersport's production is well-documented in Tulla Majot's book, *Coudersport's Glass 1900-1904* (Glass Press, 1999). The Custard Glass Society holds a yearly convention and maintains a website: www.homestead.com/custardsociety.

— *James Measell*

GLASS

Maple Leaf pattern salt and pepper shakers, green and gilt decoration, matching period lids, Northwood Glass Co., early 20th century, glass undamaged, one lid resilvered, 3-1/4" h. overall. **$460**

Jeffrey S. Evans & Associates

Four-piece table set marked Heisey, pink rose décor, good condition, no chips, cracks or repairs....... **$200**

Woody Auction

Chrysanthemum pattern butter dish, very good condition, slight gold wear around edge of bottom........ **$35**

Hewlett's Auctions

Chrysanthemum pattern three-piece table setting, Northwood Glass Co., signed, center bowl 10-3/4" l. **$90**

Constantine & Pletcher

Intaglio pattern four-piece table set, Northwood Glass Co., gold with green highlights, good condition, no chips, cracks or repairs............... **$100**

Woody Auction

Assorted tumblers, each with various decorations including gilt, staining and polychrome, including Heisey Glass Co. No. 310/Ring band, Vermont, and five others, late 19th/early 20th century, five examples undamaged, Vermont with small pattern chip, and one other specified example with small chips and flakes to edge of base, each with expected minor to moderate wear to decorations, 3-7/8" to 4" h.. **$69**

Jeffrey S. Evans & Associates

CUT GLASS

CUT GLASS IS MADE by grinding decorations into glass by means of abrasive-carrying metal or stone wheels. An ancient craft, it was revived in 1600 by Bohemians and spread through Europe to Great Britain and America.

American cut glass came of age at the Centennial Exposition in 1876 and the World Columbian Exposition in 1893. America's most significant output of high-quality glass occurred from 1880 to 1917, a period now known as the Brilliant Period. Glass from this period is the most eagerly sought glass by collectors.

American Brilliant Cut Glass

American Brilliant cut glass two-part punch bowl, clear, matching patterned stand, Stars and Crosshatched Bars pattern, signed in base, J. Hoare & Co., late 19th/early 20th century, bowl with overall minute wear, rim with significant inner rim chip, stand with moderate and small chips and minor flakes to foot, 9-1/8" h. overall, 10-1/8" dia. rim, stand 4-3/4" h., 7-1/2" dia. base.......................... **$173**

Jeffrey S. Evans & Associates

American Brilliant cut glass cheese dish, colorless, Hobstar pattern, late 19th/early 20th century, excellent overall condition, base rim with minute flakes, cover undamaged, 7-1/4" h. overall x 8-3/4" dia. base............. **$127**

Jeffrey S. Evans & Associates

American Brilliant cut glass vase, No. 763/Tampa, colorless, ovoid top and notched stem, circular foot, Pitkin & Brooks Glass Co., late 19th/early 20th century, undamaged, 11-3/4" h. overall. **$345**

Jeffrey S. Evans & Associates

American Brilliant cut glass emerald green cut to clear bowl, Hobstar, Strawberry Diamond, Star and Fan Motif, embossed sterling rim, good condition, 2" x 10-1/2"......................... **$900**

Woody Auction

American Brilliant cut glass rolled rim bowl, rare Grecian pattern by Hawkes, good condition, 4" h. x 12" dia. **$2,250**

Woody Auction

GLASS

Sinclaire American Brilliant cut glass bowl, intaglio fish and seaweed decor, signed, good condition, 2" x 9". **$225**

Woody Auction

American Brilliant cut glass water pitcher, prism cut body with elaborate sterling acorn spout, good condition, 8". **$600**

Woody Auction

American Brilliant cut glass handled rum jug, engraved floral motif, Hobstar cut stopper, triple notched handle, good condition, 7". **$350**

Woody Auction

American Brilliant cut glass bowl with elaborate sterling rim, Hobstar and Strawberry Diamond Gothic arch design, sterling rim with embossed acorn leaf and branch design by Shreve & Co., good condition, 3" x 15". **$3,200**

Woody Auction

American Brilliant cut glass tri-corner bowl, Gloria pattern by Pitkin & Brooks, good condition, 3" x 9-1/2". **$800**

Woody Auction

American Brilliant cut glass two-part punch bowl, Hobstar, Nailhead Diamond, Strawberry Diamond, Star and Fan motif, good condition, 9" x 12". **$350**

Woody Auction

American Brilliant cut glass rolled rim compote, pattern #100 by Elmira, large scalloped Hobstar foot, notched teardrop stem, good condition, 13" x 9-1/2". **$400**

Woody Auction

American Brilliant cut glass round tray, Bubble Flower pattern by W.C. Anderson, good condition, 11-1/2". **$1,000**

Woody Auction

Tuthill American Brilliant cut glass round dish, Athena pattern, signed, good condition, 6". **$250**

Woody Auction

Pair of American Brilliant cut glass oval cologne bottles, Grecian pattern by Hawkes, ornate embossed silver twist tops, good condition, 6" .. **$900**

Woody Auction

American Brilliant cut glass Flemish jug with sterling spout, pattern #50 by Dorflinger, Hobstar base, notched handle, embossed floral spout with monograms on left and right sides of spout, good condition, 11-3/4".............. **$3,000**

Woody Auction

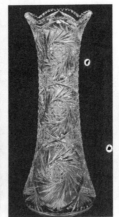

American Brilliant cut glass corset-shaped floor vase, large Pinwheel design with Hobstar, Button and Fan highlights, attributed to Quaker City, good condition, 22"........**$650**

Woody Auction

TOP LOT!

Pair of American Brilliant cut glass pitchers, cranberry cut to clear, Prism and Panel motif, clear ribbed handles, sterling spouts, good condition, 9-3/4".............. **$3,750**

Woody Auction

American Brilliant cut glass cologne bottles, colorless, each globular bottle with swirled Daisy and Button pattern, each with unmarked repoussé decorated stopper that appears to be sterling silver, possibly Hawkes or Hoare, fourth quarter 19th century, excellent condition, one bottle with shallow chip to pattern, other with minute flake to inner mouth, 6" h. overall, 4-1/4" h. bottles, 4-1/2" dia. overall. **$1,035**

Jeffrey S. Evans & Associates

Rare American Brilliant cut glass hanging "basketball" light globe, Hobstar center with finely cut prism body separated by Hobstar chain, thick heavy blank, good condition, 10-1/2" x 10". **$500**

Woody Auction

Four pieces of American Brilliant cut glass, American, late 19th/early 20th century, decanter, tall vase, ewer with sterling silver spout with beaded rim and biscuit jar with monogrammed sterling lid, tallest 14-1/4" h. **$923**

Cowan's Auctions, Inc.

Bohemian Cut Glass

Bohemian black cut to clear covered goblet with three amber etched vignettes of courting scene, old mill, and elk in woods, knopped top shows wildlife, foot shows examples of German or Dutch architecture, circa 1900, large chip to edge of foot, flakes to interior rim of lid, 12-1/4" h.....**$431**

Thomaston Place Auction Galleries

Bohemian covered goblet with wheel cut decoration of wraparound landscape and deer, knopped lid with pheasant in scrub, faceted edge to lid and foot, circa 1880, fine condition, 11-1/4" h.............**$259**

Thomaston Place Auction Galleries

Bohemian glass covered urn, cranberry cut to clear with etched frosting, depicting elk in forest, 19th century, with large domed lid with faceted knop, good condition, 16-1/4" h.............**$316**

Thomaston Place Auction Galleries

Bohemian amber cut to clear tall vase, eight-sided with flared neck, lobed top, Honeycomb pattern bottom, Starburst foot, circa 1900, fine condition, 12-3/4" h.............**$230**

Thomaston Place Auction Galleries

Bohemian pedestal vase, cranberry cut to clear, by Carl Goldberg, signed on base, game birds and starbursts, circa 1900, 11-1/2" h. x 7-3/4" dia. **$316**

Thomaston Place Auction Galleries

Bohemian wheel-cut celery green to clear goblet of deer in forest, with faceted stem and foot, shaped bubble in stem, circa 1910, single tiny flake to rim, 7-1/8" h............................**$259**

Thomaston Place Auction Galleries

Bohemian cobalt cut to clear large bowl with ornate brass four-footed mount, rim with shaped lugs, circa 1900, rim nips to glass, 5-1/2" x 16"..**$230**

Thomaston Place Auction Galleries

GLASS

Other Cut Glass

Cut overlay and gauffered smoke bell, ruby to clear, central leaf and berry vine with double row of thumbprints above and below, applied colorless glass ring hanger, Boston & Sandwich Glass Co. and others, 1850-1880, chip to wafer below hanger, otherwise undamaged, 8-1/2" h. x 6-1/4" dia. **$115**

Jeffrey S. Evans & Associates

Two-color cut glass vase, green to pink, cylindrical form with rock crystal type floral and scroll cutting above arches and panels, mounted in sterling silver flared base marked "HAWKES / STERLING" underneath, T. G. Hawkes & Co., first quarter 20th century, undamaged, 9-1/4" h. x 2" dia.................**$1,495**

Jeffrey S. Evans & Associates

Lorenz Brothers footed oval vase in emerald green cut to clear, signed on foot, decorated with peacock on face, reducing lenses on back and sides, circa 1920s, fine condition, 14" x 6-3/4" x 4-3/4"......**$633**

Thomaston Place Auction Galleries

Floral pattern colored cut glass plate, amethyst to clear, five-petal star flowers, blossoms, and leaves surround star-cut center, 20th century, undamaged, 8-1/4" dia. **$219**

Jeffrey S. Evans & Associates

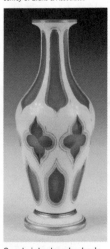

Sandwich glass barber's bottle in white cut to ice blue with gilt work, in Gothic revival form, circa 1850, wear to gilding, lacks stopper, 8-3/4" h. **$144**

Thomaston Place Auction Galleries

Edwardian English cranberry cut to clear goblet with knopped lid, Gothic vine decoration, scene with deer in forest, cartouche uncut with monogram, circa 1905, fine condition, 9" h..**$201**

Thomaston Place Auction Galleries

Pictorial cut glass water pitcher, colorless, tankard form with daisies and ferns flanking portrait of Native American chief in full headdress, facet-cut handle and star-cut base, first quarter 20th century, undamaged except for shallow chip to underside of spout that does not affect rim profile, some light residue and spots of rust in base, 9-5/8" h....**$460**

Jeffrey S. Evans & Associates

Engraved and cut square pickle caster, colorless jar with notch-cut corners, each side and cover with foliate engraving, star-cut base, fitted in quadruple-plate stand with bail handle and lion masks, marked for Meriden Silver Plate Co. and numbered 611, fourth quarter 19th century, cover with chip to underside of one corner, several minor flakes, 10" h. overall, 4-5/8" sq. base. **$150**

Jeffrey S. Evans & Associates

GLASS

CZECHOSLOVAKIAN GLASS

THE COUNTRY OF CZECHOSLOVAKIA, including the glassmaking region of Bohemia, was not founded as an independent republic until after the close of World War I in 1918. The new country soon developed a large export industry, including a wide range of colored and hand-painted glasswares such as vases, tableware, and perfume bottles. Fine quality cut crystal or Bohemian-type etched wares were also produced for the American market. Some Bohemian glass carries faint acid-etched markings on the base.

With the breakup of Czechoslovakia into two republics, the wares produced between World Wars I and II should gain added collector appeal.

Lemonade set in Czechoslovakia glass, pitcher with five matching glasses in flame orange-red with black pinstriping, hand-painted enamel decoration of peacocks, circa 1920, good condition, 11" and 5-1/2" h. **$345**

Thomaston Place Auction Galleries

Kralik Bohemian iridescent purple ovoid vase with string decoration, pinched sides, small flared neck, circa 1900, fine condition, 6-3/4" h. **$374**

Thomaston Place Auction Galleries

Czechoslovakia glass vase, red to black striated, possibly Ruckl, satin finish, fine condition, original flaw in side, 12" h.........**$115**

Thomaston Place Auction Galleries

Czechoslovakia glass vase in chipped ice surface, orange to green striation, pinched side, possibly Loetz, stamped "Czechoslovakia" in white ink on underside, fine condition, 8-1/2" h...**$230**

Thomaston Place Auction Galleries

GLASS

Loetz

Loetz vase in Maximia pattern with bulbous body and squared pinched neck, olive green pattern lines against gold iridescent background, unsigned, very good to excellent condition, 5-3/4" h.......... **$1,883**

James D. Julia, Inc.

Loetz compote, gilt bronze Art Nouveau stand with oil spot gold glass insert with ruffled edge, set with button onto three-footed tapered round base ending in sprays of flowers, Austrian, circa 1890, unmarked, fine condition, 9-3/4" h. x 10" dia............. **$978**

Thomaston Place Auction Galleries

Loetz vase in Medici pattern with green glass body with trefoil mouth and light gold iridescence with purple highlights, platinum iridescence with blue and purple highlights, very good to excellent condition, 3" h................... **$593**

James D. Julia, Inc.

Amber-colored Loetz vase with squat body and pinched sides, in Aeolus pattern with raised wave design highlighted with light blue iridescence with pink and purple highlights, unsigned, very good to excellent condition, 4-1/4" h. x 4-1/2" dia. **$425**

James D. Julia, Inc.

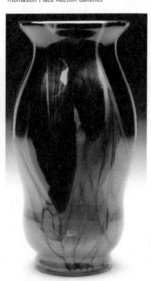

Loetz vase in Phanomen pattern with clambroth-colored body with gold and platinum iridescent pulled feather design descending from lip, four pinched sides, signed in polished pontil "Loetz Austria," 5-1/2" h., very good to excellent condition....... **$2,963**

James D. Julia, Inc.

Loetz vase in Titania pattern with green swirled decoration extending from foot against striated brown translucent background, random internal blue threading, unsigned, very good to excellent condition, 6" h. **$1,837**

James D. Julia, Inc.

Loetz vase in Formosa pattern with raised threaded design encircling green translucent glass body, iridescence with purple highlights, rolled tri-corn rim, unsigned, very good to excellent condition, 5-1/4" h. **$474**

James D. Julia, Inc.

GLASS

Loetz vase in Cytisus pattern with dark blue design at foot shading to salmon at lip, dark blue decorated with wave design and random gold and blue iridescent spots, blue highlighted with red iridescence within wavy design, unsigned, very good to excellent condition, 6-1/4" h. **$4,740**

James D. Julia, Inc.

Miniature Loetz vase in Silberiris pattern overlaid in silver with dogwood flowers connected by branches in Art Nouveau style and cased with pink interior, silver impressed "L Sterling" (La Pierre Mfg. of International Silver), excellent condition, 3-1/2" h. **$400**

Mark Mussio, Humler & Nolan

Loetz art glass centerpiece, iridescent gold oil glazed low bowl with three-lobed standing flared rim, string decorated, unmarked, circa 1900, rare form, fine condition, 5-1/2" x 12". **$1,035**

Thomaston Place Auction Galleries

Loetz Secessionist vase in ornate brass frame displaying mask of maiden framed by fancy collar, verre-de-soie marine blue slightly ribbed and drizzled on neck with lime green pulled into swag-like position, excellent original condition, 13-3/4" h. **$600**

Mark Mussio, Humler & Nolan

Loetz vase with yellow/green body decorated with gold iridescent Argus pattern, purple and blue highlights, unsigned, fleabite to inside lip, otherwise very good to excellent condition, 4-1/2" h. **$425**

James D. Julia, Inc.

Loetz vase with stout neck bound by black vines with three stems terminating with leaf pods and attached to body, slight cypriot body, graphite in color, decorated with veins of aqua from rim to polished pontil, excellent original condition, 9-1/4" h. **$1,500**

Mark Mussio, Humler & Nolan

Loetz glass centerpiece, ruffled and crimped bowl in iridescent green with pale plum interior, set on Jugendstil bronze tripod base with floral spray brackets, arched braces, circa 1890, Austrian, unmarked, fine condition, 12-3/4" h. x 10-1/2" dia........... **$920**

Thomaston Place Auction Galleries

Loetz vase in Papillon pattern with bulbous body and pinched sides, platinum iridescence with blue and gold highlights, green glass body, unsigned, very good to excellent condition, 7-3/4" h. **$356**

James D. Julia, Inc.

Loetz glass centerpiece, three-stem Art Nouveau bronze stand with reticulated domed base with finial, vine swags supporting pinched green bowl with caramel interior, Austrian, circa 1890, glass unmarked, ground pontil, bronze marked 4205, fine condition, 9-1/2" h. overall, 9" dia., bronze 11-1/2" w. **$633**

Thomaston Place Auction Galleries

Loetz center bowl in iridescent green with four applied gold handles, canted sides, ground pontil, circa 1900, fine condition, 4-1/2" h. x 10-1/2" dia........... **$374**

Thomaston Place Auction Galleries

Moser

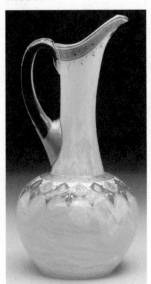

Moser decorated ewer, yellow and white swirled and striated glass body decorated with band of enameled stylized flowers topped by gilded band with enameled jewels, matching gilded band adorns lip of ewer, piece finished with applied and decorated amber glass handle, ewer signed on underside "Moser 125," very good to excellent condition, 11-3/4" h. **$1,481**

James D. Julia, Inc.

Moser vase with Amberina body with allover enamel decoration of flowers, stems and leaves with butterflies and flying insects surrounding vase, center enameled with figure of European courtier, very good to excellent condition with some wear to gilding on lip, 13" h. **$5,333**

James D. Julia, Inc.

Moser footed and lidded jar in green with gold, silver and bronze decoration of Roman general in chariot being crowned with laurel wreath, signed "BERNDT," circa 1910, fine condition, 10-1/2" h. x 5-3/4" dia. **$288**

Thomaston Place Auction Galleries

Moser decorated tea set, rare, with translucent enameled flowers covering body of each piece with gilded background and trim, set consists of teapot, four cups and saucers, six dessert plates, serving tray and covered creamer, very good to excellent condition, teapot 7-3/4" h., tray 12" dia. **$3,555**

James D. Julia, Inc.

TOP LOT!

Moser gift set in original presentation box, sapphire blue set of six cups and saucers with gold and hand-decorated with pink enamel flowers and bluish foliage, 1-3/4" taster cup or receptacle for sugar cubes, nick to one saucer, water marks on case, cups 1-3/4", flower petal saucers 4-5/8" dia............. **$750**

Mark Mussio, Humler & Nolan

Moser decorated ruby glass box with enamel flowers, stems, leaves and butterflies on sides and top, brass mounted feet, handles, collar, lock plate and original key, very good to excellent condition with wear to gilding on lid, 5-1/4" w. x 5-1/4" h. x 3-1/4" d. **$1,481**

James D. Julia, Inc.

Moser salamander pitcher, amber glass heavily decorated with enameled flowers, stems and leaves with butterflies, insects and winged dragon, clear glass gilded spout and neck terminating into heavy drippings, neck decorated with band of enameled flying insects, pitcher finished with gilded and enameled salamander handle extending around side of pitcher, very good to excellent condition with wear to gilding on neck and spout, 11" h. **$6,075**

James D. Julia, Inc.

Moser cranberry cornucopia samovar, rare, enameled ferns on body and front, glass mounted on original silver-plated frame on white marble platform, clear glass stopper at top and brass spigot at bottom, unsigned, very good to excellent condition, 12" h. x 10" l... **$1,422**

James D. Julia, Inc.

Moser square decorated plate, four corner gilded panels with colored flowers and birds in flight, each panel surrounded by floral bands, plate finished with center gilded medallion with large blue flower surrounded by floral band, very good to excellent condition with minor roughness to edge, 8" sq. **$593**

James D. Julia, Inc.

Moser opalescent decorated bowl shading to pink with wide band of enamel oak leaves surrounding shoulder of bowl with gold and yellow branches and stems, small applied glass acorns, signed on underside in gold "921 Moser D180," very good to excellent condition, 8" dia. x 6" h. **$2,133**

James D. Julia, Inc.

Moser lay-down perfume with clear twisted glass body with cased cranberry interior, enameled with colored decoration following twisted design, faceted gilt neck and original stopper, very good to excellent condition with some wear to gilding, 7" l...**$948**

James D. Julia, Inc.

GLASS

DAUM NANCY

DAUM NANCY FINE GLASS, much of it cameo, was made by Auguste and Antonin Daum, who founded a factory in 1875 in Nancy, France. Most of their cameo and enameled glass was made from the 1890s into the early 20th century.

Cameo glass is made by carving into multiple layers of colored glass to create a design in relief. It is at least as old as the Romans.

Rare gourd vase with textured mottling in red, yellow, and blue against internally decorated background of mottled brown, green, tan, and yellow, applied green stem handle wraps around body of gourd, signed on side with engraved signature "Daum Nancy" with Cross of Lorraine, very good to excellent condition, 11-3/4" h....**$10,665**

James D. Julia, Inc.

Rare cameo vase with multicolor mottled foot with golden wheat cameo stalks against frosted background with bumblebees, signed on side in cameo "Daum Nancy," very good to excellent condition, 17-1/8" h......**$4,860**

James D. Julia, Inc.

Monumental vase with cameo and enamel flowers, stems and leaves in green, amber, and yellow with red berries against mottled background of brown shading to yellow, cameo and enamel decoration circles vase, signed on side in black enamel "Daum Nancy" with Cross of Lorraine, very good to excellent condition, 18-1/2" h. **$4,148**

James D. Julia, Inc.

GLASS

$

TOP LOT!

Vase with cameo wind-blown trees with black and gray enameling, green enameled ground against pink shading to frosted sky, signed on underside with engraved signature "Daum Nancy" with Cross of Lorraine, very good to excellent condition, 6-1/2" h. **$4,740**

James D. Julia, Inc.

Mold-blown cameo vase with green mottled molded trees against mottled orange and yellow background with steeple and buildings and wheel-carved shrubbery, signed on bottom with engraved signature "Daum Nancy" with Cross of Lorraine, very good to excellent condition, 11-1/2" h.... **$6,518**

James D. Julia, Inc.

Vase with Impressionistic wooded scene with red, pink, mauve, and green foliage against mottled white and silver background, slightly flared and ruffled lip, signed on underside with engraved and gilded signature "Daum Nancy" with Cross of Lorraine with engraved and gilded palm frond, very good to excellent condition, 15-3/4" h. **$3,851**

James D. Julia, Inc.

Monumental vase with blackbirds against background of falling snow, birds shown in various stages of flight as well as resting on snow-covered trees against mottled sky blue background, signed on underside "Daum Nancy" with Cross of Lorraine to underside of foot, very good to excellent condition, 28" h........ **$30,800**

James D. Julia, Inc.

Tall cameo glass vase enamel-decorated with winter scene, 1900s, base etched "DAUM NANCY" with Cross of Lorraine, 11" x 4-1/2". **$5,938**

Rago Arts

Vase on bun foot, body cameo decorated with orange berries on green vine over mottled yellow, pink, and orange backdrop, cameo signed on side, excellent condition, 8" h.... **$1,300**

Mark Mussio, Humler & Nolan

Ewer with deciduous trees and snow-covered ground with orange and yellow mottled background, applied glass orange mottled handle and iridescent stopper with birds in flight, signed on underside "Daum Nancy" with Cross of Lorraine, wear to enameling and roughness to bottom of applied glass handle, 7" h......................... **$1,778**

James D. Julia, Inc.

GLASS

Vase with cameo and enamel seagulls against setting sun with carved ocean waves below and sea turtle against opalescent and frosted background, setting sun and lip of vase highlighted with gilding, signed on underside in gold enamel "Daum Nancy" with Cross of Lorraine, very good to excellent condition, 7-3/4" h. $13,628

James D. Julia, Inc.

Vase with cameo and enameled apple blossoms with shaded green leaves and brown stems against mottled orange to yellow background, signed on side in cameo "Daum Nancy" with Cross of Lorraine, very good to excellent condition, 7" h.................. $2,963

James D. Julia, Inc.

Cameo pillow vase of sunset by lake with sailing vessels and tree, obverse with harbor, trees and boats against orange/yellow sky, cameo signature on side, excellent condition, 4-3/8" x 7". $1,100

Mark Mussio, Humler & Nolan

Cameo bowl with vitrified glass cameo leaves, stems and flowers surrounding body in red, orange, yellow and green against frosted background, matching cameo decoration on interior, two heavy applied teardrop handles, signed on side in cameo near rim "Daum Nancy" with Cross of Lorraine, very good to excellent condition, 7" w................... $533

James D. Julia, Inc.

Miniature vase with enameled spring scene with yellow and green trees along shoreline with buildings in distance against striated background, signed on underside in black enamel "Daum Nancy" with Cross of Lorraine and initials "L.W.," very good to excellent condition, 1-3/4" h. $608

James D. Julia, Inc.

Inkwell with brown leaves and stems and blue berries against green to cream background, matching lid, signed on side with engraved signature "Daum Nancy" and Cross of Lorraine, very good to excellent condition, fleabite to bottom edge of lid, 4-3/4" w. x 3" h............. $3,555

James D. Julia, Inc.

Rose bowl with cameo trees set against shaded background of yellow to orange, each tree enameled, enameled snow-covered ground around bottom, signed on underside in black enamel "Daum Nancy" with Cross of Lorraine, very good to excellent condition, 2-3/4" h.......... $1,126

James D. Julia, Inc.

Covered box with vitrified glass, cameo leaves, stems and berries circling box and covering domed lid, cameo decoration in green, yellow, orange, and brown and set against frosted mottled blue shading to yellow background, signed on side with engraved signature "Daum Nancy" with Cross of Lorraine, very good condition with flake on inside lip of box, 5-1/4" dia. x 2-3/4" h. $2,548

James D. Julia, Inc.

DEPRESSION GLASS

DEPRESSION GLASS is the name of colorful glassware collectors generally associate with mass-produced glassware found in pink, yellow, crystal, or green in the years surrounding the Great Depression in America.

The homemakers of the Depression-era were able to enjoy the wonderful colors offered in this new, inexpensive glass dinnerware because they received pieces of their favorite patterns packed in boxes of soap, or as premiums given at "dish night" at the local movie theater. Merchandisers, such as Sears & Roebuck and F. W. Woolworth, enticed young brides with the colorful wares that they could afford even when economic times were harsh.

Because of advancements in glassware technology, Depression-era patterns were mass-produced and could be purchased for a fraction of what cut glass or lead crystal cost. As one manufacturer found a pattern that was pleasing to the buying public, other companies soon followed with their adaptation of a similar design. Patterns included several design motifs, such as florals, geometrics, and even patterns that looked back to Early American patterns like Sandwich glass.

Adam pattern, pink covered casserole. **$80**

As America emerged from the Great Depression and life became more leisure-oriented again, new glassware patterns were created to reflect the new tastes of this generation. More elegant shapes and forms were designed, leading to what is sometimes called "Elegant Glass." Today's collectors often include these more elegant patterns when they talk about Depression-era glassware.

Depression-era glassware is one of the best-researched collecting areas available to the American marketplace. This is due in large part to the careful research of several people, including Hazel Marie Weatherman, Gene Florence, Barbara Mauzy, Carl F. Luckey, and Kent Washburn. Their books are held in high regard by researchers and collectors today.

Regarding values for Depression glass, rarity does not always equate to a high dollar amount. Some more readily found items command lofty prices because of high demand or other factors, not because they are necessarily rare. As collectors' tastes range from the simple patterns to the more elaborate patterns, so does the ability of their budget to invest in inexpensive patterns to multi-hundreds of dollars per form patterns.

For more information on Depression glass, see *Warman's Depression Glass Identification and Price Guide*, 6th Edition, or *Warman's Depression Glass Field Guide*, 5th Edition, both by Ellen T. Schroy.

GLASS

American Pioneer pattern, pink salad plate. .. **$12.50**

American Sweetheart pattern, red serving plate. **$350**

Anniversary pattern, crystal butter dish. **$20**

Aunt Polly pattern, blue vase, 6-1/2" h. **$40**

GLASS

Beaded Block pattern, vaseline lily bowl, 4-1/2" dia. **$60**

Vaseline sugar with two handles. **$40**

Block Optic pattern, pink candlesticks...........**$45 pr.**
Green ice bucket. **$40**

Bowknot pattern, green sherbet.........................**$25**

Candlewick pattern, crystal cake stand, three-bead stem **$95**

GLASS

Capri pattern, azure blue snack plate with cup. .. **$15**

Cherryberry pattern, iridescent batter bowl. **$20**

Cherry Blossom pattern, pink footed pitcher. **$115**

Coronation pattern, pink soup bowl. **$16**
Pink plate. **$4.50**

Colonial pattern, pink divided grill plate. **$27.50**

Crocheted Crystal pattern narcissus bowl. **$42**

GLASS

Crow's Foot pattern, amber tumbler...................**$35**

Dogwood pattern, pink sherbet..............................**$30**

Daisy pattern, green cereal bowl........................**$12**

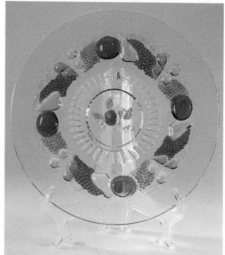

Della Robbia pattern, luster stain torte plate......**$65**

Doric pattern, pink vegetable bowl. **$45**

Doric and Pansy pattern, ultramarine cup..........**$14.25**

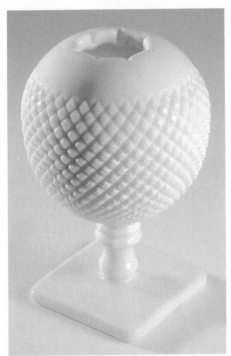

English Hobnail pattern, milk white ivy bowl. **$25**

Floral and Diamond Band pattern, green creamer.
....**$20**

Fairfax pattern, azure blue comport **$30**

Floragold pattern, iridescent salt and pepper
shakers..**$55**

Florentine No. 1 pattern, pink 8-1/2" dia. berry
bowl **$28**

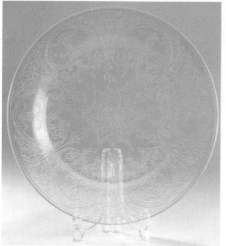

Horseshoe pattern, yellow sandwich plate. **$24.50**

Mayfair Open Rose pattern, ice blue pitcher. **$195**

Laurel pattern, jade green berry bowl................ **$30**

Moondrops pattern, red candlesticks with wings.
....**$100 pr.**

Mayfair Federal pattern, amber cup................ **$8.50**
Amber saucer... **$4.50**

New Century pattern, crystal covered casserole... **$85**

Miss America pattern, pink cup.......................... **$30**
Saucer..**$8**

GLASS

Parrot pattern, amber sherbet. **$21.50**

Princess pattern, green candy dish. **$45**

Peacock & Wild Rose pattern, green comport. ... **$100**

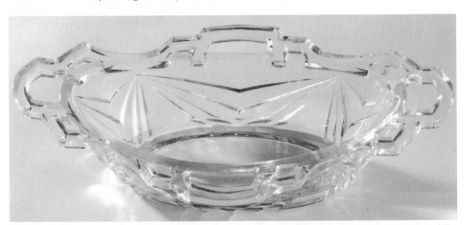

Pyramid pattern, yellow pickle dish. **$65**

GLASS

Radiance pattern, red cordial............................$45

Round Robin pattern, green cup $8
Green saucer..$2

Royal Lace pattern, cobalt blue sherbet. $45
Metal holder..$12

Ripple pattern, Jewel Turquoise berry bowl.........$12

Sandwich pattern, Hocking, pink 8-1/4" dia.
bowl. $28

Rosemary pattern, amber cream soup. $18

GLASS

Sharon pattern, pink butter dish. **$60**

Sunflower pattern, green ashtray. **$16**

Teardrop pattern, crystal champagne glass. **$10**

Twisted Optic pattern, green covered flat candy jar. **$40**

Victory pattern, green with gold edge cheese and cracker plate. **$45**

Wexford pattern, crystal decanter, 11-3/4" h. **$20**

GLASS

DUNCAN & MILLER

DUNCAN & MILLER GLASS CO., a successor firm to George A. Duncan & Sons Co., produced a wide range of pressed wares and novelty pieces during the late 19th century and into the early 20th century. During the Depression era and after, the company continued making a wide variety of more modern patterns, including mold-blown types, and also introduced a number of etched and engraved patterns. Many colors, including opalescent hues, were produced during this era, and especially popular today are the graceful swan dishes they produced in the Pall Mall and Sylvan patterns.

The numbers by the pattern name indicate the original factory pattern number. The Duncan factory was closed in 1955.

Large Sandwich basket, colorless, with applied handle, mid-20th century, undamaged, 9" h. overall, 14-1/2" x 18". **$127**

Jeffrey S. Evans & Associates

No. 800/Heavy Finecut pickle caster, vaseline (uranium), polished table ring, fitted in quadruple-plate stand marked for Warner with tongs, Geo. Duncan & Sons, fourth quarter 19th century, undamaged except for minor pattern flake, 10-3/4" h. overall, jar 4-3/8 h., 3-1/8" dia. base. **$161**

Jeffrey S. Evans & Associates

Button Arches No. 39 ruby-stained water pitcher, colorless, extensive engraving including Odd Fellows "Triple Links No. 53" lodge, Geo. Duncan & Sons Co./Duncan and Miller Glass Co., late 19th/early 20th century, excellent condition, undamaged, 10-5/8" h. overall. **$259**

Jeffrey S. Evans & Associates

Barred Oval No. 15004 table articles, colorless, cruet with appropriate stopper and cut-and-shut mark, creamer, and tray, Duncan & Miller Glass Co. and Geo. Duncan & Sons, late 19th/early 20th century, good condition, small chips and flakes to base of one tumbler and to rim of tray, otherwise undamaged, 2-1/8" to 7-1/8" h. overall. **$127**

Jeffrey S. Evans & Associates

DURAND

FINE DECORATIVE GLASS similar to that made by Tiffany and other outstanding glasshouses of its day was made by Vineland Flint Glass Works Co. in Vineland, New Jersey, first headed by Victor Durand, Sr. and subsequently by his son, Victor Durand, Jr., in the 1920s.

Covered jar with green coil pattern against gold iridescent background, matching lid with applied amber glass reeded finial, unsigned, very good to excellent condition, 6-1/2" h.......**$1,304**

James D. Julia, Inc.

Heart & Vine footed bowl with blue and green iridescent heart and vine decoration against gold/orange iridescent background, applied gold iridescent foot with blue highlights, yellow interior, unsigned, very good to excellent condition, 5" h................ **$830**

James D. Julia, Inc.

Lamp shaft with green King Tut pattern against gold iridescent background shading to orange/gold above shoulder, unsigned, very good to excellent condition, 6-1/2" h.......................... **$486**

James D. Julia, Inc.

Crackle glass with lava vase, rare dark blue iridescence with Moorish crackle design finished with clear glass lava drippings within crackle lines, unsigned, very good to excellent condition, 9" h. **$3,851**

James D. Julia, Inc.

Moorish crackle glass vase, round bulbous body with blue and white decoration separated by platinum iridescence in crackle lines, unsigned, very good to excellent condition, 10" h. ....**$2,000-$2,500**

James D. Julia, Inc.

King Tut vase, 1920s, signed "Durand 1700-8," 8" x 6".. **$938**

Rago Arts

Peacock Feather vase in white and blue against clear glass background shading to cobalt blue, slightly flaring neck, signed on underside in silver "V Durand 1998-12," very good to excellent condition, 12-1/4" h. **$770**

James D. Julia, Inc.

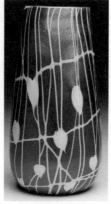

Heart & Vine vase with white heart and vine decoration against blue iridescent background, blue iridescent finish set against green glass body, unsigned, very good to excellent condition, 10-1/2" h. **$889**

James D. Julia, Inc.

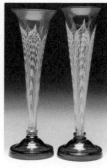

Peacock Feather vases in white and pink against clear to flashed cranberry background, unsigned, very good to excellent condition, 14" h.. **$1,067**

James D. Julia, Inc.

Torchiere with Moorish crackle glass shade with red and white decoration and gold iridescence in crackle lines, interior of shade finished with gold iridescence, shade supported by original bronze floor base with eagle talon feet, shade unsigned, base marked "Artistic Brass & Bz. WKS. N.Y.C. Pat. Appld. For," shade very good to excellent condition, base very good condition with some wear and pitting to finish, 62-3/4" h. overall. **$2,903**

James D. Julia, Inc.

Threaded Heart & Vine vase with gold and blue iridescent heart design against cream-colored background, random applied gold iridescent threading, signed on underside in silver "V Durand 20133-6," very good condition with some thread loss, 6" h. **$356**

James D. Julia, Inc.

Plate with blue pulled feather design against white background outlined in yellow and green, visible on underside of plate, top side shows yellow center with light yellow basketweave pattern encircling rim, unsigned, very good to excellent condition, 11-1/4" dia **$593**

James D. Julia, Inc.

Monumental vase in genie bottle design with vertical ribbing and blue iridescent finish, unsigned, very good to excellent condition with minor scratches to iridescence, 18-1/2" h. **$889**

James D. Julia, Inc.

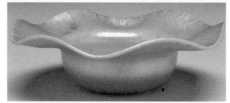

Bowl with stretched ruffled rim in gold iridescence with pink highlights, signed on underside in polished pontil "V Durand," very good to excellent condition, 6-1/4" dia. **$152**

James D. Julia, Inc.

GLASS

Threaded pulled feather vase with blue design against white background, feathers outlined in gold iridescence, random applied gold iridescent threading, interior with gold iridescence shading to yellow, unsigned, very good to excellent condition with thread loss, 7-1/2" h......... **$851**

James D. Julia, Inc.

Moorish crackle glass vase with blue and white exterior with gold iridescent crackle lines, interior of mouth finished in orange/gold iridescence, unsigned, very good to excellent condition, 9-1/4" h.................. **$948**

James D. Julia, Inc.

King Tut vase with gold iridescent design against light green background, finished on mouth and interior with orange/gold iridescence, unsigned, very good to excellent condition with minor discoloration to green background and King Tut design, 7" h........... **$608**

James D. Julia, Inc.

Lady Gay rose vase with gold iridescent King Tut pattern against rose-colored background, gold iridescent mouth, unsigned, very good to excellent condition, 9-3/4" h............. **$2,370**

James D. Julia, Inc.

Vase with iridescent leaf and vine decoration, attributed to Durand but unsigned, 11" h... **$1,560**

Cowan's Auctions, Inc.

Applied coil vase with gold iridescent pulled feather design against orange/gold iridescent background, each feather outlined in green, gold iridescent applied coil, signed on underside "V Durand" and numbered, good condition with some missing areas of applied coil, 10" h.......... **$1,304**

James D. Julia, Inc.

Heart & Vine vase with green iridescent vines and green and orange iridescent hearts against cream-colored background, inside of mouth in gold iridescence, unsigned, very good to excellent condition, 13" h.. **$1,823**

James D. Julia, Inc.

Two Heart & Vine vases, blue on gold lustre, 1920s, marked 20154-10 and 2011-12, 10-1/4" h., 12-1/4" h........... **$1,750**

Rago Arts

FENTON ART GLASS

THE FENTON ART GLASS CO. was founded in 1905 by Frank L. Fenton and his brother, John W., in Martins Ferry, Ohio. They initially sold hand-painted glass made by other manufacturers, but it wasn't long before they decided to produce their own glass. The new Fenton factory in Williamstown, West Virginia, opened on Jan. 2, 1907. From that point on, the company expanded by developing unusual colors and continued to decorate glassware in innovative ways.

Two more brothers, James and Robert, joined the firm. But despite the company's initial success, John W. left to establish the Millersburg Glass Co. of Millersburg, Ohio, in 1909. The first months of the new operation were devoted to the production of crystal glass only. Later iridized glass was called "Radium Glass." After only two years, Millersburg filed for bankruptcy.

Fenton's iridescent glass had a metallic luster over a colored, pressed pattern, and was sold in dime stores. It was only after the sales of this glass decreased and it was sold in bulk as carnival prizes that it came to be known as carnival glass.

Fenton became the top producer of carnival glass, with more than 150 patterns. The quality of the glass, and its popularity with the public, enabled the new company to be profitable through the late 1920s. As interest in carnival subsided, Fenton moved on to stretch glass and opalescent patterns. A line of colorful blown glass (called "off-hand" by Fenton) was also produced in the mid-1920s.

During the Great Depression, Fenton survived by producing functional colored glass tableware and other household items, including water sets, table sets, bowls, mugs, plates, perfume bottles and vases. Restrictions on European imports during World War II ushered in the arrival of Fenton's opaque colored glass, and the lines of "Crest" pieces soon followed. In the 1950s, production continued to diversify with a focus on milk glass, particularly in Hobnail patterns. In the third quarter of Fenton's history, the

No. 8 Water Lily and Cattails true open compote, colorless, oval bowl on low standard, with two handles , circa 1907, very good overall condition with rim chip, 7-1/2" h., 7-5/8" x 10-1/4" bowl.......... **$58**

Jeffrey S. Evans & Associates

Little Flowers carnival glass eight-piece berry set, blue, master bowl and seven individual bowls, first quarter 20th century, undamaged, 3" and 1-7/8" h., 8" and 5-1/2" dia. **$150**

Jeffrey S. Evans & Associates

GLASS

company returned to themes that had proved popular to preceding generations and began adding special lines, such as the Bicentennial series.

Innovations included the line of Colonial colors that debuted in 1963, including amber, blue, green, orange and ruby. Based on a special order for an Ohio museum, Fenton in 1969 revisited its early success with "Original Formula Carnival Glass." Fenton also started marking its glass in the molds for the first time.

The star of the 1970s was the yellow and blushing pink creation known as Burmese, which remains popular today. This was followed closely by a menagerie of animals, birds, and children. In 1975, Robert Barber was hired by Fenton to begin an artist-in-residence program, producing a limited line of art glass vases in a return to the off-hand, blown-glass creations of the mid-1920s. Shopping at home via television was a recent phenomenon in the late 1980s when the "Birthstone Bears" became the first Fenton product to appear on QVC. In August 2007, Fenton discontinued all but a few of its more popular lines, and the company ceased production altogether in 2011.

For more information on Fenton Art Glass, see *Warman's Fenton Glass Identification and Price Guide*, 2nd edition, by Mark F. Moran.

Coinspot water pitchers, cranberry and green opalescent, each with applied handle, probably first quarter 20th century, undamaged, 9-3/4" and 9-3/8" h. overall. **$230**

Jeffrey S. Evans & Associates

Silver Crest punch bowl on stand with 12 cups, bowl 15" dia. **$384**

Burchard Galleries

Orange Tree Orchard blue carnival glass water pitcher and six tumblers. **$750**

Fentonia marigold carnival glass table set, covered butter, 6" h.; spooner, 4-1/4" h.; sugar, 6-1/2" h. Partial set shown here. **$400**
Complete set (with creamer). .... **$750+**

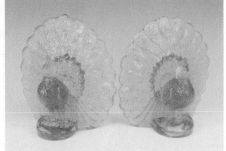

Rose peacock-form bookends, 1935, each 6" h. .. **$500**

GLASS

Orange Tree carnival glass fruit/orange bowl, marigold, raised on three scroll feet, first quarter 20th century, undamaged, 5-3/8" h., 10" dia. overall... **$138**

Jeffrey S. Evans & Associates

Salmon Run cameo glass vase, glossy Burmese with plush background, signed by Kelsey Murphy and Robert Bomkamp, numbered 22/75 under base, retired limited edition from 2010 Cameo Gallery Collection, undamaged, 8" h. **$259**

Jeffrey S. Evans & Associates

Drapery blown water pitcher, green opalescent, globular form with flared star-crimped rim and applied handle, first quarter 20th century, undamaged, body with some light scratches, 9-1/2" h. overall. **$92**

Jeffrey S. Evans & Associates

Buttons and Braids water pitcher, green opalescent, ovoid form on low foot with crimped rim, applied handle, probably first quarter 20th century, undamaged, 9-5/8" h. overall. **$161**

Jeffrey S. Evans & Associates

Buttons and Braids water pitcher, green opalescent, hexagonal-form crimped rim, applied handle, probably first quarter 20th century, undamaged, 9-1/8" h. overall. **$173**

Jeffrey S. Evans & Associates

Cranberry Coin Dot vase, excellent condition, 6-1/2" h. . **$65**

Homestead Auctions

Snow Crest cranberry glass vase, pre logo, swirl design, excellent condition, 9" h. **$53**

Homestead Auctions

Peach Crest double-crimped vases with Charleton decoration, 1940s, each 8" h. ..... **$100+ each**

Silver Crest melon-form perfume bottle with Charleton decoration by Abels, Wasserberg of New York, mid-1940s, 7" h. **$85**

FOSTORIA

THE FOSTORIA GLASS CO., founded in 1887, produced numerous types of fine glassware over the years. Its factory in Moundsville, West Virginia, closed in 1986.

Stemware, American pattern, 22 pieces including 14 clear glass wine goblets raised on hexagonal feet and eight clear glass champagne glasses with round feet, wine 6.8" h. x 3.25" dia., champagne 4.3" h. x 4" dia. **$121**

Ahlers & Ogletree Auction Gallery

American pattern clear crushed fruit jar, chips on inside of lid and exterior, scratches, 10" h. **$545**

Rachel Davis Fine Arts

Straw holder, circa 1915-1924, American pattern, original lid, excellent condition, 13" h. **$300**

Rich Penn Auctions

GLASS

Pink rose salt shaker, opaque pink with satin finish, period two-part lid, circa 1891-1894, undamaged, 1-3/4" h. overall. **$207**

Jeffrey S. Evans & Associates

No. 4183/Homespun tumblers, gold, each with trademark and original paper label, 4-5/8" h. **$46**

Jeffrey S. Evans & Associates

No. 205/Artichoke cake stand, colorless and frosted, upturned high- and low-point rim, circa 1891, undamaged with no wear to plate, 5-5/8" h. x 9-1/2" dia. **$184**

Jeffrey S. Evans & Associates

Six Versailles azure blue claret wine glasses, 5-1/2" h. **$212**

Fusco Auctions

Set of six Navarre blue magnum 16 oz. wine glasses, rarest of all Fostoria stemware, 7-1/4" h. **$638**

Omega Auction Corp.

GALLÉ

GALLÉ GLASS WAS MADE in Nancy, France, by Emile Gallé, founder of the Nancy School and a leader in the Art Nouveau movement in France. Much of his glass, both enameled and cameo, is decorated with naturalistic motifs. The finest pieces were made in the last two decades of the 19th century and the opening years of the 20th.

Pieces marked with a star preceding the name were made between 1904, the year of Gallé's death, and 1914.

Bulbous cameo glass vase, acid-etched with daisies in windowpane technique, Nancy, France, 1900s, signed Gallé on body, 6-1/2" x 8". **$2,750**

Rago Arts

Miniature vase with grapes on tendril vine, cameo signature on side, area on rim appears to have been polished, 2-1/8" h. ... **$100**

Mark Mussio, Humler & Nolan

Vase with oversized purple fuchsia and foliage in cameo over pink backdrop, marked Gallé in cameo on side, excellent condition, 4-5/8" x 4" w. **$450**

Mark Mussio, Humler & Nolan

Cameo glass vase, acid-etched with flowers, Nancy, France, 1900s, signed Gallé on body, 10" x 4-1/2".................**$2,125**

Rago Arts

Tall cameo glass vase, acid-etched with wildflowers, Nancy, France, 1900s, signed Gallé on body, 9-3/4" x 5-1/2". **$1,750**

Rago Arts

Four-color vase with foliaged tree over knoll with lake and mountain range, signature of Gallé on lower portion of body, excellent original condition, 4-3/4" h.......... **$950**

Mark Mussio, Humler & Nolan

Vase commemorating struggle for Lorraine with brown cameo thistles of Lorraine attacked by Prussian eagle, dated on front in cameo "1914" and signed in cameo "Gallé," missing original glass base and has turned wooden replacement, 14-1/2" h. **$2,430**

James D. Julia, Inc.

Cameo glass vase, yellow-green and shaded peach, banjo-form decorated with flowers and leaves, signed "Gallé" in script relief on verso, early 20th century, undamaged, 6-1/2" h. **$805**

Jeffrey S. Evans & Associates

Small acid-etched cameo glass boudoir lamp with dogwood flowers, Nancy, France, signed Gallé on base and shade, 10-1/4" x 5-1/2". **$4,375**

Rago Arts

Faience vase with central cartouche on front of vase with blue and white scene of children on shoreline with castles on opposite side of lake and mountains in background, cartouche surrounded by raised branch encircling cartouche with leaves, flowers, and fruit hanging from branch, mottled yellow and orange background, backside decorated with branch with leaves and fruit against same background, signed on underside "E. Gallé Nancy," very good to excellent condition, 6-1/2" h. **$547**

James D. Julia, Inc.

Cameo vase with green cameo leaves, stems and seedpods against russet shading to cream frosted background, signed on back in cameo "Gallé," very good to excellent condition, 7-1/2" h. **$1,007**

James D. Julia, Inc.

Covered round box, circa 1900, etched to base "Cristallerie de Emile Gallé Nancy / depose / ex. 1900" and with further inscription "Cristallerie de Gallé," rim and cover each with first standard Minerva mark and maker's mark of Henri Soufflot, Paris, compressed circular body acid-etched and enameled with iris blossoms and foliage, domed cover repoussé-decorated with spray of blossoms, 3-1/2" h. x 5-1/4" dia........... **$2,510**

John Moran Auctioneers

Vase with reddish-brown cameo ferns extending from foot to lip with transparent green stems and leaves against cream-colored background with pink hue, fire polished, signed on side with engraved signature "Gallé," very good to excellent condition with light grind marks around outer lip, probably from factory, 15-1/2" h.**$2,370**

James D. Julia, Inc.

Triangular bowl cameo carved with meadow flowers encircling circumference, cameo signed with star on corner, excellent condition, 2" x 5-3/4"........ **$225**

Mark Mussio, Humler & Nolan

Mold blown fuchsia vase with amethyst and blue fuchsia flowers and leaves against frosted yellow background, opalescent interior of mouth and cameo signature on side "Gallé," original paper label from retailer "Muebleria Caviglia 25 de Mayo 569 Montevideo," very good to excellent condition, 11-1/2" h. **$8,505**

James D. Julia, Inc.

Vase with mold blown squash blossoms and leaves in dark amber against light amber background, signed on side in raised letters "Gallé," foot broken and poorly repaired, 7-1/4" h. **$3,038**

James D. Julia, Inc.

Vase with cameo pine trees and rock outcroppings with pale purple mountains in background, against frosted yellow sky, signed on side in cameo "Gallé," very good to excellent condition, 13-3/4" h. **$2,430**

James D. Julia, Inc.

Large cameo vase with olive green and purple cameo flowers, stems and leaves against shaded purple to cream background, finished with fire polish, signed on side with Oriental style cameo signature "Gallé," very good to excellent condition, 15" h.. **$2,963**

James D. Julia, Inc.

Bottle vase cameo carved with hydrangea front and back, body molded with ridges, cameo signed with memorial star, excellent condition, 5-7/8" h. **$325**

Mark Mussio, Humler & Nolan

Cylinder-shaped cameo vase with pink frost and green ground with floral and leaf pattern in dark earthen hues, signed "Gallé" in cameo to side of vase, very good to excellent condition, 13-1/4" h. **$1,067**

James D. Julia, Inc.

Cameo banjo vase with brown and amber cameo pond with lily pads and flowers with amber-colored dragonfly, signed on side in cameo "Gallé," very good to excellent condition, 6-1/4" h. **$911**

James D. Julia, Inc.

Vase with dark brown cameo decoration of pine trees and rock outcroppings with lake and purple mountains in background set against cream shading to yellow sky, signed on side in cameo "Gallé," very good to excellent condition, 14" h. **$3,081**

James D. Julia, Inc.

GLASS

HEISEY GLASS

NUMEROUS TYPES OF FINE GLASS were made by A.H. Heisey & Co., Newark, Ohio, from 1895. The company's trademark, an H enclosed within a diamond, is known to most glass collectors. The company's name and molds were acquired by Imperial Glass Co., Bellaire, Ohio, in 1958, and some pieces have been reissued. The glass listed below consists of miscellaneous pieces and types.

No. 300/Peerless punch bowl and stand, colorless, each pieces with trademark, circa 1901, undamaged, light interior wear, 12-1/2" h. overall, 15" dia. rim.......... **$138**

Jeffrey S. Evans & Associates

Hand-enameled recessed panel candy jars, H in diamond mark, excellent condition, 13" h............... **$369**

Fine Arts Auctions, LLC

No. 356/Queen Anne toothpick holder, colorless, H in diamond trademark in base, circa 1906, undamaged, 2-1/4" h. **$288**

Jeffrey S. Evans & Associates

No. 134/Trident flower bowl, Moongleam, with appropriate colorless flower frog, excellent condition, bowl with nick under two feet, frog with light bruise to top edge, 7-1/4" x 14-1/4" x 4-3/4" h. **$104**

Jeffrey S. Evans & Associates

No. 335/Prince of Wales ruby-stained toothpick holder, colorless, circa 1902, undamaged, 2-1/2" h. **$230**

Jeffrey S. Evans & Associates

GLASS

IMPERIAL

FROM 1902 UNTIL 1984, Imperial Glass Co. of Bellaire, Ohio, produced hand-made glass. Early pressed glass production often imitated cut glass and may bear the raised "NUCUT" mark in the interior center. In the second decade of the 1900s, Imperial was one of the dominant manufacturers of iridescent or carnival glass. When glass collecting gained popularity in the 1970s, Imperial again produced carnival glass and a line of multicolored slag glass. Imperial purchased molds from closing glass houses and continued many lines popularized by others including Central, Heisey, and Cambridge. These reissues may cause confusion but they were often marked.

Cube cut tobacco pressed glass humidor, colorless, name embossed on top of finial, first quarter 20th century, undamaged, 7" h. overall ... **$115**

Jeffrey S. Evans & Associates

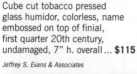

Slag glass owl handled creamer and open sugar in tan/orange, creamer approximately 3-1/2" x 3-1/2" x 2-1/4". **$58**

J. Levine Auction & Appraisal, LLC

Slag glass mint whimsy swan bowl in tan, approximately 4" x 5" x 3-1/4". **$29**

J. Levine Auction & Appraisal, LLC

Slag glass green lidded duck on nest bowl, approximately 4" h. x 4-1/2" x 3" **$29**

J. Levine Auction & Appraisal, LLC

Slag glass vase with scalloped rim in tan, approximately 5-1/4" h. x 4" dia. **$23**

J. Levine Auction & Appraisal, LLC

Caramel slag rooster on basket with satin finish on lacy base, excellent condition, no chips or cracks, approximately 8" x 7-1/2" x 6". **$35**

J. Levine Auction & Appraisal, LLC

GLASS

Slag glass neutral-toned and handled open pint pitcher with windmill motif, approximately 6-1/2" x 6-3/4" x 3-3/4".......**$52**

J. Levine Auction & Appraisal, LLC

Slag glass red-toned handled open pint pitcher with windmill motif, approximately 6-1/2" x 6-1/2" x 4"..........................**$46**

J. Levine Auction & Appraisal, LLC

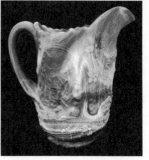

Slag glass purple-toned handled open pint pitcher with windmill motif, approximately 6-1/2" x 6-1/4" x 4"..........................**$52**

J. Levine Auction & Appraisal, LLC

Slag glass candlestick in brown, floral motif about circumference, approximately 3-1/2" h. x 4" dia. **$12**

J. Levine Auction & Appraisal, LLC

Slag glass candlestick in purple, floral motif about circumference, approximately 3-1/2" h. x 4" dia. **$12**

J. Levine Auction & Appraisal, LLC

Slag glass candlestick in red #1, floral motif about circumference, approximately 3-1/4" h. x 3-3/4" dia. **$17**

J. Levine Auction & Appraisal, LLC

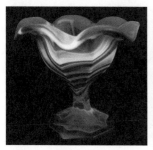

Slag glass compote, green with scalloped rim, approximately 4-1/2" h. x 5" dia.................**$29**

J. Levine Auction & Appraisal, LLC

Slag glass compote, purple with scalloped rim, approximately 4-1/2" h. x 5-1/2" dia. **$35**

J. Levine Auction & Appraisal, LLC

Slag glass footed compote, orange and red glass with crimped rim, approximately 6-1/2" h. x 6" dia.................**$35**

J. Levine Auction & Appraisal, LLC

GLASS

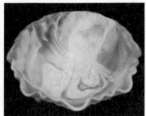

Slag glass tripod foot bowl, neutral-toned with scalloped rim and rose motif, approximately 3" h. x 8" dia. **$35**

J. Levine Auction & Appraisal, LLC

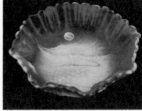

Crimped slag glass bowl with grape motif in bottom, approximately 4" h. x 10" dia. **$29**

J. Levine Auction & Appraisal, LLC

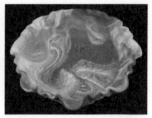

Slag glass tripod foot bowl, green toned with scalloped rim and rose motif, approximately 3-1/4" h. x 8" dia. **$35**

J. Levine Auction & Appraisal, LLC

Slag glass crimped bowl with rose motif in bottom, approximately 3" h. x 8-1/2" dia. **$29**

J. Levine Auction & Appraisal, LLC

Slag glass circular footed bowl in red tones with cuts similar to American Brilliant cut crystal, approximately 4-1/2" h. x 8-1/2" dia............................ **$35**

J. Levine Auction & Appraisal, LLC

Slag glass reticulated lidded basket bowl in neutrals with lion motif, approximately 6-1/4" x 7-1/2" x 6". **$52**

J. Levine Auction & Appraisal, LLC

Slag glass footed compote, purple hexagonal with grape motif, approximately 3-3/4" h. x 6" dia. **$23**

J. Levine Auction & Appraisal, LLC

Glass compote with cover, purple slag with satin finish, good condition with small rim chip, approximately 6-3/4" x 6-1/2". **$23**

J. Levine Auction & Appraisal, LLC

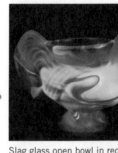

Slag glass open bowl in red with rooster motif, approximately 4-1/4" x 4-3/4" x 3"............. **$46**

J. Levine Auction & Appraisal, LLC

Glass compote, caramel slag with satin finish, excellent condition, no chips or cracks, approximately 4" x 6". **$35**

J. Levine Auction & Appraisal, LLC

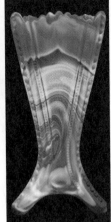

Freehand vase with orange iridescent heart and vine decoration against gold iridescent background, two applied cream-colored handles with gold iridescence near body, cream-colored applied lip, unsigned, very good to excellent condition with small flake on underside near polished pontil, 9-3/4" h... **$1,007**

James D. Julia, Inc.

Slag glass triangular vase with dots up sides in green, approximately 8-1/2" x 4-1/2" x 4". **$46**

J. Levine Auction & Appraisal, LLC

Slag glass urn in red with nude females about circumference, approximately 8" h. x 5" dia. **$58**

J. Levine Auction & Appraisal, LLC

Slag glass owl jar in purple, lidded, approximately 6-1/2" h. x 3-1/2" dia. **$40**

J. Levine Auction & Appraisal, LLC

Slag glass cruet with stopper in purple, handled, good condition, approximately 6-3/4" h. x 3" dia. **$35**

J. Levine Auction & Appraisal, LLC

Corset-shaped vase, white background with green heart and vine décor, gold iridescent interior, good condition, 10-1/4" h. **$650**

Woody Auction

Slag glass owl jar in tan/orange, lidded, approximately 4" h. x 3-1/2" dia. **$46**

J. Levine Auction & Appraisal, LLC

Slag glass large neutral-toned fluted vase with intricate cuts, slight scratches to rim on one side, approximately 10" h. x 5" dia. **$35**

J. Levine Auction & Appraisal, LLC

Two vases, one with gilt label "Imperial / Free Hand / Made in U.S.A.," other unmarked, 1920s, each of squat baluster form, iridescent glass with pulled heart and vine pattern on orange ground, rims in cobalt, overall good condition, 6" h. x 6" dia. **$600**

John Moran Auctioneers

GLASS

LALIQUE

RENÉ JULES LALIQUE was born on April 6, 1860, in the village of Ay, in the Champagne region of France. In 1862, his family moved to the suburbs of Paris.

In 1872, Lalique began attending College Turgot where he began studying drawing with Justin-Marie Lequien. After the death of his father in 1876, Lalique began working as an apprentice to Louis Aucoc, who was a prominent jeweler and goldsmith in Paris.

Lalique moved to London in 1878 to continue his studies. He spent two years attending Sydenham College, developing his graphic design skills. He returned to Paris in 1880 and worked as an illustrator of jewelry, creating designs for Cartier, among others. In 1884, Lalique's drawings were displayed at the National Exhibition of Industrial Arts, organized at the Louvre.

Calypso charger, opalescent glass, France, 1950s, M p. 306, No. 413, etched "Lalique France," 2" x 14-1/2" **$3,250**

Rago Arts

At the end of 1885, Lalique took over Jules Destapes' jewelry workshop. Lalique's designs began to incorporate translucent enamels, semiprecious stones, ivory, and hard stones. In 1889, at the Universal Exhibition in Paris, the jewelry firms of Vever and Boucheron included collaborative works by Lalique in their displays.

In the early 1890s, Lalique began to incorporate glass into his jewelry, and in 1893 he took part in a competition organized by the Union Centrale des Arts Decoratifs to design a drinking vessel. He won second prize.

Lalique opened his first Paris retail shop in 1905, near the perfume business of François Coty. Coty commissioned Lalique to design his perfume labels in 1907, and he also created his first perfume bottles for Coty.

In the first decade of the 20th century, Lalique continued to experiment with glass manufacturing techniques, and mounted his first show devoted entirely to glass in 1911.

During World War I, Lalique's first factory was forced to close, but the construction of a new factory was soon begun in Wingen-sur-Moder, in the Alsace region. It was completed in 1921, and still produces Lalique crystal today.

In 1925, Lalique designed the first "car mascot" (hood ornament) for Citroën, the French automobile company. For the next six years, Lalique designed 29 models for companies such as Bentley, Bugatti, Delage, Hispano-Suiza, Rolls Royce, and Voisin.

Lalique's second boutique opened in 1931, and this location continues to serve as the main Lalique showroom today.

René Lalique died on May 5, 1945, at the age of 85. His son, Marc, took over the business at that time, and when Marc died in 1977, his daughter, Marie-Claude Lalique Dedouvre, assumed control of the company. She sold her interest in the firm and retired in 1994.

For more information on Lalique, see *Warman's Lalique Identification and Price Guide* by Mark F. Moran.

(**Editor's Note:** In the descriptions of Lalique pieces that follow, you will find notations like "M p. 478, No. 1100" or "Marcilhac 952, pg. 428." This refers to the page and serial numbers found in *René Lalique, Maître-Verrier, 1860-1945: Analyse de L'oeuvre et Catalogue Raisonné*, by Félix Marcilhac, published in 1989 and revised in 1994. Printed entirely in French, this book of more than 1,000 pages is the definitive guide to Lalique's work, and listings from auction catalogs typically cite the Marcilhac guide as a reference.)

GLASS

Love Parakeets sculpture, "Lalique Paris" sticker on front and engraved "Lalique ® France" in script beneath, excellent condition, 7-1/2" h. **$375**

Mark Mussio, Humler & Nolan

Sirene mascot in opalescent glass with amethyst tint with gray patination, mermaid form, signed on side in raised block letters "R. Lalique," signed on side of foot in etched script "R. Lalique France," Marcilhac 831, pg. 497, very good to excellent condition, 3-3/4" h............. **$3,555**

James D. Julia, Inc.

Statuette intaglio-carved with Madonna and Child in gowns, original black wood base, script engraved "Lalique France" on side of column, excellent original condition, 13-3/8" x 1-1/2"....**$750**

Mark Mussio, Humler & Nolan

Vierge a L'enfant lumi-naire impressed with Virgin Mary holding baby Jesus, figures are frosted and seen through front of glass block that rests within metal lighted base, glass signed on side in etched block letters "R. Lalique France," Marcil-hac 1217, pg. 519, very good to excellent condi-tion, 15-1/4" h. **$1,067**

James D. Julia, Inc.

Gerardmer vase, clear glass with black patina, France, designed 1934, M p. 461, no. 10-885, etched "R. Lalique France," 9-1/2" x 6-1/4"............... **$2,250**

Rago Arts

Bacchus vase, clear and frosted glass with gray patina, France, designed 1938, M p. 469, No. 10-922, etched "R. LALIQUE FRANCE," 7" x 6".................... **$2,875**

Rago Arts

GLASS

Soucis vase, opalescent glass, France, designed 1930, M p. 447, no. 1039, etched "R. LALIQUE France," 7" x 7"............... **$1,875**

Rago Arts

Druide vase, frosted and opalescent glass with green patina, designed 1924, M p. 425, no. 937, unmarked, 7" x 7".................................... **$688**

Rago Arts

Carthage vase, deep topaz glass, France, designed 1930, M p. 440, no. 1051, etched "R. LALIQUE," 7" x 8-1/2".... **$3,000**

Rago Arts

Clos Sainte-Odile ice bucket, frosted glass, France, designed 1922, M p. 801, no. A, molded "R. LALIQUE," 9-1/4" x 8-1/4"............................. **$2,250**

Rago Arts

Espalion vase, opalescent glass with gray patina, France, designed 1927, M p. 438, no. 996, etched 'R. Lalique France," 7" x 6".............. **$1,188**

Rago Arts

"Piriac" vase, clear and frosted glass with blue patina, France, designed 1930, M p. 447, no. 1043, etched "R. LALIQUE FRANCE," 7-1/4" x 8"..... **$1,750**

Rago Arts

Avalon vase, clear, frosted, and opalescent glass with green patina, France, designed 1927, M p. 436, no. 986, etched "R. Lalique," 6" x 6-1/4"....... **$2,125**

Rago Arts

Grenade vase, black glass with white enamel, France, designed 1930, M p. 448, no. 1045, etched "R. LALIQUE France / original sticker, Made in France no. 1045," 4-1/2" x 5".... **$2,750**

Rago Arts

Moissac vase, clear and frosted yellow glass, France, designed 1927, M p. 437, no. 992, etched "R. LALIQUE FRANCE," 5" x 6"........................... **$2,250**

Rago Arts

Chamarande vase, topaz glass, France, designed 1926, M p. 433, No. 974, unmarked, 7-3/4" x 9".................... **$2,375**

Rago Arts

Marisa vase, opalescent glass, France, circa 1927, M p. 439, no. 1002, signed "R Lalique France no 1002," 9" x 9".......... **$3,500**

Rago Arts

Palms vase decorated with palm fronds encircling entire body in amber glass, signed on underside in etched script signature "R. Lalique," Marcilhac 952, pg. 428, very good to excellent condition, 4-1/2" h.......... **$2,074**

James D. Julia, Inc.

Malesherbes vase decorated with impressed overlapping leaves surrounding body, impressed pattern in cased opalescent glass, signed on underside with etched script signature "R. Lalique France No. 1014," Marcilhac 1014, pg. 442, very good to excellent condition, 9" h............... **$2,370**

James D. Julia, Inc.

Sirenes perfume burner, opalescent glass with blue patina, France, circa 1920, M. p. 688 no. 265, etched "R. LALIQUE," 7" x 3-1/2".... **$3,125**

Rago Arts

Saint-Francois vase, frosted and opalescent glass with green patina, France, circa 1930, M. p.450, no. 1055, etched "R. LALIQUE FRANCE," 7" x 6-1/2"........................... **$1,875**

Rago Arts

Tournesols vase, electric blue glass, France, designed 1927, M p. 440, no. 1007, etched "R. Lalique France No. 1007," 4-1/4" x 4".................... **$3,125**

Rago Arts

Escargot vase, clear and frosted glass with blue patina, France, designed 1920, M p. 424, no. 931, molded "R. LALIQUE," 8-1/4" x 7-1/2".............. **$3,750**

Rago Arts

Monnaie du Pape vase, frosted amber glass, designed 1914, M p. 416, no. 897, molded "R. LALIQUE," 9" x 6-1/2".... **$3,750**

Rago Arts

GLASS

LIBBEY GLASS

IN 1878, WILLIAM L. LIBBEY obtained a lease on the New England Glass Co. of Cambridge, Massachusetts, changing the name to the New England Glass Works, W.L. Libbey and Son, Proprietors. After his death in 1883, his son, Edward D. Libbey, continued to operate the company at Cambridge until 1888, when the factory was closed. Edward Libbey moved to Toledo, Ohio, and set up the company subsequently known as Libbey Glass Co. During the 1880s, the firm's master technician, Joseph Locke, developed the now much-desired colored art glass lines of Agata, Amberina, Peach Blow, and Pomona. Renowned for its cut glass of the Brilliant Period, the company continues in operation today as Libbey Glassware, a division of Owens-Illinois, Inc.

Two-part punch bowl, Corona pattern, with seven matching punch cups, signed, good condition, no chips, cracks or repairs, 14" x 14". **$700**

Woody Auction

Diamond-Optic celery vase, deep Amberina with square, scalloped rim and polished pontil mark, late 19th/ early 20th century, undamaged, 6" h., 3-1/4" sq. rim. **$92**

Jeffrey S. Evans & Associates

Cut overlay compote, opaque black to clear, shallow bowl with silver diamond and miter pattern, raised on tall stem and foot with silver diamond band and polished pontil mark with acid stamped signature, first half 20th century, undamaged, 6-5/8" h., 6" dia. rim. **$207**

Jeffrey S. Evans & Associates

Two colorless cut glass vases, 20th century, each with flutter rim and flared foot, decorated with egrets among rushes, one with factory mark, one with paper label, each in very good condition with no cracks, chips or restorations, 18" h. **$2,640**

Skinner, Inc.; www.skinnerinc.com

MARY GREGORY

GLASS ENAMELED IN WHITE with silhouette-type figures, primarily of children, is now termed "Mary Gregory" and was attributed to the Boston and Sandwich Glass Co. However, recent research has proven conclusively that this was not decorated by Mary Gregory, nor was it made at the Sandwich plant. Miss Gregory was employed by Boston and Sandwich Glass Co. as a decorator; however, records show her assignment was the painting of naturalistic landscape scenes on larger items such as lamps and shades, but never the charming children for which her name has become synonymous. Further, in the inspection of fragments from the factory site, no paintings of children were found.

It is now known that all wares collectors call "Mary Gregory" originated in Bohemia beginning in the late 19th century and were extensively exported to England and the United States well into this century,

For further information, see *The Glass Industry in Sandwich*, Volume #4 by Raymond E. Barlow and Joan E. Kaiser, and the book *Mary Gregory Glassware, 1880-1900* by R. & D. Truitt.

Shaker, blue with enamel decoration, ribbed optic with period lid, fourth quarter 19th century, undamaged, 5" h. overall..........................**$288**

Jeffrey S. Evans & Associates

Six barber's bottles, enameled Mary Gregory-type decoration, internal stress crack in one squared bottle, 8".. **$708**

Burchard Galleries

Bitters/barber's bottles, cobalt blue, light Rib-Optic pattern to each, white enamel girl and boy figures within landscapes, each with rough pontil mark, late 19th/early 20th century, undamaged, decoration with some light pitting/wear, 8" h. **$150**

Jeffrey S. Evans & Associates

GLASS

Dot/Spot-Optic water pitcher, blue with worn gilt-decorated rim with polychrome decoration of boy and girl picking cherries, folded and crimped rim, colorless applied handle, late 19th/ early 20th century, undamaged, 9-5/8" h. overall. **$138**

Jeffrey S. Evans & Associates

Panel-Optic water pitcher, blue with white enamel decoration of young woman, bulbous base and cylindrical neck, amber applied handle, ground pontil mark, late 19th/early 20th century, undamaged, 11-1/2" h. overall...**$104**

Jeffrey S. Evans & Associates

Square Royal salt and pepper shakers, smoky gray with white enamel decoration and matching period two-part lids, fourth quarter 19th century, undamaged, 6" h. overall. **$460**

Jeffrey S. Evans & Associates

Bitters/barber's bottles, green with white enamel and gilt decoration, ball-form bottle of young boy with insect net and conical-form bottle of young girl in landscape setting, one with later ceramic stopper, one with rough and other with ground pontil mark, late 19th/ early 20th century, 7-3/4" h. x 3-5/8" dia. overall and 7-7/8" h. overall x 3-1/8" dia. overall. **$270**

Jeffrey S. Evans & Associates

Water pitchers, blue Inverted Thumbprint with deer and colorless Panel-Optic with young woman, each with crimped rims, U-shaped spouts and applied handles, late 19th/early 20th century, undamaged, 8-1/2" and 9-1/8" h. overall. **$127**

Jeffrey S. Evans & Associates

Amber hinged jewel box, gilt metal angled frame with Mary Gregory decor of woman watering plants, good condition, no chips, cracks or repairs, 4-1/2" x 6"......... **$2,124**

Woody Auction

Straw holder, Victorian blown glass, peacock blue with Mary Gregory enameling, ribbed with gold rings at top and bottom, ground lip and silverplated lid, excellent condition, 12-1/2" h. **$210**

Rich Penn

Dresser box with two keys, 4-1/2" x 5" x 2-3/4".. **$584**

Michaan's Auctions

MILK GLASS

THOUGH INVENTED IN VENICE in the 1500s, the opaque glass commonly known as milk glass was most popular at the end of the 19th century. American manufacturers such as Westmoreland, Fenton, Imperial, Indiana, and Anchor Hocking produced it as an economical substitute for pricey European glass and china.

After World War I the popularity of milk glass waned, but production continued. Milk glass made during the 1930s and 1940s is often considered of lower quality than other periods because of the economic Depression and wartime manufacturing difficulties.

Though the name would lead you to believe it, white wasn't the only color produced. "Colored milk glasses, such as opaque black, green, or pink usually command higher prices," advises *Warman's Depression Glass* author and expert Ellen Schroy. "Beware of reproductions in green and pink. Always question a milk glass pattern found in cobalt blue. Swirled colors are a whole other topic and very desirable."

The number of patterns, forms, and objects made is only limited by the imagination. Commonly found milk glass items include dishes – especially the ever-popular animals on "nests" – vases, dresser sets, figurines, lanterns, boxes, and perfume bottles.

"The milk glass made by Westmoreland, Kemple, Fenton, etc., was designed to be used as dinnerware," Schroy explains. "Care should be taken when purchasing, transporting, and using this era of milk glass as it is very intolerant of temperature changes. Don't buy a piece outside at the flea market unless you can protect it well for its trip to your home. And when you get it home, leave it sit for several hours so its temperature evens out to what your normal home temperature is. It's almost a given if you take a piece of cold glass and submerge it into a nice warm bath, it's going to crack. And never, ever expose it to the high temps of a modern dishwasher."

So how do you tell the old from the new? Schroy says many times, getting your hands on it is the only way to tell: "Milk glass should have a wonderful silky texture. Any piece that is grainy is probably new. The best test is to look for 'the ring of fire.' Hold the piece of milk glass up to a good light source and see if there is a halo of iridescent colors right around the edge; look for reds, blues and golds. This ring was caused by the addition of iridized salts into the milk glass formula. If this ring is present, it's probably an old piece." She does caution, however, that 1950s-era milk glass does not have this tell-tale ring.

Old milk glass should also carry appropriate marks and signs, such as the ring of fire; appropriate patterns for specific makers are also something to watch for, such as Fenton's Hobnail pattern. Collectors should always check for condition issues such as damage and discoloration. According to Schroy, there is no remedy for discolored glass, and cracked and chipped pieces should be avoided as they are prone to further damage.
—*Karen Knapstein, Print Editor,* Antique Trader *magazine*

Pressed milk glass curtain tiebacks, American, 19th century, set of four, two opalescent, 4-1/2" dia. each. **$92**

Cowan's Auctions

GLASS

Chick on pedestal salt shaker, opaque white with polychrome decoration and period lid, C.F. Monroe Co., circa 1903, minute wear to polychrome decoration, otherwise undamaged, 2-5/8" h. overall. **$633**

Jeffrey S. Evans & Associates

Online Resources:

• Milkglass.org is an informational website. It includes historical and identification details, in addition to a collection of categorized links to milk glass items for sale on the Internet (primarily eBay).

• The National Westmoreland Glass Collectors Club's mission is to promote the appreciation for the artistry and craftsmanship of Westmoreland glass and to continue the preservation of this important part of American history. (westmorelandglassclub.org)

Westmoreland milk glass swan creamer, 5-1/2" l. x 5-1/4" h... **$12**

Homestead Auctions

Boar's head covered dish, opaque white/milk glass, on ribbed base, applied red glass eyes, 1888 patent date on lid interior and under base, Atterbury & Co., fourth quarter 19th century, mint condition, 5-1/2" h. overall, 6-1/8" x 9-3/8" overall rim. **$1,380**

Jeffrey S. Evans & Associates

Butcher occupational milk glass bay rum barber bottle, hand-painted decoration of butcher's cart, E.S. Gallagher Bay Rum, 10".................................... **$708**

Burchard Galleries

Bohemian glass girandoles, each of baluster form in milk glass with enameled floral and bird decoration, hung with prisms, 11-1/2" h... **$344**

Leslie Hindman Auctioneers

GLASS

$

MT. WASHINGTON

A WIDE DIVERSITY OF GLASS was made by the Mt. Washington Glass Co. of New Bedford, Massachusetts, between 1869 and 1900. It was succeeded in 1900 by the Pairpoint Manufacturing Co. Throughout its history, the Mt. Washington Glass Co. made different types of glass including pressed, blown, art, lava, Napoli, cameo, cut, Albertine, Peachblow, Burmese, Crown Milano, Royal Flemish, and Verona.

TOP LOT!

Overlay biscuit barrel with lava wave applied to lower body with small glass beads embedded, upper area with apple blossom branch raised from surface over mother-of-pearl backdrop, silver dome cover embossed with seashells and flowers and impressed "MW13" within, excellent original condition.............................. **$150**

Mark Mussio, Humler & Nolan

Rare Royal Flemish vase with Egyptian scene with Egyptian man riding camel and another walking beside with pyramids in background, medallions of Egyptian motif on back, two applied and decorated gilded handles, unsigned, very good to excellent condition, 14-1/4" h. **$18,960**

James D. Julia, Inc.

GLASS

Crown Milano biscuit container with fiddlehead ferns in two shades of raised gold with gold seed stems in between, floral embossed cover with figural butterfly on top and lid impressed "MW 534" underneath, excellent condition, 5-3/4" h............. **$200**

Mark Mussio, Humler & Nolan

Royal Flemish biscuit jar with three ducks in flight in front of stylized sun with three additional ducks on reverse, silverplated rim, handle and lid, lid stamped on underside "MW 4404," very good to excellent condition with ear to silverplating, 6-1/2" h...... **$3,555**

James D. Julia, Inc.

Burmese ribbed three-piece condiment set, glossy finish, pillar salt and pepper shakers with matching period two-part lids and cruet with matching stopper, fitted in quadruple-plate stand marked for William Rogers Mfg., Co. and numbered 1579, circa 1885-1895, glass undamaged, cruet with minor high-point wear, each lid with normal wear, one with enlarged holes, stand undamaged, condiments 3-3/4" to 6-7/8" h. overall, stand 7-1/8" h. overall................................. **$431**

Jeffrey S. Evans & Associates

Pillar-ribbed/ribbed three-piece condiment set, opal, glossy finish, salt and pepper shaker and mustard pot, each with polychrome floral decoration, period two-part hinged lids, Hartford Silver Plate Co., numbered 192, fourth quarter 19th century, undamaged, condiments 3-7/8" h. overall, stand 7-3/8" h. overall........ **$230**

Jeffrey S. Evans & Associates

Diamond Quilt air-trap mother-of-pearl satin glass cracker jar, shaded rose with gilt flowering tree and butterfly, inscribed "667/4 / P102" beside partially polished pontil mark, quadruple-plate rim, bail handle, and cover marked "2557 / 22" to underside, circa 1886-1890, undamaged with minor wear to decorations, wear to handle plating, 6-3/8" h. rim, 5" dia......................... **$316**

Jeffrey S. Evans & Associates

No. 522 Crown Milano cracker jar, opal with polychrome floral decoration and gilt scrolls, 10-lobe melon form, marked with crown over "CM" trademark under base, quadruple-plate rim, bail handle, and cover with embossed crab, marked "MW / 4415/b" to underside, circa 1891-1895, excellent undamaged condition, 5" h. rim, 5" dia......................... **$575**

Jeffrey S. Evans & Associates

Ostrich egg muffineer with floral bouquets against faux Burmese backdrop, 4-1/2" h.; tomato muffineer with white flowers and enamel accents over pale yellow with pierced relief floral cover, 3"; and fig salt and pepper shakers with floral patterns, 2-1/2"; flat chip to inside rim of one shaker, otherwise excellent original condition. **$325**

Mark Mussio, Humler & Nolan

Chick head salt shakers, opal, pale blue and rose grounds, each with polychrome enamel decoration, one lid with gilt decoration, fourth quarter 19th century, one shaker with flake from loss of decoration, remainder undamaged, 2-1/8" h. overall.. **$748**

Jeffrey S. Evans & Associates

Cockleshell salt and pepper shakers, opaque white with pale blue shading, plush/satin finish, each with polychrome floral decoration and matching period lids, fourth quarter 19th century, one shaker with flake to rim, hidden by lid, one lid with corrosion, 2-5/8" h. overall. **$690**

Jeffrey S. Evans & Associates

Palmer Cox Brownie salt and pepper shakers, opal, glossy finish, each with transfer decoration on front and reverse, matching period lids, fourth quarter 19th century, excellent condition, each with flakes/roughness to rim, hidden by lids, one shaker with minute flake to body, 2-3/8" h. overall............. **$805**

Jeffrey S. Evans & Associates

Tomato salt and pepper shakers, opal, shaded blue, plush/satin finish with polychrome autumn leaf and berry decoration, matching period two-part lids, fitted in period quadruple-plate figural stand with leaf and tomato ornamentation, illegible maker's mark on base, possibly Meriden Britannia Co. and numbered 059, fourth quarter 19th century, excellent condition overall, glass undamaged, minor losses to polychrome decoration, one lid with imperfections, shakers 1-5/8" h. overall, stand 5-1/8" h. overall. **$690**

Jeffrey S. Evans & Associates

Pink lava glass toothpick holder, inlaid shards of turquoise, blue, amber, and red, bulbous body of toothpick with square mouth with light purple lip, very good to excellent condition, 2-1/4" h. **$10,073**

James D. Julia, Inc.

GLASS

MURANO

IN THE 1950S, the American home came alive with vibrant-colored decorative items, abstract art, and "futuristic"-designed furniture. The colorless geometry of the 1930s was out.

Over the last decade, mid-century design has once again gained favor with interior decorators, magazines, shows, and stores dedicated solely to this period. The bold colors and free-form shapes of mid-century modern Italian glass are emblematic of 1950s design. This distinctive glass has become a sought-after collectible.

Prices realized at auction for 1950s glass have seen a resurgence. However, there are still many items readily available and not always at a premium.

Italian glass can be found in many American homes. In fact, it is likely that some of the familiar glass items you grew up with were produced in Italy – the candy dish on the coffee table with the bright colors, the ashtray with the gold flecks inside. Modern glass objects from Italy were among the most widely distributed examples of 1950s design.

As with any decorative art form, there are varying levels of achievement in the design and execution of glass from this period. While you should always buy what you love, as there is never a guarantee return on investment, buying the best representation of an item is wise. In considering modern Italian glass, several points make one piece stand above another.

Pitcher-form vase, glass with metallic inclusions and pigments, Giulio Radi (attribution), possibly Arte Vetraria Muranese, second half 20th century, 10-1/2" x 5" dia.......................... **$3,000**

Rago Arts

Tall arcobaleno vase, Anzolo Fuga (attribution) (1914-1988), possibly Arte Vetraria Muranese, second half 20th century, Sommerso glass, internal murrine, unmarked, 20" x 10".................... **$7,500**

Rago Arts

Tall pulegoso vase, Anzolo Fuga (attribution) (1914-1988), possibly Arte Vetraria Muranese, second half 20th century, unmarked, 17-3/4" x 7"............................... **$4,375**

Rago Arts

GLASS

Two pulegoso vases, Anzolo Fuga (attribution) (1914-1988), possibly Arte Vetraria Muranese, second half 20th century, blown glass with applied aventurine piastre, unmarked, 13-1/2", 15-1/2". **$9,375**

Rago Arts

Two glass vases (red and blue) with murrine and lattimo decoration, Anzolo Fuga (attribution) (1914-1988), possibly Arte Vetraria Muranese, second half 20th century, unmarked, 16" x 5" ea... **$8,125**

Rago Arts

Large tapering cased glass vase with bifurcated rim, Anzolo Fuga (attribution) (1914-1988), possibly Arte Vetraria Muranese, second half 20th century, unmarked, 20" x 12-1/2" dia. **$3,375**

Rago Arts

Italy has a centuries-old tradition of glassmaking, an industry whose center is the group of islands known as Murano in the lagoon of Venice. The most recognized and desirable Italian glass comes from three companies: Seguso, Venini, and Barovier & Toso.

Italy offers a vast array of talented glass artists. Top end collectors seem to favor Carlo Scarpa from Venini, Napoleone Martinuzzi (who worked at Venini from 1925-1932), and Dino Martens of Aureliano Toso. You can expect to pay several thousand dollars for a fine piece by one of these artists.

For slimmer collecting budgets, good quality examples by other artists are available and more affordable. Alfredo Barbini and Fulvio Biaconi (for Venini) are two of them. While some of their work does command top dollar, many of their pieces are priced for the novice collector.

A few mid-century designs can still be found that could prove to be sleepers in the near future. Look for Inciso vases by Venini, Aborigeni pieces by Barovier & Toso, and Soffiati examples by Giacomo Cappellin. Each of these designs is totally different from the other, yet all are reasonably priced in today's market.

Collectors should be aware that the most popular glass form is the vase, with glass sculpture following next in line. Popular sculptural forms include male or female nude figurals and pasta glass animals by Fulvio Biaconi.

Whether from the original manufacturer or another firm, Murano glass now being reproduced includes Sommerso designs, Barbini glass aquariums, and bowls along with Oriente designs. Venini lamps have also been reproduced. No doubt there will be more reproductions to come.

Perfume bottle in good condition with hand-painted gilt accents, sticker present on bottom, good condition, approximately 5" h. x 2-3/4" dia. **$81**

J Levine Auction & Appraisal LLC

GLASS

$

NORTHWOOD GLASS CO.

NORTHWOOD GLASS CO. was founded by Harry Northwood, son of prominent English glassmaker John Northwood, who was famous for his expertise in cameo glass.

Harry emigrated to America in 1881 and, after working at various glass manufacturers, formed the Northwood Glass Co. in 1896 in Indiana, Pennsylvania. In 1902 he created H. Northwood and Co. in Wheeling, West Virginia. After Northwood died in 1919, H. Northwood and Co. began to falter and eventually closed in 1925.

Northwood produced a wide variety of opalescent, decorated, and special effect glasses, and colors like iridescent blue and green, which were not widely seen at the time.

Northwood No. 285/Aurora toothpick holder, rubina with floral plate etching, panel optic, factory polished rim, circa 1890, undamaged with mold roughness to inner rim, 2-1/8" h. **$115**

Jeffrey S. Evans & Associates

Alaska water pitcher, vaseline (uranium) opalescent, late19th/ early 20th century, undamaged, 7-1/4" h. overall..............**$196**

Jeffrey S. Evans & Associates

TOP LOT!

Poinsettia water pitcher, cranberry opalescent, tankard form on low foot with plain rim and colorless applied reeded handle with pressed fan design to upper terminal, circa 1902, undamaged, spots of undissolved metal and stones under lower handle terminal, as made, 13" h. overall.......**$1,265**

Jeffrey S. Evans & Associates

Blown Twist nine-panel mold sugar shaker, blue opalescent, with period lid, fourth quarter 19th century, undamaged, lid with some surface rust, 4-5/8" h. overall. **$184**

Jeffrey S. Evans & Associates

Carnelian/Everglades cruet, vaseline (uranium) opalescent with appropriate but ill-fitting stopper, fourth quarter 19th century, excellent condition overall, cruet with normal flakes/ roughness to interior flange, stopper extension with normal chipping, 7" h. overall **$92**

Jeffrey S. Evans & Associates

Chrysanthemum Swirl syrup pitcher, blue opalescent, applied handle and period lid, Northwood Glass Co./Buckeye Glass Co., circa 1890, undamaged, lid with some light surface rust and old repair to hinge, 6-7/8" h. overall.....**$150**

Jeffrey S. Evans & Associates

Coin Spot nine-panel mold syrup pitcher, colorless opalescent, applied handle, period lid, circa 1894, undamaged, interior with large potstone, as made, 6" h. overall.............**$46**

Jeffrey S. Evans & Associates

Daisy and Fern syrup pitcher, cranberry opalescent, bulbous form with colorless applied handle, period Peerless lid with patent information, circa 1900, excellent condition, body with short scratch, 7" h. overall **$219**

Jeffrey S. Evans & Associates

Diamond Spearhead syrup pitcher, dark blue opalescent, period lid, circa 1902, small crack to tip of handle at upper terminal, possibly as made, otherwise undamaged, 5-5/8" h...........................**$259**

Jeffrey S. Evans & Associates

Jeweled Heart/Victor cruets, blue with gilt decoration and green, each with original stopper, fourth quarter 19th century, each with normal roughness to inner flange, green stopper with fire-polished chip to extension, 7-1/2" and 7-3/4" h. overall **$150**

Jeffrey S. Evans & Associates

Northwood No. 333/Leaf Mold covered sugar bowl, canary/vaseline (uranium) with cranberry and opal spatter, lid with molded vaseline (uranium) finial, pattern introduced in 1891, undamaged with normal light mold roughness to inner flange of cover and rim of bowl, 5-1/2" h....**$546**

Jeffrey S. Evans & Associates

Northwood No. 263/Leaf Umbrella sugar shaker, cased turquoise/blue, period lid, pattern introduced in 1889, undamaged with some normal light medial wear and small manufacturing chip to rim, 4-1/2" h. overall................**$127**

Jeffrey S. Evans & Associates

Opaline Brocade/Spanish Lace water pitcher, cranberry opalescent, squat form with seven-point star rim, colorless, applied handle, late 19th/early 20th century, undamaged, 8-3/4" h. **$460**

Jeffrey S. Evans & Associates

Opaline Brocade/Spanish Lace tumbler, green opalescent, tapered form, factory polished rim, National Glass Co. and Dugan Glass Co., circa 1899-1908, undamaged, 4" h. **$161**

Jeffrey S. Evans & Associates

Paneled Sprig sugar shaker, colorless with granite finish, green stain and gilt decoration, period lid, fourth quarter 19th century, undamaged, lid with light dent, 4-5/8" h. overall. **$127**

Jeffrey S. Evans & Associates

Royal Ivy sugar shaker, cased yellow-green and pink spatter, period lid, fourth quarter 19th century, undamaged, lid dented, 4-1/8" h. overall. **$288**

Jeffrey S. Evans & Associates

Northwood No. 287/Royal Ivy syrup pitcher, cased yellow-green and rose/pink spatter, colorless applied handle, period lid, circa 1890, undamaged, lid with short splits, 6-1/2" h. overall. **$345**

Jeffrey S. Evans & Associates

Quilted Phlox miniature lamp, cased green, matching patterned ball shade, period burner, late 19th/early 20th century, undamaged, 7" h. to top of shade, 2-1/2" dia. base. **$316**

Jeffrey S. Evans & Associates

OPALESCENT GLASS

OPALESCENT GLASS is one of the most popular areas of glass collecting. The opalescent effect was attained by adding bone ash chemicals to areas of an item while still hot and refiring the object at tremendous heat. Both pressed and mold-blown patterns are available to collectors. *Opalescent Glass from A to Z* by the late William Heacock is the definitive reference book for collectors.

Beatty Swirl water pitcher, blue opalescent, Beatty & Sons, fourth quarter 19th century, undamaged, 7-5/8" h. overall. **$150**

Jeffrey S. Evans & Associates

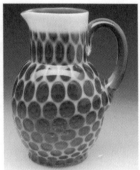

Big Windows water pitcher, deep cranberry opalescent, barrel form with circular plain rim, colorless applied handle with lightly pressed fine ribs to upper terminal, Buckeye Glass Co., 1878-1896, undamaged, 9-1/4" h. **$575**

Jeffrey S. Evans & Associates

Bubble Lattice syrup pitcher, blue opalescent, transparent blue applied handle with pressed feather pattern to upper terminal, period lid, Buckeye Glass Co., fourth quarter 19th century, undamaged, normal mold roughness, 6-5/8" h. overall. **$127**

Jeffrey S. Evans & Associates

Blown Twist nine-panel mold sugar shaker, green opalescent, with period lid, Northwood Glass Co., late 19th/early 20th century, undamaged, light wear to body, rim roughness as made, hidden by lid, lid with two enlarged holes, 4-3/4" h. overall. **$138**

Jeffrey S. Evans & Associates

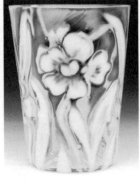

Daffodil tumbler, green opalescent, Northwood trademark under base, Northwood Glass Co., circa 1903, undamaged, 3-7/8" h. **$184**

Jeffrey S. Evans & Associates

Buttons and Braids tumbler, green opalescent, tapered side with factory polished rim, Jefferson Glass Co., circa 1905, undamaged, 3-3/4" h. **$69**

Jeffrey S. Evans & Associates

GLASS

Findlay Onyx syrup pitcher, ivory onyx with platinum flowers, opalescent applied handle, period lid with patent information, Dalzell, Gilmore & Leighton Co., Findlay, Ohio, circa 1889, undamaged, lid with denting to interior rim and minute corrosion, 7-1/8" h. overall.....**$316**

Jeffrey S. Evans & Associates

Diamond-Optic apothecary/straw jar base, pale vaseline (uranium) opalescent, bulge base, factory polished rim, late 19th/ early 20th century, undamaged, upper ring with potstone, as made, 11-1/2" h. x 3-5/8" dia. base.....**$288**

Jeffrey S. Evans & Associates

Reverse Swirl four-piece condiment set, vaseline (uranium), cranberry, blue, and colorless opalescent, two shakers, mustard pot, and oil bottle with colorless paneled stopper, fitted in unmarked nickel-plated stand, late 19th/early 20th century, oil bottle with flake to top edge of mouth, stopper with two flakes, blue shaker with rim chip and crack hidden by lid, remainder undamaged, condiments 3-1/8" to 5-1/4" h. overall. **$173**

Jeffrey S. Evans & Associates

Twist-Blown water pitcher, green opalescent, tankard form on low foot, five-scallop rim and applied reeded twist handle, Northwood Glass Co. and others, circa 1892 to 1900, very good condition overall with light residue to body, annealing check and scattered tool marks below rim, 10-1/2" h. overall. **$161**

Jeffrey S. Evans & Associates

Ribbed Opal Lattice celery vase, cranberry opalescent, circa 1888, undamaged, small area of undissolved metal, as made, 6" h. **$138**

Jeffrey S. Evans & Associates

Opaline Brocade/ Spanish Lace water pitcher, vaseline (uranium) opalescent, shouldered form with three-section crimped and ruffled rim, applied vaseline (uranium) reeded handle, National Glass Co., early 20th century, undamaged, 9-1/2" h...........................**$690**

Jeffrey S. Evans & Associates

Hobbs No. 333/ Windows water pitcher, sapphire opalescent/ blue opalescent, square rim, blue applied handle with pressed feather design to upper terminal, polished pontil mark, Hobbs, Brockunier & Co., fourth quarter 19th century, undamaged as made, part of polished pontil mark with annealing check and interior with broken bubble, 8-3/4" h. ...**$230**

Jeffrey S. Evans & Associates

Drapery blown water pitcher, green opalescent, tankard form on low foot with plain rim and applied handle, Northwood Glass Co. and others, circa 1900-1910, undamaged, 11-5/8" h. overall...**$431**

Jeffrey S. Evans & Associates

GLASS

Daisy and Fern beverage articles, blue opalescent, ball-form water pitcher with square-form rim with three crimps on each side and transparent blue applied handle, and two tumblers, Northwood Glass Co., late 19th/early 20th century, pitcher undamaged, each tumbler with minute rim flakes, 8-3/8" and 3-3/4" h. overall............................ **$161**

Jeffrey S. Evans & Associates

Chrysanthemum Swirl celery vases, colorless opalescent and blue opalescent, factory polished rim, Northwood Glass Co., circa 1890, undamaged, 6-1/2" h. **$138**

Jeffrey S. Evans & Associates

Diamond Spearhead four-piece table set, canary/vaseline (uranium) opalescent, covered butter, covered sugar, spooner, and creamer, Northwood Glass Co./National Glass Co., circa 1902, undamaged except for minute flake to sugar cover, several light scratches to spooner, 4-1/4" to 6-3/4" h.. **$345**

Jeffrey S. Evans & Associates

Findlay Floradine covered sugar bowl, ruby with opalescent flowers and satin finish, Dalzell, Gilmore & Leighton Co., circa 1899, excellent condition overall, base with moderate chip to inner rim and flakes/roughness, cover with less than expected roughness, 4-1/4" h. **$633**

Jeffrey S. Evans & Associates

Christmas Snowflake ribbed water pitcher, colorless opalescent, colorless applied handle with pressed leaf design to upper terminal, Northwood Glass Co./Dugan Glass Co., circa 1895, undamaged, 8-7/8" h. overall.....**$259**

Jeffrey S. Evans & Associates

Quadruple Diamonds juice tumbler, green opalescent, tapered form, late 19th/ early 20th century, undamaged, 3-3/8" h..........................**$230**

Jeffrey S. Evans & Associates

Polka Dot West Virginia mold sugar shaker, cranberry opalescent, tapered bulbous base, period lid, West Virginia Glass Co., circa 1894, undamaged, normal manufacturing chipping/roughness to rim, 5" h. overall. ...**$345**

Jeffrey S. Evans & Associates

Big Windows master berry bowl, ruby opalescent/cranberry opalescent, circular form, Buckeye Glass Co., 1878-1896, undamaged with normal flakes/roughness to rim, interior of base with some manufacturing imperfections, 2-1/2" h., 7" dia. rim... **$104**

Jeffrey S. Evans & Associates

GLASS

$

Seaweed/Coral bitters/ barber's bottle, colorless opalescent, polished pontil mark, later pour spout, Hobbs, Brockunier & Co., circa 1890, undamaged, interior residue, 7" h..........**$288**

Jeffrey S. Evans & Associates

Swirling Maze tumbler, green opalescent, factory polished rim, Jefferson Glass Co., circa 1905, excellent condition overall, minor flake and mold roughness to rim, 4" h............**$288**

Jeffrey S. Evans & Associates

Swastika Indiana mold syrup pitcher, cranberry opalescent, globular body with short neck and colorless applied handle, period hinged lid, Dugan Glass Co., circa 1904, undamaged, light rust to lid, 5-3/4" h. overall, 4-1/2" h. to top of neck...................**$5,750**

Jeffrey S. Evans & Associates

Stars and Stripes bitters/ barber's bottle, cranberry opalescent, two rows of stars, lower end of stripes flow to right above stars, plain base, period pour spout, Beaumont Glass Co., circa 1899, undamaged, 7" h. ..**$316**

Jeffrey S. Evans & Associates

Swastika nine-panel mold syrup pitcher, green opalescent, slight foot, with applied handle and period lid, Dugan Glass Co., circa 1907, undamaged, 5-3/4" h. overall. **$3,738**

Jeffrey S. Evans & Associates

TOP LOT!

Swastika water pitcher, cranberry opalescent, globular form with square crimped rim and colorless applied handle, Dugan Glass Co., circa 1904, undamaged, 9" h........................**$6,900**

Jeffrey S. Evans & Associates

Swirl seven-piece water set, rubina opalescent, ball-form pitcher with three-point crimped rim and colorless applied handle and six tumblers, late 19th/early 20th century, pitcher undamaged with medial wear and several short scratches, tumblers with polished rims, pitcher 8" h., tumblers 3-1/2" to 3-5/8" h. **$196**

Jeffrey S. Evans & Associates

Target Swirl items, peach opalescent, two footed tumblers and basket with applied handle, late 19th/early 20th century, undamaged, 5-1/2" and 5" h. **$489**

Jeffrey S. Evans & Associates

PAIRPOINT

ORIGINALLY ORGANIZED in New Bedford, Massachusetts, in 1880 as the Pairpoint Manufacturing Co. on land adjacent to the famed Mt. Washington Glass Co., Pairpoint first manufactured silver and plated wares. In 1894, the two famous factories merged as the Pairpoint Corp. and enjoyed great success for more than 40 years. The company was sold in 1939 to a group of local businessmen and eventually was bought out by one of the group, who turned the management over to Robert M. Gundersen. Subsequently, it operated as the Gundersen Glass Works until 1952 when, after Gundersen's death, the name was changed to Gundersen-Pairpoint. The factory closed in 1956. After that, Robert Bryden took charge of the glassworks, at first producing glass for Pairpoint abroad and eventually, in 1970, beginning glass production in Sagamore, Massachusetts. Today the Pairpoint Crystal Glass Co. is owned by Robert and June Bancroft. They continue to manufacture fine quality blown and pressed glass.

Two Puffy boudoir mold-blown Balmoral lamp shades, both reverse-painted with butterflies on floral ground, one with Pairpoint Corp. stamp to lower outer edge, one with minor flake to edge, 3-1/2" x 5-3/4" dia. **$2,280**

Skinner, Inc.; www.skinnerinc.com

Stemware, colorless, seven engraved with Denmark pattern and one engraved with Wellington pattern, each raised on tall stem with swirl-cut upper knop, silverplate foot marked "C01610" above Pairpoint and diamond trade mark, with "E.P.N.S" below, circa 1925, undamaged, 7-1/8" h. x 2-5/8" dia. rim and 7-3/8" h. x 2 7/8" dia. rim...... **$460**

Jeffrey S. Evans & Associates

Two Opalware containers for sweet biscuits, hand-decorated with poppies or flowers, pierced silverplate collars, one with pierced handle, both covers marked with Pairpoint "P in diamond" logo with registration numbers that match handwritten number beneath each container, excellent condition except for usage dings and minor wear to metal, 5-1/2" h. each.............**$150**

Mark Mussio, Humler & Nolan

Three egg flat-end salt shakers, opaque white, plush/satin finish with polychrome hen decorations and matching period lids, fourth quarter 19th century, glass undamaged, two with frozen lids, 2-1/4" h. overall................**$345**

Jeffrey S. Evans & Associates

GLASS

Ambero vase, reverse-painted fall scene with cottage, two figures and trees, textured exterior surface, signed "Ambero / W" under base, circa 1915, interior with loss of paint in base below figures, normal short interior scratches and exterior scuffs, 12" h. x 4-3/4" dia. rim. **$219**

Jeffrey S. Evans & Associates

Wickham engraved vase, green, deep cylindrical bowl with flanged rim, raised on star-cut foot, circa 1925, undamaged, 12" h. x 5-1/8" dia. rim. **$127**

Jeffrey S. Evans & Associates

Vintage engraved candlesticks, deep cobalt blue, shape 1600 with hollow stems, each with No. 192 engraving and polished pontil mark, circa 1925, undamaged, 10-5/8" h. **$374**

Jeffrey S. Evans & Associates

Waterford engraved covered urns, colorless and amber, shape A-292, each with polished pontil mark, circa 1925, undamaged, 10" h. overall, urn 6-1/4" h. **$374**

Jeffrey S. Evans & Associates

Round hinged dresser box, blue tones with gold poppy décor, marked Pairpoint, good condition, 2-3/4" x 7-1/4". . **$200**

Woody Auction

Candlesticks in amethyst, wheel carved with grapes on vine, leaves on stems, vines on bases and beaded patterns on holders, excellent condition, 7-7/8" h. **$350**

Mark Mussio, Humler & Nolan

Decorated Opalware dresser box, satin finish with polychrome floral decoration and gilt decorated scrolls, diamond trademark under base, fourth quarter 19th century, undamaged, normal wear, 4-1/4" h. overall. **$115**

Jeffrey S. Evans & Associates

Adelaide pattern rose cut-to-clear glass vase, late 19th/early 20th century, chalice-form with crosshatched register to rim and thumbprints to body on bubble-ball stem and circular foot, unsigned, 12" h. **$600**

Skinner, Inc.; www.skinnerinc.com

PATTERN GLASS

THOUGH IT HAS NEVER BEEN ascertained whether glass was first pressed in the United States or abroad, the development of the glass-pressing machine revolutionized the glass industry in the United States, and this country receives the credit for improving the method to make this process feasible. The first wares pressed were probably small flat plates of the type now referred to as "lacy," the intricacy of the design concealing flaws.

In 1827, both the New England Glass Co., Cambridge, Massachusetts, and Bakewell & Co., Pittsburgh, took out patents for pressing glass furniture knobs; soon other pieces followed. This early pressed glass contained red lead, which made it clear and resonant when tapped (flint). Made primarily in clear, it is rarer in blue, amethyst, olive green, and yellow.

By the 1840s, early simple patterns such as Ashburton, Argus, and Excelsior appeared. Ribbed Bellflower seems to have been one of the earliest patterns to have had complete sets. By the 1860s, a wide range of patterns was available.

In 1864, William Leighton of Hobbs, Brockunier & Co., Wheeling, West Virginia, developed a formula for "soda lime" glass that did not require the expensive red lead for clarity. Although "soda lime" glass did not have the brilliance of the earlier flint glass, the formula came into widespread use because glass could be produced cheaply.

Basket match/toothpick holder, translucent powder blue, slightly tapered form with rope-edge rim and concave base, no factory polishing, Boston & Sandwich Glass Co. and probably others, 1850-1870, undamaged, 1-5/8" h. x 1-5/8" dia. rim.....................**$127**

Jeffrey S. Evans & Associates

Bird and Strawberry goblet, colorless with blue, green, and red stain, early 20th century, undamaged, wear to decoration, 6-1/2" h. **$1,150**

Jeffrey S. Evans & Associates

Beaded Triangle/Royal salt and pepper shakers, chocolate, with near-matching period lids, Royal Glass Co., Marietta, Ohio, circa 1902-1903, excellent condition overall, 3-3/8" h. overall. **$345**

Jeffrey S. Evans & Associates

Bellflower-Single Vine molasses jug/syrup, opaque white, small-size ovoid body with vine flowing left, applied solid handle, plain base, period Britannia hinged lid without markings, probably Midwestern, third quarter 19th century, short, light crack to body off upper handle terminal, lid hinge slightly loose, 5-7/8" h. overall, 4-5/8" h. neck, 2-3/8" dia. base. **$92**

Jeffrey S. Evans & Associates

GLASS

Bringing Home the Cows water pitcher, colorless, Dalzell, Gilmore & Leighton Co., fourth quarter 19th century, undamaged, 10-5/8" h. overall. $518

Jeffrey S. Evans & Associates

Bulging Loops water pitcher, opal cased pink, colorless applied handle, polished pontil mark, Consolidated Glass Co., fourth quarter 19th century, undamaged, one panel with scratches, 9-1/4" h. overall.....$161

Jeffrey S. Evans & Associates

Bull's Eye with Fleur De Lys goblets, set of six, colorless lead glass, undamaged, 6-1/4" h. $403

Jeffrey S. Evans & Associates

OL-12A Cornucopia and Scroll oval open salt, light fiery opalescent, serrated large-scallop rim, probably very to extremely rare color, Boston & Sandwich Glass Co., 1830-1850, minor mold roughness to rim interior, 1-3/8" h. x 2-3/8" x 3-3/8"...$431

Jeffrey S. Evans & Associates

Cable spoon holder, translucent starch blue, scalloped six-fan rim, circular foot with cable edge, Boston & Sandwich Glass Co., third quarter 19th century, light flake to one low edge of outer rim, small potstone with light bruise at edge of one panel, shallow chip to foot edge at mold line, likely as made, 5-3/4" h. x 3-5/8" dia. overall rim, 3" dia. foot. $374

Jeffrey S. Evans & Associates

Forget-Me-Not sugar shaker, opaque mottled butterscotch, period lid, Challinor, Taylor & Co., pattern introduced 1885, undamaged, lid with light denting, 3-3/4" h. overall. $633

Jeffrey S. Evans & Associates

Lacy Eagle and Constitution oval dish, colorless, sides divided into eight stippled panels with alternating reserves of shield-breast American eagle and sailing ship believed to represent USS Constitution, scallop rim, rope surrounding plain table ring, possibly Boston & Sandwich Glass Co., 1830-1840, flake to one scallop and small open bubble to another scallop, 1-1/2" h. x 3-7/8" x 6-1/4"...$431

Jeffrey S. Evans & Associates

Lacy Gothic Arch sugar bowl and cover, translucent blue, octagonal bowl with four different arch designs and plain rim, raised on circular foot, matching cover with four arch designs and hexagonal finial on small platform, Boston & Sandwich Glass Co. and probably others, 1840-1850, bowl with light top-rim flake, cover with filled chip and flake on outer rim, shallow chip to finial, and some flaking to platform and under rim, 5" h. overall, 3-1/2" h. rim x 5-1/8" dia. overall rim, 2-7/8" dia. foot. **$1,380**

Jeffrey S. Evans & Associates

No. 263 Leaf Umbrella syrup pitcher, ruby/cranberry, colorless applied handle, period lid with patent information, Northwood Glass Co., pattern introduced 1889, undamaged, 6-5/8" h. overall.................. **$219**

Jeffrey S. Evans & Associates

Lacy Acanthus Leaf and Shield sugar bowl, rare deep blue with mottled opaque white striations, octagonal bowl with plain rim and alternating design elements, raised on circular foot, lacking cover, Boston & Sandwich Glass Co., 1835-1850, mold roughness, 3-1/2" h. x 5-1/8" dia. overall rim, 2-3/4" dia. foot. **$316**

Jeffrey S. Evans & Associates

TOP LOT!

Loop/Leaf pair stand lamps, deep brilliant peacock green, each dome-top six-loop font with lower double step and knop extension, raised on octagonal baluster-form standard and square base, wafer construction, pewter fine-line collars and double-tube whale oil burners, Boston & Sandwich Glass Co. and possibly others, 1840-1860, excellent condition, 9-3/4" h. to top of collars, 3-1/8" sq. base......................... **$9,775**

Jeffrey S. Evans & Associates

BT-4D Lafayet Steamboat open salt, deep cobalt blue, marked "B. &. S. / GLASS. / Co" on stern and "SANDWICH" on interior base, rare, Boston & Sandwich Glass Co., 1830-1845, above average condition, rim with small top-edge chip at rear and chipping/mold roughness to interior of stern, minor mold roughness to keel, no other damage, heavy high-point wear, 1-5/8" h. x 2" x 3-5/8"....... **$546**

Jeffrey S. Evans & Associates

CD-4 Lyre covered salt, colorless, on four scrolled feet, variant cover with beads on rim interior arranged 10 x 20 x 10 x 20, extremely rare, Boston & Sandwich Glass Co., 1835-1845, cover with minor flake to underside of one corner, base with crack in one corner, 2-3/4" h. overall, 2" x 3-1/8" dia. base.................................. **$748**

Jeffrey S. Evans & Associates

Pigs in Corn left bent husk goblet, colorless, fourth quarter 19th century, undamaged, 6" h. .. **$288**

Jeffrey S. Evans & Associates

GLASS

No. 484/Croesus seven-piece water set, amethyst with gilt decoration, pitcher and six tumblers, Riverside Glass Works, late 19th/early 20th century, undamaged, pitcher and rims of tumblers with wear to gilt decoration, 11-1/8" and 3-3/4" to 4" h. overall. **$184**

Jeffrey S. Evans & Associates

Rose in Snow seven-piece water set, amber, pitcher with applied handle and six goblets, Bryce Brothers Co., late 19th/early 20th century, light scratches, inclusions as made, small chip to outer edge of lip on pitcher, normal light wear/roughness to rims of three goblets, otherwise undamaged, pitcher 8-5/8" h., goblets 5-3/4" h. each........... **$69**

Jeffrey S. Evans & Associates

Swirled Feather and Sawtooth compotes, colorless, each bowl raised on Horn of Plenty high-standard base, wafer construction, Boston & Sandwich Glass Co. and others, third quarter 19th century, one with flake under base, other with heavy interior wear, 6-3/4" h., 8-3/4" and 9" dia......... **$69**

Jeffrey S. Evans & Associates

Thousand Eye table articles, colorless opalescent, milk pitcher and creamer, fourth quarter 19th century, undamaged, 6-3/4" h. rim x 4" dia. foot, and 5-1/2" h. rim x 3-1/8" dia. foot. **$81**

Jeffrey S. Evans & Associates

SL-1 Shell open salt, deep peacock green, shaped rim, extremely rare, possibly Boston & Sandwich Glass Co., 1835-1850, small chip to one base corner and shallow chip to side of base, 1-5/8" h., 2" x 3". **$1,035**

Jeffrey S. Evans & Associates

Squirrel water pitcher, colorless, with twig handle, fourth quarter 19th century, foot with annealing crack and small chips/flakes, some as made, 8-1/2" h. overall. **$316**

Jeffrey S. Evans & Associates

Worcester handled footed tumbler, deep cobalt blue lead glass, medium goblet-form bowl with six patterned panels and applied cobalt blue handle, raised on plain circular foot with polished pontil mark, probably Boston & Sandwich Glass Co., 1850-1875, undamaged, 3-3/4" h., 3-1/8" dia. rim, 2-3/8" dia. foot.. ...... **$1,093**

Jeffrey S. Evans & Associates

PEACH BLOW

SEVERAL TYPES OF GLASS lumped together by collectors as Peach Blow were produced by half a dozen glasshouses. Hobbs, Brockunier & Co., Wheeling, West Virginia, made Peach Blow as a plated ware that shaded from red at the top to yellow at the bottom and is referred to as Wheeling Peach Blow. Mt. Washington Glass Works produced a homogeneous Peach Blow shading from rose at the top to pale blue in the lower portion. The New England Glass Works' Peach Blow, called Wild Rose, shaded from rose at the top to white. Gundersen-Pairpoint Co. also reproduced some of the Mt. Washington Peach Blow in the early 1950s, and some glass of a somewhat similar type was made by Steuben Glass Works, Thomas Webb & Sons, and Stevens & Williams of England. New England Peach Blow is one-layered glass and the English is two-layered.

Another single-layered shaded art glass was produced early in the 20th century by New Martinsville Glass Mfg. Co. Originally called Muranese, collectors today refer to it as New Martinsville Peach Blow.

Three vases, small yellow vase with geometric designs, tall vase with floral decorations and applied decoration to rim, and small vase with rose decorations and crimped opening, tallest 8-1/2". **$461**

Cowan's Auctions, Inc.

Wheeling Morgan vase, strong color, Hobbs, Brockunier & Co., good condition, 8"....**$500**

Woody Auction

Four Wheeling items, Hobbs, Brockunier & Co., late 19th century, all with cream-colored linings, polished pontils, and without marks, three with glossy finish; bottle-form vase, 8-3/8" h., double gourd-form vase, 7-1/8" h., decanter with applied amber handle, crack to upper handle joint, 7-1/8" h.; and matte finish pitcher with applied amber handle, 5-1/2" h. **$1,020**

Skinner, Inc.; www.skinnerinc.com

GLASS

Goblet with pink shading to white with matte finish, Gundersen-Pairpoint Co., very good to excellent condition, 6-1/2" h. **$415**

James D. Julia, Inc.

Coral/Peach Blow No. 4 decanter, glossy, with applied and twisted reeded handle and appropriate stopper, Hobbs, Brockunier & Co., fourth quarter 19th century, decanter undamaged, stopper with bruise to extension, 9-1/2" h. overall..... **$518**

Jeffrey S. Evans & Associates

Vases, glossy finish, gourd form with Jules Barbe gilt decoration, one with dragonfly and other with two bees, each raised on low foot with polished pontil mark, Thomas Webb & Sons, circa 1885, undamaged, some wear to gilding on feet and rims, 6-1/2" h. **$489**

Jeffrey S. Evans & Associates

Acid finish vase, gold enamel floral décor, Thomas Webb & Sons, good condition, 8".. **$325**

Woody Auction

Biscuit jar with silverplate lid and bail, gold enamel floral décor, Thomas Webb & Sons, good condition, 7".. **$275**

Woody Auction

Cased oval vase, gold and silver enamel floral décor, Harrach, good condition, 9-1/2"................... **$175**

Woody Auction

Satin vase, applied frosted glass leaf, branch and cherry décor, Stevens & Williams, good condition, 7".......... **$950**

Woody Auction

Two vases, butterfly and branch gold enamel décor, Thomas Webb & Sons, good condition, 10"...... **$650**

Woody Auction

GLASS

PHOENIX GLASS

THE PHOENIX GLASS CO., Beaver, Pennsylvania, was established in 1880. Known primarily for commercial glassware, the firm also produced a molded, sculptured, cameo-type line from 1930s until 1950s.

Drape water pitcher, cranberry opalescent, bulbous form with square rim, colorless applied reeded handle, polished pontil mark, fourth quarter 19th century, undamaged, 8-1/4" h. overall.....................**$920**

Jeffrey S. Evans & Associates

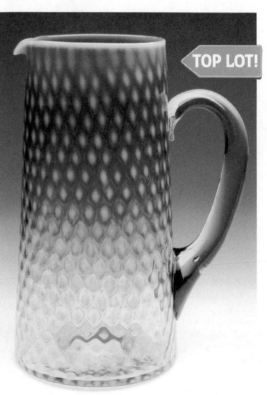

TOP LOT!

Herringbone air-trap mother-of-pearl satin glass tumbler, shaded butterscotch, polychrome-enamel and gilt floral decoration, ground pontil mark, fourth quarter 19th century, undamaged, small bruise at pontil mark, as made, 3-3/4" h. **$150**

Jeffrey S. Evans & Associates

Diamond-Optic water pitcher, ruby die-away in opal sensitive blue with opalescent diamond pattern, tankard form with circular plain rim, blue applied handle with opal to upper terminal and ruby die-away to lower terminal, polished pontil mark, circa 1883-1885, undamaged except for small area of several light scratches, 9" h............................**$4,313**

Jeffrey S. Evans & Associates

Stripe-Optic creamer, cranberry opalescent, ball-form with circular rim, colorless applied reeded handle, polished pontil mark, 1880-1894, body with small imperfection and neck with tool mark, 5-1/2" h......**$104**

Jeffrey S. Evans & Associates

Spot-Optic craquelle ice tub, cranberry opalescent, circular form with circular plain rim and two tab handles, circa 1883-1885, undamaged, 4-3/4" h. overall, 8" dia. **$219**

Jeffrey S. Evans & Associates

Flying Geese vase, pillow form body in matte red, trio of geese front and back with mother-of-pearl luster, excellent original condition, 9-1/4" x 12" w. .. **$100**

Mark Mussio, Humler & Nolan

Dot-Optic tumbler, reverse rubina opalescent, factory polished rim, fourth quarter 19th century, undamaged with minor mold roughness, 3-3/8" h. **$150**

Jeffrey S. Evans & Associates

Spot-Optic creamer, ruby die-away in opal sensitive blue with opalescent diamond pattern, ball form with circular neck and plain rim, applied pale blue plain handle, polished pontil mark, fourth quarter 19th century, undamaged, 4-3/4" h. **$633**

Jeffrey S. Evans & Associates

Grasshopper pillow vase, 7" h. **$185**

Cowan's Auctions, Inc.

Diamond-Optic craquelle water pitcher, cranberry opalescent, tankard form with circular plain rim and colorless applied handle, polished pontil mark, circa 1883-1885, excellent condition, flake/roughness to body above lower terminal, 8-1/2" h. **$920**

Jeffrey S. Evans & Associates

Spot-Optic craquelle water pitcher, cranberry opalescent, tankard form with circular plain rim and colorless applied handle, polished pontil mark, circa 1883-1885, excellent condition, rim with minute nick, 7-1/2" h. **$518**

Jeffrey S. Evans & Associates

GLASS

QUEZAL

IN 1901, MARTIN BACH AND THOMAS JOHNSON, who had worked for Louis Tiffany, opened a competing glassworks in Brooklyn, New York, called the Quezal Art Glass and Decorating Co. Named for the quetzal, a bird with brilliantly colored features, Quezal produced wares closely resembling those of Tiffany until the plant closed in 1925. In general, Quezal pieces are more defined than Tiffany glass, and the decorations are more visible and brighter.

Floriform glass vase with pulled feather decoration, New York, 1900s, etched QUEZAL, 10" x 6".......**$1,875**

Rago Arts

Shade with yellow pulled feather design ascending from ruffled lip with dragged loop descending from fitter, creamy opalescent background, interior in gold iridescence, signed in fitter "Quezal," very good to excellent condition, 4-5/8" h. x 5-1/4" dia. **$356**

James D. Julia, Inc.

Small compote with gold iridescent finish with pink and purple highlights on foot and blue highlights at rim, signed on bottom in polished pontil "Quezal," very good to excellent condition, 4-3/4" h. x 5-1/4" dia.....................**$152**

James D. Julia, Inc.

Pair of shades decorated with zipper pattern in gold iridescence with purple highlights against cream-colored background, each signed on fitter "Quezal," very good to excellent condition, 4-1/4" h.........**$474**

James D. Julia, Inc.

Pair of shades with vertically ribbed bodies with white iridescent finish and five-row band of wavy gold iridescence, both finished on interior in gold iridescence with red highlights and signed on inside of fitter "Quezal," signatures somewhat sloppy, possibly added after production, very good to excellent condition, 5-1/8" h., 2-1/4" fitters.................**$385**

James D. Julia, Inc.

Stem vase in teardrop form, iridescent gold finish, marked inside pontil "Quezal, G83," fine condition, 9-1/2" h.........**$201**

Thomaston Place Auction Galleries

GLASS

SANDWICH GLASS

NUMEROUS TYPES OF GLASS were produced at the Boston & Sandwich Glass Co. in Sandwich, Massachusetts, on Cape Cod, from 1826 to 1888. Founded by Deming Jarves, the company produced a wide variety of wares in differing levels of quality. The factory used free-blown, blown three-mold, and pressed glass manufacturing techniques. Both clear and colored glasses were used.

Jarves served as general manager from 1826-1858, and after he left, emphasis was placed on mass production. The development of a lime glass (non-flint) led to lower costs for pressed glass. Some free-blown and blown-and-molded pieces were made. By the 1880s the company was operating at a loss, and the factory closed on Jan. 1, 1888.

Pressed Petal and Loop candlesticks, electric/copper blue, each six-petal socket with hexagonal extension, raised on hexagonal knop and seven-loop circular base with rough pontil mark, wafer construction, Boston & Sandwich Glass Co. and others, 1840-1860, excellent condition, shallow chip to underside of one socket petal and minor flake under base, 6-3/4" h. x 4-3/8" dia. base. ...**$1,265**

Jeffrey S. Evans & Associates

Pressed Twisted Loop vase, amethyst, deep conical bowl with six loops twisted to right, gauffered eight-petal rim, raised on compressed knop, octagonal baluster-form standard and square base, wafer construction, 1840-1860, flake to one lower base corner and flake under base, 11" h., 5" dia. overall rim, 3-1/8" sq. base. **$4,888**

Jeffrey S. Evans & Associates

Pressed Cavalier pomade jar, translucent starch blue, marked "E . T . S & Co / NY" under base, top hat produced from Sandwich Pressed Prism Panel toy tumbler, 1850-1870, excellent condition, base rim with small chip, flake and light edge bruise, potstone in back of body causing small bruise, flake to one foot, rim of hat polished, 4-1/8" h. overall. **$2,760**

Jeffrey S. Evans & Associates

Pressed Tulip vase, emerald green, deep octagonal bowl with flared rim, panels continue to peg extension, raised on flared, octagonal base, wafer construction, 1845-1865, light flake under base, 10" h. x 5-5/8" dia. overall rim, 4-3/4" dia. overall foot.... **$3,450**

Jeffrey S. Evans & Associates

GLASS

Pressed oval inkstand, vaseline (uranium) stand with scallop-and-point shell-like tray centering plateau with two holes for original inkwell and sander, original nickel-plated covers, possibly 1870-1890, flakes around holes, covers undamaged with some wear to plating, 3-1/2" h. overall, stand 6" x 8"............................ **$1,093**

Jeffrey S. Evans & Associates

Pressed "French ink" stand, sapphire blue, stand with two shell-form receivers centering plateau with two holes for original inkwells, fitted with original brass covers, ribs and rays under base of stand, 1870-1880, excellent condition, wells undamaged, stand plateau with top-edge flake at each end, chip to outer edge and chipping/flaking around holes, covers undamaged, 3-1/2" h. overall, stand 6-5/8" x 7-3/8"...... **$2,415**

Jeffrey S. Evans & Associates

Pressed Eye and Scale hand candlestick/chamber stick, peacock blue, thick-lipped hexagonal socket applied with thick hand-formed wafer to Eye and Scale plate, applied ring-form handle with lower curl, rough pontil mark under base, 1830-1850, 3" h., 4-3/4" dia. plate. **$9,775**

Jeffrey S. Evans & Associates

Pressed Hexagonal candlesticks, peacock green, each urn-shape socket with two steps below rim and double-knop extension, raised on compressed knop and hexagonal ringed standard and base with slight step, wafer construction, probably 1840-1860, minor flakes, 7-1/2" h. x 3-7/8" dia. overall base.... **$4,313**

Jeffrey S. Evans & Associates

Pressed Petal and Columnar candlesticks, yellow-green/vaseline (uranium), each six-petal socket with lower extension, raised on fluted columnar standard and double-step square base, wafer construction, Boston & Sandwich Glass Co. and possibly others, 1850-1865, one with chip to base corner, 9-1/8" h. x 3-5/8" sq. base. **$489**

Jeffrey S. Evans & Associates

Pressed Hexagonal and Circular candlesticks, forest green, each urn-shape socket with two steps below rim and double-knop extension, raised on hexagonal baluster-form standard stepped to circular panel-top base, wafer construction, Boston & Sandwich Glass Co. and Patrick F. Slane's American Glass Co., South Boston, 1840-1860, 6-7/8" h. x 3-3/4" dia. base. **$3,450**

Jeffrey S. Evans & Associates

Pressed Dolphin double-step candlesticks, yellow (uranium), each six-petal socket with lower extension, raised on medium dolphin-form standard and square base, wafer construction, probably 1845-1870, 9-3/4" h. x 3-5/8" sq. base. **$690**

Jeffrey S. Evans & Associates

GLASS

$

STEUBEN

FREDERICK CARDER, an Englishman, and Thomas G. Hawkes of Corning, New York, established the Steuben Glass Works in 1903 in Steuben County, New York. In 1918, the Corning Glass Co. purchased the Steuben company. Carder remained with the firm and designed many of the pieces bearing the Steuben mark. Probably the most widely recognized wares are Aurene, Verre De Soie, and Rosaline, but many other types were produced. The firm operated until 2011.

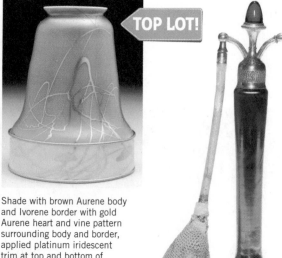

TOP LOT!

Shade with brown Aurene body and Ivorene border with gold Aurene heart and vine pattern surrounding body and border, applied platinum iridescent trim at top and bottom of border, unsigned, very good to excellent condition with minor roughness to fitter rim, 5-1/2" h., 2-1/4" fitter................ **$3,318**

James D. Julia, Inc.

Iridescent blue atomizer with cobalt blue acorn finial, short surface scratches, irregular coloring on stem, erroneously signed L.C.T. with number, dehydrated netted squeeze bulb, original to perfume, 9-3/4" h. **$325**

Mark Mussio, Humler & Nolan

Blue Aurene pedestal three-handled bowl, signed, good condition, 6"................... **$1,400**

Woody Auction

Silverina center bowl in Flemish blue with diamond patterns and silver flecking, six sides angled outward, later acid-stamped Steuben after leaving factory, excellent condition, 4-1/4" x 10-1/4"................**$700**

Mark Mussio, Humler & Nolan

GLASS

Calcite darning ball, gold Aurene decoration, rough open pontil end, unsigned, circa 1916, undamaged, 6-1/2" l. **$690**

Jeffrey S. Evans & Associates

Brown Aurene shade with applied intarsia border with brown and white entwined wavy lines against gold iridescent background with platinum and blue highlights, signed on fitter rim with gold fleur-de-lis stamp "Steuben," very good to excellent condition, 4" h. **$889**

James D. Julia, Inc.

Candlestick with hollow blown stem in amber glass with applied blue lip to edge of foot and bobeche, unsigned, very good to excellent condition, 15" h. **$326**

James D. Julia, Inc.

Pomona green covered jar, circa 1935, urn-form with scale pattern decoration, raised on hexagonal foot, interior of lid acid-stamped Steuben, minor fleabites to interior rim of lid, 13-1/4" h.. **$1,020**

Skinner, Inc.; www.skinnerinc.com

Oriental jade glass lamp within original metal mounts produced by Crest Lamp Co., Chicago, four winged griffins steady base and surround of upright acanthus leaves, ribbed glass body, cut out "laughing" mask finial, double sockets with original chains with Bakelite pulls, excellent original condition, 35" h.. **$1,500**

Mark Mussio, Humler & Nolan

Shade with green pulled feather design descending from fitter, gold iridescent diamond-quilted background, ruffled rim and gold iridescent interior, unsigned, very good to excellent condition with minor roughness to fitter, 4-1/4" h., 2-1/4" fitter. **$711**

James D. Julia, Inc.

Shade with gold iridescent hooked feather design descending from fitter against Ivorene background, vertically ribbed body, interior with gold iridescence, signed on fitter with silver fleur-de-lis mark, very good to excellent condition, 4-1/2" h., 2-1/4" fitter. **$533**

James D. Julia, Inc.

GLASS

Green jade and alabaster vase in shape 938, etched with exotic crested birds in flowering branches repeated three times about circumference, excellent original condition, 8-7/8" h. ... **$425**

Mark Mussio, Humler & Nolan

Cluthra vase in amethyst in shape 2683 with script logo acid-stamped within polished pontil, sand inclusion on side, excellent original condition, 8-1/8" h. **$750**

Mark Mussio, Humler & Nolan

Three-prong tree trunk vase with blue Aurene finish with gold, platinum, and pink highlights, unsigned, very good to excellent condition, 6-1/4" h. **$1,244**

James D. Julia, Inc.

Gold Aurene trumpet vase with ruffled top, signed and numbered "Aurene 2712," fine condition, 10-3/4" h. **$431**

Thomaston Place Auction Galleries

Blue Aurene bulbous vase, strong color, signed, good condition, 10-1/2" h. **$1,800**

Woody Auction

Modernist clear vase with eight-lobed base, cone-shaped body, 1950s, signed on underside, fine condition, 10" h. **$259**

Thomaston Place Auction Galleries

Art Deco Lotus acid-etched vase, plum jade, shape 6078, circa 1924, blossoms and leaves on scrolled ground, polished base, fleur-de-lis acid-stamped relief signature at lower edge, undamaged, 6-3/4" h. x 8" dia. overall. **$2,415**

Jeffrey S. Evans & Associates

TIFFANY GLASS

TIFFANY & CO. was founded by Charles Lewis Tiffany (1812-1902) and Teddy Young in New York City in 1837 as a "stationery and fancy goods emporium." The store initially sold a wide variety of stationery items, and operated as Tiffany, Young and Ellis in lower Manhattan. The name was shortened to Tiffany & Co. in 1853, and the firm's emphasis on jewelry was established.

The first Tiffany catalog, known as the "Blue Book," was published in 1845. It is still being published today. In 1862 Tiffany & Co. supplied the Union Army with swords, flags and surgical implements.

Charles' son, Louis Comfort Tiffany (1848-1933) was an American artist and designer who worked in the decorative arts and is best known for his work in stained glass. Louis established Tiffany Glass Co. in 1885, and in 1902 it became known as the Tiffany Studios. America's outstanding glass designer of the Art Nouveau period produced glass from the last quarter of the 19th century until the early 1930s. Tiffany revived early techniques and devised many new ones.

For more on Tiffany, please see "Lighting."

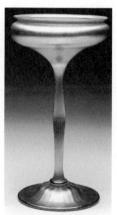

Gold candle lamp with white glass insert, 7" dia. ruffled shade with pastel halo about shoulder and stretch border and engraved "L.C.T." on fitter, swirl base with magenta highlights with cut star aperture on side and signed "L.C.T." beneath, 11-3/4" combined height................ **$600**

Mark Mussio, Humler & Nolan

Two pastel wine glasses, one with yellow foot and hollow blown stem supporting pink cup with vertical panels of white opalescence leading to white opalescent lip, signed on underside "LCT" and numbered; one with green foot and hollow blown stem with raspberry pastel cup with vertical panels of white opalescence and white opalescent lip, signed on underside "LCT Favrile"; both very good to excellent condition, 7-3/4" h............. **$770**

James D. Julia, Inc.

Gold favrile compote with gold iridescent ribbed inverted saucer foot supporting slender translucent amber stem flaring into gold iridescent bowl of compote, interior in gold iridescence with pink, blue and green highlights, signed on underside "L.C. Tiffany Favrile," very good to excellent condition with minor scratches to iridescence on foot, 11-1/4" h. **$1,215**

James D. Julia, Inc.

$

Pastel compote in aqua, morning glory blossom, ribbed spool and ball stem and slight cupped base, signed "L.C.T. Favrile," numbered P18 in base center, excellent condition, bowl 6". **$275**

Mark Mussio, Humler & Nolan

Tulip shade with gold favrile, damascene decoration on exterior with pink and blue highlights, signed on fitter rim "L.C.T. Favrile," very good to excellent with small flake on fitter, 5" h., 2-1/4" fitter ... **$1,896**

James D. Julia, Inc.

TOP LOT!

Rare scarab inkwell, patinated bronze, Favrile glass, clear glass, 1900s, stamped "TIFFANY STUDIOS NEW YORK 1501," 2-1/4" x 3-1/2". **$25,000**

Rago Arts

Pair of aqua pastel water goblets with slender reed stems mounted on cupped bases with opal pattern, engraved "L.C.T. Favrile" on bottom, excellent condition, 8-5/8". **$550**

Mark Mussio, Humler & Nolan

Finger bowl and undertray carved with beaded festoons and engraved "L.C.T.," tray reflects magenta, excellent condition, bowl 2-1/4" x 4-3/8", tray 1-1/4" x 6". **$375**

Mark Mussio, Humler & Nolan

Cabinet vase with squat body with pulled pigtail design around body, gold iridescence with highlights of purple and blue at shoulder and neck, signed on underside "L.C.T. K500" with original Tiffany paper label with Tiffany Glass & Decorating Co. logo in center, very good to excellent condition, 2-1/2" h. **$948**

James D. Julia, Inc.

Miniature flower form vase with wide ruffled rim in iridescent gold, engraved "L.C.Tiffany-Favrile, 9389," excellent condition, 4-3/4" h. **$325**

Mark Mussio, Humler & Nolan

Compote with blue iridescent finish with platinum, pink and purple, interior intaglio carved with flowers and vines, signed on underside "L.C.T. Favrile 1212," very good to excellent condition, 4-1/4" h. x 8-1/4" dia. **$1,094**

James D. Julia, Inc.

Favrile bowl with pulled pigtails encircling side, gold iridescence with purple, blue and green highlights on interior, signed on underside "L.C.T.," very good to excellent condition, 4-1/2" dia. **$320**

James D. Julia, Inc.

Pair of finger bowls and underplates with ruffled rims, gold iridescence with strong purple and pink highlights, all pieces signed "LCT," very good to excellent condition, bowls 4-3/4" dia., plates 5-3/4" dia. **$593**

James D. Julia, Inc.

Gold favrile shade with vertically ribbed body with low flaring shoulder and slightly ruffled rim, gold iridescence with pink and platinum highlights, signed on fitter rim "LCT," very good to excellent condition, 5-1/2" h., 2-1/4" fitter. **$577**

James D. Julia, Inc.

Pastel plates with borders in aqua with spread of opal spokes in center, slight scalloping to edges, engraved "L.C. Tiffany Favrile" on back, excellent condition, 11" dia. **$550**

Mark Mussio, Humler & Nolan

Vase with green heart and vine decoration against gold iridescent background, decorated with millefiori flowers covered with gold iridescence, signed on underside "L.C. Tiffany Favrile 9620D," very good to excellent condition, 5-1/4" h. **$1,600**

James D. Julia, Inc.

Vase with cylindrical, vertically ribbed body with flaring shoulder in pulled feather design ascending from foot, each feather outlined with gold iridescence, cream-colored background shading to gold/orange iridescence at lip, signed on underside "L.C. Tiffany Favrile," very good to excellent condition with irregular and missing iridescence on interior of mouth, most likely from making, 9-1/2" h .. **$1,778**

James D. Julia, Inc.

Covered jar with cylindrical body with squared shoulder and slightly flaring lip, jar and matching lid in gold iridescence with pink highlights, finial on lid with wheel-carved flower on top, signed in polished pontil "L.C. Tiffany Inc. Favrile 3352N," very good to excellent condition, 7-1/2" h. **$1,823**

James D. Julia, Inc.

Pastel goblet with green foot and hollow blown stem supporting pink blown cup with vertical ribbing shading to opalescent at lip, unsigned, very good to excellent condition, 9" h. **$365**

James D. Julia, Inc.

Gold favrile miniature vase with gold iridescent finish with wave pattern and vertical zipper design, green, purple, and pink highlights, signed on underside "LCT K748," very good to excellent condition, 2-3/4" h. **$851**

James D. Julia, Inc.

Thermometer with etched metal grapevine design against green slag glass background, beaded trim and brown patina with green highlights, signed "Tiffany Studios New York 1013," very good to excellent condition, 8-3/4" x 3-3/4". **$1,541**

James D. Julia, Inc.

Double gourd-shaped vase with gold iridescent pulled design topped by gold iridescent wavy line, white slightly iridescent background, signed on inside of fitter rim "L.C.T. Favrile," very good to excellent condition with minor roughness to fitter rim, 4-3/4" h., 2-1/4" fitter. **$711**

James D. Julia, Inc.

Picture frame with acid-etched pine needle pattern with caramel slag glass backing and oval opening for photo, gold patina, signed on back "Tiffany Studios New York 917," very good to excellent condition with minor discoloration to patina, 12" x 14" overall, opening 8-1/4" x 10-1/4"............. **$1,762**

James D. Julia, Inc.

Five-piece pine needle desk set, large inkwell with caramel slag glass backing #847, small square inkwell with caramel slag glass #845, notepad with caramel slag glass #1022, penwipe with caramel slag glass #981, and upright matchbox holder #958, all pieces signed "Tiffany Studios New York," both inkwells with original inserts, each piece with light brown patina, overall very good to excellent condition, notepad with solder repair to hinge, large inkwell 7" dia.............**$1,215**

James D. Julia, Inc.

Favrile trumpet vase in iridescent gold, engraved "L.C. Tiffany-Favrile" and numbered 138P 1764, excellent original condition, 5-5/8" h............. **$300**

Mark Mussio, Humler & Nolan

Two flower and trellis boxes: Box with etched metal flower and trellis pattern on sides and top with striated green and white glass backing, top and sides finished with double rows of beaded trim, four ball feet, signed on underside "Tiffany Studios New York," 7" w. x 7" d. x 2-1/2" h.; box with etched metal flower and trellis pattern on sides and top with beaded trim and four ball feet, etched metal design backed by emerald green striated glass, signed on underside "Tiffany Studios New York"; 4-1/2" w. x 3-3/8" d. x 3/4" h.; both very good to excellent condition. **$1,185**

James D. Julia, Inc.

TIFFIN

A WIDE VARIETY of fine glasswares were produced by the Tiffin Glass Co. of Tiffin, Ohio. Beginning as a part of the large U.S. Glass Co. early in the 20th century, the Tiffin factory continued making a wide range of wares until its final closing in 1984. One popular line called "Black Satin" included various vases with raised floral designs. Many other acid-etched and hand-cut patterns were also produced over the years and are very collectible today. The three *Tiffin Glassmasters* books by Fred Bickenheuser are the standard references for Tiffin collectors.

Etched and gilt partial service, 58 pieces (three shown), 11 large water goblets, 13 medium wine glasses, eight sherbets, 10 large champagne glasses, three small champagne glasses, eight large cordials, and five small cordials, largest water goblets 8" h. **$5,228**

Kaminski Auctions

Fruit basket lamp, mold blown puffy glass shade with apples, pears, bananas, grapes, and plums, cast white metal base with gilt painted finish with four dolphin figures, filigree and inverted domical bowl with single socket in base, shade in excellent condition with no chips, cracks or losses, 12" h. x 7-1/2" dia. ...**$272**

Fontaine's Auction Gallery

Silver-overlay decorated Amberina cupped dahlia vase, satin finish, shape no. 151, floral garland band with cameo tassels below rim, Tiffin Glass Co./ U.S. Glass Co., circa 1925, undamaged, 10-3/4" h. **$81**

Jeffrey S. Evans & Associates

Figural parrot lamp, base repair, 13". **$125**

Woody Auction

Figural parrot lamp, enameled finish, base in black colored glass, small chip on base near threads, 13". **$677**

Fox Auctions

GLASS

$

WAVE CREST

NOW MUCH SOUGHT AFTER, Wave Crest was produced by the C.F. Monroe Co., Meriden, Connecticut, in the late 19th and early 20th centuries. It was made from opaque white glass blown into molds, then hand-decorated in enamels, and metal trim was often added. Boudoir accessories such as jewel boxes, hair receivers, etc., predominated.

TOP LOT!

Square footed hinged dresser box, Egg Crate mold, dark brown background with yellow floral decor, embossed cherub head feet, fancy new lining, banner mark, good condition, 6-1/2" x 6-1/2"............ **$1,000**

Woody Auction

Rococo footed vase, opal with pale blue ground and polychrome enamel daisy decoration on both sides, beaded rim, gilt-metal base with four feet, flag trademark under base, late 19th/ early 20th century, undamaged, 10-1/8" h. x 1-7/8" dia. rim.......**$259**

Jeffrey S. Evans & Associates

Large Egg Crate satin dresser box hand-decorated with Cupid with bow and arrows by seashore, floral bouquets on cover and base with pink enamel scroll and green backdrop, ornate metal mounts with pierced shoulder pads and base with lion mask feet, unmarked, excellent condition, 6" x 6-1/2"...................**$600**

Mark Mussio, Humler & Nolan

Metal-rimmed photograph holder with pink roses, stamped with red shield mark, possibly original silk liner, 2-1/2" x 4"; metal mounted bud vase with wild roses, stamped "Wavecrest Trade Mark," 6-3/8" h.; both in excellent condition........ **$275**

Mark Mussio, Humler & Nolan

Round hinged dresser box, puff mold, light green with open white segments, pink and blue floral highlights, white enamel beaded tapestry, original lining, banner mark, good condition, 3-1/2" x 7"........................**$250**

Woody Auction

Hooked Rugs

BEGINNING ABOUT A CENTURY-AND-A-HALF AGO, men and women created hooked rugs to warm their hearths and homes. These folk art floor coverings, which were originally made to cover dirt floors, were fashioned out of ingenuity and frugality and are now highly valued in collectors' and decorators' markets.

Wool rug hooking is thought to have begun in Canada's easternmost provinces and in the Northeast United States. Fabric scraps no longer suitable for clothing were cut into strips and hooked by varying techniques into a burlap ground in patterns. The end result – whether simple or complex, geometric, floral or pictorial – was only limited by the artisan's skill and imagination.

The earliest hooked rugs date from the early-to-mid-19th century; these early rugs are most often found in museums and historical societies.

Laura Fisher, proprietor of the Fisher Heritage gallery in New York, has several hundred vintage and antique quilts in her inventory, ranging from the mid-19th century through the 1950s. When asked about what hooked rug collectors gravitate toward, Fisher said some people prefer early rugs with animals, which can fetch high prices at auction.

Hooked rug of checkerboard, 20th century, inscribed "White to Play & Win," 36-1/2" x 40".......................**$660**

Pook & Pook, Inc.

"The earlier and folksier, the more valuable," she said. "Other people love early 19th century florals that were popular in Maine and Canada. The flowers are raised, clipped and sheared so the rug has a three-dimensional quality." These rugs often have a center bouquet set within a scrollwork border.

Wool hooked rugs became widely popular in the third quarter of the 19th century. Some entrepreneurs saw the growing interest in this home activity and recognized that there would be a demand for pre-designed rug patterns, especially for rug hookers who were unsatisfied with their own artistic skills.

Edward Sands Frost of Biddeford, Maine, Ralph Burnham of Ipswitch, Massachusetts, and Ebenezer Ross of Toledo, Ohio, were three such entrepreneurs. Frost (1843-1894) was one of the earliest commercial hooked rug pattern makers. By creating pre-stamped patterns on burlap with sheet metal stencils, he expanded and transformed the homemade rug hooking industry, making rug hooking a viable cottage industry – an industry that helped fishing communities survive harsh Atlantic winters.

Probably the most noteworthy cottage industry name in the Atlantic region – and therefore some of the most prized hooked mats and rugs by collectors – is Grenfell Industries, which produced thousands of high-quality mats and rugs, many with regional themes such as wintertime, polar bears, fishermen and nautical; geometric designs were also created, but they are more rare.

Shortly after the turn of the 20th century, an English missionary, Dr. Wilfred T. Grenfell, saw the need for struggling communities in Canada to supplement the local fishing industry in the off-season. Recognizing the locals' extraordinary needlework skills (settlers brought mat hooking from England and Scotland), he established a mission based in St. Anthony, Newfoundland, Canada, to generate revenue for Labrador and northern Newfoundland residents: Material kits and patterns were distributed to home workers who then created mats, rugs and other textile products. Those products were then sold through stores and catalogs.

The original Grenfell Industries mats are distinctive because they were made using dyed silk stockings instead of wool; the artisans were so skilled that they were able to use every hole in the backing, sometimes achieving 200 stitches per square inch. Each finished piece was inspected to assure quality and workmanship standards were met.

Hooked rug in Oriental pattern, early 20th century, 54" x 36".... **$360**

Pook & Pook, Inc.

After peaking in the 1920s, the Great Depression hit Grenfell Industries hard. Sales and donations lagged and supplies were depleted. World War II caused supply and transportation challenges, as well as rising costs. After the war, silk stockings were no longer available.

Mat hooking continues today in St. Anthony by the independently owned Grenfell Handicrafts, which produces contemporary mats from original, copyrighted Grenfell patterns.

Other traditional designs manufactured a century ago also are still available and popular with contemporary rug hookers. Because hooked wool rugs were made in the home for personal use, seldom can they be traced back to the original maker or pinned down to an exact date; rarely do antique hooked rugs come with such detailed provenance. There are clues to a rug's age and value, however.

Hooked rugs generally fall into three different age categories. The first is antique: 100 years old or more. These rugs can command anywhere from a few hundred to thousands of dollars, depending upon the design, age, condition, provenance and other factors.

"Collectible" or "vintage" hooked rugs – rugs that are typically 25 to 75 years old – are often priced at less than $100 and come in an unlimited variety of styles and designs. One can pick up a collectible hooked rug for a fraction of what a true "antique" rug would cost.

Falling into the collectible rug category, "Hutchinson rugs are highly desirable and collectible," Fisher says. James and Mercedes Hutchinson designed their own rugs from the 1920s-1940s to sell to the public at auction. They are often humorous, with funny observations about relationships, poems and epigrams. Hutchinson rugs are one example of vintage rugs sometimes bringing extraordinary prices.

Pearl McGown rugs from the 1950s are also coveted by collectors. "Like Grenfell," Fisher says, "McGown rugs are extremely fine and beautiful." McGown, who was from West Amesbury, Massachusetts, wrote many books, taught people how to dye their own rag strips, and created the reverse lock stitch, making the back of a rug look as wonderful as the front. Fisher says McGown produced hundreds of patterns and trained women as

Hooked rug of potted flower with double border, 20th century, 37-1/2" x 36-1/2".............. **$360**

Pook & Pook, Inc.

rug hooking educators to share her techniques with a wider audience. McGown's granddaughter is involved with organizing contemporary rug hooking events.

Contemporary hooked rugs are newer than 25 years old. However, just because a contemporary hooked wool rug doesn't have a significant amount of age, doesn't mean it's not valuable. Each rug is still a handmade, unique work of art. Like collecting any contemporary art, the price paid for a piece will be as appreciation and recognition of the skill and design of the rug artist.

Fisher cautions that there are hooked rugs being made in China and India today, made by companies capitalizing on the interest in old, folk-art type rugs. How do you tell the difference?

"There's a different technique of manufacturing," Fisher said. "Most international imports are hooked on monk's cloth cotton weave backing rather than burlap. Burlap is the foundation of choice for the majority of hooked rugs that are antique and vintage, either American or Canadian. Rug hookers today use monk's cloth cotton because it doesn't crack and dry like burlap."

Also, a lot of Eastern import rugs have a thick latex backing. They feel and handle differently than vintage or antique rugs. Fisher elaborates: "They have a heavy feel that old rugs don't have. New England rug restorers in the 1950s used a different kind of latex."

Another detail that will help in determining if a hooked rug is old or new: Old rugs were made with rag strips; new imported rugs are usually made with wool yarn. And if they happen to be made with rag strips, it's cotton knit rather than wool. Old rugs were made with scrap fabric; there's a variation in color. Wear, use, air and environment all affect the color.

"Variegation in color and age patina give antique rugs a visual liveliness that so far no one has been able to match in manufacturing," Fisher explains. "A new-made rug has a flatter appearance ... There's no substitution for age."

Jessie Turbayne, author of *The Complete Guide to Collecting Hooked Rugs: Unrolling the Secrets*, as well as seven other books on hooked rugs, has been buying, selling, collecting, and restoring hooked rugs for nearly 40 years. She recommends focusing on a particular type or age of hooked rug when starting a collection, "Buying just for the sake of buying is unwise and costly."

A respected authority on rug values and care, Turbayne teaches rug hooking and restores anywhere from 200 to 400 hooked rugs per year for museums, collectors and antiques dealers in her Massachusetts workshop. She estimates about 90 percent of the restoration work is hand stitching, sometimes using fine surgical needles.

Turbayne says people often don't know what they're buying. If they bring a rug to her for repair, she advises the potential client of the rug's value and its estimated restoration cost. Though she has executed restorations anywhere from $10 to $20,000, a typical restoration runs $100-$300.

The possibility of expenses incurred in restoring hooked rugs shouldn't dissuade collectors. As Turbayne says, "As functioning art, they are equally at home hung on walls as placed on floors." These handcrafted works of folk art add color, texture and warmth to any décor.

—*Karen Knapstein, Print Editor,* Antique Trader Magazine

James L. and Mercedes Hutchinson hooked rug with people and dogs, inscribed "Must I Always Cook For My Husband's Kin," 33-1/2" x 51".... **$840**

Pook & Pook, Inc.

American hooked rug of dove in flight with branch in its mouth and variegated scroll background, 19th century, 33" x 36-1/2"........................ **$1,920**

Pook & Pook, Inc.

Hooked rug of tabby cat, 20th century, 35-1/2" x 49".. **$3,840**

Pook & Pook, Inc.

Hooked rug, "Reflection in Red and Blue," early 19th century, found in Indiana, 48" x 31".... **$1,320**

Pook & Pook, Inc.

Hooked rug, farmhouse, barn and well, 19th century, all wool, hooked on burlap, purchased in Maine, 31-1/2" x 54-1/2". **$900**

Thomaston Place Auction Galleries

TOP LOT!

Hooked rug of recumbent leopard, dated 1943, 35-1/2" x 89"... **$4,080**

Pook & Pook, Inc.

Floor runner, woven from fabric scraps in twisted strips of reds, blacks, blue/green, and cream/whites, alternating every 2" to 6" in pattern, Canterbury Shakers, 1850-1870, 16' 6" l. x 2' 2" w. **$1,298**

Willis-Henry Auctions

Hooked rug, "Blue Snowflake," circa 1900, 36" x 26"... **$840**

Pook & Pook, Inc.

Hooked rug of cottage scene, 20th century, with trees in foreground, 9" x 16"......................... **$540**

Pook & Pook, Inc.

Hooked rug, "Fisherman's House," with fish in pond and chicken, late 19th century, 28" x 41".... **$2,040**

Pook & Pook, Inc.

Room-sized hooked rug, floral arrangement over parti-colored field, scrolled edge, brown/black border, Waldoboro, Maine, 7' x 68"............. **$1,100**

Thomaston Place Auction Galleries

Hooked rug with central tulip and heart flanked by floral trailing vine and potted flower border, 20th century, 32" x 52". **$3,120**

Pook & Pook, Inc.

Pennsylvania hooked rug with bird and floral panels, early 20th century, 58" x 38"........... **$1,140**

Pook & Pook, Inc.

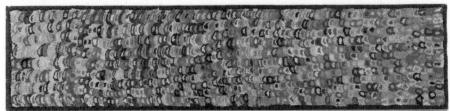

Hooked rug in abstract scale pattern, 20th century, 18-3/4" x 80"...**$1,140**

Pook & Pook, Inc.

Illustration Art

EXPOSURE PLAYS AN IMPORTANT ROLE in collector demand and values for illustration art, which has proven itself over the last decade as one of the most popular and dynamic art genres in the country.

Take for instance "Hello Everybody!," a calendar illustration originally produced for Brown & Bigelow in the late 1920s. Artist Rolf Armstrong created the carefree pastel on

Rolf Armstrong (American, 1889-1960), "Hello Everybody!," Brown & Bigelow calendar illustration, circa late 1920s, pastel on board, 27" x 37". As one of Armstrong's most iconic works, this artwork appeared as a calendar illustration, on playing cards, as the cover for *College Humor* magazine, 1929, as an illustration in the book *Pin Up Dreams: The Glamour Art of Rolf Armstrong,* and in various advertisements...**$30,000**

board of a young lady with a bright smile at the nexus of the Roaring '20s and the Great Depression. Popular reaction was enthusiastic. The artwork appeared as a calendar illustration, on playing cards, puzzles, a die-cut advertising sign for Orange Kist soda pop, and as the cover for the March 1929 edition of *College Humor* magazine. According to Janet Dobson's *Pin Up Dreams: The Glamour Art of Rolf Armstrong*, early works such as "Hello Everybody!" defined the vision of feminine beauty for the next 40 years and earned Armstrong the title of "Father of the Pin-Up Artists." The exposure and reputation of the artist generated strong demand when the original work finally came up for auction in 2013 when its sale price was pushed to $30,000.

"Hello Everybody!" represents the type of subject matter that is attracting mainstream attention.

"It's really what we think of as classic images in all genres that speak directly and powerfully to a specific time period – whether it's a 1940s *Saturday Evening Post* cover, 1950s science-fiction paperback cover, or 1960s Gil Elvgren calendar pin-up," says Todd Hignite, director of illustration art at Heritage Auctions, the world's largest auctioneer of illustration art and related works.

Interestingly, as the market for illustration art matures, auctioneers are reclassifying works as American fine art and offering works by artists with household names along with other artists such as Grandma Moses, Leroy Neiman or the Wyeths. Norman Rockwell's works now routinely bring in excess of $2 million at auction, but his early illustration art, steeped in sentimentality and strong national pride may be found for less than $100,000.

"Well-known artists such as Rockwell did indeed work in advertising – many illustrators did – and it's certainly less expensive than a magazine cover by the same artist," Hignite says.

Although industry watchers are excited to see many illustration artists make the leap from illustration art to American fine art, there are dozens – perhaps thousands – of artists whose identity is still lost but whose art still lives on. Currently these works are anonymously attributed simply as "American artist," but that doesn't mean research has stopped looking into the identity of these artists. Scholars have been given a boost in recent years thanks to collectors who remain fascinated by various styles.

"The scholarship and research in the field is very active and between exhibitions, publications, and more dealers handling the work, is increasing all the time – but there's still a lot of work to be done in terms of identifying art," Hignite says. "Oftentimes artists didn't sign their paintings, and if their style isn't immediately identifiable, there's a good deal of digging to do. Much of the best research actually comes from devoted fans and collectors, who doggedly put together extensive checklists and track down publication histories, check stubs from publishers, biographies, etc., to try and enhance our understanding of the history."

This confluence of awareness, appreciation, and a growing nostalgia for mid-century works have more than doubled values for pieces offered just a few short years ago. Gil Elvgren's original pin-up art from the collection of author Charles Martignette was sold at auction beginning in 2009 for amounts ranging from $40,000 to $60,000. However, purchase offers are now hovering between $120,000 to as much as $155,000 for the works.

Hignite credits the increase to a matter of supply and demand: "I think simply the opportunity to see a steady supply of great art by Elvgren has increased the demand," he says. "If you see one of his paintings in person, there's no question of his painting talent, and collector confidence increases as we see such a steady growth and consistent sales results."

–*Eric Bradley*

Rolf Armstrong (American, 1889-1960), "The Enchantress," Brown & Bigelow calendar illustration, oil on canvas, 80" x 60"............**$81,250**

Heritage Auctions

Robert Riggs (American, 1896-1970), "Ringing of the Bell," oil on panel, 23" x 10-1/2" **$4,375**

Heritage Auctions

American artist (20th century), "The Old Woman Who Lived in a Shoe," story illustration, gouache on board, 13" x 20-3/4". **$125**

Heritage Auctions

Garth Williams (American, 1912-1996), "Beneath a Blue Umbrella," page design artwork, 1990, set of original artwork for each page design (24 pages and 72 items total) of book including pen and watercolor on paper main design, pen overlay, and pen on paper original drawing of image, watercolor on paper, main works 13" x 9". Provenance: From estate of Garth Williams..... **$4,218**

Heritage Auctions

American artist (20th century), "Woman in a Pink Hat," magazine cover, oil on canvas laid on board, 23-1/2" x 17-3/4"............. **$187**

Heritage Auctions

American artist (20th century), "Baby Coons," Norcross Greeting Card Collection, gouache and tempera on board laid on card stock, 6-3/4" x 5-1/2". **$62**

Heritage Auctions

American artist (20th century), "Bubble Bath Girl," Norcross Greeting Card Collection, watercolor and gouache on paper laid on card stock, 6" x 5". ... **$69**

Heritage Auctions

Bill Randall (American, b. 1911), "Cinderella," *The American Magazine* story illustration, gouache and tempera on board, 15" x 11"..**$1,250**

Heritage Auctions

Charles Showalter (American, 1919-2005), Nesbitt's advertisement, "a soft drink made from real oranges," offset lithograph on paper, 24" x 35-1/2"... **$275**

Heritage Auctions

ILLUSTRATION ART

$

TOP LOT!

Joseph Christian Leyendecker (American, 1874-1951), "Honeymoon," *The Saturday Evening Post* cover, July 17, 1926, oil on canvas, 28-1/4" x 21-1/4". **$194,500**

Heritage Auctions

Edgar Church, "Put Your Shoulder to the Wheel and Help!" circa 1944, World War II-era illustration original art (circa 1944), ink on coquille paper, 14" x 11". **$1,314**

Heritage Auctions

Tom Lovell (American, 1909-1997), "Couple Lounging," probable magazine story illustration, oil on canvas, 24-1/2" x 30-1/2". **$5,625**

Heritage Auctions

Rafael Desoto (American, 1904-1992), "The
Killer Waits," *New Detective* pulp cover, May
1945, oil on board, 22" x 16"....................**$13,750**

Heritage Auctions

Harold W. McCauley (American, 1913-1977),
"The Floating Robot," *Fantastic Adventures*
pulp magazine cover, January 1941, oil on
canvas board, 24" x 18"...........................**$13,750**

Heritage Auctions

Gil Elvgren (American, 1914-1980), "Lucky
Dog" (Dog Gone Robber), Brown & Bigelow
calendar illustration, 1958, oil on canvas,
30-1/4" x 24"...**$173,000**

Heritage Auctions

Stevan Dohanos (American, 1907-1994), "The
Future Fireman," *The Saturday Evening Post*
cover, Nov. 14, 1953, new record for artist, oil
on board, 39" x 31". **$106,250**

Heritage Auctions

ILLUSTRATION ART

Frank R. Paul (American, 1884-1963), "The Ideal," *Wonder Stories* pulp magazine cover, September 1935, oil on canvas, 22" x 16"..**$11,875**

Heritage Auctions

Robert Hilbert (American, 20th century), "Who Is Going to Do the Dishes?," *The American Weekly Magazine* cover, Nov. 21, 1954, gouache on board, 16-1/2" x 13-1/2"............................ **$2,250**

Heritage Auctions

William Medcalf (American, 20th century), "Along the North Shore," Brown & Bigelow calendar illustration, oil on board, 30" x 40"............. **$2,000**

Heritage Auctions

American artist (20th century), "Hilda Clark Holding a Flower," probable Coca-Cola advertisement, oil on board, 19-1/2" x 14-1/2". **$687**

Heritage Auctions

American artist (20th century), "'Honored' All Over...Atlas Tire Warranty," Atlas Tire advertisement, oil on unstretched canvas, 13-1/4" x 37-1/4". **$312**

Heritage Auctions

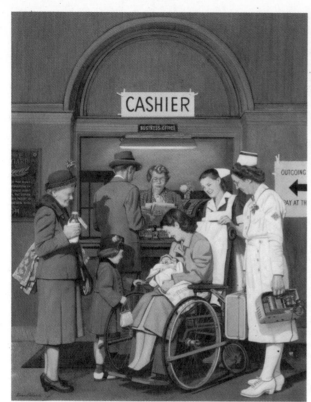

Stevan Dohanos (American, 1907-1994), "Checking Out," *The Saturday Evening Post* cover, Oct. 22, 1949, gouache and casein on board, 37-1/2" x 29-1/2"..**$32,500**

Heritage Auctions

Ron Balaban (American, 20th century), "1955 Oldsmobile Starfire," oil on canvas, 24" x 36" **$2,250**

Heritage Auctions

Edgar Church, "Menace," 1919, pulp illustration original art, gouache on board, 10" x 14".................................... **$956**

Heritage Auctions

John Collins, "New Jersey Seashore," circa 1950, Pennsylvania Railroad poster original artwork, gouache illustration, The Art Directors Club of Philadelphia 14th annual exhibition of advertising art label on verso, 27" x 16-1/2"........................... **$3,200**

Rago Arts & Auction Center

Tom Barber (American, 20th century), "Scarlet Tears," *Weird Tales #1* paperback cover, 1980, oil on canvas laid on masonite, 16-1/2" x 11".. **$1,187**

Heritage Auctions

John Philip Falter (American, 1910-1982), "Antique Store Accident," *The Saturday Evening Post* cover, June 20, 1959, oil on board, 23" x 21-1/2"..**$74,500**

Heritage Auctions

Virgil Finlay (American, 1914-1971), "The Flying Saucer," *Fantastic Universe Science Fiction Digest* cover, February 1958, oil on board, 12-1/4" x 8-3/4"............................. **$8,125**

Heritage Auctions

Arthur Saron Sarnoff (American, 1912-2000), "Playing Slots," oil on board, 20" x 30"..**$4,062**

Heritage Auctions

Laurence Herndon (American, b. 1883), "The Land of Hidden Men," *Blue Book Magazine* pulp cover for Edgar Rice Burroughs' tale, "The Land of the Hidden Men," May 1931, oil on canvas, 27-1/2" x 26-1/2". **$43,750**

Heritage Auctions

John Collins, "New York – Always Exciting!" Pennsylvania Railroad poster original artwork, circa 1950, gouache illustration, 40" x 24-1/2". **$6,400**

Rago Arts & Auction Center

Garth Williams (American, 1912-1996), "The Gingerbread Rabbit," group of five, page 3, 14, 21, 22 and frontispiece illustrations, 1964, pen on paper, 13-3/4" x 10-1/4"........... **$2,000**

Heritage Auctions

Jessie Willcox Smith (American, 1863-1935), "Two Children Praying," child's prayer book interior illustration, 1929, ink and watercolor on board, 10" x 12". **$5,000**

Heritage Auctions

JEWELRY

Jewelry

JEWELRY HAS HELD a special place for humankind since prehistoric times, both as an emblem of personal status and as a decorative adornment worn for its sheer beauty. This tradition continues today. We should keep in mind, however, that it was only with the growth of the Industrial Revolution that jewelry first became cheap enough so that even the person of modest means could win a piece or two.

Only since around the mid-19th century did certain forms of jewelry, especially pins and brooches, begin to appear on the general market as a mass-produced commodity and the Victorians took to it immediately. Major production centers for the finest pieces of jewelry remained in Europe, especially Italy and England, but less expensive pieces were also exported to the booming American market and soon some American manufacturers also joined in the trade. Especially during the Civil War era, when silver and gold supplies grew tremendously in the United States, did jewelry in silver or with silver, brass or gold-filled (i.e., gold-plated or goldplate) mounts begin to flood the market here. By the turn of the 20th century all the major mail-order companies and small town jewelry shops could offer a huge variety of inexpensive jewelry pieces aimed at not only the feminine buyer but also her male counterpart.

Inexpensive jewelry of the late 19th and early 20th century is still widely available and often at modest prices. Even more in demand today is costume jewelry, well-designed jewelry produced of inexpensive materials and meant to carefully accent a woman's ensemble. Today costume jewelry of the 20th century has become one of the most active areas in the field of collecting and some of the finest pieces, signed by noted designers and manufacturers, can reach price levels nearly equal to much earlier and scarcer examples.

Jewelry prices, as in every other major collecting field, are influenced by a number of factors including local demand, quality, condition and rarity. As market prices have risen in recent years it has become even more important for the collector to shop and buy with care. Learn as much as you can about your favorite area of jewelry and keep abreast of market trends and stay alert to warnings about alterations, repairs or reproductions that can be found on the market.

For more information on jewelry, see *Warman's Jewelry Identification and Price Guide*, 5th edition.

Early Victorian carved coral and gold suite, pendant-pin with carved red coral designed as acorns, cherries and branches, set in 14k gold, pinstem and "C" catch on reverse, 2-1/2" x 1-1/2"; earrings designed for pierced ears in carved red coral in cascading flower design, set in 14k gold, ear wire hook, 2-1/4" x 3/4"; matching pair of pins with carved red coral designed as single rose bud, set in 14k gold, pinstem and "C" catch, 1-1/2" x-1/2", 39.85 g. **$597**

Heritage Auctions

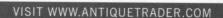

LATE GEORGIAN

Georgian topaz brooch, 18th century, designed as floral and foliate motifs and set throughout with faceted foil-back topaz, silver mount, 3-1/4" w... **$3,851**

Skinner, Inc., www.skinnerinc.com

Georgian ruby and diamond ring, circa 1820, collet-set with cushion-cut rubies and old mine-cut diamonds, floral and foliate shoulders, ribbed shank, silver and gold mount, size 8... **$533**

Skinner, Inc., www.skinnerinc.com

Memorial ring, 14k gold and inkwork, late 18th century, depicting mourning woman by urn under motto, "Not Lost But Gone Before," enamel shank reading: "John Dunbar OBt 23 Sep 1775 AEt 38," in antique box, repair, size 8 .... **$652**

Skinner, Inc., www.skinnerinc.com

VICTORIAN

Early Victorian gold and coral ring and earrings, 14k gold, 9.1 g., coral earring drops, 36 mm, and lever backs for pierced ears, ring size 5-3/4 ..... **$388**

Heritage Auctions

Early Victorian antique silver and Scottish agate earpendants on wires, each drop set with agate bands, ribbed scroll tops, and engraved accents, 2" l. **$652**

Skinner, Inc., www.skinnerinc.com

Early Victorian portrait pin, unmarked gold, tests 14k, 7.1 grams, 30 mm x 34 mm, two chips on top right sides on edges, portrait with some wear.. **$131**

Heritage Auctions

Victorian Scottish agate dirk brooch set with various agates and jasper, with shaped citrine highlights, engraved silver mount, 3-1/4" l.................. **$711**

Skinner, Inc., www.skinnerinc.com

Mid-Victorian diamond, hair and gold mourning locket-pendant, rose-cut diamonds set in 18k gold, opens to reveal lock of hair, engraved "Augusta John May 24th, 1871," 2" x 1-1/8".................................. **$507**

Heritage Auctions

Renaissance Revival Limoges enamel brooch depicting helmeted figure with flowing hair against landscape with trees and castle, gold mount with split pearl accents, 1-1/8" dia **$474**

Skinner, Inc., www.skinnerinc.com

Unmounted early Victorian Scottish shell portrait cameo depicting gentleman's profile, 45 mm x 35 mm x 3.50 mm, bottom edge of cameo inscribed, "N. 185 King," reverse inscribed, "N. 185, J. C. King, Boston, 28th May 1849." Attributed to John Crookshanks King (1806-1882), a Scottish-born machinist and sculptor, who immigrated to the United States in 1829. He was actively modeling busts and cameos of important public figures in New Orleans from 1837 to 1840, prior to continuing his craft in Boston **$179**

Heritage Auctions

Mid-Victorian shell cameo gold pendant-brooch, shell cameo 54 mm x 41 mm, depicting lady's profile, set in textured 14k gold frame, bail, pinstem and "C" catch on reverse, 25.45 g., 2-5/8" x 2".. **$896**

Heritage Auctions

Mid-Victorian black onyx, seed pearl and gold suite, pendant with rectangular and drop-shaped black onyx, set in 14k gold, pinstem and "C" catch on reverse, 1-3/4" x 1-3/4"; matching pair of earrings designed for pierced ears, set in 14k gold, shepherd's hook, 2-1/2" x 3/4"; pendant with oval-shaped black onyx, 36 mm x 45 mm, seed pearls ranging from 3.50 mm to 1.50 mm, set in 14k gold, pinstem and catch on reverse, 1-1/2" x 1-3/4"; 41.05 g. **$597**

Heritage Auctions

Renaissance Revival silver brooch and earpendants, brooch Austro-Hungarian, set with green beryls and pastes, reverse with engraved accents, hallmarks, earpendants set with rose-cut diamonds spaced by pearls, brooch 1-1/4", earrings 1-1/8".............. **$474**

Skinner, Inc., www.skinnerinc.com

Three early Victorian mourning pins: two oval, one gold with turquoise with hair glass frame on back, one gilt with braided hair; one smaller gold oval drop with hair and back frame engraved with heart, cross and anchor **$75**

Heritage Auctions

Victorian 14k gold and enamel bracelet, woven bracelet with slide and terminal in black tracery enamel, foxtail fringe, adjustable length........... **$652**

Skinner, Inc., www.skinnerinc.com

Three early Victorian pins, one rose gold with pearls and mine-cut diamond, one rose gold with hair cross, one gilt pin with pearls. **$310**

Heritage Auctions

Mid-Victorian cameo hardstone on black onyx pin and earrings, heavy gold frames, 36.8 g., cameo pin with bale, 50 mm x 40 mm, screwback earrings, 29 mm x 25 mm, with 20-mm chain drop.................**$750**

Heritage Auctions

Mid-Victorian cameo and gold pendant-brooch, oversized ivory cameo measuring 63 mm x 48 mm x 8.75 mm, depicting Tatiana, Queen of Fairies, from William Shakespeare's "A Midsummer Night's Dream," within 14k yellow gold frame; cameo carved in high relief, inscribed on backside, "HB 1669"; collapsible pendant bail, pinstem and catch on reverse, 42.30 g., 2-1/2" x 2" **$956**

Heritage Auctions

American Victorian sterling chatelaine, late 19th century, Rococo Revival brooch-form body suspending five oval link chains holding sterling Renaissance Revival notepad with celluloid pages, retractable pencil, heart-shaped monogrammed locket, round mirror, and rectangular etui; sold together with silver-plated mesh purse. **$459**

Skinner, Inc., www.skinnerinc.com

ARTS & CRAFTS/ART NOUVEAU

Brooch, "Deux Figurines Dos a Dos," France, 1913, silver foil-backed glass, gilt metal, stamped LALIQUE with cipher, 1/2" x 2-1/4" x 1-1/4"... **$2,000**

Rago Arts & Auction Center

Brooch with winged figure, France, 1910s, patinated and silver foil-backed glass, gilt metal, stamped LALIQUE with cipher, 1/4" x 1-1/4" dia.. **$1,250**

Rago Arts & Auction Center

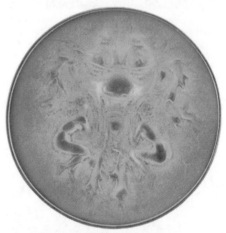

Brooch, "Le Baiser," France, circa 1905, patinated and silver foil-backed glass, gilt metal, metal stamped LALIQUE with cipher, raised signature to glass, R. LALIQUE, 1/2" x 2-1/4" x 1-1/2"..... **$3,125**

Rago Arts & Auction Center

Brooch, "Deux Figurines et Masque," France, 1912, patinated and silver foil-backed glass, gilt metal, stamped LALIQUE FRANCE, 1/2" x 1-3/4" dia **$2,375**

Rago Arts & Auction Center

Brooch, "Quatre Cabochons Bleuets," France, circa 1900, silver foil-backed glass, gilt metal, stamped LALIQUE with cipher, 1/2" x 3" x 1"............ **$3,500**

Rago Arts & Auction Center

Art Nouveau 18k gold locket-brooch of elegant lady with high collar and floral hat, rose-cut diamond accents, opening to compartment, signed Holy Frs, 1-1/4" l. **$652**

Skinner, Inc., www.skinnerinc.com

Arts & Crafts 14k gold, sapphire and diamond ring, centering old European-cut cognac diamond, four old European-cut diamonds, and sapphire melee, foliate mount, indistinct maker's mark, size 5-1/4 .... **$2,133**

Skinner, Inc., www.skinnerinc.com

Art Nouveau sapphire, pearl, and gold swag necklace, French, with sapphire cabochons and button pearls, set in 18k yellow gold, French hallmarks, 9.50 g. **$717**

Heritage Auctions

Art Nouveau diamond, demantoid garnet, plique-à-jour enamel, platinum-topped gold brooch with European-cut diamond 6.30 mm x 6.20 mm x 3.80 mm, weighing approximately 0.95 carat, oval-shaped demantoid garnets weighing approximately 1.65 carats, plique-à-jour enamel in green and lavender, native-cut diamonds set in platinum-topped 14k gold, pinstem and "C" catch on reverse. Marked AH for August Wilhelm Holström, Fabergé workmaster, Russian hallmarks, 12.70 g., 1-3/4" x 1-1/2"...........**$5,975**

Heritage Auctions

Art Nouveau diamond, pearl and enamel necklace, native and rose-cut diamonds, button pearls, royal blue enamel applied on 18k gold, stationed by 18k gold chain............... **$597**

Heritage Auctions

Art Nouveau diamond and gold bracelet, full-cut diamonds approximately 0.40 carat, set in 18k gold, French hallmarks, 36.83 g., 7-7/8" x 1/2"..... **$3,000**

Heritage Auctions

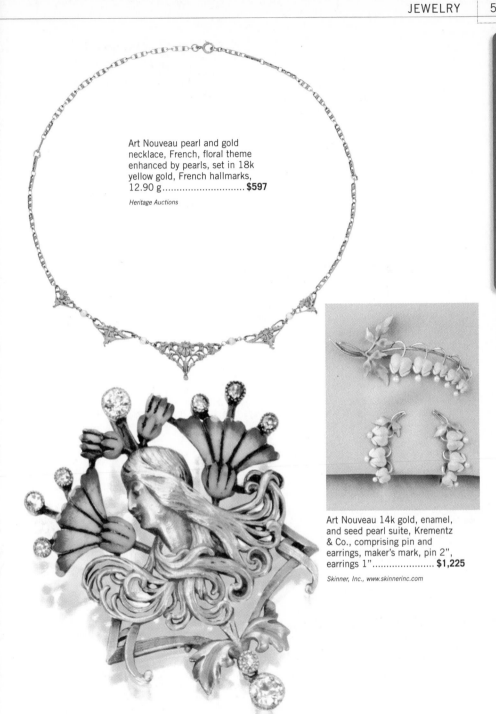

Art Nouveau pearl and gold
necklace, French, floral theme
enhanced by pearls, set in 18k
yellow gold, French hallmarks,
12.90 g............................**$597**

Heritage Auctions

Art Nouveau 14k gold, enamel,
and seed pearl suite, Krementz
& Co., comprising pin and
earrings, maker's mark, pin 2",
earrings 1"......................**$1,225**

Skinner, Inc., www.skinnerinc.com

Art Nouveau gold, diamond, and enamel pendant, circa 1900,
designed as female figure with long flowing hair within lotus flowers
applied with pink and green ombré enamel, accented by old
European-cut diamonds weighing approximately .40 carat..........**$6,875**

Sotheby's

Group of antique and Art Nouveau 14k gold, gem-set, enamel and pearl jewelry, top row from left: gold, peridot, and split pearl pin; gold, amethyst, and seed pearl pin; middle: gold and cabochon amethyst chain, 48-3/8" l.; bottom: gold, peridot, freshwater pearl, and enamel lavaliere, 16-1/2" l **$1,500**

Doyle New York

Group of antique and Art Nouveau gold, enamel, pearl, and gem-set jewelry, 14k, clockwise from top left: amethyst, enamel, pearl, and diamond pendant-brooch; green enamel and pearl leaf pin; locket with one old mine-cut diamond; gold and diamond heart locket; miniature portrait enamel pendant-brooch **$1,375**

Doyle New York

Art Nouveau diamond, cultured pearl, enamel, and gold jewelry: black velvet choker with enamel and freshwater pearl elements in 14k gold; enameled flower brooch centering one freshwater pearl, 14k gold; enameled flower brooch with old European-cut diamond weighing approximately .05 carat, freshwater pearls, in 14k gold; 13.20 grams; choker 13" x 1"; one flower brooch 3/4" dia.; other flower brooch 1" x 7/8" **$750**

Heritage Auctions

EDWARDIAN

Edwardian diamond and platinum brooch, European-cut diamonds weighing approximately 4 carats, set in platinum, pinstem and catch, marked Gattle for E. M. Gattle, 19.33 g., 2" x 1-3/4" **$2,500**

Heritage Auctions

Edwardian seed pearl sautoir, woven strap suspending tassel with platinum and rose-cut diamond cap, 42" l., tassel 2-3/4" **$6,000**

Skinner, Inc., www.skinnerinc.com

Edwardian necklace, pearl, diamond, green stone, platinum and gold, strand of pearls with clasp with European-cut diamonds weighing approximately 0.45 carat, surrounded by green stones, set in platinum-topped 14k gold, 8.70 g., 20". **$750**

Heritage Auctions

Edwardian diamond and platinum-topped gold brooch, European-cut diamonds weighing approximately 1.50 carats, set in platinum-topped gold, pinstem and catch, 6.97 g., 2-1/2" x 1/2" **$750**

Heritage Auctions

Edwardian onyx and diamond dress set, France, pair of cufflinks and two shirt studs, each designed as onyx disk with platinum and rose-cut diamond basketweave motifs, 18k gold mounts, maker's mark and guarantee stamps **$1,800**

Skinner, Inc., www.skinnerinc.com

Edwardian platinum lorgnette, hinged and spring loaded, opens to reveal two circular-shaped spectacles, handle with flower design in platinum with black cord with 14k white gold clasp, 24.50 g. **$418**

Heritage Auctions

Edwardian diamond and gold pendant-brooch, French, pear-shaped diamond weighing approximately 0.90 carat, mine- and rose-cut diamonds, set in 18k white gold, 18k yellow gold pinstem and "C" catch on reverse, French hallmarks, total diamond weight approximately 3.50 carats, 17.20 g., 2-11/16" x 1-5/8" **$2,629**

Heritage Auctions

Edwardian fire opal and diamond ring set with cushion-cut opal approximately 14 mm x 11.70 mm x 5.10 mm, framed by rose-cut diamonds, rose-cut diamond shoulders, platinum-topped 18k gold mount, approximate size 5-1/2 (sizeable) **$5,100**

Skinner, Inc., www.skinnerinc.com

FINE JEWELRY

Diamond, blue enamel and gold bangle bracelet, Tiffany & Co., circa 1960, single-cut diamonds weighing approximately 1 carat, set in 18k white gold, blue enamel applied on 18k yellow gold, 6-1/2" l............**$2,270**

Heritage Auctions

Smokey quartz and gold bangle, circa 1970, emerald-cut smokey quartz 14 mm x 10 mm, set in 18k yellow gold, concealed box clasp with figure-eight safety, 7" x 1" **$5,377**

Heritage Auctions

Diamond and platinum pendant-brooch, circa 1950, full-cut diamonds weighing approximately 4 carats, baguette-cut diamonds weighing approximately 0.60 carat, set in platinum, retractable bail, pinstem and catch on reverse, total diamond weight approximately 4.60 carats, 1-3/4" x 1-1/2"... **$2,125**

Heritage Auctions

Turquoise, sapphire and gold bracelet, circa 1950, turquoise cabochons and round-cut sapphires set in 18k yellow gold, tongue-in-groove clasp with two figure-eight safeties, 7-1/4" x 1/2"......... **$4,780**

Heritage Auctions

Diamond and gem-set patriotic brooch, circa 1920, designed as ring of full-cut diamonds flanked by fancy-cut rubies and sapphires, platinum-topped 18k gold mount, 1-1/2" **$1,800**

Skinner, Inc., www.skinnerinc.com

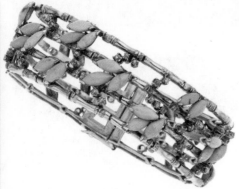

Ruby, turquoise and gold bracelet, circa 1950, bamboo themed, round-shaped rubies weighing approximately 1.60 carats, marquise-shaped turquoise cabochons, set in textured 14k gold, 6-1/2" x 1".. **$1,673**

Heritage Auctions

Diamond bracelet, France, circa 1940s, set with three old European-cut diamonds weighing approximately 1, 0.90, and 0.85 carats, with old European- and single-cut diamonds, approximate total weight 17 carats, rhodium-plated silver mount, French maker's mark and guarantee stamp, 7-1/4" l **$9,600**

Skinner, Inc., www.skinnerinc.com

Diamond and gold hinged bangle bracelet, Van Gogh, circa 1960, full-cut diamonds weighing approximately 0.70 carat, set in 14k white gold, applied on heavily textured 14k yellow gold, marked Van Gogh, 6-1/4" x 5/8".................. **$2,390**

Heritage Auctions

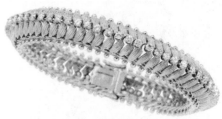

Diamond and gold bracelet, circa 1960, full-cut diamonds weighing approximately 3 carats, set in 18k white gold atop 18k gold links, 51.02 g., 7-1/8" x 1/2"... **$5,312**

Heritage Auctions

Turquoise and gold bracelets, circa 1960, fashioned with rope motif of turquoise beads measuring 3 mm, wire wrapped around textured 18k yellow gold links, forming soft bangles, box clasps with safeties, 7" x 1/2" **$2,151**

Heritage Auctions

Ruby, diamond and gold bracelet, circa 1960, full-cut diamonds weighing approximately 1.75 carats, alternating with round-cut rubies weighing approximately 2 carats, framed by Florentine finished 14k yellow gold chevron-shaped links, 7" x 3/4".. **$836**

Heritage Auctions

Diamond and platinum double-clip brooch, circa 1950, full-cut diamonds weighing approximately 1.40 carats, single-cut diamonds weighing approximately 5.90 carats, baguette-cut diamonds weighing approximately 2.35 carats, set in platinum, clip mechanisms on reverse; clips are joined by box catch with hinged locks. Total diamond weight for assembled double-clip brooch is approximately 9.65 carats; combined dimensions 2" x 2"...................................... **$5,000**

Heritage Auctions

Diamond, turquoise, cultured pearl, and gold brooch, circa 1950, round and oval-shaped turquoise cabochons ranging from 11.10 mm x 8.15 mm to 7 x 6.90 mm, cultured pearls ranging from 6.50-6 mm to 5.50-5 mm, full- and single-cut diamonds weighing approximately 0.20 carat, set in 18k white and yellow gold, pinstem and catch on reverse, 3-1/2" x 1-3/4". **$1,015**

Heritage Auctions

Diamond and pink and green gold brooch, 14k pink and green gold, 10.1 g., 47 mm x 30 mm, center diamond approximately .50 carat **$593**

Heritage Auctions

Multi-stone and gold brooch, circa 1970, designed as butterfly, modified rectangular-shaped citrine 27 mm x 17.85 mm x 11.60 mm and weighing approximately 33 carats, colored gemstones of varying shape and size, garnet, peridot, amethyst, citrine, and pink tourmaline, set in open wirework 14k yellow gold frame. **$448**

Heritage Auctions

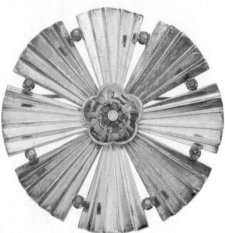

Retro ruby, diamond and two-tone gold brooch, circa 1940, flower design, round-cut rubies, single-cut diamond, set in 14k pink and yellow gold, pinstem and catch on reverse, 2-3/16" x 2-3/16".. **$478**

Heritage Auctions

Diamond and gold brooch, circa 1960, full-cut diamonds weighing approximately 1.10 carats, set in 18k gold, clip mechanism on reverse, 2-1/2" x 1-1/2".. **$687**

Heritage Auctions

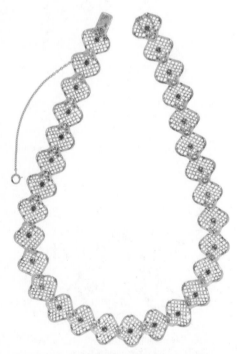

Diamond and gold dress set, circa 1960, includes one pair of cufflinks with full-cut diamonds, set in hand-engraved 14k gold, with three matching shirt studs; cufflinks 1-1/4" x 3/4"; shirt studs 1-1/8" x 7/16"... **$597**

Heritage Auctions

Sapphire and gold necklace, Ruser, circa 1960, round-cut sapphires weighing approximately 1.75 carats, set in 14k yellow gold openwork honeycomb links, concealed clasp with safety chain, signed Ruser, 15"... **$1,792**

Heritage Auctions

Gold and cultured pearl "fireworks" earclips, 18k, Tiffany & Co., signed, 1-1/8" **$1,020**

Skinner, Inc., www.skinnerinc.com

Diamond and gold earrings, circa 1960, organic, full-cut diamonds weighing approximately 1.20 carats, set en tremblant in 18k white gold against textured three-dimensional 18k yellow gold background, omega clips on reverse, designed for non-pierced ears, 1-1/4" x 1" **$1,045**

Heritage Auctions

Citrine and gold earrings, Paloma Picasso, Tiffany & Co., circa 1970, each with oval-shaped citrine weighing approximately 9.50 carats, bezel set in 18k yellow gold, omega clip back on reverse, marked Paloma Picasso for Tiffany & Co., 15/16" x 13/16" **$1,912**

Heritage Auctions

Bakelite bracelet, Flamand, Paris, gold tone cuff with green Bakelite and white stone surmount, signed, box inscribed, "Ma petite etoile Gina Taybery (?)," split to Bakelite, 6" interior circumference. In the 1930s, Flamand made several Bakelite bracelets as promotional devices for films, including one model for Josephine Baker's *ZouZou*... **$652**

Skinner, Inc., www.skinnerinc.com

Eleven-strand coral bead Torsade necklace with gold and diamond clasp, 18k, coral beads approximately 3 mm to 3.6 mm, 17-7/8" l ... **$1,625**

Doyle New York

Retro ruby, diamond, platinum and gold ring, circa 1940, full- and single-cut diamonds weighing approximately 0.50 carat, set in platinum, round-cut rubies, 3 mm and weighing approximately 1.80 carats, set in 14k pink gold, 1" x 3/4"..... **$507**

Heritage Auctions

Carnelian and 14k gold pendant-necklace, Walter Lampl, circa 1930s, pendant carved and pierced to depict mouse and berries, suspended from ribbed and polished circular links with floral and foliate carnelian tablets, signed WL, 15-1/2", drop 2-3/4" **$1,541**

Skinner, Inc., www.skinnerinc.com

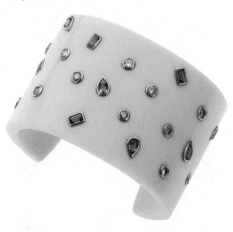

Colored diamond, smoky quartz, Bakelite and gold cuff bracelet, full-cut brown diamonds weighing approximately 2.25 carats, pear- and rectangular-shaped smoky quartz weighing approximately 3.90 carats, bezel set in 14k gold, inserted into Bakelite, 7" x 1-7/8" **$1,195**

Heritage Auctions

Star ruby, diamond, and platinum ring, circa 1950, oval-shaped star ruby, 8.10 mm x 7 mm x 3.80 mm and weighing approximately 2.30 carats, single-cut diamonds weighing approximately 0.55 carat, set in platinum, size 6-1/2 (sizeable)...... **$806**

Heritage Auctions

Kitchenware

EVERYONE KNOWS THAT THE KITCHEN is the hub of the home. So when the wildly successful "Downton Abbey" series streamed across television screens, the show's Edwardian kitchen became a visual primer on class and comfort in our increasingly uncertain times.

That vision not only riveted viewers to each "Downton Abbey" installment, but the show's anti-snobbery theme created a new market niche for antique kitchen collectibles.

When stoic butler Mr. Carson chides housekeeper Mrs. Hughes about a new-fangled electric toaster, antique dealers nationwide said vintage toasters flew off the shelves.

"We simply could not believe how much interest 'Downton Abbey' has sparked in antique kitchen utensils," said Rege Woodley, a retired antique dealer in Washington, Pennsylvania. "I sold one of my antique rolling pins to my neighbor for $100 because it looked like the one used by Mrs. Patmore, the cook in 'Downton Abbey.'"

Pat Greene, owner of Nothing New Antiques, said she is excited about all the "Downton Abbey" fuss and hopes her antique kitchenwares fetch some lasting prices, too. "My rolling pins usually go for $5 to $10, but I'm seeing a big rush on my cookie cutters," said Greene of Pittsburgh.

Mary Kirk of New Alexandria, Pennsylvania, said she collects old antique cookbooks and was especially interested in trying to prepare some of the food served in the "Downton Abbey" show. "I am extremely interested in trying to prepare the eggs poached with spinach – a dish

Silver-plated meat dome with handle, body of dome with botanical pattern, 19th century...**$170**

A.H. Wilkens Antiques & Appraisals

that poor young kitchen maid Daisy had to prepare during one show scene," said Kirk, a retired librarian. Because of the show's lengthy shooting schedule, producers have reported that most of the food served during production consists of light salads.

Jimmy Roark of Nashville, Tennessee, said he has not seen as large a rush for his kitchen collectibles as a result of the show. "What I see is a more gradual demand for these items," said Roark, who operates a small antique collectible shop in his garage. "I sell a lot of my cookie cutters, antique wooden bowls, and vintage mixer beaters during the holidays."

Still, the "Downton Abbey" magic continues to seed interest in a broad swath of antique kitchen utensils and artifacts from Bennington mixing bowls to turn-of-the-century tiger wood rolling pins.

Stephen White of White &White Antiques & Interiors of Skaneateles, New York, said interest in vintage antique kitchenware remains steady. At the ninth annual Antique Show at Oakmont Country Club March 9-10, 2013, near Pittsburgh, kitchenwares were front and center with collectors. The show, a benefit for the Kerr Memorial Museum, sports a broad mix of antiques for all ages.

White was quick to feature his rare whale ivory crested Nantucket rolling pin valued at $425. "I have unusual kitchen antiques from hand food choppers to copper pots," said White.

Other dealers at the Oakmont show featured kitchen antiques from old historical companies instrumental in the economic growth of western Pennsylvania.

"When you think of Pittsburgh, you can't escape the long history that the H.J. Heinz Co. has here," said Toni Bahnak of Candlewood Antiques in Ardara, Pennsylvania. "We have rare old vinegar bottles and ketchup bottles that denote an era when the Heinz Co. made its own glass," said Bahnak.

And industry experts say ketchup and pickle collectibles will continue to soar in value because of the recent business deal that saw the H.J. Heinz Co. announce a $23.3 billion deal to be purchased by Warren Buffett's Berkshire Hathaway and 3G Capital, which was co-founded by Jorge Lemann, one of Brazil's richest men.

Even before the blockbuster deal was announced, some Heinz memorabilia collectors

Group of three Holt Howard lidded containers for Russian, French and Italian salad dressings, circa 1950s, excellent condition. **$219**

Midwest Auction Galleries

Eggbeater, silver No. 3, embossed glass measure with cast iron mechanism, excellent condition, 13" h. x 4" sq.. **$175**

Rich Penn Auctions

Modern Kitchen Collectibles

The diverse area of kitchenware/household objects offers a world of collecting opportunities. Your interests may lead you to antique rarities more than 100 years old or to items of more recent manufacture. Any and all territory should be considered fair game. As with other collectibles, your primary motivation should be your individual likes and preferences.

There is a great deal of interest in kitchenware and related items from 35 to 60 years old; these objects rekindle old memories and represent a different, less-complicated era for many. They represent a broad spectrum of kitchen items and cooking activities. These include just about every task you would want to try to master in your kitchen of yesteryear. There are gadgets of all types and all sorts of accessories, sets, holders, and miscellaneous gizmos. Most of the items are non-electrical and small in scale.

For more information on kitchen collectibles, see *Spiffy Kitchen Collectibles* or *Warman's Kitschy Kitchen Collectibles Field Guide*, both by Brian S. Alexander.

reported that their antique bottles and jars were fetching higher prices than normal.

"I had one of my antique vinegar bottles sell for about $225 and I think I could have gotten more for it," said Ruth Oslet, an antique collector from Waynesburg, Pennsylvania. She sold it to a marketing executive who collects business memorabilia.

Tom Purdue, a long-time collector of food company antiques, said history and nostalgia play an important role in what people remember and want to save for their modern kitchens. "I can remember the distinct smell of my grandmother's old pickle jars and Heinz horseradish in her musty old kitchen where she used a hand pump to wash dishes," said Purdue, an 89-year-old former blacksmith from Wheeling, West Virginia.

The ever-expanding business reaches back to 1869 when Henry John Heinz and neighbor L. Clarence Noble began selling grated horseradish, bottled in clear glass to showcase its purity. It wasn't until 1876 that the company introduced its flagship product, marketing the country's first commercial ketchup.

Large copper cooking pot made in Austria in 19th century, with lid plus two iron handles, fair condition, with signs of age and use, superficial scratches, pot 10-1/4" h. x 8-2/3" dia....... **$235**

Auctionata

Not all history, though, is tied to corporate America. Family memories still stoke the embers of home cooking although many young people today find fast food the fuel of the future.

"I still have my family's old cornbread recipe and I use it all the time," said Elizabeth Schwan, gallery director for Aspire Auctions in Pittsburgh.

Schwan, who scans the country for antiques, admits she has a soft spot for old kitchen utensils. "Flower-sifters, antique copper mixing bowls, and rolling pins were all part of my heritage because my family grew up on a Kentucky farm," Schwan said. "I can still smell the homemade bread and jams."

And like most farm families, the kitchen served as a meeting place and refuge from a long day's work. "Between verbal debates about what to plant on the south flats, we would help our parents churn butter and chop wood for the old country stove," said Myrtle Bench, 91, of Washington, Pennsylvania.

But as a young America turned from the agricultural frontier in the late 1890s and began to embrace a manufacturing economy, automation replaced handcrafts, and the kitchen became a new testing ground for a variety of modern gizmos like the automatic dishwasher.

The automatic dishwasher was a toy for the rich when an electric model was introduced on 1913 by Willard and Forrest Walker, two Syracuse, New York brothers who ran a hardware store when they were not tinkering with kitchen machines. The new dishwasher sold for $120 (the equivalent of $1,429 in today's dollars), a hefty premium over the $20 the Walkers charged for their popular hand-cranked model and also more expensive than a gasoline-powered washer the brothers put on the market in 1911.

"You can still find some of the old hand-crank washers, but I like to spend my time finding kitchen utensils that reflect how people prepared their food," said Dirk Hayes, a freelance cook from Uniontown, Pennsylvania. "I love watching 'Downton Abbey' because the kitchen scenes really give you a flavor of how the food was prepared. I never had that kind of staff, but it's fun to dream," said Hayes, who collects rolling pins and antique carving knives.

—*Chriss Swaney*

Two pewter flagons, distressed condition, shorter flagon beefeater style, circa 1680, with collar of plain drum later shaped to form spout, flared flat base, single-curve handle with ownership triad RCA, 9-3/4" h.; taller flagon with late 17th century Charles I style "bun" lid with pseudo hallmarks, lower incised lines to tapering drum, ovulo molded foot and hollow base, and single-curve handle with shield terminal, 11-1/2" h. **$1,046**

Bonhams

Crandall and Godley hand-crank mixer, New York, circa late 19th century to early 20th century, iron and tin, side-mounted crank operates internal beaters, 12" h. **$90**

Garth's Auctioneers & Appraisers

Clarice Cliff geometric-pattern duck stand and four eggcups, stand with printed Bizarre facsimile signature mark, cups with Newport Pottery marks only, two eggcups with tiny enamel flakes to top rims. ... **$674**

Fine Art, Antiques & Collectables

Art Deco green ceramic enameled coffee set from Mexico, 20th century, octagonal coffee pot (shown), lidded sugar and creamer and four cups with four saucers that depict figures of men, women, burros and dog in tropical landscape, minor flakes, glazing cracks and firing flaws. **$177**

Brunk Auctions

Vintage coffee grinder with wooden base and drawer. **$35**

Farmer Auctions

Late 19th century springerle maple rolling pin, American or European, shallow carved grid with animals, plants, figures and sets of initial, 16" l. **$147**

Garth's Auctioneers & Appraisers

Cheese strainer with bentwood rim and punched rawhide base, circa 19th century, age splits, 3-1/2" h. x 19" dia. **$30**

Garth's Auctioneers & Appraisers

Charles II triple-reed pewter charger, circa 1675, hallmarks to rim of Anthony James, London, together with unrecorded touchmark, crowned rose mark to rear side, 23-1/4". **$1,682**

Bonhams

English silver-plated egg cruet set with four eggcups and coordinating spoons, footed tray with slots that hold each spoon in place, fluted eggcups with twisted design in body of cup and pedestal base. **$138**

A.H. Wilkens Antiques & Appraisals

Glazed redware muffin pan, 12" w. x 17-1/2 l. **$190**

Alderfer Auction & Appraisal

Dazey Churn No. 40 butter churn and one-quart butter churn, taller churn 14" h. ... **$100**

Clars Auction Gallery

Two oblong and two square lidded refrigerator dishes, pink Depression glass, no distinguishing marks; square boxes 4-1/4" sq. x 3-1/4" h., each box with roughness on interior lid rim, rectangular dishes 8-1/2" l. x 4-1/4" w. x 3-1/4" h., age-appropriate wear, each lid with minor roughness and chips on bottom of rim. **$60**

Dargate Auction Galleries

18th century William And Mary wooden dough box, rectangular canted sides with dovetail joints, raised on block-and-turned supports, with removable lid, 29" h. x 42" w. x 22" d. **$188**

Doyle New York

Collection of string holders and three advertising-themed match safes, American, late 19th century/early 20th century: Juicy Fruit and Universal Stoves and Ranges safes each 4-3/4" h. x 3-1/4" w.; Elmer Benson Dry Goods safe 5-1/4" h. x 2-1/4" w.; string holder advertises Sunny Monday laundry soap, Gold Dust washing powder and Fairy soap, 8-1/4" h. x 8-1/2" w. **$420**

Garth's Auctioneers & Appraisers

Seven 19th century English pewter measures, three half-pints, one gill and three smaller sizes ranging from 2" h. to 3-3/4" h. **$235**

Garth's Auctioneers & Appraisers

Cobalt blown-glass canister with tin lid, American, mid-19th century, 6-3/4" h. x 3" dia... **$147**

Garth's Auctioneers & Appraisers

American butter churn with dasher and lid, pine stave-construction with original green paint, latter 19th century, 22" h. **$323**

Garth's Auctioneers & Appraisers

Treenware mortar and pestle with traces of red paint and three rolling pins, one smooth-surfaced pin made of curly maple wood, one grooved-surface lefse pin, and one ravioli rolling pin, American, 19th/early 20th century. **$240**

Garth's Auctioneers & Appraisers

Small redware pie plate decorated with tulip pattern in two-tone slip, including green, American, mid-19th century, entire rim colored in, with overspray, edge flakes, 8" dia. **$720**

Garth's Auctioneers & Appraisers

Wooden flour sifter raised on cut-out feet, good condition with moderate wear to frame, 12-1/2" h. x 11" d. x 9" w... **$184**

Jeffrey S. Evans & Associates

Universal No. E9410 Sweetheart Electric Toaster, circa 1920, nickeled metal and Bakelite with expected wear to finish, original tag remains under base, 8-1/2" h. **$184**

Jeffrey S. Evans & Associates

Pink and white vertically striped cotton apron, knee length, ties at waist, patch pocket. Provenance: From the estate of Greta Garbo..................... **$1,000**

Julien's Auctions

Eight-footed Rookwood pottery trivet, #1212, circa 1952, with Rookwood mark, with Rookwood pottery creamer (dated 1954) and sugar bowl style #1947, signed, areas of crazing on trivet, trivet 5-3/4" sq. x 3/4" h.. **$123**

Gray's Auctioneers

Victorian cast-iron bottle opener, Champion, marked "Made in USA." **$225**

Grogan & Co.

Wooden kitchen tools including maple bread board with wheat-pattern carved decorations around edges, screw-cap acorn-form nutmeg grater, and two Shaker-style biscuit cutters, 19th to 20th century, grater with cracks and losses, other pieces in excellent condition, board 11-3/4 dia. **$115**

Jeffrey S. Evans & Associates

Early 20th century American graniteware pudding mold, lobed mold with "Agate L&G Mfg Co" mark stamped on mold, 4-1/4" h. x 8-3/4" l. x 6-3/4" w. **$24**

Garth's Auctioneers & Appraisers

Blue enamelware kitchen utensil set, first-quarter 20th century, dipper, ladle and skimmer, each with hooked handle, hanging on matching wall rack, very good condition, with few losses to enamel at edges, 21" x 12-1/2".......... **$173**

Jeffrey S. Evans & Associates

Signed "Chatham" wrought iron and cast iron waffle iron, long scissor-like handles with hooking lock, old natural surface, good, as-found condition, light rust and pitting, circa 1800-1850, 28-1/2" l.. **$35**

Jeffrey S. Evans & Associates

Early 20th century hand-crank ice cream maker, American, stave-constructed bucket with original green paint and cast-iron crank, bale handle, 13-1/2" h. **$47**

Garth's Auctioneers & Appraisers

Juice-O-Mat aluminum juicer, Rival Mfg Co., mid-20th century, American, 8-1/2" h. x 6" w. at base............**$25**

Garth's Auctioneers & Appraisers

Three 19th century American wrought iron broilers and trivet, revolving broilers 14", 23" and 25" l., handled trivet 23-1/2" l. **$540**

Garth's Auctioneers & Appraisers

Wrought iron kitchen utensils, American, 19th century, Ladle, fork, spatula and pan, 13" l. to 22" l. **$150**

Garth's Auctioneers & Appraisers

Thames black Americana figural pottery grease jar, metal handle on yellow hat serves as jar's lid, jar styled to look like clown, raised on three feet, Patent Pending and Thames sticker on bottom, crazing through glaze and paint loss consistent with age, 5" h. x 5" dia. **$94**

Midwest Auction Galleries

Rare Clarice Cliff Gibraltar pattern conical sugar sifter, gilt printed Lawleys retailer's mark, small firing crack, minor scuffs to enamels, 5-1/2 h....**$835**

Gorringes

Six toasters in varying styles. **$100**

Grogan & Co.

Holt Howard Pixieware lidded cocktail condiment containers for olives, cherries and onions, circa late 1960s, mint condition, each container 5" h.....**$196**

Midwest Auction Galleries

Five cast iron cooking implements, including waffle iron, muffin tin and broiler, 20th century, good overall condition with some rust, broiler 16" l..**$58**

Jeffrey S. Evans & Associates

Double-sided carved wooden cake board, one side with running horse wearing saddle and ornate foliage, other with bust of "Leopold" and cupid medallion, age cracks and insect damage, 19th century, 13" h. x 23-1/4" l............................ **$546**

Jeffrey S. Evans & Associates

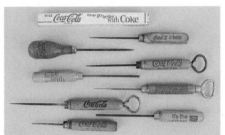

Group of eight Coca-Cola ice picks, three with bottle openers on opposite end, excellent condition with light wear overall, largest 11" l. **$84**

Morphy Auctions

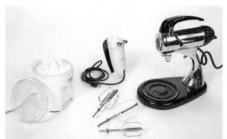

Sunbeam Mixmaster stand mixer with two chrome beaters. Provenance: From the estate of Greta Garbo **$100**

Julien's Auctions

Two sets of matching turned ivory pepper grinders and salt shakers, 20th century, tallest 4-1/4" h., 2" dia... **$369**

New Orleans Auction Galleries

Cast iron kitchen implements including two potato peelers and two cherry seeders, fair to good condition with some rust, late 19th to early 20th century, 6-1/2" to 10". **$184**

Jeffrey S. Evans & Associates

Five 19th century Pennsylvania sheet-iron figural cookie cutters, including wood chopper, man with hat, and reindeer with large eye, each with pierced back, very good condition overall, largest 9" x 4-1/4".. **$374**

Jeffrey S. Evans & Associates

Opaque white refrigerator-form salt and pepper shakers with matching grease jar, early 20th century, undamaged, shakers 3" h., grease jar 5" h... **$127**

Jeffrey S. Evans & Associates

American nine-drawer spice box with lollipop-form splash (split) pierced for hanging, late 19th century, each drawer with porcelain and brass pull, 18" h. x 13" w. $236

Midwest Auction Galleries

Antique cast iron wood fire cookstove, "Magee Clinton" No. 88 by Magee Furnace Co., Boston, Massachusetts, late 19th/early 20th century, approximately 71" h. x 43" w. x 32-1/2" d. $1,200

O'Gallerie

Vintage European cookstove with blue ceramic tiles. $210

Sandwich Auction House

Hamilton Beach teal enamel and chrome mixer, circa 1930s-1940s, very good overall condition, six mixer cups in 18/8 heavy-duty stainless steel, one is original, plus larger-size mixer, 18-1/4" h. $59

Midwest Auction Galleries

Enterprise coffee grinder, fourth quarter 19th century, side wheels signed "Enterprise Mfg. Co., Philadelphia U.S.A., Pat'd Dec. 9, 1873," 12-1/4" h. x 10" w. x 8-3/4" d. $338

New Orleans Auction Galleries

Hinged ice cream mold shaped like golfer, pewter, golfer's face (including mustache) and button-down jacket, knickers and plaid socks, circa 1920s.................$48

PBA Galleries Auctions & Appraisers

Sunkist electric juicer, circa 1920s-1930s, works, very good condition, with general medium plating loss and wear, 16" h..$210

Morphy Auctions

Large levered ice cream scoop by S. Geer Co., excellent working condition, 14-3/4" l..$72

Morphy Auctions

Wooden plunger-style butter mold with wheat stalk pattern, excellent condition, 4-1/2" dia. $96

Morphy Auctions

KITCHENWARE

Six pewter and tin ice food molds, early 20th century, six-rabbit chocolate mold, 8-3/4" h. x 9" w.; tin rooster chocolate mold, 12-1/2" h. x 7" w.; tin rabbit chocolate mold, 7-1/4" h. x 5-1/4" w.; pewter pear-form ice cream mold, 3-1/2" h.; pewter apple-form ice cream mold marked CG, 2-1/4" h.; pewter lemon-form ice cream mold marked Schall & Co., 3" h. x 3" w................... **$153**

New Orleans Auction Galleries

Three yellowware mixing bowls with spouts, circa 1910, various patterns, one bowl with white interior, some chips and hairline cracks, 12" to 14" dia... **$400**

Thomaston Place Auction Galleries

Yellowware lobster match safe, impressed AT, striker located inside lid, 5-1/2" l. **$110**

William H. Bunch Auctions

Josef Hoffman hand-hammered brass tray, signed with impressed manufacturer's mark to underside (Wiener Werkstatte JH Made In Austria), circa 1925, 14-1/2" w. x 7" d. x 2-1/4" h. **$2,750**

Wright Auctions & Appraisers

Assorted cast iron cooking implements, including Eureka folding griddle and Triumph broiler, late 19th century/early 20th century, good condition overall with some minor rust, griddle 5-1/2" x 14"... **$35**

Jeffrey S. Evans & Associates

Three-piece ceramic canister set in graduated sizes, Torquay pattern, each canister with wooden top and brass feet, coordinating decorated trivet, marked "MacKenzie-Childs, Ltd., 1983, Aurora, New York."... **$600**

Northgate Gallery

Set of three Russel Wright Oceana carved and stained maple serving trays, Klise Woodworking, United States of America, 1935, branded signature to underside of each, largest 15" w. x 15" dia. x 1-1/4" h...................................... **$4,688**

Wright Auctions

Beldings National oak icebox with paneled front, sides and back, various applied carvings and beveled oval mirror, corner columns with roaring lion heads and large paw feet, brass maker's tag, excellent condition, 56" h. x 29" w. x 19" d. **$3,300**

Rich Penn Auctions

Twenty pieces of kitchen-related pottery, seven glazed and sponge-decorated pottery pitchers, 11 glazed and banded yellow ware kitchen bowls, glazed ovoid redware jug with cover, and small glazed redware jug with handle. **$325**

Skinner, Inc., www.skinnerinc.com

Art Deco-styled universal waffle iron. **$28**

Theodore Bruce Auctions

One embroidered organza apron and two lace-trimmed aprons, 1800s era............................. **$20**

The Gallery at Knotty Pine

English copper and metal plate warmer, W.A.S. Benson, circa 1900, fitted with scalloped, D-shaped copper panel supporting two metal trivets raised on out-set legs, 22" h. x 12" d. x 11" w. **$200**

Stair Auctioneers & Appraisers

Mid-20th century Sunbeam Mixmaster with beaters and two glass mixing bowls. **$50**

Theodore Bruce Auctions

Chrome and Bakelite spherical coffee urn by Manning-Bowman, Meriden, Connecticut, circa 1935, missing cord, percolator stem, grounds basket, some discoloration to Bakelite at base, 14-1/2" h. **$225**

Thomaston Place Auction Galleries

Lighting

COLORED GLASS LOOKS BEAUTIFUL when it's illuminated, and therein lays the problem. In the case of leaded glass, or stained glass lamps, even poorly designed, cheaply made examples look attractive when the lights go on, making it critically important to be able to look beyond the pretty colors when determining any lamp's aesthetic, structural and intrinsic value.

Despite less than acceptable condition, some lamps will retain a good portion of their value due to their pedigree. A rare Tiffany or Duffner & Kimberley lamp, for instance, will still hold great value despite conditions that would otherwise render an unknown maker's lamp depreciated.

Here are 10 things you should consider when looking at or buying a leaded glass lamp. These are not the end-all and be-all of qualitative evaluations, but should form a reliable framework to better recognize quality in leaded glass lamps.

Overall Beauty

This may seem obvious, but a lamp can display beauty in any number of ways; it can be colorful (the most disarming of qualities); it can be pretty (again, sometimes disarming); it can be fascinating (due to the glass pattern or design); or it can be downright stunning when all of the visual characteristics of its shape, design, color, pattern, and aesthetics gel into one harmonious delight.

Design Excellence

Conscientious lamp designers instinctively address certain design conventions when outlining artwork to be translated onto a three-dimensional lamp mold. One primary consideration is how the design assumes the shape of the lamp. Are large flat pieces of glass expected to span a tight curvature of the form, or are the pieces sized to

Illus. 1

assume the shape gracefully, giving the impression that the glass is bent? Poor designers overlook this condition, resulting in lamps whose surfaces seem rough, jagged and harsh to the touch.

Lamp designs are based on components such as border, background, primary image, secondary image, support elements (stems and flower buds, for instance), and geometrics. Any number of these can be combined to create a design. The more intelligent the use of these elements, the more elegant the result, be it a pure geometric or an intensely naturalistic design (Illus. 1).

Another design factor to consider is flow. Does the design sit comfortably on the shape of the lamp? Are lead lines jagged or out of character with the rest of the design? Are there areas of awkward dead space between design elements? If the design repeats itself,

LIGHTING

which many do, are the repeats balanced and seamless? A simple spinning of the shade on its base will tell. In more elaborate designs, do the elements such as borders and geometric areas enhance the viewing experience or do they compete with the primary imagery, whatever that may be? A basic sense of these relationships is helpful when evaluating the many aesthetic properties of lamp design.

Choice of Glass

Strong, contrasting colors can be attractive. For the longest time, production lamp manufacturers were aware that combining a neutral background glass such as bone, beige or amber, some pretty opal colors for flower or image glass, and a strong leaf green was a slam dunk of successful color selection. I can't begin to tell you how many leaded glass lamps have been crafted over the last century using this simple recipe of coloration. Compare a lamp of this caliber (Illus. 2) with one where the selection of color, tone and texture is sensitive and painterly (Illus. 3).

Illus. 2

Illus. 3

Types of Glass

Two major types of glass dominate the leaded glass lamp landscape: mass-produced, machine-made glass and hand-rolled or art glass. Both are opalescent rather than translucent. Machine-made glass appears very uniform and consistent in color. It portrays very little variance of depth, tone or movement; it tends to look flat. Although some examples have good light to dark areas, machine-made glass provides a very two-dimensional visual experience. Hand-rolled art glass, in which case no two pieces of glass can ever be the same due to their handcrafted nature, when carefully selected portrays all of the values and visual excitement of a well-executed painting. Depth, shadow, intense light to dark transitions and strong movement of color within the individual pieces of glass prove a very satisfying, dimensional visual experience. At its best, you can easily forget that you are looking at glass.

Structural Integrity

You must judge a lamp not only when it is lit and at its most disarming, but also when it is unlit and off its base, when all of its scars, warts and flaws are visible and tangible. A well-crafted lamp should feel sturdy and substantial when in hand – not flimsy. If light pressure to the widest expanse of the shade results in flexing, it is reasonable to believe that the shade has not been properly reinforced during construction. Proper reinforcement here would consist of a rod or thick wire of brass or copper set and soldered onto the bottom edge. This also applies to the upper opening or aperture of the shade. If the lamp is built to sit on a ring or base support, and has a opening at the top to accommodate such, this area of the lamp should be properly reinforced with a strong band of metal preferably made of copper or brass and be intact. The aperture of the lamp should also be free from any damage that may render the opening a threat to the safety of the lamp (Illus. 4).

If the lamp has a finial or heat cap fastened to its aperture, that fitting should be properly fastened to a metal reinforcement at the opening and not simply to the copper-foiled glass border. The latter usually results in the cap or finial pulling away from the shade in reaction to heat from lightbulbs building up at the top of the shade. If this occurs, it is possible that the lead/tin solder used in securing the fitting could gradually soften and fail. The full weight of the shade pulling down on this joint compounds the problem. This type of repair or restoration can prove expensive, especially if the damage includes the upper row of glass. Ideally, support should come from underneath the aperture. It is important to remember that the most vulnerable parts of any leaded glass lamp are its aperture and bottom edge.

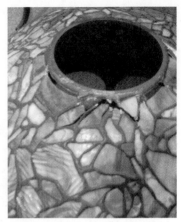

Illus. 4

Quality Craftsmanship

Many skills come together in the construction and crafting of a leaded glass lamp: glass cutting, glass shaping, copper foiling, assembly, soldering and finishing, among others. Knowing how to examine the execution of each of these component skills is necessary to evaluate not only the quality of a leaded glass lamp but also its physical condition and the possibility for any restoration or repair.

First and foremost: Are the individual pieces of glass cut and shaped accurately? If examining a geometric lamp, or section of a lamp that includes geometrics, do the resulting leaded lines line up, or are the crossing lines mismatched or carelessly assembled? Are curved lines smooth? Are border pieces either at the top or bottom, or both, set straight? A skillful glass cutter or glazier is careful to create pieces that accurately reflect the pattern or template used without creating pieces that have irregular edges or are bigger or smaller than the template. Additionally, a skillful assembler will position each glass piece carefully – in its proper position according to the established design.

Illus. 5

Each piece of glass in a leaded glass lamp has its edges wrapped with a thin copper foil to facilitate assembly. This foil should be applied so the resulting lead lines are consistent in size. Lead lines that vary from thin to wide or are unusually wide throughout are telltale signs of shoddy workmanship, or areas of poor repair technique (Illus. 5).

A lead/tin-based solder is used to join each piece of glass to its neighbor and to fill the gaps between each piece of glass with a smooth, slightly mounded bead of solder. Rough, blotchy, lumpy or inconsistent solder lines are, again, a sign of shoddy workmanship, or if isolated, signs of less-than-professional repair or restoration (Illus. 6). The character of the lead lines should be

Illus. 6

LIGHTING

consistent throughout the shade. It should be noted that many lamp makers favor the outside, or "show" side, of the shade, and the quality of the lead lines may vary from the inside to the outside of the shade, reflecting this preference.

Patina and Finish

Patina is the color produced on the metal surfaces of the lamp, i.e., the lead lines, top and bottom edges and any added components to the lamp such as filigree or finials. Patina finishes will vary from light to dark brown, to a combination of brown and green (this finish being, historically, the most desirable) to black. On a well-preserved lamp, or one that has been professionally repaired or restored, the patina color will be consistent throughout. The color should be uniform, and there should be no areas where the patina color is either missing or wrong.

Base and Shade Proportions

The marriage of shade and base should be pleasing to the eye. Most importantly, does the shade sit properly on its base? Does it seem to tilt to the left or right? This could be a sign of damage or the shade's aperture joint being compromised. Such defects are subject to expensive repair. Beyond that, is the marriage a good one? Simply put, the diameter of the shade in relation to the height and width of the base should not look extreme or unsteady in any way (Illus. 7).

Illus. 7

Comparison to Other Examples

Many leaded glass lamp designs were made in multiples utilizing the same design, templates and mold to make similar models that differed in color and mood. Comparisons to the same models by the same maker are useful in determining whether the item in question lives up to or surpasses those it compares to. A little research through auction catalogs and books is indispensable when making these comparisons.

Provenance

Finally, where did the shade come from? Can its history be traced? Is it a contemporary shade or a reproduction? Has it been repaired or restored? Was the work done by a well-known craftsperson or a hobbyist? The availability of this information would certainly be valuable.

Developing a working knowledge of leaded glass lamps and how they are designed and constructed is an ongoing process. These few guidelines are a good place to start to ensure that your choice and/or purchase of a leaded glass lamp – whether privately, through a gallery, or at auction – will be an informed and intelligent one.

—Joseph Porcelli, Porcelli Studio

Illustrations 1 and 3 courtesy James D. Julia, Inc. Illustrations 2, 4, 5, 6, 7 courtesy Porcelli Studio.

EARLY LIGHTING

LIGHTING

Panel-Optic peg lamp, cranberry urn-form font with yellow enamel scroll decoration, brass candlestick stem, No. 2 period collar, late 19th/early 20th century, 13-3/4" h. to top of shade, 3" sq. base..**$192**

Jeffrey S. Evans & Associates

Paneled miniature finger lamp, light purple, footed, period burner, fourth quarter 19th/early 20th century, 7-5/8" h......**$36**

Jeffrey S. Evans & Associates

Molded satin glass miniature lamp, cased dark to light rose, hexagonal ribbed and pinched waist font on circular base, matching colored umbrella-form shade with fleur-de-lis pattern and crimped rim, period No. 1 collar, fitted with period Kosmos slip burner, shade ring, and chimney, late 19th/early 20th century, 12-1/2" to top of shade...........**$216**

Jeffrey S. Evans & Associates

Sheet-iron Ipswitch Betty lamp, crimped-rim tray with attached strap ring handle, cylinder-form stem on saucer base, original chain with hook and pick, 19th century, 10-3/4" h. x 6-1/4" dia. base. **$108**

Jeffrey S. Evans & Associates

Pressed Loop/Leaf stand lamps, deep peacock green, each dome-top six-loop font with lower double step and knop extension, raised on octagonal baluster-form standard and square base, wafer construction, pewter fine-line collars and double-tube whale oil burners, 1840-1860, 9-3/4" to top of collars...........**$10,200**

Jeffrey S. Evans & Associates

Mini skater's lantern, brass frame with medium amethyst globe, very good to excellent condition, 7" h. **$316**

James D. Julia, Inc.

Ribbed swirl air-trap mother-of-pearl satin glass miniature lamp, light green to yellow and raspberry to greenish yellow, conical crimped-top shade, base with polished pontil mark, period Spar Brenner type burner marked "The Silber Light Comp," attributed to Stevens & Williams, fourth quarter 19th/early 20th century, 9" to top of shade. **$4,800**

Jeffrey S. Evans & Associates

Bisque skeleton figural miniature lamp, fired décor in lavender, black, gray and light blue shadowing, head serves as shade with green glass eyes, base with lavender collar and tie, period burner and chimney, fourth quarter 19th/early 20th century, 5-1/2" to top of shade. **$1,920**

Jeffrey S. Evans & Associates

LIGHTING

$

Pierced and punched sheet-iron candle lantern, cylindrical form with strap handle, large circles with bars and dots within large framed pattern, conical-form top with additional socket fitting for external candle, hinged door with hasp and single socket to interior, 19th century, 16" h. **$228**

Jeffrey S. Evans & Associates

TOP LOT!

Burmese acorn and oak leaf miniature lamp, plush finish, decorated in green, rust, brown and yellow, squat base with matching ball shade, period Spar Brenner type burner marked "The Silber Light Comp" and chimney, attributed to Thomas Webb & Sons, fourth quarter 19th/early 20th century, 6-1/4" to top of shade........ **$4,200**

Jeffrey S. Evans & Associates

English cameo miniature, rare white, pink and citron double overlay, conical shape shade decorated with daisies and butterfly, squatty base decorated with flowering vine and butterfly, raised on three frosted applied feet, polished pontil, burner marked "The Silber Light Comp," attributed to Stevens & Williams, fourth quarter 19th/early 20th century, 7-3/4" to top of shade. **$15,600**

Jeffrey S. Evans & Associates

Tiffany candlestick and shade, bronze candlestick with tripod legs with lily pad feet resting on bronze disc, candlestick supports reactive glass shade with vertically ribbed body and gold iridescent finish, when lit, shade displays brick red color in loops and swirls, 20-3/4" to top of shade........ **$3,259**

James D. Julia, Inc.

Brass and tin miner's safety lamp, brass plaque marked "Protector Lamp & Lighting Co. Ltd.,: Eccles Manchester type M. C. 40, No. 38," 9-1/2" h. **$242**

Conestoga Auction Company

Diamond Quilt air-trap mother-of-pearl satin glass miniature lamp, cased yellow, matching crimped-top ball shade, base with three applied frosted feet and polished pontil mark, period Spar Brenner type burner marked "The Silber Light Comp," fourth quarter 19th/early 20th century, 7-3/4" to top of shade. **$4,500**

Jeffrey S. Evans & Associates

Pattern-molded with satin finish peg lamp, cased dark to light yellow, melon form with fleur-de-lis pattern, No. 1 collar, fitted with period setup comprising Zimmerman & Co. No. 1 slip burner, shade ring, and dark to light yellow umbrella-form shade with swirled ribbed and acanthus pattern, late 19th/early 20th century, 4-7/8 h. with shade. **$270**

Jeffrey S. Evans & Associates

Victorian cranberry hobnail glass oil lamp light fixture with adjustable height, 19th century, with original fittings and electrified modifications, 38" h. x 17" w. **$400**

Gray's Auctioneers

Antique kerosene/oil lamp, light green pattern glass, 9-1/2" h. $50

TW Conroy, LLC

Anker light lantern, hand blown glass, early 20th century, approximately 16" h. $121

Estate Auction Co.

Victorian table lamp with brass and jewels in green, yellow, blue, red, and amethyst, 17" h., shade approximately 9-1/2" dia..............$100

Beane's Antiques & Photography

Brass masthead light, 19th century, 21"...$207

Kaminski Auctions

Nautical anchor light, Clark Brothers, London, 22" h. $118

Kaminski Auctions

Victorian hanging oil lamp lighting fixture, glass body and shade with adjustable chains to raise and lower height, decorated with floral motif, prisms, 34" h. $60

Cleveland Auction Co.

Fairy lamp on peg stand, cut glass shade and stem in cross hatch pattern, lamp rests on square stepped brass foot, finished with Clarks Cricklite base marked "Clarks Patent Trademark Cricklite," 13" h.....$243

James D. Julia, Inc.

Cornelius & Co. solar lamps with brass stepped base with ruffled and ribbed floral shaped stem supporting white opalescent shaft with applied light blue ribbing, finished with solar lamp font with applied brass tag "Cornelius & Co. Philad. July 24th. 1849 Patent April 1st. 1845," each lamp with frosted cut to clear reproduction shade, 31" h. $1,955

James D. Julia, Inc.

Bohemian glass fluid lamp with marble double step foot with vertically ribbed brass stem supporting Bohemian etched glass font decorated with three cartouche designs with crisscross pattern within, each separated by woodland scene, one with deer, one with grouse, and one with gazebo, 14" h. $122

James D. Julia, Inc.

Cut overlay fluid lamp with cut overlay font of red cut to white cut to clear, font rests on brass stem supported by double step marble base, 12-3/4" h. $178

James D. Julia, Inc.

Early railroad lantern with blue lights, signed D.L. & WRR (Delaware, Lackawanna & Western Railroad), together with Dietz NY railroad lantern. **$210**

Hyde Park Country Auctions

Two art glass oil lamps with swirled opalescent bodies, gold and blue opalescence with pink and blue highlights, each lamp signed "Fiske," one 5-1/2" dia. and other 6-1/4" dia. **$237**

James D. Julia, Inc.

Fairy lamp epergne with clear crystal inverted saucer foot supporting brass stem that houses two vases and leads to fairy lamp, vases clear blown glass with single band of applied rigaree, fairy lamp with clear shade and topped by original silk shade with wooden bead dangles, shade marked on inside metal fitter "Cricklite," 17" h. **$1,126**

James D. Julia, Inc.

Princess feather footed finger lamp, light blue, molded handle, No. 1 Taplin-Brown collar, fitted with period No. 1 slip burner and chimney with bead top, late 19th/early 20th century, 5-5/8" to top of collar, 3-5/8" base. **$510**

Jeffrey S. Evans & Associates

Rare mini lamp, blue satin diamond quilt mother-of-pearl shade and base, each shade from darker blue at top to lighter blue at base, base with applied, frosted crystal feet, fitted with foreign burner, very good to excellent condition, 9-1/2" high........................**$830**

James D. Julia, Inc.

Double Rayo hanging lamp, single support arm descending from ceiling cap branching into two arms to support font and double burners, font decorated with Greek key pattern surrounding shoulder, finished with nickel plating and marked on flame spreaders "Rayo Patented November 20th 94 March 24th 96 February 28th 05," with two milk glass shades, 36" w. x 37" h. **$296**

James D. Julia, Inc.

Blue acanthus fluid lamps, blue fonts with acanthus leaf decoration encircling bodies, stepped brass stems atop square white marble blocks, 9-1/4" h. **$830**

James D. Julia, Inc.

ELECTRIC LIGHTING

LIGHTING

$

Pairpoint Puffy desk lamp with round silver-plated platform with incised ivy decoration that supports brass arm leading to shade with blue and pink flowers surrounded by green stylized leaves set against yellow and white latticework background, shade signed on interior "The Pairpoint Corp," 15" h........ **$3,000-$4,000**

James D. Julia, Inc.

TOP LOT!

Pittsburgh table lamp with lighting base, Native American at river's edge, circa 1915, obverse-painted milk glass, patinated metal, two sockets, unmarked, 21-1/2" x 16"................. **$6,080**

Rago Arts and Auction Center

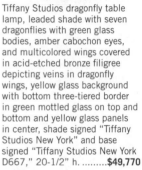

Tiffany Studios dragonfly table lamp, leaded shade with seven dragonflies with green glass bodies, amber cabochon eyes, and multicolored wings covered in acid-etched bronze filigree depicting veins in dragonfly wings, yellow glass background with bottom three-tiered border in green mottled glass on top and bottom and yellow glass panels in center, shade signed "Tiffany Studios New York" and base signed "Tiffany Studios New York D667," 20-1/2" h. **$49,770**

James D. Julia, Inc.

Painted metal five-light chandelier, bamboo form, wired for electricity, 22" h. **$192**

Susanin's Auctions

Early ornate stained glass desktop electric two-light lamp, cast iron base with marbleized rose glass, signed by Rainaud, 21" h. **$720**

Victorian Casino Antiques

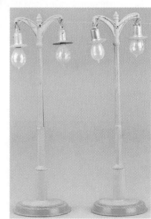

Marklin street lamps, matching pair, green painted die-cast poles, yellow and brown tin bases, double nickel-plated lamps, electric lighted, 12-3/4" h.....................................**$1,173**

Bertoia Auctions

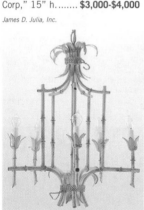

Pair of Tiffany-style stained glass electric three-light table lamps, stained glass bell shades and stained glass on ornate metal leaf bases, floral scenes, 28" h. ea.......**$540**

Victorian Casino Antiques

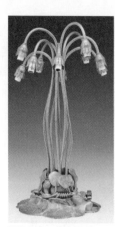

Duffner and Kimberly open top lamp, circa 1910, cast bronze arms extending from glass to middle, which supports Duffner shade ring, top and bottom ovals in mauve, diamonds in granite-backed yellow, larger panels in amber, three-socket brass base with bell-shaped finials on pulls, 24" h.... **$1,337**

Louis J. Dianni, LLC

Tiffany Studios 10-light lily lamp base, lily pad foot with 10 arching stems terminating in flower design shade holders, base finished with gold dore, signed on bottom "Tiffany Studios New York 381," 20-1/2" h............ **$7,000-$9,000**

James D. Julia, Inc.

Tiffany Studios prism lamp, etched metal shade dome on bronze shade ring with openwork wave design, ring decorated with 63 translucent gold iridescent Tiffany prisms, metal shade dome signed "Tiffany Studios New York S1147," base signed "Tiffany Studios New York 362," 27-1/2" h..................... **$28,440**

James D. Julia, Inc.

Pairpoint nautical table lamp with Spanish galleon on heavy seas with other sailing ships in background and seagulls flying above, original Pairpoint dolphin base with silver finish, shade artist signed "C. Durand," base signed "Pairpoint" with Pairpoint logo and "D3076," 21-1/2" h. **$4,148**

James D. Julia, Inc.

Bronze figural owls lamp, original dark brown patina, 13" dia. x 24" h............... **$2,900**

Metropolitan Galleries at Shaker Square

Wiender Werkstatte table lamp, hammered finish on foot, legs and shade top with silver plating over brass, 18" h............. **$4,000-$6,000**

James D. Julia, Inc.

Jefferson scenic reverse-painted lamp, signed on top ring and inside lower edge and numbered, 22" h....................... **$2,000**

Grand View Antiques & Auction

Arts & Crafts floral decorated jardinière lamp, signed Eva E. Adams, Altan Art Club, Chicago, 25" h.... **$1,045**

Kaminski Auctions

LeVerre Francais boudoir lamp in prunes pattern with brown cameo prunes and leaves against mottled red/orange background, brown cameo decoration and foot with random green mottling, lamp signed "LeVerre Francais," 14" h........................ **$1,067**

James D. Julia, Inc.

Porcelli Studios leaded lamp, allover floral pattern against background of mottled midnight blue/green confetti glass, shade signed on upper border panel "Porcelli," base signed but illegible, 24" h..**$10,000-$12,000**

James D. Julia, Inc.

Handel double student lamp, round stepped foot and column-shaped stem supporting two curving arms that hold sockets and shade holders, two leaded glass shades with caramel slag curtain border, green diamond-shaped border around shoulder and caramel slag geometric top, 19" h. **$2,430**

James D. Julia, Inc.

Wilkinson table lamp, shade with pink and yellow pond lilies in bloom repeating four times around shade against aqua background, Wilkinson base with four pad feet and incised onion design around platform, base signed "Wilkinson Co. Brooklyn, NY," 27-3/4" h................. **$2,187**

James D. Julia, Inc.

French iron and art glass lamp, hand-hammered iron base in diamond Art Deco design with center internally decorated art glass shade with green mottling shading from pink to cream, base unsigned, attributed to Edgar Brandt, 12-3/4" h...**$2,000-$4,000**

James D. Julia, Inc.

◄ Tiffany-style butterfly banker lamp with floral pattern in green, pink, blue, green, and white, shade with more than 100 hand-cut pieces of stained glass, each individually cut, wrapped in fine copper foil and soldered together, 13" h......**$236**

Windsor Auction House

Signed Tiffany stained glass table lamp, swirling oak leaf pattern, shade signed "7467-Tiffany Studios, New York," bronze base signed "Tiffany Studios, New York 358," 22-1/2" h. **$27,000**

Wooden Nickel Antiques

Parasol leaded lamp, Suess Ornamental Glass Co., early 20th century, parasol shade of green striated glass on Art Nouveau patinated bronze base with three sockets and acorn finial pull chains, 22" h. .. **$3,341**

Louis J. Dianni LLC

Octagonal Art Deco lamp shade on bronze lamp base, shade marked Hettier & Vincent, France, 8-1/4 h. x 7" dia.....**$123**

Kaminski Auctions

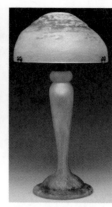

Pairpoint Puffy table lamp with apple tree shade with clusters of apples and apple blossoms with butterflies and bumblebees flying above, background decorated with shaded blue and green apple leaves and apple branches, original Pairpoint tree trunk base, shade unsigned, base signed "Pairpoint" with Pairpoint logo and "3092," 24" h.. **$20,738**

James D. Julia, Inc.

Daum Nancy internally decorated table lamp of mottled brown, green, and amber against cream-colored background, base fitted with hammered iron spider, shade signed on side with engraved signature "Daum Nancy France" with Cross of Lorraine, base unsigned, 24" h. **$4,148**

James D. Julia, Inc.

Suess leaded glass floor lamp, red and pink flowers with green and white leaves encircling side of shade from irregular border to shoulder, top of shade in random panels of tan and white striated glass with yellow sunburst extending from top rim, 63" h. **$14,220**

James D. Julia, Inc.

Franz Bergman Viennese lamp with two figures, signed and stamped, 19th century, 16-1/8" h. x 6-1/2" dia. **$3,200**

Kaminski Auctions

Victorian Arts & Crafts slag glass lamp, 24-1/2" h., base 7-3/4", shade 18-1/2" dia............**$375**

Applebrook Auctions & Estate Sales

Tiffany Studios nautilus lamp, bronze mermaid with torso extending out of water with arms raised holding nautilus shell, gold textured patina, signed on backside next to switch "Tiffany Studios New York," 15-3/4" h. **$12,443**

James D. Julia, Inc.

Gorham leaded lamp, closed top dome shade with band of stylized shields encircling bottom edge against striated amber and cream background of geometric panels, top of shade decorated with green leaded glass stylized flower, 18-1/2" h........................ **$2,370**

James D. Julia, Inc.

Revere leaded table lamp, leaded conical shade with red and green flowers interspersed with striated green leaves and stems against background of cream, red and green, tree trunk base with three-socket cluster and brown patina with green highlights, unsigned, 24" h. .... **$8,500-$12,000**

James D. Julia, Inc.

Tiffany Studios zodiac desk lamp, harp base supports bronze shade with incised geometric design surrounding skirt, shade signed in fitter notch "Tiffany Studios 1415," base signed "Tiffany Studios New York 661," 13-1/2" h.**$2,000-$3,000**

James D. Julia, Inc.

Pittsburgh reverse-painted lamp with three panels separated by vertical raised and textured ribbing, each panel with scenic painting of rivers, meadows, and forests against purple sky with clouds, cast metal base with bellflower decoration surrounding foot and acanthus leaf decoration on stem, base signed "PLB & Co," 16" h.................**$500-$700**

James D. Julia, Inc.

Handel lamp with reverse-painted shade of exotic birds with yellow, purple, orange, and blue feathers against black background with flowers in green, yellow, pink, and orange, shade signed "Handel 7026" and artist signed "Broggi," base signed "HANDEL," 25-1/4" h. ...**$11,850**

James D. Julia, Inc.

Handel and Rookwood table lamp, shade with chipped ice exterior and band of raised outlined stylized flowers encircling skirt, shaded rose color with white interior, Rookwood base with closely matching color and impressed stylized flower design at corners, shade signed "Handel 381/7047 #11," 22-1/2" h. **$4,148**

James D. Julia, Inc.

Tiffany Studios tulip lamp, vertically ribbed foot leading to organic twisted three-arm stem, arms curve downward to meet socket and shade holders, base finished with brown patina with red highlight, each shade signed "L.C.T." and base signed "Tiffany Studios New York 339," 16-1/4" h...................... **$8,000-$12,000**

James D. Julia, Inc.

Jefferson lamp with reverse-painted shade of orange poppies and green leaves encircling bottom of shade against yellow background with bumblebees and dragonflies, shade signed "2614 Jefferson R," 23" h. **$6,518**

James D. Julia, Inc.

Pairpoint reverse-painted table lamp, Garden of Allah design with garden walls, statues atop stairways, water fountain, and foliage with clouds in background, shade painted in blue, purple, green, and magenta, shade signed "Pairpoint Corp." and artist signed "Fred F 1934," three-arm, two-socket base of Art Nouveau styling on marble foot, very good to excellent condition with minor wear, silver-plated base tarnished, shade 16" dia. x 21" h. overall. **$2,015**

James D. Julia, Inc.

Magic & Illusion

MAGIC IS AN ANCIENT ART with a rich history. The earliest reported magic trick – the ball and cups trick – began thousands of years ago, around 1700 B.C. Books on magic began to be published in the 16th century, and the first magic theater opened in London in 1873. Since then the mysterious and mystical accessories of the world of magic have earned a following among collectors.

Magic – or stage magic, as it is technically called – is a performing art that entertains audiences by staging tricks, effects, or illusions of seemingly impossible feats using natural means. The person who performs these illusions or tricks is called a magician or illusionist, prestidigitator, conjuror, mentalist, or escape artist.

No discussion of magic is complete without mentioning Harry Houdini, the great escape artist who performed in the early 1900s and is considered to be one of the most famous magicians in history, or the fictional boy wizard, Harry Potter, who made magic a household word in today's culture.

Collectors are interested in the history of magic as a performing art and the magicians who performed it. They collect books, posters, tokens, apparatus, printed ephemera (programs, tickets, broadsides, etc.) about magic as well as photos, letters, and other memorabilia about past and present performers. In 2014 the collection of magic memorabilia from modern master of illusion Le Grand David of Beverly, Massachusetts, was brought to market by Kaminski Auctions. Nearly all of the 275 lots were sold, realizing total sales of more than $150,000.

Rick Heath, Le Grand David, "Always a Wonder to Remember" porcelain magician figures poster, acrylic on canvas, 43" h. x 25" w.; a replica was made to honor Spectacular Magic Co.'s 500th Beverly, Massachusetts performance on Jan. 18, 1981. .... **$1,476**
Kaminski Auctions

The most well known club for collectors of magic is the Magic Collectors' Association, founded in 1949 in New York City by several prominent collectors of that era. It has members throughout North America, England, Europe, and Australia.

Rick Heath, "Ducks and Butterflies," acrylic on board, depicting Marco the Magi, Le Grand David, Seth the Sensational, ducks and butterflies, first painted poster done by Heath in horizontal format, circa August 1983, 35" h. x 64" w **$1,045**

Kaminski Auctions

Chest of Enchantment illusion used to make someone magically appear, hand-painted wood and canvas mounted on wood, fabric mounted on wood in interior, scenes of Japanese figures, birds and flowers, on wheels, 51" h. x 38" w. x 45" d. **$1,107**

Kaminski Auctions

Set of six linking metal rings and corduroy bag from personal set of Marco the Magi (Cesareo R. Pelaez), used to perform at Cabot St. Cinema Theatre in Beverly, Massachusetts, 12" dia **$3,198**

Kaminski Auctions

Two banners, "Le Grand David Magic Company," hand-painted acrylic on canvas, white lettering against black background, 3' 11" h. x 9' 11" w.; "Le Grand David Magic Company," hand-painted wood with green curtain and genie lamp, 2' 5" h. x 8' w.; both hung in Cabot St. Cinema Theatre lobby in Beverly, Massachusetts.............................. **$246**

Kaminski Auctions

Sword Box, hand-painted wood with bats against red background, includes wig Marco the Magi wore and two puppets, 4' 3" h. x 2' 10" sq.; performed in first show at Cabot St. Cinema Theatre in Beverly, Massachusetts. Marco the Magi would climb in, doors would close, swords would be stuck through sides with pole down center of roof, doors would open and Marco would be gone, doors would close, and Marco would reappear inside.
.... **$2,214**

Kaminski Auctions

Broom Suspension illusion built by Abbott's Magic Co., original base, broom, and gimmick, 48" l. First broom suspension used in show at Cabot St. Cinema Theatre in Beverly, Massachusetts and one of few illusions performed at both Cabot St. Cinema Theatre and Larcom Theatre. **$861**

Kaminski Auctions

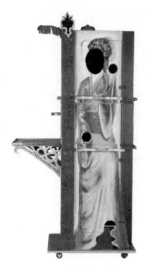

Robert Harbin's Zig Zag illusion, three hand-painted wooden sections depicting Marco's figure in kimono dress, includes two blades, 6' 7" h. x 2' 4" w.; Marco the Magi would get into cabinet, blades would be inserted by Le Grand David, and middle section would be shifted to the side. **$676**

Kaminski Auctions

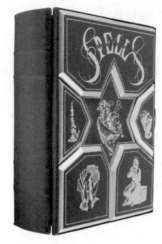

Large wooden box, cover with various magic images below the word "Spells," circa 1980s, opens to reveal spring and secret back panel that also opens, inside label reads "Collectors / Workshop / Crafters of Fine Magic Apparatus," used by son of famous Harry Blackstone, Sr., a contemporary of Harry Houdini, 15" x 11" x 5".................... **$750**

Heritage Auctions

New Haven, Petrie & Lewis, circa 1924, with prepared cards and instructions, general wear evident and one peg in platform in need of resoldering, good condition, 54" h.; three cards selected from deck placed in nickeled houlette at top of ladder, cards then cascade down ladder, filling bowl at base, except for three selected cards that remain on rungs of ladder, each at a different position. **$2,600**

Potter & Potter

Dragon illusion table, hand-painted wood with green and yellow dragons on black background, similar construction to Le Grand David's Zombie table, 43" h. x 26-1/4" dia........................ **$676**

Kaminski Auction

Light box or shadow box illusion, wooden base on casters below wooden framed top with paper sides, hand-drawn dragons on paper, 73" h. x 32" x 33" assembled; box appeared empty until Le Grand David broke through paper siding to surprise audience......................... **$1,107**

Kaminski Auctions

Two hand-painted die boxes, one with cherry blossom branches on orange background, one with gold phoenixes on red background, each with two die that appear to shift from one compartment to another by magician who make them disappear altogether, larger box 7" h. x 11-1/4" w. x 8-3/4" d.......... **$799**

Kaminski Auctions

MAGIC & ILLUSION

Breakapart Vanish illusion with two sets of rolling stairs and bamboo poles, six panels, hand-painted with floral and geometric designs on red background, 43" h. x 28" w. x 29" d. assembled; person would climb up stairs, enter vanishing box and disappear... **$615**

Kaminski Auctions

The Barrel Transposition, hand-painted wood by members of Spectacular Magic Co., 3' 11" h. x 2' w.; person would get into one barrel, be put end to end with second barrel, then would pass through bars into second barrel..................................... **$922**

Kaminski Auctions

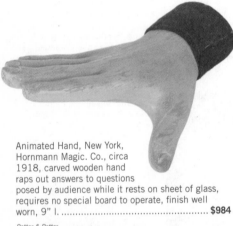

Animated Hand, New York, Hornmann Magic. Co., circa 1918, carved wooden hand raps out answers to questions posed by audience while it rests on sheet of glass, requires no special board to operate, finish well worn, 9" l. **$984**

Potter & Potter

David F. Bull, "Marco the Magi's Production of Le Grand David and his own Spectacular Magic Company," bronze, depicting broom suspension when Le Grand David would be levitated on stage by Marco the Magi (Cesareo R. Pelaez); signed in bronze "Bull 1984" and foundry mark, "1984 White Horse Production Inc. 1/3 TX," 24" h. x 54" w. x 36" d., including wooden base, housed in Cabot St. Cinema Theatre's upper lobby. Provenance: From Marco the Magi's Le Grand David Spectacular Magic Show of Cabot St. Cinema Theatre and Larcom Theatre, Beverly, Massachusetts... **$3,198**

Kaminski Auctions

Twelve-panel screen, each panel numbered on back, hand-painted dragon in clouds, artists Rick Heath and Bill Balkus, on casters, 7' h. x 31" w. ea. Provenance: From Marco the Magi's Le Grand David Spectacular Magic Co. of the Cabot St. Cinema Theatre and the Larcom Theatre of Beverly, Massachusetts... **$8,350**

Kaminski Auctions

MAGIC & ILLUSION

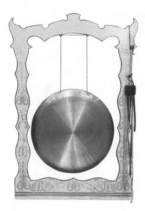

Symphonic gong and mallet, hand-painted wood frame, metal frame, hanging gong, frame 58-1/2" h. x 40" w. x 24" d., gong 27-1/2" dia.; in early years Marco the Magi would strike this gong to begin his show **$861**

Kaminski Auctions

"Marco the Magi Presents Le Grand David Spectacular" by Rick Heath, acrylic on board, depicting Samurai, housed in lobby of Cabot St. Cinema Theatre in Beverly, Massachusetts, 59" h. x 34" w. overall **$676**

Kaminski Auctions

"The Book of Life," based on Fu Manchu illusion, hand-painted muslin canvas over wooden frames with metal support beams, in style of a book with 10 painted pages/panels, dragon on front panel, characters in Spectacular Magic Co. follow, on casters and wooden base, 95" x 70" w. x 29" d.; acted as credits at end of performance, used for three to five years at Larcom Theatre. Provenance: From Marco the Magi's Le Grand David Spectacular Magic Co. of the Cabot St. Cinema Theatre and the Larcom Theatre of Beverly, Massachusetts...**$10,000-$12,000**

Kaminski Auctions

Combination of two Okito illusions, Hi Strung and The Mandarin's Dream, hand-painted wood with Asian-inspired dragons, flowers, and lions, all panels painted, 9' 2" h. x 59" sq.; three boxes are placed within pagoda and Marco the Magi (Cesareo R. Pelaez) appears when door is opened; this was the closing act of Le Grand David's Spectacular Magic Co., performed in every show at the Cabot St. Cinema Theatre in Beverly, Massachusetts.... **$8,000-$10,000**

Kaminski Auctions

Robert Harbin, vanishing flowers and vase illusion; two vases, flowers, and stand for one set, other set is original handmade vase and flowers from early years of Le Grand David, stand 29" h. x 10-1/4" dia., 55" h. overall **$2,337**

Kaminski Auctions

Will Goldston's More Exclusive Magical Secrets, Will Goldston, London, 1921, publisher's maroon morocco stamped in gold, illustrated, thick 4to, boards chipped and scuffed, spine worn, with clasp, lacking key, fair condition. **$276**

Potter & Potter

"Magician with Card Fans" sculpture by Italian artist Toni Moretto, magician with card fans on either side of his head, standing in front of table laden with props, magic books at his side and one in his back pocket, circa 1995, 9-1/2" x 7". **$738**

Potter & Potter

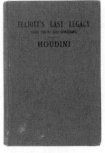 

Magic books: *Houdini's Book of Magic and Party Pastimes*, New York: Stoll & Edwards, 1927, first edition, 32 pages, pictorial paper over boards, rubbing to binding, creasing to front board, soiling to rear board; *Elliott's Last Legacy*, New York: Adams Press, 1923, first edition, 322 pages, inserted frontispiece and errata slip, publisher's full red cloth, lettered in black, rubbing, soiling to binding; and *Houdini's Paper Magic*, New York: Dutton, 1922, first edition, second printing, 206 pages, frontispiece inserted, publisher's full red cloth, lettered and ruled in black, dust jacket rubbed with short closed tears and small chips, previous owner's signature in book.................. **$200**

Heritage Auctions

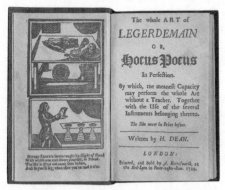

The Whole Art of Legerdemain or, Hocus Pocus in Perfection, Henry Dean, circa 1722, "By which, the meanest Capacity may perform the whole art without a Teacher. Together with the use of the several instruments belonging thereto. This like never in print before." London: modern calf, period-style binding, frontispiece, woodcuts in text, 12mo, very good condition, drop spine box; one of five examples known...**$30,750**

Potter & Potter

Breslaw's Last Legacy or, The Conjuror Unmasked by Philip Breslaw, London, 1792, 10th edition, paper-covered boards with paper spine label, engraved frontispiece, 12mo, boards worn, frontispiece depicts "Droll trick of a Cambridge Scholar" described on page 33 .... **$8,610**

Potter & Potter

MAGIC & ILLUSION

Monumental-sized Matter Through Matter, based on Okito illusion design, hand-painted details on wood and canvas, depicting Japanese tearoom, peacocks, and floral designs on red form, 75" h. x 39" w. x 33" d **$2,460**

Kaminski Auctions

Aldine's The Boy's Own Magic & Trick Books, circa 1894-1895, London, complete set in eight volumes, each describing a separate subject, all related to magic tricks, sleight of hand, allied entertainments and experiments, each volume in colored pictorial wrappers, wraps chipped and worn, some foxed, in drop-spine box; scarce, one of perhaps two complete files known of this series **$2,952**

Potter & Potter

Fu Manchu duck production illusion, hand-painted wood with Japanese garden scenes, 49" h. x 28" w. x 25" d.; black shade pulls out from top to cover box and duck would appear................... **$1,968**

Kaminski Auctions

Discoveries and Practice in Astrology Magic Witchcraft and the Occult Sciences by [unknown], Astrologer of the 19th Century, Ars longa, Vitae brevis, 267 pages, final blanks, with manuscript material, 12 blank pages within pagination, five pages throughout with hand-coloring, page 51/52 missing, bound in contemporary half brown calf over marbled boards, rebacked to style in modern full brown calf, spine tooled in blind and lettered in gilt in compartments, six raised bands, marbled end leaves, some minor wear to binding, author's name cut from title page and crossed out on dedication page, approximately 14.75" x 9" **$4,062**

Heritage Auctions

"The Séance of Wonders Conducted by Dr. Zomb" (Ormond McGill), Mason City, Iowa, Central Show Print, circa 1945, two sheet (38" x 58") three-color poster advertising spook show and magic show, tear in lower margin affecting printer's name, old folds................................... **$276**

Potter & Potter

New Fortune Book, or Conjurer's Guide; the Only Real Fortune-Teller, Glasgow, circa 1800, pictorial wrappers, illustrations in text, 24mo, ex-libris Trevor Hall, wrappers detached and chipped, otherwise good condition **$799**

Potter & Potter

Magician Howard Thurston's dressing room door sign, American, circa 1927, fiberboard-type signed with name "Howard Thurston" in metallic silver on blue metallic background, sign 9-1/2" x 1-3/4", framed with conservation glass and photo of Thurston to overall size of 16-1/2" x 23". Provenance: Letter accompanying sign states, "This was obtained from Thomas Chew Worthington... Thurston would hang this little sign on his dressing room door in theatres...as a good luck charm according to Thomas Chew Worthington III."..... **$7,000**

Potter & Potter

Fantastic Silks of Morocco, Indiana, Pennsylvania, Bob Kline, circa 1989, vanishing box shows wear, cabinet 16-1/2" x 28"; three silks are removed from sword suspended in cabinet, vanish, then reappear tied to sword still in cabinet.............................. **$475**

Potter & Potter

Herrmann the Great Co. double-sided playbill, American, circa 1898, pictorial broadside outlining performance of Leon and Adelaide Herrmann and depicting levitation, portraits of Herrmann dynasty of magicians, and decapitation illusion, corners and margins repaired, 6-7/8" x 20-3/4"............. **$3,600**

Potter & Potter

Early Victorian-era magic set, English, circa 1890, 11 turned wooden props, including large examples of millet bell and barrel, transposition vases, millet vases, card box, awl, tin funnel and cups, all housed in original partitioned box, box and pieces show wear, overall good condition, 17-3/4" x 13" x 3". .... **$1,400-$1,600**

Potter & Potter

Glass Penetration, New Haven, Petrie & Lewis, circa 1940, with display stand and spike, hallmarked, very good condition, rare, 10-1/4" x 12"; steel spike penetrates sheet of glass housed in hardwood frame, perhaps only known example........................... **$1,900**

Potter & Potter

Decapitation automaton, Switzerland, Zdenka, contemporary, bisque heads and custom-made clothes, 14-3/4" h.; doll moves fan in front of her face, her head vanishes, appears in die in front of doll, then reappears on doll's head **$2,000**

Potter & Potter

MAGIC & ILLUSION

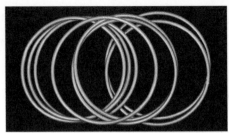

Harry Blackstone, Sr.'s linking rings, American, 1930s, set of eight heavy rings used by Blackstone in his famous illusion show, well worn from use, 10" dia., accompanied by letter of provenance from former owner to Bill King, in which he states rings were given to him by Blackstone, Sr. at Empire Theater in Fall River, Massachusetts, in late 1930s... **$1,200**

Potter & Potter

Mildred & Rouclere souvenir pocket mirror, Pennsylvania, Reading Ribbon Badge Co., circa 1909, celluloid-backed mirror with bust portrait of famous mind-reading duo in red frame with text "Mildred and Rouclere In Mildredism," 56mm dia.. **$1,722**

Potter & Potter

Harry Houdini jail cell escape photo, Los Angeles, 1918; he sits in prison cell wearing cuffs, leg irons, and shackles; stamps on verso from *Photoplay* magazine, used to publicize Houdini's serial movie, "The Master Mystery," very good condition, 8" x 10" **$461**

Potter & Potter

New Break-Apart Die Box, Los Angeles, F.G. Thayer, circa 1930, two double doors, shell, and 3" solid die, die shows light wear, cabinet near fine condition; solid die vanishes from wooden cabinet; two compartments of cabinet are physically detached from each other, die is heard to "slide" from one half to other, then it vanishes, reappearing in a borrowed hat **$1,353**

Potter & Potter

Duke Tricks with Cards trade cards, New York: The Giles Co. Lithographers, circa 1887, complete set of 24 numbered cards, lithographed fronts, methods for each effect described on versos of different cards, several with rounded corners or light wear, overall very good condition, originally packaged with Duke's Honest Long Cut tobacco, one of the scarcest sets of similar trade cards packaged with Duke's tobacco products **$4,182**

Potter & Potter

Maps & Globes

MAP COLLECTING is slowly growing in visibility thanks to recent discoveries and sales of historically important maps. In 2010, a rare copy of George Washington's own map of Yorktown sold for more than $1.1 million. And a copy of "Theatrvm civitatvm et admirandorvm Italiae" (Theater of the Cities and Wonders of Italy), published in 1663 by the atlas maker Joan Blaeu of Amsterdam, was exhibited with much fanfare during the 2012 San Francisco Antiquarian Book Print and Paper Fair. It's asking price: $75,000.

Top of the market aside, map collecting remains a surprisingly affordable hobby when one considers most made in the early 19th century are hand-colored and represent the cutting edge scientific knowledge at the time. Most examples from the last 400 years are available for less than $500, and engravings depicting America or its states may be owned for less than $150. Larger maps are usually worth more to collectors.

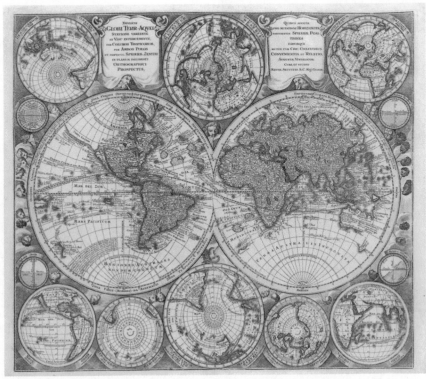

Matthaeus Seutter, "Diversi Globi Terr-Aquei," Augsburg, circa 1730, hand-colored, double-page engraved..**$2,640**

Swann Auction Galleries

Miniature ivory terrestrial globe, Great Britain, 19th century **$2,640**

Swann Auction Galleries

Victorian terrestrial globe and compass in mahogany stand, W. & A.K. Johnston, Edinburgh, Scotland and London, circa 1891, brass mount within calendar and zodiac outer rim, mounted on mahogany tripod base with incurved legs centering compass, marks: 18 INCH, TERRESTRIAL GLOBE, BY W. & A.K. JOHNSTON, Geographer, Engravers & Printers, TO THE QUEEN, 1891, EDINBURGH & LONDON; significant yellowing to globe surface, rubbing, water and sun damage to rim separating at joints, 41" high x 23" diameter **$5,000**

Heritage Auctions

Henry Schenck Tanner, "United States of America," Philadelphia, 1829 ..... **$8,400**

Swann Auction Galleries

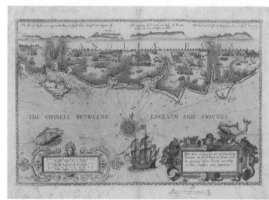

Lucas Jansz Waghenaer, "The Sea Coastes of England," London, 1588 ..... **$1,080**

Swann Auction Galleries

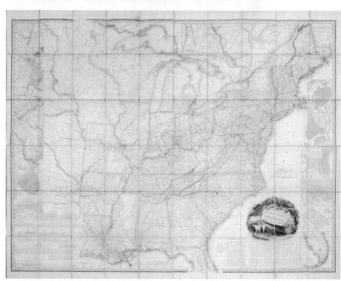

"United States of America" folding engraved map, dated 1829, one of the largest early maps of America, hand-colored in outline, 60 sections backed onto linen and edged with blue silk ribbon, marbled boards, gilt-lettered spine, engraved by H.S. Tanner, with vignette cartouche of deer in bucolic setting. **$8,000**

Heritage Auctions

Music Memorabilia

THE STATE OF THE HOBBY for those who collect music and related memorabilia is healthy. Before the economy went south in 2008, multiple buyers might be in the market for a pricey item, such as a fully signed photo of The Beatles. The resulting bidding battle could drive the price up to $10,000. These days, fewer people are looking for that type of item to begin with, and those who are interested likely would pay less for it, too. Instead, buyers are gravitating toward low- to mid-price lots that previously might not have been considered for auction. And the acts that buyers are interested in aren't necessarily your parents' favorites.

Artists from the late 1970s and 1980s, especially hard rock, heavy metal and pop acts, are poised to be the next generation of headlining acts for collectors. Guns N' Roses, Motley Crüe, Bon Jovi, U2, Prince, and Madonna are prime examples.

And just as the desired artists are changing, so, too, are some of the items that are being collected. Concert posters are practically nonexistent because there isn't much of a need for them anymore. Also on the endangered species list: ticket stubs, printed magazines, handbills, and promotional materials.

On the other hand, T-shirts have come into their own. And those reports you've heard about the pending demise of vinyl records in the wake of digital formats? Don't believe them. Vinyl is far from dead. Of 1960s artists, vinyl is a prime collectible, and collectors of '80s bands or artists are just as intrigued and as interested in vinyl as the previous generation.

One key piece of advice: Don't look at music memorabilia as an investment. Build a collection around your passion.

Here are some tips on collecting music memorabilia: Strive to acquire items that are in the best condition possible and keep them that way. Put a priority on provenance. Weigh quantity and rarity. Take advantage of opportunities geared toward collectors, such as Record Store Day. Refine the focus of your collection and don't try to collect everything. And think before you toss. Good-condition, once-common items that date back before World War II — like advertising posters, Coca-Cola bottles, 78 RPM records, and hand tools —are cherished by collectors today.

–*Susan Sliwicki, editor,* Goldmine
magazine

Ivory-toned handbag with black plastic handle, black trim and gold-toned metal clasp, pair of sepia-toned images showing The Beatles in collarless jackets appears on either side of clasp, band members' facsimile signatures appear beneath clasp, "Under License With NEMS Enterprises Ltd." written at bottom of bag's front, 10-1/2" x 12"................................ **$1,875**

Julien's Auctions

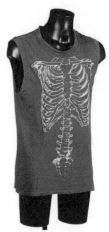

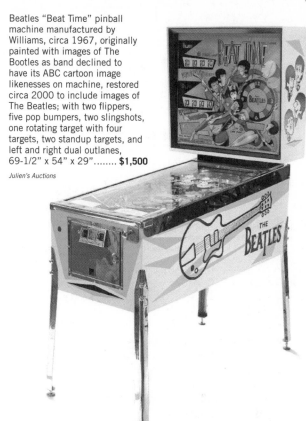

Beatles "Beat Time" pinball machine manufactured by Williams, circa 1967, originally painted with images of The Bootles as band declined to have its ABC cartoon image likenesses on machine, restored circa 2000 to include images of The Beatles; with two flippers, five pop bumpers, two slingshots, one rotating target with four targets, two standup targets, and left and right dual outlanes, 69-1/2" x 54" x 29"........ **$1,500**

Julien's Auctions

Black T-shirt with green skeleton design worn by Christopher Guest (portraying Nigel "Tuffy" Tufnel) in 1984 movie "This is Spinal Tap," with two color stills from movie and certificate of authenticity..................... **$7,883**

Bonhams

Federico Maquahe custom-designed red "jumper" dress worn onstage by The B-52's Kate Pierson during band's "Cosmic Thing" tour, size 2/4, with letter of provenance from Pierson. **$8,531**

Gotta Have Rock and Roll

Early black and white publicity photographs (one shown) of Cream, (bass player Jack Bruce, drummer Ginger Baker, guitarist Eric Clapton), circa 1967: six 8" x 10" photographs taken by David Winston and stamped on back with photographer's details; three taken of band onstage at Whisky A Go Go, taken by Out of Sight, Inc., and two large vintage prints of Jack Bruce, 11" x 14. Provenance: The Janet Bruce Collection. **$404**

Bonhams

Elvis Presley shot and then inscribed and gifted this miniature RCA TV and clock radio from his home at Graceland to Charlie Hodge. Hodge, a friend, army buddy and stage director of Presley, was staying at Graceland, watching TV, when Presley came into his room and observed Robert Goulet performing on "The Tonight Show" with Johnny Carson. Presley drew his gun and shot a hole through the screen; the bullet exited the top of the unit. Elvis then wrote, "F**k Robert Gouley if he can't take a joke. E.P.," and told Hodge to sell the TV; 13-1/4" x 9" x 7".....................**$14,495**

Gotta Have Rock and Roll

Elvis Presley-themed charm bracelet and earrings, excellent condition bracelet, 6" l., suspends figural hound dog wearing top hat, heart shape with diagonal line and text "Heart Break," guitar, and 1-1/8" brass luster frame holding black and white photo beneath cello cover with small text on photo "Best Wishes Elvis Presley," with pair of mint condition screw-back earrings with same brass luster framed portrait as on bracelet........ **$127**

Hake's Americana & Collectibles

Lock of Rolling Stones' lead singer Mick Jagger's hair from 1960, in small paper envelope inscribed that it was Mick Jagger's hair after being washed and trimmed by Chris at Rose Hill Farm, with statement of provenance **$6,468**

Bonhams

The Beatles, 1962, original Brian Epstein-issued tour itinerary **$2,531**

Backstage Auctions

OTIS REDDING
Volt Records Recording Artist

Otis Redding signed 8" x 10" glossy publicity photo by Phil Walden Artist and Promotions, signed in red ink "Respect — Otis Rerdding to Carol," light handling wear, small area of surface paper lift at bottom border.......................... **$1,898**

Hake's Americana & Collectibles

Led Zeppelin, 1970, 35 black and white negatives from Los Angeles concert, with full rights **$1,770**
Backstage Auctions

Neil Young and The Squires, 1965, set of five original concert photos. **$796**
Backstage Auctions

Original promotional poster for The Sex Pistols' 1977 single "God Save the Queen," mimics record album's cover image, Union Jack flag in background with defaced portrait of Queen Elizabeth II in center, black banner with "God Save the Queen" covers her eyes, black banner with "Sex Pistols" covers her mouth, 27" x 39" **$1,152**
Julien's Auctions

Eight framed pictures, photos and cabinet cards, circa 1880-1920, depicting American female violinists, good condition, 10-1/2" x 8-1/2" framed.. **$100**
Skinner, Inc., www.skinnerinc.com

Beatles-signed waitress summary form in black ink, very good condition **$5,857**
Gotta Have Rock and Roll

MUSIC MEMORABILIA

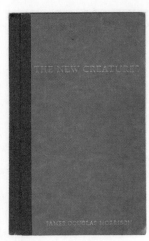

First edition of Jim Morrison's book, *The New Creatures*, self-published by Morrison in 1969, very good condition, flexible board covers and gilt lettering on front, 5-1/2" x 9", only 100 copies printed **$2,988**

Gotta Have Rock and Roll

Beatles Beat Seat vinyl-covered foam cushion designed to look like a record, with images of "The Fabulous Beatles" at label area in center of top of cushion, bottom side shows image of Ringo Starr and his facsimile signature in label area, sides have generic record and musical instrument images and small holes for air to escape; made in England by Unitrend, Ltd., 1964; very fine condition overall with scattered aging and dust soiling and light wear to vinyl top and bottom surfaces, 14" dia. x 3" d................ **$1,207**

Hake's Americana & Collectibles

Apple Records dartboard, black and green, circa late 1960s, 18" dia. Provenance: The Harrison Family Collection **$2,627**

Bonhams

"The Beatles Show" program signed on cover by John Lennon and George Harrison, 1963, from a performance at Odeon Cinema in Southport that also featured Fourmost, Gerry and The Pacemakers, Tommy Wallis and Beryl, Sons of the Piltdown Men, Tommy Quickly, Gary and Lee and Billy Baxter; program includes other performer signatures on inside pages, accompanied by certificate of authenticity from Tracks, Ltd., 10-1/2" x 8".................... **$3,840**

Julien's Auctions

Purple agate stone ring, size 6-1/2, worn by Jimi Hendrix, very good condition, approximately 1" l. x 3/4" w...................... **$6,599**

Gotta Have Rock and Roll

Red, white, and blue poster promoting Frank Sinatra's week-long 1953 engagement at Moss' Hippodrome in Birmingham, England, with Bill Miller at piano, 15" x 10" **$1,280**

Julien's Auctions

Thorens TD 124/11 belt-driven turntable and EMI Stereoscope professional amplifier owned and used by John Lennon at Apple Corps office from 1968-1971...**$6,400**

Julien's Auctions

Collection of 12 concert tour programs from late 1960s: Tamla Motown Show (signed inside by Diana Ross, Martha and the Vandellas, Smokey Robinson and the Miracles, Tony Marsh, Stevie Wonder, and Earl Van Dyke); 1965 Fall Spectacular; Kenny Rogers & The First Edition; Gladys Knight & The Pips; The Spinners; Mr. Dynamite James Brown; Beach Boys Concert at The Famous London Palladium (1968); Temptations; Dick Clark: Tom Parker Presents Dick Clark's Young Worlds Fair (signed on cover by members of The Robbs); Where the Action Is; Where the Action Is Summer Edition; and Where the Action Is Caravan; fine or better condition. **$1,875**

Heritage Auctions

Beatles embossed metal lunch box by Aladdin, with 6-1/2" metal thermos with plastic cup, ©1965 NEMS Enterprises, Ltd., graphics on all sides show Beatles performing and individual portraits of each member, facsimile signatures on lid, scattered traces of wear and aging to rim edges, light wear/oxidation to metal latch, handle and interior, very fine condition. **$482**

Hake's Americana & Collectibles

Beatles Disc Go 45 RPM record storage cases, each 7-1/2" dia. x 8-1/2" h., matching Beatles portraits and facsimile signatures on fronts, produced by Charter Industries ©1966 NEMS Enterprises Ltd., some scattered surface wear. Purple and olive green cases, total: .... **$214** Red, yellow, and light blue (shown) cases, total: **$230**

Hake's Americana & Collectibles

Beatles pink and white striped sleeveless shift dress with jewel neckline, printed with portraits of The Beatles with musical notes and The Beatles' logo, label reads "The Beatles-Dress Authorized Design," size 40. .... **$2,812**

Julien's Auctions

1965 American Folk/Blues Festival original poster signed in blue ballpoint pen by Big Mama Thornton and Mississippi Fred McDowell, folded in sixths, 2" tear at top mended with clear tape, two pinholes in each corner and two on each side, 23-3/4" x 33-1/4"... **$1,283**

Gotta Have Rock and Roll

Beatles vinyl brunch bag produced by Aladdin Industries, Inc., ©1965 NEMS Enterprises Ltd., zippered top and carrying handle, Beatles' portraits and facsimile signatures, near mint condition, 8" x 8" x 4" **$1,139**

Hake's Americana & Collectibles

Alice Cooper doll in original box, excellent condition......... **$40**

Gotta Have Rock and Roll

Sterling silver 1973 Playboy All-Star Jazz and Pop Poll Award presented to Eric Clapton by *Playboy Magazine*, in black leather case, Playboy bunny logo on front with text reading in part "Winner," engraved on back "Eric Clapton / Guitar / 1973 / Readers' Winner," hallmark reads "Sterling / Playboy," 2-1/2" dia **$1,000**

Heritage Auctions

Eric Clapton's stage-used guitar strap gifted to friend and Crossroads Centre co-founder Richard Conte, very good condition. **$1,075**

Gotta Have Rock and Roll

John Lennon's white Working Class Hero T-shirt, given to Cyrinda Foxe, one-time wife of Aerosmith frontman Steven Tyler, good condition, shows signs of wear **$4,000**

Gotta Have Rock and Roll

Honorary badge from New Jersey State Constables Association presented to Elvis Presley in 1970s; he later gifted it to his cousin, Harold Loyd; very good condition, 2-1/4" dia **$550**

Gotta Have Rock and Roll

Aug. 5, 1982, *Rolling Stone* magazine cover signed in black felt-tip pen by all five members of The Go-Go's: drummer Gina Schock, bassist Kathy Valentine, lead vocalist Belinda Carlisle, lead guitarist and keyboardist Charlotte Caffey, and rhythm guitarist Jane Wiedlin, very good condition **$150**

Gotta Have Rock and Roll

Thin Lizzy-Phil Lynott, 1978, 105 black and white negatives from New York concert, with full rights.....**$944**

Backstage Auctions

The Rolling Stones, 1975, Dallas Cotton Bowl rare concert slides **$836**

Backstage Auctions

The Clash silk-screened glossy-paper poster advertising release of band's 1977 studio debut and May 8, 1977, concert at Electric Circus in Manchester, England; with album cover art in black and white, "The Clash" and "New Album" text in fluorescent pink type; rolled with some light handling wear, small tears. **$329**

Hake's Americana & Collectibles

Striped scarf and pin worn by Jimi Hendrix in studio and on tour in late 1967 and early 1968, with letter of provenance from Nancy Reiner, Hendrix's friend and girlfriend of Hendrix's manager, Michael Jeffrey. **$888**

Gotta Have Rock and Roll

Diana Ross Motown dolls; doll made by Ideal in gold lamé gown with original box, marked 1969 Motown Inc.; doll made by Mego Corp. in silver lamé gown with original box marked 1977 Motown Record Corp.; both boxes bent and creased due to age, dolls in excellent condition, 17" and 11" h., respectively...**$500**

Heritage Auctions

The Beatles, 1968, "Yellow Submarine" original production art drawing. **$650**

Backstage Auctions

Sex Pistols, 1977, "God Save the Queen" original J. Reed promo flag...**$885**

Backstage Auctions

Paul McCartney-Wings, 1976, rare Houston concert slides...**$885**

Backstage Auctions

Set of 66 Elvis Presley Topps gum cards, fronts with color photos, backs with "Ask Elvis" text or information related to film "Love Me Tender"; card no. 2 has unused record collector's checklist; copyright 1956, Elvis Presley Enterprises, Bubbles, Inc. copyright on back, trace of margin aging/corner tip wear to some, collection in excellent to near mint condition overall, each 2-1/2" x 3-1/2"..**$419**

Hake's Americana & Collectibles

Package of Zig-Zag rolling papers signed by pop/ spoken word artists Cheech Marin and Tommy Chong, very good condition..............................**$250**

Gotta Have Rock and Roll

Complete 1964 Beatles button set, plus vending machine insert paper, 7/8" lithos by Greenduck; each carries text on curl "Seltaeb 1964," some with pinpoint rub marks, all in excellent condition, set near mint to mint, insert paper 4" h., reads "Get Your Beatles! Buttons Here!" **$210**

Hake's Americana & Collectibles

Michael Jackson, "Thriller" glove party invitation, 1984 .... **$514**

Backstage Auctions

Unrestored German A1 movie poster for "A Hard Day's Night" (Atlas Film, R-1981) with good color, fine-plus condition, folded, extra vertical creases on left side, 23-1/2" x 33" **$60**

Heritage Auctions

Concert poster for Willie Nelson's 1985 Fourth of July Celebration at Southpark Meadows in Austin, Texas (Pace Concerts) with image of Nelson by artist Danny Garrett, fine plus condition, unrestored with horizontal folds from being flattened while rolled, 22" x 39" **$185**

Heritage Auctions

Sleeveless shift dress on black and white dotted fabric, keyhole neckline and black piping trimming neckline and armholes, each Beatle's portrait printed in column, on diagonal, with George on top by neckline, followed by John, Paul and Ringo on skirt, Beatles' logo and band members' facsimile signatures printed on white guitar parallel to faces, hangtag present, no other labels included, size 36................ **$875**

Julien's Auctions

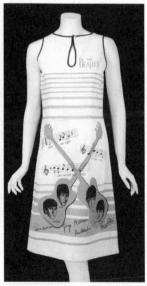

Blue and white sleeveless shift dress with keyhole neckline and black piping trimming neckline and armholes, printed with portraits of The Beatles on tan guitar shapes, The Beatles' facsimile signatures and musical notes and lyrics including "Hold Me Tight" and "I Wanna Hold Your Hand," no labels included, hangtag present, size 40.................. **$625**

Julien's Auctions

Native American Artifacts

OUR INTEREST IN Native American material cultural artifacts has been long-lived, as was the Indians' interest in many of our material cultural items from an early period.

During recent years, it has become commonplace to have major sales of these artifacts by at least four major auction houses, in addition to the private trading, local auctions, and Internet sales of these items.

Anthropologists have written millions of words on American Indian cultures and societies and have standardized various regions of the country when discussing these cultures. We have been fascinated with the material culture of Native Americans from the beginning of our contact with their societies. The majority of these valuable items are in repositories of museums, universities, and colleges, but many items that were traded to private citizens are now being sold to collectors of Native American material culture.

Native American artifacts are now acquired by collectors in the same fashion as any material cultural item. Individuals interested in antiques and collectibles find items at farm auction sales (an especially good place for farm family collections to be dispersed), yard sales, estate sales, specialized auctions, and from private collectors trading or selling items. The most wonderful of all sources is the Internet, especially online auction sales. There is no shortage of possibilities in finding items; it is merely deciding where to place one's energy and investment in adding to one's collection.

Native American artifacts are much more difficult to locate for a variety of reasons

Native American Indian Hupa basket, Northern California, early 1900s, 6"...**$275**
The Artifact Co.

including the following: scarcity of items; legal protection of items being traded; more vigorous collecting of artifacts by numerous international, national, state, regional, and local museums and historical societies; frailties of the items themselves, as most were made of organic materials; and a more limited distribution network through legitimate secondary sales.

However, it is still possible to find some types of Native American items through the traditional sources of online auctions, auction houses in local communities, antique stores and malls, flea markets, trading meetings, estate sales, and similar venues. The most likely items to find in the above ways would be items made of stone, chert, flint, obsidian, and copper. Most organic materials will not have survived the rigors of a marketplace unless they were recently released from some estate or collection and their value was unknown to the previous owner.

For more information on Native American collectibles, see *Warman's North American Indian Artifacts Identification and Price Guide* by Russell E. Lewis.

Native American or Oceanic bottleneck woven basket from early 1900s, finely shaped and tightly woven, from Seminole Chief Joe Dan Osceola's museum collection, certificate of authenticity, 12" x 14" **$750**

Pangaea Auctions

Paint-decorated covered splint basket, probably made by Eastern Woodland tribe, late 19th/early 20th century, round-over-square form, painted with yellow, blue, green, and red striped bands, 7-1/8" h. x 13" dia... **$123**

Skinner, Inc., www.skinnerinc.com

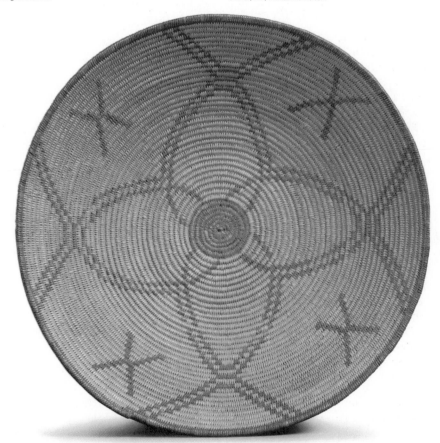

Apache coiled geometric tray of flaring form, woven in willow and devil's claw, with circular medallion in basin enclosed by foliate motif, surmounted by crisscross designs in open field, all beneath darkened rim, 13-7/8" dia...**$625**

Sotheby's

Zuni polychrome bowl painted in basin with massive red quartrefoil, 6" h. x 12" dia........ **$3,125**

Sotheby's

Pinedale geometric bowl, 13th century, painted in black against white slip with overlaying panels of zigzag bands, 4-3/4" w. x 11-3/8" h............. **$1,000**

Sotheby's

Acoma polychrome pictorial bowl, painted in orange and dark brown against chalky white slip, with pair of parrots beneath band of stylized feathers, 4-1/2" h. x 7" dia. **$875**

Sotheby's

TOP LOT!

Eagle Woman effigy pipe, LeFlore County, Oklahoma, found during 1933-1935 Pocola excavations, stone great pipe with traces of copper "guilding," 8-5/8" l **$290,000**

Tony Putty Artifacts

Colima dog effigy, Colima, Mexico, circa 1 AD, solid, painted face, 15" **$1,900**

Tony Putty Artifacts

Horn effigy jar, Bradley Place, Arizona, solid, minor rim repair, 5-5/8" **$500**

Tony Putty Artifacts

Turtle effigy, Colima, Mexico, circa 1 AD, solid, engraved, 10-1/2" **$750**

Tony Putty Artifacts

Zuni polychrome mug, painted in red and dark brown against cream slip, with heartline deer, attributed to We'Wha (1848-1896), 8" h **$2,125**

Sotheby's

Dora Tse Pe (b. 1939), San Ildefonso, decorated overall with highly polished red slip, carved on shoulder with encircling avanyu, inset with plaque of turquoise at eye, signed on base "Dora 94," 7" h **$1,000**

Sotheby's

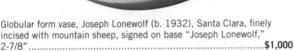

Globular form vase, Joseph Lonewolf (b. 1932), Santa Clara, finely incised with mountain sheep, signed on base "Joseph Lonewolf," 2-7/8" **$1,000**

Sotheby's

Globular form vase, Maria Martinez (1887-1980), San Ildefonso, decorated with polished gunmetal black slip, signed on base "Maria Poveka 1264," 3-1/4" h **$1,000**

Sotheby's

Globular form vase, Grace Medicine Flower (b. 1938), Santa Clara, decorated overall with polished red slip, finely incised in sgraffito technique with avanyu, signed on base "Grace Medicine Flower," 5-1/2" h **$875**

Sotheby's

Early and rare Tabira polychrome canteen from Salinas Pueblos, possibly Las Humanas Pueblo, of massive scale, painted in two shades of matte brown against grayish slip, with a bird, its head in profile, wings and tail feathers spread, and talons extended, 11-1/2" h. x 12-3/8" w **$5,000**

Sotheby's

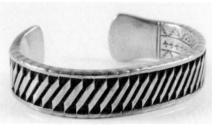

Heavy sterling silver cuff bracelet with deeply engraved decoration by Native American Creek Seminole maker Kenneth Johnson, intricate carved designs to interior and exterior surfaces, marked "Creek Seminole," "KJ," "Hand Made," and "Sterling," 3" x 2-1/4" **$450**

Thomaston Place Auction Galleries

Four pieces of silver and turquoise jewelry: canteen marked "TKW," pendant marked "G.," squash necklace, and bracelet; from upstate New York museum, necklace 19" l **$550**

Cottone Auctions

Rare Pawn Zuni sterling inlay bracelet, vintage stone-to-stone inlay of turquoise, onyx, coral, and mother-of-pearl, cardinal in mother-of-pearl cabochon with silver leaf designs and five turquoise cabochons, five silver beads along base of cabochon, triple band, artist signed "Velz," 2-1/4" w. **$100**

Desert West Auction Services

Ring, solid sterling silver with large oval turquoise, size 6-1/4, top of ring is 1-1/2" l **$105**

Linda Roberts Jewelry

Buckskin dress, machine sewn with fringe decoration, one side lacking leather tie, 2 lbs., 55-1/4" l. x 21-1/2" w. under arms. **$125**

Austin Auction Gallery

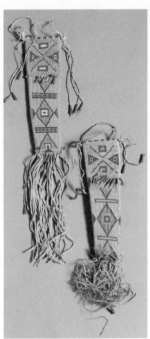

Two Sioux beaded and fringed hide woman's knife sheaths of tapering section, tanned buffalo hide, each sinew sewn and lazy-stitched in typical colors of glass beadwork, one against yellow ground, other against light blue ground, with typical geometric motifs, trimmed with tin cone pendants, 10-1/4" l. each................................ **$3,125**

Sotheby's

Pueblo gourd rattle, Arizona, circa early 20th century, used in Pueblo dance rituals, painted in red, white, blue and yellow, handle wrapped in old gauze-like fabric, custom stand, 11-1/2" h........................... **$750**

Artemis Gallery LIVE

Large ladle, Jeddito, California, 1275 to 1400 CE, black on orange, deep bowl decorated with arrows and other geometric patterns, handle with series of wide vertical and horizontal hash marks, small opening at end for suspending, 12" l. x 5" w. Provenance: Ex-Fort Knox Artifacts Gallery, Scottsdale, Arizona **$225**

Artemis Gallery LIVE

Beaded and fringed hide gauntlets of tanned deer skin, stitched in typical colors of glass beadwork with floral sprays, 14" l **$500**

Sotheby's

Handmade Shoshone war shirt, tight beadwork strips, 1940-1950s, beadwork on both sides, hide dyed with blue and reds **$725**

North American Auction Co.

Handmade cape by Montana Cree, worn over dress or shirt for ceremonies, heavy moose hide fringe and construction on 1800s trade cloth white muslin with tight glass trade beadwork of spinning wheel and floral design believed to be added later, cape from mid-to-late 1800s, beadwork from 1910-1930s, 27" x 17" and 6" fringe on side. **$225**

North American Auction Co.

Blackfoot war shirt, pony beadwork across both shoulders and arms, made of brain tanned and painted hide arms with 1800s tradecloth shirt with two long bead strips over shoulders and two long bead strips over arms, 1920-1950s, 72" across arms and 28" down torso area **$450**

North American Auction Co.

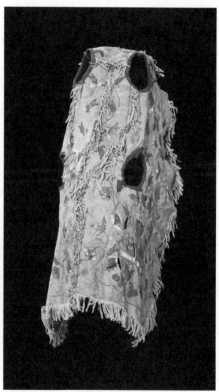

Apache beaded hide tab-toe moccasins, sewn in black, white, red, dark blue and greasy yellow glass beadwork, with narrow strips enclosing parallelograms above soles and on vamps, legs stitched with columns of chevrons flanking concentric circles connected by fine stripe, 24" h **$7,500**

Sotheby's

Santee Sioux horse mask, rare, quilled in leaf and flower pattern, sewn in sections with fringe along both seams and edges, tradecloth edged eye and ear holes, custom display stand included, originally full-size vest that was converted, probably during 1890s............................... **$7,500**

Brian Lebel's Old West Auction

Gros Vente beaded and fringed hide ceremonial man's moccasins, each thread sewn in red, pumpkin, light and dark blue beadwork against white ground, with series of diamonds on sole with typical geometric designs on edge, vamp and cuff, trimmed with cut hide panel, remains of yellow ochre on tongue, 10" l **$2,500**

Sotheby's

Arapaho beaded hide man's moccasins, each sinew sewn in typical colors against white lazy-stitched glass beadwork ground, with stylized butterfly motifs on cuff, vamp overlaid with beaded split-forked tongue, 10-1/2" l **$2,750**

Sotheby's

Sioux pipe bag, brain tanned hide, tin cone dangles, 16" with fringe **$2,750**

Tony Putty Artifacts

Beaded bag, Plains type, with U.S. flags in beadwork, 9" overall including fringe. **$400**

The Artifact Co.

Beaded bag, Plains type, mostly purple and green beads, excellent condition, slightly over 12" with fringe **$250**

The Artifact Co.

Photograph of Chippewa elder in dress with root-ball club, likely taken in New York State or Canada at turn of the 20th century, mounted on card larger than stated dimension, 3-7/8" x 5-1/2" **$30**

The Artifact Co.

Photograph of woman in dress with woven shawl, name on back says "Annie Kills-Twice," a Sioux woman born around 1881 in South Dakota, photo probably taken around 1900, 3" x 4-1/8" **$5**

The Artifact Co.

Colored lithograph of "Mah-To-Toh-Pa" by George Catlin (1796-1872), "The Mandan Chief (from Catlin's N.A. Indian Collection)," Day and Haghe Lith to the Queen, 17-1/2" x 12-1/2" **$2,280**

Skinner, Inc., www.skinnerinc.com

Jose De La Cruz Medina (1935-1968), Apache Crown or Spirit Dancer, ink and pencil on paper, signed "JC Medina" in lower left corner, 19-1/4" x 14-3/4"...**$625**

Sotheby's

Hand-carved stone platform pipe, excellent condition, rare, with certificate of authenticity signed by Chief Joe Dan Osceola and Seminole tribe, 9-1/2" l. x 2-1/4" w. x 3" d **$90**

Pangaea Auctions

Catlinite pipe stone, circa late 1800s, with certificate of authenticity signed by Chief Joe Dan Osceola and Seminole tribe, 4-1/2" l. x 2" w. x 1" d **$90**

Pangaea Auctions

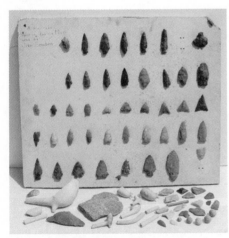

Artifacts dug from ground in Hadley, Massachusetts, around 1920, by John Bemben, display board with approximately 42 arrowheads plus box of random pieces including more arrowheads, pipe fragments, and lead ball bullets.
.... **$225**

Stanton Auctions

Hopewell Period carved red steatite stone pipe in crescent form with small beaver sitting atop, bowl behind his back, sticker on base with "Ashland, County, Ohio, Hopewell, Around 400 BC," 3" l. x 2-1/4" h. Provenance: Ex-Knox Artifacts, Scottsdale, Arizona, ex-J.J. Klejman Gallery New York, New York, ex-Stanley R. Grant Collection........................... **$250**

Artemis Gallery LIVE

Two hardstone full-groove axe heads, well formed with deep groove, hardstone bell pestle, both from Ohio River Valley, 4-1/2" h. x 3-1/4" dia. and 6" h. x 5" w **$100**

Rich Penn Auctions

Navajo Han al Chadi woven blanket, circa 1885, native wool, second phase chief blanket, certificate of appraisal attached, 63-1/2" h. x 47" w. **$7,000**

Kaminski Auctions

Wool rug, early to mid-20th century, serrated diamonds along with other designs, 3 lbs., 42" l. x 21-1/2" w. **$70**

Louis J. Dianni, LLC

Navajo wearing blanket in Chief's Third Phase Design, Red Mesa, composed of nine diamond elements overlaying striped panels in red, black, brown and white, typical banded background, 61" x 64" **$4,400**

Leslie Hindman Auctioneers

Wool rug, early to mid-20th century, multicolored serrated diamonds, each corner with hanging strands of red and gray wool, 3 lbs., 44" l. x 27" w. **$175**

Louis J. Dianni, LLC

Oddities

THESE COLLECTIBLES fall in the "weird and wonderful" category of unusual items.

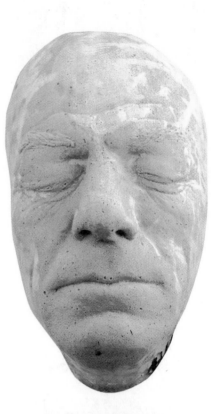

Life mask taken of actor Glenn Strange by the Universal makeup department for his career-making role as Frankenstein's monster in the film "House of Frankenstein" (Universal, 1944). Strange, a bit player who worked his way up in B films playing "heavies" in everything from science fiction to Westerns, eventually replaced Boris Karloff as Frankenstein's monster.
.... **$60**

Blacksparrow Auctions

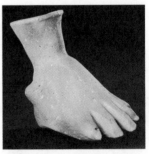

Flared-neck foot effigy bottle, Poinsett Co., Arizona, one of rarest forms of Mississippian, Southern cult iconography, 4-1/2" h. x 5-1/2" l. **$7,000**

Dan Morphy Auctions, LLC

Brass jockey scale, made by W & T Avery, Birmingham, England, circa 1850, with weights, 100" h. x 68" w. x 57" d **$8,500**

Red Baron Antiques

ODDITIES

Taxidermy alligator holding ashtray, mounted on board, loss to 1" section on tail, small amount of deterioration in corner of mouth, 9-1/4" w. x 18" d. x 18-1/4" h **$200**

Roland New York

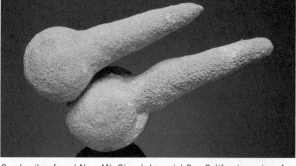

Sand spikes found Near Mt. Signal, Imperial Co., California, grains of sand cemented by calcite, 4" x 6" x 2-1/4" **$3,125**

Heritage Auctions

Four African knives: So/Lokele knife, small Lozi form with wood sheath, Ngombe knife, and two-bladed form with wood hilt, up to 19" l **$420**

Skinner, Inc., www.skinnerinc.com

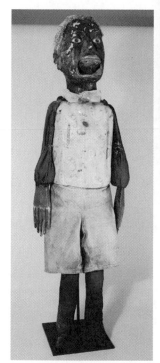

Early ventriloquist dummy, American, circa 1890, wood, composition, fabric, and leather, overall very fine condition, leather on lower chin missing.............................. **$800**

The RSL Auction Co.

Taxidermy elephant foot umbrella and cane stand, Victorian era, with collection of eight canes or walking sticks, four glass and four wood, one with carved ivory dog's head finial, longest 35-1/2"; stand 19-1/2" h. x 12" x 16"..............**$800**

Burchard Galleries, Inc.

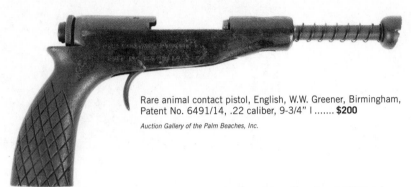

Rare animal contact pistol, English, W.W. Greener, Birmingham, Patent No. 6491/14, .22 caliber, 9-3/4" l **$200**

Auction Gallery of the Palm Beaches, Inc.

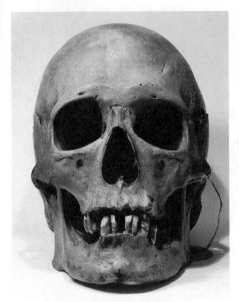

Skull from Late Period Egyptian mummy, circa 664-30 BC, brownish color from oils used in embalming process, museum tag on skull, Ex Wistar Institute of Anatomy and Biology, collected in 18th-19th century, 7-5/8" l **$4,000**

Ancient Resource, LLC

Famous cartographic oddity showing Europe in shape of woman, circa 1580. The representation of Europa Regina, or Queen of the World, was first drawn by Jonannes Bucius in 1537. This simplified version appeared in several editions of Munster's *Cosmography* from 1580 onwards. Spain forms the crown and head, France and Germany the neck and bust, Bohemia the heart, Italy the left arm holding an orb (Sicily) and Denmark the right arm holding a scepter with Britain as the flag. The remainder of the figure is a flowing robe with Greece and Russia at the feet. It has been argued that instead of a woman, the map represents Charles V of Spain, modeling a Europe that had Spain as its crown, or that it symbolizes a Habsburg-dominated Europe; 10-1/4" x 6-1/2" **$450**

PBA Galleries

Carved ivory and wood cigar cane with hidden compartment, circa 1900, ivory handle carved as burning cigar held by brass mounts and collar, bamboo shaft with brass ferrule to tip, handle pulls away from shaft to reveal hidden brass sleeve with storage compartment for two cigars, 35-3/4" l.............. **$2,375**

Heritage Auctions

ODDITIES

Carved wood and metal rattle, circa late 19th century, with animal and avian features done in blend of traditional and folk art styles, detailed with small metal studs and red and black with gold pigments, custom stand, 12" l............. **$9,000**

Skinner, Inc., www.skinnerinc.com

Reconstructed egg of Madagascan elephant bird, *Aepyornis maximus*, 12" h. **$1,200**

Skinner, Inc., www.skinnerinc.com

Iron handcuffs, 19th century, impressed "HART" on each side.. **$98**

Skinner, Inc., www.skinnerinc.com

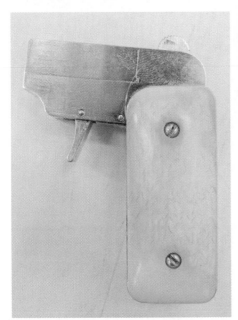

Lady's "lipstick gun," 1930s, bone handle and gold stainless, 22 caliber, 2-1/4" w. closed, 2-1/2" open **$1,900**

Red Baron Antiques

Carved oak gargoyle from Main Line, Philadelphia, 7" h. x 7" w. x 5-1/2" d **$600**

Red Baron Antiques

Horse race gaming wheel with odds changer on black wooden base with pull-out game layout, eagle finial, 40" h **$1,100**

Victorian Casino Antiques

Dogon carved wood mask, stylized form with pierced triangular eyes, pointed ears, and scoop-shaped projection from top of head, weathered patina, 22" h **$521**

Skinner, Inc., www.skinnerinc.com

Designer cone-shaped bar in maple with multiple hidden drawers, 33-1/2" h. x 21-1/2" dia. **$300**

Red Baron Antiques

Early lodge skull with on/off switch on bottom to control battery-operated lightbulb, eyes once functioned, some old poems and chants on top and back of piece, good condition, 6-3/4" h. **$225**

Dan Morphy Auctions, LLC

Lithographed paper and wood toy of William Jennings Bryan, leading American politician in the 1890s until his death in 1925. Body and head of Bryan are one piece with separate cutout arms and legs attached, front and back are identical, assuming it originally came with some strings, which wrapped around the hands and could be manipulated with a wooden stick to make the figure move; 5-1/2" h. **$106**

Heritage Auctions

Heart attack paddle, wooden with velveteen paddle, shoots when hits surface and scares victim, for Masonic initiation, fires 32 caliber blank, 23" l. **$900**

Red Baron Antiques

Wooden jointed horse model with articulated neck, circa 1950, wooden stand, repair to base, excellent condition, 16" l. **$10**

Dan Morphy Auctions, LLC

Six Neoclassical plaster casts of feet, 20th century, tallest 15" h. **$750**

Heritage Auctions

Pygmy mammoth tooth, *Mammuthus primigenius*, Wrangle Island, Siberia, gray, black, and brown coloring, root section, wear to upper grinding surface of tooth, 2" x 1-3/8" x 2-1/4". **$1,000**

Heritage Auctions

Rare 1¢ gumball machine, "The Comet," 20" h. x 14" w. x 13" d. **$4,000**

Red Baron Antiques

World War II Japanese "rabbit-ear" binocular telescope with original canvas carrying case and tripod support, adjustable, 12" h. x 3-1/2" w. x 3-1/2" d. closed **$275**

Red Baron Antiques

Paperweights

ALTHOUGH PAPERWEIGHTS had their origin in ancient Egypt, it was in the mid-19th century that this art form reached its zenith. The finest paperweights were produced between 1834 and 1855 in France by the Clichy, Baccarat, and St. Louis factories. Other weights made in England, Italy, and Bohemia during this period rarely match the quality of the French weights.

In the early 1850s, the New England Glass Co. in Cambridge, Massachusetts, and the Boston & Sandwich Glass Co. in Sandwich, Massachusetts, became the first American factories to make paperweights.

Popularity peaked during the classic period (1845-1855) and faded toward the end of the 19th century. Paperweight production was rediscovered nearly a century later in the mid-1900s. Baccarat, St. Louis, Perthshire, and many studio craftsmen in the United States and Europe still make contemporary paperweights.

Rookwood double goose paperweight, designed by Sallie Toohey, cast in 1935, ivory mat glaze, impressed with Rookwood symbol, date and shape 1855, excellent original condition, without crazing, 4-1/4".............. **$225**

Mark Mussio, Humler & Nolan

Baccarat pompon paperweight, pink pompon flower blossom, bud and green leaves surrounded by garland of red, white, and green millefiori canes, star cut base, signed with "B 1992" signature/date cane, 3" dia. x 2-1/4" h. Provenance: Barry Schultheiss Collection. **$632**

James D. Julia, Inc.

Weedflower paperweight, rose-color petals with blue dots and goldstone arranged six over six, red, white, and blue rods, cog and goldstone center cane, detached green stem and leaves surrounded by swirled spatter, colorless ground, slightly concave base with slightly protruding ground pontil mark, Boston & Sandwich Glass Co., possibly by Nicholas Lutz, 1870-1887, good as-found condition, chip to underside of base, light scratches/wear and minute dings, 2-1/4" h. x 3-1/2" dia....... **$690**

Jeffrey S. Evans & Associates

St. Louis millefiori close pack newel post with complex multicolored canes, signed with "SL 1974" signature/date cane, original metal hardware, 3-1/2" dia. x 7" h. Provenance: Barry Schultheiss Collection. **$805**

James D. Julia, Inc.

Orient & Flume paperweight, circa 1978, signed translucent iridescent dragonfly and flower motif, no box, approximately 2.75" h. x 3" dia. **$184**

J Levine Auction & Appraisal, LLC

Silvered bronze paperweight, French table sculpture in form of mouse nibbling corner of book titled *Joueurs de Paris*, initialed "AA" and dated 1867 on spine, plaster filled, worn, handling patina, 1-1/2" x 3" x 2". **$690**

Thomaston Place Auction Galleries

Pressed glass novelty paperweights, colorless, each with encased dancing turtle, one with frosted hand holding weight, both with original base cover, one with printed "Patent applied for" label, possibly Gillinder & Sons, fourth quarter 19th century, undamaged, 3" dia. x 4-1/4" l. **$288**

Jeffrey S. Evans & Associates

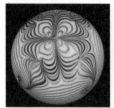

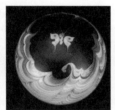

Northern star art glass paperweight, circa 1976, signed S. Smeyers, no box, approximately 2" h. x 2.75" dia. **$92**

J Levine Auction & Appraisal, LLC

Lundberg Studios iridescent swirled paperweight with butterfly, circa 1976, signed, no box, 2.25" h. x 3" dia. **$207**

J Levine Auction & Appraisal, LLC

Vandermark egg-shaped glass paperweight in blue and neutral swirled motif, signed, dated 1977, no box, approximately 3" h. x 2.75" dia. **$63**

J Levine Auction & Appraisal, LLC

Satava jellyfish paperweight displaying purple ribbed jellyfish, engraved "Satava" and numbered 3009-12, excellent condition, 5" h. **$250**

Mark Mussio, Humler & Nolan

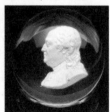

Charles Kaziun miniature pedestal paperweight, millefiori canes surrounding central duck cane on opaque blue ground, gold-foil "K" underneath, weight angled forward on colorless pedestal with polished pontil mark, 1960-1989, undamaged, 2" h. x 1-1/4" dia. **$230**

Jeffrey S. Evans & Associates

Pairpoint lampwork pedestal paperweight, purple and white narcissus with four wide and four narrow green leaves, six cut windows, engraved vintage pattern under foot, "1974 / #98" on polished pontil mark and embedded blue and white "P" in base of weight, circa 1974, undamaged, 4-3/4" h. x 3-5/8" dia. foot. **$173**

Jeffrey S. Evans & Associates

Almeric Walter Pate De Verre paperweight with light blue fantail pigeon standing atop mottled brown and blue pedestal, signed on side with impressed signature "A. Walter Nancy," very good condition with nick to tail feathers, 3-1/2" h. ... **$122**

James D. Julia, Inc.

Antique Benjamin Franklin sulphide paperweight, colorless ground, thin portrait bust with no markings, similar to bust used by Clichy, flat polished base, possibly New England Glass Co., 19th century, undamaged, polished surface, 1-3/4" h. x 2-3/8" dia. **$345**

Jeffrey S. Evans & Associates

Perfume Bottles

ALTHOUGH THE HUMAN SENSE OF SMELL isn't nearly as acute as that of many other mammals, we have long been affected by the odors in the world around us. Science has shown that scents or smells can directly affect our mood or behavior.

No one knows for certain when humans first rubbed themselves with some plant or herb to improve their appeal to other humans, usually of the opposite sex. However, it is clear that the use of unguents and scented materials was widely practiced as far back as Ancient Egypt.

Some of the first objects made of glass, in fact, were small cast vials used for storing such mixtures. By the age of the Roman Empire, scented waters and other mixtures were even more important and were widely available in small glass flasks or bottles. Since that time glass has been the material of choice for storing scented concoctions, and during the past 200 years some of the most exquisite glass objects produced were designed for that purpose.

It wasn't until around the middle of the 19th century that specialized bottles and vials were produced to hold commercially manufactured scents. Some aromatic mixtures were worn on special occasions, while many others were splashed on to help mask body odor. For centuries it had been common practice for "sophisticated" people to carry on their person a scented pouch or similar accoutrement, since daily bathing was unheard of and laundering methods were primitive.

Commercially produced and brand name perfumes and colognes have really only been common since the late 19th and early 20th centuries. The French started the ball rolling during the first half of the 19th century when D'Orsay and Guerlain began producing special scents. The first American entrepreneur to step into this field was Richard Hudnut, whose firm was established in 1880. During the second half of the 19th century most scents carried simple labels and were sold in simple, fairly generic glass bottles. Only in the early 20th century did parfumeurs introduce specially designed labels and bottles to hold their most popular perfumes. Coty, founded in 1904, was one of the first to do this, and they turned to René Lalique for a special bottle design around 1908. Other French firms, such as Bourjois (1903), Caron (1903), and D'Orsay (1904) were soon following this trend.

People collect two kinds of perfume bottles—decorative and commercial. Decorative bottles include any bottles sold empty and meant to be filled with your choice of scent. Commercial bottles are any that were sold filled with scent and usually have the label of the perfume company.

The rules of value for perfume bottles are the same as for any other kind of glass—rarity, condition, age, and quality of glass.

The record price for perfume bottle at auction is something over $310,000, and those little sample bottles of scent that we used to get for free at perfume counters in the 1960s can now bring as much as $300 or $400.

For more information on perfume bottles, see *Antique Trader Perfume Bottles Price Guide* by Kyle Husfloen.

R. Lalique "Bouchon Fleurs de Pommier" perfume bottle, circa 1919, clear/frost glass, inverted drapery pattern, tiara stopper molded both sides in openwork apple blossom motif, Lalique mark on stopper, 5-1/2". $17,220

Perfume Bottles Auction

German chatelaine scent bottle, 18th century, hand finished crystal, inner stopper, ornate silver mounts of angels and putti, silver and makers marks, bottle 3-3/8". $2,214

Perfume Bottles Auction

German enamel scent bottles, circa 1725, silver mounts, screw caps with rings, scenes of couples in garden settings, very slight wear, 3-1/8"........$799

Perfume Bottles Auction

Daum-Nancy scent bottle, circa 1900, hand-finished art glass, graduated peach hue, enameled and gilt relief decoration, gilt metal mounts, Daum-Nancy mark, 6"............$1,230

Perfume Bottle Auctions

Pair of German character perfume bottles, 1920s, thin porcelain, glazed detail, marked Germany, 1-3/4"...$246

Perfume Bottles Auction

Pyramid perfume bottle, 1920s, black glass with gilt detail, partial label, metal stopper fittings with glass insert and dauber, 6-3/4". $399

Perfume Bottles Auction

Emile Gallé perfume bottle, circa 1900, enameled pale blue-green art glass, English sterling silver hinged mount, stopper, molded Gallé mark, 4-1/4".......$4,920

Perfume Bottles Auction

DeVilbiss atomizer, dated 1926, clear/frost pale yellow Cambridge glass, acid-etched leaf and berry motif, gilt detail, gilt metal hardware, black glass finial, 9-1/4"....... **$9,840**

Perfume Bottles Auction

DeVilbiss atomizer, 1925, Fry opalescent art glass, reverse-painted blue foot, engraved drape motif, brass fittings, 6-5/8".
.............................**$676**

Perfume Bottles Auction

Goebel "crown top" perfume bottle, 1920s, decorated white porcelain, metal top/cork seal, Goebel mark, 4-3/4"...................**$369**

Perfume Bottles Auction

Monpelas A la Violette perfume bottle and stopper, 1830, clear bright aqua glass, unusual six-part mold, base label, early gold lithography, rare, 5".
.............................**$615**

Perfume Bottles Auction

A. Jollivet Salon Charme Caressant perfume bottle and stopper, 1927, pale green opaque glass, sharkskin finish, blue green patina, 4-1/8".
.............................**$738**

Perfume Bottles Auction

Czechoslovakian perfume bottle and stopper, circa 1930, clear/frost deep amethyst crystal, dauber stub, small nick to stopper edge, Czechoslovakia in line, 6-3/8"...................**$676**

Perfume Bottles Auctions

Grenoville Byzance perfume bottle and stopper, 1935, black glass, chromed metal cover, 2-1/8"..........**$799**

Perfume Bottles Auction

Ingrid Czechoslovakian perfume bottle and stopper, circa 1930, deep smoky gray crystal, stands on three feet, fish motif, dauber, Ingrid label, 7"............. **$1,476**

Perfume Bottles Auction

Ingrid Czechoslovakian floriform perfume bottle and stopper, circa 1930, clear/frost amber crystal, floral pattern, dauber, MIC in oval, 5-5/8".
.........................**$1,230**

Perfume Bottles Auction

Czechoslovakian atomizer, circa 1930, clear/frost crystal, translucent enamel detail, gilt metal hardware, MIC in lines, 5-1/2"...................**$369**

Perfume Bottles Auction

Limoges enamel scent bottle, circa 1870, gold mounts, glass stopper, shaped as hinged etui box, gold mark D&V, 3". **$1,230**

Perfume Bottles Auction

American perfume atomizer in cut crystal, circa 1880, figural silver screw top, youth on shell holding dolphin, detailed hands and face, 8". **$2,091**

Perfume Bottles Auction

Gorham chatelaine scent bottle, circa 1900, sterling silver, hand chased images of Poseidon and Amphitrite among sea creatures, screw cap, Gorham marks, bottle 3-1/4". **$1,1,68**

Perfume Bottles Auction

English double-end scent bottle, circa 1880, red crystal, silver screw cap and pressure cap marked GB, 5-1/2". **$338**

Perfume Bottles Auction

Moser Bohemian perfume bottle, circa 1900, cranberry crystal, flashed stopper, molded overall floral motif, gilt and enameled detail, 5-1/8". **$1,045**

Perfume Bottles Auction

Richard cameo glass atomizer, circa 1900, cut leaf and pod design, burgundy color glass on white ground, original gilt metal fittings, Richard mark, 9-1/4". **$492**

Perfume Bottles Auction

Bohemian art glass atomizer, circa 1910, cameo cut red to clear/ frost central band, metal fittings, original hose and ball, 7-1/4". **$615**

Perfume Bottles Auction

Ota telephone atomizer, 1920s, black glass, metal fittings, carved wooden receiver, replaced hose and ball, bottom molded: Ota-Paris, 8-1/4". **$1,845**

Perfume Bottles Auction

Perfume bottle charm, 1930s, 14K yellow gold (7.9 dwt), screw cap, hanging chain, marked 14K, 3/4". **$553**

Perfume Bottles Auction

◄ Bohemian figural perfume bottle pendant, 1920s, silver and gold finished metal case, glass with jewels, head moves, filigree metalwork holds four pins and tiny glass bottle, bottle 3/4". **$1,968**

Perfume Bottles Auction

Czechoslovakian perfume bottle and stopper, circa 1930, blue crystal, dauber, jeweled and enameled metalwork at neck and all around, 7-1/2"......................................**$12,300**

Perfume Bottles Auction

Czechoslovakian perfume bottle, circa 1930, pink crystal, gilt metalwork collar, jeweled bib front/back, stopper head, glass dauber, Austria in metal, 5".........................**$984**

Perfume Bottles Auction

Depinoix Lubin Au Soleil perfume bottle and stopper, circa 1912, frost glass, molded lizard chasing fly, enameled detail and label, 5-3/4"................**$1,476**

Perfume Bottles Auction

R. Lalique D'Orsay Chypre perfume bottle and stopper, 1927, molded Art Deco floral design, black patina, Lalique mark, 2-1/2". **$922**

Perfume Bottles Auction

Baccarat design, Schiaparelli Sleeping, circa 1938, figural perfume bottle, clear glass, red flashed stopper, gilt detail, label, figural box, 6-1/2" ..**$430**

Perfume Bottles Auction

Czechoslovakian perfume bottle and openwork stopper, circa 1930, clear/frost crystal, dauber stub, Czechoslovakia in oval, 6-3/4". **$676**

Perfume Bottles Auction

Schiaparelli Si figural perfume bottle and stopper, 1958, gilt and enameled glass, plastic hangtag label, gold foil box, named for Juliette Greco Song, 4-3/4"..**$738**

Perfume Bottles Auction

Baccarat Grenoville Victrix perfume bottle and stopper, clear/frost crystal, molded label, gray patina, numbered, 1-3/4".............................. **$1,599**

Perfume Bottles Auction

R. Lalique Gabilla Le Lilas perfume bottle and stopper, circa 1925, frost glass, molded floral surface, rose patina, Lalique mark, box (lacking tassel), 3-5/8"...**$3,075**

Perfume Bottles Auction

Petroliana

PETROLIANA COVERS a broad range of gas station collectibles from containers and globes to signs and pumps and everything in between.

As with all advertising items, factors such as brand name, intricacy of design, color, age, condition, and rarity drastically affect value.

Beware of reproduction and fantasy pieces. For collectors of vintage gas and oil items, the only way to avoid reproductions is experience: making mistakes and learning from them; talking with other collectors and dealers; finding reputable resources (including books and websites), and learning to invest wisely, buying the best examples one can afford.

Oldsmobile Used Cars sign, "Safety Tested," 42". **$4,250**

Marks can be deceiving, paper labels and tags are often missing, and those that remain may be spurious. Adding to the confusion are "fantasy" pieces, globes that have no vintage counterpart, and that are often made more for visual impact than deception.

How does one know whether a given piece is authentic? Does it look old, and to what degree can age be simulated? What is the difference between high-quality vintage advertising and modern mass-produced examples? Even experts are fooled when trying to assess qualities that have subtle distinctions.

There is another important factor to consider. A contemporary maker may create a "reproduction" sign or gas globe in tribute of the original, and sell it for what it is: a legitimate copy. Many of these are dated and signed by the artist or manufacturer, and these legitimate copies are highly collectible today. Such items are not intended to be frauds.

But a contemporary piece may pass through many hands between the time it leaves the maker and winds up in a collection. When profit is the only motive of a reseller, details about origin, ownership, and age can become a slippery slope of guesses, attribution, and – unfortunately – fabrication.

As the collector's eye sharpens, and the approach to inspecting and assessing petroliana improves, it will become easier to buy with confidence. And a knowledgeable collecting public should be the goal of all sellers, if for no other reason than the willingness to invest in quality.

For more information about petroliana, consult *Warman's Gas Station Collectibles* by Mark Moran.

PETROLIANA

Atlantic Motorboat Oil counter-top display with round quart metal can, "Brand New Power." **$525**

Greyhound sign with graphics, 24" x 40"..........**$450**

Mileage Gasoline sign, tire in motion logo, 14" x 20". **$400**

Oldsmobile Service flange sign, porcelain, 16" x 22". **$900**

Oliver Farm Implements sign, "Plowmakers for the World," with logo, 14" x 48"...................**$2,200**

Studebaker Rockne Authorized Service Genuine Parts sign, with logos. **$3,500**

Speedwell Motor Oil flange sign, porcelain, "Running Made Easy" logo. **$600**

Porsche Stuttgart sign, classic crest, 1960s. **$4,500**

Packard Cup Grease by Wolverine Lubricants five-pound metal can **$375**

Reliable Premium Regular 13-1/2" lenses in original Capco globe body. **$7,700**

TOP LOT!

Beacon Security Gasoline die-cut sign, "A Caminol Product" lighthouse, 48" x 30", likely finest known..................$55,000

BMW convex sign, classic logo, prewar, 24".....................$2,250

Harbor Petroleum Products die-cut sign, double-sided porcelain, seaplane graphics............$8,250

Golden West Oil Company sign, blue mountains graphics ... $2,700

John Deere self-framed sign, new old stock, embossed, two-legged deer, 42" x 38". $375

76 Outboard Fuel Gasoline sign, 11-1/2"..............................$350

North Dakota Route 28 highway sign, 15" x 15". $375

Certified Garages of America Association and Authorized Member by Invitation metal sign................................. $3,700

Vespa Service scooter sign with logo, 31".........................$1,500

Shell shark-tooth shape sign, 48" x 48"........................$1,750

Ford sign, mid-size oval, 23" x 33"...................................$950

POSTCARDS

Postcards

IN THE FIRST HALF OF THE 20TH CENTURY, postcards were cheap, often one cent and rarely more than five cents on the racks. Worldwide exchanges were common, making it possible to gain huge variety without being rich.

Those days are gone forever, but collectors today are just as avid about their acquisitions. What postcards are bestsellers today? The people most likely to have the pulse of the hobby are dealers who offer thousands of cards to the public every year.

Ron Millard, longtime owner of Cherryland Auctions, and Mary L. Martin, known for running the largest store in the country devoted exclusively to postcards, have offered some insights into the current state of the market. Each dealer has taken a son into the business, a sure sign of the confidence they have in the future of postcard collecting.

Real photo postcards of the early 1900s are highly rated by both dealers. Martin, who sells at shows as well as through her store, reports that interest in rare real photos is "increasing faster than they can be bought."

Millard, whose Cherryland Auctions feature 1,800 lots closing every five weeks, indicates that real photos seem to be "holding steady with prices actually rising among the lower-end real photos as some people shy from paying the huge prices they have been bringing ... Children with toys and dolls have been increasing and also unidentified but interesting U.S. views."

Cherryland bidders have also been focused on "advertising cards, high-end art cards, Halloween, early political, and baseball postcards." Movie stars, other famous people and transportation, especially autos and zeppelins, also do very well. Lower-priced cards with great potential for rising in value include linen restaurant advertising, "middle range" holidays, and World War I propaganda.

Millard also says vintage chromes, especially advertising, is "really starting to take off with many now bringing $10 to $15. (These were $1 cards a few years ago.)"

At one time, foreign cards were largely ignored by collectors, but online sales have broadened the international market. In Millard's experience, "The sky is the limit on any China-related." A few months ago Cherryland had a huge influx of new bidders from Australia, and the number from Asia is also increasing.

"Hooty the Owl" image advertising Quaddy Playthings Mfg. Co., divided back, monochrome, used, minor corner wear and creasing on edges, near fine to very fine condition. **$20**

Cherryland Postcard Auctions

POSTCARDS

Martin sees hometown views as the most popular category, with real photo social history, dressed animals, and Halloween also in high demand. She reports, "We see a lot of interest in military right now, and I don't believe it has really peaked yet." Social history from the 1950s and '60s also does well. She's encouraged by the number of new and younger collectors at postcard shows.

Fantasy photo, circa 1911, copyright Martin, "Watermelons Grow Big in Iowa," Indianola, Iowa, used, divided back, fine condition. **$22**

Cherryland Postcard Auctions

Will anyone want your postcards when you're ready to sell? It's a valid question, and our two experts have good advice for anyone with a sizeable accumulation, say 500 or more postcards.

Auctions are one good option, both for direct purchases and consignments. Millard is always looking for quality postcards to offer collectors worldwide. His firm can handle collections of any size from small specialized to giant accumulations, and is willing to travel for large consignments. Active buying is a necessity for dealers to keep their customers supplied, which should reassure collectors that their cards will have a ready market. Contact Millard at CherrylandAuctions@charter.net or www. Cherrylandauctions.com.

Martin suggests that collectors go back to some of the dealers who sold them cards when they're ready to sell. Her firm is always willing to buy back good quality cards. She also sees reputable auction houses as a good avenue, and strongly suggests, "They should never be sold as a very large group if they can be broken down into different subject matter or topics." Martin can be contacted at marymartinpostcards@gmail. com.

Both experts agree there's an active demand for quality collections. That would exclude postcards in poor condition, a caution for collectors expanding their holdings. Look for the best and pass up damaged and dirty cards.

Billions of postcards were produced in the last century on practically every topic imaginable. As collections become more specialized, new subjects are sure to attract attention. Many outstanding collections were put together with moderate expense by people who were among the first to recognize the value of a new collecting area.

As an example of an area yet to be fully explored, the photographers who made postcards possible haven't been widely collected in their own right. Many were anonymous, but some, like Bob Petley, famous for Western views as well as comic humor, attract attention. The Tucson Post Card Exchange Club has made a specialty of gathering and listing the output of its "favorite son." No doubt there are fresh, new specialties just waiting to be discovered.

Postcard collectors love history, appreciate fine art, enjoy humor, and above all, are imaginative. There's every indication that today's favorite topics will be joined by new and exciting ones in the future.

— *Barbara Andrews*

POSTCARDS

$

TOP LOT!

1910 real photo advertising Mertes & Breitenfelt Druggists, Hartford, Wisconsin, real photo of store interior with portraits, very fine condition. **$200**

Cherryland Postcard Auct

1926 Sesquicentennial Expo, "Fokker the Seventh," Commander Byrd's flight, white border, near very fine condition. **$11**

Cherryland Postcard Auctions

Artist signed comic "Greetings from Coney Island," copyright 1907, divided back, monochrome, wearing on corners, fine condition. **$7.50**

Cherryland Postcard Auctions

Tinted photogravure advertising Mangel Florist of Chicago, Albertype publisher, divided back, near very fine condition **$17**

Cherryland Postcard Auctions

Hawaii, Pineapple Plantation, Island Curio Co., used, copyright 1911, divided back, monochrome, cancel on front, some wearing on corners, fine condition. **$10**

Cherryland Postcard Auctions

Novelty hand-drawn on U.S. Gov't Postal, U.S. Military 1898 Spanish-American War, used, copyright 1898, fine condition...........................**$65**

Cherryland Postcard Auctions

POSTCARDS

Young child illustration advertising Elgin's Watches, of Prospect, Ohio, circa 1914, divided back, near very fine condition. **$15**

Cherryland Postcard Auctions

Rocking Horse & Soldiers, real photograph, European publisher, circa 1914, creasing on corner, fine to very fine condition. **$15**

Cherryland Postcard Auctions

Fantasy Monsters, circa 1907, copyright Helen Stilwell Car #241/3, divided back, used, monochrome, near fine to very fine condition. **$35**

Cherryland Postcard Auctions

Amsterdam Donald Duck series, Disney, copyright 1967, wear on corners, near fine condition. **$5**

Cherryland Postcard Auctions

Halloween, AMP Pub., copyright 1909, divided back, embossed, some wear to corner, near fine to very fine condition...**$8**

Cherryland Postcard Auctions

INSIDE INTEL

BEST ADVICE: Linen cards (1930s-1950s) are big, but it's the eye candy collectors pay for. The most expensive cards are in demand. Most of my new customers I find through eBay. Shows are still fun to do; you get personal contact with collectors. Some people say eBay hurt the collectibles business, but I think it created more collectors, and it changed what it meant to call something rare.

HOT OR NOT: My youngest customers are on eBay, and they are buying color chrome cards (Photochrom) from the 1950s and 1960s. Even though they didn't grow up during that time they are drawn to that nostalgia.

HOT

— *Tony Meager,*
Dealer, Matchsets Vintage Postcards & Photography
matchsets.com

Tinted printed photo, Yankee Stadium, New York, copyright 1929, used, near very fine condition. $15

Cherryland Postcard Auctions

Lacrosse team, real photo, Hoboken, New Jersey, copyright 1913, used, monochrome, writing on front and some wear to corners, fine to very fine condition..$50

Cherryland Postcard Auctions

Train depot, real photo, Richland, New York, copyright 1908, near very fine condition. $55

Cherryland Postcard Auctions

Chinatown, San Francisco, California, used, copyright 1915, monochrome, creasing on edges, near fine to very fine condition. $11

Cherryland Postcard Auctions

New Year with Snowman, Belgian publisher, copyright 1935, #3151 very fine condition. $12

Cherryland Postcard Auctions

Jack in the Box, art by E. Colombo, Italian publisher, part of series from 1941-1942, fine to very fine condition......$15

Cherryland Postcard Auctions

World War I Red Cross Wohlfahrtskarte Mail Call, artist signed, used, copyright 1917, Stuttgart Bahnhof cancellation stamp, wear to corners, fine condition. $23

Cherryland Postcard Auctions

A Proud Mother, artist signed Louis Wain, London publisher, #1472, circa 1907, monochrome, divided back, used, minor corner wear and edge creasing, near fine to very fine condition. ...$100

Cherryland Postcard Auctions

4th of July, P. Sander publisher, copyright 1910, divided back, embossed, major back thinning and creases, fine condition. $12

Cherryland Postcard Auctions

Motorcycle with sidecar advertising Mobiloel Oil, German publisher, early Continental, very fine condition. $30

Cherryland Postcard Auctions

Posters

A POSTER IS a large, usually printed placard, bill, or announcement, often illustrated, that is posted to advertise or publicize something. It can also be an artistic work, often a reproduction of an original painting or photograph, printed on a large sheet of paper.

Vintage posters are usually between 20 and 50 years old and must be original and not copies or newer reproductions.

The value of a vintage poster is determined by condition, popularity of the subject matter, rarity, artistic rendering, and the message it conveys.

"Breakfast at Tiffany's" (Paramount, 1961): Rare large format poster shares similar artwork with one sheet; Audrey Hepburn in her iconic black Givenchy gown, pearl necklace, and diamond hair jewelry; artwork by renowned poster artist Robert McGinnis; cleaned and touched up to minimize appearance of tears, chips, and pinholes in borders, creasing, rolled, fine/very fine condition, 30" x 40" **$5,378**

Heritage Auctions

"Home Made Home" (RKO, 1951), one sheet: Walt Disney's Goofy encounters difficulties with paint, blueprints, and a saw while attempting to build his dream home; slight fold and crossfold separation, light handling wear, very fine condition, 27" x 41"... **$1,195**

Heritage Auctions

POSTERS

MOVIE POSTERS

"The African Queen" (United Artists, 1952), insert:
Humphrey Bogart and Katharine Hepburn star
in John Huston film, adapted from novel by C.S.
Forester, in which the two travel down an African
river during World War I to destroy a German
battleship; professionally restored tear from top
border into background, tear from right border
into background, small holes in borders and red
background, chip in upper right corner, some paper
loss in image at center fold, borders airbrushed,
fine+ condition on paper, 14" x 36" **$837**

Heritage Auctions

"The African Queen" (United Artists, 1952),
one sheet: Humphrey Bogart won an Oscar for
portraying a drunken riverboat captain who
embarks on a mission with a spinster (Katharine
Hepburn) to sink a German battleship during World
War I; some color touchup to upper center point in
"R" of title, pinhole in each corner, upper border
airbrushed, fine/very fine condition on linen, 27" x
41" **$2,271**

Heritage Auctions

"International House" (Paramount, 1933), CGC graded lobby card: Comedy starring W.C. Fields, George Burns, and Gracie Allen, rare, CGC graded 9.4, near mint condition, 11" x 14" **$2,390**

Heritage Auctions

"International House" (Paramount, 1933), CGC graded lobby card: Scene with car and W.C. Fields, George Burns, Gracie Allen, Stuart Erwin, Lumsden Hare, and Franklin Pangborn, extremely scarce, CGC graded 8.0, very fine condition, 11" x 14".. **$3,585**

Heritage Auctions

"My Little Chickadee" (Universal, 1940), one sheet, Style B: Written by both W.C. Fields and Mae West, it is said the two stars disliked each other; piece missing in upper border into upper tag line, piece missing from upper left corner into red field, minor chipping in upper horizontal fold to left of West's head, chipping in center horizontal fold above West's and Field's credit, piece missing in left border just below West's name that extends into red field, professional restoration, fine- condition on linen, 27" x 41"................................. **$3,585**

Heritage Auctions

"Tarzan the Fearless" (Principal Distributing, 1933), one sheet, Chapter 1, "The Dive of Death": Olympic swimmer Larry "Buster" Crabbe stars in one of his first major roles as legendary Ape Man, based directly on an Edgar Rice Burroughs story; prior to restoration, small tears and tiny chips in borders, which have been airbrushed, professional touchup to folds, only all-art stone litho poster for serial, fine/very fine condition on linen, 27" x 41" **$2,629**

Heritage Auctions

"The Acid Eaters" (FPS Ventures, 1968), one sheet: Cult classic dealing in exploitation of sex, drugs, and rock and roll in the late 1960s, produced by David Friedman, one of his last films as an independent, near mint-condition, 28" x 41-3/4"...**$1,165**

Heritage Auctions

"One Cab's Family" (MGM, 1951), one sheet: Directed by Tex Avery, story about two taxicabs whose son has ambitions to become a hot rod, very fine+ condition on linen, 27" x 41"...........................**$837**

Heritage Auctions

"Star Wars" (20th Century Fox, 1977), one sheet, Mylar advance: Printed in 1976, with title design that would be changed for all posters to follow, making this a rare and collectible item; minor creases and light handling wear, rolled, very fine+ condition, 27" x 41"................................. **$1,195**

Heritage Auctions

"The New Adventures of Batman and Robin" (Columbia, 1949), one sheet, Chapter 13, "The Wizard's Challenge": Second serial to feature characters played by Robert Lowery and John Duncan, based on Bob Kane's legendary character, art of heroes with image of villain in inset photo; prior to restoration, poster had two extended tears from right border into title and image areas, fine+ condition on linen, 27" x 41"........................**$1,912**

Heritage Auctions

"A Day at the Races" (MGM, 1937), midget window card: The Marx Brothers star with Maureen O'Sullivan, who tries to save her medical facility with the help of a vet (Groucho) posing as a doctor with his accomplices; established Marx Brothers artist Al Hirschfeld provided art; top imprint area professionally replaced, small tears in right border addressed, touchup work to lower border, fine condition, 8" x 14" ... **$2,629**

Heritage Auctions

"The War of the Worlds" (Paramount, 1953), one sheet: H.G. Wells' classic alien invasion tale earned an Academy Award for its special effects; poster with alien hand reaching from dark skies toward a couple; prior to restoration, slight paper loss at center crossfold, small hole in palm of alien hand in image, and small chips in horizontal fold, fine condition on linen, 27" x 41".

.... **$3,466**

Heritage Auctions

"Godzilla" (Trans World, 1956), one sheet: Image of towering Godzilla (Gojira in Japan) laying waste to everything in his path; prior to restoration, poster had tears in upper, right, and lower borders, tear in upper border that extended into background, separations in upper and lower crossfolds, and chip in left border at center horizontal fold, touchup work to folds, fine/very fine condition on linen, 27" x 41" **$2,390**

Heritage Auctions

"Lumber Jack-Rabbit" (Warner Brothers, 1954), one sheet, 3-D style: Looney Tunes cartoon directed by Chuck Jones, Bugs Bunny matches wits with Paul Bunyan and his 4,600 ton dog, Smidgen, very fine+ condition on linen, 27" x 41" **$1,195**

Heritage Auctions

"Dillinger: Public Enemy No.1" (Midland Film Co., 1934), one sheet: J. Edgar Hoover commissioned this propagandic newsreel to make the FBI's killing of John Dillinger more heroic; rare poster was part of four-wall campaign by makers; backed on Kraft paper, poster shows pinholes in image, smudging, wrinkling, and misfold at lower horizontal fold, fine+ condition, 27" x 41" **$2,629**

Heritage Auctions

"Devil's Harvest" (Continental, 1942), one sheet: "The Smoke of Hell!" directed by Ray Test, 1940s anti-drug film; tear in imprint area, which, along with borders and white portions of image, have been airbrushed, touchup work to folds, fine condition on linen, 27" x 41"... **$1,673**

Heritage Auctions

"Vertigo" (Paramount, 1958), three sheet: Posters for Alfred Hitchcock's tale of obsession are among the most collectible for any Hitchcock film; artwork by Saul Bass; professional restoration with some color retouch done to white areas of borders and lower credits as well as orange background enhanced to diminish some sun fading, very good+ condition on linen, 41" x 81" **$7,768**

Heritage Auctions

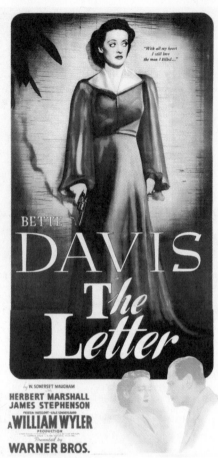

"The Letter" (Warner Brothers, 1940), three sheet: This adaptation of W. Somerset Maugham's play finds Bette Davis entangled in web of lies and deceit; full-length image of Davis with the murder weapon; 1/2" added to airbrushed borders, professional restoration to pinholes in corners and tear in white background in lower section, touchup work to folds, fine/very fine condition on linen, 41-1/2" x 79" **$6,573**

Heritage Auctions

"The Nightmare Before Christmas" (Touchstone, 1993), lenticular one sheet, advance 3-D style: Produced and written by Tim Burton, directed by Henry Selick; produced in limited quantity, made of photographic material laminated onto Plexiglass to create three-dimensional effect, known as barrier strip image in industry; light surface scratches, very fine+ condition, 27" x 40" **$4,183**

Heritage Auctions

POSTERS

$

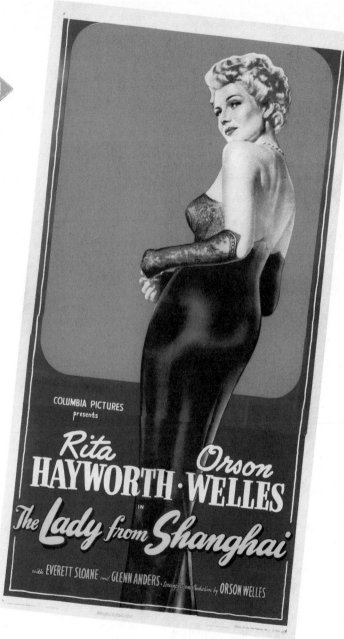

TOP LOT!

"The Lady from Shanghai" (Columbia, 1947), three sheet: Rita Hayworth as devious Elsa Bannister embodies the ultimate femme fatale in Orson Welles' film noir classic; professional restoration to surface paper loss on verso, at top crossfold, and small chip in Hayworth's chest, touchup applied to folds and top left corner and upper right background chips, fine/very fine condition on linen, 41" x 80"
.... **$8,963**

Heritage Auctions

TRAVEL POSTERS

Come to Britain for Golf, Rowland Frederick Hilder (1905-1993), lithograph in colors, printed by W.S. Cowell Ltd., London, backed on linen, 25-1/2" x 20" **$2,086**

Dreweatts & Bloombury

Deutsche Lufthansa/Luftreisen, 1935, Julius Ussy Engelhard (1883-1964), paper, framed, with woman waving from steps as she boards plane, Chromolitho-Kunstanstalt, Munich, 40-1/2" x 24-3/4". **$875**

Swann Auction Galleries

New England, United Air Lines, anonymous, offset lithograph in colors, not backed, 40" x 25". **$367**

Dreweatts & Bloombury

Discover South Africa, lithograph in colors, printed by Rotogravure, backed on linen, 40" x 25"..... **$918**

Dreweatts & Bloombury

Bermuda, Pan Am, by Ray Ameijide, offset lithograph in colors, backed on linen, 42" x 28" **$3,171**

Dreweatts & Bloombury

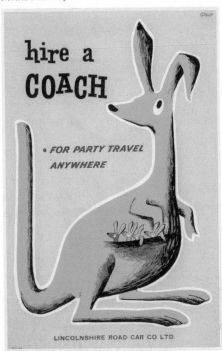

Qantas travel poster for Japan, circa 1960, artwork by Harry Rogers, linen backed, 38" x 29".........**$412**

Mossgreen Auctions

Hire a Coach, lithograph in colors, not backed, 30" x 20"..**$200**

Dreweatts & Bloombury

See the Land of the Vikings, 1937, Swedish, artwork by Ben Blessum, printed by Bortzells, Essette, Stockholm, linen backed, 39" x 25"... **$584**

Ewbanks

San Francisco Fly TWA, David Klein, offset lithograph in colors, not backed, 40" x 25"...... **$117**

Dreweatts & Bloombury

Superbagnères–Luchon/Sports d'Hiver, 1929, standout piece for Leonetto Cappiello (1875-1942), one of his few travel posters, 39" x 24"........... **$3,750**

Swann Auction Galleries

PROPAGANDA POSTERS

Rare war-date propaganda poster aimed at separatist sentiments of Ukrainian Cossacks, marked at bottom: "W.Z. 96125 (D. ofs.) 1943)," Cossack in red shirt, blue pants and black boots, holding in each hand green-complexioned caricature of orthodox Jew and grimacing commissar, at bottom: "Cossacks, now is the time to save your family and country! Time to toss off the yoke which we have upon us!"; 25-1/4" x 33-3/4"... **$3,250**

Alexander Historical Auctions, LLC

China Leading the World to Higher Heights, by James Kwabena Anane, 30-1/2" x 20". **$350**

Material Culture

Soviet Russian propaganda poster, 1942, of British Prime Minister Winston Churchill's face on bulldog's body, 11-3/4" x 16-3/8".................... **$12**

Pioneer Auction Gallery

POSTERS

Iconic American propaganda poster from World War I promoting Victory Liberty Loan, by artist Clyde Forsythe, American soldier with spoils of war: three German helmets, shattered buildings and barbed wire behind him, with exclamation, "And they thought we couldn't fight"; 30-1/2" x 41"........**$140**

Alexander Historical Auctions, LLC

Let's Give Him Enough and On Time, by Norman Rockwell (U.S. Government Printing Office, 1942). The United States found itself unprepared for war after the Japanese bombed Pearl Harbor, due to weapon shortages; poster showcases a soldier in a frayed uniform with a weapon nearly exhausted of its ammo; Rockwell's only work featuring a soldier in battle; his other art depicts soldiers on the homefront or in light-hearted situations; 28-1/2" x 40". **$896**

Heritage Auctions

Quilts

EACH GENERATION MADE QUILTS, comforters and coverlets, all intended to be used. Many were used into oblivion and rest in quilt heaven, but for a myriad of reasons, some have survived. Many of them remain because they were not used but stored, often forgotten, in trunks and linen cabinets.

A quilt is made up of three layers: the top, which can be a solid piece of fabric, appliquéd, pieced, or a combination; the back, which can be another solid piece of fabric or pieced; and the batting, which is the center layer, which can be cotton, wool, polyester, a blend of poly and cotton, or even silk. Many vintage quilts are batted with an old blanket or even another old, worn quilt.

The fabrics are usually cotton or wool, or fine fancy fabrics like silk, velvet, satin, and taffeta. The layers of a true quilt are held together by the stitching, or quilting, that goes through all three layers and is usually worked in a design or pattern that enhances the piece overall.

Pennsylvania Broken Star quilt, circa 1900, 83" x 93"..**$420**

Pook & Pook, Inc.

Quilts made from a seemingly single solid piece of fabric are known as wholecloth quilts, or if they are white, as whitework quilts. Usually such quilts are constructed from two or more pieces of the same fabric joined to make up the necessary width. They are often quilted quite elaborately, and the seams virtually disappear within the decorative stitching. Most wholecloth quilts are solid-colored, but prints were also used. Whitework quilts were often made as bridal quilts and many were kept for "best," which means that they have survived in reasonable numbers.

Wholecloth quilts were among the earliest type of quilted bedcovers made in Britain, and the colonists brought examples with them according to inventory lists that exist from colonial times. American quiltmakers used the patterns early in the nation's history, and some were carried with settlers moving west across the Appalachians.

Appliqué quilts are made from shapes cut from fabric and applied, or appliquéd, to a background, usually solid-colored on vintage quilts, to make a design. Early appliqué quilts dating back to the 18th century were often worked in a technique called *broderie perse*, or Persian embroidery, in which printed motifs were cut from a piece of fabric, such as costly chintz, and applied to a plain, less expensive background cloth.

Appliqué was popular in the 1800s, and there are thousands of examples, from

QUILTS

exquisite, brightly colored Baltimore Album quilts made in and around Baltimore between circa 1840 and 1860, to elegant four-block quilts made later in the century. Many appliqué quilts are pictorial with floral designs the predominant motif. In the 20th century, appliqué again enjoyed an upswing, especially during the Colonial Revival period, and thousands were made from patterns or appliqué kits that were marketed and sold from 1900 through the 1950s.

Victorian Flying Geese crazy quilt, 70" x 67". **$420**
Pook & Pook, Inc.

Pieced or patchwork quilts are made by cutting fabric into shapes and sewing them together to make a larger piece of cloth. The patterns are usually geometric, and their effectiveness depends heavily on the contrast of not just the colors themselves, but of color value as well. Patchwork became popular in the United States in the early 1800s.

Colonial clothing was almost always made using cloth cut into squares or rectangles, but after the Revolutionary War, when fabric became more widely available, shaped garments were made, and these garments left scraps. Frugal housewives, especially among the westward-bound pioneers, began to use these cutoffs to put together blocks that could then be made into quilts. Patchwork quilts are by far the most numerous of all vintage-quilt categories, and the diversity of style, construction and effect that can be found is a study all its own.

Dating a quilt is a tricky business unless the maker included the date on the finished item, and unfortunately for historians and collectors, few did. The value of a particular example is affected by its age, of course, and educating yourself about dating methods is invaluable. There are several aspects that can offer guidelines for establishing a date. These include fabrics; patterns; technique; borders; binding; batting; backing; quilting method; and colors and dyes.

In recent years many significant quilt collections have appeared in the halls of museums around the world, enticing both quilters and practitioners of art appreciation. One of the most noted collections to become a national exhibition in 2014 was the Pilgrim/Roy Collection. The selection of quilts included in the "Quilts and Color" exhibition, presented by the Museum of Fine Arts in Boston, was a mix of materials and designs, represented in nearly 60 distinct 19th and 20th century quilts.

For more information on quilts, see *Warman's Vintage Quilts Identification and Price Guide* by Maggi McCormick Gordon.

QUILTS

Amish Diamond in Square quilt, early 20th century, 77" x 80". **$800**

Pook & Pook, Inc.

Star of Bethlehem quilt, late 19th century, 83" x 82". **$960**

Pook & Pook, Inc.

Pennsylvania floral appliqué quilt, circa 1900, 78" x 74".................................... **$492**

Pook & Pook, Inc.

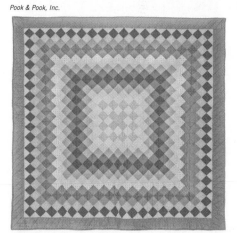

Trip Around the World quilt, circa 1900, 66" x 66".. **$780**

Pook & Pook, Inc.

Pieced and appliqué crib quilts, 19th century, with central star surrounded by quilted garland within sawtooth border, 34" x 34". **$3,600**

Pook & Pook, Inc.

QUILTS

Appliqué World's Fair quilt, dated 1933, showing a century of American progress, 68" x 82". **$1,920**

Pook & Pook, Inc.

Appliqué chintz Tree of Life quilt, circa 1820, 101" x 95". Provenance: Descended in the Bennett family of Maryland........................... **$4,029**

Pook & Pook, Inc.

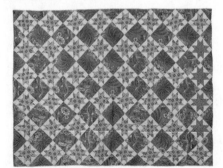

Virginia chintz Star quilt, circa 1840, signed verso Julia Martin, 59" x 77". **$770**

Pook & Pook, Inc.

New England quilted linsey woolsey bedspread, early 19th century, 89" x 84"....................... **$1,126**

Pook & Pook, Inc.

Pieced geometric quilt, early 20th century, 79" x 78". **$711**

Pook & Pook, Inc.

Wake County, North Carolina Log Cabin quilt, 19th century, with lace border, 84" x 84"......... **$369**

Pook & Pook, Inc.

QUILTS

$

Pieced and appliqué patriotic quilt, mid-20th century, 91" x 76"..................... **$1,007**

Pook & Pook, Inc.

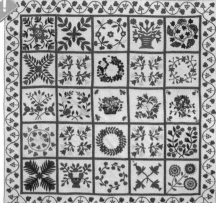

Schoolhouse quilt, early 20th century, 74" x 91"....................... **$360**

Pook & Pook, Inc.

Baltimore appliqué and trapunto album quilt, dated 1851, with 25 floral decorated panels within a trailing vine and berry border, 104" x 106"...**$13,200**

Pook & Pook, Inc.

Commemorative appliqué quilt, 1683-1983, Germans to America: 300 Years of Immigration, 88" x 100".. **$510**

Pook & Pook, Inc.

Virginia chintz Star quilt, circa 1840, signed verso Julia Martin, 59" x 77". **$770**

Pook & Pook, Inc.

Reedsville, Pennsylvania Amish star quilt, early 20th century, 78-1/2" x 79"............................ **$456**

Pook & Pook, Inc.

Virginia Pineapple Log Cabin quilt, circa 1920, with zigzag border, 76-1/2" x 78-1/2". **$474**

Pook & Pook, Inc.

Records

BEFORE YOU CAN FIGURE OUT a record's worth, you need to grade it. When visually grading records, use a direct light, such as a 100-watt desk lamp, to clearly show all defects. If you're dealing with a record that looks worse than it sounds, play grade it. You also need to assess the condition of each sleeve, cover, label and insert. Think like the buyer as you set your grades. Records and covers always seem to look better when you're grading them to sell to someone else than when you're on the other side of the table, inspecting a record for purchase. If in doubt, go with the lower grade. And, if you have a "still sealed" record, subject it to as many of these same grading standards as you can without breaking the seal.

Goldmine Grading

MINT (M): Absolutely perfect. Mint never should be used as a grade unless more than one person agrees the item meets the criteria; few dealers or collectors use this term. There is no rule for calculating mint value; that is best negotiated between buyer and seller.
- Overall Appearance: Looks as if it just came off the manufacturing line.
- Record: Glossy, unmarred surface.
- Labels: Perfectly placed and free of writing, stickers, and spindle marks.
- Cover/Sleeve: Perfectly crisp and clean. Free of stains, discoloration, stickers, ring wear, dinged corners, sleeve splits, or writing.

NEAR MINT (NM) OR MINT MINUS (M-): Most dealers and collectors use NM/M- as their highest grade, implying that no record or sleeve is ever truly perfect. It's estimated that no more than 2 to 4 percent of all records remaining from the 1950s and 1960s truly meet near mint standards.

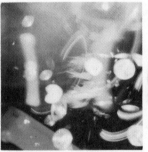

The Beatles, "Happy Christmas 1969," Beatles Fan Club-U.K., EX/NM Flexi-Disc with cover design by Richard Starkey (aka Ringo Starr) and Zak Starkey. **$138**

Heritage Auctions

- Overall Appearance: Looks as if it were opened for the first time. Includes all original pieces, including inner sleeve, lyric sheets, inserts, cover and record.
- Record: Shiny surface is free of visible defects and surface noise at playback. Records can retain NM condition after many plays provided the record has been stored, used and handled carefully.
- Labels: Properly pressed and centered on the record. Free of markings.

• Cover/Sleeve: Free of creases, ring wear, cut-out markings and seam splits. Picture sleeves look as if no record was ever housed inside. Hint: If you remove a 45 from its picture sleeve and store it separately, you will reduce the potential for damage to the sleeve.

VERY GOOD PLUS (VG+) OR EXCELLENT (EX+): Minor condition issues keep these records from a NM grade. Most collectors who want to play their records will be happy with VG+ records.

• Overall Appearance: Shows slight signs of wear.

• Record: May have slight warping, scuffs or scratches, but none that affect the sound. Expect minor signs of handling, such as marks around the center hole, light ring wear, or discoloration.

• Labels: Free of writing, stickers or major blemishes.

• Cover/Sleeve: Outer cover may have a cut-out mark. Both covers and picture sleeves may have slight creasing, minor seam wear or a split less than 1" long along the bottom.

VERY GOOD (VG): VG records have more obvious flaws than records in better condition, but still offer a fine listening experience for the price.

• Overall Appearance: Shows signs of wear and handling, including visible groove wear, audible scratches and surface noise, ring wear, and seam splits.

• Record: Record lacks its original glossy finish and may show groove wear and scratches deep enough to feel with a fingernail. Expect some surface noise and audible scratches (especially during a song's introduction and ending), but not enough to overpower the music.

• Labels: May have minor writing, tape, or a sticker.

• Cover/Sleeve: Shows obvious signs of handling and wear, including dull or discolored images; ring wear; seam splits on one or more sides; writing or a price tag; bent corners; stains or other problems. If the record has more than two of these problems, reduce its grade.

VERY GOOD MINUS (VG-), GOOD PLUS (G+), OR GOOD (G): A true G to VG- record still plays through without skipping, so it can serve as filler until something better comes along; you can always upgrade later. At most, these records sell for 10 to 15 percent of the near mint value.

• Overall Appearance: Shows considerable signs of handling, including visible groove wear, ring wear, seam splits and damaged labels or covers.

• Record: The record plays through without skipping, but the surface sheen is almost gone, and the groove wear and surface noise is significant

• Labels: Worn. Expect stains, heavy writing, and/or obvious damage from attempts to remove tape or stickers.

• Cover/Sleeve: Ring wear to the point of distraction; dinged and dog-eared edges; obvious seam splits and heavy writing (such as radio station call letters or an owner's name).

FAIR (F) OR POOR (P): Only outrageously rare items ever sell for more than a few cents in this condition – if they go at all. More likely, F or P records and covers will end up in the trash or be used to create clocks, journals, purses, jewelry, bowls, coasters or other art.

• Overall Appearance: Beat, trashed and dull. Records may lack sleeves or covers (or vice versa).

• Record: Vinyl may be cracked, scratched and/or warped to the point it skips.

• Labels: Expect stains, tears, soiling, marks and damage – if the label is even there.

• Cover/Sleeve: Heavily damaged or absent.

–Susan Sliwicki, editor, Goldmine *magazine*

Picture Sleeves and 45s

Tom Jones, "I Who Have Nothing" b/w "Stop Breaking My Heart," Parrot Records 45-40051, VG+ 45 with picture sleeve, 1970.........................**$13**

Jerry Lee Lewis, "The Great Ball of Fire" EP, Sun Records (EPA-107), VG+ 45 with VG picture sleeve, 1957.............**$32**

The Mamas & The Papas, "California Dreamin'," Dunhill (D-4020), EX picture sleeve only, 1965. ....**$400**

The Rolling Stones, "(I Can't Get No) Satisfaction" b/w "The Under Assistant West Coast Promotion Man," London 45-9766, 45 with picture sleeve (no grade given), 1965........**$150**

Connie Francis, "If I Didn't Care" b/w "Toward the End of the Day," MGM (K12769), VG 45 with VG picture sleeve, 1959.................................**$125**

Johnny Mathis, "Misty" b/w "The Story of Our Love," Columbia 4-41483, VG+ 45 with VG+ picture sleeve, 1959.............**$30**

The Temptations, "My Girl" b/w "(Talkin' 'Bout) Nobody But My Baby," Gordy (G-7038), VG+ 45 with VG+ picture sleeve, 1964.................................**$100**

The Rolling Stones, "Heart of Stone" b/w "What a Shame," London (45-9725), VG+ 45 with VG/VG+ picture sleeve............................**$383**

RECORDS

78s

Roy Orbison, "Ooby Dooby" b/w "Go! Go! Go!," Sun 242, NM 78 RPM, 1956................... **$325**

Heritage Auctions

Prisonaires, "Just Walking in the Rain" b/w "Baby Please," Sun 186, EX 78 RPM, 1953...... **$250**

Heritage Auctions

Ma Rainey, "Lost Wandering Blues" b/w "Dream Blues," Paramount 12098, G 78 RPM, 1924................................. **$375**

Heritage Auctions

◀ The Flamingos, "I Only Have Eyes For You" b/w "At the Prom," End 1946, EX 78 RPM, 1959.................................... **$94**

Heritage Auctions

LPs

Ray Conniff, "The Happy Beat," CBS (SBPG 62132) VG+/EX stereo LP, U.K. pressing, 1963........ **$15**

John Coltrane, "Blue Train," Blue Note (BLP 1577), NM mono LP, 1959. .... **$287**

Barbra Streisand, "Barbra Streisand," Columbia (PCQ 39801), VG+ quadraphonic LP, 1974.................................... **$37**

Led Zeppelin, "Led Zeppelin III," Atlantic (SD19128), still-sealed LP, 1970; "Led Zeppelin IV," Atlantic (SD19129), still-sealed LP, 1971; "Houses of the Holy," Atlantic (SD7255), still-sealed LP, 1973; all in at least NM condition. **$1,625**

Heritage Auctions

Glen Campbell, "Glen Campbell's Greatest Hits," Capitol (C1832), still-sealed LP with light ring wear, minor scrapes and small holes in shrink wrap. **$40**

The Doors, "The Doors," VG album cover signed in black ink by drummer John Densmore, guitarist Robby Krieger and keyboardist Ray Manzarek (d. May 20, 2013)................... **$175**

Gotta Have Rock and Roll

Herb Alpert & The Tijuana Brass, "Whipped Cream & Other Delights," A&M Records (SP 4110), still-sealed stereo LP, 1965, cover with slight corner rounding. **$27**

Sonny Rollins, "Saxophone Colossus," Acoustech Mastering/Prestige 7079, factory-sealed 45 RPM two-LP set, 2004. .... **$350**

Elvis Presley, "Aloha From Hawaii Via Satellite," RCA (SAR-9392-93), Japanese pressing, VG LP, with original RCA poster......................... **$200**

Gotta Have Rock and Roll

Bill Haley and His Comets, "Shake Rattle and Roll," Decca 5560, EX/VG 10" LP (1955).**$213**

Heritage Auctions

Bruce Springsteen, "Greetings From Asbury Park, NJ," VG album cover signed in black ink by Bruce Springsteen and inscribed and signed in blue ink "Love Clarence Clemons" by longtime E Street Band saxophonist (d. June 18, 2011). **$330**

Gotta Have Rock and Roll

Roy Clark, "The Lightning Fingers of Roy Clark," Capitol (ST 1780), NM stereo LP, 1963, sleeve EX+ condition, includes original Capitol Records inner sleeve. **$20**

RECORDS

Promotional Records

Long considered to be forbidden fruit for collectors, promotional records are considered fair game to buy and sell – regardless of any warnings printed on their labels – thanks to a ruling by the U.S. Ninth Circuit Court of Appeals. Although many promos are identical to the final releases save for a cut-out, different label or a promo sticker, they still hold an appeal to collectors. For starters, promo records are run in limited quantities and distributed to only a select few – artists, managers, deejays, reviewers, company executives – who might not even open the record, let alone listen to it. In the 1980s, many labels used Quiex II vinyl to press promo records, which was considered to be closer to audiophile quality than the vinyl used for stock copies. Some promo versions feature alternate versions, unreleased tracks, a different run order or even different cover artwork, all of which can boost a record's desirability and value. If all other things are equal, though, expect the value of a promo pressing to mirror that of the stock pressing.

Led Zeppelin, "Stairway to Heaven" (stereo) b/w "Stairway to Heaven" (mono), Atlantic (PR-175), VG+ 45 with VG+ picture sleeve, 1972........... **$307**

Rush, "Rush 'N' Roulette," Mercury (MK-185), 12" EP, 1981, label printed "Promotional Copy Not For Sale," with two-minute excerpts from Rush songs including "Tom Sawyer," "Closer to the Heart," "Spirit of Radio," "The Trees," "Red Barchetta," and "Spirit of Radio," no grade given. **$41**

Elvis Presley, "Special to DJ's USA," RCA (45-76), promotional EX 45 with picture sleeve, 1960. RCA issued this single to promote Elvis' second greatest hits album, "50,000,000 Elvis Fans Can't Be Wrong." **$1,500**

Bruce Springsteen, "Born to Run," Columbia Records, white-label advance promotional copy, EX/NM LP, 1975, with red promo card and lyric sheets. **$1,250**

Spotlight on The Beatles

Beatlemania started with a bang on Feb. 9, 1964, when the Fab Four performed on "The Ed Sullivan Show" for the first time. The band's records remain in demand among record collectors and generations of music fans.

The Beatles, "Love Me Do" b/w "P.S. I Love You," Oldies (OL-151), 45 RPM single, 1964, inscribed and signed "Love Me Do, Andy White" in black ink; White was the drummer who played on the recorded single............... **$175**

Gotta Have Rock and Roll

The Beatles, "4-by The Beatles," Capitol 5365, EX/NM EP, 1965, with songs from U.S. album "Beatles '65." **$238**

Heritage Auctions

The Beatles, "I'll Get You," Swan 4152, EX 45 RPM one-sided single, white-label promo, 1964 .... **$625**

Heritage Auctions

The Beatles, "Can't Buy Me Love" b/w "You Can't do That," Capitol 5150, 45 RPM U.S. picture sleeve, 1964, picture sleeve EX+ condition, record NM condition. **$441**

The Beatles, "Songs, Pictures and Stories of the Fabulous Beatles," Vee-Jay (VJ 1092), EX LP, stereo, 1964 .... **$750**

Heritage Auctions

Salesman Samples

SALESMAN SAMPLES came into use in the mid-to-late 19th century, becoming one of many categories of modern miniatures utilized by various professionals. Traveling salesman, like architects, engineers, and filmmakers, utilized scaled models to demonstrate or better understand the operation of a full-size or large-scale device.

In the early 20th century most salesman samples were working samples, which sometimes added to their misidentification as toys. However, in most cases salesman samples measured 1:6 or 1:8 scale, making them larger than the average toy. Plus, almost every salesman sample had a name engraved, etched, or painted somewhere on it.

The salesman sample came into fashion as an aid for traveling salesmen pitching products to retailers who were considering a purchase. It allowed the salesmen to sell larger-size products limited by the ability to transport the item from town to town. If a retailer was able to keep a salesman sample for a while, he could then use it to market the merchandise to potential customers.

Source: "A Brief History of Modern Miniatures," by Lisa Robinson, The San Lorenzo Valley Museum.

Lightning protection: Electra Protection Co. demonstration case that used electric charges to simulate lightning for company's line of lightning rods; using wooden buildings affixed with rods and wires, the demonstrator would press a button and despite a spark, buildings would come away unscathed; with Samsonite snakeskin case, very good to near excellent condition, electrics untested, larger case 22-1/2" l. x 16" h. x 9" d. **$4,740**

James D. Julia, Inc.

Replica of gold medal crafted for 1984 Summer Olympic Games in Los Angeles, gold-plated, identical in design to those presented to Carl Lewis and Mary Lou Retton except for word "Sample" stamped on each side, pristine condition, 2.5" dia. Provenance: From personal collection of a former Josten's employee............ **$1,912**

Heritage Auctions

Aermotor of Broken Arrow, Oklahoma, advertising on tail of windmill, 17-3/4" h............**$240**

Morphy Auctions

Four-prong working agitator washer by Columbia, name stenciled on barrel portion, original condition, circa 1920, 18-1/2" h..........................**$600**

Morphy Auctions

Jergens lotion coin-op dispenser, Art Deco-styled wall mount in original case with original lock, key and decals, 1¢ mechanism, manufactured by Lotion Dispenser Corp., Rock Island, Illinois, circa 1937, near excellent condition, hard shell case 6-1/2" w. x 19-1/2" h. x 7-1/4" d......................**$711**

James D. Julia, Inc.

Jump spark-style cigar lighter by National Selling Co., Allentown, Pennsylvania, circa 1900, 7-1/2" h. **$2,400**

Morphy Auctions

Coca-Cola cooler, circa 1939, with closed front panel with small scuffs and scratches, central area paint chipping around logo hidden behind panel, chipping on cap catcher, minor paint flakes and chips at edges of cooler and lid, original books inside, very good condition, 12-1/4" l. **$1,400**

Morphy Auctions

Cast iron sample of Buck's Stoves & Ranges, St. Louis, circa 1900, 23" l. **$960**

Morphy Auctions

Samsonite suitcase with six different finishes, three cigar humidors in form of steamer trunks, and three miniature suitcases in graduated sizes stamped "Made in Czechoslovakia" on interior, fair to good condition with separations between finishes on Samsonite case and areas of loss on humidors, largest 15-1/2" l. x 10-1/2 h.. **$486**

James D. Julia, Inc.

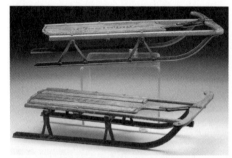

Miniature Kiddo & Fleetwing sleds, one stenciled "KIDDO" in red with surrounding green pinstripe, front steering bar with remains of stenciling, second sled stenciled "FLEETWING" with black pinstriping throughout; Kiddo sled has remains of original semi-gloss shellacked finish, very good condition, 17-1/2" l., Fleetwing sled has repair to top steering bar, good to very good condition, 19" l. **$1,837**

James D. Julia, Inc.

Large wooden model seeder with brass accents and two handles with covered boxes on left and right to hold seed, depressing levers on handles sift seeds down through plow-shaped chute, depositing them in ground; good to very good condition, 20-1/2" l. x 14-1/2" w. x 9" h. **$1,718**

James D. Julia, Inc.

Reaper with original carrying case; when rolled, gear mechanism to right of driver connects to chain-driven forked jointed arm that sweeps around, grabbing cut hay from brass sickle bar, which is fluffed and churned by two-part brass paddle to wagon that would follow alongside; formed brass saddle seat rests on springs to left of hand lever that raises and lowers jointed wooden tow bar, smaller lever on floor in front of driver activates brake, third lever at front of platform engages gear mechanism; hinged platform can be flipped up to view gear arrangement underneath, gear box stamped on right "J. F. Werner Model Maker & Machinist 62 Centre St N.Y."; with original wrench and small canister of loose parts; housed within original formed metal carrying case with fitted wood inserts, very good to near excellent condition, 16" w. x 13" d. (excluding tow bar) x 6" h. **$10,665**

James D. Julia, Inc.

Barn door with original carrying case, walnut hanging door with nickel-plated hardware in dovetailed wooden carrying case with metal plaque reading "The Dayton Mfg Co Dayton Ohio USA," near excellent condition with minor scrapes and scuffs, interior in near mint condition, 17-1/2" l. x 11-1/2" h. **$1,458**

James D. Julia, Inc.

SALESMAN SAMPLES

Washing machine with original carrying case, large cubicle nickel-plated tub in pine frame topped with nickel-plated hardware, locking hinged top, inverted nickel-plated cone agitator activated by hand lever that works treadle-type mechanism with offset wheel that raises and lowers agitator while rotating it a quarter turn, two glass viewing windows on front and back of machine, original leather felt-lined carrying case, near excellent condition with minor chips, smooth operation of gears and components, case in very good condition overall with alligatoring and some loss to leather, 10" w. x 10-1/4" d. x 15" h. **$2,607**

James D. Julia, Inc.

Grain, seed, and bean cleaner, dual-action machine in pine framework stenciled on two sides "Grain, Seed and Bean Cleaner" and "Manufactured by A. T. Ferrell & Co. Saginaw, Mich" on front, cast iron hand crank (missing handle) shakes series of mesh screens while belt drive churns and separates product within drum, expelling it below; overall good to very good condition, missing one small board forming base and other minor chips, scratches and loss to finish, 29" l. x 23" h. x 13-1/2" w. **$711**

James D. Julia, Inc.

Rare Winchester metallic cartridge display board in wood grain factory box, picture of Winchester New Haven factory inside lid, cartridge compartment with light green background, contains 52 cartridges ranging from BB to .405 Winchester Soft Point, each cartridge marked with caliber below it, top middle reads, "SAMPLES OF / WINCHESTER METALLIC CARTRIDGES / THE W BRAND / TRADE MARK / MADE FOR ALL KIND OF FIREARMS," compartment bordered with wood quarter round, case in rare "wood grain" marked in silver "WINCHESTER / CARTRIDGES / THE W [in red] BRAND / TRADE MARK" on lid, 16-1/4" w. x 9-1/8" d. x 1" h. **$3,600**

Rock Island Auctions

Jack O'Lantern Hot-P-Nuts vendor in leather case/trunk with stack of agreement papers for placing machines on location, most likely from 1920s, aluminum-based with glass sides and aluminum top, machine heated peanuts and store merchant scooped out desired amount to customer; all original as-found very fine condition, aluminum with light oxidation, 11" h. **$830**

James D. Julia, Inc.

Science & Technology

WHEN COLLECTORS THINK VINTAGE TECHNOLOGY, they're not thinking of a first-generation iPad or a rotary telephone. The number of science and technology collectors is on the rise, as are the opportunities at auction. For the first time, all top-tier mainstream auction houses held a science and technology auction last year, and several mid-tier auction houses kept pace.

Several years ago, the science auction was a rare occurrence. When Christie's held an all-science auction in 2006, the collecting public didn't know quite how to respond. A wood crate of Thomas Alva Edison's personally owned lightbulbs failed to sell at a $250,000 estimate. The bulbs were used to prove Edison invented the electric bulb in 1890, 10 years after he was awarded a U.S. patent.

The market has changed significantly since then. Seven years later, a piece of vintage technology just as historically important as Edison's bulbs sold at public auction for an astounding $671,000. The sale of a vintage Apple 1 computer, one of the first computers created by Apple co-founders Steve Jobs and Steve Wozniak, set a new record in early 2013.

A survey of the major auction houses shows the science and technology category is now estimated at $15 million across several categories and collecting subsets. Rocks, gems, and minerals are a growing section, natural history auctions offer everything from meteorites to dinosaur skeletons, and laboratory equipment items from the late 19th century are now collected as mechanical works of art.

In particular, mechanical scale models are one subset that is attracting new collectors, especially those in their 20s and 30s. Already gaining mainstream media attention, collectors of mechanical models are attracted by their eye appeal and a rare window of affordability.

"These are things you can put on your desk or in your man cave, and anyone who walks in is going to say, 'That's fantastic,'" says Nick Dawes, a vice president at Heritage Auctions, Dallas, as quoted in *ForbesLife* magazine. Dawes introduced a series of branded Gentleman Collector auctions at Heritage and in early 2014 managed the sale of the Glenn Reid Collection of Mechanical Models. Once on display in Reid's Detroit-area museum, the collection is filled with nearly 500 lots of German driving school models and fine specimens of model steam engines, salesman samples, and scale model cars. One of the more curious items offered in the collection was an 1841 model of the annular compound steam engine. The well-preserved Victorian

Barometer, late 19th century, non-working, 43-1/2" h. **$312**

Heritage Auctions

Twentieth century technology items: Charleville crank jack, Palmer-Lowe Accelerbrake that combined accelerator and brake in one pedal, dated 1936, nickel Ashton Valve Co. pipe assembly, Steeple form Boyles air pump ventilator, brass water pump, and others, ranges from 8" h. to 19" h...**$414**

James D. Julia Auctioneers

model was filed with a patent office by British engineer Joseph Maudsley (1801-1861), best known as the inventor of the dual-cylinder "Siamese" engine. Reid's collection also held interesting and obscure "tools of the trade" so to speak, as a cased portable steam boiler gauge kit and a Ricardo's Indicator calibration device, designed to verify pressure in systems, was offered in its original oak case, circa 1920. The entire collection sold for more than $1.2 million.

The Reid collection is just one of the large collections that came to market in the last year or two. In April 2013, collector/dealer/scholar Elli Buk's enormous vintage technology collection made headlines for its depth and breadth. The eight-day auction included more than 2,000 objects, 30 categories, and served as a survey of more than 200 years of human invention and innovation. It was marvelous.

"This was the first time anyone, including Elli's closest friends and family, had ever seen the collection in its entirety," auctioneer Michael Grogan said. "The collector response to the exhibition and auction was a combination of awe and enthusiasm."

The discovery of the auction was an Edison electric light two-wire meter system, sold with a Thompson Watt Hour Meter, which together brought $30,000 against a $200 low estimate. The elated collector who won the lot was bidding in the room and told the auctioneer that he had been searching for this Edison item for 30 years. A Page's horizontal double-beam axial engine soared well beyond its $500 low estimate to sell to a European phone bidder for $25,200. One of Buk's prized possessions, an observatory-size Henry Fitz telescope, circa 1850, sold to a telescope expert for $19,200; in addition, a Howard & Co. gold bullion scale fetched $19,200. The auction grossed more than $1.9 million dollars and attracted bidders from 15 countries.

As the science and technology category grows, some auctioneers and dealers often fold scientific or technological items with more generally recognized items such as maritime collectibles or watches. Collectors would do well to subscribe to auction house newsletters or catalogs, if only to monitor values, descriptions and estimates. The science and technology category is a new frontier as a fresh demographic worldwide starts collecting.

—Eric Bradley

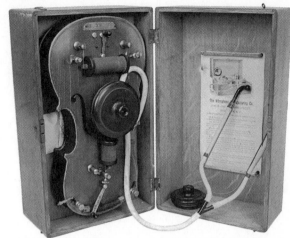

Quack device, Violin Vibrophone, circa 1900, marks: The Vibrophone Manufacturing Co. Brooklyn, New York; device survives as rare medical quack device thought to cure tinnitus, a disorder manifested by the perception of sound within the ear that is not heard externally. Provenance: From the Elli Buk Collection...................................**$3,382**

Grogan & Company, Fine Art Auctioneers and Appraisers

Telescope, circa 1850, signed H. Fitz, New York, accompanied in wooden case 8' l., lens 7-1/2" dia., 9' h. overall, including stand. Henry Fitz (1808-1863), a Newburyport, Massachusetts, native, was the first important American telescope maker. From 1840-1855, Fitz made 40 percent of all telescopes sold in the United States and manufactured 80 percent of all astronomical telescopes. Provenance: From the Elli Buk Collection. **$19,200**

Grogan & Company, Fine Art Auctioneers and Appraisers

Leavitt pumping engine, live steam exhibition scale model built to represent a massive American steam-powered waterworks pump designed by Erasmus Darwin Leavitt, circa 1895, exceptional detail, finished with complex gearing operated by central ship's wheel, on wood stand with table base, 16" x 27" x 15"..**$4,375**

Heritage Auctions

Edison desk model fan with plaque bearing number 100026, circa early 20th century, original condition, 12" x 10-1/2" x 9". **$3,250**

Heritage Auctions

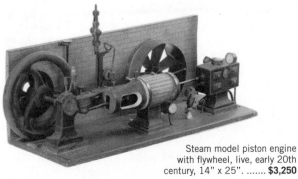

Steam model piston engine with flywheel, live, early 20th century, 14" x 25". **$3,250**

Heritage Auctions

SCIENCE & TECHNOLOGY

$

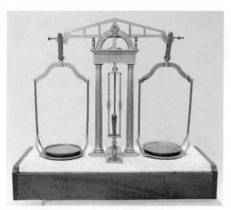

Gold bullion scale, circa late 19th century, stamped U.S. Gold Standard Balance, E. Howard & Co., Boston, Mass; full jeweled, on mahogany and marble base, 30" h. Edward Howard, described as a technological genius, first opened the E. Howard Clock Co. in Roxbury, Massachusetts, where he manufactured clocks, gold scales and precision instruments. In 1858, Howard formed a partnership with Charles Rice and renamed the company E. Howard & Co. Provenance: From the Elli Buk Collection. **$19,200**

Grogan & Company, Fine Art Auctioneers and Appraisers

Page's double-beam axial engine model, 13" l. Provenance: From the Elli Buk Collection.....**$25,200**

Grogan & Company, Fine Art Auctioneers and Appraisers

Scale model Beam winding engine, late 19th century, made of brass and wood, 31" x 11" x 23"..**$6,250**

Heritage Auctions

TOP LOT!

Electrical apparatus: Thompson watt hour meter, General Electric Co., with Edison electric light two-wire meter system. Provenance: From the Elli Buk Collection...**$30,000**

Grogan & Company, Fine Art Auctioneers and Appraisers

Three sample engines: Internal combustion engine, nickel-plated cutting machine on wooden base, and wood and metal steam engine with locking beam and large flywheel, largest: 21" l. x 22" h. x 10" d. **$1,944**

James D. Julia Auctioneers

$

Trilobite fossil, *Crotallocephalina benziregensis*, Devonian, Djebel Issmour area, Anti-Atlas Mountains, Morocco, 3-1/2" x 1-1/4" x 3/4"; trilobites were one of the first life forms to develop complex eyes. . **$656**

Heritage Auctions

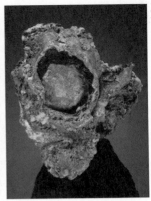

Native copper from Keweenaw Peninsula, Michigan, specimen in rounded, hollow structure of metallic copper called a "skull," rounded exterior conceals sharp dodecahedral copper crystal, 3" x 2" x 1-1/2" **$23,750**

Heritage Auctions

Icthyosaur fossil, Posidonienschiefer, Holzmaden, Germany, plate 59" x 34"; approximately 150-90 million years ago, ichthyosaurs were marine reptiles that filled the same ecological niche as modern dolphins. **$34,000**

Heritage Auctions

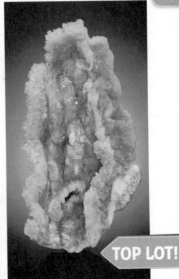

TOP LOT!

Rose and smoky quartz, Lavra Berilo Branco, Sapucaia do Norte, Galiléia, Doce Valley, Minas Gerais, Brazil, nicknamed "La Madona Rosa," discovered in 1950, exceptionally large, world record for most valuable mineral specimen ever sold at public auction, 15-1/5" x 8"....**$662,500**

Heritage Auctions

Stibnite, Lushi Mine, Lushi Co., Sanmenxia Prefecture, Henan Province, China, 15 major crystals among smaller ones, radiating out from common base, 9" x 10" x 4". **$40,625**

Heritage Auctions

SCIENCE & TECHNOLOGY

Nine cross-section cable samples, 19th century, Europe, Air Space Cable 4 Wire Isle of Wight Telephone, Zandvoort Cable 4 Wire, and Deep Sea Cable 6 Wire Standard Type, all housed in glazed hinged lid box, 12" w. x 12" d. x 5" h. **$1,845**

Skinner, Inc., www.skinnerinc.com

Globe, circa 1920, made by H. Hughes & Son, cased, depicting star charts, constellations, etc., 8" h. **$2,031**

Heritage Auctions

Reflecting telescope, circa 18th century, made by Watkins, London, England, 28" x 24"........................ **$4,375**

Heritage Auctions

Hugh Powell pillar microscope, 1841, large scale, marked Hugh Powell, London, 1841, 23" h. Provenance: From the Elli Buk Collection. **$10,455**

Grogan & Company, Fine Art Auctioneers and Appraisers

Brass propeller anemometer, airplane form with aluminum propeller, mounted to allow 360 degree rotation, tail to keep propeller pointed into wind, on heavy mounting plate with seven electrical connections, 30" h. Anemometers are also known as aerovanes as they tell both wind speed and direction from one unit. **$923**

Skinner, Inc., www.skinnerinc.com

Dual Burner A-B Lyth brass and mahogany compensating binnacle, 20th century, brass hood with circular viewing lens enclosing gimbaled compass marked A-B Lyth Stockholm, brass wings supporting red and green painted compensating spheres above octagonal mahogany base, 54-1/2" h. . **$615**

Skinner, Inc., www.skinnerinc.com

Telegraph instruments, late 19th and early 20th century, including two Signal Electric Mfg. Co., Federal Enterprises, Inc. pony relays, Bunnell & Co., Western Electric sounding relays, two Vibroflex, and two others. **$400**

Skinner, Inc., www.skinnerinc.com

Legrandite, Ojuela Mine, Mapimí, Mun. de Mapimí, Durango, Mexico, bright yellow crystals, parallel spray of golden blades over 1" l. fan out from matrix of reddish-brown limonite, 3-1/2" x 1-1/2" x 1"..$93,750

Heritage Auctions

Four medical apparatuses, boxed blood transfuser by Madison Kip Corp., boxed Davidson Pneumothorax Apparatus by J. Sklar, and two other transfusers, one by C.M. Sorenson Co........ **$62**

Skinner, Inc., www.skinnerinc.com

Fluorite, baryte, sphalerite and calcite, Elmwood Mine, Carthage, central Tennessee, Ba-F-Pb-Zn Dist., Smith County, 10-1/2" x 9-3/4" x 6"...........**$125,000**

Heritage Auctions

Stormoguide display model, circa 1927, Taylor Instruments Companies, Rochester, New York, marks: TAYLOR INSTRUMENT COMPANIES, ROCHESTER, N.Y., DES. PAT. 99184, © 1927, INTERNATIONAL COPYRIGHT 1927 BY TAYLOR INSTRUMENTS COMPANIES, original face set in chromed metal frame attached to black lacquered stepped base by semi-circular support, 18" h.......................... **$1,375**

Heritage Auctions

McIntosh MC275 tube amplifier and Marantz Model 10B tuner, 20th century, other components include McIntosh preamplifier model C22, pair of B&W DM7 loudspeakers, Marantz five-disc CD player CC-48, Bang & Olufsen turntable, Tanberg TR 2080 AM/FM stereo receiver, and pair of Bose 601 loudspeakers. **$6,765**

Skinner, Inc., www.skinnerinc.com

Sextant, 19th century, American, marks: A. PRINCE, PHILADELPHIA, in wood box, 12" h.. **$687**

Heritage Auctions

10 **Things** You Didn't Know About
Collecting Rocks, Gems, Minerals

1 Collectors of rocks, gems and minerals (rockhounds) are an organized and active group with two magazines that have served the community for more than 40 years. *Rocks & Minerals* magazine has published articles on the topic of mineralogy since 1926, while *Rocks & Gems* magazine has served fans of the hobby for 41 years.

2 A large rose and smoky quartz, measuring 15-1/2" x 8", sold for $662,500 during Heritage Auctions' Nature & Science Signature Auction June 2, 2013, part of the largest fine mineral collection ever to appear at auction. Discovered in a small mine in Brazil sometime between 1959 and 1972, it is referred to as the "La Madona Rosa" for its resemblance to modern day images of the Virgin Mary.

A linarite mineral sample fetched $158,500 at the Nature & Science Auction.

Heritage Auctions

3 There were more than 200 rock, gem and mineral shows in the United States between July and December 2013. Show information can be found at both *Rock & Gems* (www.rockngems.com) and *Rocks & Minerals* (www.rocksandminerals.com) websites.

4 The Smithsonian Museum of Natural History houses a collection with about 350,000 mineral specimens and 10,000 gems – one of the largest collections in the world.

5 A linarite specimen, a rarely seen copper mineral, discovered during a dig in New Mexico in 1979, sold for $158,500 during Heritage Auctions' Signature Auction on June 2, 2013.

6 Worldwide, there are more than 80 mineral museums or museums with a significant gems and minerals exhibit/collection. More than half of all the mineral museums in the world are located in North America.

7 Examples of metallurgy (d. Art and science of extracting metals from their ores and modifying the metals for use) date back more than 7,000 years, based on the discovery of jewelry made from forged copper.

8 Rock and mineral collecting tours are starting to experience mainstream popularity. These expeditions attract participants from various backgrounds and levels of collecting experience. Companies like Geology Adventures (www.geologyadventures.com) offer these types of collecting adventures stateside and abroad.

9 A sample of ore, from the famous Cripple Creek mining region of Colorado, sold for $2,375 during Heritage Auction's Nature & Science Signature Auction June 2, 2013. The high-grade sample is a gray wall rock that sandwiches a ribbon of purple flurite that cuts through brassy, bladed crystals of calaverite: gold telluride.

10 There are hundreds of rock and mineral collecting clubs in the United States. A great portal to locating collecting clubs in your area is http://www.gemandmineral.com/states.html.

— Compiled by Antoinette Rahn

Sources: *Collecting Rocks, Gems and Minerals, Webster's Dictionary,* www.rockngem.com, Smithsonian National Museum of Natural History – Department of Mineral Sciences (www.mineralsciences.si.edu), Heritage Auctions (www.ha.com), American Geoscience Institute (www.agiweb.org/smmp/museums.htm), Geology Adventures (www.geologyadventures.com), The Gem and Mineral Exploration Co. (www.gemandmineral.com), *Rocks & Gems* magazine, *Rocks & Minerals* magazine.

Silver

STERLING SILVER (STANDARD SILVER) is an alloy made of silver and copper and is harder than pure silver. It is used in the creation of sterling silver flatware (silverware) as well as tea services, trays, salvers, goblets, water and wine pitchers, candlesticks and centerpieces. Coin silver is slightly less pure than sterling.

The value of silver has seen steady growth since the first indications of the Great Recession in late 2008. From a low of $8.92 in November 2008, silver prices topped out

Silversmithing in America goes back to the early 17th century in Boston and New York and the early 18th century in Philadelphia. Boston artisans were influenced by English styles, New Yorkers by Dutch. American manufacturers began to switch to the sterling standard about the time of the U.S. Civil War.

at $48.48 in May 2011 and hit a plateau between $25 and $35 in late 2012 and early 2013. Silver prices are so high that in some cases the auction value of an antique or collectible silver object is nearly identical to the prices paid for scrap silver. This presents a quandary for newly inherited silver and a looming threat for unique works produced by craftsmen: High melt prices threaten objects whose designs enhance its value among collectors or institutions.

"For those of us dedicated to the world of antiques and art, the idea of scrapping is difficult to take, but we know that it is an option for people looking to generate income

Bailey & Co. coin silver elephant entree dishes, two cushion-shaped covered dishes with deep ruffled rim above acanthus joints to ball and paw feet, chased floral and applied ruffle lid, detachable cast Indian dressed elephant finials, circa 1850, one piece has yellow lacquer, monograms EMC, oval mark Bailey & Co., Chestnut St., #13G (?), eagle-u-shield mark, 12-1/2" x 9-1/2" x 6-1/4", 153.6 troy oz. **$18,750**

Rago Arts

from unwanted objects," said Skinner Auctioneers, Inc. CEO Karen Keane on the Skinner blog. "But with all things being equal, before making that decision, we encourage investigating selling your silver at auction rather than melting it down."

Take, for example, the American Gorham silver martelé vase #1838. Although highly decorative, the vase looks similar to many silver vases produced at the turn of the 20th century. In the hands of a novice, the 34.6 troy oz. piece would have been scrapped out for $722 based on mid-2014 spot silver prices. According to the Gorham archives, production of vase #1838 began on March 29, 1899, and required 38 hours to produce, plus an additional 34 hours of chasing. That's nearly a full two weeks of labor for one vase. Martelé is softer and

SILVER

purer (950/1000 parts of silver than sterling's 925/1000 parts) in order to make the silver more malleable and easier to work by hand. Each martelé object begins as a flat piece of silver, raised with hammering to the desired shape before being passed on to the chaser. The finished pieces show hammer marks because they were not buffed. Rather than fall victim to the smelter, this martelé silver vase brought $22,500 at Heritage Auctions in 2013.

This is but one reason why it's important to take a piece of silver to an auction house for inspection before you consider a dealer or scrap metal buyer. A seller should know both the spot silver price as well as the historical or decorative price in order to make the best decisions. Some dealers do not deal in silver weight and couldn't care less about current spot silver prices.

In addition to relatively high silver melt values, older silver objects suffer another threat. American dealers often lament that young buyers are turned off by the thought of owning silver. It's seen as a high-maintenance object. What they may not know is that fine silver of some quality actually improves in value if it's used rather than stored.

What silver objects are likely to increase in value? High quality silver objects from American name-brand makers, such as Gorham, Tiffany, Towle, Stieff, and Reed & Barton, remain desirable and represent a solid purchase. Functional pieces will survive longer than those that are purely decorative.

There exist a number of excellent resources on the topic of sterling silver. The most famous continues to be *Discovering Hallmarks on English Silver* by John Bly. This 1968 book was recently re-released in 2008 by Shire Publishing and remains the mainstay for English hallmarks. Flatware is well covered in *Warman's Sterling Silver Flatware*, 2nd edition, by Phil Dreis. However, a 21st century generation of resources is available on tablets and tablet personal computers: Dealer Steve Freeman developed a free app for iPad users offering a free library of hundreds of images of English silver maker's marks. The SilverMakers app was released in March 2012 and offers an easy way to find marks based on the object's intended use, marks, and even silver content.

Portuguese Second Standard (.833) silver swan centerpiece, second quarter 20th century, by Manuel Alcino Figueiredo Moutinho, active 1936- 1987, Porto, retailed by W. A. Sarmento, Lisbon, detailed bird with poseable articulated neck and glass eyes, wings hinged and opening to reveal jardinière opening in body, 16-1/2" h. x 7-1/2" w. (23" with wings open) x 22" l., 97.41 troy oz.
.... **$6,150**

New Orleans Auction Galleries

Prussian .750 silver-covered punch bowl and ladle, 1848- 1854, by HWL Wilm, Berlin, oval melon-form bowl mounted with elaborate opposing rococo scroll handles with twining acanthus, waisted collar and acanthus-mounted rim, fitted domed lid with gallery en suite, tall knopped finial, gilt interior, raised on conforming waisted stem and foot en suite with applied rococo scroll banding, body with applied armorial of sun, 15-1/2" h. x 15-3/4" l. x 10" w., with original ladle, 14-3/4" l., 104.24 troy oz. **$6,500**

New Orleans Auction Galleries

George III silver repoussé chinoiserie tea caddy, round form on four mask and paw feet, rococo chasing bracket scenes of Chinese nobility at leisure, recumbent Chinese figural finial, armorial crest, John Crouch, London 1812, 5-1/2" x 5-1/2", 17.7 troy oz. **$1,625**

Rago Arts

Continental silver Renaissance Revival vase, waisted cylinder with mythological masks among fruit and strap ornaments, circa 1900, 11-3/8" x 5-3/4", 26.13 troy oz. **$750**

Rago Arts

Unusual large Peruvian silver box, 19th century, repoussé floral decoration, sloping lid with armorial of Charles I of Spain, large paw feet, 10" h. x 18-5/8" w. x 15" d., 184.08 troy oz., 12 lb., 10 oz. **$4,500**

Crescent City Auction Gallery

Edwardian silver novelty porcupine pincushion by Levi & Salaman, Birmingham 1904, loaded marks clear, five shallow bruises to body, rubbing to texture of body down backbone, one foot slightly bent, 2-3/4" l. **$428**

Dreweatts & Bloomsbury Auctions

French silver wine cooler, strapped tulip form with figural satyr handles, Bacchus medallions, gilt interior, Pointaburet, Paris, 19th century, marked Pointaburet, A. Paris, #65094 31, Minerva head, 15-3/4" x 9-3/4", 98.24 troy oz. **$6,250**

Rago Arts

Gorham "Puritan" silver coffee pot, circa 1925, 32", 394 troy oz.; built to scale for promotional use, this vessel was displayed in the office of the chairman of the board, Gorham, deaccessioned from the sample archives of Lenox-Gorham.**$18,750**

Rago Arts

Set of 12 Italian silver chargers, Buccellati, Milan, Italy, circa 1950, inset center and pinched rim with banded border, marks: BUCCELLATI, STERLING, ITALY, 12" dia., 292.4 oz.**$11,250**

Heritage Auctions

Gorham engraved sterling hip flask, cushion form, inscribed Trenton Princeton FTPCC 1774 on sporran below crested helmet, crossed sword and rifle and flags, marked for J.E. Caldwell, 1881, 4-1/2" x 4-3/4", 5.9 troy oz.............. **$531**

Rago Arts

Tiffany & Co. coin silver revolving railroad cruet, square boxcars on drum-shaped plateau, chased repoussé grape vine foot, applied cast vine border and loop handle, six cars support Gothic style cut crystal vessels, on car with hinged lid, John Moore, 1853, Tiffany & Co. arched mark above Gothic "M" in oval, #505, cars marked NH, H&S, most likely New Haven, Hartford and Springfield Railroad, 14-1/2"; 73 troy oz. **$15,000**

Rago Arts

Silver shaped square salver by Harrods, Ltd., London 1935, with raised molded border and four pad feet, 34 cm l., 46.15 oz. **$955**

Dreweatts & Bloomsbury Auctions

SILVER

Pair of silver hexagonal spill vases and comport by Walker & Hall, Sheffield 1917, spill vases with tapering stems and hexagonal spreading feet, 30 cm h., comport 22 cm l., 43.05 oz. **$741**

Dreweatts & Bloomsbury Auctions

Rare Victorian silver shaped rectangular "castle top" card case by Nathaniel Mills, Birmingham 1852, cover with Dublin International Industrial Exhibition building of 1853 amidst scrolls, flowers and foliage, reverse with scrolls, flowers and foliage, central cartouche engraved "Mary," in original leather covered case, 4" l. .... **$4,000-$6,800**

Dreweatts & Bloomsbury Auctions

Silver-filled figure of Labrador by Camelot Silverware Ltd., Sheffield 1990, shaped oval base engraved "J. Spouse," marks clear, slightly rubbed to high points, 15 cm l. **$198**

Dreweatts & Bloomsbury Auctions

Victorian silver twin-handled comport and cover by Joseph Angell I and Joseph Angell II, London 1845, foliate knop to domed cover, whole pierced with tapering panels of stylized palmettes and scrolls, tapering stem and step molded pedestal, embossed with leaves and palmettes, blue glass liner, marks rubbed to base, three sections of repair to lid, two sections of repair to base, high points to lid, finial rubbed, glass liner in good order, 8" h., 14.6 oz. .... **$273-$409**

Dreweatts & Bloomsbury Auctions

George III silver mounted coconut cup by Peter, Ann & William Bateman, London 1799, rim with single thread, pedestal base with circular foot threaded to rim, marks clear to base but rim marks rubbed to maker's mark and duty mark badly stamped, some fine surface cracks, rim mount secure, 4-7/8" h. .... **$409-$682**

Dreweatts & Bloomsbury Auctions

Edwardian silver octagonal tea kettle, stand and burner by Goldsmiths & Silversmiths Co., Ltd., London 1904, with composition and double scroll handle, banded finial to domed cover and body engraved "MJB," octagonal stand with four scroll legs and four pad feet, marks to body are slightly rubbed, light scratches overall, handle is worn, engraving is crisp, cover sits well, 43.4 oz. **$658**

Dreweatts & Bloomsbury Auctions

Edwardian silver mounted cut glass claret jug, probably by William Devenport, Birmingham 1906, shell finial to flat cover, flattened C-scroll handle, all engraved with scrolling foliage and geometric bands, marks are clear, engraving is crisp, minor chips to edges of glass, slight movement to hinge cover, slight overlapping to one side, 9-1/2" h. .... **$341-$477**

Dreweatts & Bloomsbury Auctions

Set of six silver gilt cauldron salt cellars by The Goldsmiths & Silversmiths Co. Ltd., London 1927, with gadrooned borders, engraved with crest above motto, on three lion mask and paw feet, 4" dia.; six King's pattern salt spoons by The Goldsmiths & Silversmiths Co. Ltd., London 1927, 46.25 oz., crest and motto are those of Russell, which pertains to the Dukes of Bedford and other noble branches of that Russell family. .... **$955-$1,356**

Dreweatts & Bloomsbury Auctions

Silver and silver gilt child's handled cup, Gorham Manufacturing Co., Providence, Rhode Island, circa 1909, repoussé scene of children's band marching, C-scroll reeded handle, gilt interior, monogrammed to underside HCL III 1909, marks: (lion-anchor-G), STERLING, A 4708, 2-1/4" h., 3.4 oz. **$375**

Heritage Auctions

American silver reticulated centerpiece with gilt silver-plated liner and basket, circa 1910, everted reticulated rim, chased stylized floral and foliate band to center of tapering body, raised on conforming reticulated foot, marks: STERLING, 14-1/2 IN, PATENTED 5/18-1909, 5024/47, 8" h. x 14" w., 53.5 oz. (weighable silver)........ **$2,500**

Heritage Auctions

American silver figural inkwell with glass liner, circa 1900, helmet opens at face mask to reveal clear glass inkwell, ending in four lobed spreading feet, monogrammed LD, marks: (man in profile-anchor-O), STERLING, 4-1/2" h., 8.3 oz. **$812**

Heritage Auctions

Silver repoussé ginger jar, S. Kirk & Son Co., Baltimore, circa 1910, flowers and two landscape scenes on textured ground, monogrammed E du LB to underside, marks: S. KIRK & SON CO, 925/1000, 13T, 4" h., 6 oz. **$1,375**

Heritage Auctions

German silver-colored singing bird musical box by Adolf Meyer, Frankfurt am Main, post 1886, .800 standard, early 20th century, shaped rectangular case operated by bird lever in front releasing oval-engraved cover, revealing pierced interior with colored feathered bird, rectangular cam-operated movement with barrel, latch wheel and bellows, 4-1/8" w. .... **$950-$1,300**

Dreweatts & Bloomsbury Auctions

Vanderbilt pattern silver bottle opener, Tiffany & Co., New York, designed 1884, typical form, textured ground with lion in foliage to one side, coat of arms and man battling beast to other, marks: TIFFANY & CO., STERLING, STAINLESS, 6" l., 3.8 oz. **$687**

Heritage Auctions

Silver and silver gilt olive spear spoon, Gorham Manufacturing Co., Providence, Rhode Island, designed 1885, naturalistic fruited olive twig handle with stepped spear to one end and pierced shaped spoon to opposite end, marks: (lion-anchor-G), STERLING, 267, 11-1/2" l., 2.2 oz. **$594**

Heritage Auctions

SILVER

Italian silver figural table ornament, squirrel with silver gilt acorns, Buccellati, Milan, Italy, 20th century, squirrel on hind legs holding two silver gilt acorns on branch, in lavorazione a pelo or "hair-like" technique, marks: MARIO BUCCELLATI, BUCCELLATI, 925, 5, (effaced), 3" h., 4.7 oz. **$1,750**

Heritage Auctions

Italian silver figural table ornament of seated monkey, Buccellati, Milan, Italy, circa 1970, in lavorazione a pelo or "hair-like" technique, marks: BUCCELLATI, ITALY, 800, 4" h., 8.3 oz........................ **$2,375**

Heritage Auctions

Indian silver and silver gilt handled cup, circa 1900, tapering cylindrical cup with stylized chased repoussé flowers to body, S-form handle with thumb rest, double-banded rope and plain border and foot, hammered bottom, unmarked, 3-1/2" h., 5.1 oz. **$262**

Heritage Auctions

Chinese export silver model of junk or warship by Luen Hing, Shanghai, circa 1900, two masts with unfurled sails, sailors and equipment on the deck, on wooden base carved and pierced as waves, marks to base are clear, some ropes contrilling sails are detached but most appear to be present, anchor wire is loose, fine holes to inside section of stern that suggests there were small appendages of silver now not present, mounting of three figures is loose, slight bend in one sail, surface of wood base has been rubbed by silver polish, 7-5/8" l., 8.4 oz. Luen Hing worked from 231 Szechuan Road, Shanghai from circa 1880 to 1925.....**$130-$225**

Dreweatts & Bloomsbury Auctions

Silver rooster with hinged wings, 20th century, naturalistically modeled in erect posture, marks: GERMANY, 800, (crown), (partially effaced horse), (effaced mark), 8-5/8" h., 18.3 oz...................... **$1,875**

Heritage Auctions

American coin silver card case attributed to Leonard & Wilson, Philadelphia, circa 1850, case of shaped rectangular-form with hinged lid, one side with chased repoussé depiction of Trinity Church, New York and architectural landscape chased within cartouche to reverse, with repoussé decoration of scrolling flowers and foliage throughout, unmarked, 3-1/2" h. x 2-1/2" w., 1.6 oz.......... **$312**

Heritage Auctions

American silver and silver gilt mounted glass flask, circa 1900, ovoid, silver mounted base and removable lid, repoussé decoration of female mask with undulating hair ending in flowers and fruit, lid opens to reveal conforming clear glass flask with silver screw top and gilt visible to base interior, marks: STERLING, 4-3/4" h........... **$531**

Heritage Auctions

CHINESE EXPORT SILVER

In the world of antique silver, Chinese export silver is probably one of the least known yet largest major silver categories in the world. It can rival the work of the finest European and American silversmiths of the 18th and 19th centuries, much of it deemed museum quality. In the world of antique silver, no other category has been so consistently buoyant in terms of values achieved at auction.

Adrien von Fescht

Chinese export silver was produced in China from 1785 to 1940, a period of 150 years with thousands of silversmiths involved in the production. It is also one of the most complex silver categories to understand, given there was a total absence of any official assay system in China, which resulted in a total nonconformity to the marking of silver. In fact, the only constant to be found in Chinese export silver is the absence of conformity.

With a 1,200-year history of silver making through successive Imperial dynasties, Chinese export silver emerged as a definable silver category and movement towards the latter part of the 18th century, following a century of creating extraordinary items of silver for royal households and aristocracy across Europe.

By the mid-18th century, Emperor Qianlong had relented somewhat by creating the Canton System – a highly regulated construct that confined approved foreign merchants to a tiny stretch of land outside of the city walls at Canton. Although tea, opium, silk, and later porcelain were the main focus of the "China trade," merchants were quick to recognize the ability of Chinese silversmiths to produce high quality silver at a considerably lower cost to that of Britain and America. Chinese export silver was born.

Shen Chang two-handled covered figural standing cup, circa 1900, marks: MLW, (workshop mark for Shen Chang), dragon head finial atop stepped domed lid with chased repoussé decoration, dome with swirling dragons's body circled by band of grapevines and lowest step with stylized foliage, 13-1/2" h. x 9-1/2" w., 37.7 oz............ **$22,500**

Heritage Auctions

Early pieces were high-quality copies of English and American Georgian silver. Much of the Chinese silver created prior to this time was unmarked, as was the custom. In the hierarchy of Chinese society, an artisan was in the lower pecking order even if they were superb masters of their art. When the export trade took off, many Chinese silversmiths adopted what became known as "pseudo-hallmarks." Almost all early Chinese export silver carried marks that, until the latter part of the 20th century, were considered by collectors to be the marks of the maker. The reality was that merchants bought or ordered silver items from retail silversmiths, and the main mark was that of the retailer. Often, a secondary mark in Chinese characters is the mark of the artisan who worked on the item. Artisans were itinerant and worked in silver workshops that supplied the retailers. It is common to see the same artisan mark alongside several different retailer marks.

Towards the mid-19th century, after a standoff between the British and the Chinese now referred to as the first Opium War, China was rapidly defeated by the British fleet and an agreement between the Imperial Court and Queen Victoria was set by the Treaty of Nanking in 1842. As a result, the Canton System was dismantled, the British won the right to trade freely with China, and Hong Kong was ceded to them.

By the latter third of the 19th century, the number of retail silversmiths had mushroomed, as had the level of production. The earlier Georgian pieces went through a metamorphosis, arriving at silver with Western forms overtly decorated in the high Chinese style. This, too, was in the

SILVER

context of high Victorian style where neo-classicism gave way to the brash, busy, eclectic style the Victorians craved.

In short, in the hundred years leading up to 1940, vast amounts of Chinese export silver left the shores of China. With the impending outbreak of World War II and the Japanese invasion of China and Hong Kong, many foreign residents made a speedy retreat with their goods and chattels.

Chinese export silver was created as a direct result of political history and national protectionism. No other silver category comes with 1,200 years of silver-making history preceding it. As such, Chinese export silver and its forebears are remarkable vehicles for demonstrating the evolution of Chinese culture and style across a wide spectrum of disciplines.

— *Adrien von Ferscht*

Three-piece square tea service by Tien Shing, Hong Kong, circa 1870-1925, teapot with curved bamboo finial on flush fitting circular cover, top engraved with bamboo, simulated bamboo handle and spout, sides chased with figure in landscape or birds amidst prunus boughs, bracket feet, cream jug and sugar basin with parcel gilt interiors, pot 7-1/2" l., 30.3 troy oz. **$8,150**

Drewatts & Bloomsbury Auctions

Three-piece tea service on tray by Gem Wo, Canton, second half 19th century, crabstock finials, handles and teapot spout, relief decorated with prunus blossom and butterflies, shaped oblong tray similarly engraved, raised border with conforming relief decoration, teapot 10-1/4" l., tray 18-1/2" l., 104.95 oz..........................**$11,050**

Drewatts & Bloomsbury Auctions

Brush pot, Leeching, Hong Kong, Canton and Shanghai, circa 1860, marks: LEECHING, STERLING, traditional form, probably intended for use as vase, with chased repoussé decoration depicting battle within landscape scene against textured ground, banded rim and foot, central blank shield-form cartouche, 5" h., 10.9 oz. **$3,000**

Heritage Auctions

Silver gilt filigree lidded urns attributed to Canton silversmith Pao Ying. From the same stable as much of the Chinese silver filigree items in State Hermitage Museum in St. Petersburg, much of which belonged to Catherine the Great..........**$40,600**

Drewatts & Bloomsbury Auctions

Flask, maker unknown, 20th century, marks: (characters), textured with etched dragon decoration, octagonal lid, 5-3/8" h., 6.11 troy oz. **$625**

Heritage Auctions

Adrien von Ferscht is regarded as the foremost expert in Chinese export silver. He is an Honorary Research Fellow at University of Glasgow [Scottish Centre for China Research & School of Culture and Creative Arts] and cataloged *Chinese Export Silver Makers' Marks*, now published in a third edition digital format, the most detailed reference guide for the silver category with information on over 100 makers.

Qianlong gilt filigree pedestal lidded vases, unmarked, in style of Pao Ying, circa 1780-1840, Canton, domed lids and ovoid bodies decorated with filigree flowers, foliage and fruits, all on woven ground, stems with ball knops on octagonal bases with fretwork edges and feet, 6" h., 9.2 troy oz. $28,860

Drewatts & Bloomsbury Auctions

Vases, Canton maker S, circa 1870, baluster form with undulating rim and waisted neck, chased repoussé decoration depicting two male figures presenting child to third in landscape setting with birds, circular foot tapering to segmented standard, marks: S, 85, (maker's marks), 8" h., 16.1 oz. $3,250

Heritage Auctions

Compote, Luen Wo, Shanghai, circa 1890, marks: LUEN WO, (maker's mark), SHANGHAI, pedestal compote with lotus-form bowl with nine lobed peaked petals, each with chased repoussé and applied design of foliage and flowers with birds, center bowl supported by three dragons that emanate from central baluster column, 7-1/8" h. x 7" w., 19.5 oz. $5,625

Heritage Auctions

Purse, Hung Chong & Co., Canton and Shanghai, circa 1900, marks: HC, (maker's mark), hinged with repoussé decoration of dragon in clouds swirling around central engraved circular cartouche set against planished ground, reverse decorated with repoussé foliate motif of bamboo centering quatrefoil cartouche with Chinese characters, gilt interior, heavy link chain, monogrammed on front FPS, 3-1/2" h., 5.4 oz. $1,250

Heritage Auctions

Teapot, Wo Shing [Wong Hsing], Canton, circa 1820-1860, pseudo English mark for this maker with figure of Chinese mandarin seated cross-legged as finial of domed lid, tree shrew amongst fruited vine border and shell and foliate rim, capped scroll handle with conforming decoration, lobed baluster body embossed with panels of figures amidst landscapes and gardens, head of mythical beast at bottom of spout, four foliate and paw feet, 9-1/4" h., 44.8 troy oz....$11,375

Drewatts & Bloomsbury Auctions

Cup, Kecheong, Canton, circa 1840, marks: KHC, (three partially effaced pseudo English marks), tapering cylindrical cup with figures in Chinese attire and in various pursuits, banded rim and foot, figural serpentine-form S-scroll handle mounted to rim at snout and body at claw feet, medallion at top center of cup inscribed "S. Heber Dana From his Uncle Rich d. P. Dana 1842," 4-1/4" h., 10.57 troy oz. $1,750

Heritage Auctions

Pair of ceremonial columns models, [Huabiao] by Bao Xiang, Beijing, circa 1880, each with mythical den long [aka hou] seated upon removable dew-collecting plate, column, with dragon amidst clouds above waves in semi-relief and "cloud board," on hexagonal waisted plinth, square base enclosed by balustrade of reticulated dragons confronting flaming pearl on lower panels, 11-1/2" h., 27 troy oz, rare. $5,095

Drewatts & Bloomsbury Auctions

Sports

PEOPLE HAVE BEEN SAVING sports-related equipment since the inception of sports. Some of it was passed down from generation to generation for reuse; the rest was stored in closets, attics, and basements.

Two key trends brought collectors' attention to sports collectibles. First, decorators began using old sports items, particularly in restaurant décor. Second, collectors began to discover the thrill of owning the "real" thing.

There are collectible items representing nearly every sport, but baseball memorabilia is probably the most well-known segment. The "national pastime" has millions of fans, with enthusiastic collectors seeking out items associated with players such as Babe Ruth, Lou Gehrig, and others who became legends in their own lifetimes. Although baseball cards, first issued as advertising premiums for bubble gum and other products, seem to dominate the field, there are numerous other items available.

Sports collectibles are more accessible than ever before because of online auctions and several auction houses that dedicate themselves to that segment of the hobby. Provenance is extremely important when investing in high-ticket sports collectibles. Being able to know (and prove) the history of the object may greatly enhance the value, with a premium paid for items secured from the player or directly from their estate.

Babe Ruth's Official Baseball Game, 1948.. **$180**
Legendary Auctions

SPORTS

1904 Honus Wagner sheet music by William J. Hartz, "Husky Hans, a Stirring March and Two-Step," 9-3/4" x 12-3/4"................................. **$270**

Legendary Auctions

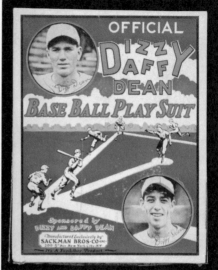

1930s Official Dizzy and Daffy Dean Base Ball Play Suit by Sackman Bros. Co., original box shown, contents included jersey, pants, cap and belt. **$775**

Legendary Auctions

1948 Cleveland Indians World Series pennant, only offered at the 1948 World Series.............. **$214**

Memory Lane, Inc.

"1909 Pittsburg N.L. Champions" team composite pinback, available only during 1909 World Series, celluloid, 2-1/8"... **$1,135**

Legendary Auctions

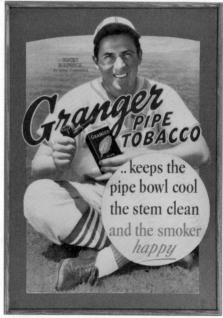

Ducky Medwick, 1930s, Granger Pipe Tobacco advertising display, 23" x 32"......................... **$480**

Legendary Auctions

1940s Trophy Official League baseball novelty radio, AM tuning, 9-1/2" h.................. **$500**

Legendary Auctions

Golf great Phil Mickelson-signed 2010 Masters flag.... **$382**

Collect Auctions

Barry Sanders-signed full-size Detroit Lions Riddell helmet................................ **$243**

Collect Auctions

1960s "Fred A Kail" New York Giants figure, ceramic, 10" h. **$200**

Legendary Auctions

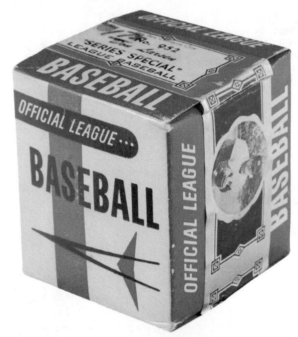

1950s Don Larsen Official League baseball, unopened in original box **$1,006**

Goldin Auctions

Early 1900s laced leather basketball from James Naismith days **$390**

Legendary Auctions

Notre Dame 1929 National Champions banner, heavy felt, 17-1/2" x 35" **$3,325**

Goldin Auctions

SPORTS

Negro League team Cuban Stars real photo postcard with Jose Mendez, circa 1909, 3-1/2" x 5-1/2"..**$6,325**

Hake's Americana & Collectibles

1949 Leaf Gum Co. promotional football poster for Leaf football cards, 8-1/2" x 13-3/8"........................... **$2,370**

Robert Edward Auctions

University of Pennsylvania "Beat Penn-State" button, dated Nov. 1, 1919, with back paper by Phila Badge and spring pin holding four ribbons, 2-1/4".............................. **$190**

Hake's Americana & Collectibles

Circa 1935 watch depicting pitcher Dizzy Dean, chrome plated with original metal link band, one of first watches to feature a baseball player, 1-1/4" x 1-1/4".................. **$633**

Hake's Americana & Collectibles

Jackie Robinson Daily Dime Register Bank, tin litho, 1950, 2-1/2" x 2-1/2" x 5/8"........ **$366**

Hake's Americana & Collectibles

1993 Daytona 500 champion ring won by Dale Jarrett, manufactured by Herff Jones, 10K gold, size 12-1/2, 45 points worth of small diamonds......................... **$2,390**

Legendary Auctions

1888 original stock certificate representing two shares for the Boston Base Ball Association, 8-1/2" x 5-1/4" **$325**

Collect Auctions

SPORTS

Hardcover copy of *The Four Winners, the Head, the Hands, the Foot, the Ball* signed by author Knute Rockne, printed in 1925 by The Devin-Adair Co **$1,856**

Collect Auctions

Program for 1912 World Series between Boston Red Sox and New York Giants, first World Series played at Fenway Park **$5,950**

SCP Auctions

Gary Carter signed and used knee brace, inscribed "The Kid." **$771**

Goldin Auctions

1860 *Base Ball Player's Pocket Companion*, Third Revised Edition, rules of game, 35 pages, 3-3/4" x 5-1/2" **$8,963**

Heritage Auctions

1991 American Bowling Congress 300 Game ring produced by Balfour, 10k gold................ **$508**

Legendary Auctions

Rawlings Gold Glove Award presented to Edgar Renteria, approximately 17-1/2" l. x 6-1/2" w. x 16" h **$9,815**

Goldin Auctions

Goose Gossage's 2008 National Baseball Hall of Fame induction plaque issued to the legendary closer at his induction ceremony in 2008..........................**$16,560**

SCP Auctions

Stub from March 2, 1962, the night Wilt Chamberlain scored 100 points for the Philadelphia Warriors basketball team...**$10,755**

Heritage Auctions

1940s Joe Louis figural desk clock, base caption reads, "Joe Louis World Champion," 12-1/4" x 8-3/4" x 3-3/4"...**$330**

Legendary Auctions

Muhammad Ali tribute button from event held at Apollo Theatre on April 13, 1979, produced by N.G. Slater, reads "Harlem Roasts the Champ," 3-1/2" dia..........................**$127**

Hake's Americana & Collectibles

Mickey Mantle's *Bengal Tales* high school yearbook, 56 pages, hardbound, class of 1948 at Commerce (Oklahoma) High School...............................**$650**

Legendary Auctions

Replica jersey signed by NBA Hall of Famer Wilt Chamberlain....................**$1,673**

Legendary Auctions

2001 University of Miami National Champion trophy, offered to players and university officials, 6" x 5" x 14".....**$4,922**

Goldin Auctions.

Black and white photo of Bill Russell shooting over Wilt Chamberlain, signed by Russell, 16" x 20"..........................**$150**

Collect Auctions

SPORTS

$

1943 St. Louis Cardinals Old Judge Coffee calendar celebrating St. Louis Cardinals 1942 World Series championship (with Stan Musial) **$450**

Legendary Auctions

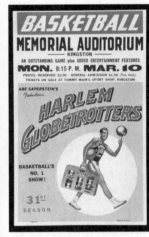

1957 Harlem Globetrotters advertising broadside, 14" x 22" **$270**

Legendary Auctions

History of Colored Base Ball by Sol White, published in 1907, first and most noteworthy book about the Negro Leagues. **$10,158**

Heritage Auctions

TOP LOT!

Jesse Owens' 1936 Olympic gold medal from Berlin games; only documented gold medal among four originals awarded to Owens during those games ....**$1.47 million**

SCP Auctions

SPORTS

Pair of Converse shoes worn in late 1980s by Boston Celtics legend Larry Bird, signed **$6,845**

SCP Auctions

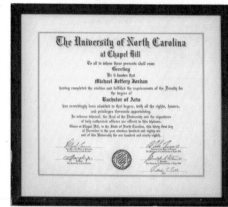

Michael Jordan's University of North Carolina diploma, formerly on display in Chapel Hill, North Carolina, restaurant called Michael Jordan's 23..........**$20,786**

Goldin Auctions

Red Auerbach 1961 Pro Basketball Coach of the Year cup presented by The Touchdown Club of Columbus, Inc., silver, 7-1/4" h. x 9" w........ **$2,163**

Goldin Auctions

Early 1950s Gordie Howe game-used Detroit Red Wings hockey jersey **$33,089**

Goldin Auctions

1910 Philadelphia As World Series champions advertising mirror, 2-3/16" dia.....................**$1,390**

Goldin Auctions

SPORTS

Michael Jordan 1984-1998 Chicago street banner, approximately 30-1/2" x 98"........... **$900**

Goldin Auctions

Hulk Hogan match-worn and signed trademark yellow boots with inscription, "These are my real boots with my real blood on them from MSG." **$6,544**

SCP Auctions

1940s original photo of Earl Louis "Curly" Lambeau, founder, player, and first coach of the Green Bay Packers, 8" x 10".................. **$20**

Collect Auctions

Early baseball holder counter display rack, holds up to 18 baseballs, 11-1/2" h........ **$1,219**

Goldin Auctions

Michael Phelps-signed USA swim cap **$685**

Goldin Auctions

1933 KOOL Cigarettes Washington Nationals vs. New York Giants World Series line score advertising display, Brown & Williamson Tobacco Co., 36" x 13-1/2".. **$636**

Goldin Auctions

Stamps

STAMP COLLECTING, called philately, is generally accepted as the world's oldest hobby, dating to the introduction of prepaid adhesive stamps to indicate the payment of mailing fees in Great Britain in 1840. The Universal Postal Union, an international postal watchdog and clearinghouse, estimates that 30 million people around the world collect stamps today, and retail sales in the hobby total $10 billion annually.

It is safe to say no two collections are alike. An entire library of books on the hobby would be needed to cover all its nuances.

The first government postage stamps in the United States were authorized to take effect July 1, 1847. In

1957 4¢ 48-Star Flag..........................$.40 unused; $.20 used

Great Britain, where stamps originated seven years earlier, the first issues featured a portrait of the long-sitting Queen Victoria. But in America, Congress decided to bypass the president, James K. Polk, in favor of two giants of the nation's founding, President George Washington, whose image graced the 10-cent stamp (designated by a Roman "X"), and statesman Benjamin Franklin, who also happened to be the United States' first postmaster, on the 5-cent stamp.

The subjects on U.S. stamps represent famous people, places and events of our nation's past or, in many issues of recent years, popular culture. Call it nostalgia, appreciation or education, history plays a major role in many collections.

From the fine engraving of early intaglio stamps to the full-color gravure of today, the printer's art is on display in stamps. From tiny secret marks used to distinguish some early stamps to almost microscopic nicks and spots to hidden images that can be seen only with special lenses, stamps carry an array of attractions for the technophile.

Some stamp subjects, such as scenes from our national parks, are original art, created especially for the medium of the postage stamp. Others are exquisitely detailed, tiny reproductions of larger originals. Artists themselves have been commemorated on stamps. A collector could concentrate entirely on this aspect, but visually every stamp collection is essentially an artistic display of its owner's creation.

For more information on U.S. stamps, see *Warman's U.S. Stamps Field Guide*, 3rd edition, by Maurice D. Wozniak.

STAMPS

1908-1909 10¢ Washington, yellow. ..... **$90 unused; $2.50 used**

1857-1861 5¢ Jefferson, brick red .. **$25,000 unused; $2,300 used**

1897-1903 4¢ Lincoln, rose-brown. ...... **$40 unused; $2.50 used**

1847 5¢ Franklin, red-brown. .... **$6,000 unused; $600 used**

Second Bureau Issue $2 James Madison, dark blue. ... **$1,500 unused; $225 used**

1949 3¢ Edgar Allan Poe. .... **$.60 unused; $.20 used**

1992 20¢ Love Envelope & Heart...... **$1.60 unused; $.20 used**

1986 22¢ American Folk Art Carved Figures, block of four. .... **$4.95 unused**

1922-1926 5¢ Theodore Roosevelt, dark blue. .... **$33.50 unused; $.20 used**

1999 33¢ Arctic Animals, strip of five................................ **$7 unused**

1918 $5 Franklin, deep green and black, unwatermarked paper, Perforation 11. .... **$425 unused; $53 used**

1851-1857 12¢ Washington, black.
$4,000 unused; $375 used

1902-1903 8¢ Martha Washington (first woman on a definitive U.S. stamp), violet-black.
$55 unused; $3 used

1958-1959 Lincoln Sesquicentennial 4¢ Statue of Lincoln. .... **$.50 unused; $.20 used**

2004 37¢ John Wayne. ..... **$1.50 unused**

1998 22¢ Uncle Sam, self-adhesive, coil.
....**$.90 unused; .25 used**

1986 Fish Booklet, pane of five.
.... **$15.95 unused**

1972 8¢ Mail Order Business.
.... **$.60 unused; $.20 used**

1984 20¢ Christmas, Santa Claus. ..**$1.25; $.20 used**

1863-1866 2¢ Jackson
.... **$300 unused; $40 used**

2001 34¢ Porky Pig.
$1.20 unused; $.20¢ used

2005 37¢ Jim Henson & The Muppets sheetlet, panel of 11 stamps. .... **$15 unused**

TOOLS

Tools

TOOL COLLECTING is nearly as old as tools themselves. Certainly it was not long after Stone Age man used his first stone tool that he started watching for that special rock or piece of bone. Soon he would have been putting tools away just for the right time or project. The first tool collector was born!

Since earliest man started collecting tools just for the right time or project, many other reasons to collect have evolved. As man created one tool, he could then use that tool to make an even better tool.

Very quickly toolmakers became extremely skilled at their craft, and that created a new collecting area – collecting the works of the very best makers. In time toolmakers realized that tools were being purchased on the bases of the quality of workmanship alone. With this realization an even more advanced collector was born as toolmakers began making top-of-the-line tools from special materials with fine detailing and engraving. These exquisite tools were never intended for use but were to be enjoyed and collected. Many of the finest tools were of such quality that they are considered works of art.

So many tools exist in today's world that many tool collectors focus on one special category. Some of the most popular categories to collect fall into the general areas of: function, craft or trade, personal connection, company or brand, patents, and investments.

For more information on tools, see *Antique Trader Tools Price Guide* by Clarence Blanchard.

Evendens beading tool, brass and maple handle, 4-1/4" l...$48
John McInnis Auctioneers

Stanley No. 45 plane, original wooden box, includes additional cutters with blades. **$113**

Scheerer McCulloch Auctioneers, Inc.

Keuffel & Esser Co. surveying tool, New York, serial No. 52091, Wye level No. 5111, 11-1/4" x 6-1/2". **$45**

Garth's Auction

Butterfield Co. bicycle screwplate tap and die set, original, box. **$201**

Copake Auction, Inc.

Stanley No. A4 smoothing plane, aluminum, Sweetheart trademark on cutting iron, clean, complete, 9" l. **$201**

Martin J. Donnelly Auctions

American Shear & Knife Co. knife, Woodbury, Connecticut, ebony handle, single spey blade. **$144**

Martin J. Donnelly Auctions

Friend H. Dickinson carpenter's slick, Higganum, Connecticut, early style turned handle, clean, usable, 3-1/2" w. **$259**

Martin J. Donnelly Auctions

Leetonia Tool Co. box, "Leetonia, Ohio, USA. Manufacturers of drills and tools for coal, clay and metal mines / Tools for the hardware and marine trade." **$18**

Holabird Western Americana Collections

Ludwig Oertling wantage rod, London, England, dual loops in brass sliding gauge, maker mark and "Inland Revenue" on body. **$259**

Martin J. Donnelly Auctions

Spear & Jackson dovetail saw, Sheffield, England, blade 10", open handle, total 14-1/2" l. **$104**

Martin J. Donnelly Auctions

Smoothing plane, brass and rosewood, blade support iron marked Alex Mathieson and Glasgow, blade marked GV & H Stormont, base 9-1/8" l. **$193**

Dickins Auctioneers, Ltd.

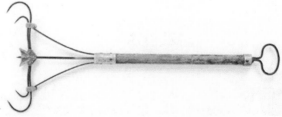

Spring gaff hook, probably E.T. Holtz, Shell Lake, Wisconsin, hollow wooden handle with spring that opens and closes spiked jaws, 38-1/4" l. **$575**

Lang's Auction

TOOLS

Facet tool, maker unknown, cast iron and brass diamond, marked "17" on arm, 7-1/2" x 15-1/2" x 7-1/4"..................**$60**

Burchard Galleries, Inc.

Stanley shoe-buckle block plane No. 110, type 2, cast iron, approximately 90 percent of original black japan finish, no cracks or chips...............**$276**

Martin J. Donnelly Auctions

Bridge City Tool Co. No. BS5 bevel, Portland, Oregon, limited edition, factory engraved "D.B. Wing," original box, new condition, 6-1/2" l..............**$259**

Martin J. Donnelly Auctions

Davis & Cook level, Watertown, New York, cast iron, patent mark on level vials, Dec. 7, 1886, Gustavus Cook, Watertown, 12" l. **$720**

Martin J. Donnelly Auctions

Millers Falls Co. miter box, Millers Falls, Massachusetts, cast iron, small size, with Henry Disston & Sons tenon saw....**$345**

Martin J. Donnelly Auctions

Jo. Fuller quarter-round molding plane, Providence, Rhode Island, 18th century, owner mark "R.C. Starr," with 3/4" yellow-birch round and 1/4" beech edge bead.........**$173**

Martin J. Donnelly Auctions

European bearded ax, cutting edge 11", rib pattern forged at neck, later wooden handle 31" l..**$316**

Martin J. Donnelly Auctions

American Lock Crank Co. automatic lock crank, Milwaukee, patented March 25, 1884, Tracy L. Paine, Milwaukee, 4-1/2" l..............**$81**

Martin J. Donnelly Auctions

C. Fisher round molding plane, Windsor, Vermont, beech, yellow-birch body, extra bold imprint, excellent condition, sheared wedge finial. **$184**

Martin J. Donnelly Auctions

Millers Falls Co. No. 15 sweep bit brace, Millers Falls, Massachusetts, non-ratchet, 85 percent of original nickel plating, 5"...................**$201**

Martin J. Donnelly Auctions

Early bowl adze, 9-1/2" cutting edge, early round handle, 10" l. **$219**

Martin J. Donnelly Auctions

Screw-type eyelet press, Germany, marked "D.R.M.," acorn finials on screws, 8-1/2" l. **$92**

Martin J. Donnelly Auctions

Block plane, early, cast iron, solid brass bridge, beech infill and wedge, 5-1/2" l. **$196**

Martin J. Donnelly Auctions

Farrier's gauge, marked "Made in England," solid brass, protractor graduations on beveled arm, 6" l. **$87**

Martin J. Donnelly Auctions

Ohio Tool Co. No. O20 adjustable compass plane, Auburn, New York, 60 percent of original nickel plating, complete, usable, 9-1/2". ... **$150**

Martin J. Donnelly Auctions

B. Freeth & Co. wooden brace, Sheffield, England, spring lock chuck, maker mark on chuck, maker attributed to 1818-1820, 14-1/2" l. **$86**

Martin J. Donnelly Auctions

Goodell Co. apple parer, Antrim, New Hampshire, patented March 18, 1884, by William A.C. Oaks, Antrim, then assigned to Goodell, 11" l. ... **$276**

Martin J. Donnelly Auctions

William J. Young & Sons surveyor's compass, Philadelphia, needle 7", complete, vernier adjust, both original sighting vanes, 17" l. **$604**

Martin J. Donnelly Auctions

Large pair of early wooden dividers, beech, hand-forged ram's horn nut, 40" l. **$150**

Martin J. Donnelly Auctions

Large early log hammer, marked with letter V and number 7, 29-1/4" l. **$288**

Martin J. Donnelly Auctions

North Brothers Manufacturing Co. No. 555 ratchet-action breast drill, Philadelphia, ratchet mechanism patented Dec. 15, 1908, by George O. Leopold, Philadelphia, 18" l. **$161**

Martin J. Donnelly Auctions

Griffin Rug Machine rug-making tools, nine pieces, original box, instructions, extra parts......... **$35**

Saco River Auction Co.

Bailey, Chany & Co. No. 3 vertical-post plane, Boston, complete, original, 98 percent of original japan finish, rare, 18" l. **$3,105**

Martin J. Donnelly Auctions

Edwin W. Foster turntable smoothing plane, Central Park, New York, patented Jan. 29, 1907, national marketer Oliver Woodworking Machinery Co., Grand Rapids, Michigan, probable maker Ohio Tool Co., 9-3/4" l. **$1,955**

Martin J. Donnelly Auctions

Stanley No. 50 plane body section, Miller patent Sept. 17, 1872, original gold-wash finish, excellent condition, 11" l. **$1,840**

Martin J. Donnelly Auctions

Jensen combination dado, rabbet and fillister plane, patented May 14, 1872, by Conrad Jensen, Boston, "C. Jensen" and patent date on toe, rare, 11-1/2" l................. **$3,220**

Martin J. Donnelly Auctions

Ce. Chelor gunstock molding plane, Wrentham, Massachusetts, yellow birch, original wedge, "A1" imprint, rare, 10" l........................ **$2,300**

Martin J. Donnelly Auctions

Hubbard Hardware Co. folding rule, Middletown, Connecticut, pitch filled, two fold, 24" l. Hubbard produced rules from 1864 to 1877 when the company's assets were liquidated during a national financial panic. **$633**

Martin J. Donnelly Auctions

Carroll Thomas multipurpose combination tool, Lincoln, Illinois, plane, bevel, level, try square, marking gauge, patented Jan. 10, 1882, rare, well preserved, 10" l........ **$1,610**

Martin J. Donnelly Auctions

R. H. Smith & Co. five-button crosscut hand saw, St. Catharines, Ontario, Canada, 10 pont, blade 23", marked "Successors to J. Flint." **$1,093**

Martin J. Donnelly Auctions

Toys

THE COLLECTIBLE TOY MARKET has undergone some considerable changes during the last 15 years as major collectors sold their holdings and the Internet brought collectors together like never before. The toy market remains a bright spot as longtime collectors open their toy boxes to scores of collectors in America and overseas. But one collector who has no plans to sell is Ron Sturgeon, owner of DFW Elite Toy Museum in Fort Worth, Texas.

Sturgeon opened his 3,000-piece collection to the public for free, with rotating exhibits of salesman samples to toy racecars and memorabilia related to the Indianapolis 500. A museum was the next logical step for the collector, who started with his first purchase of a Marklin truck and trailer at a Sotheby's toy auction in London in 1985. He spent $250 on the toy as a souvenir of his trip and a fitting addition to his collection of 60 antique cars.

He says the toy hobby changed dramatically with the arrival of the Internet.

"Lots of great toys have been exposed by the Internet and eBay, although toy shows have suffered in attendance," says Sturgeon, whose museum houses one of the largest public collections of automotive toys and models in the world. It includes 1950s-era battery-operated toys to land speed record cars and even ship models from legendary collector Malcolm Forbes.

Edwards' Big League Table Baseball, circa 1915, working mechanical baseball game, base runners circle diamond with crank-powered chain, 26" x 26" x 5" particle board "stadium." **$10,755**

Heritage Auctions

Sturgeon says the museum is one way to educate and entertain the public while also raising money for his preferred charity, the King Charles Cavalier Rescue Group. Other collectors who may also own a large collection may struggle to share with the world without a similar museum format, he says. "I think it's hard without a business attached. I think that does lead to frustration and sell-offs."

Sturgeon proudly displays an important Fischer Father Christmas car. The 10-1/2" rare tin litho shows Father Christmas at the wheel with a small feather tree and die-cut figures, including a teddy bear, situated in the clockwork car. The scarce concept car is part of a trio of rare Santa cars in the collection, including an example by German toymaker Tippco and a Japanese-made CK car.

Exceptional items such as these easily find new homes in a market such as the one we see in 2015. Toys too numerous to count change hands regularly on eBay. The variety of antique toys to be found is staggering, although it's not always certain this venue brings the best prices for collectors.

The new Best Offer option on eBay allows buyers to negotiate sale prices with sellers. A scan of recent antique and vintage toy completed items lists over a three-month period show that more than

Mickey Mouse Circus Train, 1935, Lionel, #1536, windup O gauge train set, original box with locomotive (#1508), stoker tender car (with shoveling Mickey), Mickey Mouse Circus car (#1536), Circus Dining Car (#1518), and Mickey Mouse Band car (#1536), tracks (two straight sections and six curved), paper circus tent, large Mickey Mouse barker composite figure, and assorted cardboard cutout pieces, box 11-1/4" x 17" x 2-1/4".......................... **$9,858**

Heritage Auctions

half of the sales were completed with this function. That means buyers are generally not seeing fair market values when they visit the site, and the site's completed item listing does not show the final price the piece sold for.

It's more important than ever to research your purchases before you dive headfirst into a collection. It's easy to overspend in the antique and vintage toy hobby and easier still to get stung by reproductions and fantasy pieces. Work with a trusted auction house or, better yet, a reliable and honest mentor who can show you the ropes of this fascinating and dynamic hobby.

–Eric Bradley

TOYS

Toy truck, World War II-era people mover made by Hausser, Germany, clockwork halftrack with folding gray cloth top, 11 composition soldiers, exchangeable "Hausser" marked rubber tires (including two spares), original windshield, manual turn indicators, and rubber treads, excellent condition, 14" l. **$5,975**

Heritage Auctions

Muhammad Ali Bop Bag punching bag, 1976, original box, with two children's boxing gloves, each issued in 1976.........**$80**

Heritage Auctions

Noisemaker, cap-shooting Official Batman Bat Grenade, 1966, pair, with original store display cards, very good condition. **$250**

Heritage Auctions

Danger Girl action figures, 1999, McFarlane Toys, set of three carded action figures with detailed dioramas: Abbey Chase, Sydney Savage, and Natalia Kassle; excellent unopened condition. **$35**

Heritage Auctions

Toy pistol, Buck Rogers Atomic Pistol U-238, 1946, Daisy, gold-finish metal toy ray gun, flint still produces spark when trigger is pulled, fine condition. **$173**

Heritage Auctions

Masuyama Rickshaw EPL 773, Lehmann, circa 1930, lithographed and hand-painted tin, working clockwork, original box, nearly mint condition, 7-1/2" l. **$5,800**

Auction Team Breker

Pull toy, jointed figure of Mickey Mouse sitting on back of horse, 1930s, made in Italy, rare, very good condition, 3" x 8-1/2" x 6-7/8" h............ **$765**

Hakes Americana & Collectibles

Pull toy, Popeye, 1939, Fisher Price, Toy No. 488, Popeye with 1929 King Features Syndicate, Inc. copyright on leg, character holds drumsticks and stands in front of large can of "Spinach – Come and Get It!" 9-7/8" h. **$600**

Hakes Americana & Collectibles

Toy Buick saloon, circa 1950s, Märklin, #8001, maroon die-cast car with aluminum wheels and rubber tires, original box with tiny hole punched on side panel as produced so buyers could see car color, car produced in variety of colors, box 4-7/8" l........ **$230**

Hakes Americana & Collectibles

Playset, Disneyland, circa 1961, Marx Happi-Time set #5995, original Sears Allstate box, set includes character figures of Mickey Mouse, Minnie Mouse, Donald Duck, Goofy, Pluto and Ludwig, plus 18 others and 12 animals, box 21" x 27-1/2" x 7".............. **$556**

Hakes Americana & Collectibles

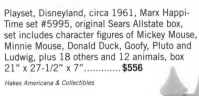

Sorry! The Fashionable English Game, Parker Brothers, circa 1930s, containing 16 pieces, deck of cards, and instruction booklet, very good condition, 5" x 4" box................................ **$28**

Heritage Auctions

United States Educational Toy Money game, Milton Bradley & Co., patent date of March 20, 1877, original box, with imitation coins and currency: 11 1872 cents, nine 1867 two-cent pieces, 15 1870 shield nickels, 14 1875 dimes, 11 1876 quarters, five 1875 halves, five 1878 Morgan dollars, two 1853 quarter eagles, one 1862 three-dollar piece, one 1883 half eagle, two 1880 eagles, and two 1873 Open 3 twenties. **$500**

Heritage Auctions

TOYS

Sturditoy oil truck, circa 1925, pressed steel, 25" l. Provenance: Formerly in Palumbo and Kaufman toy collections. **$15,340**

Bertoia Auctions

Walkie-talkies, circa 1950s, Space Patrol Space-A-Phones, Ralston premium, 4-1/2" h. black and white hard plastic phones with original box and catalog. **$192**

Hakes Americana & Collectibles

Toy drum, 1939, J. Chein & Co., copyright Paramount Pictures, with characters from animated film "Gulliver's Travels," 5" d. x 13" dia. **$115**

Hakes Americana & Collectibles

Battleship "Cincinnati," circa 1912-1915, Märklin 2nd Series, 34" l. **$78,880**

Bertoia Auctions

Science kit, Atomic Energy Lab by A.C. Gilbert, U-238, complete and intact, box with full-color graphics, excellent condition, 25" l. x 16-1/2" w. x 5" d. One of the most sought after science toys rarely offered for sale; due to its complexity it sold for $49.50 in 1951. ....**$2,962**

James D. Julia Auctioneers

Locomotive, Boucher #2500, passenger set. **$25,960**

Bertoia Auctions

TOYS

Toy ring, 1933, likely issued at time of Paramount Pictures 1933 "Alice in Wonderland" movie, each side of ring with three heart-shaped designs, young child size 2.5. ....**$379**

Hakes Americana & Collectibles

Toy pails: Disney toy sand pail set of three with 7" Mickey Mouse Picnic pail made by Ohio Art in fine condition, 6" Mickey's Garden pail in fine condition, and 3-1/2" Mickey pail; two 3" Mickey "Ice Cold Drinks" pails, one in very good condition in red, other fine condition with green interior, made by Ohio Art; 1949 Disneyland 3" pail that originally held candy, made by Overland, in fine condition; and 1937-era Ohio Art Mickey Mouse shovel, fine condition. **$1,700**

Heritage Auctions

TOYS

INSIDE INTEL

WHAT'S CHANGED: Lots of great toys have been exposed by the Internet and eBay, although toy shows have suffered in attendance. [We are] continuing to look for interesting pieces, but trying to be a lot more selective as we don't have much display room left.

COLLECTING TIP: The original box the toy came in almost always increases the value of the toy by a minimum of 25 percent. Boxes can easily double the value of rarer, older toys. There are no known examples of some toys with their original boxes, and to find one of them with a box could possibly even triple its value.

— Ron Sturgeon
Owner of DFW Elite Toy Museum
Fort Worth, Texas
dfwelitetoymuseum.com

HOT

On display at the DFW Elite Toy Museum in Fort Worth, Texas, this Fischer Father Christmas car is one of three Santa-related automotive toys on display from owner Ron Sturgeon's 3,000-piece collection. The car, one of a handful known to exist, often brings in excess of $25,000 at auction.

DFW Elite Toy Museum

This Marklin truck and trailer, now on display at the DFW Elite Toy Museum of Fort Worth, Texas, was purchased during a Sotheby's auction in London in 1985 for $250.

DFW Elite Toy Museum

Large Bing tin toy limousine no. 10376/4, Gebrüder Bing, Nuremberg, Germany, circa 1912, hand-japanned tin, working clockwork motor, beveled glass windows, steerable front wheels, brake, opening doors, rubber tires, molded driver's seat, produced by hand in small numbers for luxury market, 18-1/2" l............................**$15,000**

Auction Team Breker

Motorcycle, Wilhelm Krauss, Nuremberg, Germany, circa 1923, lithographed tin, crank for friction drive, marked "KW," very good condition, 7-9/10" ...**$12,500**

Auction Team Breker

Motorcycle No. 1106, China, circa 1930, lithographed tin, working clockwork, rare, near mint condition, 7-1/2" l **$15,400**

Auction Team Breker

Mickey the Magician wind-up figure by Linemar, tinplate, with original box. **$4,100**

Bertoia Auctions

Horse-drawn coupe No. 8425/1, Märklin, circa 1909, hand-painted tin, glass windows, nickel-plated lanterns, imitation upholstery, two opening doors, horse on wheels with leather bridle and fur coating, 18-1/2" x 5-3/4" x 7" overall. **$8,600**

Auction Team Breker

TOYS

Answer Game calculating robot, circa 1963, Ischida/Japan, mostly tin, working adding machine, 14" h.............. **$1,200**

Auction Team Breker

Battleship "Maine," series 1, Märklin, German, mint condition, 30-1/2" l..**$64,900**

Bertoia Auctions

Pabst Beer boxcar, Märklin gauge 1, German...........................**$21,240**

Bertoia Auctions

Primus tinplate clockwork roller skater, Lehmann, German, circa 1915.............................**$14,160**

Bertoia Auctions

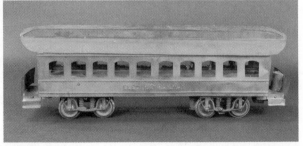

Carlisle & Finch Electric Railway Interurban train car, brass body with embossed sides, 19" l. **$12,980**

Bertoia Auctions

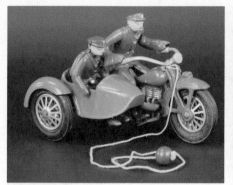

Motorcycle and sidecar, Vindex, cast iron, green with khaki driver and rider, production run of less than two years, 8-1/2" l. **$25,960**

Bertoia Auctions

Mickey and Minnie Mouse clockwork motorcycle, Tipp & Co..**$56,050**

Bertoia Auctions

Santa in open roadster, CK, pre-1940s, Japan, decorated with Christmas images, 7" l.........**$37,760**

Bertoia Auctions

Limousine, Carette, circa 1912, German, tinplate, 16" l. **$21,240**

Bertoia Auctions

Winky Robot, circa 1950s, made by Tonezawa, Japan, working condition, Vari-Vue flicker/flasher discs for eyes, giving robot appearance of winking as he walks, with original box, 9-1/2" h. **$635**

Hakes Americana & Collectibles

Transistor Radios

The most collectible and historic transistor radios were made in America from 1955 to 1960 and Japan from 1956 to 1963. An easy way to date a transistor radio of this period is to look for small triangles or circles between the 6 and 7 and the 12 and 16 on the dial. These are Civil Defense (CD) marks, which appeared on all radios manufactured or sold in the United States from 1953 to 1963.

At the height of the Russian Red Scare, the United States enacted the CONELRAD program, establishing two civil defense frequencies, 640 and 1240 kilohertz. During times of emergencies, all stations except the CONELRAD stations at 640 and 1240 AM would cease operations (note that some Japanese radios made by Sharp and Hitachi during the late 1950s left out the CD marks).

American companies were the first out of the solid-state-radio gate with the release of the Regency TR-1 in 1954 (it sold well into 1955 and 1956 as the redesigned TR-1G and TR-4). As a transistor radio collector I think it's important to have one example of this historic radio in your collection. Depending on color, they run between $300 and $1,000. Basic ivory and grey cabinets bring less money than the "mandarin" red and black models.

For a brief period the TR-1 was released in very attractive pearlescent pink and light blue colors as well as swirled, jade green, and mahogany. These later examples command top dollar on the secondary marker. Early Zenith radios like the Royal 500 series are also worthy of having in a collection. The first Royal 500 was hand wired and had a metal chassis. The fifth generation Zenith 500 was the 500H. It has a large oval speaker and is considered to be the best sounding/performing portable transistor radio.

Other collectible American-made radios are from RCA, General Electric, Admiral, Motorola, Magnavox, Philco, Raytheon, Arvin, Sylvania, and Emerson. American radios tend to be slightly larger than their Japanese counterparts. Most U.S. radios are considered "coat pocket"-sized – too big for your shirt pocket. Many were also larger, leather-clad portable sets like the Zenith Royal 750 and Raytheon 8TP-1.

The Emerson 888 series is one of the most popular and attractive coat pocket radios. Emerson released several models in this series from 1958 to 1960, such as the Vanguard, Pioneer, Explorer, Satellite, and Atlas – all named after various U.S. space programs. These radios can be found in great numbers today, and are terrific looking and often reasonably priced (typically from $20 to $100, depending on condition).

The first Japanese transistor released was Sony's TR-55, an incredibly rare find today. But it was the Sony TR-63 that created the greatest stir. Released in 1957, it was considered the world's first truly pocket-sized radio and was the first to utilize all miniature components. It was also the first Japanese radio to be imported into the United States (several other early Sony radios were sold in Canada in 1956). Even examples with cracks or chips can fetch $400. Mint condition models are considerably more valuable.

Toshiba, Hitachi, Sharp, Standard, Sanyo, Matsushita (Panasonic), Mitsubishi, Aiwa, Realtone, Global, and Zephyr soon arrived on North American shores. Small, affordable and colorful, these radios were an immediate hit with the youth market. The simultaneous arrival of imported pocket radios and rock 'n' roll conspired to change the electronics industry forever.

By the late 1950s and early 1960s, many American companies had opted to have their

TRANSISTOR RADIOS

Lafayette FS-91, nine transistors, reverse-painted dial in Art Deco style, marketed as "Mighty 9." .... **$50-$90**

Mitsubishi 6X-300, Japan, almost identical to Silver 6TR-100, maker Shirasuna Denki. .... **$40-$70**

Zephyr ZR-620, six transistors, Japan, circa 1960-1961, Zephyr name on dial painted on outside, chevron frames tuning window, similar to Harpers GK-631. .... **$30-$75**

radios made in Japan but retained their American brand names, such as Trancel, Penny's, Channel Master, and Bulova. Even giants like Zenith, RCA, Motorola, Philco, and G.E. had their radios made in Japan. They could no longer compete with the lower prices and more attractive designs coming from Asia.

One of the classic features of Japanese radios is reverse-painted plastic. Reverse (back) painting was a popular method of ornamenting transistor radios between 1958 and 1962. By painting all artwork on the inside of the clear plastic dial cover, there would be no wear or damage to the most attractive features of the radio. A smooth protective surface remained on the outer dial.

This process also gave the radio a three-dimensional appearance. The depth and palette of colors was breathtaking. Gold on white, black accents, bright red and powder blue along with geometric shapes like starbursts, chevrons, jet wings, diamonds and parallel lines make reverse-painted radios visually stunning and highly sought after by collectors. Makers like Toshiba and Crown were exceptional with their creative use of reverse painting.

Even Japanese radios without reverse painting are highly collectible. The Sony TR-610, with its sleek cabinet and round speaker grill, spawned a host of imitators like the Realtone TR-1088 "Comet." These radios can be found in abundance today and range in price from $50 to $150, depending on condition and color.

In your travels you may even encounter pocket radios called "Boy's Radios." Japanese firms were hit with both a domestic export tax and a North American import tax on any AM radio having three or more transistors. To avoid the expense, Japanese manufacturers in the 1960s developed AM radios that operated on two transistors. They were marketed as "toys" rather than electronic devices, thus sidestepping the taxes.

These radios would either have Boy's Radio or Two Transistors prominently and proudly displayed on the cabinet. In many cases, the cabinets were identical to "real" radios with six transistors. Performance was less than stellar, but these radios could still pick up local stations. Teenagers were swayed by price and appearance; performance was low on their list. Today Boy's Radios often range in value from $25 to $70.

With any transistor radio from the 1950s or early 1960s, it seems the brighter the color the higher the price. Cool 1950s shades like robin's egg/powder blue, sea foam green and bright red or yellow command higher prices. Black and ivory cabinets are considered less attractive by some and may reduce a radio's value on the collector market.

Of course condition is key in valuing a radio as well. Finding a radio with its original box, leather case, earphones, owner's manual, and warranty card/sales slip will inflate worth. Be sure to examine the cabinet closely when making a purchase. Small hairline cracks or chips are often found in the corners.

TRANSISTOR RADIOS

Zephyr AR-600, six transistors, Japan, circa 1958-1959, unusual design for pocket radio, circle and arrow inside reverse-painted dial, similar to Trylon and Perisphere (1939 World's Fair), maker Aiwa........... **$50-$90**

Zephyr ZR-930, nine transistors, Japan, reverse-painted dial, shield-shape grille, blue cabinet, kickstand on back allows radio to sit upright, also branded as Londal.......................... **$60-$90**

Harper's GK-631, six transistors, Japan, small dial window framed by sideways oversized chevron inset within reverse-painted circle, similar to Zephyr ZR-620. .... **$50-$90**

Mitsubishi 6X-145, six transistors, Japan, circa 1959, reverse-painted dial, starburst intersects tuning indicator, possible maker Shirasuna Denki Manufacturing Co. ....**$40-$80**

Global GR-711, Japan, circa 1959-1960, gold reverse-painted dial, shield-shape speaker grille, available in red, black, light blue, beige (looks pink), ivory, and hard-to-find lavender, also branded as a Zephyr. .... **$40-$80**

Global GR-100, 10 transistors, Japan, starburst motif with fake diamond inset, vertical slide rule dial, tapered cabinet. .... **$50-$90**

Some collectors refuse to buy damaged radios. Others are not troubled by buying less than perfect examples. Restoring and repairing are an option. If you want to keep a radio historically accurate, I recommend not changing its electronic components.

During the 1970s radio design experienced a renaissance. Bright colors and cool shapes made a comeback (perhaps inspired by disco, mood rings and the excesses of the decade). Panasonic released several radios that are highly collectible today, such as the Panapet and Toot-A-Loop. They can be found at flea markets or online auctions ranging in price from $10 to $50. Be prepared to spend more if you find one in its original box.

—*Michael Jack*

Inflicted with the collecting disease, Michael Jack has more than 1,100 transistor radios in his collection. He owns everything from the world's first transistor radio, the Regency TR-1, to the extremely rare Sony TR-5 (a redesign of Sony's very first radio). Jack also has many classic "Made in the U.S.A." sets and the best of "Made in Japan" models. By day, Michael is a recording engineer and music producer (see www.recordandmix.ca.). To view more of his radios, go to: http://www.flickr.com/people/transistor_radios/

TRANSISTOR RADIOS

Prince Pearl, "Transistr" misspelled on dial, uses cylindrical Toshiba. .... **$60-$90**

Electra YTR-603, six transistors, circa early 1960s, similar to Sony TR-610, Electra has brushed metal facade, also branded as Browni. .... **$20-$30**

Toshiba 6TP-309, six transistors, reverse-painted dial, nicknamed "Deep Vee" because of large chevron that frames tuning window, Seabreeze name at bottom left of speaker grille denotes Toronto company, ivory cabinet at lowest end of price range, black in middle, lime green-yellow at top....**$150-$400+**

Channel Master 6509, six transistors, Japan, circa 1959-1960, similar to Sony TR610, red and black cabinet, maker Sanyo. **$20-40**

Realtone TR-803 Valiant, seven transistors, circa 1960-1961, tiny pocket radio (3" x 2") nicknamed "The Blade" by collectors, also branded as Hudson, Cronovox, and Supreme....................**$140-$200**

Truetone Eight Transistors White, slide-rule dial, speaker grille resembles TV screen, usually found as Realtone Lancer (TR-1820) but also released as SounDesign and GM Sportsman, Truetone brand produced for Western Auto................. **$15-$25**

ITT Starburst, six transistors, starburst on grille, maker Nippon Electric Co......... **$20-$40**

Motorola X-11R, six transistors, circa 1959, first Motorola radio made in Japan, chassis same as some Danube, Hoffman, Monarch, Ambassador, and Lafayette models, R in model number denotes cabinet color, maker Tokai. .... **$20-$30**

Realtone TR-8611 Constellation, six transistors, large gold chevron and porthole dial window. .... **$20-$30**

Gold-Tone, four transistors, primitive and boxy look of earlier Japanese set, model number and maker uncertain. .... **$30-$60**

Sony TR-74, Japan, 1957, cabinet front and back identical, large ivory lattice speaker grille with old-style Sony logo in center, produced for two years, in burgundy only, originally retailed for $124.95, rare. ....**$300-$450**

Toshiba 5TP-90, silver reverse-painted dial with starburst. .... **$30-$50**

Toshiba 6TP-309A, in ivory, gray, and black. ....**$60-$100**

Regency TR-4, circa 1957, redesign of Regency TR-1 (world's first commercially released transistor radio, released Oct. 18, 1954) with less-expensive aluminum dial. ....**$150-$250**

Crown TR-777, reverse-painted panel with gold chevron, designer speaker grille, Crown Radio Corp., originally known as Asahi Radio Manufacturing Co., Ltd. ....**$175-$250**

Mantola M4-D, circa 1957, same as Regency TR-4, aluminum dial with spinning atom graphic, Mantola brand produced for B.F. Goodrich Co. ....**$150-$250**

Hoffman T-P410, California, circa 1957, Sony-made cabinet also used on Sony TR-6, also available in black (K-P410), desert sand (B-P410), calico red (R-P410), and circus pink (P-P410). ....**$600-$1,000**

Marconi Constellation, Montreal, sold in United States as Emerson Satellite, leather clad, chassis same as Emerson 888 Pioneer. .... **$50-$90**

Sony TR-86, eight transistors, circa 1958, about 100,000 sold, eclipsed by popular TR-610 (more than 500,000 sold). .....**$80-$130**

Chic 9, nine transistors, reverse-painted dial with gold starburst, Chic logo on grille, same as Kowa KT-91, similar to Lafayette FS-91, Zephyr ZR-930, Summit S-900, Monarch 90 and Crown TR-999......................**$100-$200**

Eureka KR-6TS35, circa 1958, early Koyo, reverse-painted dial, maroon plastic cabinet, angled brass nameplate, same as Polyrad KR-6T2, Koyo KTR-621 and Electrometric KR-6TS35. .... **$50-$80**

Commodore Super Deluxe, eight transistors, lots of reverse painting....................... **$30-$50**

RCA GP-336, Japan, circa 1959, same as Channel Master 6503, cloisonné badge on bottom left of speaker grille displays "His Master's Voice" logo, maker Sanyo. .... **$30-$50**

Gloritone HT-881, early 1960s, purple and lavender cabinets, reverse-painting around tuning dial and large silver chevron. .... **$40-$70**

Windsor 6T-220, six transistors, reverse painted on front, maker Fuji High Radio Frequency Lab Co., Ltd. (also produced Constant, Crestline, Vulcan, and Jupiter brands). .... **$30-$50**

Linmark T-80, eight transistors, Japan, early 1960s, starburst and reverse-painted dial, imported by Shapiro Trading Co. of New York and Los Angeles, same as Air Chief 4C54 (produced for Firestone Tire & Rubber Co.) and Capehart T8-201............................. **$40-$70**

Sanyo 6515B Super Fringe, eight transistors, Japan, also branded as Channel Master. .... **$20-$40**

Continental TR-682, six transistors, Japan, upper reverse-painted dial framed by two gold chevrons and crown design above peephole dial window, chrome speaker grille. .... **$25-$50**

Vintage Fashion

Peacock blue silk corset, heavily boned with brass busk and 35 pairs of back-lacing eyelets, blue embroidered flossing and coarse linen lining, front ties on shoulder straps, very good condition, six small holes in silk, bust 30+", waist 18-1/2+", full length 13-1/2". **$2,160**

Augusta Auctions

THROUGHOUT HISTORY, women have adorned themselves with the likes of found objects to create a look or style that is unique to them. Carryall bags and footwear were made from the hides of last night's dinner. It was quickly discovered that the head needed to be protected from the elements, so a good fur pelt became the most ideal source for warmth. In the tropics, raffia or straw hats were created to shield one from the sun. It was only a matter of time before these utilitarian items were artistically adapted by the individual wearer, and "fashion" began.

Changes in fashion over the next few millennia were insignificant compared to the past couple of centuries. People were generally clothed in full-length garb with little variation in accessorizing.

It wasn't until the industrial revolution that we had the ability to mass produce items that would affect the buying and selling of fashionable frills. The more a machine could crank out, the less pricey these items became.

Of course, the best hats and shoes continue to be those of the handmade variety, but these goods are justifiably costly and may not be affordable to all. Mass production allows manufacturers to lower the cost of their goods to the consumer since there is an exceedingly unlimited supply.

Men and women alike utilize the availability of accessories to express their individuality. A businessman carefully chooses his tie so as not to offend his clients, whereas a salesman might choose a loud, showy one to attract customers. A woman of this same status might have a chic designer handbag on her arm or perhaps drape a graceful scarf around her neck.

The history of fashion is a mirror to the future. Nearly every style has already been done in some form and is reproduced with variations today. The popularity and demand for vintage pieces are growing because clothing and accessories are great collectibles that are also a good investment. Many factors come into play when assessing value. When shopping vintage fashion, keep the following in mind:

Popularity: How well known the designer is affects the price.

Condition: Collectors tend to want the original design condition with no modifications or repairs.

Relevance: The piece should be a meaningful representation of a designer's work.

When you're hot, you're hot: As a trend develops, it is shown in fashion magazines, and the original vintage pieces go up in value (and plummet when it goes out of favor).

Location: Prices fluctuate from one geographic region to another.

Value: The appeal of vintage fashion items has greatly increased over the last few years. Our rule of thumb is to buy quality.

For more information on vintage fashion, see *Warman's Handbags Field Guide* by Abigail Rutherford, *Vintage Fashion Accessories* by Stacy LoAlbo, and *Warman's Shoes Field Guide* by Caroline Ashleigh.

Balenciaga couture strapless cocktail dress, circa 1950s, black lace over silk chiffon, chiffon upper bodice panel extends to back as two streamers that meet in bow, labeled "Balenciaga," inner tape marked "50097," very good condition, bust lining taken in, chiffon behind right shoulder mended, bust 30", waist 23", hips 34"............................. **$660**

Augusta Auctions

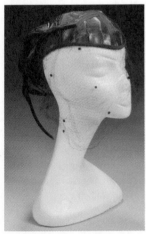

Lederer crocodile hat sold by Saks Fifth Avenue, New York, with brown feather plume, three leather-topped hatpins and brown netting, Paris, mid-20th century. **$277**

Skinner, Inc., www.skinnerinc.com

Cotton butterfly-print party dress, fitted bodice with halter neck, full circle skirt with attached crinoline petticoat and one beaded and sequined butterfly on skirt and bodice, excellent condition, bust 33", waist 25", 47" l. **$2,400**

Augusta Auctions

Ladies' high lace boots, circa 1900, red with Louis heel, excellent condition, 9-3/4" l. x 10-1/4" h. **$3,000**

Augusta Auctions

Chanel black leather ladies' cutaway-style pumps, European size 36-1/2 (approximately U.S. size 5), original dust covers and box, bow and keyhole detail on toe box.......................................**$74**

Skinner, Inc., www.skinnerinc.com.

Red, green and white geometric-patterned knit wool ladies' swimsuit with overskirt and solid green undershorts, circa 1925-1930, label reads "Knit-Well Swimming Suit," missing belt, very good condition, hole on shoulder, bust 34", waist 30", 33" l **$660**

Augusta Auctions

Black and white striped silk faille strapless ball gown with princess seams, full skirt and black velvet and chiffon trailing-rose trim, circa 1950s, very good condition, three pulls near hem, bust 30", waist 22", 53" l. overall. **$510**

Augusta Auctions

Black gabardine Adrian skirt suit with label, jacket ties at waist, with padded shoulders and two flap pockets, circa 1940s, excellent condition, bust 38", waist 26", jacket 25" l., skirt 28-1/2" l.....**$1,140**

Augusta Auctions

Men's white cotton duck cloth Palm Beach suit, circa 1940, double-breasted jacket with three pockets, cuffed pants with button fly, labeled "Palm Beach Ch 45," jacket 40", inseam of slacks 31-1/2". ..**$150**

Augusta Auctions

Chanel red caviar leather shoulder bag with perforated initial detail on both sides of exterior, zip closure with gold CC ball zipper pull, gold chain straps, red leather interior, good to very good condition, light fading to one side of exterior, small tear to one corner and wear to other, interior shows light signs of use, internal brand code has been scratched off, 11-1/2" w. x 14" h. x 1" d....................**$500**

Heritage Auctions

Christian Dior shoulder-length white kid gloves, deadstock, mid-20th century, two self-covered buttons at wrist, inside stamped "7-1/2, Made in France, Modele de Christian Dior, Exécuté par Lionel Le Grand," paper Neiman Marcus label marked "$39.95," pristine condition, 32-1/2" l. **$1,200**

Augusta Auctions

Cartier black patent leather bag with flap, top handle and coordinating leather turn-lock closure, Cartier logo embossed on exterior, interior lined with Cartier black monogram fabric and with one zipper pocket, very good condition, exterior leather with light wear to corners of bottom of bag, mild creasing on flap and scuff marks on exterior, interior in very good to excellent condition, includes original Cartier dust bag, 11" w. x 9" h. x 3" d...............**$263**

Heritage Auctions

Single-shoulder swimsuit with attached overskirt, circa 1950s, dark blue cotton sateen covered in blue silk chiffon printed with dark blue flowers, label marked "Sand Castle," includes matching sleeveless cover-up with tie at neck, excellent condition, bust 34", waist 24", 27" l. to skirt hem. **$150**

Augusta Auctions

Bottega Veneta gray wool pinstripe bag with chain-link handle and frame, snap closure with Bottega name across closure tabs, interior black fabric with one zip pocket, excellent condition, no visible signs of wear to exterior, slight scratching to silver hardware at closure, with small mirror, 8-1/2" h. x 8" w. x 4-1/2" d. **$194**

Heritage Auctions

Yellow crepe flapper dress with scoop neck, beaded drop waist and flared skirt, silver-tone beads and rhinestones, circa 1920s, probably American, ladies' size 4 to 6.......................**$369**

Skinner, Inc., www.skinnerinc.com

Two men's hats (one shown), blond beaver high hat with cream silk hat band and tan leather crown facing, circa 1850-1860, very good condition, crown dented, some fur loss, brim 1-5/8" w., crown 5-3/4" h.; black riding hat with narrow rolled brim, leather facing and silk lining stamped "Sweet & Butts Providence RI," very good condition, crown edge worn.................. **$540**

Augusta Auctions

Louis Vuitton "Noe PM" drawstring shoulder bag in blue Epi leather, black interior shows some wear as does bottom trim, 10-3/4" h. x 15-1/2" w. x 16-2/3" d. **$300**

Austin Auction Gallery

Yves Saint Laurent leopard-patterned pony-hair tote with ivory leather trim and studs on base, black satin interior with one slip pocket and one zipper pocket, original dust bag, very good to excellent condition with light wear to handle and wear to base studs, 17" w. x 13" h. x 5" d., 5" handle drop. **$513**

Heritage Auctions

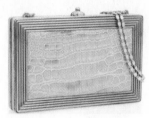

Judith Leiber cream-colored crocodile clutch, box-style bag with push-lock closure and gold hardware, gold metallic leather interior, gold chain strap that can be tucked in or worn out with bag, excellent condition, exterior with pen mark on one side, interior with scratch to leather, 7" w. x 4-1/2" h. x 1" d......................... **$1,025**

Heritage Auctions

Henry Beguelin olive green crocodile embossed leather tote bag with ruching on sides, brushed gunmetal hardware, brown leather straps and loose flap-top closure, linen interior with two slip pockets, attached mini wallet, excellent condition, includes dust bag and authenticity card, 14" w. x 10" h. x 5" d.................. **$500**

Heritage Auctions

Salvatore Ferragamo brown leather handbag with gold-tone clasp and detachable brown leather shoulder strap, 8-1/4" h. x 10-1/2" w.. **$308**

Skinner, Inc., www.skinnerinc.com

Gucci metallic bronze leather horse bit shoulder bag with matching shoulder strap and gold hardware, hidden magnetic closure and large horse bit detail on front exterior, interior brown canvas and one zip pocket, excellent condition, light scratching to hardware, small marks on lower front and rear exterior, 13" w. x 10" h. x 2" d. **$263**

Heritage Auctions

Hermès yellow and green "Automobile" silk scarf by Joachim Metz, excellent condition, 35" sq............................... **$263**

Heritage Auctions

Christian Dior classic monogram canvas clutch bag, gold-tone clasp closure, leather interior, good overall condition, hardware at top of bag scuffed and faded, interior with small scratches, exterior with light staining, 11" w. x 5-1/4" h. x 1" d. **$123**

Heritage Auctions

Watches

COLLECTING TIMEPIECES is not a new fad, but one enjoyed by men and women, the young and old alike. Essentially, there is something for everyone. Whether you collect by maker, by style, or by the type of movement, you can find watches to fit any budget.

Most everyone has a watch. They were given as graduation gifts from high school or college, something that was handed down to you from a family member, or potentially a gift received from a company you work for. By collecting watches, not only do you have a fun collectible, but it also has function.

Over the last 100+ years, millions of watches have been produced. Some were made for the masses, others made in very small quantities for a select few. There are dealers that specialize in watches, but they can also be found at flea markets, garage sales, auctions, on the Internet and at antique shops. Collecting creates an opportunity for you to have a watch for every occasion. You can have a watch to wear to work, one when out on the town, another one to use while participating in sports, and finally, an everyday watch.

The values placed on the watches illustrated in this section are market value, representing what they have recently sold for privately or at auction. Values can fluctuate due to numerous variables. How a watch is sold, where it is sold, and the condition all play a big role in the value.

The Internet has helped collectors identify watches worn by their favorite celebrity, worn on the moon, in a car race, in their favorite action film, etc.

One of the not-so-positive aspects of Internet collecting is the sheer volume of reproductions out there posing as authentic watches. They turn up everywhere, with links to professionally designed Websites offering the best of the best for a discount, or up for bid on an Internet auction. You must keep in mind the old saying, "If it looks too good to be true, it probably is."

For more information on watches, see *Warman's Watches Field Guide* by Reyne Haines.

Modele Depose chronograph C13356-2214525, two-tone with diamond bezel and diamond numbers, includes paperwork and original case, excellent condition. **$3,250**

Morphy Auctions

Vacheron & Constantin stainless steel automatic bracelet watch with date "222." **$25,000**

Bonhams

Rare silver openface watch Series I, No. 164, 1860s, Charles Fasoldt, Albany, New York, signed on escape wheel bridge as "C.Fasoldt / Albany. N.Y." on third wheel bridge as "Pat.Feb.1.1859 / Apr.5.1865 No.164." and under balance as "and patent applied for."
......................................**$18,750**

Bonhams

Gentleman's Heuer Camaro, circa 1970, manual wind 7730 17-jewel Valjoux movement, signed Heuer Leonidas SA. on bridge, silvered dial with two subsidiary dials for running seconds and 30-minute recording, white metal hands with luminous inserts and faceted indexes, polished and brushed finish steel case with screw-down case back and twin pushers flanking crown, 37mm. **$900**

Cowan's Auctions

Rare Louis XV-style 18k yellow gold, keyless pocketwatch, circa 1890, bezel cast and chased, domed back cover decorated with scene of St. George and the Dragon and motto S.Georgivs. Eqvitvm. Patron vs., interior of case back decorated with scene of Christ on ship in rough sea, hinged gold cuvette, radial blue Roman numerals on oval white enamel reserves, outer white enamel minute ring with blue dot and baton markers, blued steel Louis XV hands, case and movement signed Patek Philippe & Co. Geneve, 46mm dia **$16,000**

A.B. Levy's

Watch in form of padlock in gold and silver decorated with clear stones, obverse with lower porcelain dial with Arabic numerals, upper circular decoration now missing, on cobalt and white enameled ground with gold birds and foliage, verso with winder below moon and flower motif on cobalt enameled ground, 19th century, enameling unstable with significant loss to reverse with three missing stones, crystal and one hand missing, rusting to remaining hand and lower frame, 1-3/4" x 1" .. **$5,500**

Cordier Auctions

Must de Cartier silver gilt wristwatch, two-piece screw-down case with silvered dial, Arabic numerals and tapering hands, on black strap, in Cartier pouch, with guarantee and booklets, case 32mm including lugs..................................**$461**

Dreweatts & Bloomsbury Auctions

Rolex Cosmograph 14k gold chronograph wristwatch and bracelet with aftermarket dial, circa 1966.
....$45,000

Bonhams

Gentleman's Blancpain Villeret triple-date moon phase automatic wristwatch, 18● yellow gold, 23-jewel caliber 6511, serial number 268, Girard-Perregaux black leather band. $5,000

Bonhams

TOP LOT!

Bulgari Tubogas lady's 18k gold wristwatch, circa 1980, two-piece screw-down case with silvered dial, Arabic 12 and 6, baton numerals and hands, 17-jewel movement, integral 18k gold coiled block link bracelet, Bulgari case, movement functioning, light scratches overall, good condition, 130g .. $6,910

Dreweatts & Bloomsbury Auctions

Patek Philippe perpetual calendar chronograph, 18k white gold, mechanical movement with moon phases, AM/PM indicator and leap year indicator, silvered dial with hours, minutes and chronograph features, sub second dial at 9:00, power reserve 55 hours, Patek Philippe strap with 18k white gold deployment buckle, sapphire case back, water resistant to 30m/100ft, with original box and paperwork dated 2006, 40mm dia......$110,000

A.B. Levy's

Two pocketwatches: Roskopf silver-colored pocketwatch, four-piece hinged case with white dial, enameled numerals and outer red Arabic 24-hour ring, engine-turned decoration to reverse, Swiss cylinder movement, case 5.5cm dia.; Roskopf base metal pocketwatch, three-piece hinged case with white dial, enamelled numerals and outer red Arabic 24-hour ring, with foliate decoration throughout and rearing horse motif to reverse, Swiss cylinder movement, case 5.3 cm dia.............................$198

Dreweatts & Bloomsbury Auctions

Wright & Craighead 18k gold open-face keyless wind pocketwatch, hallmarked London 1896, three-piece hinged case with monogrammed back cover, white dial with black Roman numerals, blued steel spade hands and subsidiary seconds dial, English lever movement, movement functioning, engraving crisp, light scratches, case 48mm.. **$905**

Dreweatts & Bloomsbury Auctions

Rolex nickel open-face pocketwatch, circa 1940, three-piece screw-down case engraved with War Department "B 4720," white dial with black Arabic numerals, blued steel hands and subsidiary seconds dial, 15-jewel Rolex movement, movement functioning, dial, case and movement signed Rolex, number on case is B. 4720, case 45mm dia **$313**

Dreweatts & Bloomsbury Auctions

Rolex Precision lady's 18k gold wristwatch, two-piece case set with eight graduated diamonds, shaped dial with baton hands, 18-jewel Rolex movement, on integral 18k gold woven bracelet, light scratches to clasp and back of case, mark to dial at 2 o'clock, movement functioning, diamonds are original setting, clasp signed "Rolex SA," 2.4cm w. x 16.5cm l., 77 g.............. **$3,620**

Dreweatts & Bloomsbury Auctions

Eton lady's 18k gold wristwatch, two-piece case with silvered dial, Arabic and dart numerals and Dauphine hands, 17-jewel movement, on integral woven bracelet with ladder snap clasp. **$823**

Dreweatts & Bloomsbury Auctions

Swiss open-face fob watch, four-piece hinged case with enamel portrait of girl to back cover, white enamel dial with black Roman numerals and Breguet hands, suspended on fancy link chain, case 34mm. **$461**

Dreweatts & Bloomsbury Auctions

WATCHES

Omega Constellation gentleman's stainless steel wristwatch, circa 1966, ref. 168.004, two-piece screw-down case with silvered dial, raised Arabic numerals, baton hands and date aperture, 24-jewel Omega automatic movement adjusted to five positions and temperature, on brown strap, movement functioning, light scratches overall, numerals with signs of loss, case 40mm including lugs.................................. **$527**

Dreweatts & Bloomsbury Auctions

Vacheron & Constantin gentleman's 18k white gold wristwatch, circa 1970, ref. 6351, no. 499187, two-piece case with silvered dial, baton numerals and hands, 17-jewel Vacheron Constantin movement, adjusts to heat and cold, isochronism, and five positions, on black strap, buckle stamped "0.750, AW, Depose, Swiss," strap seems to be stamped "Audemars Piguet," movement functioning, light scratches overall, case 37mm l. **$2,470**

Dreweatts & Bloomsbury Auctions

Omega lady's dress watch, circa 1973, ref. 511.417, two-piece oval case with matte silvered dial, baton numerals and hands, 17-jewel Omega movement, black lizard skin strap, Omega box, movement functioning, light scratches to glass and case, signs of wear to strap, case 32mm including lugs.................................. **$362**

Dreweatts & Bloomsbury Auctions

Tag Heuer gentleman's stainless steel Chronometer wristwatch, two-piece screw-down case with rotating bezel, white dial with raised Arabic numerals, luminous Mercedes hands, three subsidiary dials running seconds, hours and minutes, date aperture, on white strap, in Tag Heuer case with guarantee and instruction booklet, 37-jewel movement (automatic), movement not functioning, strap stamped "Hirsch Pure," case 46mm including lugs.......... **$494**

Dreweatts & Bloomsbury Auctions

Universal gentleman's 18k gold wristwatch, two-piece case with silvered dial, Arabic 12 o'clock and dart numerals and Dauphine hands, 17-jewel Universal bumper automatic movement, on block link bracelet with ladder snap clasp, case 43mm including lugs... **$988**

Dreweatts & Bloomsbury Auctions

Aquastar Regate gentleman's stainless steel wristwatch, circa 1970, two-piece screw-down case with silvered dials, five circular apertures at 12 o'clock, changes color every five minutes, blue, red, and silver, blued steel cathedral hands and orange center seconds fly back hand, 17-jewel Aquamaster automatic movement, on blue rubber strap, movement functioning, new case gasket, light scratches to case, case 45mm including lugs. **$790**

Dreweatts & Bloomsbury Auctions

Rolex Oyster Royal gentleman's wristwatch, circa 1948, two-piece screw-down case and crown with silvered dial, luminous Arabic numerals, skeleton luminous hands and subsidiary seconds dial, 15-jewel Rolex movement, Rolex balance and overcoil balance spring, on blue-striped strap, movement functioning, marks to glass, light scratches to case, case 38mm including lugs.................................... **$694**

Dreweatts & Bloomsbury Auctions

Omega DeVille Co-Axial Chronometer gentleman's stainless steel wristwatch, circa 2006, two-piece open back screw-down case with silvered dial, baton numerals, luminous lance hands, subsidiary dials running seconds and power reserve, 29-jewel Omega Co-Axial automatic movement, cal. 2627, no. 81670329, on brown strap with fold-over clasp, Omega box with outer card packaging, guarantee and instruction booklet, movement functioning, glazed open back, 35mm dia. excluding crown, case 49mm including lugs. **$1,810**

Dreweatts & Bloomsbury Auctions

Harwood gentleman's silver wristwatch, circa 1928, three-piece case with rotating bezel to wind set, silvered dial with skeleton Arabic numerals and skeleton hands, 13-jewel Swiss movement with Harwood self-winding mechanism, patent no. 106583, on black leather strap, signs of wear to strap, light scratches to case, case 36mm including lugs. **$494**

Dreweatts & Bloomsbury Auctions

Lady's Rolex Oyster Perpetual Date, model 6917, circa 1981, stainless and 14k yellow gold, 26mm, champagne dial with gold markers, jubilee bracelet, fluted gold bezel, Rolex logo on crown, fits up to 7" wrist .. **$1,300**

Cowan's Auctions

Gentleman's 14k yellow gold Longines Automatic, caliber 19AS wristwatch, circa 1958, serial number 10405302, 17-jewel movement marked LXW, screw-back Star Watch case, aftermarket brown leather strap **$600**

Cowan's Auctions

Gentleman's Movado wristwatch, circa 1940, stainless steel case with screw-down back, apertures for day and date, outer ring and red arrow hand for date indication, gold hands, polished circular case with two circular push buttons for date and month adjustment, auxiliary seconds hand, rose gold bezel and lug surface. **$700**

Cowan's Auctions

Rewel Nivaflex lady's 18k gold wristwatch, two-piece case with silvered dial, Arabic and baton numerals and subsidiary dial, on 18k gold block link bracelet with ladder snap clasp, case 31mm including lugs **$461**

Dreweatts & Bloomsbury Auctions

Lady's 18k yellow gold Lady of Lyons hunter case pocketwatch, porcelain face with auxiliary seconds hand at six o'clock position, 39.3 dwt **$420**

Cowan's Auctions

Pair of Cartier 18k yellow gold small model gentleman's Tank wristwatches, Cartier, one mechanical, one quartz, cases complete including sapphire crowns, crystals scratch free. **$2,100**

Cowan's Auctions

Chinese duplex hunter case pocketwatch, silver, stamped 18 with crown above, blued hands, matching case and movement serial numbers (37572), 10-jewel hand-engraved movement ... **$550**

Cowan's Auctions

Rare and unusual Patek Philippe silver open-face keyless lever watch with center seconds, signed Patek Philippe & Co. No. 74382, gilt-finished lever movement, 18 jewels, bimetallic compensation balance, wolf's tooth winding, silver cuvette, silvered chased dial with Roman numerals on blank cartouches, outer Arabic five minute divisions, raised scroll and foliage decorated center, pink gold Louis XV hands, sweep center seconds, circular case with chased and engraved scroll and floral decorated bezel and band, back centered by chased and embossed scene depicting St. George and the Dragon and inscription S. Georgius Equitum Patronus in high relief, inside with inscription In Tempestate Securitas and a ship in full sail with sleeping Christ and two apostles, cuvette signed by maker and numbered, dial signed PP & Co. GENEVE, 47mm dia **$6,000**

Cowan's Auctions

WATCHES

French 18th century verge fusee gold pocketwatch with gold, diamond and enameled chatelaine, open face watch with porcelain dial, gold scrolled hands, Roman numerals and outer minute ring, marked "Arthur" for Jean Arthur (French, 1730-1810), gilt full plate verge fusee movement with pierced and engraved balance bridge and marked "Arthur Paris No. 431," 18k gold case, tested 14k gold chatelaine of three panels connected by chains, top panel with circular and star enameling in white, blue and cobalt centered with 20-point round diamond, middle panel with 13-point diamond, lower oval panel with central hairwork under convex glass surrounded by 23 diamonds and cobalt and white enameling engraved verso "E. Powel" and ending in twin enamel topped tassel drops, glass fob seal and small globe with hardstone cameo base, in original fitted silk-lined case, includes key, 1-3/4" dia., chatelaine 8-1/2" l **$7,500**

Cordier Auctions

Lady's platinum Art Deco Hamilton wristwatch, 22-jewel Hamilton 757 movement, white dial with silver markers, 14 baguette diamonds weighing approximately .50 carats and 42 single-cut diamonds weighing approximately 1.50 carats, linked band in 14k white gold with 24 single-cut diamonds weighing approximately .50 carats, 11.8 dwt. without movement, approximately 2.50 carats total weight. **$750**

Cowan's Auctions

Lady's 14k white gold Hamilton wristwatch containing two round full-cut diamonds weighing approximately .40 carats, 16 round full-cut diamonds weighing approximately .80 carats, and 32 single-cut diamonds weighing approximately .80 carats, 22-jewel Hamilton 757 movement, room for seven more diamonds on band, approximately 2.0 carats total diamond weight, 11.4 dwt., 5.75" l. **$650**

Cowan's Auctions

Lady's Rolex silver gilt and enamel ball pendant watch, signed Rolex, circa 1950, nickel-finished lever movement, mono-metallic balance, white enamel dial with Arabic numerals, translucent blue enamel case on guilloche background, gilt accents, hung from bar pin enameled "TT," .95" dia **$300**

Cowan's Auctions

World War II Collectibles

DURING THE NEARLY SEVEN DECADES since the end of World War II, veterans, collectors, and nostalgia-seekers have eagerly bought, sold, and traded the "spoils of war." Actually, souvenir collecting began as soon as troops set foot on foreign soil. Whether Tommies from Great Britain, Doughboys from the United States, or Fritzies from Germany, soldiers eagerly looked for trinkets and remembrances that would guarantee their place in the historic events that unfolded before them. Helmets, medals, Lugers, field gear, daggers, and other pieces of war material filled parcels and duffel bags on the way back home.

As soon as hostilities ended in 1945, the populations of defeated Germany and Japan quickly realized they could make money selling souvenirs to the occupation forces. The flow of war material increased. Values became well established...a Luger was worth several packs of cigarettes, a helmet, just one. A Japanese sword was worth two boxes of K-rations, an Arisaka bayonet was worth a Hershey's chocolate bar.

German SS field tunic
.... **$12,000-$14,000**

History Hunter.com

Over the years, these values have remained proportionally consistent. Today, that "two-pack" Luger might be worth $5,000 and that one-pack helmet, $1,500. The Japanese sword might fetch $1,200 and the Arisaka bayonet $95. Though values have increased dramatically, demand has not dropped off a bit. In fact, World War II collecting is the largest segment of the miltaria hobby.

Surprisingly, the values of items have been a closely guarded secret. Unfortunately, the hobby has relied on paying veterans and their families far less than a military relic is worth with the hope of selling later for a substantial profit. This attitude has given the hobby a bad reputation.

The advent of the Internet, though, significantly leveled the playing field for sellers and buyers. No longer does a person have to blindly offer a relic for sale to a collector or dealer. Simply logging onto one of several Internet auctions will give the uninitiated an idea of value.

But a little information can be dangerous. The value of military items resides in variation. Whether it is a difference in manufacturing technique, material or markings, the nuances of an item will determine the true value. Don't expect 20 minutes on the Internet to teach you these nuances. Collectors are a devoted bunch. They have spent years and hundreds, if not thousands, of dollars to establish the knowledge base that enables them to navigate through the hobby.

For more information on World War II collectibles, see *Warman's World War II Collectibles*, 3rd edition, by John Adams-Graf.

UNIFORMS AND FOOTWEAR

► French summer uniform belonging to Gen. Charles Noguès ... **$2,680**

Hermann-Historica.de

German reversible winter jacket in autumn camouflage .... **$2,000-$3,000**

Hermann-Historica.de

► USN naval aviator's M-445A fleece flying jacket ....**$255-$285**

AdvanceGuardMilitaria.com

British Royal Tank Regiment lieutenant colonel's battledress jacket ....**$200-$385**

AdvanceGuardMilitaria.com

◄ British Royal Field Artillery lt. colonel's tunic and breeches..**$145-$195**

AdvanceGuardMilitaria.com

USMC 2nd Marine regiment
colonel's jacket...........**$345-$395**

AdvanceGuardMilitaria.com

German special issue
Panzer clothing for
an Oberleutnant .. **$4,288**

Hermann-Historica.de

U.S. Army Nurses Corps M1940
blue uniform jacket.....**$195-$245**

AdvanceGuardMilitaria.com

British RAF 1941 Pattern flying boots .....**$285-$345**

AdvanceGuardMilitaria.com

WORLD WAR II COLLECTIBLES

HEADGEAR

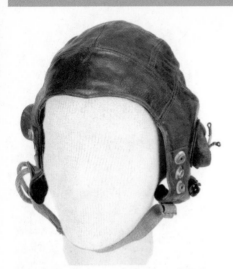

British RAF flying helmet, Type C ....**$250-$325**

AdvanceGuardMilitaria.com

Luftwaffe leather LKpW101 flight helmet,
complete set with earphones, microphone and
goggles ....**$700-$800**

AdvanceGuardMilitaria.com

Free French Foreign Legion helmet..........**$500-$650**

Hermann-Historica.de

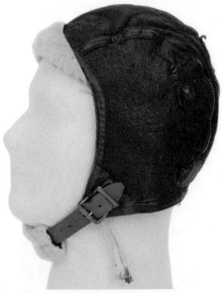

AAF B-6 fleece flight helmet...................**$115-$150**

AdvanceGuardMilitaria.com

Hitler Youth 1936 Pattern cap ....**$550-$700**

Hermann-Historica.de

Japanese Army helmet .... **$650-$950**

AdvanceGuardMilitaria.com

USMC M1 helmet and liner with World War I-era EGA **$595**

AdvanceGuardMilitaria.com

Panzer officer's visor cap .... **$1,000-$1,200**

Hermann-Historica.de

USN flat hat .... **$15-$25**

AdvanceGuardMilitaria.com

Luftwaffe Fallschirmjäger helmet, Normandy camouflage .... **$4,000-$6,000**

AdvanceGuardMilitaria.com

WORLD WAR II COLLECTIBLES

ACCOUTREMENTS

French Model 1935 ammunition pouch ...... **$15-$25**

AdvanceGuardMilitaria.com

French "Blitzkrieg" pilot's goggles .... **$165-$225**

AdvanceGuardMilitaria.com

U.S. shotgun ammunition pouch .... **$265-$325**

AdvanceGuardMilitaria.com

Japanese Infantry front
ammunition pouch ...... **$100-$125**

AdvanceGuardMilitaria.com

British No. 4A mine detector in wooden transit
chest .... **$200-$400**

Heritage Auctions

Luftwaffe cockpit airspeed indicator .... **$75-$95**

AdvanceGuardMilitaria.com

Italian mess kit with capture document **$40**

AdvanceGuardMilitaria.com

Heer folding 1938 Pattern entrenching shovel and carrier ....$265-$365

AdvanceGuardMilitaria.com

Third Reich political field canteen .... $25-$45

AdvanceGuardMilitaria.com

Luftwaffe field lantern...........$145-$165

AdvanceGuardMilitaria.com

Wehrmacht air raid siren ....$195-$265

AdvanceGuardMilitaria.com

Japanese aviator's goggles with box $345

AdvanceGuardMilitaria.com

Japanese air raid
siren.............**$165-$225**

AdvanceGuardMilitaria.com

Japanese Army officer map
case .... **$65-$85**

AdvanceGuardMilitaria.com

Soviet M1939 knapsack with kit pouches .... **$300-$365**

AdvanceGuardMilitaria.com

U.S. Army Pacific Theater
camouflage jungle
pack.........................**$200-$245**

AdvanceGuardMilitaria.com

U.S. enameled canteen and cup
set ....**$235-$265**

AdvanceGuardMilitaria.com

U.S. Army Issue Type E 6 x 30 Power binoculars.. **$50-$95**

AdvanceGuardMilitaria.com

USN/USMC doctor's field surgical kit.......... **$55-$95**

AdvanceGuardMilitaria.com

1st Marine Division portable telephone............................ **$135**

AdvanceGuardMilitaria.com

USN summer aviator's gloves.................. **$155-$195**

AdvanceGuardMilitaria.com

World War II-era Sperry S-1 precision bombsight........... **$1,175**

Heritage Auctions

MEDALS

Third Reich Iron Cross,
I Class .... **$200-$400**

AdvanceGuardMilitaria.com

U.S. Purple Heart Medal,
ribbon bar and lapel
button .... **$65-$95**

AdvanceGuardMilitaria.com

French Order of the Legion of
Honor .... **$65-$80**

AdvanceGuardMilitaria.com

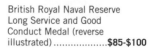

British Royal Naval Reserve
Long Service and Good
Conduct Medal (reverse
illustrated) .... **$85-$100**

AdvanceGuardMilitaria.com

Japanese Order of the
Sacred Treasure, III
Class .... **$520-$675**

AdvanceGuardMilitaria.com

Special Contributors and Advisors

The following collectors, dealers, sellers, and researchers have supported the *Antique Trader Antiques & Collectibles Price Guide* with their pricing and contacts for nearly 30 years. Many continue to serve as a valuable resource to the entire collecting hobby, while others have passed away. We honor all contributors past and present as their hard work and passion lives on through this book.

Andre Ammelounx

Mannie Banner

Ellen Bercovici

Sandra Bondhus

James R. and Carol S. Boshears

Bobbie Zucker Bryson

Emmett Butler

Dana Cain

Linda D. Carannante

David Chartier

Les and Irene Cohen

Amphora Collectors International

Marion Cohen

Neva Colbert

Marie Compton

Susan N. Cox

Caroline Torem-Craig

Leonard Davis

Bev Dieringer

Janice Dodson

Del E. Domke

Debby DuBay

Susan Eberman

Joan M. George

Roselyn Gerson

William A. and Donna J. Gray

Pam Green

Linda Guffey

Carl Heck

Alma Hillman

K. Robert and Bonne L. Hohl

Ellen R. Hill

Joan Hull

Hull Pottery Association

Louise Irvine

Helen and Bob Jones

Mary Ann Johnston

Donald-Brian Johnson

Dorothy Kamm

Edwin E. Kellogg

Madeleine Kirsh

Vivian Kromer

Curt Leiser

Gene Loveland

Mary McCaslin

Pat Moore

Reg G. Morris

Craig Nissen

Joan C. Oates

Margaret Payne

Gail Peck

John Petzold

Dr. Leslie Piña

Joseph Porcelli

Arlene Rabin

John Rader, Sr.

Betty June Wymer

LuAnn Riggs

Tim and Jamie Saloff

Federico Santi

Peggy Sebek

Steve Stone

Phillip Sullivan

Mark and Ellen Supnick

Tim Trapani

Jim Trautman

Elaine Westover

Kathryn Wiese

Laurie Williams

Nancy Wolfe

Contributors by Subject

Advertising Items: Eric Bradley
Barbie: Steve Evans/Susan Sliwicki
Books: Kristine Manty
Bottles: Michael Polak
Clocks: Antoinette Rahn/Donald-Brian Johnson
Cloisonné: Arlene Rabin
Compacts & Vanity Cases: Roselyn Gerson
Country Store: Donald-Brian Johnson/Antoinette Rahn
Dolls: Kristine Manty
Disney Collectibles: Tom Bartsch
Hooked Rugs: Antoinette Rahn/Karen Knapstein
Kitchenwares (vintage): Chriss Swaney/Susan Sliwicki
Electric Lighting: Joseph Porcelli/Tom Bartsch
Early Lighting: Donald-Brian Johnson/Tom Bartsch
Records: Susan Sliwicki
Salesman Samples: Antoinette Rahn
Samplers: Donald-Brian Johnson
Sports: Tom Bartsch
Steins: Andre Ammelounx
Toys: Eric Bradley
Vintage Clothing: Nancy Wolfe/Madeleine Kirsh/Susan Sliwicki
Watches: Antoinette Rahn
World War II: John Adams-Graf

CERAMICS

Abingdon: Elaine Westover
American Painted Porcelain: Dorothy Kamm
Amphora-Teplitz: Les and Irene Cohen
Bauer Pottery: James Elliott-Bishop
Belleek (American): Peggy Sebek
Belleek (Irish): Del Domke
Blue & White Pottery: Steve Stone
Blue Ridge Dinnerwares: Marie Compton and Susan N. Cox
Brayton Laguna Pottery: Susan N. Cox
Buffalo Pottery: Phillip Sullivan
Caliente Pottery: Susan N. Cox
Catalina Island Pottery: James Elliott-Bishop
Ceramic Arts Studio of Madison: Donald-Brian Johnson
Clarice Cliff Designs: Laurie Williams
Cleminson Clay: Susan N. Cox
deLee Art: Susan N. Cox
Doulton/Royal Doulton: Reg Morris, Louise Irvine and Ed Pascoe
East Liverpool Potteries: William and Donna J. Gray
Fine Art: Kristine Manty
Flow Blue: K. Robert and Bonne L. Hohl
Franciscan Ware: James Elliott-Bishop
Frankoma Pottery: Susan N. Cox
Fulper Pottery: Karen Knapstein
Gonder Pottery: James R. and Carol S. Boshears
Gouda: Antoinette Rahn
Haeger: Donald-Brian Johnson

Hall China: Marty Kennedy
Haviland: Karen Knapstein
Hedi Schoop: Donald-Brian Johnson
Harker: William A. and Donna J. Gray
Hull: Joan Hull
Ironstone: General – Bev Dieringer; Tea Leaf – The Tea Leaf Club International
Limoges: Karen Knapstein
Majolica: Michael Strawser
McCoy: Craig Nissen
Mettlach: Andre Ammelounx
Noritake: Tim Trapani
Old Ivory: Alma Hillman
Overbeck: Karen Knapstein
Pacific Clay Products: Susan N. Cox
Phoenix Bird & Flying Turkey: Joan Collett Oates
Pierce (Howard) Porcelains: Susan N. Cox
Quimper: Sandra Bondhus
Red Wing: Gail Peck
Royal Bayreuth: Mary McCaslin
Rozart Pottery: Susan N. Cox
R.S. Prussia: Mary McCaslin
Russel Wright Designs: Kathryn Wiese
Satsuma: Melody Amsel-Arieli
Schoop (Hedi) Art Creations: Susan N. Cox
Shawnee: Linda Guffey
Shelley China: Mannie Banner, David Chartier, Bryand Goodlad, Edwin E. Kellogg, Gene Loveland, and Curt Leiser
Stoneware and Spongeware: Bruce and Vicki Waasdorp
Sumida Gawa: Karen Knapstein
Vernon Kilns: Pam Green
Warwick China: John Rader, Sr.
Zeisel (Eva) Designs: Kathryn Wiese
Zsolnay: Federico Santi/ John Gacher

GLASS

Animals: Helen and Bob Jones
Carnival Glass: Jim and Jan Seeck
Crackle Glass: Donald-Brian Johnson
Depression Glass: Ellen T. Schroy
Fenton: Helen and Bob Jones/Mark F. Moran
Fire King: Karen Knapstein
Higgins Glass: Donald-Brian Johnson
Milk Glass: Karen Knapstein
New Martinsville: Helen and Bob Jones
Opalescent Glass: James Measell
Paden City: Helen and Bob Jones
Phoenix Glass: Helen and Bob Jones
Schneider Glass: Donald-Brian Johnson
Sugar Shakers: Scott Beale
Wall Pocket Vases: Bobbie Zucker Bryson

SPECIAL CONTRIBUTORS   789

Pricing, Identifications, and Images Provided By:

LIVE AUCTION PROVIDERS

AuctionZip
113 West Pitt St., Suite C
Bedford, PA 15522
(814) 623-5059
www.auctionzip.com

Artfact, LLC
38 Everett St., Suite 101
Allston, MA 02134
(617) 746-9800
www.artfact.com

LiveAuctioneers, LLC
2nd Floor
220 12th Ave.
New York, NY 10001
www.liveauctioneers.com

AUCTION HOUSES

A-1 Auction
2042 N Rio Grande Ave., Suite E
Orlando, FL 32804
(407) 839-0004
a-1auction@cfl.rr.com
http://www.a-1auction.net/

Allard Auctions, Inc.
P.O. Box 1030
St. Ignatius, MT 59865
(406) 745-0500
(800) 314-0343
www.allardauctions.com

American Bottle Auctions
2523 J St., Suite 203
Sacramento, CA 95816
(800) 806-7722
americanbottle.com

American Pottery Auction
Vicki and Bruce Waasdorp
P.O. Box 434
Clarence, NY 14031
(716) 759-2361
www.antiques-stoneware.com

Antique Helper Auction House
2764 East 55th Pl.
Indianapolis, IN 46220
(317) 251-5635
www.antiquehelper.com

Apple Tree Auction Center
1616 West Church St.
Newark, OH 43055-1540
(740) 344-4282
www.appletreeauction.com

Artingstall & Hind Auctioneers
9312 Civic Center Dr., #104
Beverly Hills, CA 90210
(310) 424-5288
www.artingstall.com

Arus Auctions
www.arusauctions.com
arusauctions@gmail.com
(617) 669-6170

ATM Antiques & Auctions, LLC
811 SE US Hwy. 19
Crystal River, FL 34429
(352) 795-2061
(800) 542-3877
www.charliefudge.com

Auction Team Breker
Otto-Hahn-Str. 10
50997 Köln (Godorf), Germany
02236 384340
www.breker.com

Belhorn Auctions, LLC
2746 Wynnerock Ct.
Hilliard, OH 43026
(614) 921-9441
auctions@belhorn.com
www.belhorn.com
www.potterymarketplace.com

Bertoia Auctions
2141 DeMarco Dr.
Vineland, NJ 08360
(856) 692-1881
www.bertoiaauctions.com

Bonhams
7601 W. Sunset Blvd.
Los Angeles, CA 90046
(323) 850-7500
www.bonhams.com

Brunk Auctions
P.O. Box 2135
Asheville, NC 28802
(828) 254-6846
www.brunkauctions.com

**Bunte Auction Services
and Appraisals**
755 Church Rd.
Elgin, IL 60123
(847) 214-8423
www.bunteauction.com

Charles Miller Ltd.
Suite 6 Imperial Studios
3/11 Imperial Rd.
London, England
SW6 2AG
+44 (0) (207) 806-5530
www.charlesmillerltd.com

Charlton Hall Auctioneers
912 Gervais St.
Columbia, SC 29201
www.charltonhallauctions.com

Cherryland Postcard Auctions
Ronald & Alec Millard
P.O. Box 427
Frankfort, MI 49635
(231) 352-9758
CherrylandPostcards.com

Christie's New York
20 Rockefeller Plaza
New York, NY 10020
www.christies.com

Cincinnati Art Galleries
225 East Sixth St.
Cincinnati, OH 45202
www.cincinnatiartgalleries.com

Clars Auction Gallery
5644 Telegraph Ave.
Oakland, CA 94609
(510) 428-0100
www.clars.com

The Coeur d'Alene Art Auction
8836 North Hess St., Suite B
Hayden, ID 83835
(208) 772-9009
www.cdaartauction.com

John W. Coker, Ltd.
1511 W. Hwy. 11E
New Market, TN 37820
(865) 475-5163
john@antiquesonline.com
www.antiquesonline.com

Collect Auctions
(888) 463-3063
collectauctions.com

Conestoga Auction Co.
768 Graystone Rd.
Manheim, PA 17545
(717) 898-7284
www.conestogaauction.com

Constantine & Pletcher
1321 Freeport Rd.
Cheswick, PA 15024
(724) 275-7190
Fax: (724) 275-7191
http://www.cpauction.info
sold@cpauction.info

Cordier Auctions
1500 Paxton St.
Harrisburg, PA 17104
(717) 731-8662
www.cordierantiques.com

Cowan's Auctions
6270 Este Ave.
Cincinnati, OH 45232
(513) 871-1670
www.cowanauctions.com

CRN Auctions, Inc.
57 Bay State Rd.
Cambridge, MA 02138
(617) 661-9582
www.crnauctions.com

Dargate Auction Galleries
326 Munson Ave.
McKees Rocks, PA 15136
(412) 771-8700
Fax: (412) 771-8779
www.dargate.com

DGW Auctioneers & Appraisers
760 Kifer Rd.
Sunnyvale, CA 94086
www.dgwauctioneers.com

Dickins Auctioneers Ltd.
Calvert Rd.
Middle Claydon
Buckingham, England
MK18 2EZ
+44 (129) 671-4434
www.dickinsauctioneers.com

Doyle New York
175 E. 87th St.
New York, NY 10128
(212) 427-2730
www.doylenewyork.com

Dreweatts & Bloomsbury Auctions
24 Maddox St.
London, England W1S 1PP
+44 (207) 495-9494
http://www.dreweatts.com/

Elite Decorative Arts
1034 Gateway Blvd., #108
Boynton Beach, FL 33426
(561) 200-0893
www.eliteauction.com

Fine Arts Auctions, LLC
324 S. Beverly Dr., #175
Beverly Hills, CA 90212
(310) 990-2150
www.fineartauctionllc.com

Frasher's Doll Auction
2323 S. Mecklin Sch. Rd.
Oak Grove, MO 64075
(816) 625-3786

Fontaines Auction Gallery
1485 W. Housatonic St.
Pittsfield, MA 01210
www.fontainesauction.net

Forsythes' Auctions, LLC
P.O. Box 188
Russellville, OH 45168
(937) 377-3700
www.forsythesauctions.com

Fox Auctions
P.O. Box 4069
Vallejo, CA 94590
(631) 553-3841
Fax: (707) 643-3000
foxauctions@yahoo.com
www.foxauctionsonline.com

J. Garrett Auctioneers, Ltd.
1411 Slocum St.
Dallas, TX 75207
(214) 683-6855
www.jgarrettauctioneers.com

Garth's Arts & Antiques
P.O. Box 369
Delaware, OH 43015
(740) 362-4771
www.garths.com

Glass Works Auctions
Box 180
East Greenville, PA 18041
(215) 679-5849
www.glswrk-auction.com

The Golf Auction
209 State St.
Oldsmar, FL 34677
(813) 340-6179
thegolfauction.com

Great Gatsby's Antiques and Auctions
5180 Peachtree Industrial Blvd.
Atlanta, GA 30341
(770) 457-1903
www.greatgatsbys.com

Grogan & Co.
22 Harris St.
Dedham, MA 02026
(781) 461-9500
www.groganco.com

Guyette, Schmidt & Deeter
24718 Beverly Rd.
St. Michaels, MD 21663
(410) 745-0485
Fax: (410) 745-0487
decoys@guyetteandschmidt.com
www.guyetteandschmidt.com

GWS Auctions, LLC
41841 Beacon Hill # E
Palm Desert, CA 92211
(760) 610-4175
www.gwsauctions.com

Ken Farmer Auctions and Appraisals
105 Harrison St.
Radford, VA 24141
(540) 639-0939
www.kfauctions.com

Hake's Americana & Collectibles
P.O. Box 12001
York, PA 17402
(717) 434-1600
www.hakes.com

Hamilton's Antique & Estate Auctions, Inc.
505 Puyallup Ave.
Tacoma, WA 98421
(253) 534-4445
www.joe-frank.com

Norman Heckler & Co.
79 Bradford Corner Rd.
Woodstock Valley, CT 06282
www.hecklerauction.com

Heritage Auctions
3500 Maple Ave.
Dallas, TX 75219-3941
(800) 872-6467
www.ha.com

Hess Fine Auctions
1131 4th St. N.
St. Petersburg, FL 33701
(727) 896-0622
www.hessfineauctions.com

Hewlett's Antique Auctions
PO Box 87
13286 Jefferson St.
Le Grand, CA 95333
(209) 389-4542
Fax: (209) 389-0730
hewlettsdirect@sbcglobal.net
http://www.hewlettsauctions.com/

Holabird-Kagin Americana
3555 Airway Dr., #308
Reno, NV 89511
(775) 852-8822
www.holabirdamericana.com

Homestead Auctions
3200 Greenwich Rd.
Norton, OH 44203
(330) 807-1445
www.homesteadauction.net

Bill Hood & Sons Art & Antique Auctions
2925 S. Federal Hwy.
Delray Beach, FL 33483
(561) 278-8996
www.hoodauction.com

Humler & Nolan
The Auctions at Rookwood
225 E. Sixth St., 4th Floor
Cincinnati, OH 45202
(513) 381-2041
Fax: (513) 381-2038
info@humlernolan.com
www.humlernolan.com

iGavel Auctions
229 E. 120th St.
New York, NY 10035
(212) 289-5588
www.igavelauctions.com

Ivy Auctions
22391 Hwy. 76 E.
Laurens, SC 29360
(864) 682-2750
www.ivyauctions.com

Jackson's International Auctioneers & Appraisers
2229 Lincoln St.
Cedar Falls, IA 50613
jacksonsauction.com

James D. Julia, Inc.
P.O. Box 830
203 Skowhegan Rd.
Fairfield, ME 04937
(207) 453-7125
jamesdjulia.com

Jeffrey S. Evans & Associates
2177 Green Valley Ln.
Mount Crawford, VA 22841
(540) 434-3939
www.jeffreysevans.com

John Moran Auctioneers
735 West Woodbury Rd.
Altadena, CA 91001
(626) 793-1833
www.johnmoran.com

Julien's Auctions
9665 Wilshire Blvd., Suite 150
Beverly Hills, CA 90210
(310) 836-1818
www.juliensauctions.com

Kaminski Auctions
564 Cabot St.
Beverly, MA 01915
(978) 927-2223
Fax: (978) 927-2228
http://www.kaminskiauctions.com/

Kennedy Auctions Service
160 West Court Ave.
Selmer, TN 38375
(731) 645-5001
www.kennedysauction.com

Legend Numismatics
P.O. Box 9
Lincroft, NJ 07738
(800) 743-2646
www.legendcoin.com

Legendary Auctions
17542 Chicago Ave.
Lansing, IL 60438
(708) 889-9380
www.legendaryauctions.com

Los Angeles Modern Auctions
16145 Hart St.
Van Nuys, CA 91406
(323) 904-1950
www.lamodern.com

Leslie Hindman Auctioneers
1338 West Lake St.
Chicago, IL 60607
(312) 280-1212
www.lesliehindman.com

Louis J. Dianni, LLC Antiques Auctions
May 1-Oct. 15:
982 Main St., Suite 175
Fishkill, NY 12524
Oct. 20-April 15:
1304 SW 160th Ave., Suite 228A
Sunrise, FL 33326
https://louisjdianni.com

Love of the Game Auctions
P.O. Box 157
Great Meadows, NJ 07838
loveofthegameauctions.com

Manitou Auctions
205 Styer Dairy Rd.
Reidsville, NC 27320
(336) 349-6577
www.manitou-auctions.com

Manor Auctions
2415 N. Monroe St.
Tallahassee, FL 32303
(850) 523-3787
Fax: (850) 523-3786
www.manorauctions.com

Mark Mattox Auctioneer & Real Estate Broker, Inc.
3740 Maysville Rd.
Carlisle, KY 40311
(859) 289-5720
http://mattoxauctions.com/auctions/

Martin J. Donnelly Antique Tools
5523 County Rd. 8
Avoca, NY 14809
(607) 566-2617
www.mjdtools.com

Matt Maring Auction Co.
P.O. Box 37
Kenyon, MN 55946
(507) 789-5227
www.maringauction.com

Material Culture
4700 Wissahickon Ave.
Philadelphia, PA 19144
(215) 849-8030
www.materialculture.com

Matthews Auctions
111 South Oak St.
Nokomis, IL 62075-1337
(215) 563-8880
www.matthewsauctions.com

McLaren Auction Service
21507 Highway 99E
Aurora, OR 97002
(503) 678-2441
www.mclarenauction.com

McMasters-Harris Auction Co.
P.O. Box 755
Cambridge, OH 43725
www.mcmastersharris.com

Michaan's Auctions
2751 Todd St.
Alameda, CA 94501
(510) 740-0220
www.michaans.com

**Michael Spooner & Son
Estate Auctioneers**
501 Golden Ave.
Ottawa, Ontario K2A 2E6
Canada
(613) 722-8321
www.spoonerauctions.com

Midwest Auction Galleries
925 North Lapeer Rd.
Oxford, MI 48371
(877) 236-8181 or (248) 236-8100
Fax: (248) 236-8396
sales@midwestauctioninc.com
www.midwestauctioninc.com

Mile High Card Co.
7200 S. Alton Way, Suite A230
Centennial, CO 80112
(303) 840-2784
www.milehighcardco.com

Dan Morphy Auctions
2000 N. Reading Rd.
Denver, PA 17517
(717) 335-3435
morphyauctions.com

Mohawk Arms, Inc.
P.O. Box 157
Bouckville, NY 13310
(315) 893-7888
www.militaryrelics.com

Mosby & Co. Auctions
5714-A Industry Ln.
Frederick, MD 21704
(240) 629-8139
www.mosbyauctions.com

Neal Auction Co.
4038 Magazine St.
New Orleans, LA 70115
(504) 899-5329
www.nealauctions.com

Nest Egg Auctions
30 Research Pkwy.
Meriden, CT 06450
(203) 630-1400
www.nesteggauctions.com

New Orleans Auction Gallery
1330 St. Charles Ave.
New Orleans, LA 70130
www.neworleansauction.com

Nico Auctions
4023 Kennett Pike, Suite 248
Greenville, DE 19807
(888) 390-0201
www.nicoauctions.com

Noel Barrett Vintage Toys @ Auction
P.O. Box 300
Carversville, PA 18913
(215) 297 5109
toys@noelbarrett.com
www.noelbarrett.com

North American Auction Co.
78 Wildcat Way
Bozeman, MT 59718
(800) 686-4216
northamericanauctioncompany.com

Northeast Auctions
93 Pleasant St.
Portsmouth, NH 03801
(603) 433-8400
Fax: (603) 433-0415
contact@northeastauctions.com
www.northeastauctions.com

**O'Gallerie: Fine Arts, Antiques and
Estate Auctions**
228 Northeast 7th Ave.
Portland, OR 97232-2909
(503) 238-0202
www.ogallerie.com

Omaha Auction Center
7531 Dodge St.
Omaha, NE 68114
(402) 397-9575
www.omahaauctioncenter.com

Omega Auction Corp.
1669 W. 39th Pl.
Hialeah, FL 33012
(786) 444-4997
www.omegaauctioncorp.com

**Pacific Galleries Auction House
and Antique Mall**
241 South Lander St.
Seattle, WA 98134
(206) 441-9990
Fax: (206) 448-9677
www.pacgal.com

Past Tyme Pleasures
39 California Ave., Suite 105
Pleasanton, CA 94566
www.pasttyme1.com

PBA Galleries
133 Kearny St., 4th Floor
San Francisco, CA 94108
(415) 989-2665
www.pbagalleries.com

Phoebus Auction Gallery
18 East Mellen St.
Hampton, VA 23663
(757) 722-9210
www.phoebusauction.com

Pioneer Auction Gallery
14650 SE Arista Dr.
Portland, OR 97267
(503) 496-0303
bidpioneer@aol.com
www.pioneerantiqueauction.com

Pook & Pook, Inc.
463 East Lancaster Ave.
Downingtown, PA 19335
(610) 269-4040
info@pookandpook.com
www.pookandpook.com

Potter & Potter Auctions
3759 N. Ravenswood Ave., #121
Chicago, IL 60613
(773) 472-1442
info@potterauctions.com
www.potterauctions.com

Premier Auction Galleries
12587 Chillicothe Rd.
Chesterland, OH 44026
(440) 688-4203
Fax: (440) 688-4202
jessemathews@pag4u.com
http://www.pag4u.com

Don Presley Auction
1319 West Katella Ave.
Orange County, CA 92867
(714) 633-2437
www.donpresley.com

Preston Hall Gallery
2201 Main St., Suite #820
Dallas, TX 75201
(214) 718-8624
www.prestonhallgallery.com

Profiles in History
26901 Agoura Rd., Suite 150
Calabasas Hills, CA 91301
(310) 859-7701
www.profilesinhistory.com

Purcell Auction Gallery
2156 Husband Rd.
Paducah, KY 42003
(270) 444-7599
purcellauction@bellsouth.net
http://www.purcellauction.com/

Quinn's Auction Galleries
360 S. Washington St.
Falls Church, VA 22046
(703) 532-5632
www.quinnsauction.com

Rago Arts & Auction Center
333 N. Main St.
Lambertville, NJ 08530
(609) 397-9374
www.ragoarts.com

Red Baron's Antiques
8655 Roswell Rd.
Atlanta, GA 30350
(770) 640-4604
www.rbantiques.com

Richard Opfer Auctioneering, Inc.
1919 Greenspring Dr.
Lutherville-Timonium, MD 21093
(410) 252-5035
www.opferauction.com

Rich Penn Auctions
P.O. Box 1355
Waterloo, IA 50704
(319) 291-6688
www.richpennauctions.com

RM Auctions
One Classic Car Dr.
Blenheium, Ontario
N0P 1A0 Canada
+1 (519) 352-4575
www.rmauctions.com

Robert Edward Auctions
P.O. Box 7256
Watchung, NJ 07069
(908) 226-9900
www.robertedwardauctions.com

Rock Island Auction Co.
7819 42 St. West
Rock Island, IL 61201
(800) 238-8022
www.rockislandauction.com

RR Auction
5 Route 101A, Suite 5
Amherst, NH 03031
(603) 732-4280
www.rrauction.com

Saco River Auction Co.
2 Main St.
Biddeford, ME 04005
(207) 602-1504
www.sacoriverauction.com

Scheerer McCulloch Auctioneers
515 E Paulding Rd.
Fort Wayne, IN 46816
(260) 441-8636
www.smauctioneers.com

SCP Auctions, Inc.
32451 Golden Lantern, Suite 308
Laguna Niguel, CA 92677
(949) 831-3700
www.SCPauctions.com

Seeck Auction Co.
Jim and Jan Seeck
P.O. Box 377
Mason City, IA 50402
www.seeckauction.com

SeriousToyz
1 Baltic Pl.
Croton on Hudson, NY 10520
(866) 653-8699
www.serioustoyz.com

Showtime Auction Service
22619 Monterey Dr.
Woodhaven, MI 48183-2269
(734) 676-9703
www.showtimeauctions.com

Skinner, Inc.
357 Main St.
Boston, MA 01740
(617) 350-5400
www.skinnerinc.com

Sloans & Kenyon Auctioneers and Appraisers
7034 Wisconsin Ave.
Chevy Chase, MD 20815
(301) 634-2330
www.sloansandkenyon.com

Sotheby's New York
1334 York Ave.
New York, NY 10021
(212) 606-7000
www.sothebys.com

Specialists of the South, Inc.
544 E. Sixth St.
Panama City, FL 32401
(850) 785-2577
www.specialistsofthesouth.com

Stanley Gibbons
399 Strand
London, England
WC2R 0LX
Tel: +44 (0)207 836 8444
www.stanleygibbons.com

Stefek's Auctioneers & Appraisers
18450 Mack Ave.
Grosse Pointe Farms, MI 48236
(313) 881-1800
www.stefeksltd.com

Stephenson's Auctioneers & Appraisers
1005 Industrial Blvd.
Southampton, PA 18966
(215) 322-6182
www.stephensonsauction.com

Stevens Auction Co.
301 North Meridian St.
Aberdeen, MS 39730-2613
(662) 369-2200
www.stevensauction.com

Strawser Majolica Auctions
P.O. Box 332
Wolcottville, IN 46795
www.strawserauctions.com

Sullivan & Son Auction, LLC
1995 E. County Rd. 650
Carthage, IL 62321
(217) 743-5200
www.sullivanandsonauction.com

Swann Auction Galleries
104 E 25th St., # 6
New York, NY 10010-2999
(212) 254-4710
www.swanngalleries.com

Teel Auction Services
619 FM 2330
Montabla, TX 75853
(903) 724-4079
jteelenterprises@aol.com
www.teelauctionservices.com

Theriault's – The Doll Masters
P.O. Box 151
Annapolis, MD 21404
(800) 638-0422
www.theriaults.com

Thomaston Place Auction Galleries
51 Atlantic Hwy.
Thomaston, ME 04861
(207) 354-8141
www.thomastonauction.com

John Toomey Gallery
818 North Blvd.
Oak Park, IL 60301
(708) 383-5234
http://johntoomeygallery.com

Tory Hill Auction Co.
5301 Hillsborough St.
Raleigh, NC 27606
(919) 858-0327
www.toryhillauctions.com

Tradewinds Antiques & Auctions
24 Magnolia Ave.
Manchester-by-the-Sea, MA 01944
(978) 526-4085
www.tradewindsantiques.com

Treadway Gallery, Inc.
2029 Madison Rd.
Cincinnati, OH 45208
www.treadwaygallery.com

Turkey Creek Auctions, Inc.
13939 N. Hwy. 441
Citra, FL 32113
(352) 622-4611
(800) 648-7523
www.antiqueauctionsfl.com

Vero Beach Auction
492 Old Dixie Hwy.
Vero Beach, FL 32962
(772) 978-5955
Fax: (772) 978-5954
verobeachauction@bellsouth.net
www.verobeachauction.com

Victorian Casino Antiques Auction
4520 Arville St., #1
Las Vegas, NV 89103
(702) 382-2466
www.vcaauction.com

Weiderseim Associates, Inc.
PO Box 470
Chester Springs, PA 19425
(610) 827-1910
www.wiederseim.com

Philip Weiss Auctions
74 Merrick Rd.
Lynbrook, NY 11563
(516) 594-0731
www.weissauctions.com

William J. Jenack Estate Appraisers & Auctioneers
62 Kings Highway Bypass
Chester, NY 10918
(877) 282-8503
info@jenack.com
www.jenack.com

Witherell's Art & Antiques
300 20th St.
Sacramento, CA 95811
(916) 446-6490
witherells.com

Woodbury Auction, LLC
50 Main St. N.
Woodbury, CT 06798
(203) 266-0323
info@woodburyauction.com
www.woodburyauction.com

Woody Auction
317 S. Forrest St.
Douglass, KS 67039
(316) 747-2694
www.woodyauction.com

Wright
1440 W. Hubbard St.
Chicago, IL 60642
(312) 563-0020
www.wright20.com

Zurko Promotions
115 E. Division St.
Shawano, WI 54166
www.zurkopromotions.com

Additional Photographs and Research Provided By:

45cat.com, an online archive dedicated to the magic of the vinyl 7" single; Belleek Collectors International Society, www.belleek.ie/collectors-society; CAS Collectors, www.cascollectors.com and www.ceramicartstudio.com; International Perfume Bottle Association, www.perfumebottles.org; National Association of Warwick China & Pottery Collectors; popsike.com, Rare Records Auction Results; Red Wing Collectors Society, www.redwingcollectors.org; and Tea Leaf Club International, www.tealeafclub.com.

Index

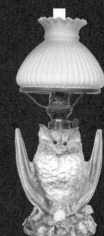

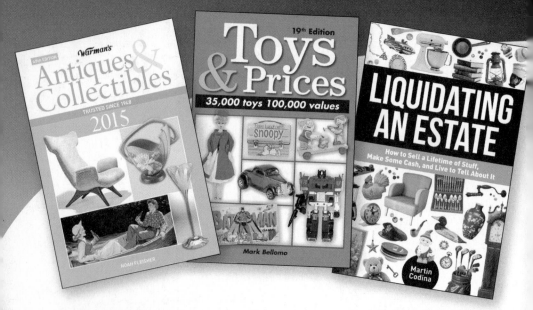
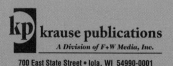